DICTIONARY OF
AUTOMOBILE
ENGINEERING

PETER COLLIN PUBLISHING

English edition editorial team
Rupert Livesey
Robin Sawers
Liz Greasby

Advisor
Dave Whitehouse
Department of Engineering, Kingston College

German edition editor
Dr Peter A. Schmitt

First published in Great Britain 1996 by

Peter Collin Publishing Ltd

1 Cambridge Road, Teddington, Middlesex, TW11 1DT

Based on the English text of
PONS Fachwörterbuch der Kfz-Technik (englisch-deutsch)
published by Ernst Klett Verlag in Germany
© Copyright Ernst Klett Verlag & Peter Collin Publishing Ltd 1996

British Library Cataloguing in Publication Data
A catalogue record for this book is available from the British Library
ISBN 0-948549-66-1

Text computer typeset by Tradespools Ltd, Frome, Somerset
Printed in Finland by WSOY, Finland
Cover design by Gary Weston

DICTIONARY OF
AUTOMOBILE
ENGINEERING

LIBRARY
RUGBY COLLEGE

WITHDRAWN

Titles in the series

(see back of this book for full title list and information request form)

Also Available

Workbooks for teachers and students of specialist English:

Check your

PREFACE

This dictionary aims to provide the basic vocabulary of terms used in the motor vehicle industry, covering not only bodywork, engines, electrical parts, fuels but also general terms used in vehicle maintenance as well as driving. American English usage is covered as well as British English.

The main words and phrases are defined in simple English, and in some cases the definitions have been expanded by explanatory comments.

Number Compounds

+ve plate *noun* = POSITIVE PLATE

-ve plate *noun* = NEGATIVE PLATE

12-point *noun* = BIHEXAGON

12-point socket *noun* socket of a spanner or wrench to fit a standard hexagon nut or bolt head (NOTE: also called **bihexagon socket)**

12-valve (engine) *noun* three-cylinder engine with four valves per cylinder (e.g. Daihatsu), or a six-cylinder engine with two valves per cylinder, or a four-cylinder engine with three valves per cylinder, i.e. two inlet valves and one exhaust valve

13-inch wheel *noun* wheel with a rim 13 inches in diameter

13-way connector *noun* electrical connection between the towing vehicle and a trailer or caravan with 13 contacts

16-valve (engine) *or* **16V** *noun* four-cylinder engine with four valves per cylinder; *(compare* FOUR-VALVE)

1P rim *noun* = ONE-PIECE RIM

2-point (seat) belt *noun* seat belt fastened at two locations, usually a lap belt

2-star petrol *noun* lowest petrol grade (no longer available) (NOTE: also called **regular)**

20-valve (engine) *noun* five-cylinder engine, as used by Audi, with four valves per cylinder

3+O *noun* three-speed gearbox with overdrive

3-panel panoramic mirror *noun* rearview mirror with two convex-glass outer panels to eliminate blind spots on right- and left-hand sides

3-point static belt *noun* 3-point seat belt without automatic belt retractor, now obsolete

3-point (seat) belt *noun* combined lap-shoulder belt fastened at three points, usually with an automatic retractor; *(compare* 2-POINT (SEAT) BELT)

3-star petrol *noun* intermediate petrol grade (no longer available)

4+O *noun* four-speed gearbox with overdrive

4-arm wheel nut wrench *noun* a cross-shaped tool with sockets for four different sizes of wheel nut at the ends of its arms (NOTE: US English is **4-way lug wrench)**

4-star (petrol) *noun* premium petrol grade, leaded and usually 98 octane

4-way lug wrench *noun* US = 4-ARM WHEEL NUT WRENCH

4wd *or* **4WD** *adjective & noun* = FOUR-WHEEL DRIVE

4x2 *noun & adjective* = TWO-WHEEL DRIVE

4x4 *noun & adjective* = FOUR-WHEEL DRIVE

5-star (petrol) *noun* top petrol grade, leaded and 100 octane (not often available)

50K (certification) test *noun* catalyst durability test, which involves the selection of a representative fleet of vehicles with EPA approval and the successful completion of

50,000 miles within the set emission standards and with a very well-defined service procedure

COMMENT: the test is preceded by a prognosis to ensure an 80% likelihood of meeting the emission standards at 50,000 miles, based on the emission levels at 4,000 and 5,000 miles

7-pin socket *noun* socket for the electrical connection between the towing vehicle and a trailer or caravan with 7 contacts

Aa

A = AMPERE

AA = AUTOMOBILE ASSOCIATION

AAA = AMERICAN AUTOMOBILE ASSOCIATION

A-arm *noun US* = WISHBONE

abrasion *noun* removal of surface material from any solid, through frictional action

◊ **abrasive** *noun* substance used for the removal of matter; **abrasive cleaner** = cleaner which removes a certain amount of the surface; **abrasive disc** = rotating disc of a sanding or grinding tool; **abrasive paper** = paper with a rough surface for the removal of matter

ABS = ANTI-LOCK BRAKING SYSTEM; **ABS override button** = button which cuts out the anti-lock braking system, for drivers who want to take threshold braking into their own hands; **ABS relay valve** = electrically operated valve controlling the air pressure in an ABS system

abut *verb* to make contact, especially of gear teeth

◊ **abutment** *noun* **(a)** part which another part comes up against so that its motion is stopped; a more formal word for 'stop' **(b)** making of contact, especially by gear teeth; **when tooth-to-tooth abutment occurs** = when gear teeth make contact

◊ **abutting edge** *noun* edge of a panel where it joins another, i.e. near spot-weld joints

COMMENT: the panels must be flat one on top of another, and the edges are often smoothed with hard solder

AC = ALTERNATING CURRENT

a/c = AIR-CONDITIONING

A/C (dimensions) *noun* width across the corners (of a hexagon, square drive, etc.)

ACC = ACCELERATE (NOTE: used mostly on cruise controls)

accelerate *verb* to go faster or make faster *the car accelerated to 50 mph* (NOTE: opposite is **decelerate**); **accelerated test procedure** = test which has been made quicker, by leaving out or shortening certain items; **accelerating agent** = ACCELERATOR (a)

◊ **acceleration** *noun* increase of speed; **the car has brisk acceleration from 0 to 50** = the car can increase its speed quickly from a standing start to 50 mph; **sluggish acceleration** = increasing speed slowly; **acceleration enrichment** = providing a richer fuel/air mixture during acceleration, when a richer mixture is needed to provide extra power and a smooth response (NOTE: opposite is **deceleration**)

◊ **accelerator** *noun* **(a)** chemical agent which makes a reaction happen more quickly, for instance in plastics production an additive which promotes the hardening process of resins (NOTE: opposite is **retarder**) **(b)** pedal which controls the opening of the throttle (NOTE: US English is **gas pedal**); **depress the accelerator** *or* (*informal*) **step on the accelerator** = cause the throttle to open to make the vehicle go faster; **ease up on the accelerator** = reduce the throttle opening to go less fast; **take one's foot off the accelerator** = close the throttle in order to slow down (NOTE: also called **accelerator pedal** *or* **throttle pedal**); **accelerator interlock** = connection between the accelerator pedal and the automatic transmission; **accelerator pedal** = ACCELERATOR (b); **accelerator pump** = carburettor device that improves acceleration by injecting an additional amount of fuel when the accelerator pedal is depressed; *(see illustration 11)*

acceptance test *noun* test of a part or assembly for acceptable quality

access *noun* means of reaching something *access to the fuses is through a flap on the* *dash* **access hole** = hole through which something can be reached, also a hole through which sealant is injected into cavities

accessories *noun* additional items of equipment which can be fitted to a vehicle or used with a basic tool

accident damage *noun* damage to the bodywork of a vehicle resulting from an accident

accumulator *noun* (a) storage battery, especially for an electrically driven vehicle (b) pressure reservoir for a suspension system with automatic levelling (c) part of a hydraulic system which is charged by the fluid pump, absorbs fluctuating fluid delivery, stores fluid at pressure, and can provide a rapid flow of fluid under pressure

| COMMENT: in the hydraulic control system of an automatic transmission, accumulators are used to delay the pressure build-up in the application of a brake band or clutch to make the operation smoother

accumulator battery *noun* = STORAGE BATTERY

◊ **accumulator-drier** *noun* device on the low side of an air-conditioning system, usually at the evaporator outlet on the bulkhead which stores excess refrigerant and removes moisture from the refrigerant; it consists of a tank, a filter, a drying agent and a vapour return tube; *(compare* RECEIVER-DRIER) *(see illustrations 34, 35)*

◊ **accumulator system** *noun* system in an automatic transmission comprising a hydraulic accumulator controlled by a valve, and a running time throttle

◊ **accumulator valve** *noun* valve controlling a hydraulic accumulator

AC generator *noun* = ALTERNATOR

acid rain *noun* rain containing pollutants from industrial waste and vehicle exhaust gases dissolved in the atmosphere

Ackermann steering *noun* form of double-pivot steering in which the front wheels turn on kingpins and are connected by inclined steering arms and a track rod, so arranged that the inner wheel turns through a greater angle than the outer; **Ackermann angle** = toe-out or toe-in with the wheels in the straight-ahead position; **Ackermann axle**

= fixed-position, steerable front axle with two pivot points, one on each end of the axle, with vertical kingpins

| COMMENT: the projected centrelines of the inclined steering arms meet in the centre of the vehicle, in line with the rear-axle centreline; this is the Ackermann steering centre

across corners = A/C

◊ **across flats** = A/F

acrylate *noun* polymer, such as ethyl acrylate, used in rubber toughening

acrylic (paint) *noun* paint with pigments mixed in a solution based on acrylic resin; **acrylic finish** = finish using acrylic paints, often a two-pack finish; **acrylic resin** = any thermoplastic synthetic polymer made by the polymerization of acrylic derivatives such as acrylic acid, ethyl acrylate, and methacrylate, used for adhesives, protective coatings, and finishes

ACT = AIR CHARGE TEMPERATURE

activated carbon *noun* highly porous carbon, usually in pellet form, granular, or powdered, characterized by fine pores resulting in a very large surface area per unit volume, hence able to adsorb gases, fluids, etc. (NOTE: also called **activated charcoal**); **activated carbon canister** = filter which adsorbs fuel vapours from the tank and fuel system when the engine is not running, and when the engine is running is regenerated by purging the charcoal bed with hot air, using engine vacuum to draw the released vapours into the intake air stream

| COMMENT: typically, the activated carbon canister or filter is mounted on the side of the engine bay and contains about 600 grams of activated carbon; three hoses are attached to it, one leading to the fuel tank, the other two to the carburettor

activated charcoal *noun* = ACTIVATED CARBON; **activated charcoal trap** = ACTIVATED CARBON CANISTER

◊ **activator** *noun* material or mixture added to an accelerated curing system to enhance the effect of the vulcanization accelerator in tyre production

◊ **active braking time** *noun* time required to come to a standstill after the brakes have been applied, i.e. not including the driver's reaction time

◊ **active noise control (system)**
noun = ANTI-NOISE SYSTEM

◊ **active safety** *noun* active measures
taken to prevent accidents, such as more
powerful brakes and safer handling
characteristics (NOTE: opposite is **passive
safety**)

◊ **active suspension** *noun* suspension
system which uses microprocessors to control
electronically adjustable shock absorbers
which adapt automatically to the road surface
and load

actuate *verb* to bring a part into operation;
the valve is actuated pneumatically = the
valve is made to move by air pressure; **an
actuating lever** *or* **switch** = a lever or switch
which brings a part into operation

◊ **actuator** *noun* controlling or operating
device, e.g. a vacuum mechanism for opening
flaps in air-conditioning systems; **actuator
arm** = arm connecting the diaphragm to the
contact breaker platform in a vacuum advance
mechanism (NOTE: also called **diaphragm
link**)

adapter *or* **adaptor** *noun* device for
connecting two parts of different sizes,
especially an accessory for joining a socket
and a drive handle with different size drives;
adapter plate = plate which allows the
mounting of a different part from the original;
(*compare* TRANSFER PLATE)

additive *noun* substance added to fuel or
engine oil to enhance its performance and to
improve its properties, such as upper cylinder
lubricant

adhere *verb* to remain attached or stick (to
something) *the two layers of paint must
adhere to one another; a film of lubricant
adheres to the surface of the bearing*

◊ **adhesion** *noun* ability to remain
attached (to something), especially the ability
of a tyre to grip the road surface *we must
improve the adhesion of the top coat to the
primer; aquaplaning causes loss of
adhesion between the tyre and the road*

◊ **adhesive** *noun* substance used to join
together two or more solids so that they form a
single piece, such as resins, formaldehyde,
glue, cement, etc. *two-pack epoxy-based
adhesives can form a strong bond* **adhesive
bonding** = joining together of two or more
solids by the use of glue, cement, or other
adhesives; **adhesive tape** = sticky tape
usually with one shiny side and one side

coated with adhesive; **adhesive weight** = a
small lead weight used to balance a wheel
*adhesive weights are stuck onto the wheel
rim opposite a heavy area (compare
CLIP-ON WEIGHT)*

adiabatic *adjective* neither losing nor
gaining heat, therefore thermally efficient;
adiabatic engine = engine which makes the
best use of combustion heat by reducing heat
loss due to coolant

adjust *verb* to put (something) into the
correct position; **adjust the ignition timing** =
cause the spark to occur at the correct moment

◊ **adjustable** *adjective* that can be
changed or made different *a steering wheel
adjustable for height or a height-adjustable
steering wheel* **adjustable shock absorber** =
shock absorber which can be made harder or
softer; **adjustable spanner** = open-ended
spanner with a single smooth jaw that can be
adjusted to fit nuts and bolts of different sizes
(NOTE: also called **monkey wrench**)

◊ **adjuster** *noun* device for moving
something into a different or the correct
position; **seat adjuster** = mechanism for
moving a seat backwards and forwards;
adjuster cam = cam in a drum brake which
acts on the shoes to take up the adjustment,
i.e. bring the shoes closer to the drum

◊ **adjusting gauge** *noun* tool such as a
feeler gauge used to check distances and
clearances between parts for adjustment
purposes; **adjusting screw** = screw for
altering e.g. the idling speed of the engine or
for brake adjustment; **adjusting shim** = shim
for reducing clearances especially in
adjusting valve tappets; **adjusting sleeve** =
sleeve on the end of the tie rod which shortens
or lengthens it to increase or reduce toe-out

◊ **adjustment** *noun* **(a)** altering or
correcting the position of something or the
position or value achieved *the correct
mixture can be obtained by a simple
adjustment; pinking usually means that the
adjustment of the ignition is wrong* **(b)**
possibility of altering or correcting the
position of something; clearance or play;
there is no adjustment left = the adjusting
screw or nut is at the end of its travel; **to take
up the adjustment** = to obtain the correct
position, usually by reducing a clearance

A-drier *noun* paint drier with heating
elements below the stoving line

COMMENT: with the new A-driers the
bodywork no longer passes through the oven
on the same level as the entry and exit, but

rather two storeys higher. The hot air accumulates at the top and can no longer escape as was previously the case

adsorption *noun* bonding of a solid with a gas or vapour which touches its surface (NOTE: opposite is **desorption**)

◊ **adsorption canister** *noun* = ACTIVATED CARBON CANISTER

advance 1 *verb* to cause (something) to occur earlier; **to advance the spark** *or* **ignition** *or* **timing** = to cause the spark and therefore combustion to occur earlier **2** *noun* extent to which the ignition spark is made to occur earlier; **the ignition needs more advance** = the spark is occurring too late (NOTE: opposite is **retard**)

◊ **advance capsule** *noun* = VACUUM ADVANCE (UNIT)

◊ **advance curve** *noun* curve showing how the amount of ignition advance increases with the speed of the engine and/or the vacuum in the inlet manifold

◊ **advanced** *adjective* **(a)** *(of ignition)* occurring early; **the ignition is (over-) advanced** = the spark is occurring (too) early (NOTE: opposite is **retarded**) **(b)** *(of product, design)* incorporating new ideas, in line with the latest thinking

◊ **advance weight** *noun* either of the two weights in a centrifugal advance mechanism

aeration *noun* foaming due to the introduction of air into hydraulic fluid or the oil of a shock absorber

aerial *noun* long metal tube for receiving radio signals (NOTE: US English is **antenna**)

aerodynamic *adjective* (i) relating to the flow of air round a moving body; (ii) *(of a car, bodywork, etc.)* streamlined, offering low wind resistance **the new XYZ has aerodynamic lines** *or* **a good aerodynamic shape** **a high level of aerodynamic noise** = a lot of noise caused by wind resistance of body parts

◊ **aerodynamics** *noun* **(a)** branch of dynamics dealing with the motion of air and with the forces acting on bodies moving through the air **(b)** aerodynamic properties; **the poor aerodynamics of early cars resulted in wastage of power** = early cars had too much wind resistance which wasted power (NOTE: sense (a) is singular, sense (b) is plural)

aerofoil *noun* wing-like structure, used on racing cars to achieve negative lift or downforce

A/F = AIR/FUEL; **three-way catalytic converters demand close A/F control** = the air/fuel mixture has to be carefully controlled when using three-way catalytic converters

A/F (dimensions) *noun* width across the flats (of a hexagon, square drive, etc.)

A-frame *noun* A-shaped chassis frame, typically of a trailer or caravan

afterburning *noun* completion of the combustion of incompletely burnt mixture in the exhaust system; **CO and HC levels can be reduced by afterburning** = emissions of carbon monoxide and hydrocarbons can be reduced by burning incompletely burnt mixture

aftercooler *noun* heat exchanger in a diesel engine which cools the intake of air before it enters the cylinders

COMMENT: in tandem turbocharger systems, an aftercooler may be used to cool the air between the second stage turbocharger and engine, in addition to an intercooler between the first stage turbocharger and second stage turbocharger

aftermarket 1 *noun* sale of accessories and spare parts after a vehicle has been purchased **2** *adjective* sold after a vehicle has been purchased; **aftermarket equipment** = accessories and fittings added by the vehicle's buyer; **aftermarket overdrive** = overdrive fitted subsequently and not as original equipment; **aftermarket rustproofing** = rustproofing undertaken by the buyer, not by the manufacturer

after-start enrichment *noun* enrichment of the air/fuel mixture on starting the engine, especially in electronic fuel injection systems, regulated by the electronic control unit; it is reduced either at a fixed rate or as engine temperature increases

aged catalyst *noun* catalyst which has been used (NOTE: opposite is **fresh catalyst**)

◊ **age-hardening** *noun* hardening of aluminium or metal alloys as a result of ageing

◊ **ageing** *noun* a change of characteristics in some metals after heat treatment or cold working

aggressive agent or **medium** noun corrosive material which attacks metals

agitation cup noun type of paint pot for spray guns fitted with an integral agitator

◊ **agitator** noun device for mixing paint by shaking

a.h. = AMPERE-HOUR

AH rim noun rim design able to run with a flat tyre and with increased safety in case of sudden air loss

COMMENT: a double hump of variable cross section along the bead seat prevents the tyre beads from sliding into the rim well, which is particularly important when cornering, when lateral forces try to dislodge the tyre bead

aimer noun tool for aiming headlights

◊ **aiming** noun adjusting the direction of headlight beams; **aiming screw** = screw for aiming headlights

air noun mixture of gases forming the atmosphere; **put some air in the tyres** = inflate the tyres; **there is too much air in the mixture** = the mixture is too weak

air bag noun bag in the fascia region which inflates on impact and thus saves the occupants of the vehicle from injury caused by being thrown against the interior structure in a collision; **air bag module** or **unit** = the air bag plus inflator and cover; **air bag restraint system** = system using an air bag to restrain occupants in a collision (NOTE: this is also called a **passive restraint system**)

COMMENT: the air bag is usually made of polyamide fabric, sometimes coated with neoprene on the inside, but this coating is omitted on newer bags to facilitate recycling

air bellows noun rubber vessel or sleeve filled with compressed gas or air to act as a compression spring in air suspensions

◊ **air brake** noun brake mechanism in which compressed air acting on a piston or diaphragm is used to apply the brakes; mainly found in commercial vehicles

◊ **airbrush** noun precision spray gun for detailing and custom paintwork

◊ **air charge temperature (ACT)** noun temperature of the air sucked into the carburettor or fuel injection system

◊ **air cleaner** noun = AIR FILTER

◊ **air compressor** noun device for supplying compressed air, e.g. for paint spraying or in an air brake system

◊ **air-conditioned** adjective provided with air-conditioning **we drove through the desert in air-conditioned comfort**

air-conditioning noun system of filtering air and keeping it at a desirable temperature and humidity level; (see illustration 35)

COMMENT: an automotive air-conditioning system cools, cleans, and dehumidifies air before the air enters, or re-enters, the passenger compartment. There are two basic types of air-conditioners: the receiver-drier type and the accumulator type, and their major components are: compressor, condenser, evaporator and receiver-drier or accumulator. Operation of an air-conditioning system (specifically of the compressor) consumes engine power and increases fuel consumption

air-cooled adjective cooled by a current of air as opposed to water, etc. **finning is used in air-cooled engines to help dissipate the heat generated by combustion** (NOTE: opposite is liquid-cooled)

◊ **air correction jet** noun jet admitting air into the emulsion tube of a carburettor; (see illustration 11)

◊ **air cushion** noun = AIR BAG

◊ **air dam** noun spoiler under the front bumper to reduce wind resistance

◊ **air deflector** noun US = AIR SHIELD

◊ **air duct** noun any passage conducting air, particularly for heating and ventilation; (see illustration 34)

◊ **air filter** noun device for filtering dust and dirt out of the air drawn into the carburettor or fuel injection system through the air intake; (see illustration 3); **air filter element** = element of absorbent paper or felt inserted into the air filter, which catches dirt and dust in the air drawn into the engine

◊ **airflow** noun flow of air past a moving object, especially a vehicle, or through a duct **items projecting into the airflow increase wind resistance** (see illustration 34); **airflow sensor** = sensor in an electronically controlled fuel injection system which has a flap that is deflected by the intake air and thus governs the amount of fuel delivered; it also incorporates a temperature sensor; (see illustration 14)

air/fuel (A/F) adjective relating to the combination of air and fuel in the charge for combustion; **a lean** *or* **rich air/fuel mixture** = a mixture containing little *or* a lot of fuel in relation to air; **variations in the air/fuel ratio** = variations in the amount of fuel in relation to air, more air resulting in a lean or weak mixture, less air in a rich mixture

air gulp system *noun* system in vehicles with secondary air injection or induction, which prevents an over-rich mixture being supplied to the inlet manifold during deceleration, resulting in unburnt fuel being carried over to the hot exhaust system where it causes uncontrolled detonations

COMMENT: the air gulp system prevents these detonations by admitting fresh air to the inlet manifold during deceleration by means of a valve controlled by engine vacuum (the air gulp valve), whose vacuum signal is governed by a solenoid and a thermovalve to ensure that its action does not interfere with enrichment of the mixture when starting from cold

air hold fitting *noun* special tool for work on OHV-engines used to keep valves closed by means of air pressure

COMMENT: the air hold fitting is screwed into the sparking plug and air is applied to hold the valves in place. It allows, for example, valve seal or valve spring replacement without removing the cylinder head

air horn *noun* motor horn in which a blast of compressed air is forced through a reed

◊ **air induction** *or* **injection system** *noun* secondary air system without an air pump, using aspirator valves and the pulse air principle to introduce fresh air into the exhaust system to promote afterburning of unburnt hydrocarbons and carbon monoxide; *(see illustration 6)*; **air injection manifold** = duct inside or a tube outside the cylinder head feeding secondary air into the exhaust ports

◊ **air intake** *noun* opening through which air enters, especially for the carburettor or fuel injection system, for the radiator or for the heating and ventilating system; *(see illustration 34)*

◊ **airless spraying** *noun* spraying process in which the coating material is not atomized by a stream of air, but is subjected to high pressure, which causes it to pass through a jet or nozzle allowing it to be atomized and projected onto the surface to be coated; **airless spray gun** = spray gun used for airless spraying

◊ **air line** *noun* **(a)** pipe, hose or duct which conveys air or vacuum *disconnect the air line*

from the inlet manifold to the brake servo **(b)** compressed air supply for inflating tyres, driving compressed air tools, etc. *an air line can be used to blow the plugs dry*

◊ **air micrometer** *noun* precision control for adjusting the air quantity delivered by a spray gun

◊ **air outlet** *noun* opening from which air exits, especially for ventilation and demisting; *(see illustration 34)*

◊ **air pressure** *noun* **(a)** pressure exerted by air, e.g. on the diaphragm of a brake servo **(b)** = ATMOSPHERIC PRESSURE **(c)** = TYRE PRESSURE

air ratio *noun* air/air ratio, i.e. the ratio of the actual intake air volume to the air volume theoretically needed for complete combustion of the fuel content of the air/fuel mixture

COMMENT: the air ratio is designated by the Greek letter lambda; for an ideal or 'stoichiometric' air/fuel mixture, the air ratio lambda is 1

air receiver *noun* = AIR TANK

◊ **air scoop** *noun* air intake facing forwards on the bonnet or some other part of the bodywork for high pressure ventilation or cooling

◊ **air select valve** *noun* valve in a two-stage catalytic converter with secondary air injection, which is solenoid-operated and is triggered by the electronic control module to direct air to the exhaust valve ports or to the midbed catalytic converter, depending on operating conditions

◊ **air sensor** *noun* sensor which monitors the air quality inside the car, checks it for the presence of pollutants, and operates flaps to cut off the external air to the air conditioning system if the pollutant concentration is too high

◊ **air shield** *noun* sloping panel on the roof of a vehicle, especially a commercial vehicle or trailer, intended to improve airflow; *(see illustration 1)* (NOTE: US English is **air deflector)**

◊ **air shock absorber** *noun* shock absorber incorporating a rubber boot filled with compressed air serving as an auxiliary pneumatic spring; mainly used for level control purposes on the rear axle of a vehicle, e.g. when towing heavy trailers

◊ **air silencer** *noun* device usually incorporated in the air filter to cut out induction hiss

◇ **air spring** *noun* = AIR BELLOWS

◇ **air suspension** *noun* vehicle suspension in which air or gas in compression is the principal or only spring medium (NOTE: also called **pneumatic suspension)**

◇ **air tank** *noun* container for compressed air, especially for a compressor

◇ **air transformer** *noun* device connected between compressor and spray gun to provide clean spraying air and regulate the oil pressure

◇ **air volume** *noun* quantity of air

Al = ALUMINIUM

ALAP *(short for)* as low as possible

ALARA *(short for)* as low as reasonably achievable

alarm (system) *noun* theft protection system, which typically provides the following functions: exterior and interior protection; locking the boot and bonnet; making the ignition system inoperative

COMMENT: sensing is by contacts and motion detectors; arming and disarming is by means of key, push buttons, or remote-control transmitter; if triggered by unauthorized entry or tampering, most alarms sound the car horn or an extra siren; typically, the alarm is reset after some minutes to prevent battery drain

alarmed *adjective* protected by an alarm *even if the car is alarmed, it is not safe to leave it in this street*

Alfin *adjective* with fins of light alloy bonded to a basic steel structure after the Alfin process *Alfin brake drums; Alfin cylinder barrels (for air-cooled engines)* **Alfin process** = process to permanently bond light metal alloy to steel, initially developed by the Fairchild Engine and Airplane Corporation

al fresco driving *noun* driving in an open car with the hood down

align *verb* to bring into line or be in line (with something) *the holes must be correctly aligned before inserting the bolt; the input shaft aligns with the output shaft*

◇ **aligning punch** *noun* tool used to align holes, e.g. for inserting a screw or bolt, or to centre round components with other parts

◇ **alignment** *noun* state of being in line or act of bringing into line *check the alignment of the two shafts* **alignment mark** = mark, e.g. on a timing gear or camshaft pulley, which must be brought into line with another mark to give the correct position

alkaline battery *noun* secondary battery using an alkaline electrolyte (dilute potassium hydroxide) and used for driving electric cars

◇ **alkaline degreasing** *noun* removal of any greasy substances with an alkaline solution *alkaline degreasing and zinc phosphating are employed to give improved adhesion and corrosion protection to the paint coats*

all-alloy engine *noun* engine in which the cylinder head, block, crankcase and sump are all of light alloy

◇ **all-aluminium body** *noun* body shell made almost entirely of aluminium

Allen key *noun* key (in effect a spanner) for recessed hexagon screws and bolts, consisting of a bar with a right angle bend and six flats in the end; **Allen screw** = type of recessed hexagon screw

all-enveloping body *noun* passenger car body style generally used today, combining wings, headlamps and radiator grille into one smooth body line

COMMENT: it superseded the traditional pre-war style for popular models with separate wings and headlights shortly after World War II, being first introduced pre-war on some sports and racing cars

alligator clip *noun* US = CROCODILE CLIP

all-out braking *noun* using the maximum braking effort available; **the car loses directional stability under all-out braking** = the car tends to swerve when the brakes are applied as hard as possible

alloy *noun* **(a)** any metallic substance of various elements **(b)** any light metal, typically aluminium; **alloy piston** = piston made primarily of aluminium

alloy wheels *or (informal)* **alloys** *noun* wheels made of light alloy, mainly aluminium but also magnesium, for sports and other high-speed cars

COMMENT: the lighter weight of alloy wheels permits the use of thicker sections promoting stiffness and distributing stresses over a wider area, and also reduces the unsprung weight of a car. The increased rim width possible with alloy wheels allows the fitting of wider tyres, thus improving roadholding. Alloy castings and forgings are good conductors of heat and so disperse the heat generated by tyres and brakes more quickly than steel wheels

all-steel body *noun* body shell made almost entirely of steel, as opposed to a body with a wooden frame and panels made of steel or aluminium

◇ **all-terrain** *adjective* for use on any kind of surface; **all-terrain tyre** = tyre mainly for off-road vehicles; **all-terrain vehicle** = OFF-ROAD VEHICLE

◇ **all-weather tyre** *noun* tyre suitable for use in rain and on snowy or icy roads as well as in warm and dry conditions

◇ **all-wheel drive** *noun & adjective* = FOUR-WHEEL DRIVE; **all-wheel steering** = = FOUR-WHEEL STEERING

alternating current (AC) *noun* a continuous electric current that periodically reverses direction (NOTE: opposite is **direct current**)

alternator (ALT) *noun* generator which produces three-phase alternating current inside its stator windings; *(see illustration 3)*; **alternator charging light** = warning light on the instrument panel, which comes on when the alternator is not charging

COMMENT: as the car's electrical system requires a DC supply (to charge the battery), the alternator includes diodes to convert the AC to DC. With the ignition switched on and the engine not running, the alternator charging light comes on because current is being drawn from the battery; it will go out when the engine is started as long as the alternator is working. If it does come on when the engine is running, it means that either the alternator or its drive belt has failed

altimeter *noun* instrument showing height above sea level

alumina *noun* form of aluminium oxide used as substrate for ceramic catalysts; **alumina beads** = tiny beads of alumina used in some catalytic converters

aluminium (Al) *US* **aluminum** *noun* silvery lightweight metallic element resistant to corrosion; **aluminium alloy** = metal containing aluminium mixed with another metal or metals; **aluminium wheel** = ALLOY WHEEL

◇ **aluminized** *adjective* coated with aluminium or aluminium paint

◇ **aluminum** *noun US* = ALUMINIUM

AM = AMPLITUDE MODULATION

ambient air *noun* air outside and surrounding the vehicle

◇ **ambient temperature** *noun* outside temperature; **ambient temperature switch** = switch which delays compressor action in an air-conditioning system when the outside temperature is low

ambulance *noun* vehicle designed for carrying sick or injured people *he was taken to hospital in an ambulance*

ammeter *noun* instrument for measuring (in amperes) the electrical current flow in a circuit

amp = AMPERE

amperage (rating) *noun* strength of an electric current in amperes, used e.g. for marking fuses *when replacing a burnt fuse, use only a fuse of the correct amperage*

◇ **ampere** *noun* the basic unit for measuring electric current, usually abbreviated to amp *a discharge of 3 amp (ere)s*

◇ **ampere-hour (a.h.)** *noun* unit of the quantity of electricity flowing in one hour through a conductor carrying a current of 1 ampere; **a 36 a.h. battery** = a battery with a capacity of 36 ampere-hours; **ampere-hour capacity** = quantity of electricity which a battery can deliver under given conditions such as temperature, rate of discharge, and final voltage, depending on the number of plates used

amplifier *noun* device used to produce a larger electrical signal, as to amplify sound signals in radios, etc.; **ignition amplifier** = device used to increase the electrical signal in an electronic ignition system

COMMENT: in car stereo systems, the amplifier is usually built into the integrated radio-cassette and/or CD player. Only very high-power systems have separate amplifiers, which are usually installed in the boot

amplitude modulation (AM) *noun* form of radio transmission in which the frequency of the carrier wave is unchanged, but its amplitude varies in accordance with the input signal

analogue cluster *noun* instrument panel display using dials and numbers (NOTE: opposite is **electronic cluster)**

analyzer *see* ENGINE ANALYZER

ANC *(short for)* at no extra cost

anchorage *noun* fixing point for a seat belt, seat or other stress-bearing item which is not part of the structure

anchor bolt *noun* = THROUGH BOLT

ancillaries *noun* components placed close to or fitted on the engine, such as alternator, power steering pump, supercharger, fuel pump and water pump, and driven by the engine

COMMENT: driving the ancillaries consumes engine power; the additional power required to drive the ancillaries is roughly equal to the difference between SAE and DIN horsepower specifications

aneroid-type thermostat *noun* thermostat consisting of a metallic bellows partially filled with acetone, alcohol or similar volatile liquid

COMMENT: when the coolant surrounding the bellows reaches the operating temperature of the engine (typically 80-90°C) the liquid will boil, evaporate, and expand the bellows, which opens the valve which admits coolant to the radiator. This type of thermostat is not adequate for pressurized coolant systems, as system pressure counteracts the expansion of the bellows; the more usual kind is the wax-type thermostat

angle grinder *noun* power tool (either electric or driven by compressed air) with abrasive discs, especially for removing old paintwork and smoothing the surface prior to spraying

◊ **angle-nose pliers** *noun* pliers with jaws having a right-angle bend, for gripping e.g. items in a recess, etc.

◊ **angle of lock** *noun* angle between the line through the centre of a wheel seen from above when taking a corner and the same line when going straight

◊ **angle parking** *noun* parking at an angle to the pavement or parking line (NOTE: also called **echelon parking)**

◊ **angle screwdriver** *noun* screwdriver usually having two blades at either end, both at right angles to the shank

◊ **angular motion** *noun* = ROTATION

anisotropy *noun* having different mechanical properties when measured in different directions

anneal *verb* to treat (a metal, alloy, or glass) with heat and then cool it to remove internal stresses and to make the material less brittle

◊ **annealing furnace** *noun* oven or furnace with controllable atmosphere in which metal, an alloy, or glass is annealed

annular *adjective* in the form of a ring; **annular gap** = circular gap

◊ **annulus (gear)** *noun* hollow gearwheel in the form of a ring with either internal teeth, as in epicyclic or planetary transmissions, or external teeth

anode *noun* positive electrode in an electrolytic cell

◊ **anodic coating** *or* **film** *or* **oxide layer** *noun* protective, decorative, or functional coating, formed in an anodizing process

◊ **anodize** *verb* to deposit a hard, non-corroding oxide layer on (aluminium or light alloy)

◊ **anodizing** *noun* process by which a hard, non-corroding oxide layer is deposited on aluminium or light alloys; **anodizing bath** *or* **tank** = tank in which the anodizing process is performed

ANS = ANTI-NOISE SYSTEM

ANSI *(short for)* American National Standards Institute

antenna *noun US* aerial

anti-chip coating *noun* resilient intermediate coat between the primer and the top coat, applied to protect the body shell from chipping damage caused by gravel or stones; **anti-chipping primer** *or* **filler** = a resilient primer protecting the paintwork from chipping caused by gravel or stones

◊ **anti-corrosion** *adjective* combating and protecting against corrosion, especially rust *anti-corrosion agent* or *material* or *primer* or *system* or *treatment* anti-corrosion warranty = a warranty, usually limited to corrosion damage, valid for an average of 6 years

◊ **anti-corrosive** *adjective* inhibiting corrosion

◊ **anti-dazzle mirror** *noun* = DIPPING MIRROR

◊ **anti-dive (system)** *noun* front suspension arrangement that converts the downward force in the suspension links caused by braking into a vertical force that tends to lift the body, thus reducing dive under braking

◊ **anti-drum compound** *noun* sticky material, usually based on bitumen or rubber, applied to the inside of panels to reduce noise due to vibration or 'drumming'

antifreeze *noun* chemical, such as ethylene glycol, added to the cooling water of an engine to lower its freezing point

| COMMENT: nowadays antifreeze is kept in the engine's cooling system all year round and also contains inhibitors for protection against corrosion

antifriction bearing *noun* any bearing supporting its load on rolling surfaces, such as balls, rollers or needles, to minimize friction

anti-knock additive or **agent** *noun* petrol additive preventing premature ignition (i.e. knocking or pinking) of the mixture in the combustion chamber, e.g. tetraethyl lead or tetramethyl lead; **anti-knock index** = measure of the anti-knock properties of a petrol, particularly in North America, where it is defined as half the sum of the research octane number and motor octane number; *(compare* MON, RON)

| COMMENT: supercharged engines sometimes use water (in the form of spray or steam) or water-alcohol as an anti-knock agent

anti-lock brakes or **anti-lock (braking) system (ABS)** *noun* system installed with the brakes to prevent the wheels locking during heavy braking

anti-noise system (ANS) *noun* electronic noise attenuation system

| COMMENT: a microprocessor analyzes the driving noise in the car interior and, when certain limits are exceeded, generates the

precisely matching counter-frequencies of the noise and distributes the resulting 'anti-noise' through micro-loudspeakers into the car interior, thereby erasing the original noise

anti-rattle spring *noun* = SPREADER SPRING

◊ **anti-roll bar** *noun* steel torsion bar running across the car as part of the front and, less frequently, rear suspension layout and used to reduce body roll during cornering; *(see illustrations 27, 28)* (NOTE: not to be confused with **roll bar**, a safety feature in case the car rolls over. Note also US English is **anti-sway bar**)

◊ **anti-rust treatment** *noun* treatment of iron and steel, i.e. using sealants, for the purpose of corrosion protection (NOTE: also called **rustproofing**)

◊ **anti-skid braking system (ASBS)** *noun* = ANTI-LOCK (BRAKING) SYSTEM

◊ **anti-spin regulation (ASR)** *noun* control or prevention of wheelspin under power, normally by means of electronic sensing and in conjunction with anti-lock braking *ASR traction control system also called* ASC

◊ **anti-spray flap** *noun* = MUDFLAP

◊ **anti-squat system** *noun* rear suspension arrangement that converts the downward force caused by acceleration into a vertical force that tends to lift the rear body, thus reducing 'squat' under acceleration; *(compare* ANTI-DIVE SYSTEM)

◊ **anti-squeal shim** *noun* shim placed behind the brake piston (or behind the brake pad in disc brakes) to reduce squeal

◊ **anti-sway bar** *noun US* = ANTI-ROLL BAR

◊ **anti-theft (security) system** *noun* either an alarm system, or an additional locking device (especially for the steering wheel), or an electric circuit immobilizing the car by disconnecting the starter and/or ignition

◊ **anti-vibration mounting** *noun* flexible (typically rubber) mounting for an engine, gearbox or other mechanical item, that reduces the amount of noise and vibration passed from the item in question to the chassis

anvil *noun* (a) heavy iron block on which something is placed for forging (b) lower wheel of a wheeling machine

A-panel *noun* side panel, typically on the BMC Mini, used to bridge the gap between the rear edge of the front wing and the front edge of the doors

aperture panel *noun* large panel consisting mainly of the openings for the door(s) and window(s), usually including the rear wing; *(see illustration 1)*

apex seal *noun* sealing strip in a rotary engine which has the same gas-sealing function as a piston ring in a conventional piston engine

A-pillar *or* **A-post** *noun* upright member in front of the front door, a major structural part of the body frame

appliance *noun* = FIRE ENGINE

application *noun* **(a)** use to which something is put *the automotive applications of hydrocarbons* **(b)** putting something on(to something) *the application of primer to the bare metal*

◊ **applicator** *noun* tool for putting something onto a surface, such as a spreader for filler

◊ **apply** *verb* to put (something) on(to something) *to apply the final or top coat to the wing; zinc and cadmium can also be applied mechanically; apply some lubricant to the shaft before assembly*

apron *noun* **(a)** panel extending downwards, typically forming a skirt along the side of the car or an air dam at the front **(b)** = KICK PANEL

AQL *(short for)* acceptable quality level

aquaplaning *noun* loss of contact between the tyre and a wet road when it rides up on a layer of surface water

COMMENT: the aquaplaning phenomenon depends on vehicle speed, tyre design and condition, and the thickness of the water layer; at aquaplaning speed, the tyre can no longer disperse the water and leaves the road surface, making the brakes and steering virtually useless

aqueous solution *noun* water-based solution

arbor *noun* rotating shaft or spindle in a machine tool on which, for example, a

grinding wheel or a piece for machining is fitted

arc *verb* to jump across a gap, especially of an electric current forming a discharge *the spark arcs from one electrode to the other*

arch *noun* = WHEEL ARCH

arcing *noun* **(a)** sparking and discharge at the contact breaker points in the distributor, a cause of premature wear of the points **(b)** faulty spraying technique where the spray gun is not moved along the panel surface at a uniform distance, but is moved towards the panel when starting and is moved away again towards the end of the panel; this results in an uneven thickness of paint being applied

arc welding *noun* welding process widely used for do-it-yourself repairs (as the required equipment is fairly cheap) in which the welding current is generated by a transformer, and the circuit is closed when the electrode held in the welding rod holder touches the metal surface; the electrode burns off as the rod holder is moved along

armature *noun* **(a)** coil or coils of wire around a metal core in which electric current is induced in a generator, or in which the input current interacts with a magnetic field to produce torque in a motor; *(see illustration 37)* **(b)** movable part of an electromagnetic device, e.g. the movable iron part of a relay

◊ **armature brake** *noun* mechanical or electrical component in a starter used to stop armature movement after the starter motor has been switched off

◊ **armature shaft** *noun* shaft on which the armature is mounted in a starter or generator; *(see illustration 37)*

armour-plated *adjective* made bullet-proof, e.g. with extra-thick body panels and glass

armrest *noun* projection on the door (or the side of the car at the rear) to support the passenger's or driver's arm; in some luxury cars one is also provided in the centre of the rear seat

articulated *adjective* made in two separate sections, with a joint or coupling between them; especially of commercial vehicles consisting of a tractor or towing unit and a trailer, having a swivelling coupling giving better manoeuvrability *articulated lorry* **articulated bus** = bus in two sections, usually a single-decker, with passenger accommodation in both sections

asbestos-free *adjective* containing no asbestos; used especially of brake and clutch linings

ASBS = ANTI-SKID BRAKING SYSTEM

ASC *see* ANTI-SPIN REGULATION

ascending stroke *noun* = UP-STROKE

ASD = AUTOMATIC SLIP-CONTROL DIFFERENTIAL

ash frame *noun* body frame of ash timber which is covered with aluminium panels in a traditional style of body manufacture

aspect ratio *noun* ratio between the height and the width (e.g. of a tyre)

aspiration *noun* sucking in of the air/fuel mixture or breathing process of an internal combustion engine

aspirator valve *noun* check valve in air induction systems

COMMENT: this works according to the pulse air principle: opening when exhaust pressure is lower than the pressure in the air cleaner, allowing fresh air to be introduced into the exhaust stream; when exhaust pressure is higher than intake pressure, the valve closes, preventing the flow of exhaust gas back into the intake system

ASR = ANTI-SPIN REGULATION

assemble *verb* to put together or build up (something) from a number of parts; **assembled crankshaft** = built-up crankshaft

◊ **assembly** *noun* the process or result of putting together a number of components; **assembly line** = production line where a vehicle is progressively built up from its individual components

◊ **assy** *(short for)* assembly

ASTM *(short for)* American Society for Testing and Materials

asymmetric(al) *adjective* not having parts that correspond, not uniform (especially in distribution); **asymmetrical beam** = a headlight beam which has greater intensity on one side than the other; **asymmetric power distribution** *or* **split** = transmitting more power to the front or rear wheels in a four-wheel drive; **asymmetric rim** = wheel rim where the well is located outside the centreline of the wheel (NOTE: opposite is **symmetric rim**)

ATC = AUTOMATIC TEMPERATURE CONTROL

ATDC *(short for)* after top dead centre; *(see* TOP DEAD CENTRE)

ATE = AUTOMATIC TEST EQUIPMENT

ATF = AUTOMATIC TRANSMISSION FLUID

atmospheric corrosion *noun* gradual destruction or alteration of metals or alloys by contact with substances present in the atmosphere, such as oxygen, carbon dioxide, water vapour, and sulphur and chlorine compounds

◊ **atmospheric pressure** *noun* pressure exerted by the atmosphere at the earth's surface

atomize *verb* to produce a fine spray, e.g. of paint

◊ **atomizer** *noun* device for producing a fine spray, e.g. on a spray gun

◊ **atomizing pressure** *noun* pressure needed to atomize a liquid such as a paint

atramentizing *noun* corrosion protection process in which steel is coated with phosphate using a zinc phosphate solution at 90°C

attachment *noun* a fitting or accessory to be used in conjunction with a tool, such as a grinding disc for use with an electric drill *there is a special attachment for grinding in valves*

attack 1 *noun* example of corrosion or another damaging, especially chemical, action *a direct chemical attack on the metal surface* **2** *verb* to damage, especially by corrosion *road salt attacks the underbody*

◊ **attack angle** *noun* angle of a rear spoiler at which it is effective against lift

attendant parking *noun* parking supervised by an attendant

attenuation *noun* reduction, especially of noise or emissions

attrition *noun* process of wearing out by friction, as with pellets in catalytic converters *attrition severely reduces the useful service life of pellet-type converters*

ATV = ALL-TERRAIN VEHICLE

authorized dealer *noun* firm selling and servicing a particular make of vehicle, appointed by the manufacturer *contact your nearest XYZ authorized dealer for a test drive*

auto 1 *noun & adjective* = AUTOMATIC **2** *noun US* = AUTOMOBILE; **auto bonnet** = car cap

◊ **autochoke** *noun* = AUTOMATIC CHOKE

autoclave *noun* sealable high-pressure container used for polymerisation and in tyre production

autocycle *noun* form of light motorcycle with a small engine and pedals for starting and assisting the engine on hills; now obsolete having been superseded by the moped

autojumble *noun* bazaar-type sale of secondhand parts for old cars and especially classic and vintage cars, with stalls mostly rented by private enthusiasts, and often held in the open

COMMENT: the biggest such event in Europe is the Beaulieu (pronounced 'byoolee') Autojumble at the National Motor Museum in southern England

automatic 1 *noun* colloquial short form for automatic transmission, or a car with automatic transmission (NOTE: opposite is **manual) 2** *adjective* performing an operation by itself; **automatic advance (mechanism)** = mechanism which adjusts the advance either by means of centrifugal weights or of a diaphragm controlled by inlet manifold vacuum; **automatic air-conditioning (system)** = air-conditioning system which

automatically maintains a preset temperature; **automatic air-recirculation (control) system** = heating and ventilation subsystem which automatically switches to the recirculation mode when the pollutant levels of the air inside the vehicle exceed certain levels (e.g. in rush-hour nose-to-tail traffic), but after a certain period of recirculation (typically after 3 minutes), opens the intake air doors again to let some fresh air in, even if its quality is still questionable; **automatic choke** = device in the carburettor intake which positions the choke valve automatically in accordance with engine temperature or time; **automatic closing system** = system which automatically closes doors, windows and sunroof; **automatic frequency control** = automatic retuning of stations on the FM waveband when subject to drift; **automatic gearbox** = gearbox in an automatic transmission system which changes gear automatically; **automatic level control** *or* **levelling system** = suspension system that automatically adjusts front and rear ride heights to compensate for changes in axle loads; this can either be achieved by adding air shock absorbers to a conventional suspension system, or by incorporating the system in a sophisticated pneumatic or hydropneumatic suspension system; **automatic muting** = car radio circuit which automatically cancels noise output during tuning; **automatic seat belt** = INERTIA REEL SEAT BELT; **automatic slip-control differential (ASD)** = electronically controlled, automatic locking differential developed by Mercedes-Benz; **automatic speed control** = CRUISE CONTROL; **automatic temperature control (ATC)** = device for maintaining a constant temperature in the vehicle interior; **automatic test equipment (ATE)** = usually electronic equipment for testing ignition, wiring, fuel injection systems, etc.

automatic transmission *noun* transmission which changes the gear ratio without assistance from the driver and without interruption of power flow, the changes being governed by factors such as engine load and vehicle road speed (although the driver usually has a manual override); **automatic transmission fluid (ATF)** = special oil used in automatic transmissions

COMMENT: typical automatic transmissions use an automatic gearbox with a torque converter and planetary gears, but there are also infinitely variable transmissions which have no gears and no gearbox, such as the Variomatic system which uses a belt and an expanding pulley

automatic volume control (AVC)
noun car radio circuit which automatically
adjusts the volume to the noise level in the car

◊ **automatic wear adjuster** *noun*
device that compensates automatically for
wear, e.g. in the brakes or clutch

◊ **automatic wire stripper** *noun* wire
stripper that automatically adjusts to the size
of the wire to be stripped and removes the
insulation without damaging the wires inside

automobile *noun* dated or formal word for
motor car in British English, but still widely
used in American English; **automobile
association** = major motoring organization,
especially the Automobile Association (AA)
in Great Britain and the American
Automobile Association (AAA) in the USA;
automobile engineering = automotive
engineering; **automobile industry** = motor
industry; **automobile manufacturer** = motor
manufacturer; **automobile mechanic** =
motor mechanic; **automobile polish** = car
polish

automotive *adjective* relating to or
occurring in motor vehicles; **automotive
adhesive** = adhesive used in the manufacture
of motor vehicles; **automotive electrician** =
electrician working on and designing systems
for motor vehicles; **automotive electronics** =
applications of modern electronics to the
motor vehicle; **automotive emissions** = all
types of release into the atmosphere from
motor vehicles, including exhaust gas, fuel
and crankcase fumes, and noise; **automotive
engineering** = the design and construction of
motor vehicles; **automotive tool** = tool for
use in the construction or repair of motor
vehicles

AUX = AUXILIARY (NOTE: an abbreviation
often used to label fuses)

auxiliary *adjective* additional,
supplementary; **auxiliary brake lights** =
additional brake lights mounted at eye level in
the rear window to reduce the risk of being
run into from behind; **auxiliary drive shaft** =
secondary drive shaft driving, for example,
the fuel or water pumps or distributor; *(see
illustration 3)*; **auxiliary driving lamp** =
lamp supplementing the light from the
headlamps, such as a fog lamp or spot lamp;
auxiliary gearbox = extra gearbox used in
conjunction with the main (manual) gearbox

to provide an additional range of speeds;
auxiliary leaf = helper leaf (in a leaf spring)

AVC = AUTOMATIC VOLUME CONTROL

average 1 *noun* mean value or rate **2** *verb*
to achieve a certain mean value or rate *he
averaged 50 mph from London to
Edinburgh* **3** *adjective* found by calculating
the mean value or rate; **average speed** *or* **fuel
consumption** = the distance covered divided
by the time taken *or* the fuel used

aviation fuel *noun* fuel suitable for aircraft

awl *noun* tool with a sharp point and a fluted
blade for piercing holes

awning *noun* roof of canvas or similar
material stretched out from e.g. a caravan for
protection from the sun and rain

axis *noun* centreline about which a body can
or could rotate, or which divides a figure into
two symmetrical parts

axle *noun* transverse bar, tube, shaft or beam
which carries wheels at either end; **axle
casing** = external, basically tubular housing
containing the differential and half-shafts and
with bearings at either end for the hubs; *US*
axle housing = AXLE CASING; **axle load** =
AXLE WEIGHT; **axle stand** = tripod which is
adjustable for height and used for supporting
the vehicle for longer jobs *when working
under the car it should be jacked up and
supported on axle stands* **axle tramp** =
rocking or oscillation of an axle under heavy
acceleration or braking due to inadequate
damping; **axle tube** = that part of the axle
casing enclosing the half-shaft, or the tube
forming a tubular rigid axle; **axle weight** =
that part of the weight of a vehicle resting on
the wheels of an axle; **axle wind-up** =
rotation of the casing of a driven axle under
torsional loads due to heavy acceleration or
braking

◊ **axle drive** *noun* **(a)** FINAL DRIVE **(b)**
ring gear and pinion inside a differential cage

◊ **axle shaft** *noun* **(a)** short shaft
connecting the differential and the drive shaft
on each side in an independent suspension
layout **(b)** drive shaft, or the half-shaft in a
rigid axle

Bb

BA *(short for)* British Association; used to designate a series of fine, small diameter threads for electrical and other precision equipment

Babbitt metal *noun* alloy of tin, copper, antimony, and lead still occasionally used for bearing surfaces

baby seat *noun* seat for babies weighing up to about 20lbs, normally installed facing backwards on the front seat and allowing a half upright seating position

BAC = BLOOD ALCOHOL CONTENT

back axle *noun* rear axle, usually on a four-wheeled vehicle *there is a whine from the back axle on the overrun* **back axle ratio** = FINAL DRIVE RATIO

backbone chassis *noun* chassis based on a single central spine carrying or containing the drive train, the body shell being mounted on outriggers

backfire 1 *noun* explosion either at the wrong time in the cylinder, or of unburnt or only partly burnt mixture in the exhaust system, causing a loud bang **2** *verb* to make a loud bang as a result of unburnt or only partly burnt mixture exploding in the exhaust system or in the cylinder

◇ **backfiring** *noun* repeated backfires in the exhaust or in the cylinder *backfiring on the overrun is often a sign of faulty timing*

backflow scavenging *noun* = LOOP SCAVENGING

backing pad *noun* rubber disc on a spindle as a support for abrasive discs, polishing or buffing mops, etc.; for use with power tools

◇ **backing plate** *noun US* = BACKPLATE

backlash *noun* excessive play in a mechanical system such as gears or linkages,

due to looseness or flexing *there is backlash in the throttle linkage*

backlight *noun US* = REAR WINDOW *US* **backlight heater or defogging system** = HEATED REAR WINDOW

◇ **back panel** *noun* = REAR PANEL

backplate *noun* fixed heavy-gauge metal plate attached to the suspension and carrying the brake shoes' and brake operating mechanism of a drum brake, or the plate carrying the brake pad in a disc brake; *(see illustration 30)* (NOTE: US English is **backing plate**)

back pressure *noun* any pressure holding back the flow of the gases in an exhaust system

backrest *noun* back of a seat

back up *verb US* = REVERSE

◇ **back-up alarm** *noun US* = REVERSING WARNING SIGNAL

◇ **back-up light** *noun US* = REVERSING LIGHT

back-voltage *noun* voltage which opposes the current when the current in an inductive circuit changes and the magnetic field cuts the conductors; **self-induction back-voltage** = back-voltage produced by self-induction; this induced electromotive force opposes the change in current, restricting it if the current is increasing and enhancing it if the current is decreasing

BAC level *noun* = BLOOD ALCOHOL LEVEL

badge *noun* typically, the maker's logo in coloured enamel on chrome plate, but can also be letters or symbols indicating a particular type or model, such as V-12, 16V, Fiesta, etc.; **badge engineering** = selling what is the same car apart from a few minor changes, mainly to the appearance, as different models with different model names

◇ **badging** *noun* provision of badges *the modern tendency is towards much more restrained badging*

baffle (plate) *noun* usually transverse steel plate reducing the flow or motion of gases or liquids, e.g. in a silencer, in the sump of an engine or in a fuel tank; *(see illustration 4)*

> COMMENT: the baffles in the sump help to prevent oil surge during fast cornering, acceleration or braking

bake *verb* to dry or cure (a paint or other finish) using heat; **baking finish** = paint that requires baking for the development of desired properties; **baking temperature** = temperature at which a varnish or paint must be baked to develop desired final properties of strength and hardness

Bakelite *noun* proprietary, hard, brittle plastic used in the early days of plastics engineering, especially for electrical parts because of its good insulating properties

balance 1 *noun* state in which weight is evenly distributed *the front wheels are out of balance/not in balance* **2** *verb* to fix weights, e.g. to the rim of a wheel or to a crankshaft in order to correct weight distribution and thus reduce vibration; **balanced crankshaft** = crankshaft with extended webs to form counterbalances or a vibration damper; **balanced engine** = engine in which all reciprocating parts such as pistons and connecting rods are adjusted to exactly the same weight

> COMMENT: in general, a wheel is out of balance if its centre of gravity and axis of rotation do not coincide. Smaller wheels must be regularly balanced since their speed of rotation is much higher than that of larger wheels

balance control *noun* knob or slide control which adjusts the level of the left and right speakers of a stereo system

◇ **balance disc** *noun* balancing device in centrifugal pumps, in the form of a disc fitted to the pump shaft, which lifts when a force is generated on the underside of the disc, leaking pressure until the axial forces are balanced

◇ **balance pipe** *noun* in a twin carburettor layout, a pipe joining the inlet

tracts or choke tubes of the two carburettors to even out differences in flow

◇ **balance shaft** *noun* additional rotating shaft in the crankcase fitted with counterweights, especially in single and twin-cylinder engines, to reduce vibration

◇ **balance weight** *noun* small lead weight fitted to the wheel rim to restore wheel balance

◇ **balancer** *noun* = WHEEL BALANCER

◇ **balancing** *noun* adjustment of incorrect and uneven weight distribution; **balancing weight** = BALANCE WEIGHT

> COMMENT: a wheel balancing machine determines the degree and the location of the wheel imbalance, which is then restored by clipping or sticking small lead weights onto the rim flange opposite a heavy portion of the wheel. An out-of-balance wheel may set up serious vibrations which can affect steering control even at moderate speeds

bald tyre *noun* tyre on which the tread is completely worn away

balk ring *noun* = BAULK RING

ball *noun* **(a)** spherical part, e.g. in a ball bearing or a ball and socket joint **(b)** = TOWBALL

◇ **ball-and-nut steering** *noun* = RECIRCULATING BALL STEERING

◇ **ball and socket (joint)** *noun* = BALL JOINT

ballast ignition system *noun* ignition system incorporating a ballast resistor connected in series with the coil primary winding and bypassed when the starter is operated, ensuring improved cold starting performance and spark efficiency; **ballast resistor** = resistor in which the resistance increases as the current passing through it increases, used in motor vehicles to control the output from the coil at high engine speeds and provide a better spark for starting

ball bearing *noun* most common type of antifriction bearing, comprising two rings or races between which hardened steel balls run in tracks, and able to absorb both axial and radial loads; **ball bearing puller** = puller for removing ball bearings that sit on a shaft and in a housing

◇ **ball cage** *noun* circular frame which holds the balls in place in a ball bearing

◊ **ball end hexagon screwdriver** *noun* screwdriver with a ball-type hexagon tip allowing it to be used at an angle of up to 30° from the screw head

◊ **ball joint** *noun* mechanical coupling in which a ball on the end of one part moves freely within a recessed spherical socket in the end of another, often used in suspension and steering linkages; **ball joint separator** = tool for forcing out ball or tapered joints, either in the form of a simple fork with wedge-shaped jaw which is struck with a hammer to separate the joint, or a tool using direct pressure from a screw or screw-activated lever action to split the joint

balloon tyre *noun* name for a low pressure tyre when introduced in the 1920s, which also had a width the same as its height, giving a generally wider section than the previous high pressure beaded edge tyres

ball peen hammer *noun* hammer with a head having one flat and one rounded end

◊ **ball socket** *noun* recessed spherical socket for receiving the ball in a ball joint

◊ **ball valve** *noun* non-return valve comprising a recessed spherical seating into which a ball fits to cover a hole, closing if the flow of liquid is reversed; *(see illustration 11)*

BAL RES = BALLAST RESISTOR

band brake *noun* brake consisting of a steel band with a friction lining passing round a drum, which contracts and grips the drum when the brake is applied

> COMMENT: in modern vehicles, band brakes are confined to planetary gear trains in automatic transmissions, where they hold individual members of the gear sets

bandwidth *noun* range of audio frequencies an audio component such as a car stereo can handle

> COMMENT: generally speaking, the wider the bandwidth or frequency range, the better the reproduction; typical car stereos feature a range of about 35-18,000 Hz

banger *noun* (*informal*) old, cheap and well-worn car, which may however still be serviceable; **banger racing** = racing beat-up old saloons from which the glass and trim has been removed on small tracks, with aggressive driving and frequent contact between the cars

banjo *noun* **(a)** type of right-angled union for a pipe or flexible hose, comprising a ring-shaped piece on the end of the pipe through which a threaded hollow bolt is passed **(b)** drum-shaped central part of an axle casing containing the differential; **banjo axle** = rear axle with a drum-shaped differential casing

bar *noun* unit of pressure; one bar equals 100 kilopascals or 14.5 pound-force per square inch; (*compare* TYRE PRESSURE)

bar clamp *noun* tool with a fixed head and a sliding foot for clamping purposes

bare shell *noun* body shell that has been dismantled completely, including removal of all hinged parts

barometric pressure sensor *or* **BARO** *noun* sensor in an engine management system providing information on ambient barometric pressure for the adjustment of mixture etc., which is important for the maintenance of good engine performance at different altitudes

barrel *noun* main tubular section of a carburettor including the air intake and choke tube

◊ **barrel tappet** *noun* hollow barrel-shaped tappet

barrier cream *noun* special cream recommended for use when working on cars to reduce soiling of the hands and prevent skin infections or allergic reactions when working with substances such as oils, thinners, paints, etc.

◊ **barrier effect** *noun* the effect produced by coatings shielding especially metal surfaces from corrosive agents

◊ **barrier paint** *noun* primer which isolates a top coat from a surface or other finish with which it is incompatible

base *noun* lowest supporting part of a usually upright member, or bottom layer or coating in a paint system

◊ **base and clear system** *noun* paint finish consisting of a coloured base coat, especially a metallic finish, and a clear coat of lacquer. *base and clear systems should be applied in an exceptionally clean environment*

◇ **base coat** *noun* first coat in a paint system, either an undercoat or primer, or a coloured coat to be covered in a coat of clear lacquer

◇ **base material** *noun* material under a coating or which is to be coated

◇ **base metal** *noun* metal under a coating or which is to be coated; **base metal attack** = corrosion of the metal under a finish

baseplate *noun* strong metal plate which forms the base of something *a distributor baseplate*

basic ignition setting *or* **timing** *noun* position to which the ignition is set, which is then varied by the automatic advance system

◇ **basic price** *noun* minimum list price of a certain car model, to which must be added any tax or extras, the charge for delivery, number plates, etc.

◇ **basic timing** *noun* = BASIC IGNITION TIMING

basket case *noun* *(informal)* old car, often in a dilapidated condition, partly or completely dismantled and lacking certain parts, so that it requires a total restoration involving considerable expense and effort

bastard *noun* = COARSE-CUT FILE

batch *noun* **1** number of things produced as a group *the first batch of the new model has been sent out to the dealers* **2** mixture of natural and/or synthetic rubbers with various ingredients, such as fillers, chemicals, and vulcanizing agents, used in tyre production

bath *noun* process of immersion or the container used *the objects to be galvanized are immersed in a bath of molten zinc*

battery *noun* on most cars, a lead-acid storage battery, usually of 12 volts; **to disconnect** *or* **isolate the battery** = remove the leads from the battery terminals; **the battery is flat** *or* **dead** = there is no current left in the battery; **check the battery and top up if necessary** = check the level of the battery acid in the battery cells and add distilled water to restore the level if needed

COMMENT: small cars and American cars used to use 6 volt batteries, while diesels use two 12 volt batteries in series; today most car batteries are maintenance-free, i.e. do not require topping up

battery acid *noun* fluid in the cells of a car battery, in fact sulphuric acid

◇ **battery capacity** *noun* = AMPERE-HOUR CAPACITY

◇ **battery case** *noun* housing made of polypropylene used to accommodate the cells of a battery with their plates and separators, and the battery acid

◇ **battery charge** *noun* condition of the battery in relation to the amount of current stored in it (NOTE: also called **state of charge**); **battery charge indicator** = instrument showing the state of charge of the battery; **battery charger** = device which can be plugged into the mains and connected to a storage battery to restore its state of charge; **battery charging station** = centre with high capacity battery chargers for recharging batteries, especially of electric cars

◇ **battery compartment** *noun* separate space provided for the battery, usually under the bonnet but sometimes below the rear seat or in the boot

◇ **battery condition** *noun* = BATTERY CHARGE

◇ **battery connector** *noun* plug on battery-powered vehicles to connect the batteries to a charging station

◇ **battery cover** *noun* one-piece cover permanently sealed to the battery case and with common batteries provided with one opening for each of the individual cells for filling and topping-up purposes; such openings are usually closed by plugs but are absent on modern maintenance-free batteries

◇ **battery discharge controller** *noun* device on vehicles with electric motor drive, which triggers a warning indicator and/or turns off the power supply when battery voltage drops below a certain minimum level; **battery discharge indicator** = instrument on vehicles with electric motor drive which indicates battery charge condition in percent of full charge

◇ **battery earth** *noun* earth provided by a braided earth strap or a heavy-duty cable leading from the negative terminal (or exceptionally, in positive earth systems, from the positive terminal) to a suitable point on the body or chassis

◇ **battery filler** *noun* device with a suction ball which can suck up liquid and discharge it into the battery

◇ **battery fluid** *noun* = BATTERY ACID

◇ **battery ignition (system)** *noun* general term for any battery-powered ignition system where battery voltage is stepped up to ignition voltage by an ignition coil or transistorized ignition unit

◇ **battery master switch** *noun* switch which disconnects the battery completely and cuts off power to all electrical components

◇ **battery post** *noun* round terminal on a battery to which a cable is attached, usually by a clamp (NOTE: to avoid confusion, the positive post is usually of larger diameter than the negative post)

◇ **battery state indicator** *noun* = BATTERY CHARGE INDICATOR

◇ **battery terminal** *noun* terminal on the battery either in the form of a post or a lug with a hole; also used sometimes to mean the clamp on the end of the cable

◇ **battery tester** *noun* **(a)** voltage meter or hydrometer for checking the state of charge of a battery **(b)** instrument for checking the condition of the battery cells

◇ **battery tray** *noun* metal ledge supporting the battery, usually on the side of the engine bay

baulk ring *noun* part in a synchromesh gearbox which prevents a gear being engaged too soon

bayonet cap *noun* cylindrical base of an electric light bulb, usually with two pins projecting on either side, which engage in J-shaped slots to lock the bulb securely in its socket; **bayonet fitting or socket** = socket with either twin contacts or a single contact and J-shaped slots on either side to receive the pins of the bulb

BDC = BOTTOM DEAD CENTRE

bead *noun* **(a)** the part of a tyre which is shaped to fit the rim, made of steel wires wrapped and reinforced by the plies of the tyre **(b)** any small ball-like part, such as the glass beads used in bead blasting or the pellets used in certain catalytic converters

◇ **bead base** *noun* the part of the tyre bead in contact with the rim bead seat; *(compare* BEAD HEEL, BEAD TOE)

◇ **bead blasting** *noun* cleaning process using glass beads that is fairly slow, but gives a high quality finish since paint and contamination can be removed without affecting the critical tolerances of parts being blasted

◇ **bead core** *noun* ring of steel wires in the tyre bead

◇ **beaded edge** *noun* edge of a body or upholstery panel wrapped around a wire or other stiffening medium; **beaded edge tyre** = early form of high-pressure tyre with projecting beads

◇ **beader** *noun* power tool for forming beads on the edges of body panels

◇ **bead heel** *noun* portion of the tyre bead in contact with the rim flange

◇ **beading** *noun* forming a step in the middle of a panel, not at the edge, which creates a shallow indentation to reinforce the panel

bead seat *noun* portion of the wheel rim below the rim flange providing radial support to the bead of the tyre; *(see illustration 33)*

| COMMENT: with tubeless tyres it is particularly important to keep the bead seat areas free of rust and rubber deposits, since in this case the bead seat is the air sealing element

bead seat mat *noun* seat cover made of a network of wood beads

◇ **bead separation** *noun* separating the tyre bead from the wheel rim

◇ **bead toe** *noun* bottom portion of the tyre bead in contact with the rim bead seat

◇ **bead unseating** *noun* shifting of the tyre bead from its seat on the wheel rim, often resulting in the tyre leaving the rim altogether

beam axle *noun* now used for any rigid axle, but the original sense was a non-driven axle formed of an I-section beam

beam indicator *noun* light on the instrument panel which comes on usually only when the main headlight beam is in use

bearing *noun* device which supports or positions a usually rotating or reciprocating part such as a shaft, especially in such a way that little or no friction results *the big-end bearings are in the form of shells (compare* ANTIFRICTION BEARING)

◇ **bearing assembly** *noun* assembly of more than one bearing for the same component, where more than one load has to be supported

◇ **bearing block** *noun* part accommodating a bearing, consisting of a lower shell with a straight surface suitable for installation on flat surfaces, and an upper shell which is bolted to the lower one quite often against the clamping surface; *(see illustration 6)*

◊ **bearing cage** *noun* circular frame which holds the balls or rollers in place in a ball or roller bearing

◊ **bearing cap** *noun* rigid, semicircular part which encloses and holds the outer shell of a shell bearing, as in the main bearings or big-end bearings of an engine; *(see illustration 9)*

◊ **bearing clearance** *noun* space between the bearing surface and its journal; **check the con rod for big-end bearing clearance** = check the gap between big-end and crankpin

◊ **bearing cone** *noun* **(a)** = TAPER ROLLER BEARING **(b)** inner race in an adjustable axial or radial ball bearing

◊ **bearing cup** *noun* = BEARING SHELL

◊ **bearing face** *noun* face of a nut or bolt head which bears against the surface of the part which it joins to some other part

◊ **bearing housing** *noun* housing for a bearing, such as the centre section of a turbocharger which supports the compressor and turbine housings and the shaft to which the compressor and turbine wheels are attached; *(see illustration 10)*

◊ **bearing material** *noun* metal layer forming the surface of a plain bearing, typically of white metal *replace the bearing if the bearing material shows signs of wear*

◊ **bearing puller** *noun* tool used to remove different types of bearings by pulling action

◊ **bearing race** *noun* in ball or roller bearings, one of two steel rings between which the balls or rollers run in tracks

◊ **bearing separator** *noun* special tool used to separate double bearings or close fitting gears, especially when a conventional jaw-type puller cannot be used, having bevelled edges which allow insertion behind the bearings and gears to be separated

◊ **bearing shell** *noun* one of a pair of thin semicircular steel cups lined with an alloy such as copper-lead or lead-indium, which together enclose a shaft or other rotating member, and are held in a circular housing which can be divided into two halves; *(see illustration 9)*

◊ **bearing spread** *noun* diameter slightly greater than that of the housing with which almost all main and big-end bearings

are manufactured; this means that the bearing shell has to be forced into place, and so cannot rotate; there is also total contact between its back and the housing (NOTE: this is also called an **interference fit**)

◊ **bearing surface** *noun* area of the bearing actually in contact with the shaft or other member being supported

bed *noun* flat area used as a support

◊ **bed in** *verb* to make parts fit together accurately; **it takes a while for new brake pads to bed themselves in** = new brake pads have to wear slightly to be a perfect fit on the discs

◊ **bedding-in oil** *noun* engine oil for use when running in new bearings

beefed-up *adjective (informal)* made stronger, e.g. for heavy loads *the GT model has beefed-up suspension*

Beema *or* **Beemer** *noun (informal)* = BMW

Beetle *noun (informal)* the original rear-engined Volkswagen

bell housing *noun* circular housing between the crankcase and gearbox containing the flywheel and clutch, or the torque converter in the case of automatic transmission

belt *noun* **(a)** loop of strong material passed round two or more pulleys and transmitting drive from one to the other, such as a fan belt or timing belt **(b)** = SEAT BELT **(c)** reinforcing layer or layers of steel or nylon strands in the carcass of a radial ply tyre; *(see illustration 32)*

◊ **belt anchorage** *noun* point where the end of a seat belt is attached to the body of a car *the lower belt anchorage must be reinforced*

belt drive *noun* system for transmitting power by means of a belt passing round pulleys

COMMENT: the Variomatic transmission used rubber belts and expanding pulleys to provide an infinitely variable belt drive

belted bias tyre *noun* hybrid tyre which is a mixture between cross-ply and radial-ply designs, with added belts (as in radial-ply tyres) on diagonal body plies (as in cross-ply tyres), resulting in stiffer sidewalls than with straight radial tyres

◇ **belt end** *noun* part of the seat belt carrying the buckle and attached to the floor pan, increasingly replaced by buckles attached directly to the car seat

◇ **belt line** *noun US* = WAISTLINE

◇ **belt mounting** *noun* = BELT ANCHORAGE

◇ **belt retractor** *noun* device which automatically pulls the seat belt back into its reel

◇ **belt sander** *noun* power sanding tool with a rotating belt lined with abrasive

◇ **belt slack** *noun* looseness of a belt

◇ **belt slip** *noun* slipping of a drive belt on its pulleys due to insufficient tightness, so that no power is transmitted

◇ **belt tensioner** *noun* arrangement for tightening a drive belt, often comprising an idler pulley whose position can be adjusted

◇ **belt transmission** *noun* = BELT DRIVE

◇ **belt up** *verb* to put on one's seat belt (NOTE: US English is **buckle up**)

◇ **belt webbing** *noun* strong webbing material used for seat belts

bench *noun* workbench, also used to mean a test bed for engines; **this engine delivers 250 bhp on the bench** = when tested on the dynamometer this engine can register a power output of 250 bhp

◇ **bench grinder** *noun* power grinder for mounting on a workbench, with two grinding wheels for grinding and sharpening purposes

bench seat *noun* seat in one piece stretching across the full width of the car

COMMENT: bench-type front seats were used particularly in American cars of the 1940s and '50s; combined with steering-column gear levers, they allowed three people to sit abreast in the front of the car

bench test *noun* stationary test, especially of an engine, in which it is mounted in a test bed and run for a period of time; checks being made with the aid of instruments on e.g. power output, fuel consumption and emission levels *transmissions and ancillaries such as alternators and catalytic converters can also be subjected to a bench test*

◇ **bench vice** *noun* vice for mounting on a workbench

bending pliers *noun* pliers with flat, smooth jaws used to hold sheet metal in place, e.g. for welding

◇ **bending strength** *noun* ability of a material to resist the bending moment

Bendix drive *noun* form of drive mainly used for starter motors, where a pinion is mounted on a shaft with a helical screw and rushes down the shaft into engagement with the starter teeth on the flywheel when the shaft is spun (NOTE: also called **inertia drive,** due to the heavy piston moving along the shaft under the momentum of its own weight or inertia when the shaft turns inside it); **Bendix screw** = the form of helical screw on the shaft of a starter motor; **Bendix starter** = starter motor with a Bendix drive

benzene (C_6H_6) *noun* fluid constituent of petrol

bevel differential *noun* differential which has bevel gears for its main elements, which allows the input and output shafts to be at right angles to one another; *(compare* SPUR DIFFERENTIAL)

bevel drive shaft *noun* shaft with a bevel gear at one end or both ends, used especially for driving an overhead camshaft

COMMENT: the famous racing motorcycle, the Manx Norton, had a bevel (drive) shaft to drive its overhead camshaft

bevel gear *noun* gear shaped in the form of a frustum of a cone, used to transmit motion through an angle; **bevel gear drive** *or* **transmission** = form of transmission used to drive shafts which do not align with the output shaft; *(see illustration 24)*

beverage holder *noun* circular clip for holding a beaker or glass, typically on the centre console

bezel *noun* circular metal surround or rim of an instrument, headlamp, etc.

bhp = BRAKE HORSEPOWER

bias belted tyre *noun* = BELTED BIAS TYRE

◇ **bias ply tyre** *noun* = CROSS-PLY TYRE

bicycle carrier *noun* device attached to the rear of a car, often supported on a towbar, for carrying a bicycle

big-block engine *noun US* typical large American V-8 engine of the 1960s and '70s, with a simple and robust design including cast-iron block and heads and conventional carburettors, and giving ample power and enormous torque

| COMMENT: the dream engine for American dream cars such as the Corvette and Mustang

big end *noun* end of the connecting rod which fits round the crankpin; *(see illustration 9)*; **big-end bearing** = bearing of the connecting rod on the crankpin, now nearly always in the form of replaceable shell bearings, but formerly of white metal deposited on fixed shells; **big-end bolt** = one of the bolts fixing the big-end cap to the connecting rod; **big-end cap** = the detachable end of the connecting rod which fits on the crankpin

Big Jim *noun (informal)* device for picking door locks, consisting of a flexible metal strip designed for insertion between window glass and frame, with hooks for pulling the door lock knobs

bihexagon *noun & adjective* (figure) having twelve angles; the shape of some nuts, bolt heads and their corresponding sockets; **bihexagon socket** = socket which will fit a standard hexagon bolt head or nut

◇ **bihexagonal** *adjective (of a nut, bolt head, etc.)* having twelve angles or points

bimetallic corrosion *noun* corrosion of two different metals exposed to an electrolyte while in electrical contact; *(see also* GALVANIC CORROSION)

Bimmer *(informal)* = BMW

binder *noun* non-volatile portion of a paint, which binds or cements the pigment particles together, and the paint film as a whole to the material to which it is applied

binding *noun* **(a)** rubbing of brake shoes against the drum or of brake pads against the

disc **(b)** strip material turned over along the edge of a carpet or mat

binnacle *noun* cluster of instruments and/or switches mounted in a usually circular casing fixed on or near the steering column

bio-degradable *adjective* capable of being made to rot by bacteria

bit *noun* part of a tool for boring or cutting, especially the interchangeable tip of a drill or the blade of a screwdriver; **bit adapter** *or* **holder** = tool with a female square drive at one end to accept a socket drive handle and a female hexagon drive at the other end to accept hexagon bits

bituminous paint *noun* black or dark-coloured tarry paint which contains bitumen; used for the protection of exposed metal parts

BL = BRITISH LEYLAND

black box *noun (informal)* **(a)** = CRASH RECORDER **(b)** = CONTROL UNIT

◇ **black chromium plating** *noun* electrolytic deposition of a black chromium layer for decorative purposes

◇ **blackening** *noun* = BULB BLACKENING

blade *noun* straight, narrow flat part, such as the end of a screwdriver, the part of a windscreen wiper in contact with the windscreen, or one of the vanes of a rotor or impeller; **blade connector** = plain metal tongue for forming electrical connections; **blade rubber** = rubber strip fitted into the arm of a windscreen wiper

◇ **bladed impeller** *noun* rotating member of a centrifugal pump fitted with blades or vanes

blanking piece *or* **plate** *noun* usually flat piece of metal closing off an aperture

◇ **blanking plug** *noun* rubber plug for filling holes in the bodywork, such as drain holes in the floorpan

blast cleaning *noun* removal of corrosion, dirt, scale, etc., by a blast of abrasive particles; *(compare* SAND-BLASTING)

bleed *verb* to drain fluid from (a hydraulic system), usually to remove any air which may have found its way in *after fitting the new brake pipe, you will have to bleed the brakes* **bleed(er) screw** = screw which when slacked off allows hydraulic fluid to escape; *(see illustrations 30, 31)*; **bleed(er) valve** = valve which when opened allows hydraulic fluid to escape

◊ **bleeding** *noun* **(a)** process of draining a certain amount of fluid from a hydraulic system **(b)** paint fault where pigment from the original or base colour dissolves in the top coat and becomes visible as a stain of a different colour

blind rivet *noun* = POP RIVET

◊ **blind spot** *noun* area not visible from the driver's seat; **there is a large blind spot to the rear quarter** = it is impossible to see from the driver's seat what is diagonally to the rear, even using the mirror

blister *noun* bubble in the paintwork, caused by trapped moisture or air under the paint or by rust

◊ **blistering** *noun* formation of blisters due to rust or air or moisture trapped under the paint

COMMENT: when the paint film is subjected to abrupt changes in temperature, the trapped moisture expands and builds up pressure, which weakens the adhesion between coats and causes blisters to form

BLMC *(short for)* British Leyland Motor Corporation

block *noun* = CYLINDER BLOCK

◊ **blocking ring** *noun* = BAULK RING

◊ **block sanding** *noun* sanding the bodywork with a sanding block which gives even sanding pressure

blood alcohol (level *or* **content)** *noun* amount of alcohol in the blood due to drinking

blooming *noun* formation of an undesired thin surface film or a milky white haze or mist on paintwork, which can occur when paint is applied during humid, cold conditions and is caused by moisture being trapped in the wet film

blow 1 *verb* to become defective, either by leaking or burning through; **the silencer** *or* **exhaust gasket is blowing** = gases are leaking from the silencer *or* exhaust gasket;

the short circuit caused the fuse to blow = the fuse burnt through because of the overload caused by the short circuit **2** *noun* leak of air or gases, e.g. from the exhaust

◊ **blowback** *noun* forcing back of some of the air/fuel mixture through the carburettor due to a sticking valve or as a result of the inlet valve closing late

◊ **blow-by** *noun* leakage of compressed air/fuel mixture and burned gases (from combustion) past the piston rings into the crankcase

◊ **blowdown** *noun* escape of gases between the opening of the exhaust valve and the piston reaching bottom dead centre, or in a two-stroke engine between exhaust port opening and transfer port opening; **blowdown period** = in a two-stroke engine, the period between exhaust port opening and transfer port opening which should be sufficiently long to allow time for the cylinder pressure to drop below crankcase pressure, so that the exhaust gases can be expelled more easily

◊ **blower** *noun* **(a)** *(informal)* = SUPERCHARGER **(b)** fan for an interior heating and ventilating system, or more rarely for an air-cooled engine; **blower switch** = switch for the fan of a heating and ventilating system

◊ **blow gun** *noun* pressure-fed spray gun with a wide nozzle used to blow out crevices, dust off large areas, etc.

◊ **blowlamp** *noun* tool giving an intense flame for burning off paint, brazing and soldering, and heating lead filler (NOTE: US English is **blow torch**)

◊ **blown** *adjective* **(a)** defective and leaking in the case of a gasket, burnt through in the case of a fuse *a blown head gasket is easily identifiable by thick white exhaust smoke* **(b)** *(informal)* = SUPERCHARGED

◊ **blow-off valve** *noun* spring-loaded valve that prevents excessive boost pressure in a turbocharger or supercharger

◊ **blow out** *verb* to clean (a blocked pipe, etc.) by blowing or passing air under high pressure through it

◊ **blow-out** *noun* puncture in which the tyre bursts and often leaves the rim

◊ **blow-over** *noun* respray of doubtful quality, often poorly prepared and carelessly masked

◊ **blowtorch** *noun US* = BLOWLAMP

blue smoke *noun* exhaust smoke indicating too rich a mixture

BMC = BRITISH MOTOR CORPORATION

BMEP = BRAKE MEAN EFFECTIVE PRESSURE

BMW *noun* German make of car, the letters standing for Bayerische Motorenwerke

board *noun* = PRINTED CIRCUIT BOARD; **board test** = test of a printed circuit board

boat trailer *noun* trailer for carrying a boat

bodge 1 *noun (informal)* a hasty botched-up repair, not carried out with the proper tools or materials **2** *verb (informal)* to do work badly, not using the proper tools or materials *a bodged job*

bodily harm *or* **injury** *noun* physical injury caused, for example, in an accident

body *noun* **(a)** main visible upper structure of a vehicle, as opposed to the chassis and running gear **(b)** main part or housing, e.g. of a silencer **(c)** shank of a bolt

◇ **body assembly** *noun* building up of the body from its various components and panels

◇ **body builder** *noun* = COACHBUILDER

◇ **body-coloured** *adjective (of bumpers, etc.)* painted in the same colour as the body; *(compare* COLOUR-CODED)

◇ **body component** *noun* structural part of the body

◇ **body construction** *noun* manufacture of a vehicle body; **built according to the principles of unitary body construction** = made as a monocoque with no separate chassis

◇ **body file** *noun* hand tool for smoothing body panels by removing material from the surface, e.g. on filled areas, consisting of a file blade held in an adjustable holder that may be adapted to convex or concave surfaces

◇ **body filler** *noun* = FILLER (a)

◇ **body flange** *noun* point on the body where two panels overlap, forming a small step, e.g. at the windscreen aperture or along other spot-weld joints

◇ **body framing** *noun* assembly of the body components

◇ **body glass** *noun* windows and windscreen of a car

◇ **body hammer** *noun* hammer for knocking out dents

◇ **body-in-white** *noun* bare body shell after welding but before painting

◇ **body jack** *noun* hydraulic device for providing the force to push or pull damaged body parts into shape, either directly or via straightening equipment, e.g. pulling beams

◇ **body lead** *noun* alloy consisting of lead and tin used to fill dents and seams in the body panels so that a smooth surface is achieved, which is heated with a torch and then spread on the body area to be filled as soon as it becomes plastic

◇ **body panel** *noun* flat or curved body part made of sheet metal

◇ **body rattle** *noun* noise in the bodywork, usually caused by loose parts, badly fitting doors or bonnets, items shifting in the boot, etc.

◇ **body repair** *noun* repair to the bodywork of a car made necessary by accident damage or corrosion; **body repair shop** = workshop specializing in body repairs

◇ **body roll** *noun* rolling of a vehicle's body when cornering

◇ **body sealer** *noun* elastic paste applied to the body to seal body joints, often having silicon rubber as its basic component

◇ **body shell** *noun* the bare skeleton of a vehicle, stripped of all running gear, fittings, accessories and detachable panels; *(compare* BODY-IN-WHITE, BARE SHELL)

◇ **body shop** *noun* **(a)** body assembly shop in a factory **(b)** = BODY REPAIR SHOP

◇ **body side moulding** *noun* strip along the side of the body, usually of plastic or hard rubber but sometimes with decorative metal trim, for stiffening and protection against side impacts

◇ **body spoon** *noun* tool with a flat, contoured working surface, used for slapping out dents, and also in place of dollies when direct access to the rear of the panel is obstructed by the internal frame structure

◇ **body stripe** *noun* ornamental strip along the bottom of the side of the body, usually on sports cars and including the make and/or model name in large letters

◇ **body styling kit** *noun* package of additional parts such as spoilers, air dams and side skirts, which can simply be bolted on in most cases, intended to give the car a more sporty appearance and improve the aerodynamics

◇ **body tub** *noun* bare body shell minus all removable panels such as doors and wings on cars featuring a separate chassis, which is lowered onto the chassis during assembly

◇ **bodywork** *noun* complete body structure mounted on the chassis of vehicles with separate chassis, and the complete assembly of sheet metal panels for cars of unitary construction

bogie *noun* assembly of four wheels on two axles with common suspension, usually on heavy commercial vehicles and trailers; *(see also* TANDEM AXLE)

boil *verb* to bubble and change partly to vapour due to heat, said of engine coolant and colloquially of a car or its engine, also of brake fluid *the car or engine boiled because the radiator was blocked*

◇ **boiling point** *noun* temperature at which a liquid boils *silicone brake fluid has a high boiling point*

bolster *noun* supporting pad, e.g. in a seat or seat back, or a load-supporting beam in a commercial vehicle

bolt *noun* piece of metal bar with a screw thread and a usually hexagonal head, for use with a nut or for screwing into a part with a matching female thread

◇ **bolt-on** *adjective* easily attached or mounted by means of bolts or screws; *(informal)*; **bolt-on goodies** = additional accessories usually fitted to the outside of the car, which are often unnecessary, such as extra lamps, spoilers, etc.; **bolt-on kit** = kit of parts, e.g. for transistorized ignition or for body panels, which the owner can fit himself; **bolt-on wing** = wing that is simply bolted on and not welded

bond 1 *noun* state of adhesion *two-pack epoxy adhesives give a strong bond* **2** *verb* to join by means of an adhesive *the plastic panels are bolted and bonded to the steel structure* **bonded windscreen** = system in which the windscreen is stuck into the body shell without the addition of a windscreen rubber

◇ **bonding agent** *noun* material that provides adhesive properties

◇ **bonding method** *noun* method of joining two parts together with an adhesive

bonnet *noun* hinged cover over the engine bay, usually of metal but now often of fibreglass; *(see illustrations 1, 2)* (NOTE: US English is **hood)**

bonnet badge *noun* badge usually stating the make and sometimes the model of vehicle in the centre of the front edge of the bonnet

COMMENT: if erect (like the Mercedes star) the badge must be able to fold down to prevent injury in the case of an accident

bonnet bump rubber *or* **bonnet bumper** *noun* rubber buffer mounted on the vertical panel onto which the bonnet is lowered

COMMENT: designed to reduce closing noise of the bonnet and to prevent damage to the paintwork of the sheet metal panels that would otherwise touch each other when closed

bonnet landing panel *noun* panel onto which the bonnet is lowered; also houses the bonnet locking mechanism

bonnet liner *noun* sound-absorbing material attached to the inside of the bonnet to reduce engine noise

COMMENT: modern cars use bonnet liners made of PE, PP or PUR foam, or lightweight, very thin mouldings of special, impregnated polyester material

bonnet lock *noun* locking mechanism comprising a notched peg fixed to the front underside of the bonnet, which fits into a hole with a sliding latch in a panel above the grille

◇ **bonnet pin kit** *noun* kit which secures the bonnet of competition cars even under severe conditions, and typically consists of stainless-steel or chromium-plated scuff plates, ½in x 4in studs, nuts, washers, a selection of clips and plastic lanyards

◇ **bonnet release** *noun* cable with a handle inside the vehicle which releases the bonnet lock

◇ **bonnet (support) stay** *noun* rod which engages in a hole in the bonnet to hold it in the open position

◇ **bonnet tape** *noun* double piping with fabric covering used to keep bonnets of older-style cars from rubbing on the paintwork of the panels beneath them

booming *noun* **(a)** noise caused by interruptions to the airflow such as open windows *opening the sunroof causes quite a bit of booming, which is eliminated by opening the rear windows slightly* **(b)** low-pitched resonance, especially in the exhaust

boost 1 *noun* additional power, pressure or charge, especially the pressure from a supercharger (NOTE: also called /NX boost pressure); **to give the battery a boost** = to charge the battery when it is low (but not flat); **the supercharger is running at 10 pounds boost** = the supercharger is producing 10 pounds of pressure into the inlet manifold; **the boost comes in at 3,500 rpm** = the supercharger starts to operate at 3,500 rpm **2** *verb* to increase (power, charge, pressure, etc.), amplify (an audio signal, etc.) *engine power has been boosted to 98 bhp*

◊ **boost control valve** *noun* = BLOW-OFF VALVE

◊ **booster** *noun* amplifier unit which increases the audio signal level at the loudspeakers, fitted between the radio or stereo unit and the speakers, often mounted in the boot

◊ **booster battery** *noun* additional battery connected in series to give added power for starting

◊ **booster cable** *noun* JUMP LEAD

◊ **booster coil** *noun* additional coil which increases the strength of the spark

◊ **boost gauge** *noun* instrument indicating boost pressure

◊ **boost pressure** *noun* pressure in the intake system of supercharged engines when the supercharger operates; *(compare* BOOST 1)

◊ **boost sensor** *noun* sensor located in the choke tube which sends a signal to the ignition control unit according to pressure conditions, and the control unit then adjusts the ignition timing for optimum performance

◊ **boost valve** *noun* valve in a hydraulic system which amplifies pressure

boot *noun* **(a)** separate area for luggage behind the rear seats and mostly behind the rear window, or below the rear window in the case of fastback designs, with a hinged cover (NOTE: US English is **trunk**) **(b)** = DUST BOOT **(c)** = WHEEL CLAMP

◊ **booted version** *noun* subsequent saloon version with a boot of a model originally launched as a hatchback

◊ **boot handle** *noun* handle for opening the bootlid

◊ **bootlid** *noun* hinged cover for the boot; *(see illustration 3.2)*

◊ **boot spoiler** *noun* = REAR SPOILER

bore 1 *noun* **(a)** diameter of a cylinder, especially of a cylinder in an internal combustion engine *the capacity of an engine is calculated from its bore and stroke* **(b)** internal wall of a cylinder *if the bores are badly worn, a rebore will be necessary* **2** *verb* **to bore and stroke an engine** = to increase the bore and stroke of an engine; **to bore out an engine** = to increase the bore of an engine

◊ **bore/stroke ratio** *noun* relation of the piston stroke to the diameter of the cylinder of an engine, which provides information as to whether the engine is a short stroke or a long stroke unit; *(compare* LONG STROKE ENGINE, SHORT STROKE ENGINE, SQUARE ENGINE)

bossing mallet *noun* mallet with a pear-shaped wooden head commonly used for shaping and stretching metal over a sandbag or wooden block

botch 1 *noun* very badly executed piece of work **2** *verb* to do (a piece of work) very badly; **botched-up job** = *(informal)* very badly executed repair which is unlikely to last very long

bottle jack *noun* small hydraulic jack in the shape of a bottle

◊ **bottleneck** *noun* narrow stretch of road, or point on a road where traffic is held up

bottom 1 *adjective* lower or lowest **2** *noun* lowest point **3** *verb* **(a)** *(of suspension)* to reach the bottom end of its travel, causing a jolt *the suspension kept on bottoming on the bumpy road* **(b)** *(of a low part of a vehicle)* to make contact with the ground *the exhaust system bottomed on a hump in the ground*

◊ **bottom dead centre (BDC)** *noun* lowest point of travel of the piston in a (vertical) piston-operated combustion engine, from which the piston starts to move upwards again until it reaches the upper point of travel (top dead centre); **the inlet valve closes 60° after bottom dead centre** *or* **BDC** = the inlet valve closes at a point when measured on the flywheel 60° after the piston's lowest point (NOTE: opposite is **top dead centre** ; the corresponding point (to BDC) in a horizontally opposed or 'flat' engine is that furthest from the combustion chamber, also called **outer dead centre**)

◊ **bottom end** *noun* **(a)** all moving parts in the crankcase and their bearings, or more narrowly, the end of the connecting rod attached to the crankshaft (the big end); **the bottom end has been completely overhauled** = the crankshaft has been reground and the main and big-end bearings have been replaced **(b)** lower range of engine revolutions; **bottom end torque** = pulling power at low engine speeds

◊ **bottom gear** *noun* = FIRST GEAR

◊ **bottoming** *noun* **(a)** a suspension element reaching the end of its travel on going over a bump **(b)** contact between a low part of a vehicle and the ground

◊ **bottom tank** *noun* bottom radiator tank in a thermosyphon water-cooling system; *(compare* HEADER TANK, RADIATOR TANK)

bounce 1 *verb* **(a)** *(of valves or contact breaker points)* to chatter or bounce instead of closing properly at high speeds; *(compare* CONTACT BOUNCE, VALVE BOUNCE) **(b)** to push down and release a corner of a vehicle

| COMMENT: bouncing is necessary to test the shock absorbers, and also to settle the suspension before wheel alignment is checked or adjusted

Bowden cable *noun* control cable consisting of a wire cable in a sheath, used especially for choke, clutch, and accelerator cables

bowser *noun* tanker for refuelling especially military vehicles and aircraft

box *noun* = SILENCER (a)

boxer engine *noun* horizontally opposed or 'flat' engine, especially a flat four

box member *noun* structural part made as a box section

◊ **box section** *noun* closed panel structure of substantially square cross section, used especially to strengthen the underbody of a vehicle

◊ **box spanner** *noun* spanner in the form of a tube with one or two hexagonal socket ends for fitting over nuts and bolt heads, and with holes in the sides to accept a crossbar called a tommy bar

◊ **box van** *noun* van with a large square-sectioned enclosed area for goods behind the driver's cab

◊ **box wrench** *noun US* = RING SPANNER

◊ **boxy** *adjective (of a car body)* looking square and lumpy

boy racer *noun (informal)* low-tech and therefore low-cost car with the emphasis on sporty looks, but not necessarily very fast or powerful

| COMMENT: examples include the old Ford Capri and some of the 'hot hatches'; also often applied to an old car of no great performance which has been tuned and done up to look sporty with spoilers, alloy wheels, etc.

B-pillar *or* **B-post** *noun* upright member behind the front door supporting the roof and carrying the striker plate for the front door and, in the case of four-door models, the hinges for the rear door

brace *noun* part providing support or reinforcement between two or more components

◊ **bracing** *noun* **(a)** *(action)* stiffening by means of braces **(b)** brace; part used to provide support

bracket *noun* support usually made from metal strip for a part carried on or suspended from a vehicle, such as a fog lamp or exhaust system

braided hose *noun* usually rubber pipe covered in woven material or braided wire, for fuel lines or brake hoses

brake 1 *noun* **(a)** mechanism for slowing or stopping a vehicle in motion, or for holding it when standing still; **to put on** *or* **apply the brakes** = to brake; **to stand on the brakes** = *(informal)* to brake hard **(b)** device for measuring the power of an engine; **to test an engine on the brake** = to find out how much power an engine develops (NOTE: the device used nowadays is called a **dynamometer) (c)** = SHOOTING BRAKE **2** *verb* to operate the brakes in order to slow down; **to brake hard** = to press hard on the brake pedal

◊ **brake adjuster** *noun* device in a drum brake system for moving the shoes in relation to the drum; **brake adjusting spanner** = special spanner with a square cutout to fit over a square adjuster projecting from the brake backplate (NOTE: US English is **brake wrench**); **brake adjusting tool** = lever-type tool for use on drum brakes with star wheel adjustment, which fits through a slot in the backplate to turn the star wheel and adjust the clearance between the brake shoe and the drum

◇ **brake band** *noun* device used to hold one of the three turning members of the planetary gear set in an automatic gearbox stationary in order to change gear ratios, being replaced in more modern designs by, for example, multiple-disc clutches; *(see illustration 21)*

◇ **brake bleeder** *noun* workshop equipment used to bleed air from hydraulic brake, clutch or steering systems on vehicles

◇ **brake cable** *noun* wire cable used to operate the brakes in some mechanical brake systems, still used for trailers and for the handbrake on most cars

◇ **brake caliper** *noun* assembly in a disc brake system fitting over the disc and containing the pistons which act on the brake pads, which in turn press on the disc *brake calipers may be fixed, sliding or floating (see illustration 31)*

◇ **brake cylinder** *noun* = WHEEL CYLINDER

◇ **brake disc** *noun* flat metal disc in a disc brake system, mounted on a wheel hub and rotating with the wheel until acted on by the brake pads; *(see illustrations 31, 37)* (NOTE: US English is **(disc) brake rotor)**

◇ **brake dive** *noun* dipping of a car's front end or lifting of the rear end when the brakes are applied, due to a load transfer from the rear to the front suspension (NOTE: opposite is **squat)** *(compare* ANTI-DIVE)

◇ **brake drum** *noun* metal drum mounted on a car hub to form the outer shell of the brake, against which the brake shoes press to slow or stop rotation of the drum and wheel; *(see illustration 30)*

◇ **brake fade** *noun* loss of friction in the brakes and thus of stopping power due to overheating

◇ **brake failure** *noun* complete failure of the brakes to function

brake fluid *noun* special thin oil used in hydraulic brake systems to transmit force through a closed system of pipes (i.e. brake lines); **brake fluid reservoir** = usually a translucent plastic tank located either directly on top of the master cylinder or on a higher level for easier access, which contains two

chambers in dual-circuit braking systems, and may include a level sensor; *(see illustration 29)*

COMMENT: brake fluid must fulfil various stringent requirements: boiling point above 290°C, freezing point lower than -60°C; chemically inert to the materials used in the braking system; lubrication effect under all operating conditions; and resistant to ageing. However, brake fluid is also hygroscopic (i.e. collects moisture from the air), toxic, and attacks the car body finish, and since the presence of moisture in the brake fluid reduces dramatically the boiling point (the temperature of brake discs may reach 700°C), the brake fluid should be changed about every year

brake horsepower *noun* power developed by an engine which is measured by a brake or dynamometer; often abbreviated as bhp; *(compare* SAE GROSS BHP, SAE NET BHP)

◇ **brake hose** *noun* flexible, reinforced high-pressure hose, used to connect the fixed brake pipes to the brake assemblies that move up and down with the wheels; *(see illustration 31)*

◇ **brake light** *noun* red rear light activated when the foot brake is applied; usually integrated in a tail light assembly (NOTE: also called **stop light)**

◇ **brake line** *noun* = BRAKE PIPE

◇ **brake lining** *noun* curved strip of friction material usually containing asbestos attached to a brake shoe; **riveted** *or* **bonded brake linings** = brake linings attached to the brake shoes with rivets or glued on with adhesive; *(see illustration 30)*

◇ **brake mean effective pressure (BMEP)** *noun* average pressure in the cylinders of an engine divided by its mechanical efficiency, i.e. the ratio of the power actually delivered at an output shaft to the power developed in the cylinders; used as an indication of torque

◇ **brake pad** *noun* pad of friction material on a steel plate that is brought into contact with the disc under heavy pressure in a disc brake; *(see illustration 31)*; **brake pad wear indicator** = either a mechanical system which produces a screeching, squealing, or scraping noise when the pads are worn, as the metal indicators contact the brake discs, or an electrical system in which worn pads close an electric circuit that illuminates a warning light on the instrument panel

◇ **brake pedal** *noun* pedal on the floor of a vehicle in front of the driver which operates the brakes; **spongy brake pedal** = lack of normal resistance when the pedal is pressed, often due to air in the hydraulic system; **brake pedal travel** = free movement of the brake pedal before resistance is felt

◇ **brake pipe** *noun* steel pipe used to carry the brake fluid

◇ **brake pulling** *noun* pulling to left or right as a result of uneven braking effort

◇ **brake rotor** *noun US* = BRAKE DISC

◇ **brake servo (unit)** *noun* apparatus which supplements the driver's physical effort in providing most of the force required for braking, usually using vacuum from the inlet manifold

◇ **brake shoe** *noun* curved part in drum brake systems with T-shaped cross section, made of sheet steel or an alloy casting, to which the brake lining is riveted or bonded with adhesive (NOTE: the term 'brake shoe' is often used for the complete shoe-and-lining assembly); **brake shoe return spring** = spring whose ends are attached to two brake shoes, bringing them back into the off position after the brake has been applied; *(see illustration 30)*

◇ **brake test** *noun* test of braking efficiency, typically as part of a roadworthiness test

◇ **brake warning light** *noun* light which can serve several purposes, such as indicating a low fluid level in the brake fluid reservoir, a malfunction in one of two separate braking circuits, excessive wear of brake pads or linings, or when the handbrake is applied with the ignition switched on

◇ **brake wrench** *noun US* = BRAKE ADJUSTING SPANNER

braking *noun* operation or functioning of the brakes; **to skid under heavy braking** = to skid when the brakes are applied hard; **braking distance** = distance required for a vehicle to come to rest from the point where the brakes are first applied; *(compare* STOPPING DISTANCE); **braking effort** *or* **force** = retarding power of a brake or brakes *the braking effort or force on the two front wheels must be even* **braking performance** = behaviour of the brakes when operated or amount of braking effort available; **braking ratio** = distribution of braking effort between the front and rear wheels; **braking system** = complete set of braking equipment

COMMENT: a vehicle may have more than one braking system; in addition to the main or service braking systems, there are secondary braking systems, parking braking systems, and (on lorries) additional retarding braking systems, and automatic braking systems

brass punch *noun* brass tool used to drive bearing races, bushes, etc. in and out

◇ **braze** *verb* to join two metal surfaces by fusing a layer of brass or high-melting solder between them

break *verb* **(a)** to separate into several parts; **to break (up) a car for spares** = to take a car to pieces so that the parts can be used to repair other cars **(b)** to separate; **points break 5° before TDC** = the contact breaker points open (and the spark occurs) 5° before top dead centre

break away *verb (of a vehicle)* to leave the desired line of travel due to loss of adhesion, especially when cornering

◇ **breakaway** *noun* leaving the desired line due to loss of adhesion, especially when cornering *if a deflated tyre leaves the rim this can result in immediate breakaway*

break down *verb* **(a)** *(of a mechanism or vehicle)* to cease to operate *we or the car broke down miles from anywhere* **(b)** *(of insulation)* to lose its effectiveness

◇ **breakdown** *noun* **(a)** failure of a mechanism or a vehicle *we suffered a complete breakdown of the electrical system or a complete electrical breakdown* **(b)** *(of insulation)* loss of effectiveness; **breakdown across the sparking plug insulator causes missing** = if the insulation of the sparking plug becomes faulty, that cylinder will stop firing or fire only intermittently

◇ **breakdown recovery (service)** *noun* towing or transporting broken-down vehicles to a garage for repair or to the owner's home; **breakdown service** = service providing on-the-spot assistance, repairs where possible and recovery where repair is not possible; **breakdown truck** = vehicle equipped for towing or sometimes transporting disabled vehicles

breaker *noun* **(a)** person who breaks up cars and sometimes other vehicles which are worn out or no longer roadworthy and will sell any reusable parts *breaker's yard* **(b)** in radial tyres, an additional cushioning layer between the belt layers and the tread, in cross-ply tyres between the carcass and the tread **(c)** = CONTACT BREAKER; **breaker-**

triggered transistorized ignition (system) = transistorized ignition system whose distributor is the same as that of a coil ignition system, but whose contact breaker switches only the control current of the transistor, not the primary current; usually not fitted as original equipment (NOTE: opposite is **breakerless transistorized ignition (system)**; **breaker-type distributor** = distributor with a contact breaker in conventional coil ignition systems (NOTE: opposite is **breakerless distributor**)

◇ **breaker cam** *noun* cam that turns on the distributor shaft and has as many lobes as there are engine cylinders

◇ **breakerless** *adjective* having no contact breaker; **breakerless distributor** = distributor in an electronic ignition system with a pulse generator instead of a contact breaker (NOTE: opposite is **breaker-type distributor**); **breakerless transistorized ignition (system)** = electronic ignition system with a pulse generator such as a magnetic or Hall effect pick-up instead of a contact breaker, processing the signals generated in an electronic control unit

break in *verb US* = RUN IN

breakover *noun* area of a dent in a panel where the sheet metal is actually buckled into the opposite direction of the normal shape

COMMENT: this area is highlighted by the fact that the paint flakes off more heavily. The breakover condition requires careful straightening as the outline of the damage will otherwise remain visible

break time *noun* period during which the contact breaker points remain open (NOTE: opposite is **dwell period**)

break up *verb* to dismantle a vehicle and sell the parts (NOTE: US English is **part out**)

breathalyse *or* **breathalyze** *verb* to give (a driver) a breathalyser test

◇ **breathalyser** *or* **breathalyzer** *noun* device into which a driver blows to determine the amount of alcohol in his breath (and thus in his blood); **breathalyser** *or* **breathalyzer test** = test given by the police to find out how much alcohol a driver has drunk

breather *noun* passage to the open air from an enclosed space, especially the crankcase, to provide ventilation

breath test *noun* = BREATHALYSER TEST

BRG = BRITISH RACING GREEN

bridge igniter *noun* device for detonating the air bag

bright *adjective (of finish or plating)* shiny and reflecting much light (NOTE opposite is **matt**)

Brinell hardness *noun* hardness measured in a test by hydraulically pressing a hard ball under a standard load into the specimen

British Association *see* BA

◇ **British Leyland (BL)** *noun* former name for the Rover Group

◇ **British Motor Corporation (BMC)** *noun* former name for the Rover Group, before it became British Leyland

◇ **British Racing Green (BRG)** *noun* dark green, formerly used as the official British racing colour

◇ **British Standard Fine (BSF)** *noun* screw thread which was formerly that most commonly used in British automotive engineering

◇ **British Standards Institution (BSI)** *noun* organization preparing and issuing British standard specifications

◇ **British Standard Whitworth (BSW)** *noun* coarse screw thread still widely used for light applications

brush *noun* **(a)** paintbrush **(b)** rubbing electrical contact for use with rotating members, especially commutators in starters, alternators or generators; **brush holder** = in a starter motor, generator or alternator the part holding the carbon brushes and providing guidance for the spring-loaded brushes to maintain their contact with the commutator or slip ring; *(see illustration 36)*; **brush spring** = spring holding a carbon brush in contact with the commutator or slip ring

BSF = BRITISH STANDARD FINE

◇ **BSI** = BRITISH STANDARDS INSTITUTION

◇ **BSW** = BRITISH STANDARD WHITWORTH

BTDC *see* TOP DEAD CENTRE

B thread *noun* = INTERNAL THREAD

bubble *noun* small blister in the paintwork

◇ **bubble car** *noun* ultra-small car type popular in the 1950s, with glass all round and a particularly bulbous shape to provide maximum interior room within a diminutive body, and often a front door ahead of the driver, e.g. on the BMW Isetta, Heinkel Trojan, etc.

bucket seat *noun* rigid seat with slightly raised sides to give the passenger or driver lateral support; mainly used in sports cars

◇ **bucket tappet** *noun* round tappet shaped like a bucket and fitting over the end of the valve stem, also holding the end of the valve spring

buckle 1 *noun* locking metal clasp of a seat belt **2** *verb (of metal)* to crumple up

◇ **buckle up** *verb (informal US)* = BELT UP

buffeting *noun* sort of severe, pulsating draught as experienced when driving at high speeds with the windows open, or in convertibles with the top down

buffing *noun* smoothing and polishing of a surface by means of a rotating flexible wheel to the surface of which fine, abrasive particles are applied in liquid or paste form; **buffing wheel** = wheel covered in soft cloth or lambswool, often as a special accessory for power tools, impregnated with polishing compound and used to produce a high gloss on painted or polished metal surfaces

build quality *noun* quality of workmanship and materials in the construction of a vehicle

◇ **build up** *verb* **(a)** to raise (a surface), often to restore the original contour *deep dents can be built up with lead; the worn shaft can be built up with weld or metal spraying* **(b)** to assemble or put together from parts; **built-up crankshaft** = crankshaft made from separate parts rather than cast or forged in one piece

bulb *noun* gas-filled, glass envelope (often pear-shaped if not actually pear-sized) containing a thin metal filament which lights up when an electric current is passed through it; **bulb blackening** = blackening of the bulb glass due to metal vapour deposition, often indicating that the bulb is about to fail; **bulb holder** = usually a bayonet socket for a light bulb (NOTE: US English is **lamp socket**)

bulkhead *noun* panel at the rear of the engine compartment that spans the full width of the body and extends vertically from the scuttle down to the front edge of the floorpan or the toeboard; also used for the panel behind the rear seat separating the passenger cabin from the boot; *(see illustration 2)* (NOTE: US English is **dash panel**)

bull bar *noun* upward extension of a bumper to protect lights and (at the front of the car) the grille; *(compare NERF BAR)*

◇ **bull horn** *noun* horn that bellows like a bull and moos like a cow

bump and rebound *noun* the two stages of suspension movement requiring damping

bumper *noun* previously a separate metal bar or blade at the front or rear of a vehicle, now a reinforced impact-absorbing plastic moulding faired in to the bodywork, with the purpose of protecting bodywork and absorbing impacts, at least at low speeds; **the queue stretched bumper to bumper as far as the eye could see** = there was no break in the endless line of traffic; **bumper bar** = usually tubular or curved section separate bumper; **bumper blade** = usually flat or slightly curved section, basic separate bumper without overriders, etc.; **bumper bracket** = mounting bracket for the bumper assembly, fixed to the body or chassis, now often designed to give way to a certain extent on impact; **bumper filler** = small panel between the bumper bar and the body shell, usually a plastic moulding; **bumper horn** = OVERRIDER; **bumper insert** = rubber strip inserted across the width of modern bumpers; **bumper iron** = BUMPER BRACKET

bumping out *noun* first step in the panel beating process, in which the panel is roughly brought back into shape with a straightening hammer; **bumping blade** *or* **file** = tool used for slapping out slight or moderate dents, with or without the backing support of a dolly, having blade serrations which hold the metal within the area of contact to avoid stretching; **bumping hammer** = hammer for coarse hammer work on bodies, used with dollies; **bumping spoon** = SPRING BEATING SPOON

bump start 1 *noun* method of starting a car with a flat battery, by pushing it or letting it run down a hill and then letting in the clutch in second gear **2** *verb* to start a car using a bump start (NOTE: only possible on a car with a manual gearbox)

◊ **bump steer** *noun* effect observed when the movement of the suspension caused by hitting a bump or hole in the road acts on the steering to turn the wheels slightly sideways, which makes the car veer to one side; this can be felt by the driver, as it causes some kick-back at the steering wheel

◊ **bump stop** *noun* rubber buffer which limits the extent a vehicle suspension can move on hitting a bump

burning *noun* **(a)** erosion or eating away, especially of contact breaker or sparking plug points or exhaust valves **(b)** = COMBUSTION

burnishing *noun* polishing process for metal, usually using a fine abrasive on a buffing wheel

burnt *adjective (of points or valves)* eroded or eaten away *burnt valves cause loss of compression*

burr *noun* rough edge or other small projection on metal

◊ **burr walnut** *noun* wood veneer used for dashboards and door cappings in luxury cars; *(compare* ZEBRAWOOD)

burst *verb (of tyre)* to explode and lose all its air very suddenly

bus *noun* **(a)** *(short for omnibus)* vehicle for carrying a fairly large number of passengers, usually for payment, over a set route and with a fixed time schedule; **single-decker bus** = bus with one storey or deck; **double-decker bus** = bus with two storeys or decks; *(compare* COACH) **(b)** busbar

◊ **busbar** *noun* rod or other electrical conductor carrying a large current at a

constant voltage and connecting several circuits

bush *US* **bushing** *noun* thin metal sleeve fitted into a circular hole and acting as a bearing for a shaft or similar inserted into it; *(compare* SLEEVE, PLAIN BEARING) *(see illustration 37)*

butterfly nut *noun* = WING NUT

◊ **butterfly (valve)** *noun* throttle valve in a tube, especially a carburettor air intake, comprising a disc pivoted along its diameter

butt joint *or* **weld** *noun* welded joint where the panels or other parts to be joined do not overlap

> COMMENT: when butt-welding heavier gauge steel, the edges of the sheets to be joined should be chamfered along the weld seam

button head *noun* = ROUND HEAD (BOLT)

buttressed thread *noun* screw thread with one vertical and one inclined flank

bypass 1 *noun* **(a)** road going round and thus avoiding a town or other congested area **(b)** means such as a passage through which the flow of a liquid or gas is redirected in place of its original or main course **2** *verb* to go round (an object) so as to avoid it

◊ **bypass air screw** *noun* screw on the airflow sensor of a fuel injection system, for adjusting the amount of air in the mixture

◊ **bypass filter** *noun* type of oil filter through which only part of the total lubricant passes (approximately 10-20%), the rest being supplied directly to the lubricating points

◊ **bypass valve** *noun* valve which, when open, directs the flow of a liquid or gas through a bypass; such as the wastegate in the exhaust of a turbocharger system

Cc

C (a) *(short for)* celsius *or* centigrade **(b)** = COULOMB **(c)** = COMFORT

◇ **C-4 system** *noun* = COMPUTER-CONTROLLED CATALYTIC CONVERTER

cab *noun* **(a)** = TAXI(CAB) **(b)** enclosed part at the front of a commercial vehicle for the driver and passenger(s)

◇ **cabin** *noun* = PASSENGER COMPARTMENT; **cabin-forward design** = passenger car design with a relatively short front end, and footwells extending up to the front axle, providing added passenger space

cable *noun* **(a)** assembly of insulated electrical conductors, usually wires, laid together, often around a central core and surrounded by a heavy insulation, for heavy duty applications such as battery cables; **cable clamp** = device for connecting cables to their terminals, especially battery cables to the terminal posts *cable clamps should be tight on the terminal posts and free of corrosion* **cable covering** = outer layer, now nearly always of plastic, serving as electrical insulation for cables **(b)** assembly of wire strands twisted together used for a pulling or sometimes a pushing or twisting action, either without a sheath (as in some brake cables), or with a sheath as in control cables and drives such as speedometer cables *the handbrake cable is stretched and will eventually break* **cable brake** mechanical brake operated by levers and a cable, either unsheathed or a Bowden type, now only used for a handbrake or on a trailer; **cable guide** = tube section bolted or spot-welded to a part of the body such as the floorpan for routeing an operating cable, e.g. for a bonnet release; **cable-operated** = brought into operation by a cable *cable-operated brakes or clutch*

cabriolet *noun* convertible with a soft top and windows, usually a four-seater (NOTE: usually only applied to continental models)

CACIS = CONTINUOUS AC IGNITION SYSTEM

CAD *(short for)* computer-aided design

cadence braking *noun* emergency braking method in which the driver rapidly depresses and releases the brake pedal

cadmium-plated *adjective* covered in a coating of cadmium

COMMENT: cadmium plating is often used to protect aluminium and its alloys, and also on steel especially for bolts and nuts

CAE *(short for)* computer-aided engineering

◇ **CAL** *(short for)* computer-aided lighting

Cal-look *noun* US special style of body modifications that originated in California and is performed mostly on smaller cars, e.g. VW Beetle, including the removal of all chrome except perhaps one side trim strip, paintwork mostly in bright shades such as yellow, light blue, red, etc., and possibly chrome-plated dual tubular or blade-type bumpers

calibration *noun* marking the measuring units on an instrument or checking their accuracy

caliper *or* **calliper** *noun* **(a)** measuring tool with two legs usually mounted in a slide on a measuring bar, for internal and external measurement; some designs allow depth and step measurement as well; the different types include vernier calipers, dial calipers, or digital calipers **(b)** = BRAKE CALIPER; **caliper frame** = casting that holds the brake caliper, either directly bolted to the suspension or to an adapter

◇ **caliper gauge** *noun* = CALIPER (a)

cam *noun* **(a)** rotating part with a projection or projections (called lobes) used to push another part at precisely defined intervals *the cam in the distributor has one lobe for each cylinder* **(b)** *(informal for)* camshaft; **twin cam engine** = engine with two camshafts

◇ **cam-and-lever** *or* **cam-and-peg steering** *noun* steering system in which a conical peg mounted on a lever engages in a helically cut groove on a cylindrical drum; **cam-and-roller steering** = steering system in which a tapered disc or a set of discs/rollers engage with a helically cut, tapered groove on a cylindrical drum

◊ **cam angle** *noun* = DWELL

◊ **cam belt** *noun* = TIMING BELT

◊ **cam chain** *noun* = TIMING CHAIN

◊ **cam design** *noun* = CAM PROFILE

◊ **cam face** *noun* surface of a cam; **measure the cam face from nose to heel** = measure the cam's surface from the highest point to the lowest

◊ **cam follower** *noun* **(a)** part of the valve operating gear of a four-stroke engine, located between the cam and the pushrod or valve stem - possibly equipped with a roller mechanism - in a manner to prevent lateral forces acting on either the pushrod or valve stem **(b)** = TAPPET

◊ **cam heel** *noun* lowest point of a cam opposite the lobe (NOTE: also called **base circle**)

◊ **cam lobe** *noun* projecting part of a cam which pushes on a pushrod, valve stem, or follower, etc. *wear on the cam lobes leads to loss of performance due to reduced valve lift*

◊ **cam lubricator** *noun* device, often in the form of a wick, for lubricating the contact breaker cam in the distributor

◊ **cam profile** *noun* exact shape of the cam face which determines the rate and extent of valve lift, i.e. how fast and how far the valve opens, and all other aspects of valve behaviour during the opening and closing process

◊ **cam roller** *noun* rotating wheel acting as a cam follower

camber *noun* **(a)** angle formed by the plane of the wheel to the perpendicular as viewed from the front; **positive camber** = wheel leaning outwards at the top; **negative camber** = wheel leaning inwards at the top **(b)** slightly arched contour of a road or other surface; **adverse camber** = slope on the outside of a bend which throws a vehicle off the desired line **(c)** curvature of a leaf spring

camper *noun* motorized caravan, with a body in appearance like a van, built on a small to medium-sized commercial vehicle chassis and offering sleeping, cooking and other facilities

◊ **camping trailer** *noun* **(a)** trailer containing camping equipment or fitted with a tent which can be erected on arrival at the desired camping site **(b)** *US* = CARAVAN

camshaft *noun* shaft carrying the cams which operate the valves usually of a four-stroke engine and rotating at half engine speed; *(see illustration 6)*; **camshaft bearing** = bearing (usually a plain bearing) which supports the camshaft; **camshaft drive** = connection between crankshaft and camshaft - either via gears, chain, drive belt, shaft or eccentric shaft - that ensures the required speed ratio of 1:2; **camshaft drive belt** = TIMING BELT; **camshaft drive sprocket** = sprocket mounted on the crankshaft to drive the camshaft via the timing chain; **camshaft end play** = free lateral movement of the camshaft *move the camshaft towards and away from the thrust bearing to determine the end play* **camshaft housing** = housing for one of the camshafts of a twin overhead camshaft engine mounted on top of the cylinder head, and containing the camshaft and usually also the tappets; *(see illustrations 4, 5, 7)*; **camshaft journal** = part of the camshaft running in one of its bearings; **camshaft pulley** = pulley on the end of the camshaft for the camshaft drive belt; **camshaft sprocket** = sprocket mounted on the camshaft, driven by the timing chain which in turn is driven by the crankshaft

COMMENT: the function of an engine camshaft is to control the entry and exit of the air/fuel mixture in relation to the position of the piston in the cylinder

can *noun* tube in a canned motor pump which insulates the motor winding

candela *noun* basic unit of luminous intensity

candy paint job *noun* (*informal US*) custom paintwork using a transparent colour medium applied over the base coat, which adds translucence and richness to the paint, especially all shades of red

canned motor pump *noun* glandless pump with a special type of submersible or 'canned' motor, whose stator winding is insulated from the fluid pumped by a tube, the so-called can

COMMENT: canned motor pumps ensure safe pumping with a guarantee of no leakage, as they require no shaft seal to insulate the motor

cannibalize *verb* to take parts from (a vehicle) to fit to another vehicle

canning *noun* insertion of the catalyst element into the converter shell of a catalytic converter.

cantilever spring *noun* **(a)** leaf spring mounted upside down and fixed to the vehicle at its mid-point, (now obsolete) **(b)** = QUARTER-ELLIPTIC LEAF SPRING

cantrail *noun* = ROOF RAIL

canvas top *noun US* soft top for an open car, especially one made of a natural fabric

cap *noun* **(a)** protective cover, usually round and such as can be screwed or twisted on, e.g. radiator cap, petrol cap **(b)** base of a light bulb which fits into the socket

capacitor *noun* assembly of one or more pairs of conductors separated by insulators, able to store an electric charge where there is a voltage difference; **capacitor discharge ignition (CDI) (system)** = electronic ignition system whose ignition energy is stored in the electrical field of a capacitor, which discharges via the ignition transformer when a thyristor is triggered at the ignition point

COMMENT: capacitors can be used for a variety of purposes in motor vehicles, for instance as suppressors to prevent radio interference or as a storage element for electronic ignition systems; a CDI system allows the use of surface-gap sparking plugs

capacity *noun* **(a)** amount which can be contained in a container such as a fuel tank, sump, radiator, etc., and by extension the swept volume of an engine **(b)** output of an electric motor or other electrical apparatus **(c)** volume of fluid handled through a pump, usually in gallons per minute

◇ **capacity rating** *noun* = RATED CAPACITY

capillary (tube) *noun* tube with a very small bore used for temperature gauges

cap nut *noun* nut whose outer end is closed, covering the thread

capping *see* DOOR CAPPING

capstan screw *noun* screw with a round head with a hole or holes passing through it, into which a tommy bar is inserted for tightening or loosening

capstat *noun* wax-type thermostat at the base of the jet of a SU carburettor, which expands and reduces fuel flow when the underbonnet temperature rises; *(compare* TEMPERATURE COMPENSATOR)

captive *adjective* permanently located in the desired position; **bolt with captive plain washer** = bolt with a plain washer trapped under its head; **captive nut** = nut inserted in a sheet metal cage spot-welded to the body in an inaccessible position, so that the item fixed to it can easily be removed

car *noun* **(a)** *US* = TRAMCAR **(b)** = PASSENGER CAR; **car accident** = CAR CRASH; **car alarm (system)** = alarm system; **car banger** = *(informal)* person or organization that fakes car accidents and repair bills in order to get the repair money from insurance companies; **car banging** = *(informal)* insurance fraud involving fake car accidents and repair bills; **car blind** = blind for the rear window to prevent dazzle from following vehicles' headlights; **car burglar** = person who steals things from cars; **car cap** = waterproof cover for the roof, windscreen and windows; **car care product** = preparation or article for cleaning, polishing and preserving especially the bodywork and interior; **car cover** = cover shaped to fit a car, usually waterproof for use outdoors, but can also be for protection against dust and condensation during storage; **car crash** *see* CRASH; **car insurance** = MOTOR INSURANCE; **car key** = key for the ignition, boot, doors or petrol cap, etc.; **car park** = area or building where cars may be parked; **car phone** = cellular telephone installed in a car; **car polish** = polish for the exterior paintwork of a car; **car radio** = radio receiver for use in a car; **car sponge** = large sponge for washing a car; **car stereo** = combination of a stereo radio with a cassette player or sometimes with a CD player, for use in a car; **car tax** = tax added to the price of a new car, or tax payable annually or six-monthly for using a car on the road; **car test** = ROAD TEST; **car theft** = stealing cars or stealing items from cars; **car thief** = person who steals cars; **car tyre** = tyre suitable for a passenger car; **car wash** = **(a)** drive-in, automatic facility for washing a car **(b)** car cleaning agent for adding to water, containing a detergent and usually a wax; **car wax** = non-abrasive polish containing wax for protecting a car's finish

caravan *noun* mobile home especially for recreational purposes, for towing behind a car or commercial vehicle, usually with two wheels (NOTE: US English is **camping trailer, mobile home**)

◇ **caravanning** *noun* travelling with a caravan, usually as a holiday

carb *noun* = CARBURETTOR

carbon *noun* **(a)** black material with good electrical properties of conductivity **(b)** deposit which forms in the combustion chamber, on the piston crown and to a lesser extent in the inlet and exhaust ports, resulting from incomplete combustion especially of oil

◇ **carbon black** *noun* engineering material, used as filler in plastic mouldings and in tyres, where it improves the mechanical properties of tyre rubber and produces, as a side effect, the typical black colour

◇ **carbon brush** *noun* rubbing electrical contact in the form of a carbon block or rod which bears against another member, such as a commutator, collector ring or slip ring, to provide passage for an electric current, e.g. from an external source to the armature of a motor, as in a starter, or from the rotor of an alternator via slip rings to an external circuit; *(see illustrations 36, 37)*; **carbon brush spring** = BRUSH SPRING *(see illustration 37)*

carbon build-up *or* *deposits noun* residues of burnt oil deposited in the combustion chamber, on the piston top and elsewhere in the course of the combustion process

COMMENT: carbon build-up can cause loss of performance where it occurs, for instance on the valve stems, causing the valves to stick or not to close properly

carbon-core leads *noun* HT or ignition leads with a tiny diameter core of carbon or graphite

◇ **carbon dioxide (CO₂)** *noun* colourless, odourless, non-toxic gas, a natural constituent of the atmosphere and a product of breathing and some combustion processes

carbon fibre *noun* thin, light and very strong fibre of pure carbon, used as a reinforcement with resins, metal and other materials

COMMENT: the term is also used for plastics containing carbon fibre, which are extremely strong and light and consequently have been used for the frames of racing cars, and also,

due to their resistance to high temperatures, for the blades of turbines

carbon fouling *noun* blocking of the points of a sparking plug by carbon, often causing intermittent firing or complete failure

◇ **carbon knock** *noun* type of engine knock in internal combustion engines, caused by uncontrolled ignition as a result of carbon deposits in the combustion chamber, especially in old engines

◇ **carbon monoxide (CO)** *noun* poisonous but colourless and odourless gas resulting from incomplete oxidation or combustion of carbon, which is one of the three major pollutants found in the exhaust of spark ignition engines

◇ **carbon pin** *noun* spindle-shaped carbon brush in the centre of the distributor cap, bearing on the centre of the contact breaker arm

◇ **carbon tracking** *noun* formation of a leakage path for current, e.g. inside the distributor cap, where there are carbon deposits

carburation *US* **carburetion** *noun* mixture of fuel which has been vaporized with air in the correct proportions for combustion in an internal combustion engine *precise carburation is the key to emission control*

COMMENT: carburation is actually a general term for the generation of the A/F mixture required in an internal combustion engine, i.e. including both carburation in carburettors and by fuel injection systems, but it is sometimes used only with respect to carburettors, in contrast to fuel injection

carburetion *noun US* = CARBURATION

carburetor *noun US* = CARBURETTOR

carburettor *or* **carburetter** *US* **carburetor** *noun* conventional, mechanical device in the engine fuel system, mixing fuel with air to produce a combustible mixture which is supplied to the inlet manifold

COMMENT: carburettors are less suited for emission control by catalytic converters than fuel injection systems, which can adjust the air/fuel ratio more precisely to the prevailing conditions

◇ **carburettor barrel** *noun* the main air passage through the carburettor

◇ **carburettor engine** *noun* engine fitted with a carburettor as opposed to fuel injection (NOTE: opposite is **fuel injected engine**)

◇ **carburettor icing** *noun* formation of ice deposits in the carburettor intake during very damp and cool, but not freezing weather

◇ **carburettor throat** *or* **carburettor venturi** *see* VENTURI

carburization *noun* process of increasing the carbon content of steel to produce a desired degree of hardness, yielding high carbon steel

carcass *noun* basic structure of a tyre consisting of various plies of cord (made of rayon, nylon, polyester or steel), which are impregnated with rubber; *(see illustration 32)*

COMMENT: there are two ways to apply the plies which form the carcass, on the bias and radially, which result respectively in cross-ply and radial-ply, or simply radial, tyres

cardan joint *noun* most common type of a universal joint, in which two yokes mounted on the two parts to be coupled, usually a shaft and a driving or driven member, are connected with pivots to the arms of a cross-shaped piece

◇ **cardan shaft** *noun* shaft fitted with universal joints at each end

cargo area *noun* US load area of an estate car or pick-up truck

carpeting *noun* carpets made to fit the front and rear footwells, and also the boot in better equipped models

carriage bolt *noun* mushroom-headed bolt with a square neck which holds it in position in a square hole

cart spring *noun* *(informal)* = LEAF SPRING

carvac *noun* small, easily portable vacuum cleaner that can be plugged into the cigarette lighter of a car

casing *noun* **(a)** cover passing all the way round a piece of equipment, such as an electric motor **(b)** tyre, especially in its basic form before the tread has been moulded on

cassette compartment *noun* built-in cassette storage space; **cassette player** = unit

for playing audio cassettes, usually incorporated in a stereo unit

cast 1 *verb* to produce (a metal part) by pouring molten metal into a sand or metal mould **2** *adjective* produced by pouring molten metal into a sand or metal mould *cast crankshaft/camshaft/piston* **cast-alloy wheel** = one-piece wheel, as opposed to two-piece and three-piece forged wheels, produced using the low-pressure die casting process, which offers a great degree of design flexibility as to the styling of the wheel disc; *(compare* ALLOY WHEELS); **cast aluminium** = aluminium alloy made by pouring the molten metal into a sand or metal mould

caster *noun* US = CASTOR

cast iron *noun* iron with a high carbon content and also containing much cementite or graphite, so that it is unsuitable as wrought iron

castle nut US **castellated nut** *noun* hexagon nut with slots cut in the top of each face, two of which are lined up with a hole in the bolt or stud and a split pin inserted to prevent loosening *castle nuts have been largely superseded by self-locking nuts*

◇ **castle section** *noun* panel with fairly shallow strengthening humps that are, however, deeper than normal stiffening ribs, e.g. in floorpans featuring beaded or offset areas

castor US **caster** *noun* **(a)** inclination or angle from the vertical of the kingpin or steering axis on the ground between the extended vertical axis through the wheel centre and the point where the extended steering axis would meet the ground (NOTE: also called **castor angle) (b)** distance on the ground when viewed from the side, between the point of contact of the tyre (which is also the extended vertical axis through the wheel centre) and the point where a line through the inclined kingpin (or the extended steering axis) would meet the ground (NOTE: also called **castor offset, trail)**

◇ **castor action** *noun* self-centring action resulting from castor which brings the steered wheels back to the straight ahead position

◇ **castor angle** *noun* = CASTOR (a)

◇ **castor offset** *noun* = CASTOR (b)

cat *noun* *(informal)* = CATALYTIC CONVERTER

catalyst *noun* **(a)** substance that changes the rate of a chemical reaction without itself being used up; in a catalytic converter the element which reduces the toxicity of the exhaust gases **(b)** special agent added to a plastic body filler or resin or two-pack paint to speed up the setting process of the basic material applied

◊ **catalyst bed** *noun* layer of catalyst-coated material such as pellets or ceramic in a catalytic converter through which the gases pass *the two-stage converter receives additional air between the catalyst beds*

◊ **catalyst charge** *noun* catalyst-coated materials such as pellets or ceramic in a catalytic converter

◊ **catalyst coating** *noun* = CATALYTIC LAYER

◊ **catalyst container** *noun* = CONVERTER HOUSING (b)

◊ **catalyst contamination** *noun* loss of catalytic efficiency caused by contaminating deposits

◊ **catalyst degradation** *or* **deterioration** *noun* loss of catalytic efficiency *use of leaded petrol or overheating of the converter will result in irreparable catalyst degradation*

◊ **catalyst efficiency** *noun* = CATALYTIC EFFICIENCY

◊ **catalyst indicator** *noun* indicator light in the instrument panel that illuminates after a certain mileage, e.g. after 25,000 miles, to remind the driver that the catalytic converter should be replaced; some older designs used a mechanical signal

◊ **catalyst substrate** *or* **support** *noun* base material carrying the catalytic layer or coating

catalytic converter *noun* device shaped like a silencer for exhaust emission control installed in the exhaust system as close to the engine as possible, in which a catalyst-coated substrate is enclosed in a sheet metal canister of stainless steel, protected against vibration by wire mesh, its lower shell being provided with a heat shield; *(see illustration 19)*

COMMENT: converters can be classified into different types according to: **1. Function:** oxidizing, reducing, three-way converters; **2. Number of beds:** single-stage, two-stage converters; **3. Substrate:** ceramic, metal converters; **4. Support:** bead-type, monolithic converters; **5. Catalyst:** precious or non-precious metal catalysts; **6. Fuel:** converters for leaded or unleaded fuel; **7. Usage:** main, primary converters; **8. Quality of exhaust gas:** computer-controlled, open-loop catalytic converter

catalytic activity *noun* rate at which a given catalytic converter purifies the exhaust gas stream, usually expressed as a conversion rate

◊ **catalytic efficiency** *noun* effectiveness of the catalyst in purifying the exhaust gases

catalytic layer *noun* very thin layer of a catalyst, usually consisting of platinum metals, supported by a ceramic or metal carrier material

COMMENT: the processes which occur on the catalytic layer are based on heterogeneous catalysis, i.e. the catalysis between solid catalyst molecules and gaseous molecules of the exhaust gas stream, and take place in three major steps: **1.** adsorption of the gas molecules at the active surface, the rate of adsorption being dependent on the surface area; **2.** chemical reaction between adsorbed gas molecules and between gas molecules and catalyst molecules; **3.** desorption of the reaction products

cathode *noun* negative electrode in an electrolytic cell

◊ **cathodic electropainting** *or* **cataphoretic painting** *noun* process used to apply the first coat of paint to car bodies involving positively charging paint particles, in which the cleaned metal parts to be coated are immersed in a tank of electrodeposition paint, and the current is then turned on, so that the positively charged particles are attracted by the negative metal parts

◊ **cathodic protection** *noun* protecting a metal from electrochemical corrosion by using it as the cathode of a cell with a sacrificial anode

caustic etching *noun* removal of metal by dipping aluminium parts in caustic soda

cavitation *noun* formation and subsequent collapse of vapour-filled cavities in a liquid, such as bubbles, vapour-filled pockets or a combination of both

cavity *noun* **(a)** empty space in a body structure, either in a box section or a double-skinned area **(b)** holder and contact for fuses

◊ **cavity sealant** *noun* sealant used for protecting cavities against rust, usually consisting of film-forming oils, waxes, solvents and rust inhibitors

CB (a) = CONTACT BREAKER **(b)** = CITIZENS' BAND; **CB radio** = citizens' band radio, both the form of communication on certain frequencies between drivers (particularly American truck drivers in the 1970s and '80s) and the receiver/transmitter used for this

CBR process *noun* controlled burn rate, a method of improving fuel economy by controlling/accelerating the fuel burn rate

cc = CUBIC CENTIMETRES

> COMMENT: the usual unit of measure for the capacity of an engine; 1,000cc are equal to 1 litre

C-clamp *noun* screw-activated locking clamp with long, C-shaped jaws

CCS = CONTROLLED COMBUSTION SYSTEM

CDI = CAPACITOR DISCHARGE IGNITION

CD player *noun* device for playing compact discs

Cd value *noun* coefficient of drag, a characteristic indicating the resistance of a given car body to air flowing against its front, at high speeds, which is measured in a wind tunnel, and unlike drag as such, depends only on the shape or outline of the body, not on the cross-sectional area, and being a coefficient, has no unit of measurement

cell *noun* **(a)** system of negative and positive plates for storage of electricity, either used singly or in combination to form a battery **(b)** combustion chamber of a rotary piston engine

cellular phone *noun* portable, wireless telephone, introduced in 1983 in the USA and mainly used as a car phone

cellulose *noun* popular term for the previously almost universal automotive finish, which is thin and therefore suitable for spraying, fast drying and gives a hard and brilliant finish (NOTE: properly called **nitrocellulose**); **cellulose putty** = filler for minor surface imperfections

cementite (FE$_3$C) *noun* iron carbide, a very hard substance found in cast iron

central gearchange *noun* usual arrangement with the gear lever in the centre of the floor

◊ **central chassis lubrication** *noun* lubrication of all chassis components with oil or grease from one central point

◊ **central locking** *noun* locking of all doors by operating an electronic device or by turning the key in the lock of the driver's door

◊ **central-locking hub** *noun* = SPLINED HUB; **central-locking wheel** = wheel with splines in its centre which mate with splines on the outside of the hub, usually of the wire-spoke type fixed with one central nut

◊ **central reserve** *or* **reservation** *noun* strip that separates the two sides of a motorway or dual carriageway; *(compare* CRASH BARRIER)

◊ **centre** *verb* to place (a part) in a central position in relation to another part; **to centre the clutch** = to align the centre hole in the clutch plates with the end of the crankshaft, so that the gearbox shaft will fit easily into the splines

◊ **centre console** *noun* centre section of the dashboard which is extended downwards, with space for a radio or stereo unit and storage for cassettes and the like

◊ **centre differential** *noun* differential located between two drive axles to balance the speed differences between the two axles, mainly used in vehicles with permanent four-wheel drive

◊ **centre drive** *noun* engine design with power take-off between the cylinders rather than at the end of the crankshaft; **centre drive plate** = INTERMEDIATE (DRIVE) PLATE

◊ **centre electrode** *noun* **(a)** electrode projecting out of the insulator nose of a sparking plug typically a compound electrode with a copper core, or a silver or platinum electrode **(b)** = CENTRE TERMINAL

◊ **centre gear** *noun* = SUN GEAR

◊ **centreline** *noun* imaginary straight line passing through the centre of, e.g. a vehicle, from front to rear

◊ **centre locking disc** *noun* = HUB CAP; **centre lock nut** = SPINNER

◊ **centre of gravity** *noun* point about which the weight of a body will act or pivot *a car with a low centre of gravity will roll less in corners*

◊ **centre pillar** *noun* = B-PILLAR

◊ **centre point steering** *noun* steering geometry layout where the steering axis cuts the wheel axis in the wheel centre plane, with no offset at the road surface

◊ **centre punch** *noun* tool with a sharp conical steel tip for punching an indentation where a hole is to be drilled

◊ **centre section damage** *noun* type of frame damage where the car is hit from the side approximately in the middle, causing the centre part of the car around the B-pillar to move inwards so that, seen from the top, the frame is no longer straight, but appears curved like a banana

◊ **centre terminal** *noun* spring-loaded carbon pin or carbon brush contact in the centre of the distributor cap acting on and forming contact with the rotor

◊ **centre tunnel** *noun* tunnel in the longitudinal centreline of the vehicle, usually but not necessarily enclosing the transmission, i.e. this tunnel may even be present on front-wheel drive cars; *(compare* TRANSMISSION TUNNEL)

centrifugal advance *noun* automatic mechanical ignition advance by means of centrifugal force, supplied by advance weights; **centrifugal advance mechanism** = automatic speed-dependent spark advance mechanism inside the distributor, controlled by centrifugal force supplied by advance weights which turn the distributor cam via yokes to advance the spark; *(compare* VACUUM ADVANCE MECHANISM)

◊ **centrifugal clutch** *noun* clutch in which the friction elements are brought into contact with the clutch face by centrifugal force so that the clutch automatically engages and disengages at a certain speed of rotation; the term is also used for a clutch mechanism that uses centrifugal force to apply a higher force against the friction plate as the clutch turns faster

◊ **centrifugal force** *noun* force which pushes a body outwards that is rotating about a centre

◊ **centrifugal governor** *noun* device controlling speed by means of centrifugal force in automatic transmissions and other applications

◊ **centrifugal oil filter** *noun* filter in which suspended solids are removed from the oil by centrifugal force created by spinning the oil at high speed in a rotating element

centrifugal pump *noun* impeller pump in which the liquid is forced, by either atmospheric or other pressure, into a set of rotating vanes constituting an impeller

COMMENT: the impeller discharges the liquid at a higher pressure and a higher velocity at its periphery, with the major portion of the velocity energy then being converted into pressure energy by means of a diffusing device; a centrifugal pump is more suitable for handling large volumes of liquids than a positive-displacement pump

centrifugal weight *noun* weight in a governor or other controlling device which is thrown outwards by centrifugal force as speed increases and thus causes a control rod to be moved or pressure to be exerted

ceramic honeycomb *noun* interior of a monolithic converter which supports the catalyst

cetane rating *or* **number** *noun* measure of the ignition quality of diesel fuel, or how high a temperature is required to ignite it (the lower the cetane number, the higher the temperature required)

CFCs *or* **CFC gases** *noun* = CHLOROFLUOROCARBONS

cfm *(short for)* cubic feet per minute

chafer (strip) *noun* area between the bead and sidewall of a tyre

◊ **chafing** *noun* wearing away by rubbing

chain *noun* series of flexibly connected links formed into a loop so that it can be passed over sprockets whose teeth engage in the spaces between the links, in order to transmit motion; **chain case** = metal casing completely enclosing a drive chain and its sprockets; **chain drive** = form of transmission using a chain passing over sprockets (NOTE: chain drive is still the most common form of transmission on motorcycles); **chain filter wrench** = chain wrench whose chain passes round and grips the body of an oil filter; **chain guard** = inverted L-section metal guard placed usually over the upper run of a chain; **chain hoist** = hoist for heavy objects such as engines consisting of a chain and a block and tackle; **chain pipe wrench** = chain wrench whose chain passes round and grips a pipe; **chain run** = section of a drive chain that runs between the sprockets *chain slack should be measured at the middle of the lower chain run* **chain tensioner** = component usually comprising a spring steel strip pressing on the chain, used mainly on four-stroke engines with a chain-driven camshaft and responsible for maintaining the proper chain tension; **chain wrench** = tool for loosening and tightening round or irregularly shaped objects, having a chain which is passed around the object, and a lever or key which at the same time tightens the chain and turns the object

chalking *noun* surface disintegration of the paint film, primarily due to weathering and lack of maintenance and characterized by dulling and powdering of the surface

chamber *noun* combustion chamber of a rotary piston engine, particularly where non-cylindrical, as in a Wankel engine

COMMENT: the volume of the chamber corresponds to the volume of the air/fuel mixture

chamfered *adjective* with a symmetrically bevelled surface on an edge or corner

chamois leather *noun* piece of soft bleached leather from sheep, goats, etc., used especially for drying paintwork, chrome and glass after washing (NOTE: also called informally **shammy leather**)

change 1 *verb* **(a)** to select and engage a gear (NOTE: also more fully **to change gear**. Note US English is **to shift gear**); **to change up** *or* **down** = to engage a higher *or* lower gear; **to change into second** *or* **top** = to engage second *or* top gear **(b)** to take away and put something new or different in its place *to change the oil* **2** *noun* engaging of another gear; **upward** *or* **downward change** = engaging of a higher *or* lower gear

◊ **change-speed gearbox** *noun* gearbox containing sets of gears which can be moved in and out of engagement with one another to give a number of different ratios between the speeds of the input and output shafts

◊ **change valve** *noun* valve used to change gear in an automatic gearbox, operated by rising oil pressure as the vehicle speeds up (NOTE: US English is **shift valve**)

channel section *noun* usually metal part with a U-shaped profile, e.g. in chassis members

Chapman strut *noun* form of MacPherson strut used in the rear suspension of some cars

characteristic map *noun* usually three-dimensional representation of several interdependent quantities, in most of which engine speed and load correspond to the x- and y-axes, and the third quantity, which depends on the first two, is measured against the z-axis; *(compare* IGNITION MAP, DWELL-ANGLE MAP)

charcoal canister *noun* = ACTIVATED CARBON CANISTER

charge 1 *noun* **(a)** amount of air/fuel mixture supplied to the cylinder that is available for combustion **(b)** definite quantity of electricity, such as that contained in a storage battery **2** *verb* to supply electrical charge to (a battery)

◊ **charge air** *noun* air in the air/fuel mixture; **charge-air cooling** = INTERCOOLING; **charge-air recycling (system)** = device on some turbocharger systems which serves to maintain the speed of the compressor while no boost is being delivered, so that boost is more instantly available on demand; *(compare* OVERRUN CONTROL VALVE)

◊ **charge changing** *or* **exchange process** *noun* removal of exhaust gases through the exhaust port and admission of a fresh charge through the transfer port in a two-stroke engine

◊ **charge losses** *noun* that part of the fresh charge in a two-stroke engine that short-circuits out of the cylinder during the charge changing process before the combustion process occurs and is thus lost; *(compare* SCAVENGING LOSSES)

◊ **charger** *noun* = BATTERY CHARGER

◊ **charging characteristic** *noun* charger characteristic showing the dependence of the current on the voltage during charge

◊ **charging current** *noun* electric current supplied to the battery when the charging system is operative

◊ **charging efficiency** *noun* figure indicating the mass of charge retained in the cylinder of a two-stroke engine after the ports close, divided by the actual swept volume

◊ **charging piston** *noun* additional piston formerly fitted to some two-stroke engines, designed to precompress the fresh charge and to supply it at excess pressure into the engine cylinders

◊ **charging point** *noun* = BATTERY CHARGING STATION

◊ **charging pressure** *noun* = BOOST PRESSURE

◊ **charging rate** *noun* amount of current, usually in amperes, delivered by the charging system

◊ **charging stroke** *noun* = INDUCTION STROKE

Charpy test *noun* impact resistance test in which the specimen is supported as a horizontal beam and broken by a single swing of a pendulum with the impact line midway between the supports and directly opposite the notch for notched specimens

chassis *noun* originally, and today still in heavy goods vehicles, a separate structure consisting of a frame, springs and axles forming the lower part of a vehicle, to which the bodywork is fitted, but with modern unitary construction there is no separate chassis and the term is used to refer to the running gear, i.e. suspension, including control arms, springs, shock absorbers, steering components, etc.; **chassis bracket set** = set of brackets to be welded under the sill prior to straightening the accident damage when the standard sill panel does not have a jointing flange; **chassis channel** = channel section forming a chassis member; **chassis dynamometer** = test stand for a complete car to determine, for example, its emission characteristics under a set of defined driving conditions; **chassis frame** = frame usually consisting of two longitudinal side members joined by a number of crossmembers, to which the suspension and axles are attached, in goods vehicles and formerly in cars; **chassis leg** = short channel or box section that runs along the vehicle main axis and is not a main side member but rather an auxiliary member; **chassis number** = formerly the manufacturer's number identifying a vehicle (NOTE: now called **vehicle identification number**); **chassis section** = box or channel section forming part of the chassis *liberal amounts of rust inhibitor were injected into all the chassis sections*

chatter *verb* to move jerkily especially at high speed, making only irregular contact

check 1 *noun* inspection to see whether something is all right; **an engine oil level check** = looking at the dipstick to see if there is enough oil in the sump *normally, checks are made on a warm engine* **2** *verb* to inspect (something) to see whether it is all right; **check the plugs, and replace if necessary** = take the sparking plugs out and see whether they are in good condition, if not fit new ones *check the bearings for wear*

◊ **check ball** *noun* ball in a ball-type check valve

◊ **check engine warning light** *noun* light which indicates a malfunction of the engine system

◊ **check point** *noun* **(a)** particular point on a piece of equipment where it is possible to check if there is any malfunction **(b)** place on a road where vehicles are stopped, e.g. at a frontier or on a rally

◊ **check routine** *noun* series of checks to be made when tracing a fault or when inspecting a new vehicle at the factory

check valve *noun* **(a)** non-return valve permitting flow in one direction only, widely used in emission control systems **(b)** residual pressure valve in a brake master cylinder

COMMENT: in cars with air injection, one check valve is positioned in the air line from the diverter valve to the air manifold; its purpose is to protect the air pump from backflow of exhaust gases

cheese head *noun* cylindrical head for a screw with a straight slot and straight sides

chemical brightening *or* **polishing** *noun* improvement of surface smoothness of a metal by immersion in a suitable solution

◊ **chemical toilet** *noun* portable toilet for use in caravans or when camping

childproof lock *noun* lock on rear doors which when activated prevents the door from being opened from inside the car

◊ **child restraint system** *noun* general term for child seats and accessories, often used as a synonym for child seat

◊ **child seat** *noun* combination of a seat shell, a belt system and/or an impact cushion, especially suited for children of the age groups 1 and 2

COMMENT: according to the ECE-R 44 standard, children are grouped into the following age brackets: group 0 up to 10 kg *or* up to 9 months; group 1 from 9-18 kg *or* 8 months - 4 years; group 2 from 15-25 kg *or* 4-6 years; group 3 from 22-36 kg *or* 6-12 years. The age group must be specified on a restraint system

chip *verb (of stones)* to cause damage to (paintwork) in the form of small pits

◇ **chipping** *noun* damage to paintwork in the form of small pits caused by stones being thrown against it *the front end of the car is particularly susceptible to chipping*

◇ **chipping hammer** *noun* hammer used to remove the slag from weld seams

chisel *noun* simple steel tool with a sharp end, used with a hammer to cut through metal and other materials

chlorofluorocarbons *noun* gaseous compounds used especially as propellants for aerosol cans and in refrigerants (NOTE: usually called **CFCs**)

chock *noun* = WHEEL CHOCK

choke *noun* (i) device which restricts the amount of air entering the carburettor in order to enrich the mixture when starting the engine and running cold; (ii) choke knob; **choke control** = system for actuating a non-automatic choke, usually a cable with a knob on the fascia; **choked** = **(a)** *(of engine)* running with the choke in operation **(b)** clogged; **choke knob** = knob on the fascia for operating the choke; **choke tube** = CARBURETTOR VENTURI; **choke valve** = valve restricting the amount of air or liquid admitted, especially on a carburettor; *(see illustration 11)*

chop shop *noun US* workshop or factory that specializes in replacing the standard steel roof of cars or pick-up trucks with a convertible top

chromate 1 *noun* salt or ester of chromic acid, often used as a pigment **2** *verb* to treat with a solution of a chromium compound to produce a protective coating of metal chromate; **chromate (conversion) coating** = conversion coating produced by chromating; **chromate treatment** = treatment of metal with a solution of a chromium compound to produce a protective coating of metal

chromate (NOTE: not to be confused with **chroming**)

◇ **chromatize** *verb* = CHROMATE (2)

◇ **chrome 1** *noun* **(a)** = CHROMIUM **(b)** chromium plating, or all the items that are chromium-plated on a car **2** *verb* to plate with chromium; **chrome-hardened** = *(of steel)* hardened by the addition of chromium; **chrome-plated** *or* **chromed** = CHROMIUM-PLATED; **chrome steel** = steel containing chromium for extra hardness and rust resistance; **chrome work** = all the chromium-plated items on a car body

◇ **chromic acid** *noun* electrolyte used in anodising processes for producing non-transparent, non-metallic oxide layers

◇ **chromium** *noun* hard grey metallic element used in electroplating and in steel production for extra hardness and rust resistance; **chromium-plated** = coated with a thin layer of chromium by electrodeposition for protection against corrosion, also with a thicker layer for wear resistance; **chromium plating** = process of coating metal with a layer of chromium and also the result; **satin chromium plating** = chromium plating with a soft matt sheen; **chromium steel** = CHROME STEEL

chubby screwdriver *noun* screwdriver with a very short handle and blade for use in confined spaces

chunking *noun* breaking away of pieces of the tread of a tyre

CI (a) = COMPRESSION IGNITION *CI engine* **(b)** = COIL IGNITION (SYSTEM)

CIH *(short for)* camshaft in head; **CIH engine** = type of overhead valve (OHV) engine with the camshaft enclosed in, not on top of, the cylinder head (NOTE: not to be confused with an overhead camshaft (OHC) engine)

CIM *(short for)* computer-integrated manufacturing

circlip *noun* retaining ring in the form of an incomplete circle and made of spring steel, often with eyes either side of the gap so that it can be opened for removal; *(see illustration 6)* (NOTE: US English is **snap ring**); **circlip pliers** = special pliers with jaw tips coming to a point so that they can engage in the eyes of the circlip in order to expand it for removal

COMMENT: circlips can either fit in external grooves on shafts in order to hold rotating or pivoting parts in position, or in internal grooves in housings for keeping shafts, for example, in position

circuit *noun* **(a)** course forming a complete loop over which races are held **(b)** series of electrical connections forming a complete path for the current to flow through; **circuit breaker** = protective device which can be reset; it breaks an electric circuit to prevent damage when the circuit is overloaded or overheated by excess current flow; **circuit diagram** = diagram showing the complete wiring system of a vehicle; **circuit tester** = tool often similar in appearance to a screwdriver, with a light in the handle and a crocodile clip which can be attached to a suitable earth while the point touches the part or the wire which is to be tested; if the light comes on, the circuit is live at that point

circular headlamp *noun* traditional shape of headlamp as opposed to the modern rectangular headlamp

circulating pump *noun* centrifugal pump designed to generate forced circulation of a liquid in a closed system, e.g. a water pump in an internal combustion engine

CIS = CONTINUOUS INJECTION SYSTEM

citizens' band *see* CB RADIO

city car *noun* very compact car, usually 10-12 feet in length

◇ **city cycle** *noun* = URBAN CYCLE

CL (*short for*) Comfort Luxe, denoting a model more luxurious than 'L' but not as grand as 'GL'

cladding *noun* **(a)** process of covering one material with another and bonding them together under high pressure and temperature **(b)** outer body panels fitted separately to composite wooden or tubular frames, e.g. on buses and coaches

clamp *noun* fastening which holds an item or items in its jaws by strong pressure; (*compare* G-CLAMP, WHEEL CLAMP)

◇ **clamping load** *noun* pressure on the plates in a clutch or coupling

class A thread *noun* = EXTERNAL THREAD

◇ **class B thread** *noun* = INTERNAL THREAD

classic car *noun* specifically applied to cars of the postwar era up to about 1970 or even 1980, but also used as a general term for all old cars; **the XYZ is already a classic** = the XYZ has cult status and is regarded as collectable, so that it is going up and not down in value; **a classic-car meeting** = a meeting to which enthusiasts bring their old cars to look at them and discuss them, often with a competition to decide which is the smartest (a concours); **restoration of classic cars** = putting old cars back as near as possible into as new condition

classified (ad) *noun* small advertisement in a newspaper or magazine, usually put in by a private person, e.g. with a car for sale

claw hammer *noun* hammer with two curved prongs at the back of the head for extracting nails, etc.

clay model *noun* mock-up of a new design made before an actual prototype is built; **a fully-detailed, full-size clay model** = a clay model showing all external features and which is the same size as the finished product

clean oil *noun* fresh engine oil supplied to the engine from a container; **clean oil lubrication** = lubrication system in which clean engine oil is supplied directly to the lubrication points of the engine, as in some two-stroke engines; (*compare* TOTAL-LOSS LUBRICATION)

clearance *noun* gap between two parts; **piston clearance** = gap between the piston and the cylinder wall; **valve clearance** = gap between the top of the valve stem and the tappet when the valve is closed and the tappet is not pressing on it

◇ **clearance height** *noun* **(a)** = GROUND CLEARANCE **(b)** maximum height of a vehicle such that it can pass under a bridge or similar obstruction

◇ **clearance (marker) lamp** *noun* lamp mounted on the roof of vans, lorries and other large vehicles at the left- and right-hand corners to show the maximum height and width of the vehicle

◇ **clearance volume** *noun* space remaining above the piston of an engine when it is at top dead centre

clear coat *or* **lacquer** *noun* top coat of base and clear systems

click-type torque wrench *noun* torque wrench designed to apply pre-determined torque, to which it is preset, automatically releasing once the setting is reached; the release action is normally accompanied by an audible click and/or visible signal

climate control *noun* lever or similar that controls the heater and/or air-conditioning system; **climate control system** = combined heating and air-conditioning system

◇ **climatic chamber** *noun* test chamber which can reproduce extremes of temperature and humidity, as well as artificial ultraviolet rays

climbing ability *noun* performance when climbing steep gradients

clinometer *noun* instrument used to measure the steepness of a gradient

clip-on weight *noun* small lead weight used to balance a wheel by clipping it onto the rim opposite a heavy spot of the tyre/wheel assembly; *(compare* BALANCE)

clock 1 *noun* **(a)** instrument showing time **(b)** *(informal)* = ODOMETER *or* SPEEDOMETER; **this car has 40,000 miles on the clock** = this car has covered 40,000 miles **2** *verb* to record (a speed or time), or to time (a car); **he clocked 45.68 seconds on his first run** = he covered the course in 45.68 seconds; **she was clocked at 198.2 mph over the measured mile** = she was timed at an average speed of 198.2 mph

◇ **clocking** *noun* putting back the mileage on a car's odometer, so that it shows a lower mileage than the car has in fact done (an illegal practice)

c/locking *noun* = CENTRAL LOCKING

clockwise *adverb* in the same direction as the hands of a clock *turn the lever fully clockwise*

clog *verb* to become obstructed with debris, sludge or other matter *if the passages are clogged with sludge, clean them with solvent and a long brush*

close coils *noun* coils at the end of a spring which are closer together

closed loop *noun* chain of control in which feedback, usually from a sensor or sensors, is used to regulate mixture strength, dwell angle and other engine functions by electronic means; **closed-loop control** = electronic control system using feedback to maintain correct mixture strength, etc.; *(compare* OPEN-LOOP)

COMMENT: the most effective catalytic converter systems use closed-loop control, i.e. if the oxygen sensor reads rich, the system is driven lean and vice versa

close-ratio gearbox *noun* gearbox in which there is relatively little difference between the gear ratios, so that fast changes can be made

◇ **closing cam/rocker** *noun* cam/rocker which is used to close the valve in desmodromic valve operation; unlike conventional valve control systems, in which the valves are closed by the valve spring

◇ **closing force** *noun* force necessary for closing the valves, provided by the valve springs

◇ **closing panel** *noun* panel that covers a gap in the body framework

cloth upholstery *noun* upholstery covered in a fabric as opposed to vinyl or leather

club hammer *noun* heavy hammer with a short handle for use with cold chisels, drifts, etc.

clunker *noun US (informal)* rusty old car

cluster gear *noun* layshaft and/or the set of gears mounted on it

clutch *noun* mechanism for connecting or disconnecting the drive between two shafts while they are rotating or at rest, placed between the engine and gearbox in vehicles with manual transmission, and usually mounted on the flywheel; *(see illustration 20)*

COMMENT: when starting from rest, disengaging the clutch allows a gear to be selected, and re-engaging it allows the drive to be taken up smoothly and progressively; further disengagement and re-engagement allows gears to be changed while in motion. Most cars use a single-plate, dry disc clutch of either diaphragm spring design or direct-pressure coil spring design

clutch aligning set *noun* selection of different tools used to align the clutch plate with the flywheel, usually containing a shaft, pilot bearing adapters, and tapered universal sleeves; **clutch aligning tool** = special tool, either in the form of a bar or a disc, with the aid of which clutch plate and flywheel can be precisely aligned on single disc clutches

◇ **clutch brake** *noun* device for slowing down the clutch plate and hence the gears on the input shaft in order to enable faster and quieter engagement of gears

◇ **clutch cable** *noun* operating cable from the clutch pedal to the clutch release lever; *(see illustration 20)*

◇ **clutch cover** *noun* bowl-shaped cover that houses the rotating elements of a friction clutch, anchors the clutch spring(s), and is normally attached to the flywheel

◇ **clutch disc** *noun US* = CLUTCH PLATE

◇ **clutch drag** *noun* failure of the clutch to disengage completely when the pedal is depressed, with the result that gearchanges become difficult as the driven plate and input shaft continue to rotate

◇ **clutch facing** *noun* = CLUTCH LINING

◇ **clutch fork** *noun* clutch release lever with a forked end which presses on the release bearing to disengage the clutch

◇ **clutch housing** *noun* = BELL HOUSING

◇ **clutch judder** *noun* faulty condition in which the clutch does not take up smoothly but judders during engagement

◇ **clutch lining** *noun* ring of friction material on the clutch plate

◇ **clutch pedal** *noun* pedal which operates the clutch usually either mechanically via a cable, or hydraulically

◇ **clutch plate** *noun* part of the clutch assembly which carries the clutch lining and is squeezed between the flywheel and pressure plate when the pedal is released, thus transmitting power to the gearbox input shaft; *(see illustration 20)* (NOTE: US English is **clutch disc**); **clutch pressure plate** = part of the clutch assembly which is pressed against the clutch plate by the clutch springs to transmit the drive; *(see illustration 20)*

◇ **clutch release** *or* **thrust bearing** *noun* bearing (usually a roller bearing) that

can be moved by the release lever through clutch pedal action to disengage the drive from the engine to the transmission; *(see illustration 20)* (NOTE: US English is **throwout bearing**); **clutch release lever** = lever one end of which presses on the clutch release bearing, the other being actuated mechanically or hydraulically by the clutch pedal; *(see illustration 20)* (NOTE: US English is **throwout fork, lever**)

◇ **clutch shaft** *noun* short gearbox input shaft, rotating at engine speed and coaxial with but not connected to the main shaft, which transmits power from the clutch to the gearbox

◇ **clutch slip** *noun* incomplete engagement of a clutch, so that not all the drive torque is transmitted even when the clutch pedal is fully released and the driven plate does not rotate as fast as the flywheel; engine speed increases but road speed often does not; *(compare SLIP THE CLUTCH)*

◇ **clutch spring** *noun* one of the coil springs (generally mounted in the clutch cover) which press the pressure plate against the driven clutch plate to transmit the drive

◇ **clutch stop** *noun* = CLUTCH BRAKE

C-matic transmission *noun* trade name for a semi-automatic transmission developed by Citroën

CNG = COMPRESSED NATURAL GAS

CO = CARBON MONOXIDE

coach *noun* a single-deck bus, usually with a luxurious specification, for carrying passengers over long distances, either from city to city on regular schedules or in groups on tours; *(compare BUS)*

◇ **coach bolt** *noun* bolt with a mushroom head underneath which it has a square neck which holds it in a matching square recess, e.g. in wood, so that a spanner is only needed for the nut

coachbuilder *noun* firm specializing in the production of special bodies for motor vehicles; **coachbuilt body** = separate body not forming a single structure with the chassis; **coachbuilt construction** = vehicle layout incorporating a separate chassis frame which serves as a carrier of all drive train and suspension parts, the vehicle body itself not forming an integral structural part of the vehicle; *(compare SKELETON*

CONSTRUCTION, UNITARY CONSTRUCTION)

COMMENT: very few coachbuilders making special bodies for passenger cars remain, due to the almost universal use of monocoque construction, which is only suited to large-scale production; however this is not the case with most commercial vehicles, so that there are many small specialist firms making bodywork on chassis produced by major manufacturers. Coachbuilt construction reflects the era of horse-drawn carriages, which influenced the structural layout of motor vehicles until the invention of the unitary or monocoque style of construction predominant since World War 2

coachlining *noun* thin, precisely contoured lines, especially along the whole side of the vehicle, also on motorcycle tanks, the most common colours being gold and black

◊ **coach paint** *noun* type of slow-drying, high-gloss paint used in the early days of motoring for brush-painting car bodies

◊ **coachwork** *noun* = BODYWORK

coarse(-cut) file *noun* file for the rapid removal of large amounts of material in a first rough shaping stage (NOTE: opposite is smooth file)

◊ **coarse pitch** *noun* construction of a gear or screw thread with relatively wide gaps between the teeth or threads; **coarse thread** = screw thread with relatively wide gaps between the threads, and hence fewer threads for a given length of screw

coast *verb* to run without any drive being transmitted to the wheels, either in neutral or with the clutch out

coat 1 *noun* layer of material, usually applied in liquid form, covering a surface *the top coat should be polished with buffing compound* **2** *verb* to apply a layer of usually liquid material *the bearing shells are coated with white metal*

◊ **coating** *noun* **(a)** action of applying a layer of material to a surface **(b)** = COAT (1)

cock *noun* tap or shut-off valve controlling the flow of water, for example

cockpit *noun* area comprising the driver's seat and all instruments and controls, especially in a racing car

coefficient of drag *see* CD VALUE

◊ **coefficient of friction** *noun* ratio of the force needed to slide one surface over another to the force preventing the motion

cog *noun* *(informal)* gear; **cog-swapping** = gear-changing

◊ **cogged belt** *noun* toothed belt

coil *noun* **(a)** device for generating high tension voltage consisting of primary and secondary windings around a laminated iron core (NOTE: also called **ignition coil**) **(b)** = FIELD COIL/WINDING

COMMENT: when the primary circuit is closed, current flows in the primary winding and a magnetic field builds up, which collapses when the contact breaker or a control unit interrupts the primary circuit, inducing a high tension voltage in the secondary winding which is transmitted to the sparking plug

coil chimney *noun* = COIL TOWER

◊ **coil-coating** *noun* process of coating continuous metal strips with an organic finishing system for decoration and protection

coil ignition (CI) (system) *noun* inductive ignition system with an ignition coil which stores the primary current from the battery and steps it up to ignition (high tension) voltage, which is then transferred to the sparking plugs via the distributor and HT (high tension) leads in the engine firing order.

COMMENT: conventional coil ignition systems are being increasingly superseded by breakerless transistorized ignition systems and electronic map ignition systems

coil lead *noun* HT (high tension) lead from the coil to the distributor (NOTE: US English is coil wire)

◊ **coil spring** *noun* spiral of spring steel wire, used in suspension systems and clutches and as valve springs; *(see illustrations 27, 28)*; **coil spring clutch** = clutch in which a ring of coil springs hold the pressure plate in position; **coil spring compressor** = SPRING COMPRESSOR

◊ **coil tower** *noun* top of the standard type of ignition coil in which the socket for the HT lead to the distributor is found, projecting upwards

◊ **coil wire** *noun* US = COIL LEAD

coke *noun* = CARBON (b)

◇ **coked up** *adjective* covered with a thick carbon deposit

cold-condensate corrosion *noun* corrosion of the inside of exhaust systems by direct chemical attack resulting from an acidic, aqueous solution that condenses from the exhaust gas at relatively low temperatures and collects at the cooler rear portions of the exhaust system

| COMMENT: this condition can lead to very rapid holing of the metal and failure of the exhaust, and is particularly bad where the vehicle is only used for short runs

cold cranking ability *noun* criterion for assessing the performance of a battery based on its ability to supply the considerable amount of current needed to turn the engine when cold

◇ **cold galvanizing** *noun* galvanizing with zinc-rich paint or similar, or by electroplating with zinc

◇ **cold sparking plug** *noun* sparking plug with a short insulator nose, which absorbs less heat and dissipates heat quickly; *(compare* HEAT RANGE)

◇ **cold spraying** *noun* spraying method in which the paint is diluted with so much solvent that it can easily be sprayed, the solvent evaporating after painting

cold start(ing) *noun* starting the engine from cold

| COMMENT: a cold start in winter can require as much as three times the power from the battery compared with summer conditions. To improve cold starting, particular attention should be paid to all ignition components

cold start enrichment *noun* increasing the fuel content of the air/fuel mixture to compensate for condensation losses in the intake system when the engine is cold

| COMMENT: typically, cold start enrichment is provided by a choke or cold start injectors, and is governed mechanically or electronically by engine temperature. Some electronically controlled systems provide different degrees of enrichment for cranking, immediately after starting and during warming up

cold start injector *noun* device in fuel injection systems which injects additional fuel during starter operation when the engine is cold, working in much the same way as a choke on a carburettor; *(see illustration 14)*

| COMMENT: the cold start injector is a solenoid-operated electrovalve energized by current from the starter solenoid, in which a thermo-time switch interrupts the current if the engine is hot or after the starter has been operated for more than a few seconds, in order to prevent flooding. In some systems, the cold start injector is operated intermittently by a hot-start pulse relay, to improve starting once the engine has warmed up

collapsible spare tire *noun US* = SPACE-SAVING SPARE WHEEL

◇ **collapsible steering column** *noun* steering column designed to fold or telescope in a case of frontal impact

collar *noun* **(a)** washer fitted under the head of a bolt or screw **(b)** raised area on a shaft to hold it in position, usually against a bearing; *(see illustration 37)*

collector's car *noun* usually older car which is of value to collectors; *(compare* CLASSIC CAR)

collet *noun* removable collar fitting in a groove to hold, for example, the valve spring on the valve stem

colour chart *noun* booklet containing details of paint names, codes and samples of exact colours, for the customer to choose from

◇ **colour coat** *noun* coat of paint which has the desired final colour, often but not always the top coat (in the case of two-pack finishes a clear lacquer is applied on top of it)

◇ **colour-coded** *adjective* **(a)** finished in the same colour as the main part of the bodywork *the bumpers and spoiler are colour-coded* (NOTE: also called **colour-keyed** *or* **colour-matched**) **(b)** *(of wiring, etc.)* finished in different colours to aid recognition

◇ **colour scheme** *noun* combination of colours, on the outside or inside of the vehicle *a vivid colour scheme*

column (gear)change *noun* gearchange mechanism in which the gear lever is on the steering column, just below the steering wheel (NOTE: also called **column shift** especially in the USA)

| COMMENT: this was a common arrangement in the 1950s and '60s, especially on American and other cars with bench front seats, but gave an imprecise action. Most American cars still have the selector lever for the automatic transmission on the steering column

combination *noun* vehicle made up of more than one element, especially a motorcycle and sidecar

◇ **combination pliers** *noun* typical general purpose pliers with serrated jaws, an oval recess and a wire cutter; in the USA they also have a slip joint so that the jaws can be opened wider

◇ **combination spanner** *noun* spanner with a ring spanner at one end and an open end of the same size at the other

◇ **combination valve** *noun* pressure-regulating valve in braking systems incorporating a failure warning switch and comprising two or more of the following valves: pressure-differential valve, metering valve, proportioning valve

combustion *noun* extremely rapid (but not explosive) burning of the air/fuel mixture timed to occur when the piston is at the top of its stroke, so that it is forced down to turn the crankshaft; **combustion chamber** = space between the top of the piston and the cylinder head, in which the air/fuel mixture is burned; *(see illustrations 4, 5)*; **combustion chamber recess** = area where combustion occurs in a rotary piston engine; **combustion pressure** = pressure created during the combustion of the air/fuel mixture in the cylinder, measured in pounds per square inch; **combustion residue (s)** = carbon and other deposits resulting from combustion

CO meter *noun* device for checking exhaust gases for carbon monoxide, a high level of which indicates an over-rich mixture as well as causing pollution

Comet head *noun* head with a swirl chamber for indirect injection diesel engines

Comfort (C) *noun* fairly basic car model specification; **Comfort Luxe (CL)** = slightly more luxurious specification than Comfort; *(compare* GL)

commercial vehicle *noun* vehicle for carrying goods or large numbers of passengers for money

commutator *noun* series of copper bars at one end of the dynamo or starter motor armature, electrically insulated from one another by mica; *(see illustration 37)*

COMMENT: the brushes rub against the bars of the commutator, which form a rotating connector between the armature windings and brushes

compact (car) *noun* American car category with a length of 14ft 5ins - 17ft and taking five passengers *some typical compact cars are: Alfa Romeo 164, BMW 5 series, Buick Skylark, Mercedes-Benz 200-300, Volkswagen Golf (compare* SUBCOMPACT (CAR))

company car *noun* car provided by an employer for an employee's business or private use

◇ **company logo** *noun* emblem forming the whole or part of a company's trademark

compass (display) *noun* instrument with a magnetized needle which always points to the magnetic north

COMMENT: an almost standard feature on American cars, but relatively uncommon on European models. It is very useful on the American highway system with its characteristic pattern of northbound, southbound, eastbound and westbound roads and streets; the absence of such a layout in Europe along with the relatively short distances and winding roads make an on-board car compass less useful

compensating bar *noun* = COMPENSATOR

◇ **compensating jet** *noun* jet in a fixed jet carburettor which supplies either extra air or extra fuel to maintain the correct mixture strength

compensating port *noun* small hole in the wall of a tandem master cylinder which connects the brake fluid reservoir to the pressure chamber; *(see illustration 29)*

COMMENT: in tandem master cylinders, there is a primary compensating port for the primary circuit and a secondary compensating port for the secondary circuit; the compensating port is always the second port, behind the replenishing port, as seen from the pushrod end

compensator *noun* horizontal bar which is pulled forward when the handbrake is applied at its central point, which is pivoted, while it is connected at each end to the handbrake cable, enabling equal force to be exerted on each rear brake

competition car *noun* car specially constructed for taking part in competitions, such as races, hill climbs and rallies

component *noun* part which may be either a single piece, such as a brush or bush, or an assembly such as a starter or a fuel pump; **component sharing** = the use of the same components (including major components such as engines) in different models and even in models from different manufacturers

composite propeller shaft *noun* innovative, single-piece propeller shaft made of fibre-reinforced epoxy in which the fibres are usually glass and/or carbon

compound carburettor *noun* carburettor with more than one choke (normally two - a smaller one for small throttle openings and a larger one for large throttle openings), but for fitting to a single port

◇ **compound (centre) electrode** *noun* electrode for a sparking plug with a copper core and a jacket of a nickel-based alloy

◇ **compound glass** *noun* = LAMINATED GLASS

◇ **compound motor** *noun* DC electric motor with two separate field windings, one in parallel and the other in series with the armature circuit; used as a starter motor

comprehensive insurance *noun* insurance against most risks, including third-party liability, fire, theft, and damage

compress *verb* to place under pressure or to squeeze into a small space *the piston as it rises in the cylinder compresses the mixture in the combustion chamber* **compressed air** = air at a higher than atmospheric pressure, used to drive tools and machinery; **compressed-air spray gun** = spray gun which atomizes the coating material and projects it against a surface by means of the negative pressure occurring when a stream of air enters a pipe of smaller diameter; **compressed natural gas (CNG)** *see* NATURAL GAS

◇ **compression** *noun* **(a)** compressing of the air/fuel mixture drawn into the combustion chamber before ignition takes place, either by the piston during its upward travel, or in the case of rotary engines by the reduction of the volume in the area between the rotor and the epitrochoid housing; **check the engine's compression** = turn the engine over and check that adequate resistance is felt when each piston reaches the top of its compression stroke; alternatively use a compression tester **(b)** pressing together of a spring or shock absorber; **the shock absorber**

is adjustable in both compression and rebound = it is possible to adjust the resistance of the shock absorber to both pressure and rebound

◇ **compression gauge** *noun* = COMPRESSION TESTER

◇ **compression ignition** *noun* system on which the diesel engine works, where ignition is caused by the heat of compression and not by a spark; **compression ignition engine** = DIESEL ENGINE

◇ **compression leakage** *noun* loss of compression due to the escape of gases usually past the piston and due to wear of the bores and piston rings

◇ **compression moulding** *noun* shaping of moulding material by softening it under pressure and the action of heat, and forcing it through a hole into a hollow space which it completely fills

◇ **compression ratio (CR)** *noun* ratio of the volume between the piston and cylinder head when the piston is at the bottom of its stroke (bottom dead centre) and this volume when the piston is at the top of its stroke (top dead centre) *the CR of petrol engines is usually somewhere between 8:1 and 10:1, that of diesel engines typically 23:1*

◇ **compression ring** *noun* upper piston ring of an internal combustion engine

◇ **compression spring** *noun* = COIL SPRING

◇ **compression stroke** *noun* upward stroke of the piston with both valves closed; as the piston ascends, the air/fuel mixture (in diesel engines air only) is compressed, increasing pressure and temperature of the charge before ignition

◇ **compression tester** *noun* instrument for measuring engine compression when running or cranking the engine, usually inserted in the plughole on petrol engines

◇ **compressor** *noun* **(a)** pump for increasing pressure used e.g. in air-conditioning or in forced induction (supercharging or turbocharging); *(see illustration 35)*; **compressor impeller** = impeller of a turbocharger driven by the turbine at speeds up to 160,000 rpm, which accelerates by centrifugal force the charge air which enters axially and leaves radially at very high velocity; *(see illustration 10)* **(b)** tool for compressing a coil spring, such as a valve spring

Comprex (pressure wave) supercharger *noun* supercharger using the pressure waves created by the expanding exhaust gases to compress the inlet charge

COMMENT: a belt-driven multi-vaned rotor assembly rotates at about 8,000 rpm, and combines the advantages of the immediate throttle response of a positive displacement supercharger with the thermodynamic efficiency of a turbocharger

computer-aided *adjective (of process)* in which computers are used for calculations, etc. *computer-aided design/engineering/ lighting/manufacturing*

◊ **computer-controlled** *adjective* regulated by a computer; **computer-controlled catalytic converter** = system in which exhaust emissions are controlled by close regulation of the A/F ratio and by the use of a three-way catalytic converter (NOTE: opposite is **open-loop catalytic converter**) *(compare* THREE-WAY CATALYTIC CONVERTER); **computer-controlled ignition timing** = electronic ignition system with an integral microprocessor determining the correct timing using information from crankshaft and camshaft sensors

concealed headlights *noun* headlights which are hidden under covers until required, when they are raised into position (NOTE: also called **pop-up headlights**)

concept car *noun* car incorporating new ideas, of which only one example is usually made, primarily as a design exercise, but also to impress the public; *(compare* PROTOTYPE)

concours *noun* a meeting to which enthusiasts bring their classic cars to show, including a competition to decide which is the smartest *the car is in concours condition*

condensation *noun* liquid, especially water, formed due to cooling of moist air or vapour; also the process of its formation

◊ **condense** *verb* to increase in density and (of a vapour) to become a liquid; **condensed water** = water resulting from condensation

◊ **condenser** *noun* **(a)** device in an air-conditioning system mounted in front of the car's radiator with coils in which the refrigerant vapour cools and turns to liquid; *(see illustrations 34, 35)* (NOTE: opposite is **evaporator**) **(b)** capacitor for the contact breaker of a conventional distributor

conductive *adjective* capable of conducting or carrying electricity

◊ **conductivity** *noun* ability of a material to conduct electricity (NOTE: opposite is **resistivity**)

◊ **conductor** *noun* material which conducts electricity due to the fact that it has many free electrons (NOTE: opposite is **insulator**) *(compare* SEMICONDUCTOR)

cone clutch *noun* early type of clutch in which the driving and driven elements have conical surfaces, still used in the synchronizing mechanisms of synchromesh transmissions

configuration *noun* arrangement of parts in relation to one another

conical *adjective* in the shape of a cone; tapered; **conical seat** *or* **seating** = circular seating, e.g. for a valve or sparking plug, with sloping sides

connecting rod *noun* bar forming the link between piston and crankshaft, and transmitting the force exerted by the piston to the crankshaft; *(see illustrations 3, 4, 9)*; **connecting rod bearing** = BIG-END BEARING; **connecting rod shank** = longitudinal, usually I-section, part of the connecting rod

COMMENT: the connecting rod has a big end at the bottom mounted on the crankpin, and a small end at the top which holds the gudgeon pin on which the piston is pivotally mounted

connection *noun* joining of two parts, especially parts conducting electricity *if there is no spark check for proper connections*

◊ **connector** *noun* part which joins two or more parts together

con rod *noun (informal)* = CONNECTING ROD

console *noun* small fascia and/or storage space between the front seats in a car, which may serve as a support for additional instruments

constantan *noun* nickel and copper alloy, used as resistance wire or in thermocouples

constant-mesh gearbox *noun* most commonly used transmission type in which forward gear pairs remain in mesh all the time, the driving pair being engaged by a clutch mechanism incorporating a hub and sleeve, today almost invariably laid out as a synchromesh mechanism; *(compare* SLIDING-MESH GEARBOX)

◊ **constant power distribution** *or* **split** *noun* system which ensures that the same amount of the power is always transmitted to the front and rear wheels in a four-wheel drive vehicle

constant velocity joint (CV joint) *noun* universal joint in which the driven shaft rotates at a constant speed regardless of the angle adopted, given a constant input shaft speed; *(see illustrations 23, 24)*

COMMENT: almost universally used in FWD drive shafts, but also in jointed shafts requiring minor diffraction angles. On a FWD drive shaft there are two CV joints: an inboard or inner joint of the sliding joint type, and an outboard or outer joint of the fixed type

consumption *noun* process of using up or amount used, especially of fuel or oil

contact *noun* **(a)** touching of two parts *the tyre must be kept in contact with the road* **(b)** part carrying electricity made to touch another such part for passing current, e.g. in a switch or a contact breaker *dirty contacts can lead to intermittent functioning or failure of the circuit (see illustration 37)*

COMMENT: the typical distributor has a fixed contact rigidly mounted on the contact breaker plate, and a moving contact on a pivoting arm on whose other end is a heel which is pushed out by the lobe of the distributor cam. These contacts are also called 'points'

contact area *noun* = CONTACT PATCH

◊ **contact arm** *noun* arm in the distributor on which the moving contact is mounted

◊ **contact bounce** *noun* rapid opening and closing of electrical contacts causing intermittent functioning of the circuit

◊ **contact breaker (CB)** *noun* mechanical switch as the part of the distributor of breaker-triggered ignition systems which breaks the primary current at the ignition point to provide a spark, consisting of a fixed contact or point and an arm with a moving contact or point; *(compare* CONVENTIONAL IGNITION SYSTEM); **contact breaker gap** = POINTS GAP; **contact breaker plate** = plate on which the contact breaker assembly is mounted, and

which can be rotated slightly by the vacuum or centrifugal advance mechanism; *(compare* DISTRIBUTOR BASEPLATE); **contact breaker point** = individual contact of a contact breaker

◊ **contact chatter** *noun* = CONTACT BOUNCE

◊ **contactless electronic ignition (system)** *noun* = BREAKERLESS TRANSISTORIZED IGNITION (SYSTEM)

◊ **contact patch** *noun* part of a tyre in contact with the road surface (NOTE: also called **footprint)**

◊ **contact pattern** *noun* wear pattern visible at points where two parts touch

◊ **contact point** *noun* = CONTACT BREAKER POINT

◊ **contact set** *noun* replacement contact breaker assembly for fitting when new points are required

◊ **contact spring** *noun* spring pressing on a contact to hold it in engagement, in a switch, bulb holder, etc.

contaminant *noun* dirt or other undesirable substance or pollutant *contaminants present in fuel and lubricating oil, e.g. lead, zinc, and phosphorous compounds, can block the catalyst surface and flow channels*

Continental-type fuse *noun* ceramic fuse with conical end caps, colour-coded for different values

Continuous AC Ignition System (CACIS) *noun* fundamentally new ignition system, where a high-energy AC arc burns for the entire power stroke

COMMENT: this type of ignition prevents erosion of the sparking plug electrodes and promotes better combustion of the air/fuel mixture, allowing for compliance with exhaust specifications without the use of a catalytic converter

continuous injection system (CIS) *noun* mechanical fuel injection system giving a constant supply of fuel; *(compare* K-JETRONIC)

◊ **continuously variable transmission (CVT)** *noun* transmission system in which the speed ratio of driving and driven elements is infinitely variable over the required working range, or is varied over a very large number of fixed ratios, either automatically or by manual control; (compare VARIOMATIC TRANSMISSION)

Conti tyre system (CTS) noun new tyre/wheel concept incorporating an innovative rim design with the rim flanges turning towards the wheel disc and the tyre seated on the inner surface of the rim; the tyre can be run deflated for up to 250 miles at up to 50 mph

contre pente (CP) noun (wheel) raised portion on the rim bead seat, designed to retain the tyre beads of an insufficiently inflated tyre on the rim bead seats, thereby preventing the beads from jumping into the rim well; (mainly used on passenger cars of French make); **contre pente on both bead seats (CP2)** = safety rim contour with a contre pente on both rim bead seats; (compare OUTBOARD CONTRE PENTE)

control noun **1 (a)** device used to regulate the functioning of a system, either operated by the driver by means of a lever, knob or switch, or operating automatically *cruise control; heater control; all controls must be at the driver's fingertips* **(b)** ability of the driver to make the vehicle perform as required *to lose control of a car; these tyres provide excellent control on wet roads* **2** verb to make do what is required, to regulate

◇ **control arm** noun suspension arm controlling wheel camber, especially the upper or lower wishbone

◇ **control box** noun **(a)** box containing voltage regulators and cut-out **(b)** = CONTROL UNIT

◇ **control cable** noun cable, usually in an outer sheath, running from a knob or lever to the device which it operates or regulates (NOTE: US English is **control wire**)

controlled burn rate see CBR PROCESS

controlled combustion system (CCS) noun General Motors term covering a set of emission control measures, including (i) modified combustion chamber design, (ii) high-temperature coolant systems, (iii) thermostatically controlled air cleaners, (iv) very lean A/F mixtures, (v) high idle speeds, (vi) severely retarded ignition timing, (vii) TCS and TVS

controlled vehicle noun vehicle fitted with a system for reducing exhaust emissions,

such as a catalytic converter, EGR, air injection or fuel evaporative emission control

◇ **control plunger** noun device in a fuel injection system whose up-and-down movement in the metering unit of the fuel distributor controls the open cross-sectional area of the metering ports and thus the quantity of fuel supplied to the individual cylinders

◇ **control pressure** noun pressure in fuel injection systems; pressure in an automatic transmission which acts on the command valves and is derived from line pressure or from throttle pressure

◇ **control stalk** noun spindle projecting from the steering column just below the steering wheel, on which are grouped controls for some or all of the following: lights, windscreen wipers and washers, direction indicators and horn *all functions are on one (control) stalk*

◇ **control unit** noun = ELECTRONIC CONTROL UNIT

◇ **control valve** noun valve regulating or operating a system, especially a hydraulic or vacuum control system; **control valve assembly** = casting located in the sump of an automatic gearbox, which contains most of the valves for the hydraulic control system

◇ **control wire** noun US = CONTROL CABLE

conv noun = CONVERTIBLE

conventional ignition system noun ignition system consisting of battery, ignition switch, ballast resistor, ignition coil, distributor and capacitor, contact breaker, centrifugal or vacuum advance unit, sparking plugs and ignition cables

COMMENT: when the ignition is on and the contact points are closed, current flows in the primary circuit, i.e. in the primary winding of the ignition coil, and builds up a magnetic field. At the ignition point, the contact breaker points open, the magnetic field collapses and induces a high voltage in the secondary winding of the coil. The distributor transfers this high voltage to the sparking plugs. Ignition timing is adapted to engine conditions by the centrifugal and/or vacuum advance mechanisms. Unsuitable for modern exhaust gas systems

conventional spare wheel noun spare wheel identical with the standard wheels on a car

conversion noun **(a)** changing from one state into another, e.g. of noxious gases into harmless gases **(b)** altered state of a particular system, or set of parts needed to achieve it; **manual choke conversion (kit)** = parts needed to change an automatic choke into a manually operated choke

◇ **conversion coating** *noun* metal surface coating consisting of a compound of the base metal

◇ **conversion rate** *noun* rate at which a given catalytic converter purifies the exhaust gas stream, governed by various parameters such as operating conditions and converter design

converter *noun* **(a)** = TORQUE CONVERTER **(b)** = CATALYTIC CONVERTER **(c)** = ADAPTER

◇ **converter case** *noun* assembly in an automatic gearbox comprising the impeller with the converter cover welded to it, containing the converter fluid and vane wheels and connected to the crankshaft via the drive plate and revolving at engine speed

◇ **converter cover** *noun* part in an automatic gearbox welded to the pump, with which it constitutes the converter case

◇ **converter housing** *noun* **(a)** stationary outer part of the automatic gearbox casing which houses the converter case **(b)** housing of a catalytic converter (NOTE: also called **converter shell)**

convertible *noun* car with a hood that can be folded down or a hard top which can be removed (NOTE: also called **open car)** *US* **convertible top** = soft foldable top of an open car, made of canvas or vinyl and usually including a PVC rear window; *(compare* HOOD)

coolant *noun* mixture of water and anti-freeze (usually now with corrosion inhibitors) in the cooling system *at least every two years, the engine cooling system should be drained, inspected, flushed, and refilled with fresh coolant*

◇ **coolant level warning light** *noun* light on the instrument panel which comes on when there is too little coolant in the cooling system

◇ **coolant pump** *noun* = WATER PUMP

◇ **coolant temperature sensor** *noun* sensor usually on the bottom of the radiator connected to the temperature gauge; *(see illustration 15)*

cooling fan *noun* large and powerful fan on an air-cooled engine, usually of the axial flow type, driven via a V-belt from the engine crankshaft, which supplies a large volume of cooling air to the cooling fins of the engine, and adds significantly to engine noise; *(compare* RADIATOR FAN)

◇ **cooling fins** *noun* protruding strips of flat metal cast on the cylinders of air-cooled engines (and sometimes other components) to increase the available cooling surface, and to improve heat dissipation; *(see illustration 16)*

◇ **cooling jacket** *noun* = WATER JACKET

cooling system *noun* system for keeping the temperature of an engine down to a desirable level, usually by the circulation of water with additives; *(see illustration 15)*

| COMMENT: comprises a radiator through which air passes to cool the water, hoses to connect it to the engine, water passages in the cylinder head and block, and a pump. The term almost invariably refers to a water-cooled system which should be drained, flushed and refilled every two years |

copolymer *noun* polymer produced from two different monomers

copper core *noun* central electrode of a sparking plug or the wires of an HT lead made of copper, which is an excellent conductor of electricity; **copper-cored lead** = (unsuppressed) HT lead with a copper core

◇ **copper-faced hammer** *noun* hammer with a round head made of copper, used on items which would be damaged by the use of a harder steel hammer, such as knock-off hubcaps or spinners

◇ **copper plating** *noun* applying a thin layer of copper by electrolytic deposition, especially on parts in the electrical system such as terminals and contacts

cord *noun* strong thread usually of nylon used in the carcass of a tyre

core *noun* **(a)** central part which is entirely enclosed, as in an ignition coil, a sparking plug, an electrical lead or a tyre valve **(b)** main part of a radiator below the header tank, consisting of numerous small tubes with cooling fins and gaps between for the air to pass through

◇ **core plug** *noun* sheet metal disc inserted in a hole in the water jacket of the cylinder block to prevent it from cracking if the coolant should freeze due to insufficient anti-freeze, the core plug being forced out by the pressure created by the expansion of the water when frozen; *(see illustration 3)* (NOTE: US English is **freeze plug**)

cornering *noun* negotiation of a corner or bend; **good/poor cornering (ability)** = ability/inability of a car to go round corners safely at a reasonable speed, without body roll and breakaway; **cornering forces** = forces exerted on a tyre by the slip angle when taking a corner; **cornering speed** = speed at which a corner is taken

corner panel *noun* panel used to fill a gap between larger panels or frame members meeting at an angle and to serve as a stiffener, such as those at the intersection of side- and crossmembers and the rear corner panels of rear wings

◊ **corner steady** *noun* jib-jack support for the corner of a (parked) caravan

corrode *verb* **(a)** to suffer corrosion, especially rust *the wing has corroded right through* **(b)** to cause corrosion in *leaking acid has corroded the battery tray*

◊ **corrosion** *noun* chemical process in which a metal is eaten away, such as the oxidation of iron and steel; otherwise known as rusting; **corrosion control** *or* **prevention** *or* **protection** = minimizing corrosion by coating with a protective metal, an oxide, or similar substance, or with a protective paint, or by rendering the metal passive; **corrosion inhibitor** = substance which reduces or prevents corrosion, in oils and anti-freeze as well as in coatings and paints for metal; **corrosion product** = substance formed as a result of corrosion; **corrosion resistance** = ability of metals to withstand corrosion; **corrosion warranty** = ANTI-CORROSION WARRANTY

◊ **corrosive** *adjective* causing corrosion

cost-effective *adjective* worthwhile in terms of tangible benefits produced by money spent

cost option *noun* optional extra for a new car available on payment of an additional sum *ABS brakes are available as a cost option*

Cotal gearbox *noun* kind of semi-automatic electrically operated gearbox of the preselector type, made in France before and just after the Second World War

cotter *noun* tapered pin or wedge inserted through holes in two parts such as a wheel or other part on a shaft, so as to hold the two parts firmly in position relative to one another; **cotter pin** = **(a)** SPLIT PIN **(b)** COTTER

coulomb (C) *noun* unit of electric charge, being the amount of electricity conveyed in one second by a current of one ampere

countershaft *noun* US = LAYSHAFT

countersink *verb* to enlarge the part of a hole on the surface of the material so that a conical recess is formed to take the correspondingly shaped head of a screw, which will then be flush with the surface; **countersunk bolt** *or* **screw** = bolt or screw the back of whose head is angled to conform with the angle (countersink angle) of the sides of the hole into which it is fitted; **countersunk hole** = enlarged hole with sloping sides

counterweight *noun* **(a)** weight added to the crankshaft of an engine to improve smoothness of running at low engine speeds as well as even increase or decrease of speed, usually in the form of an extension of the crank web on the opposite side from the crankpin; *(see illustration 8)* **(b)** = BALANCE WEIGHT

coupé *noun* car with closed two-door bodywork usually having a boot (i.e. not a hatchback) and sleek and sporty lines, the rear seat often being rather cramped; *(compare DROPHEAD COUPÉ)*

coupling *noun* part for joining two parts, especially shafts; **coupling sleeve** = sleeve or collar moved along the main shaft of a gearbox by a selector fork engaging in a groove on its centre and having dog clutches at either end

courtesy light *noun* interior light which comes on when the door is opened

cover *noun* **(a)** piece of material for protecting the car or part of the car (such as the seats) from dust and dirt **(b)** tyre (as opposed to the inner tube)

cowl *noun* **(a)** part of the bodywork which protects and/or provides streamlining for a usually projecting component **(b)** *US* = SCUTTLE

◇ **cowling** *noun* = COWL (a)

CP = CONTRE PENTE

C-pillar *or* **C-post** *noun* third vertical pillar of a typical saloon body shell behind the rear door and to either side of the rear window, connecting the rear of the roof to the side of the body

CR *or* **cr** = COMPRESSION RATIO

crab-tracked *adjective* having the front wheels wider apart than the rear, a chassis layout used, for instance, in the successful Frazer Nash sports car in the 1920s and '30s

cracking *noun* forming of cracks, e.g. in the sidewalls of a tyre due to hardening of the rubber, or in paintwork due to weathering of an excessively deep coat

crank 1 *noun* **(a)** arm incorporating a right angle, often mounted on a shaft **(b)** = CRANKSHAFT **2** *verb* to turn (the engine) by means of the starter or with a handle; **cranking enrichment** = provision of a richer mixture for starting the engine; **cranking speed** = speed at which the starter turns the engine

◇ **crankcase** *noun* part of the engine that houses the crankshaft (and usually the oil pump) and carries the sump, typically made of cast iron and in one piece with the engine block; *(see illustration 3)*; **the crankcase air space must be hermetically sealed** = the area below the piston of the two-stroke engine is used for pre-compression of the charge so none must escape; **crankcase breather** = vent which allows fumes and blow-by gases to escape, and reduces condensation, usually connected to the air intake of the carburettor so that the fumes can be burnt in the combustion chamber; **crankcase compression** *or* **pre-compression** = initial compression of the fueloil mixture in a two-stroke engine in the area below the pistons to enable more fresh charge to be fed into the cylinder **crankcase emissions** = pollutants allowed to escape into the atmosphere from the crankcase; **crankcase half** = one side of the crankcase where it is split down the middle, especially in single-cylinder motorcycle engines; **crankcase scavenging** = system in a two-stroke engine where the fresh charge is induced into the cylinder via the crankcase and the transfer ports; **crankcase ventilation** = circulation of air through the crankcase of a running engine to remove water, blow-by and other gases and

thus prevent oil dilution and contamination, sludge formation and pressure build-up

◇ **cranked** *adjective* having an elbow or right-angle shape in it, e.g. a starting handle or wheelbrace

◇ **crankpin** *noun* journal on which the connecting rod of a piston engine is mounted; *(see illustrations 4, 8)*

◇ **crankshaft** *noun* part of the engine connected to the pistons by connecting rods which converts the reciprocating or up-and-down motion of the pistons into rotary motion used to provide the drive to the wheels via the clutch and transmission *from the front end of the crankshaft are driven the camshaft (via a chain, cogged belt or timing gear) and the alternator or dynamo (via a belt which may also drive the fan and water pump)* *(see illustrations 3, 4, 5, 8)*; **crankshaft journal** = term usually applied to the journals running in the main bearings as opposed to those for the big-end bearings; **crankshaft position sensor** = sensor which transmits data on the exact position of the crankshaft to the engine management system for accurate ignition timing; **crankshaft pulley** = pulley on the nose of the crankshaft which may be toothed for use with a cogged belt for driving the camshaft, or recessed to accept a V-belt, or slotted to take a ribbed belt for driving the alternator or dynamo plus sometimes the fan and water pump; it may also carry timing marks; **crankshaft sprocket** = sprocket mounted on the nose of the crankshaft driving the camshaft via a timing chain

◇ **crank throw** *noun* distance between the crankpin and the axis of rotation or centreline of the crankshaft, which is equal to half the stroke

◇ **crank web** *noun* one of the pair of arms which carry the big-end journal; *(see illustration 8)*

crash *noun* collision either with another car or into some usually stationary object; **crash barrier** = barrier with longitudinal members designed to prevent a vehicle which is out of control from leaving a road or race track, or on a motorway from crossing the central reserve

◇ **crash gearbox** *noun* gearbox without any synchromesh, thus requiring double declutching (NOTE: also informally called **crash box**)

crash recorder *noun* electronic device that measures the speed and direction of a motor vehicle, as well as brake and indicator activity; **crash sensor** = sensor which triggers the air bag when a certain degree of deceleration is exceeded, i.e. in a severe frontal crash; **crash test** = controlled test in which a vehicle is propelled into a wall or another vehicle at a given speed, in order to study the effect on its structure, the effectiveness of safety belts, etc.

COMMENT: in contrast to a tachograph, a crash recorder only stores details for one minute; in the event of a crash, all the data recorded in the 60 seconds prior to the crash can be retrieved from the memory and used to reconstruct what happened

crawler noun (informal) slow-moving vehicle; **crawler gear** = extremely low gear mainly for off-road use; **crawler lane** = separate lane for heavy lorries and other slow-moving vehicles on a hill

crazing noun development of a network of fine cracks on or just under the surface of paintwork

crease noun ridge produced by folding of the metal either as part of the design or as a result of accident damage

creep noun tendency of a vehicle with automatic transmission to edge forwards when idling with drive engaged unless held on the brake

◊ **creepage** noun spreading of corrosion, especially rust, under paintwork causing blistering and flaking

◊ **creeper** noun low flat trolley made of wooden slats with castors, used by mechanics to lie on when working under a vehicle

crescent noun (in internal gear pumps) part between the inner and outer gears; (see illustration 17)

crest noun highest point of a screw thread (NOTE: opposite is **root**)

crimping noun creation of corrugations in two thin metal parts as they are pressed tightly together in order to join them, a method often used in place of soldering for electrical connections; **crimping pliers** or **tool** = tool in the form of pliers with serrated jaws especially for creating electrical connections

critical speed noun engine or shaft speed at which some unwanted phenomenon such as vibration sets in

crocodile clip noun spring clip with serrated jaws for making temporary electrical connections, as on jump leads (NOTE: US English is **alligator clip**)

crossbar noun (a) any transverse bar, especially a tie rod across the chassis, also specifically the top tube of a cycle or motorcycle frame (b) US = TOMMY BAR

◊ **cross bracing** noun strengthening ribs or other members which connect two sides of a frame

◊ **cross coat** noun paint spraying technique in which consecutive coats are sprayed at right angles to one another

◊ **cross-country vehicle** noun = OFF-ROAD VEHICLE

◊ **cross-draught carburettor** noun = SIDEDRAUGHT CARBURETTOR

◊ **crossflow cylinder head** noun cylinder head design (especially in an OHC-engine) with the inlet manifold on one side and the exhaust manifold on the other side of the head, so that inlet and exhaust valves are arranged on opposite sides of the combustion chamber, giving a wider engine but better gas flow

◊ **crossflow radiator** noun radiator in which the water flows sideways instead of vertically, and which is therefore wider than it is high, permitting a lower bonnet line

◊ **cross-head screw** noun screw whose head has a double slot in the shape of a cross, designed to accept a special screwdriver; **cross-head screwdriver** = screwdriver such as the Phillips or Pozidriv type with cross-shaped ridges in its point for cross-head screws (NOTE: opposite is **flat-bladed screwdriver**)

◊ **crossmember** noun any structural main body or chassis member mounted transversely, i.e. linking left- and right-hand side members *the front crossmember carries the front suspension*

◊ **cross-ply tyre** noun tyre in which the plies are laid diagonally, running across the carcass and crisscrossing one another at an angle of about 30-40°; (compare RADIAL TYRE)

◊ **cross-point screwdriver** noun = CROSS-HEAD SCREWDRIVER

◊ **cross scavenging** noun scavenging in a two-stroke engine with flow across the cylinder assisted by a wedge-shaped piston crown

◊ **cross section** noun view of an object when cut transversely at right angles across its centre

◊ **cross-shaft** *noun* **(a)** any transverse shaft **(b)** *US* = ROCKER SHAFT

◊ **cross-spoke wheel** *noun* modern design of alloy wheel which imitates the appearance of the classical wire wheel

◊ **cross-threaded** *adjective (of a bolt)* damaged by being inserted in a threaded hole at an angle

◊ **crosswind** *noun* wind blowing at the side of the car *the car is stable in crosswinds*

crown *noun* **(a)** top part, especially of a piston **(b)** outward curvature of an apparently flat sheet metal panel

◊ **crown wheel** *noun* larger of two gears in a bevel gear drive with teeth round its periphery facing sideways; **crown wheel and pinion** = pair of gears in the final drive of a vehicle, always found in the back axle of a rear-wheel drive layout where the pinion is on the end of the propeller shaft driving the crown wheel mounted on the differential at right angles to it, and also in front-wheel drives where the engine is not transversely mounted

cruciform frame *noun* frame with X-shaped bracing either as a chassis frame, or in a monocoque as strengthening for the floor

cruise *verb* to drive at a constant speed, using a fairly small throttle opening

◊ **cruise control** *noun* computer-controlled system which maintains a preset speed until the driver overrides the system by braking or accelerating, or by shutting it off

◊ **cruising speed** *noun* constant speed at which a car can be driven without strain

crumple zone *noun* front end (and also sometimes the rear end) of a car which is so designed that it gives way in a crash in order to absorb as much as possible of the impact

crusher *noun* machine which crushes scrapped cars into small blocks

CTS = CONTI TYRE SYSTEM *CTS wheel*

cubby hole *noun* glove compartment on older cars, often without a lid

cubes *noun (informal US)* = CUBIC INCHES

◊ **cubic capacity** *noun* volume of any enclosed space, including a cylinder or an engine; *(compare* DISPLACEMENT*)*

◊ **cubic centimetre** *noun* usual unit of measure for the capacity of an engine, almost always abbreviated to cc

◊ **cubic inch** *noun* unit of measure for the capacity of an engine used in North America, equal to 16.387 cc (NOTE: abbreviated as **cu.ins.)**

cult car *noun* car which has many enthusiastic owners, often also a classic car but not necessarily so, as it can be in current production

cup seal *noun* synthetic rubber seal with a single lip used for sealing hydraulic and pneumatic pistons; *(see illustrations 11, 30)*

◊ **cup-shaped wire brush** *noun* circular wire brush on an arbor for use with an electric drill

curb *noun US* = KERB

cure *verb (of a plastic)* to harden

◊ **curing time** *noun* time required for a plastic such as a filler or coating to harden

current regulator *noun* device for controlling the current output of a dynamo (which increases with engine speed) by opening a switch when the current exceeds a certain value, thus protecting the dynamo from damage due to excess current

custom *adjective* individually made to suit the requirements and tastes of the owner, especially as regards appearance *custom-built; custom car* **custom wheel** = special wheel with attractive styling, usually alloy, available as an aftermarket accessory, fitted mainly to make a car look more sporty; *(compare* ALLOY WHEEL*)*

◊ **customize** *verb* to alter a car to suit the requirements and tastes of the owner, especially as regards appearance

cut-and-shut *adjective (of a car)* shortened by cutting out a section of the chassis and/or bodywork

◊ **cutaway** *adjective (of a drawing or model)* with part of the external cover or casing removed to show the internal parts and how they work

◊ **cut-in speed** *noun* speed at which the dynamo has to rotate to produce a voltage which is greater than that across the battery terminals

◇ **cut-out** *noun* circuit-breaker, especially one in the charging circuit of a dynamo, whose points open when the dynamo output is less than the battery voltage, so that the battery does not drain into the dynamo

cutting compound *noun* relatively abrasive paste used to bring up the shine of paint finishes which dry dull or have gone dull due to neglect

◇ **cutting disc** *noun* abrasive wheel of an angle grinder

◇ **cutting line** *noun* line established by the factory along which welded-up assemblies must be cut when replacing a sheet metal part, in order to maintain structural strength in the finished repair

◇ **cutting torch** *noun* oxyacetylene torch for cutting through metal, used by emergency services and people dismantling vehicles

CV joint *noun* = CONSTANT VELOCITY JOINT; **CV joint boot** = rubber cover over a CV joint, often with concertina folds

CVT = CONTINUOUSLY VARIABLE TRANSMISSION

cwt = HUNDREDWEIGHT

cycle *noun* sequence of changes of state after which the system is in its original state again

◇ **cycle car** *noun* early type of lightweight car (less than 7½ cwt unladen) with a tubular frame, belt or chain transmission and fitted with a single- or twin-cylinder air-cooled engine

cylinder *noun* tubular chamber which accommodates a reciprocating piston, as in an engine or a hydraulic system

◇ **cylinder bank** *noun* one half of the V in a V-engine; i.e. one of the two rows of four cylinders in the case of a V-8

◇ **cylinder barrel** *noun* external casing of a cylinder forming a separate unit, especially of an air-cooled engine

◇ **cylinder block** *noun* cast-iron or, less frequently, cast-alloy casing containing the cylinders of an internal combustion engine, with a water jacket if water-cooled, or cooling fins if air-cooled, and usually in one piece with the crankcase; **cylinder block heater** = electric heater element in the water jacket connected to the mains which warms the coolant before the car is used, ensuring better starting and faster engine and heater warm-up

◇ **cylinder charge** *noun* quantity of fresh mixture fed into the combustion chamber prior to combustion

◇ **cylinder head** *noun* casting, on earlier engines of cast iron and on most modern engines of cast aluminium, bolted on top of the cylinder block, usually containing part of the combustion chamber(s) with the valves and the sparking plugs; *(see illustrations 4, 5, 6, 7)*; **cylinder head bolt or nut** = bolt or nut holding the cylinder head down; *(see illustration 7)*; **cylinder head gasket** = gasket located between the cylinder block and cylinder head to seal the combustion chamber and to prevent compression and coolant leaks, usually of more than one material; *(see illustration 7)*

cylinder head tester *noun* device used to detect cylinder head leakages which cause combustion gases to appear in the cooling system

> COMMENT: the gases are forced out of the cooling system then pass through a reaction chamber, where even the smallest concentration of combustion gases will cause the reaction fluid to change colour

cylinder hone *noun* special tool for use with an electric drill or air tools to hone and polish engine, clutch or brake cylinders, with a number of hone stones that adjust to different cylinder bore diameters by spring tension

◇ **cylinder liner** *noun* hard metal insert in the cylinder block forming the cylinder wall, and in which the pistons run (NOTE: also called **cylinder sleeve; compare** DRY LINER, WET LINER)

◇ **cylinder wall** *noun* internal face of the cylinder or bore

Dd

D (a) = DIESEL **(b)** = DRIVE (d) **(c)** mark on the output (live) terminal on a dynamo; *(compare* F)

damp *verb* to reduce the oscillations of (a spring, carburettor piston, etc.) or the vibration in (a crankshaft, etc.)

◊ **damper** *noun* any device which reduces oscillations (either mechanical or electrical) or vibration, such as a shock absorber in the suspension, or a vibration damper on the crankshaft; *(compare* ACCUMULATOR (c), STEERING DAMPER); **damper piston** = piston in a cylinder whose movement is restricted by a liquid or gas, which thus also restricts the movement of another member to which it is connected *hydraulic shock absorbers contain damper or working pistons* **damper springs** = springs in a clutch plate providing a cushion against sudden loads due to abrupt engagement; **damper strut** = suspension strut whose hub carrier is attached to the spring element rather than to the damper tube; *(compare* MACPHERSON STRUT)

◊ **damping force** *or* **rate** *noun* amount of damping applied by a shock absorber

dash(board) *noun* = INSTRUMENT PANEL

◊ **dashboard gearchange** *noun* gearchange layout with the gear lever mounted in and protruding from the dashboard

> COMMENT: the gears are not engaged by moving the lever around a pivot but rather by pulling and pushing and then moving the lever up and down as with a column gearchange. This arrangement was used on several French front-wheel drive cars, in particular on Citroën models such as the 2CV

dashboard plaque *noun* metal plate, typically made of brass or chromium-plated steel, awarded for attendance or winning a prize at a rally or other event, or with the supplier's name and address

◊ **dash panel** *noun* **(a)** structural panel with bracings across the width of the car on the inside of the bulkhead below the windscreen that provides the mounting locations of the dashboard; *(see illustration 1)* **(b)** *US* = BULKHEAD

dashpot *noun* small housing for a damper piston moving in oil, such as that of an SU carburettor

dazzle *noun* glare from the headlights of oncoming traffic which can momentarily blind a driver *drivers of low-built sports cars are particularly prone to dazzle*

dBA *noun* measurement of the level of sound pressure with reference to a particular circuit on a sound-level meter which reacts in a similar way to the ear

DC = DIRECT CURRENT

◊ **DC generator** *noun US* = DYNAMO

DC rim *noun* = DROP-CENTRE RIM

dead battery *noun (informal)* = FLAT BATTERY

◊ **dead axle** *noun* axle that supports weight and attached parts, but does not deliver power to a wheel or other rotating member; *(compare* LIVE AXLE)

◊ **dead centre** *noun* position of the piston either at the top or the bottom of its stroke; *(compare* BOTTOM DEAD CENTRE, TOP DEAD CENTRE)

◊ **dead pedal** *noun* footrest to the left of the clutch on some vehicles

◊ **dead space** *noun* space below the piston available for pre-compression of the incoming fresh charge of the two-stroke engine; *(compare* CRANKCASE AIR SPACE)

dealer *noun* person whose business is buying and selling cars

death rattle *noun (informal)* noise from an engine which indicates that it is likely to break down at any moment

debugging *noun* eradicating faults in a system

deburr *verb* to remove burrs from a metal surface

◇ **deburring** *noun* removing burrs from a metal surface

decal *noun* type of transfer bearing a model name or logo or other wording

decarbonize *verb* to remove carbon deposit from the piston top and combustion chambers of an engine

decelerate *verb* to slow down by taking one's foot off the throttle (NOTE: opposite is **accelerate)**

◇ **deceleration** *noun* slowing down; **deceleration fuel cut-off** = in an electronically controlled carburation or fuel injection system, cutting off the fuel supply when the engine is at operating temperature, the throttle is closed, and engine speed is above tick-over

deck *noun* **(a)** floor of a commercial vehicle, especially a bus **(b)** in an engine, top face of the cylinder block on which the cylinder head rests

◇ **deck panel** *noun* = REAR DECK PANEL

declutch *verb* to disengage the clutch; *(compare* DOUBLE-DECLUTCH)

decoke *verb* = DECARBONIZE

decompressor *noun* valve, often manually operated and mostly on old or diesel engines, which releases compression in a cylinder by allowing air to escape in order to facilitate manual starting (or kick-starting of a motorcycle)

dedicated *adjective* designed for a specific use or for a specific vehicle

De Dion axle *noun* rear-wheel drive layout with virtually semi-independent suspension, having a solid tubular crossmember attached to both wheel carriers and a single pivot point forward of the axle, the differential being attached to the chassis and thus part of the sprung mass of the vehicle; **De Dion tube** = solid tubular crossmember behind the rear axle in a De Dion layout linking the two wheel carriers

defect *noun* fault in a system or flaw in materials or a finish

◇ **defective** *adjective* faulty or flawed

defensive driving *noun* taking into account the likelihood of mistakes that could be made by other drivers and driving accordingly

deflated *adjective (of a tyre)* having lost all its air; containing no air

◇ **deflation** *noun* loss of air from a tyre

deflection *noun* movement of a member, especially part of the suspension, when subjected to a load

◇ **deflector** *noun* special piston profile used to achieve cross scavenging in earlier two-stroke engines; **deflector piston** = now obsolete piston design, featuring a profiled crown intended to help direct the incoming fresh mixture upwards to expel the burnt exhaust gas from the cylinder

defogger *noun US* = DEMISTER

deformation *noun* alteration of shape or dimensions of a body caused by stresses, expansion or contraction due to temperature or moisture change, or chemical or metallurgical changes; **deformation zone** = CRUMPLE ZONE

defroster *noun US* = DEMISTER

degradation *noun* deterioration in the condition of a material

degrease *verb* to remove the oil and grease from the surface (of a part)

◇ **degreasing** *noun* removal of grease or oil from surfaces; **degreasing agent** = usually a solvent, but can also be an alkaline solution or steam, used for removing oil and grease

dehumidifier *noun* device which absorbs moisture from the air, e.g. in a garage or in an air-conditioning system

de-ice *verb* to remove ice from the outside of a windscreen or rear window

de-icer *noun* liquid usually in the form of an aerosol spray for removing ice from windscreens and windows

de-ionized water *noun* water from which impurities have been removed by a special process, for topping up batteries; *(compare* DISTILLED WATER)

delay valve *noun* valve used in vacuum or hydraulic systems whose closing or opening action is delayed, e.g. delaying vacuum signals by about 10-30 seconds in the lines connected to the distributor vacuum advance

deliver *verb* **(a)** *(of a pump, etc.)* to pump or discharge (a liquid) **(b)** to drive (a new car) from the factory to the distributor or dealer

◇ **delivery** *noun* **(a)** discharging of a liquid from a pump, etc.; **delivery pipe/side** = outlet pipe/side; **delivery valve** = valve on the outlet side of a pump **(b)** driving a new car from the factory to the distributor or dealer; *(in advertisement)*; **delivery mileage only** = has only been driven from the factory to the dealer who is selling the car

delta configuration *noun* triangular connection of the three stator windings of an alternator; *(compare* Y-CONFIGURATION)

de luxe (DL) *adjective* better in its quality or level of equipment than the basic version *the de luxe model has air-conditioning and ABS brakes*

demist *verb* to clear the windscreen or rear window when they have misted up (or when ice has formed on the outside) (it takes longer to clear frost or ice on the outside than internal condensation)

◇ **demister** *noun* device or system for clearing a windscreen or rear window which is misted up or covered in ice; *(see illustration 34)* (NOTE: US English is **defogger, defroster**)

demonstrator *noun* car used by a dealer for test drives and sold at a reduced price after a year or less of use; **ex-demonstrator for sale** = car for sale which has been used as a demonstrator

demountable rim *noun* = DETACHABLE RIM

Denovo tyre *noun* special tyre (fitted to a special rim) which used to be made by

Dunlop, and which can be run flat for up to 100 miles at up to 50 mph; *(compare* TD RIM)

density *noun* compactness of a substance, expressed as the quotient of its mass and its volume, or mass per unit volume

dent 1 *noun* hollow or dip, e.g. in part of the body, caused by a sharp blow or impact; **to hammer out a dent** = to hammer a panel from behind where it has been dented so that the metal surface regains its correct shape **2** *verb* to cause a dent in (a body panel, etc.) *never attempt to straighten dented rims*

◇ **dent puller** *noun* tool with a powerful suction cup to pull dented doors, wings, bonnets, etc. back into shape; *(compare* PANEL PULLER)

Denver boot *noun US* = WHEEL CLAMP

deposit 1 *noun* **(a)** coating of material, especially unwanted, or layer of sediment at the bottom of a tank *remove all carbon deposits from the combustion chamber* **(b)** sum of money paid in advance as part payment *£100 deposit required for all hire purchase deals* **2** *verb* to apply (a coating of metal, etc.); **zinc is deposited electrolytically** = a layer of zinc is applied by electrolysis

depreciation *noun* loss of value due to age or deterioration

depression *noun* restricted airflow causing low pressure and a partial vacuum; *(compare* ENGINE DEPRESSION)

depth gauge *noun* measuring tool for depth measurements

◇ **depth micrometer** *noun* micrometer used for precise measuring of hole depths, recesses, keyways, and other depth measurements

◇ **depth of thread** *noun* distance from thread crest to root, measured perpendicular to the axis of the thread

derust *verb* to remove the rust from (metal parts)

derv *noun* diesel oil when used as a fuel for road vehicles (NOTE: stands for **diesel-engined road vehicle**)

descaling *noun* removal of scale or metallic oxide from metallic surfaces by pickling

design 1 *noun* arrangement of parts; form of construction **2** *verb* to arrange the parts or construction of (a car, an engine, etc.); **design engineer** = designer responsible for mechanical parts; **design feature** = particularly good or unusual aspect of a vehicle, etc.

◇ **designer** *noun* person responsible for the concept of a new car, etc.

desmodromic *adjective (of valves, valve operation)* closed as well as opened by mechanical means

COMMENT: in the desmodromic system for operating the valves of four-stroke engines, the valves are not - as is usually the case - closed by springs, but by means of an additional (closing) cam or a cable. A desmodromic system is more costly and complex than the use of conventional valve springs, but the closing motion is controlled more precisely and valve bounce is eliminated

desorption *noun* removing adsorbed material (NOTE: the opposite of **adsorption)**

detachable rim *noun* rim which is bolted to the wheel spider and can be removed to facilitate tyre changing, now mainly seen on lorries

detergent *noun* additive used in oil or petrol which either removes deposits or holds the contaminating materials in suspension (which prevents them coating sensitive surfaces such as pistons)

detonation *noun* condition in the combustion chambers that gives rise to knocking or pinking, which occurs when fuel is ignited too early and/or spontaneously, due to excessive ignition advance or low octane fuel; this results in colliding flame fronts and shock waves which can in turn cause overheating and mechanical stress; **detonation sensor** = sensor mounted near the cylinder bores in the cylinder block, used to detect engine knocking and to retard the ignition correspondingly in order to prevent engine damage

COMMENT: in engines with electronic ignition, detonation sensors automatically adjust the ignition timing for the octane rating of the fuel, allowing a car to run on lower octane fuel than is recommended

detoxed vehicle *noun* = CONTROLLED VEHICLE

detuned *adjective (of an engine)* intentionally adjusted so as to reduce power, either for economy or for greater flexibility; **a detuned road-going version** = a version of a car used for racing which has less power and is suitable for road use

dewax *verb* to remove the wax from (bodywork)

dew point *noun* temperature at which vapour begins to condense

DFC = DIGITAL FREQUENCY CONTROL

dhc = DROPHEAD COUPÉ

diagnostic centre *noun* part of a garage or workshop where diagnostic testing is undertaken; **diagnostic computer** = computer used for diagnostic testing; **diagnostic link** = connection between the diagnostic socket on the vehicle and an engine analyzer; **diagnostic socket** = socket on the vehicle connected to a diagnostic system to which an engine analyzer can be attached; **diagnostic system** = system of electronic devices on the vehicle which alert the driver when a fault occurs, and to which an engine analyzer can be connected; **diagnostic testing** = testing of a vehicle system such as the electrical system or fuel injection to detect faults, usually by means of a computerized engine analyzer

diagonal belt *noun* = SHOULDER BELT

◇ **diagonal split braking (system)** *noun* dual-circuit braking system in which each circuit brakes one front wheel and the diagonally opposite rear wheel, so that in case of failure of one circuit reasonably balanced braking can be achieved

dial *noun* usually circular face of a measuring instrument such as a gauge or speedometer

◇ **dial caliper** *noun* slide-type caliper with dial-type indicator

◇ **dial gauge** *noun* precision measuring tool for taking measurements in hundredths of a millimetre or thousandths of an inch, having a plunger or contact arm and a dial face with needle to register measurement, and used, for example, to measure taper in engine cylinders, runout of gears, or the trueness of a shaft

◇ **dial torque wrench** *noun* torque wrench which measures torque applied while the nut or bolt is is being tightened and indicates the value on a calibrated dial

diameter *noun* length of a straight line through the centre of a circular object connecting two directly opposite points on its circumference

diamonding *noun* condition where one side of the car has been shifted to the rear or front, causing the frame and/or body to be out of square, resulting in a figure similar to a parallelogram

| COMMENT: diamonding is the result of accident damage where one corner of the car is hit straight on, causing displacement to the front or rear in that side only

diaphragm *noun* thin, flexible membrane displaced under pressure, e.g. in vacuum units, often connected to a rod or other member to transmit movement

◇ **diaphragm clutch** *noun* = DIAPHRAGM SPRING CLUTCH

◇ **diaphragm link** *noun* arm connecting the diaphragm and the distributor baseplate in a vacuum advance mechanism

◇ **diaphragm pump** *noun* glandless reciprocating pump in which a flexible diaphragm is moved backwards and forwards by a solenoid or mechanically, used typically as a fuel pump on an engine

◇ **diaphragm spring** *noun* large metal disc with spring fingers formed by cutting internal radial slots, used in clutches; *(see illustration 20)*; **diaphragm spring clutch** = most common type of clutch used in modern vehicles with manual transmission, in which a diaphragm spring keeps the pressure plate in contact with the friction plate

dickey (seat) *noun* extra folding seat in the back of a two-seater, common in the 1920s (NOTE: US English is **rumble seat**)

die *noun* **(a)** tool for cutting shapes in metal, especially outside threads on pieces of round bar or similar; *(compare* TAP*)* **(b)** metal mould for casting; **die-cast** = manufactured by forcing molten metal (e.g. aluminium) into a die

dielectric *noun* material which is an electrical insulator or in which an electric field can be sustained with a minimum loss of power

diesel 1 *noun* **(a)** = DIESEL ENGINE *all diesels are fuel-injected* **(b)** diesel-engined car *my car's a diesel; diesels are twice as reliable as petrol-engined cars* **(c)** = DIESEL FUEL *my car runs on diesel* **2** *verb* = RUN ON

diesel cycle *noun* usually four-stroke cycle according to which a diesel engine operates, in which air is sucked into the cylinder and compressed at a ratio of up to 24:1

| COMMENT: the fuel is injected at the end of the compression stroke when the temperature of the compressed air has risen above the ignition temperature of the fuel, resulting in combustion, and is followed by an exhaust stroke to remove the combustion products

diesel engine *noun* compression ignition engine named after its German inventor Rudolf Diesel (1858-1913), operating on the diesel cycle and burning diesel fuel rather than petrol; *(compare* SI ENGINE*)*

| COMMENT: diesel engines thus have no ignition system, but need a high-pressure injection pump and a particularly sturdy engine to cope with the stresses resulting from the extremely high compression ratio. They offer excellent economy and reliability with relatively few poisonous fumes, but an objectionable smell and considerable noise (the famous diesel knock) at low speeds, especially when started from cold

diesel fuel *noun* light oil fuel with a relatively low ignition temperature

◇ **dieselling** *noun* = RUNNING-ON

◇ **diesel knock** *noun* noise caused by the rapid rise in pressure in a diesel engine, especially at low speeds and when cold

◇ **diesel oil** *noun* = DIESEL FUEL

◇ **diesel particulate filter** *noun* filter removing particulates from a diesel exhaust, similar in appearance to a honeycomb-type catalytic converter, but unlike the catalytic converter without any catalytic function, acting simply as a mechanical separator

◇ **diesel rattle** *noun* = DIESEL KNOCK

die stock *noun* tool used to hold and operate dies when cutting outside threads

differential *or (informal)* **diff** *noun* gear assembly between two drive shafts that permits one shaft to turn at a different speed from the other, while transmitting power; *(see* *illustration 28)*; **differential cage** *or* **carrier** = rotating metal frame that encloses the differential side gears and pinion gears inside the axle casing; **differential casing** *or* **housing** = casing for a differential, often forming part of the axle casing of a live beam axle; **differential lock** = mechanism which eliminates the action of the differential, so that both wheels can be driven for better adhesion on slippery surfaces; *(compare* LIMITED-SLIP DIFFERENTIAL); **differential pinion** = bevel pinion in the differential; **differential side gear** = bevel gear on either side of the differential into the centre of which the axle shaft fits

diffusing lens *noun* lens in a headlamp glass to help focus the beam

digital caliper *noun* slide-type caliper with digital readout

◊ **digital frequency control (DFC)** *noun* system which automatically stabilizes and/or tunes the frequency of a selected radio station

◊ **digital speedometer** *noun* speedometer which only has a digital display of the current speed, with no dial

dimmer (control) *noun* device giving gradual fading of brightness, e.g. for the instrument panel illumination

◊ **dimmer (switch)** *noun* US = DIPSWITCH

DIN *(short for)* Deutsche Industrie Norm (en): German Industrial Standard(s); **DIN bhp** = officially obsolete unit of measurement for engine power, but still frequent in everyday usage, the measurement method being comparable to SAE net bhp; **DIN mounting** = standard aperture and mounting for a radio unit in the instrument panel

dinging *noun* *(principally US)* straightening a damaged panel using hammer and dolly to bring it back into shape, after initial roughing out

diode *noun* solid-state electronic device that allows the passage of an electric circuit in one direction only, used in alternators to change alternating current to direct current for charging the battery

dip *verb* to switch (headlights) to the lower beam *you must always dip (your headlights) when there is someone coming the other way*

◊ **dipped beam** *noun* lower beam directed at the road closer to the front of the vehicle than the main beam in order not to dazzle drivers of oncoming vehicles, and also to the near side to illuminate the side of the road; achieved by switching to a second filament in the headlight bulb which is closer to the upper half of the reflector (NOTE: US English is **low beam**)

◊ **dipper (switch)** *noun* = DIPSWITCH

◊ **dipping mirror** *noun* mirror reducing annoying dazzle from the headlights of following vehicles which consists typically of two glass panes, one a mirror and one clear, the clear glass being tilted by moving a small control under the mirror which then deflects the headlight glare downwards

◊ **dipswitch** *noun* switch usually incorporated in the control stalk but sometimes foot-operated, which changes the headlights from main to dipped beam (and vice versa) (NOTE: US English is **dimmer switch)**

dipstick *noun* metal rod which when pushed home on its seating enters the oil with its bottom end, so that when withdrawn it indicates the level of the oil *the oil level must be between the minimum and maximum marks on the dipstick (see illustration 5)*; **dipstick tube** = tube on the engine block or gearbox which holds the dipstick; *(see illustration 5)*

direct-acting shock absorber *noun* = TELESCOPIC SHOCK ABSORBER

◊ **direct current (DC)** *noun* electric current flowing in one direction only (NOTE: opposite is **alternating current)**

◊ **direct damage** *noun* damage caused directly by the impact of an obstacle, i.e. more or less the damage in the actual impact area (NOTE: opposite is **indirect damage)**

◊ **direct drive** *noun* transmission mode in which engine, gearbox and propeller shaft rotate at the same speed, bypassing the reduction stages of the gearbox; *(compare* OVERDRIVE)

◊ **direct ignition (system) (DIS)** *noun* = DISTRIBUTORLESS IGNITION (SYSTEM)

◊ **direct injection** *noun* fuel injection directly into the combustion chamber, especially in diesel engines, and requiring very high injection system pressure to overcome the pressure inside the combustion chamber at the time of injection

directional stability *noun* vehicle's ability to continue moving in a straight line with a minimum of steering control, even under adverse conditions such as crosswinds *a car with poor directional stability will tend to wander*

◊ **directional tread pattern** *noun* tyre tread pattern designed to rotate in one direction only

direction indicator *noun* winking signal light on either side of the vehicle at front and rear used to indicate that the driver is about to turn right or left; **direction indicator warning light** = light on the instrument panel which flashes when the indicators are being operated; usually in the shape of a green arrow; *(compare* FLASHER UNIT)

◊ **direction of rotation** *noun* direction in which a wheel, shaft or similar turns *operating the pump in the wrong direction of rotation will result in damage*

◊ **direction of travel** *noun* direction in which a vehicle is travelling

DIS = DIRECT *or* DISTRIBUTORLESS IGNITION (SYSTEM)

disabled *adjective* **(a)** *(of vehicle)* unable to be driven due to a breakdown or accident damage **(b)** *(of driver)* lacking the use of a limb

disassemble *verb* = DISMANTLE

disc *noun* flat circular plate as used for instance in disc brakes and some clutches

◊ **disc brake** *noun* brake in which brake pads, in a vice-like caliper which is either fixed or floating, grip a revolving disc mounted on the hub in order to slow it down or to stop it; *(see illustration 27)*; **four-wheel disc brakes** = disc brakes fitted to both front and rear wheels; **disc brake gauge** = tool for measuring thickness, wear, and score depth on brake discs; *US* **disc brake rotor** = BRAKE DISC

discharge 1 *verb* **(a)** to lose or give out electric current, as from a battery; **discharged battery** = flat battery **(b)** to pour out (a liquid) as from a pump **2** *noun* giving out of electric current or pouring out of liquid

◊ **discharge indicator** *noun* = BATTERY DISCHARGE INDICATOR

◊ **discharge pipe** *noun* outlet pipe of a pump

◊ **discharge pressure** *noun* pressure exerted in a liquid pumped, expressed in psi

◊ **discharge rate** *noun* amount of current discharged, expressed in amps

◊ **discharge side** *noun* = OUTLET SIDE

◊ **discharge valve** *noun* valve on the outlet side of a reciprocating pump (NOTE: opposite is **suction valve)**

◊ **discharging current** *noun* current supplied by a storage cell or battery, whose direction is opposite to that of the charging current

discolour *verb* to alter the colour of (a finish, metal, etc.) to a colour which is not wanted

disconnect *verb* to remove the connection to (a mechanical or electrical device); **disconnect the battery** = remove the battery terminals

disc sander *noun* round, rubber disc powered by an electric drill and covered with abrasive paper for rough sanding work; *(compare* ORBITAL SANDER)

◊ **disc valve** *noun* type of rotary valve that allows the passage of fluid through an arc-shaped slot

◊ **disc wheel** *noun* simple, most common form of wheel on passenger cars and light commercial vehicles, consisting of a pressed steel disc the centre of which is bolted to the hub, and which has fixed to its periphery, the rim serving as a seat for the tyre

disengage *verb* to move (a gear, dog clutch, etc.) so that it is no longer in mesh with another matching part; **to disengage the clutch** = to let out the clutch by pressing on the clutch pedal, so that there is no connection between the engine and the gearbox

dished *adjective* offset so that the centre (of a wheel or similar) is not in line with the rim, but recessed

disk *noun* = DISC

dismantle *verb* to take (a car, engine, etc.) to pieces *partly dismantled for restoration*

displacement *noun* term used particularly in America for cubic capacity; **displacement volume** = SWEPT VOLUME

distance piece *noun* part such as a collar placed between two parts to keep them the correct distance apart

distilled water *noun* especially pure water that has been freed of dissolved or suspended solids and organisms by distillation, used, for example, to top up batteries

distortion *noun* bending and twisting out of shape *distortion of bodywork panels can be caused by the heat from welding*

distributor *noun* assembly which distributes the ignition voltage generated in the ignition coil to the sparking plugs in the firing order of the engine; *(see illustration 3)*; **distributor baseplate** = fixed plate in the body of the distributor on which the contact breaker or triggering device is mounted, and through the centre of which the distributor shaft passes; *(compare* CONTACT BREAKER PLATE); **distributor body** = bowl-like part containing the distributor shaft with the rotor arm at its top end, and, in the conventional version, the centrifugal advance mechanism and the contact breaker; **distributor cam** = cam at the top of the distributor shaft with as many lobes as there are cylinders, acting on the heel of the contact breaker arm; **distributor cap** = removable cover of the distributor, having a high-voltage centre tower for the lead from the coil, and as many regularly spaced outer towers as there are cylinders, each of these corresponding to a contact on the inside of the cap and receiving the HT lead for one of the sparking plugs on the outside; *(see illustrations 3, 4)*; **distributor clamp** = clamp which holds the distributor in position, and which can be loosened in order to turn the distributor relative to its shaft to adjust the ignition timing; **distributor rotor (arm)** = = ROTOR ARM; **distributor shaft** = drive shaft to the distributor that rotates at half engine speed and has at its top end the distributor cam and rotor arm; **distributor tower** = TERMINAL TOWER; **distributor weight** = one of the weights used in a centrifugal advance mechanism; **distributor wrench** = wrench designed for loosening and tightening the distributor clamp bolts and/or lock nuts, when adjusting, removing or installing distributors

distributorless ignition (system) (DIS *or* **DLI)** *noun* electronic ignition system without a conventional rotating distributor, using multi-spark ignition coils or one ignition coil per sparking plug

COMMENT: the ignition voltage is fed into the distributor cap via the centre tower and distributed to the HT lead terminals by the rotor arm. The conventional distributor also contains the contact breaker or a pulse generator to trigger the ignition pulse as well as the centrifugal advance mechanism and control elements of the vacuum control unit, but in modern ignition systems, the distributor has no mechanical timing devices and, in some cases, no triggering devices

dive *noun* = BRAKE DIVE

diversification *noun* varying and extending a firm's range of models and products

divert *verb* to make (air, a liquid, traffic, etc.) follow a different course *air is diverted to the air cleaner; traffic has been diverted around the accident site*

◊ **diversion** *noun* alternative route which traffic has to follow due to closure of a stretch of road for repairs, etc.

◊ **diverter valve** *noun* = AIR GULP VALVE *(see* AIR GULP SYSTEM)

divided propeller shaft *or* **propshaft** *noun* propeller shaft, usually in long chassis rear-wheel drive vehicles, which is divided into two sections with a bearing and CV joint mounted on a chassis crossmember at the central point

divider *noun* measuring tool with two straight pointed arms used to mark off and transfer measurements, e.g. on sheet metal or other metal components

DIY *(short for)* do-it-yourself; **DIY mechanic** = unqualified person who does his own repairs on his car

DL = DE LUXE

DLI = DISTRIBUTORLESS IGNITION

dlr *(short for)* dealer

DOC = DOUBLE OVERHEAD CAMSHAFTS

dog clutch *noun* simple coupling with two halves called dogs, with square projections in one that engage in square slots in the other to transmit drive, but can also be disengaged to break the drive

◇ **dog guard** *noun* grid made of tubular bars or wire mesh to keep a dog in the luggage compartment of an estate or hatchback

◇ **dogleg pillar** *noun* = C-PILLAR; **dogleg section** = irregular shaped part of the leading edge of the rear quarter panel of a four-door saloon along the wheel cutout and up to the waistline

DOHC *or* **dohc** = DOUBLE OVERHEAD CAMSHAFTS

dolly *noun* **(a)** metalworking tool, available in a variety of shapes and sizes, comprising a curved polished block of cast iron or forged steel, used to assist in forming three-dimensional shapes and in straightening dented panels, usually by holding the dolly behind the metal to be shaped and hammering the metal **(b)** trolley that supports the front wheels when a disabled vehicle is being towed

dome lamp *noun US* dome-shaped interior light

domestic *adjective (of product)* made in the country in question (NOTE: opposite is **foreign**)

donor car *noun* car from which parts are used to repair another one of the same type or to build a special or kit car

door *noun* hinged panel or flap allowing access or exit; **five-door version** = hatchback version with two doors either side and a rear tailgate

◇ **door alignment** *noun* accuracy of fitting of the door in the door aperture

◇ **door aperture** *noun* opening into which the door fits

◇ **door beam** *noun* = SIDE IMPACT BAR

◇ **door bottom** *noun* lower door area, both of the door skin and of the door frame, also the narrow horizontal lower panel of the door frame that incorporates the drain holes

◇ **door capping** *noun* moulding between the door trim panel and the window glass

◇ **door check arm** *or* **strap** *noun* device which controls the full open and holding positions of a door and prevents it from being opened too far; *(compare* DOOR STAY)

◇ **door frame** *noun* **(a)** bare skeleton of the door to which the door skin and door trim are fitted **(b)** = DOOR APERTURE

◇ **door gap** *noun* gap all round the edge of the door

◇ **door glass** *noun* glass pane filling the top half of a door, which can be lowered and raised

◇ **door handle** *noun* interior or exterior handle for opening a door

◇ **door hinge** *noun* part by which the door is attached with a pivot to the door pillar, and which allows it to swing open or shut

◇ **door hold-open spring** *noun* spring fitted to door hinges to provide a spring load to keep the door in an open position

◇ **door latch** *noun* part of the door lock which contacts the striker plate as the door is closed, and springs back when the door is fully shut to hold it in the closed position

◇ **door lock** *noun* mechanism for opening and closing the door, with a lockable cylinder for holding the door closed until opened by a key; **door lock de-icer** = fluid, usually in an aerosol, for melting ice in a door lock

◇ **door mirror** *noun* exterior, door-mounted, rear-view mirror; nowadays adjustable from inside the car

◇ **door pillar** *or* **post** *noun* one of the vertical members of the body shell ahead of and behind the doors, which also support the roof structure and reinforce the body as a whole; **door pillar switch** = small switch, typically in the lower portion of the A-pillar, whose main function is to switch on the courtesy lighting when the door is opened

◇ **door pocket** *noun* container now usually mounted on, rather than in, the door trim, for maps, dusters, cloths, etc.

◇ **door protector** *noun* strip of rubber or plastic which fits over the edge of the door to protect it from damage when opened carelessly

◇ **door seal** *noun* weatherstrip fitted to the door surround to form a seal when the door is closed

◇ **door shut (face)** *noun* edges of a door which are not visible from the outside or inside when the door is shut

◇ **door sill** *noun* = SILL (a)

◇ **door skin** *noun* large sheet metal panel of the door visible from the outside

◇ **door speaker** *noun* loudspeaker for a car stereo mounted in the door trim

◊ **door stay** *noun* device incorporated in door hinges that keeps the door in an open position and prevents it from closing under its own weight; *(compare* DOOR CHECK STRAP)

◊ **door step** *noun* top part of the outer sill, visible when the door is opened

◊ **door surround** *noun* faces of the door step, door pillars and roof section forming the door aperture

◊ **door trim (panel)** *noun* panel covered in vinyl or other material and fitted to the inside of the door

◊ **door well** *noun* cavity enclosed by the door frame, door skin and trim panel, containing the window winding mechanism and into which the window glass is lowered

DOT *(short for)* **(a)** *GB* Department of Transport **(b)** *US* Department of Transportation; **DOT 4 (brake fluid)** = brake fluid made to a particularly high specification; **DOT code** = code on tyre sidewalls made up of letters and numbers giving information on the production date of a tyre

double-acting *noun (of a shock absorber or pump)* having a piston with fluid on both sides so that in a pump one piston end performs the suction stroke while the other discharges the liquid, and in a shock absorber both upward and downward movements are damped

◊ **double-barrel carburettor** *noun* = TWIN-CHOKE CARBURETTOR

◊ **double-decker (bus)** *noun* bus with two decks or storeys, used mainly in large towns

double-declutch *US* **double-clutch** *verb* to change gear using the following technique: declutch, move the gear lever into neutral, let in the clutch, press the accelerator (when changing down) to raise the engine and gearbox rpm to the level needed in the lower gear, let out the clutch again quickly and move the gear lever into the lower gear (before the gearbox shaft rpm drop too far); when changing up there is no need to depress the accelerator when in neutral, but it is often necessary to pause in order to let the gearbox shaft speed drop to the right level

COMMENT: double-declutching is only necessary on so-called crash gearboxes without synchromesh, such as fitted to earlier cars, but still found on a few commercial vehicles; some cars still had no synchromesh on bottom gear until relatively recently

double-ended spanner *noun* open-ended or ring spanner with jaws or rings at both ends for two different sizes of hexagon

◊ **double filament bulb** *noun* light bulb with two filaments, either a headlamp bulb with one for the main beam and another above it for the dipped beam, or a stop and tail light bulb with one for the brake light and one for the rear light

◊ **double helical gear** *noun* gear with two rows of inclined teeth, each forming an open V or chevron (NOTE: also called **herringbone gear)**

◊ **double hexagon socket** *noun* = 12-POINT SOCKET

◊ **double overhead camshafts (DOC, DOHC)** *noun* two camshafts mounted on the cylinder head, one operating the inlet valves and one the exhaust valves (NOTE: also called **twin overhead camshafts)**; **double overhead camshaft engine** = engine with two overhead camshafts, a relatively costly arrangement used on high performance engines; *(see illustrations 3, 4)*

◊ **double-pivot steering** *noun* steering in which the steered wheels are pivoted on kingpins, which is the usual arrangement on motor vehicles; *(compare* ACKERMANN STEERING, SINGLE-PIVOT STEERING)

◊ **double reduction gearing** *noun* gearing in which the ratio is reduced in two stages, used especially in heavy goods vehicles

◊ **double roller chain** *noun* = DUPLEX CHAIN

◊ **double-tube shock absorber** *noun* older design of hydraulic shock absorber using two concentric tubes, one serving as the working cylinder, the other as the reservoir; *(compare* SINGLE-TUBE SHOCK ABSORBER)

◊ **double wishbone suspension** *noun* form of independent suspension most frequently used at the front of a vehicle, with upper and lower wishbones of equal length

doughnut coupling *or* **joint** *noun* flexible coupling made of rubber and shaped like a ring doughnut, used for instance between the front of the propeller shaft and the gearbox; *(see illustration 22)*

dowel (pin) *noun* pin projecting from one of two mating surfaces which fits into a corresponding hole in the other, to ensure correct location during assembly

downdraught carburettor *noun* carburettor with a vertical barrel, at the top of which is the air intake; *(compare* SIDEDRAUGHT CARBURETTOR) *(see illustration 11)*

downflow radiator *noun* traditional type of vertical radiator, with header tank and bottom tank and a system of small tubes and cooling fins in-between, the hot water entering at the top and exiting at the bottom

| COMMENT: the downflow radiator uses much vertical space and is being superseded by the lower crossflow radiator

downforce *noun* downward pressure provided, for example, by a spoiler *added downforce improves adhesion and counteracts the tendency of a car to lift at speed*

◊ **down pipe** *noun* front section of the exhaust system connected to the exhaust manifold

◊ **downshift** *noun US* = DOWNWARD CHANGE

◊ **downstroke** *noun* downward movement of the piston, either the induction stroke or the power stroke in the four-stroke cycle

◊ **downward change** *noun* gear change into a lower gear (NOTE: US English is **downshift)**

D-pillar *or* **D-post** *noun* rearmost vertical pillar in the body of an estate car, on either side of the tailgate

drag 1 *verb (of clutch)* to fail to disengage completely; *(of brakes)* to fail to come off completely when the brake pedal is released **2** *noun* **(a)** = CLUTCH DRAG **(b)** = BINDING (a) **(c)** characteristic of a car body, indicating the resistance which the body offers to the airstream; *(compare* CD VALUE)

| COMMENT:increasing the cross-sectional area of a car by factor X will increase drag by the same amount, but increasing vehicle speed by factor Y will increase drag by Y^2 with correspondingly increased engine power and fuel requirements

drag link *noun* rod which connects the drop arm or idler arm in a steering system with the steering arm

drag racing *noun* form of acceleration test in which two cars at a time accelerate down a measured quarter-mile strip

◊ **dragster** *noun* specially constructed car for drag racing, typically with a huge supercharged V-8 engine mounted well back in the chassis and extremely wide rear tyres

◊ **dragstrip** *noun* quarter-mile stretch of track for drag racing

drain 1 *verb* to empty (the sump, radiator, etc.) of a liquid *drain the sump completely before removing the oil filter* **2** *noun* passage or piece of tube which takes water away from places in the bodywork where it tends to accumulate, such as the edge of the sunroof

◊ **draincock** *noun* = DRAIN TAP

◊ **drain hole** *noun* hole drilled in the bottom of a box section or a door, to allow water that has accumulated to escape so as to prevent or delay rusting

◊ **draining tray** *noun* container used to catch oil when draining the sump, gearbox, etc.

◊ **drain plug** *noun* usually threaded plug at the lowest point of the sump, gearbox, cooling system, etc., which is removed in order to drain the oil or coolant, and typically has a recessed hexagon head; **drain plug key** *or* **spanner** *or* **wrench** = tool for removing and tightening drain plugs, e.g. on gearboxes and engine sumps, either as a multi-purpose tool with a number of different drives in the form of hexagonal or square projections at either end for different drain plugs, or as a special tool for one specific size of drain plug

◊ **drain tap** *noun* tap on the cylinder block or, on older cars, at the bottom of the radiator for draining the cooling system

draught *noun* unpleasant current of air intruding into the interior of a car; **draught excluder** = weatherstrip

drawbar *noun* two converging bars forming a V- or an A-frame at the front of a trailer or caravan, which carry the coupling for attachment to the towing vehicle

dress *verb* to give (a rough surface, flanges, etc.) the right shape by grinding or a similar process

drier *noun* **(a)** = DEHUMIDIFIER **(b)** = DRYING OVEN

drift *noun* **(a)** piece of bar or a punch used with a hammer to drive components in and out of place for removal and installation; **drift punch** = tapered tool for use with a hammer to remove and install pins, shafts, rivets, etc.; also used to align holes when inserting screws and bolts **(b)** = FOUR-WHEEL DRIFT

drill 1 *noun* **(a)** usually power-driven tool for making holes in metal, wood, plastic, etc., with a chuck that will accept bits of different sizes **(b)** = DRILL BIT **2** to make (a hole) with a drill

◇ **drill bit** *noun* piece of rod with spiral recesses cut in it and a hardened steel tip, made in different sizes for drilling different-sized holes, and inserted in the chuck of a drill

drip moulding *noun* moulding running along either side of the roof, functioning as a gutter to take water to the front or rear of the car, and prevent it from dripping into the car when the door is opened; *(see illustrations 1, 2)* (NOTE: US English is **drip rail**)

drivability *noun* general operating characteristics of a vehicle, usually rated from good to poor, and of concern to the average driver, such as flexibility and smoothness, acceleration, ease of starting and quick warm-up, as well as handling and comfort

◇ **drivable** *adjective (of a vehicle)* in a state in which it can be driven *the car was still drivable after the accident*

◇ **drive 1** *verb* **(a)** to travel in a car; **we drove to Bath** = we went to Bath by car **(b)** to control and guide (a vehicle); **she drove (the car) all the way** = she was at the steering wheel for the whole journey **(c)** to make (a wheel, shaft, etc.) turn or rotate; to propel (a vehicle); **a petrol-driven generator** = a generator for which the motive force is a petrol engine **2** *noun* **(a)** journey in a car; **it's two hours drive** = it takes two hours to get there by car; **to go for a drive** = to go out in a car for pleasure on a round trip **(b)** stretch of private road leading to a house **(c)** means of transmitting power or motion; **drive is taken through a four-speed gearbox** = power is transmitted through a four-speed gearbox; **half-inch square drive** = in a socket spanner, projection on the handle or recess in the socket half an inch by half an inch **(d)** the position (D) on the gear selector of an automatic gearbox for the forward gears

◇ **drive belt** *noun* belt passing round two or more pulleys, transmitting motion from one to the other(s)

◇ **drive chain** *noun* chain passing round two or more sprockets, transmitting motion from one to the other(s)

◇ **drive end** *noun* end of an alternator, dynamo, etc., where the pulley or gear

accepting the drive is situated; **drive end bracket** = cover housing the bearing at the drive end of an alternator, dynamo, etc.; *(see illustrations 36, 37)*

◇ **drive gear** *noun* gearwheel transmitting the drive on a component such as an oil pump; *(see illustration 17)*

drive handle *noun* tool, typically in the form of a bar, for turning sockets to loosen and tighten nuts and bolts, with a male square drive to be inserted into the female square drive of sockets for the turning operation

> COMMENT: drive handles come in a variety of shapes; some of them are specially designed for fast spinning, whereas others can provide good leverage when it is needed to free extremely tight nuts or bolts. The most common types are ratchets, jointed handles, screwdriver-type spinner handles and speeder braces

drive layout *noun* configuration of engine, gearbox and driven axle(s); *(compare* FOUR-/FRONT-/REAR-WHEEL DRIVE)

◇ **driveline** *noun* = DRIVE TRAIN

◇ **drive module** *noun* interchangeable unit providing motive power, either in the form of an electric motor and ancillaries, or an internal combustion engine with all necessary components, for alternative use in the same vehicle according to needs and conditions

◇ **drive motor** *noun* electric motor providing motive power in an electric vehicle

◇ **driven** *adjective* made to rotate by the engine or some other source of motive power; **driven axle** *or* **wheels** = axle *or* wheels to which power is transmitted to drive the vehicle; **driven plate** = central clutch plate carrying clutch linings and held under pressure between the flywheel and the pressure plate when the clutch pedal is released, and transmitting power to the gearbox input shaft via splines

◇ **drive pinion** *noun* small bevel gear on either side of the differential in mesh with the two differential pinions, and into the centre of which one of the axle shafts fits

◇ **drive plate** *noun* light plate bolted to the crankshaft to which the torque converter is attached in a vehicle with automatic transmission

◇ **drive pulley** *noun* pulley round which a belt passes for transmitting power

driver *noun* **(a)** person driving a vehicle *he's a good driver* **(b)** screwdriver-type drive handle for use with sockets

driver air bag *noun* original type of air bag, designed to protect the driver from being hurled into the steering wheel and instrument panel

COMMENT: when used as an alternative to seat belts (the original idea, conceived for the American market where drivers are less willing to wear belts than their European counterparts), the driver air bag is rather bulky and requires a relatively large steering wheel hub to accommodate it, whereas the European-style air bag (designed as a supplementary restraint system, in addition to seat belts) is less bulky and fits inconspicuously into a standard-size steering wheel

Driver and Vehicle Licensing Agency (DVLA) *noun* section of the Department of Transport responsible for keeping records of all registered vehicles, and issuing registrations and licences for vehicles as well as driving licences for drivers

COMMENT: the Agency (usually abbreviated to DVLA) is housed in the Driver and Vehicle Licensing Centre (usually abbreviated to DVLC) in Swansea, which term is often used for the authority as well

driver error *noun* mistake or mistakes made by the driver, especially as the cause of an accident

drive shaft *noun* **(a)** any shaft transmitting power, especially the jointed shaft between the differential and the road wheel in a de Dion or fully independent rear suspension layout; *(see illustration 23)* **(b)** *US* = PROPELLER SHAFT

◊ **drive sprocket** *noun* sprocket round which a chain passes for transmitting power

◊ **drive tool** *noun* any accessory for use with a socket spanner, including the drive handle

◊ **drive train** *noun* combination of all power-transmitting components from the clutch via the gearbox and propeller shaft, if any, to the final drive and axle shafts (NOTE: also called **power train**)

◊ **driveway** *noun* short drive, often leading to a garage

driving 1 *adjective* providing motive power, making a gear, shaft, etc. rotate; **driving axle** *or* **wheels** = axle or wheels responsible for propelling the vehicle (which are in fact the same as the driven axle or wheels); **driving gear** = DRIVE GEAR **2** *noun* control of a moving vehicle *driving in city traffic is wearing on the nerves*

◊ **driving conditions** *noun* situation created by the amount of traffic, the weather and state of the roads

◊ **driving habits** *noun* personal behaviour at the wheel, including typical speeds under certain circumstances, frequency, timing and smoothness of gear changes, use of the brakes and so on

◊ **driving licence** *noun* document which allows the holder to drive a certain type or types of vehicle, and is the only document required to be carried by the driver in Britain

◊ **driving lamp** *noun* = SPOT LAMP

◊ **driving mirror** *noun* rear-view mirror either in the interior of the car or mounted on the outside of the front doors

◊ **driving position** *noun* position in which the driver sits at the steering wheel, influenced by distance from the controls, angle of the seat back, etc. *the typical Italian driving position is sitting with knees well bent and arms almost straight*

◊ **driving style** *noun* manner in which one handles a car; **a sporty driving style** = includes taking corners fast, braking and accelerating hard, using high revs in every gear and changing down before corners

drop *noun* sudden reduction (of pressure, voltage, etc.)

◊ **drop arm** *noun* usually vertical arm fitted to the outer end of the rocker shaft of a steering box, whose bottom end is connected to the drag link which it pulls back or pushes forward when the steering wheel is turned; *(see illustration 25)* (NOTE: US English is **pitman arm)**

◊ **drop-centre axle** *noun* beam axle in which the main central portion of the beam is lower than the wheel centres, which was the usual layout for front axles until independent front suspension became almost universal; **drop-centre rim** = WELL-BASE RIM

◊ **drophead 1** *noun* = CONVERTIBLE **2** *adjective* having a folding hood which can be raised or lowered over the passenger compartment; **drophead coupé (dhc)** = elegant style of body mainly seen on classic cars, with two wide doors and a large hood with no windows in the side and only a small window at the rear

◊ **droptop** *noun* *(informal)* = CONVERTIBLE

drum *noun* circular container, especially a brake drum; **drum brake** = brake in which curved brake shoes press against the inner circumference of a metal drum to produce the braking action; *(compare* DISC BRAKE) *(see illustration 30)*

dry 1 *verb* to lose or make lose its wetness; **the body is then dried in an oven at 115°C =** after painting, the body shell is subjected to heat so that the paint is baked on **2** *adjective* not wet; *(of bearing, etc.)* lacking lubricant; **dry liner** *or* **sleeve =** cylinder liner or sleeve which is not in contact with the coolant

◊ **dry clutch** *noun* = SINGLE-PLATE CLUTCH

◊ **dry galvanizing** *noun* hot-dip galvanizing method in which the metal components are first immersed in a solution of flux and then dried, so that they become pre-coated with a thin film of flux, which melts in the zinc bath, to which certain metals, such as tin and aluminium, may be added to give fluidity, and in the case of tin, brightness (NOTE: opposite is **wet galvanizing)**

◊ **drying oven** *noun* enclosure where car bodies are subjected to heat in order to dry and/or bake on the paintwork

◊ **dry joint** *noun* faulty electrical joint which does not give proper contact

◊ **dry liner** *or* **sleeve** *noun* cylinder liner that is not in contact with the coolant (NOTE: opposite is **wet liner)**

dry sump lubrication *noun* main lubrication of an engine supplied from a separate oil tank, the sump containing no oil while the engine is operating; a common feature of motorcycle and racing car engines; *(compare* WET SUMP LUBRICATION)

> COMMENT: the oil drains down into the bottom of the crankcase, where it is picked up through a strainer by the return side of the oil pump and transferred to an external oil tank

dry weight *noun* weight of a vehicle without any fuel, oil, or coolant; *(compare* GROSS VEHICLE WEIGHT, KERB WEIGHT)

dual 1 *adjective* comprising two parts, which are often identical **2** *verb* to convert (a single carriageway road) into dual carriageway

◊ **dual-acting** *noun* = DOUBLE-ACTING

◊ **dual-bed catalytic converter** *noun* catalytic converter which combines two

converters (with different catalysts) in a single housing

◊ **dual carriageway** *noun* road with two separate lanes for traffic travelling in different directions, separated by a central reserve

◊ **dual-circuit braking system** *noun* hydraulic braking system that provides two separate, independent hydraulic circuits, each acting on two wheels

◊ **dual controls** *noun* second set of controls for use by a driving instructor when teaching someone to drive

◊ **dual exhaust system** *noun* = TWIN EXHAUST SYSTEM

◊ **dual ignition system** *noun* = TWIN IGNITION SYSTEM

◊ **dual-line braking system** *noun* braking system in which towing vehicle and trailer are connected by two or more brake lines

◊ **dual-piston engine** *noun* = TWIN-PISTON ENGINE; **dual-piston master cylinder** = TANDEM MASTER CYLINDER

◊ **dual-range gearbox** *noun* gearbox in a four-wheel drive vehicle with two sets of ratios, usually a higher set for road use and a lower set for off-road use

◊ **dual-tone horn** *noun* = TWO-TONE HORN

Dubonnet suspension *noun* independent front suspension and steering arrangement used in the 1930s and '40s, in which the axle beam is rigidly attached to the vehicle frame, and the kingpins carry sprung steering and suspension arms, from which the wheels are mounted on stub axles

duct *noun* passage in square-section or tubular form for ventilation, heating or cables

ductile *adjective (of a metal)* which can be bent, hammered, or drawn out into wire or sheet without fracturing

◊ **ductility** *noun* ability of a material to undergo stretching or bending without fracturing

dull *adjective (of a finish)* not shiny

dumbirons *noun* front extensions of the side members of a chassis frame in older designs, to which were fitted the front ends of the leaf springs carrying the front axle

dummy *noun* stuffed figure made to look like a human being, used, for instance, when testing cars to destruction

dump truck *noun* small truck with a tipping container in front of the driver, used on building sites

◊ **dump valve** *noun* valve for relieving pressure, such as that between the turbocharger and the carburettor in some systems

duo-servo brake *noun* servo brake with one double-end wheel cylinder and two linked self-energizing brake shoes

duplex chain *noun* chain with two rows of rollers, used especially for timing chains; *(compare* SIMPLEX CHAIN, TRIPLEX CHAIN)

durability *noun* ability to last a long time; **improved exhaust durability** = ability of an exhaust system to last longer

dust boot *noun* concertina-like rubber cover for pushrods, e.g. on brake master cylinders and shock absorbers, also for constant velocity joints; *(see illustrations 20, 22, 30, 31)*

◊ **dust cap** *noun* = VALVE CAP

◊ **dust cover** *noun* any cover for excluding dust and dirt

◊ **dust-free** *adjective* *(of paint)* sufficiently hardened to prevent dust becoming embedded in the paint film; *(compare* HARDEN)

◊ **dust sheet** *noun* sheet for covering a car when in a garage and not in use

◊ **dust shield** *noun* = SPLASH SHIELD

DVLA = DRIVER AND VEHICLE LICENSING AGENCY

◊ **DVLC** = DRIVER AND VEHICLE LICENSING CENTRE

dwell *noun* **(a)** in a contact breaker ignition system, the angle in degrees of distributor shaft rotation during which the contact breaker points remain closed; the smaller the contact gap, the larger the dwell (angle), which determines the charging time of the ignition coil (NOTE: also called **dwell angle**) **(b)** in a breakerless ignition system, the time during which the electronic control unit allows current to flow through the primary winding of the coil, which in ignition systems with a Hall generator is determined by the width of the vanes

◊ **dwell-angle control** *noun* system ensuring that dwell is sufficient for all engine conditions; **dwell-angle map** = characteristic map for electronic dwell-angle control, dependent on engine speed and battery voltage

◊ **dwell meter** *noun* instrument for measuring the dwell angle

◊ **dwell period** *noun* period during which the primary circuit is closed and primary current flows through the ignition coil, given in crankshaft or distributor shaft degrees and therefore also called dwell angle

DWS (system) *noun* deflation warning system developed by Dunlop for on-line detection of tyre pressure loss, which since tyre pressure loss reduces tyre circumference and increases wheel rpm, uses the wheel speed sensors of an existing ABS system to continuously monitor wheel speed and tyre condition, any defects triggering a warning signal

dynamic balancing *noun* method of balancing wheels and other rotating components such as crankshafts, using a machine which spins the component and detects any running out of true which indicates imbalance (NOTE: opposite is **static balancing**)

◊ **dynamic ignition timing** *noun* modern timing procedure using a timing light which is controlled by the ignition pulse for the first cylinder and whose flashing beam is directed onto the timing marks, the rotating mark appearing fixed due to the stroboscopic effect, and indicating ignition advance or retard by its position in front of or behind the fixed timing mark (NOTE: also called **stroboscopic ignition timing;** opposite is **static ignition timing)**

◊ **dynamic imbalance** *noun* lack of balance in a rotating part such as a wheel, which can cause vibration and judder

◊ **dynamic seal** *noun* oil seal between a moving and a stationary part (NOTE: opposite is **static seal)**

◊ **dynamic supercharging** *noun* pressurizing of the air/fuel mixture using the natural dynamic behaviour of the aspirated air, and not some mechanical device to compress it

dynamo *noun* electrical generator driven by the engine and producing direct current, to charge the battery and thus feed the electrical circuits (NOTE: US English is **(DC) generator**)

COMMENT: in most modern vehicles, an alternator is used in place of a dynamo

dynamometer *noun* machine for measuring the power output of an engine, either directly or at the driven wheels; *(compare* BRAKE 1b)

dynastart(er) *noun* combined dynamo and starter used on some cars in the 1920s and '30s, and more recently on two-stroke motorcycles

Ee

E = ECONOMY (GEAR)

EAC valve *noun* electric air control valve; *(compare* EAS VALVE)

COMMENT: the GM version of a diverter or air gulp valve, providing three functions in a single valve: 1. the normal diverter valve function, i.e. it diverts air on rapid increase in manifold vacuum; 2. it relieves pressure by diverting air to the air cleaner when the air injection system pressure exceeds a certain set level; 3. being solenoid-controlled, it allows air to be diverted under any desired operating mode

ear *noun* projection in the shape of an ear, usually as a lug, but also as a spoiler behind the rear windows to improve stability in side winds

early fuel evaporation (EFE) system *noun* system that heats the inlet manifold to provide a warm air/fuel mixture, reducing condensation and improving fuel evaporation, thus improving cold engine operation and reducing exhaust emissions; *(see illustration 3)*

COMMENT: an EFE system operated by engine exhaust gas responds quicker to engine heat-up than systems heated by engine coolant; some EFE systems use an electric heater in the intake duct

earth 1 *noun* return path of an electrical system, which in a motor vehicle is provided by the metal body and chassis (NOTE: US English for this is **ground**); **earth connection** = wire or other metal strip for connecting a component to the vehicle chassis or body; **earth electrode** = side electrode of a sparking plug (NOTE: opposite is **centre electrode**); **earth return** = return path of an electrical circuit, provided by an earth connection; **earth strap** = piece of braided wire for earthing the battery, with a clip for attachment to the appropriate battery terminal at one end and a terminal for connecting to the chassis or body at the other **2** *verb* to connect a circuit or a component to a metal chassis or body part, either directly or by means of a wire

easing fluid *noun* = PENETRATING OIL

east-west layout *noun* transverse positioning of the engine across the car, found in many front-wheel drive designs (NOTE: also called **transverse engine** ; the opposite is **north-south layout**)

EAS valve *noun* valve in an emission control system governing the airflow from the air pump in connection with the EAC valve; *(compare* EAC VALVE)

COMMENT: when its solenoid is energized, air is directed into the exhaust ports to increase oxidation and accelerate catalytic converter heat-up to operating temperature, and when its solenoid is de-energized, it switches airflow between the converter beds to help the oxidizing catalyst to decrease the CO and HC levels

eat (away) *verb* to corrode and remove the metal from *the front wing has been eaten away by rust*

ebonite *noun* hard black rubber compound especially one containing no filler

eccentric 1 *adjective* mounted off-centre; **eccentric drive** = drive from a point not on the axis of the driving shaft, e.g. from the outer part of a disc, so that a reciprocating or up and down motion is transmitted; used in pumps or for a camshaft drive; **eccentric rotor pump** = ROTOR-TYPE PUMP; **eccentric shaft** = shaft transmitting eccentric motion **2** *noun* part transmitting an eccentric drive, such as a disc with a provision for a drive from its outer part, or an eccentric shaft

ECE test cycle *noun* 13 minute, three-part test of automotive emissions for compliance with emission standards, adopted by most European countries, simulating urban driving conditions, i.e. involving relatively long idling periods and speeds below 35 mph, emission characteristics at cruising speeds not being considered

echelon parking *noun* parking with the nose of the car close to the kerb and at an angle to it

ECI *(short for)* electronically controlled injection

◊ **ECM** = ELECTRONIC CONTROL MODULE

ecological damage *noun* damage to the environment, usually in the form of pollution, such as that caused by vehicle emissions

◊ **ecologically harmful** *adjective* damaging to the environment *automotive exhaust gases are ecologically harmful*

economical *adjective* using only a small amount of fuel; **most cars are more economical on long runs** = most cars give better mileage per gallon when driven long distances

◊ **economizer** *noun* device for making a vehicle use less fuel, either by regulating the flow of fuel, or by admitting extra air to the air/fuel mixture (especially when cruising)

◊ **economy** *noun* (especially low) consumption of fuel, usually measured in miles per gallon; **tuned for economy** = tuned to use less fuel; **good/bad fuel economy** = low/high fuel consumption; **economy device** = ECONOMIZER; **economy gear** *or* **ratio** = high gear designed for economical cruising; **economy jet** = additional jet in a carburettor admitting extra air to the air/fuel mixture (especially when cruising)

ECS *(short for)* electronically controlled suspension

ECT *(short for)* engine coolant temperature

ECU = ELECTRONIC CONTROL UNIT

edge binding *noun* tape for binding the edges of carpets

◊ **edge protection** *noun* protection of edges against corrosion, e.g. by weatherstrips

◊ **edge trim** *noun* rubber or plastic U-section strip fitted to panel edges to protect them against chipping, etc.

Edison base *or* **screw** *noun* threaded type of base for light bulbs, with only a few automotive applications, bayonet fittings being almost universal (NOTE: opposite is **bayonet base)**

Edwardian car *noun* *(GB)* car built between 1905 and 1918

EEC = ELECTRONIC ENGINE CONTROL

EFE system *noun* = EARLY FUEL EVAPORATION SYSTEM

effective *adjective* **(a)** actual rather than theoretical or potential; **effective deflection** = deflection of a suspension system under a particular load **(b)** producing an effect; **effective stroke** = working or power stroke in a two-stroke engine

efficiency *noun* performance of a mechanical device or system, especially with regard to the amount of energy used; **braking efficiency** = braking effort as a percentage of the weight of the vehicle; *(compare* THERMAL EFFICIENCY)

EFI *or* **EFi** = ELECTRONIC FUEL INJECTION

egg-crate grille *noun* radiator grille with crisscrossing bars forming gaps which are more or less square, or sometimes hexagonal

EGR = EXHAUST GAS RECIRCULATION; **EGR valve** = part of an EGR system mounted on or near the inlet manifold and controlled by inlet manifold vacuum, which is usually closed at idle and low speeds, but opens during acceleration, admitting exhaust gas to the inlet manifold; *(see illustration 4)*

COMMENT: most EGR valves are of the single diaphragm type, some are dual diaphragm valves connected to two separate vacuum sources to more closely match EGR function to engine loads; for the same purpose, EGR valves are frequently governed by additional regulating devices

eight *noun* eight-cylinder engine, or a car fitted with one; the cylinders may be in-line (a straight eight) or in a V-layout (a V-8)

EIN = ENGINE IDENTIFICATION NUMBER

eject *verb* to push or throw out; **eject button** = button on a cassette player for taking out the cassettes

elasticity *noun* ability to recover original size and shape when deforming, especially stretching, forces are released

◊ **elastomer** *noun* elastic macromolecular material that at room temperature returns rapidly to approximately its initial dimensions and shape after substantial deformation by a weak stress and release of the stress

elbow *noun* bend in a pipe

electric *adjective* operated by or derived from electricity

◊ **electric air control valve** = EAC VALVE

◊ **electric air switching valve** = EAS VALVE

◊ **electrical** *adjective* relating to electricity; **electrical conductivity** = ability of a material to conduct electricity (NOTE: opposite is **resistivity**); **electrical screwdriver** = usually small screwdriver for use when working on the electrical system, with a thin blade and an insulated handle, also sometimes an insulated shank; **electrical spanner** = small, open-ended spanner with two jaw openings of the same size set at different angles to the handle, e.g. 15° at one end and 60° at the other; **electrical system** = combination of all wiring circuits and electrical units and equipment on a vehicle, with the exception of those in the ignition system

◊ **electric car** *noun* car whose motive power is provided by an electric motor, with the advantages of silence and lack of pollution, and the disadvantages of the weight of the batteries and the need for recharging after a relatively short distance

◊ **electric charge** *noun* definite quantity of electricity, which may be positive, as with protons, or negative, as with electrons; (*compare* COULOMB)

◊ **electric current** *noun* flow of electricity passing through a conductor

◊ **electric fuel pump** *noun* electrically powered petrol or diesel pump, drawing fuel from the tank and delivering it to the carburettor or fuel injection system

◊ **electric grid** *noun* = ELECTRICAL SYSTEM

◊ **electric mirror** *noun* external, usually door mirror which can be adjusted from inside the car

electric motor *noun* machine which changes electrical energy into usually rotational motion

COMMENT: in addition to the starter and windscreen wiper motors, which were the first electric motors to be added to automotive electrical systems about 80 years ago, modern cars include a large number of small motors for driving systems such as electric windows, aerials, sunroofs, mirrors and seat adjustment, central locking and power hoods; electric-powered cars use large motors for their drive

electric top *noun US* = POWER HOOD

◊ **electric windows** *noun* windows which are raised and lowered by electric motors, and operated by switches on the centre console or on the door (NOTE: US English is **power windows**)

electrochemical corrosion *noun* corrosion involving at least one electrode reaction

electrocoating *noun* = ELECTROPHORETIC PAINTING

electrode *noun* conductor which leads current into a gas, liquid or vacuum, such as those in a sparking plug between which the spark passes to ignite the mixture; **electrode adjusting tool** = tool used to bend side electrodes on sparking plugs for gap adjustment, usually combined with gauges for checking the gap; **electrode gap** = SPARKING PLUG GAP

electrodeposition *noun* generic term for electrolytic processes in which a metal is deposited at the cathode from a solution of its ions, such as electroplating, or in which paint is deposited in an immersion process by means of electric current

◊ **electrogalvanizing** *noun* coating of metal, especially iron or steel, with zinc by electroplating

electrolysis *noun* method by which chemical reactions are carried out by passage of electric current through a solution of an electrolyte or through a molten salt, e.g. in a starter battery

◊ **electrolyte** *noun* substance which can dissolve to yield a solution, or a solution itself able to conduct electric current, especially in an electric cell or battery *the electrolyte in a starter battery is sulphuric acid* **electrolyte level** = amount of electrolyte in a car battery, which must cover the top of the plates *if the electrolyte level is too low, it should be* *restored by adding distilled water* **electrolyte tester** = device for checking electrolyte density in a battery, and hence its state of charge

◊ **electrolytic** *adjective* relating to electrolysis or an electrolyte; **electrolytic cell** = cell consisting of electrodes immersed in an electrolyte solution for carrying out electrolysis; **electrolytic corrosion** = electrochemical corrosion causing the electrolytic removal of metal; **electrolytic deposition** = ELECTROPLATING; **electrolytic galvanizing** = ELECTROGALVANIZING; **electrolytic protection** = CATHODIC PROTECTION

electromagnetic clutch *noun* any clutch in which magnetic force is used to hold the drive in engagement, such as that in the compressor drive of an air-conditioning system

electromotive force (EMF) *noun* source of electrical energy required to produce an electric current, produced by devices such as batteries or generators and measured in volts

electron *noun* negatively charged constituent of an atom; **electron flow** = current produced by the motion of free electrons towards a positive terminal, whose direction is the opposite to that of the current

electronic *adjective* featuring semiconductors (usually transistors) as an operating medium

◊ **electronically controlled** *adjective* controlled by electronic means *electronically controlled injection; electronically controlled suspension*

◊ **electronic cluster** *noun* display showing various functions, including speedometer, tachometer, gauges, etc., using LEDs or LCD technology displaying symbols and bar graphs instead of numbers (NOTE: opposite is **analogue cluster)**

◊ **electronic control unit (ECU)** *noun* microprocessor and memory with electronic maps, forming the central part of an engine management system or of subsystems such as a fuel injection or ignition system (NOTE: also called **electronic (control) module (ECM)** *(compare* IGNITION CONTROL UNIT)

◊ **electronic engine control (EEC)** *noun* engine management system which

controls the ignition system and various other systems, including the exhaust gas recirculation and air-injection systems

◊ **electronic fuel injection (EFI** *or* **EFi)** *noun* system that injects fuel into the engine and includes an electronic control unit to time and meter the flow

◊ **electronic ignition system** *noun* term used to designate breakerless transistorized ignitions, transistorized ignitions with electronic spark timing, and sometimes mapped ignition systems

◊ **electronic navigator** *noun* = TRIP COMPUTER

◊ **electronic ride control** *noun* suspension control system comprising microprocessor-controlled, electronically adjustable air shock absorbers for automatic selection of the optimum damping characteristics depending on road surface and load conditions

◊ **electronic spark advance (ESA)** *noun* the part of an ECU that controls ignition timing and dwell angle

◊ **electronic spark control (ESC)** *or* **electronic spark timing (EST)** *noun* ignition timing by means of an ignition map, either integrated into mapped ignition systems or available as a separate module to enhance transistorized ignition systems

◊ **electronic traction control (ETC)** *noun* system for reducing wheelspin, incorporating wheel sensors; *(compare* ANTI-SPIN REGULATION)

◊ **electronic transmission control** *noun* system or module for controlling automatic transmission

electropainting *noun* = ELECTROPHORETIC PAINTING; **electropaint tank** = tank in which items are immersed for electrophoretic paint application

electrophoretic painting *noun* process used to apply the first coat of paint (primer) to car bodies; **electrophoretic primer** = paint used to prime car bodies by the electrophoretic process

COMMENT: the process involves using negatively charged paint particles (anodic electropainting) or positively charged paint particles (cathodic electropainting); the cleaned metal parts to be coated are immersed in a tank of electrodeposition paint, and the current is turned on, so that the paint particles are attracted by the positively charged paint particles

electro picker *noun* electrical door lock picker (available to key services and the police only)

COMMENT: consists basically of a vibrator with an attached steel blade; when the vibrating blade is inserted into a lock, it finds its way past the locking pins which would normally block anything but the original key

electroplate *verb* to plate (metals) by electrodeposition

◊ **electroplating** *noun* electrodeposition of metals or alloys from suitable electrolyte solutions, the articles to be plated being connected to the cathode in an electrolyte solution, and direct current introduced through the anode of the metal to be deposited

electrostatic painting *or* **spraying** *noun* painting method using the particle-attracting property of electrostatic charges, in which a direct current of approx. 100,000 volts is applied to a grid of wires through which the paint is sprayed to charge each particle, and the metal objects to be sprayed are connected to the opposite terminal of the high-voltage circuit, so as to attract the paint particles; **electrostatic powder coating (EPC)** = painting process in which the outer parts of the body shell are coated with a powder dispersion by means of cathodic immersion, and in which the cavities are coated with cathodic electropaint

electrovalve *noun* = SOLENOID VALVE

element *noun* assembly of all positive and negative plates of a single battery cell including its separators, arranged so as to start and finish with a negative plate (so that there are always negative then positive plates), because the positive plates tend to distort under discharge

Elliot axle *noun* axle design in which the axle beam terminates in a yoke or fork-shaped end which holds the kingpin; *(compare* REVERSED ELLIOT AXLE)

ellipsoidal headlight *noun* headlight with a reflector which is wider than it is high, and not circular; has replaced the parabolic reflector

embrittlement *noun* reduced toughness in plastic or metal cuased by age, heat or rough use; *see also* HYDROGEN EMBRITTLEMENT

emergency *noun* sudden, unexpected occurrence, such as a breakdown or the failure of some part, which may be dangerous and demands immediate action; **emergency brake** = secondary braking system which comes into operation when the main braking system fails; **emergency inflator** = aerosol can which inflates a punctured tyre and injects sealing compound to provide at least a temporary repair; **emergency transmitter** = transmitter no larger than a car radio, fitted inside the vehicle which enables drivers to radio for help from the security of their own cars; **emergency windscreen** = sheet of clear plastic fitted in place of a broken windscreen

emery cloth *noun* cloth coated in emery crystals for use as an abrasive on metals

EMF = ELECTROMOTIVE FORCE

Emily *noun* affectionate name for the Rolls-Royce radiator mascot, the 'Spirit of Ecstasy'

emission *noun* passing of gases and other toxic substances into the atmosphere; **emissions** = gases and other pollutants coming from a vehicle with an internal combustion engine

emission control *noun* **(a)** reduction of all types of emission from motor vehicles *the second phase of automotive emission control began in 1975 with the introduction of catalytic converters* **(b)** emission control **(system)** = any system, device or modification added onto or designed into a motor vehicle for the purpose of reducing air-polluting emissions, such as a catalytic converter

COMMENT: there are two standards for emission controls, level E for Europe and the more stringent level U for the United States

emission levels *noun* amounts of toxic substances passed into the atmosphere by motor vehicles

◊ **emission standards** *noun* specified maximum emission levels permitted from different classes of motor vehicle in different countries; **the stringent US emission standards** = the low emission levels permitted in the United States, especially in California

EMS = ENGINE MANAGEMENT SYSTEM

emulsion *noun* mixture of two liquids which do not fully mix, such as oil and water, or specifically of petrol and air in a carburettor; **emulsion tube** = part of a fixed jet carburettor, in which air is introduced into the mixture through holes to help atomize it and correct excessive richness at higher engine speeds

enamel *noun* high-gloss paint that is slower drying and therefore easier to apply than cellulose, and will cause cellulose applied over it to lift

end bracket *noun* = END COVER (PLATE)

◊ **end cap** *noun* cap covering the end of a piece of trim or of a fuse

◊ **end cover (plate)** *noun* cover containing a bearing at either end of a dynamo or alternator; *(compare* DRIVE END BRACKET*)*

◊ **end cutters** *or* **end cutting pliers** *noun* small pincers with sharp jaws for cutting and stripping wires, etc.

◊ **end float** *noun* = END PLAY

endoscope *noun* instrument used to see into the interior of hollow cavities such as box sections

end play *noun* bearing clearance in an axial direction; **check the big end bearing for end play** = check if there is any sideways movement in the big end

endurance test *noun* test of a material or system over a long period

energize *verb* to activate (a solenoid, relay, etc.) by providing sufficient energy

energy *noun* capacity for doing work, measured in joules or in the case of electrical energy, in kilowatt-hours

◊ **energy-absorbing** *adjective* able to absorb forces of impact; **energy-absorbing steering column** = safety design of steering column which telescopes on impact

◊ **energy conversion** *noun* changing of one form of energy into another or into work, such as that in the combustion process, the heat of which is used to turn the engine and thus create motion

engage *verb* **(a)** to come into contact and be locked together (with another part); **the clutch engages smoothly** = the driving and driven plates of the clutch come together and take up the drive without judder **(b)** to bring (a part) into contact with another so that it is locked to it; **to engage a lower gear** = to select a lower ratio by moving the gear lever

◊ **engagement** *noun* bringing into locking contact (e.g. of the clutch), or selection of a gear

engine *noun* energy-converting propelling unit of a motor vehicle, usually an internal combustion engine of the reciprocating-piston type, either with spark ignition (petrol engines) or compression ignition (diesel engines)

COMMENT: in British usage, there is a clear distinction between the terms engine and motor, the term motor only being used for electric power units, but in American usage it is used for all types of power unit including internal combustion engines

engine analyzer *noun* electronic engine-testing device, formerly free-standing in a cabinet, and now often hand-held and connected to the vehicle's diagnostic socket (as in the case of the diagnostic read-out box), which provides data on all aspects of the engine's state of tune; *(compare* DIAGNOSTIC SYSTEM*)*

◊ **engine bay** *noun* = ENGINE COMPARTMENT

◊ **engine block** *noun* cylinder block with integral crankcase; *(see illustrations 3, 5, 7)*; **engine block heater** = CYLINDER BLOCK HEATER

◊ **engine brake** *or* **braking effect** *noun* retarding effect of an engine when the vehicle is in gear with the throttle closed, i.e. on the overrun, which is increased by changing to a lower gear

◊ **engine capacity** *noun* swept volume of an engine

◊ **engine compartment** *noun* area into which the engine is fitted; **crowded** *or* **cluttered engine compartment** = engine compartment in which all the available space round the engine is taken up with ancillaries

◊ **engine coolant** *noun* liquid used in the engine's cooling system

◊ **engine cover** *noun* panel of metal or plastic covering the engine of a rear-engined car (NOTE: the terms **bonnet** in British usage and **hood** in American usage are only used for the cover over a front-mounted engine)

◊ **engine damage** *noun* breakage, deformation or scoring of the internal parts of an engine; **overrevving may cause engine damage** = running the engine too fast may result in, for example, seizure, a burnt piston or a dropped valve

◊ **engine depression** *noun* low pressure on the engine side of the throttle caused by piston suction in the inlet manifold

◊ **engine diagnostic connector** *noun* electrical connector for plugging in the engine analyzer, forming an interface between the engine electronic controls and diagnostic unit, and used to read the engine data as well as any fault codes stored in the memory of the engine controller

◊ **engine hoist** *noun* small crane for lifting an engine out of a motor vehicle, formerly incorporating a block and tackle, but now usually hydraulically operated; *(compare* GANTRY)

◊ **engine (identification) number (EIN)** *noun* number stamped on the engine and usually also on the vehicle identification plate, which should be quoted when ordering parts *the first two digits of the engine number give you information on the assembly plant*

◊ **engine knock** *noun* engine operating condition, accompanied by audible noise, that occurs when fuel in the cylinders is ignited too early and/or spontaneously, resulting in colliding flame fronts and shock waves which cause high thermal and mechanical stress, and can severely damage the engine

◊ **engine layout** *noun* **(a)** type of engine, with reference to the arrangement of its cylinders and their number (as in a flat four, V-twin or straight eight) **(b)** positioning of the engine in the vehicle (as in a front, mid- or rear engine, a transverse or in-line engine)

◊ **engine management system (EMS)** *noun* electronic engine control system which covers at least the functioning of the fuel injection and ignition, but may also include emission controls and self-diagnostics

◊ **engine map** *noun* = CHARACTERISTIC MAP

◊ **engine misfire** *noun* = MISFIRE

◊ **engine modifications** *noun* alterations to the specification of the engine to increase power output, improve economy, reduce emissions, etc.

◊ **engine mounting** *noun* flexible support for the engine in which an elastic medium, usually rubber, is interposed between lugs on the engine and the frame of the vehicle; *(see illustration 27)*

◊ **engine noise** *noun* amount of noise emitted by the engine when running *engine noise is more noticeable with a diesel at lower speeds*

◊ **engine oil** *noun* usually multigrade oil of lower viscosity than gear oil, used to lubricate an engine; **engine oil level warning light** = light on the instrument panel which comes on when the oil in the sump falls below a certain level

engine overhaul *noun* dismantling of the engine and restoration of the manufacturer's original tolerances by replacement of worn parts, reboring the cylinders, regrinding the crankshaft, etc.

| COMMENT: the usual indicators for the need of an engine overhaul are heavy oil consumption and poor oil pressure

engine parameters *noun* used in the context of emission controls for those engine characteristics sensitive to engine performance, such as power/bhp, general engine performance and fuel economy

◊ **engine performance tester** *noun* = ENGINE ANALYZER

◊ **engine size** *noun* = ENGINE CAPACITY

◊ **engine speed** *noun* number of revolutions per minute (rpm) at which the engine is turning; **engine speed limiter** = device acting as a governor which cuts the power when a certain number of rpm is reached; **engine speed sensor** = in most cases, a magnetic pick-up that scans the flywheel teeth and produces one output signal per scanned tooth, or a Hall generator in the distributor, whose signals are passed to the electronic control unit

◊ **engine subframe** *noun* separate frame in which the engine is mounted

◊ **engine temperature sensor** *noun* sensor used to monitor the temperature of the engine (NOTE: not identical with the /NX coolant temperature sensor) *(see illustration 4)*

◊ **engine timing** *noun* ignition and valve timing

enrichment *noun* making the air/fuel mixture richer, i.e. increasing the fuel content; **enrichment device** *or* **unit** = circuit in a carburettor providing a richer mixture, operated by engine vacuum; *(see illustration 11)*

entry-level version *or* entry model *noun* basic model suitable as someone's first car

envelope *noun* cover enclosing something entirely, such as the glass of a lamp bulb; **envelope separator** = porous plastic separator used in maintenance-free batteries to enclose the individual plates completely

environment-conscious *or* **environmentally aware** *adjective* aware of dangers and threats to the environment and taking appropriate action to avoid them; **environmentally friendly** = harmless to the environment, or causing as little harm as possible

EPA *noun US* Environmental Protection Agency, which is responsible for recommending environmental legislation and in the automotive sphere produces test cycles and estimates fuel economy

EPC = ELECTROSTATIC POWDER COATING

EP gear oil *noun* extreme pressure gear oil preventing metal-to-metal contact, used mainly in gearboxes and final drive units

epicyclic gearbox *noun* constant-mesh gearbox with several planetary gear sets made up of an internally toothed outer ring gear, several small intermediate pinions or planet gears and a large externally toothed central gear known as a sun wheel (NOTE: US English is **planetary transmission**)

COMMENT: the sets can be either fixed together (e.g. the planet carrier holding the planet gears of one set fixed to the sun wheel of another set) or coupled by means of clutches, the various gear ratios being obtained by coupling the members of the gear sets in different ways with the aid of multi-plate clutches and multi-disc or band brakes. Many automatic transmissions such as the Simpson or Ravigneaux transmissions use the epicyclic principle

epitrochoid(al) *adjective* (part of a circle) which is not on the circumference of another circle around which it turns

epoxy resin *noun* thermosetting resin based on ethylene oxide or similar materials or derivatives, used in adhesives, fillers, and primers and other finishes

EPS *(short for)* electronically controlled power steering

COMMENT: EPS is used in more expensive models, such as the BMW Servotronic system where the assistance provided alters according to the speed at which the car is travelling

equalizer *noun* **(a)** = GRAPHIC EQUALIZER **(b)** = COMPENSATOR

equal power distribution *or* **split** *noun* system in four-wheel drive vehicles which ensures that an equal amount of power is passed to the front and rear wheels

equipment *noun* devices and systems fitted to a vehicle which are either essential or optional, and either fitted by the manufacturer (original equipment) or subsequently by the owner (aftermarket equipment); **equipment package** = particular combination of equipment provided by the manufacturer

erode *verb* to remove a surface layer (by chemical action or by rubbing) *the points become eroded after a period of use*

◇ **erosion** *noun* removing a surface layer (by chemical action or wear)

ESA = ELECTRONIC SPARK ADVANCE

◇ **ESC** = ELECTRONIC SPARK CONTROL

esr *(short for)* electric sunroof

EST = ELECTRONIC SPARK TIMING

estate car *noun* private car which is essentially a saloon whose roof is extended to the rear of the car, which is more or less vertical and incorporates a tailgate, giving a large internal loading space that can be further increased by lowering the back of the rear seat (NOTE: US English is **station wagon**)

ESV = EXPERIMENTAL SAFETY VEHICLE

ETA *(short for)* estimated time of arrival

ETC = ELECTRONIC TRACTION CONTROL

etching *noun* **(a)** roughening or disintegration of the paint surface, which can occur on small patches or over a wide area, through attack from bird droppings, screen washer fluid, industrial fallout, etc. **(b)** removal of soil or the natural oxide film from an aluminium surface, giving a roughened surface which improves adhesion of the subsequent paint layer, or removal of the actual metal; **etch** _or_ **etching primer** = primer for aluminium which has an etching effect to improve adhesion **(c)** system of marking car windows with the registration number so as to deter thieves

ethanol _noun_ ethyl alcohol which is added to petrol, typically in a mixture of 10% ethanol and 90% unleaded petrol

ethyl acrylate _noun_ polymer used in toughening rubber

ethylene-glycol _noun_ thick hygroscopic liquid which is used as the main constituent of antifreeze

Euromix formula _noun_ basis for a standard test cycle covering both town driving and driving on the open road

evacuate _verb_ to remove by pushing out _the pump evacuates the air from the pipe_

evaporate _verb_ to turn into a vapour _the refrigerant evaporates by absorbing heat_

◊ **evaporation** _noun_ conversion of a liquid into a vapour; **evaporation control system** _or_ **evaporative emission control (system) (EVAP)** = system for reducing evaporative emissions by means of a sealed fuel tank, a vapour-liquid separator, a three-way valve, an activated carbon filter, and a network of interconnecting hoses

◊ **evaporative emissions** _or_ **losses** _noun_ vapours or fumes not emitted by the exhaust system, but escaping from the fuel tank, carburettor and crankcase, and accounting for about 40% of hydrocarbon emissions released by a petrol engine without emission controls

evaporator _noun_ in automotive air-conditioning systems, a heat exchanger designed to absorb heat by evaporation of a refrigerant (NOTE: opposite is **condenser**) _(see illustration 35)_

COMMENT: usually located in front of the heater core and formed of a refrigerant coil surrounded by small, thin cooling fins receiving very cool, low-pressure, atomized

liquid refrigerant from the expansion valve or orifice tube and transferring the heat from incoming fresh air or recirculated air from the passenger compartment into the refrigerant, which changes to low-pressure vapour, its outlet being connected to the compressor's suction side

EVAP system _noun_ = EVAPORATIVE EMISSION CONTROL SYSTEM

EVC = EXHAUST VALVE CLOSES

EVO = EXHAUST VALVE OPENS

ew _(short for)_ electric windows

exchange engine _noun_ overhauled replacement engine provided in exchange for a worn (but undamaged) engine, plus a charge

excitation winding _noun_ = FIELD WINDING

ex-demonstrator _noun_ car formerly used by a dealer as a demonstrator

executive car _noun_ large, powerful luxury car considered suitable for a business executive

exhaust 1 _noun_ **(a)** = EXHAUST GAS **(b)** = EXHAUST SYSTEM **2** _verb_ to push out or discharge (combustion gases) _pollutants are exhausted from the exhaust system_

exhaust back pressure _noun_ any pressure holding back the flow of the gases in an exhaust system

COMMENT: the pressure present in the exhaust system during the exhaust period of the two-stroke engine counteracts the pressure of the exhaust gases expelled from the cylinder and prevents excess velocity of the gases, since this would cause the fresh charge supplied into the cylinder at the same time to be expelled straight out of the cylinder again; excessive back pressure reduces engine power, while very low back pressure allows the fresh charge to escape before being cycled in the engine, leading to a sharp increase in fuel consumption

exhaust cam(shaft) _noun_ separate camshaft controlling the opening and closing of the exhaust valves used in twin overhead camshaft engines; _(see illustrations 3, 6)_ (NOTE: opposite is **inlet camshaft**)

◇ **exhaust chamber** *noun* part of the two-stroke exhaust system designed to maintain a specified back pressure

◇ **exhaust emission control** *noun* reduction of harmful pollutants in the gases emitted from the exhaust system; **exhaust emission control system** = general term for any system that reduces the harmful exhaust emissions of a motor vehicle, including one or all of the following systems: catalytic converter (with or without oxygen sensor air/fuel control), exhaust gas recirculation, secondary air injection or induction, and positive crankcase ventilation

◇ **exhaust emissions** *noun* gases emitted into the atmosphere through the exhaust system, or indeed any opening downstream of the exhaust ports of an engine

◇ **exhaust gas** *noun* gas which is the product of the combustion process and which is passed out of the cylinder through the exhaust valve or port into the exhaust system; **exhaust gas analyzer** = device which can establish the hydrocarbon, carbon monoxide or carbon dioxide content of the exhaust gases; used for tuning the engine or testing to see whether emission control standards are met; **exhaust gas purification (system)** = emission control system for diesel engines, which may consist of an exhaust scrubber, a diesel exhaust filter, and/or a catalytic converter; **exhaust gas recirculation (EGR)** = process in which a small portion of the exhaust gas is mixed with air in the induction tract, which has the effect of reducing the nitrogen oxides then emitted

◇ **exhaust manifold** *noun* first part of the exhaust system, usually made of cast iron, and fixed directly to the cylinder head over the exhaust ports, from which it collects the gases and passes them to the down pipe(s) connected to its outlet(s); *(see illustrations 3, 5, 19)*

◇ **exhaust note** *noun* sound coming from the end of the exhaust pipe *a pleasant or loud or sporty exhaust note*

◇ **exhaust pipe** *noun* any pipe forming part of the exhaust system

◇ **exhaust pollutants** *noun* = EXHAUST EMISSIONS

◇ **exhaust port** *noun* **(a)** *(in four-stroke engines)* short passage in the cylinder head from the exhaust valve opening to the exhaust manifold (or exhaust pipe on a typical motorcycle); *(see illustration 6)* **(b)** *(in two-stroke engines)* opening in the cylinder wall used for discharge of the spent gases into the exhaust system

◇ **exhaust scrubber** *noun* diesel exhaust gas purification system which cools the exhaust and separates nitrogen oxide and oil vapours from the gas stream

◇ **exhaust side** *noun* side of the engine where the exhaust valves and exhaust manifold are situated *the highest temperatures are on the exhaust side*

◇ **exhaust stroke** *noun* in spark ignition and diesel engines, the upward stroke of the piston when the energy of combustion is spent and the piston moves upward again, the exhaust valve opens and burned gases are forced out past the open exhaust valve

◇ **exhaust system** *noun* system in a four-wheeled motor vehicle that collects the exhaust gases and discharges them into the air, consisting of the exhaust manifold, exhaust pipe, silencer, tailpipe, and rear silencer or resonator

◇ **exhaust timing** *noun* exhaust control system developed especially for two-stroke motorcycle engines in order to enhance low and mid-range power

◇ **exhaust treatment** *noun* any measures taken to reduce the pollutant concentrations in the exhaust of an internal combustion engine released into the atmosphere

◇ **exhaust turbocharging** *noun* = TURBOCHARGING

◇ **exhaust valve** *noun* valve, usually of the poppet type and smaller than the inlet valve, in four-stroke IC engines, operated directly or indirectly by a camshaft to open during the exhaust stroke to allow the combustion gases to escape; *(see illustrations 3, 6)*; **exhaust valve closes (EVC)** = mark on a valve-timing diagram; **exhaust valve opens (EVO)** = mark on a valve-timing diagram; *(compare* IVC, IVO)

expander *noun* device in a drum brake system (either hydraulic or mechanical) which forces the shoes apart into contact with the drum

◇ **expander ring** *or* **spacer** *noun* part used in an oil-control piston ring consisting of more than one part (e.g. one upper and one lower rail) to exert a constant pressure on the ring, in order to ensure a tight seal towards the cylinder wall

◇ **expansion** *noun* increase in volume of a liquid or a gas; **expansion stroke** = POWER STROKE; **expansion tank** = overflow container for gases or liquids subject to expansion, such as fuels or more particularly coolant which expands when heated, and when cool returns to the radiator; **expansion valve** = flow-control valve located between the condenser and evaporator in an air conditioner which controls the amount of refrigerant sprayed into the evaporator; *(see illustration 35)*

Experimental Safety Vehicle (ESV) *noun* special vehicle built for research into and testing of safety features; *(compare* SID)

exploded view *noun* drawing of a mechanism or structure which shows the parts separately but approximately in the position they occupy when assembled

expressway *noun US* multilane road like a motorway, with full or partial control of access

extension bar *or* **piece** *noun* part used with socket spanners inserted between a socket and the drive handle, which allows access to nuts or bolt heads in deeply recessed or otherwise confined areas

exterior mirror *noun* = EXTERNAL MIRROR

external combustion engine *noun* engine (such as a steam engine) in which fuel is burnt outside the cylinder or cylinders, power being generated by the expansion of another liquid or gas heated by combustion

◊ **external diameter** *noun* the external diameter of a cylinder or tube

◊ **external micrometer** *noun* micrometer for measuring external diameters

◊ **external mirror** *noun* mirror attached to the outside of the vehicle, typically on the driver's or the passenger's door; *(compare* DOOR MIRROR, WING MIRROR)

external mix air cap *noun* special type of air cap for spray guns; *(compare* INTERNAL MIX AIR CAP)

COMMENT: air and fluid are mixed in the space outside the air cap, directly in front of the nozzle; the most common type of air cap

external thread *noun* thread consisting of projecting ridges on the outside of a part such as a bolt or screw (which fits into the corresponding internal thread of a nut or similar) (NOTE: also called **male thread)**

◊ **external vane pump** *noun* pump with either an elliptic rotating piston or an eccentrically mounted circular rotor; *(compare* SLIDING-VANE PUMP)

extractor *noun* special tool for extracting bearings, bushes and sleeves from housings and blind holes

COMMENT: a special collet is inserted through the bearing or sleeve and gives positive grip when expanded; pulling action is achieved with a slide hammer or a special bridge yoke

extras *noun* optional additional items either fitted by the manufacturer at the buyer's request, or fitted later by the owner, comprising either accessories such as seat covers or additional lights or built-in items such as a heated rear window or sunroof

eye *noun* circular opening or hole, such as that at the end of a leaf spring or that formed at the end of a cable

◊ **eyebolt** *noun* bolt with an eye in place of a head, through which a cable can be passed, e.g. for lifting purposes

◊ **eyelet connector** *noun* connector for electrical connections which is attached to a wire and has its ring-shaped end pushed onto a round post or threaded terminal

◊ **eyelet pliers** *noun* pliers for punching small holes, with a round stud in one jaw and a hole in the other

Ff

F (a) *(short for)* Fahrenheit **(b)** = FIELD (TERMINAL)

fabric *noun* material made from textile or man-made fibres, used e.g. in the structure of tyre casings, for covering seats, etc.; **fabric body** = simple form of lightweight bodywork in which a waterproof, cloth-backed material is stretched over a wooden framework, popular around 1930 and still used at a later date by DKW and even postwar by Lloyd; **fabric hood** *or* **top** = soft top made from a textile (such as canvas) as opposed to vinyl

fabricate *verb* to make, usually by a relatively complex process or from several parts *most body panels are fabricated from sheet steel*

face *noun* front, visible or working surface of a part (such as a valve) or a tool (such as a hammer)

◇ **facelift** *noun* minor styling modifications made to a car model which may be approaching the end of its useful life, intended to improve the appearance and thus boost sales with minimum cost, including such features as restyled headlights, larger tail lights, added trim and spoilers

facia *noun* = FASCIA

factory adjusted *adjective* set by the works when the vehicle is built (and not to be altered) *the adjustment screw is factory adjusted*

◇ **factory primer** *noun* primer coat applied to new body panels in the factory for protection during storage, which in some cases has to be removed prior to painting because of paint compatibility problems

fade *noun* = BRAKE FADE

◇ **fader** *noun* device which adjusts the sound balance of front and rear speakers in a four-speaker layout

◇ **fading** *noun* **(a)** loss of brightness or colour in a paint finish **(b)** = BRAKE FADE

failsafe system *noun* system which remains safe even when part of it fails, such as a dual-circuit brake system

fair *verb* to add a fairing to a body

◇ **fairing (panel)** *noun* additional streamlined body panel placed over a projecting part, or an integral panel also designed to give minimum drag

family car *noun* car suitable for transporting a family, usually a four-door saloon or hatchback

fan *noun* device with a number of blades mounted in a central hub, which can move air as it turns

COMMENT: used in motor vehicles to draw cooling air through the engine's radiator, and in the heater/air-conditioning system to distribute warm (or cool) air in the interior of the vehicle; modern car engines nearly all have electric fans, which are brought into operation by a thermostat only when the engine reaches a certain temperature

fan belt *noun* originally and logically, the V-belt used to drive the engine fan from a pulley on the front of the crankshaft, which also drives the dynamo or alternator and in some cases the water pump

COMMENT: the term is still sometimes used where a vehicle is fitted with an electric fan, although the belt in this case only drives the alternator (and possibly the water pump), but not of course the fan

fan blade *noun* part of the fan projecting at an angle from the central hub, which draws the air through the radiator *a radiator fan typically has four blades*

◇ **fan clutch** *noun* clutch by means of which the fan can be engaged and disengaged according to engine temperature, usually operated automatically by a thermostat

◇ **fan cooling** *noun* type of air cooling where a blower is responsible for transporting the amount of air required for the cooling of the engine past the cooling fins, which in turn dissipate the heat stored in them to the current of air flowing past them *Porsche and Volkswagen air-cooled engines use a fan cooling system*

◊ **fan pulley** *noun* pulley on the hub of the radiator fan on which its driving belt runs

fascia *noun* **(a)** = INSTRUMENT PANEL **(b)** *US* panel forming part of the external trim, such as that below the bumper

fastback *noun* sleek-looking rear end, sloping in an unbroken line, which may either be found in a hatchback with a tailgate or a saloon or coupé with a fixed rear window and bootlid *a fastback saloon or coupé*

◊ **fast charger** *noun* battery charger which can charge a battery at a rate of 40 amps or even more, used by garages and battery suppliers

◊ **fast idle** *noun* higher than normal tick-over speed of an engine when cold with the choke in operation; **fast idle cam** = cam in a carburettor which opens the throttle slightly when the choke is brought into operation, either automatically or mechanically; **fast idle screw** = screw on a carburettor for adjusting the fast idle speed; *(see illustration 13)*; **fast idle solenoid** = solenoid operating in conjunction with an automatic choke to open the throttle slightly when the choke is in operation

◊ **fast lane** *noun* outside lane on a motorway used by fast-moving traffic for overtaking

fatigue *noun* weakening of a material subjected to high stresses, which may crack or even break as a result; **fatigue limit** = maximum stress that a material can endure for an infinite number of stress cycles without breaking; **fatigue resistance** *or* **strength** = maximum stress that a material can endure for a given time without breaking; **fatigue test** = test on a material to determine the range of stress it will stand without failing, by subjecting it to rapidly varying stresses to establish its fatigue limit

fault *noun* defect which is either inherent in the vehicle as built (manufacturing fault) or which occurs during running; **fault diagnosis** = tracing of faults, greatly aided on many modern vehicles by the use of an in-built diagnostic system and an engine analyzer; **fault memory** = part of the electronic control unit and of the diagnostic system that stores faulty conditions to facilitate vehicle diagnosis; **fault reader** = device to be used in conjunction with the vehicle's diagnostic system, providing a read-out of the values measured, etc.

FBC = FEEDBACK CARBURETTOR

FE analysis *noun* = FINITE-ELEMENT ANALYSIS

featheredge 1 *noun* border of a repair area to which filler has been applied, which has been sanded to merge imperceptibly into the undamaged area **2** *verb* to sand the edges of a repaired area until they merge imperceptibly into the surrounding undamaged area

feathering *noun* **(a)** type of tyre wear in which the tread is worn down to a very thin edge **(b)** very gently pressing on the throttle or brake pedal

feather key *noun* key with parallel faces whose ends may be round or square; *(compare* SQUARE KEY)

Federal engine *noun US* engine meeting Federal emission standards and certified by the EPA for use in any state except California *all Federal engines are equipped with positive crankcase ventilation*

◊ **Federal Test Procedure (FTP)** *noun US* method of testing automotive emissions simulating typical driving conditions; *(compare* FTP TEST CYCLE)

Fédération Internationale de l'Automobile (FIA) *noun* international umbrella motoring organization to which national motoring organizations are affiliated

Fédération Internationale du Sport Automobile (FISA) *noun* the international governing body of motor sport

feed 1 *verb* to supply (fuel, oil, current, etc.) **2** *noun* supply of fuel, oil, current, etc.; **feed line** *or* **pipe** = pipe supplying a liquid or gas; **feed pump** = pump supplying, for example, fuel in regulated quantities

◊ **feedback** *noun* information in the form of a signal from a sensor, which is then used in a closed loop system to regulate the mixture strength, for example; **feedback carburettor**

(FBC) = carburettor regulated by a closed loop system providing the air/fuel mixture quality needed to operate a catalytic converter; **feedback control** = CLOSED-LOOP CONTROL

feeler gauge *noun* tool with metal feeler blades or wire feelers of various thicknesses for measuring small distances and gaps between components, e.g. valve clearances or gaps between sparking plug electrodes or contact breaker points; **feeler blade** = thin blade of spring steel of an exact thickness for measuring small gaps or clearances between parts, usually made in sets of various thicknesses pinned together at one end to form a feeler gauge; **feeler strip** = metal strip of a specific thickness from which single feeler blades can be cut, appropriate when frequent measuring is required, to avoid using worn blades

FEI = FULLY ELECTRONIC IGNITION

female *adjective* fitting inside another part, usually where two parts form a connection of some kind; **female thread** = internal thread

fender *noun* **(a)** *US* = WING **(b)** = BUMPER

Ferguson four-wheel drive (transmission) *noun* transmission system in which power is distributed through a special viscous coupling differential, 37% to the front wheels and 63% to the rear wheels

ferrous *adjective* containing iron

festoon bulb *noun* light bulb in the form of a small glass tube with caps at each end providing the contacts

FF headlight *noun* free-form headlight using a free-shape reflector; *(compare* FREE SHAPE)

F-head engine *noun* engine design with overhead inlet and side exhaust valves; *(see* IOE ENGINE)

FHP = FRICTION HORSEPOWER

FI = FUEL INJECTION

FIA *noun* Fédération Internationale de l'Automobile, international umbrella motoring organization to which national motoring organizations are affiliated

fibreglass *noun* material made from fine glass strands matted or woven and bonded with a synthetic resin (NOTE: also called **glass reinforced plastic** *or* **GRP**); **fibreglass body** = body whose shell is moulded in one piece from fibreglass *fibreglass bodies have the advantages of light weight and freedom from corrosion, and so are most often used for sports cars and minicars* **fibreglass mat** = layer of chopped but irregular individual fibreglass strands dressed with a chemical to hold them loosely together, which when a resin is applied hardens into a strong material for repairing holes, e.g. in car bodies

◇ **fibre optics** *noun* transmission of information in the form of light carried along sheathed glass fibres, used in some engine management systems and malfunction warning indicators

field coil *noun* = FIELD WINDING

◇ **field terminal (F)** *noun* the input terminal on a dynamo; *(compare* D)

◇ **field testing** *or* **trial** *noun* testing of a vehicle or component in more or less normal use

◇ **field winding** *noun* part which produces a constant-strength magnetic field in an electric motor or generator, the field core being on the stator or the rotor depending on the type of motor or generator; *(see illustration 37)*

fierceness *noun* tendency of a clutch to engage suddenly so that it is difficult to start smoothly from rest

fifth (gear) *noun* highest ratio in a five-speed gearbox

◇ **fifth wheel** *noun* **(a)** additional wheel attached to the rear of a vehicle being road-tested which drives a highly accurate speed-measuring instrument **(b)** in an articulated vehicle, the generally circular pad at the rear of the tractor unit on which the front end of the trailer is mounted and which is able to turn when a corner is being negotiated

fifty-fifty power split *noun* arrangement in a four-wheel drive transmission where equal amounts of power are delivered to the front and rear wheels

filament *noun* thin, usually tungsten wire in a light bulb which becomes incandescent when current is passed through it

file *noun* flat or rounded tool with a rough surface of hardened steel for removing metal with the aim of smoothing or shaping it; **file card brush** = brush with angled wire bristles for cleaning file threads; **file handle** = handle, now usually of plastic, which may be attached to the end of a file

filler *noun* **(a)** paste usually with a polyester base which, when mixed with a hardener, forms a surface which can be sanded smooth and is suitable for repairs to dented or rusted bodywork (NOTE: also called **filler paste**) **(b)** = PRIMER FILLER **(c)** inert material added to paper, resins, and other substances to modify their properties and improve quality; e.g. carbon black used in tyre production **(d)** orifice into which a liquid such as oil or petrol can be poured; **filler cap** = closure which covers a filler orifice; **filler neck** = funnel-shaped part with the filler orifice at its top end

◇ **filling** *noun* repairing of holes or dents in bodywork with filler paste or body lead *the seams of the welded-in panel are filled with body lead to smooth out all contours*

◇ **filling station** *noun* place where petrol, diesel, oil and other supplies for motorists are sold (NOTE: US English is **gas station**)

fillister screw *noun* setscrew with a deep rounded head

fill plug *noun* small screw-in plug in the steering box or similar, which is removed for topping up with oil

fill up *verb* to refill the fuel tank

film *noun* thin layer or coating; **film strength of an oil** = ability of an oil to withstand pressure

filter *noun* device for removing dirt or suspended particles in a liquid or in the air; **filter cartridge** *or* **element** = replaceable porous part of some oil and most air filters, made of paper, felt or fine wire mesh; **filter screen** = piece of wire mesh in a pipe used to collect dirt and foreign matter; **filter wrench** = OIL FILTER WRENCH

COMMENT: the major filters on motor vehicles are the air filter, fuel filter and oil filter; there are also many small filters used, for example, in vacuum lines and valves, such as the air filter in the brake servo unit

filtration *noun* removal of dirt or suspended particles from a liquid or the air with the aid of a filter

fin *noun* projecting thin flat part, such as the cooling fins on an air-cooled cylinder, or the large vertical member at the rear of some streamlined record-breaking cars, intended to aid directional stability; *(see illustration 16)*

final drive *noun* assembly of gears in the back axle of rear-wheel drive vehicles and in the front axle of front-wheel drive vehicles, comprising essentially the differential and crown wheel and pinion, which reduce the speed of rotation and also change its direction; **final drive ratio** = ratio between the rotational speed of the propeller shaft or drive shaft and that of the driven road wheel, the gear reduction being determined by dividing the number of teeth on the crown wheel or ring gear by the number of teeth on the drive pinion

fine *adjective* **(a)** made of very small particles *fine grinding paste/emery cloth* **(b)** *(of a thread)* having many grooves and ridges close together

finger *noun* narrow projecting part, often acting as a lever and pivoting at one end or in the middle and pressing on another part

◇ **finger-tight** *adjective* tightened only with the fingers, without using a spanner *after the accident, it was found that the wheel nuts were only finger-tight*

finish 1 *noun* general appearance or condition of a surface, either painted or unpainted *dull/shiny finish* **finish coat** = TOP COAT; **finish hammer** = hammer used for detail work in shaping a panel after it has been brought roughly into the right shape; **finish restorer** = slightly abrasive polish which cuts back and restores the colour and lustre of dull and oxidized finishes **2** *verb* to give (a surface) its final treatment, resulting in a certain appearance; **a car finished in red** = a car painted red; **finishing enamel** *or* **paint** = paint for the top coat of a painting system

finite-element analysis *or* **FE analysis** *noun* reduction of a complex structure to its basic component parts so that these can be studied in a computer, especially in a CAD (computer-aided design) process

finning *noun* arrangement of fins on a surface to aid cooling by improving the heat transfer rate, typically found on air-cooled engines

fire *verb* **(a)** to start to run *the engine fired immediately* **(b)** to ignite (the mixture)

◇ **fire appliance** *noun* = FIRE ENGINE

◇ **fireball combustion chamber** *noun* combustion chamber design developed by the Swiss engineer May and introduced on Jaguar's V-12 engine in 1981

◇ **fire engine** *noun* vehicle equipped for fire-fighting with ladders, pumps, hoses, etc.

◇ **fire extinguisher** *noun* cylinder which can spray powder, foam or a liquid onto a fire to put it out

◇ **firewall** *noun* = BULKHEAD

firing *noun* process of igniting the mixture in the combustion chamber; **firing end** = part of the sparking plug extending into the combustion chamber; **firing order** = sequence of igniting the air/fuel mixture in the cylinders of a multi-cylinder engine; **firing stroke** = POWER STROKE

> COMMENT: some typical firing orders are: 4-cylinder in-line engine: 1-3-4-2 or 1-2-4-3; flat four: 1-4-3-2; 5-cylinder in-line engine: 1-2-4-5-3; 6-cylinder in-line engine: 1-5-3-6-2-4 or 1-2-4-6-5-3 or 1-5-4-6-2-3; V-6 engine: 1-4-2-5-3-6; V-8 engine: 1-8-2-7-4-5-3-6 or 1-8-4-3-6-5-7-2

first-aid kit *noun* box containing bandages, antiseptic ointment and other basic medical requirements for treating injuries *all motorists have to carry a first-aid kit on the continent*

first (gear) *noun* lowest gear available in the gearbox, which in fact gives the highest ratio of engine speed to road speed, and consequently the highest torque at the driven wheels, and so is used for starting and climbing very steep hills

FISA *noun* Fédération Internationale du Sport Automobile, the governing body of motor sport

fit 1 *noun* way in which two parts come together, with varying degrees of tightness; **clearance** *or* **sliding fit** = parts assembled so that there is clearance between them or so that one can slide in the other **2** *verb* to fix or put into place *it is advisable to fit a new camshaft belt at 50,000 miles*

◇ **fittings** *noun* small ancillary parts for a particular system such as fuel lines

five-cylinder engine *noun* engine with five cylinders, a rare configuration because of the problems of balance

◇ **five-door** *adjective* body design typical of estate cars and most hatchbacks, with four side doors and a tailgate

◇ **five-link rear suspension** *noun* independent rear suspension layout also used on live rear axles, in which each wheel is guided by two trailing links, two transverse links and a common track rod

◇ **five-speed gearbox** *or* **transmission** *noun* gearbox with five forward speeds, the highest of which usually functions more as an overdrive for high-speed cruising

◇ **five-valve head** *noun* cylinder head with five valves per cylinder, usually three inlet valves and two exhaust valves

fixed-caliper disc brake *noun* disc brake with a caliper which cannot move, the caliper consisting of two halves which are bolted together and contain at least one cylinder and piston each

◇ **fixed-cam brake** *noun* drum brake in which the cam is rigidly mounted in the backplate

◇ **fixed-choke carburettor** *noun* carburettor in which the size of the venturi or choke tube is fixed, synonymous in practice with fixed-jet carburettor

◇ **fixed contact** *noun* stationary point in a contact breaker

◇ **fixed drive** *noun* power transmission without differential action at the driven axle or between the driven axles in a four-wheel drive layout

◇ **fixed head** *noun* non-removable cylinder head, cast in one piece with the cylinder block; found in early internal combustion engines

◇ **fixed-jet carburettor** *noun* most common type of carburettor, in which the jets and the choke are of a fixed size (NOTE: opposite is **variable-jet carburettor)**

flag down *verb* to stop (a vehicle) with a hand signal in an emergency

flagship model *noun* prestige model, the top model of a manufacturer's range

flake (off) *verb* (*of paint*) to come or peel off in thin pieces (flakes)

◇ **flaking** *noun* tendency of a paint film to lift away from the underlying surface

> COMMENT: the flakes will be smooth and often curled up at the edges, and pieces can readily be broken off. This may be limited to

the topcoat or can reach down to the base metal, and is often caused by contamination of the surface with wax, grease, etc. or failure to use proper metal conditioners

flame front *noun* edge of the combustion flame spreading from the sparking plug, which should move in a controlled pattern across the cylinder, rather than simply exploding immediately

◊ **flame glow plug** *noun* glow plug that preheats the intake air by burning a small quantity of precisely metered fuel

◊ **flame paint** *noun* special paint job applied to the front of custom cars; large flames painted in a contrasting colour, usually yellow or orange, extend halfway back from the front and gradually fade away from the A-pillar backwards

◊ **flame trap** *noun* device consisting of a valve or similar, preventing the escape of ignited blowback gases, usually located in the hose or pipe leading from the crankcase to the inlet tract

flange *noun* flat outside edge or rim of a part, by which it is often attached to another part *the flanges of two adjacent panels are the mating surfaces along which the panels are fitted to each other, often overlapping* **flange bolt** = bolt with a flanged head; **flange joint** = coupling between two shafts formed of two disc-shaped flanges on the ends of the shafts which are bolted to one another; **flange-type puller** = puller with legs that fit behind a flange on a hub or similar

◊ **flanged** *adjective* with flanges; **flanged head** = bolt head under which is a flange

◊ **flanger** *noun* tool for making a flange; **panel flanger** *see* JOGGLER

◊ **flanging** *noun* putting on a flange; **flanging tool** = BENDING PLIERS

flank *noun* **(a)** side of a screw thread, rising from the bottom of the groove to the top of the ridge **(b)** one of the two flat parts of the face of a cam

flap *noun* flat piece of material attached along one side, often by a hinge and thus forming a small door for shutting off an aperture

flared wheel arch *noun* wheel arch bent outwards around its circumference, usually to accommodate wider wheels and/or tyres

◊ **flare nut** *noun* nut fitting over the flared end of a brake or fuel pipe at a union; **flare nut**

spanner = ring spanner for use on union nuts, with one of the flats cut out allowing its end to be slipped over tubing

◊ **flaring tool** *noun* tool used to spread or form flares on pipe or tubing ends, for example, when servicing brake, fuel and cooling systems on vehicles

flash *verb* **(a)** to use one's direction indicators; **he was flashing turning left** = he had his left-hand indicator on **(b)** to switch one's headlights on and off quickly

COMMENT: care must be taken when flashing (sense (b)), as there is no standard interpretation of what a flash from the headlights signifies; e.g. a flash from a car behind could mean 'watch out, I'm coming past' or 'you may pull out in front of me'; and a flash from the an oncoming vehicle may be either a greeting or a warning

flashback *noun* = BLOWBACK

◊ **flasher** *noun* flashing direction indicator; **flasher unit** = electronic switch apparatus controlling the operation of the direction indicators, including their rate of flash; self-cancelling when the steering wheel is returned to the straight-ahead position

◊ **flashover** *noun* HT current which short-circuits over the exterior portion of the sparking plug insulator

◊ **flash point** *noun* lowest temperature at which vapours from a volatile fuel will ignite momentarily on the application of a small flame under specified conditions

◊ **flash time** *noun* time required for most of the solvent to escape from a freshly applied paint coat

flat 1 *adjective* **(a)** *(of battery)* completely discharged, so that it cannot turn the engine and the lights are at best very dim **(b)** *(of tyre)* completely deflated, especially as the result of a puncture or a leaky valve **(c)** *(of engine)* having horizontally opposed cylinders; **flat twin** *or* **four** *or* **six** *or* **eight** = engine with two *or* four *or* six *or* eight horizontally opposed cylinders **2** *noun* **(a)** level area on an otherwise rounded surface *to file flats on a round-headed bolt* **(b)** *(informal)* flat tyre **3** *verb* to give a final light rubbing down to (paintwork or filler) with fine grade sandpaper or similar, to prepare the surface for a top coat

◊ **flatbed trailer** *or* **truck** *noun* trailer or truck which has a flat load platform

◊ **flat-bladed screwdriver** *noun* normal type of screwdriver for slotted screws (NOTE: opposite is **cross-head screwdriver**)

◊ **flat file** *noun* tapered file cut on all faces and with rectangular cross section, for shaping metal; *(compare* HAND FILE)

◊ **flat hump** *noun* raised and flattened portion on the bead seat of some wheel rims which retains the beads of an insufficiently inflated tyre on the bead seat, thereby preventing the tyre beads from jumping into the rim well; *(compare* SAFETY RIM)

◊ **flat-nose(d) pliers** *noun* most common type of pliers in which the ends of the jaws are cut off short; *(compare* LONG-NOSE PLIERS)

flat pente *noun* raised portion on the bead seat of some wheel rims which retains the tyre beads of an insufficiently inflated tyre on the bead seat, thereby preventing the beads from jumping into the rim well; *(compare* SAFETY RIM)

COMMENT: this is a compromise between the contre pente and the flat hump contours and is mainly used on passenger cars of French manufacture

flat seat *noun* seat of a sparking plug which is sealed by means of a gasket

◊ **flat spot** *noun* **(a)** point during acceleration at which the engine hesitates and stops accelerating for an instant *the engine has a flat spot at 4000 rpm* **(b)** flattened area on a tyre (especially a racing tyre), usually caused by a locking brake

◊ **flat tappet** *noun* tappet with a flat contact surface towards the cam lobe; *(compare* MUSHROOM TAPPET)

◊ **flat-tip screwdriver** *noun* = FLAT-BLADED SCREWDRIVER

◊ **flat-top(ped) piston** *noun* piston with a crown which is flat and not domed

◊ **flat washer** *noun* plain washer (as opposed to a locking or spring washer)

flaw *noun* = DEFECT

fleet *noun* all the vehicles owned by a company or other organization; **fleet car** = car belonging to a company fleet, typically one driven by a sales representative which has done a high mileage; **fleet sales** = sales of cars to companies for their company fleets, which account for almost one third of the total car market in the UK

flex arm suspension *noun* rear axle design with torsionally flexible axle beam in line with the rear wheels and trailing links

◊ **flexibility** *noun* **(a)** elasticity of a material **(b)** ability of an engine to go down to low speeds in a high gear and pull away smoothly without changing down, which is governed mainly by its torque characteristics

◊ **flexible** *adjective* **(a)** able to bend without breaking; **flexible brake pipe** = pipe connecting the wheel cylinder to the rest of the system, which has to flex to allow for the up and down movement of the wheel **(b)** *(of an engine)* able to go down to low speeds in a high gear and pull away smoothly; *(compare* PEAKY)

◊ **flexible coupling** *noun* simple shaft coupling used where only small angles of misalignment between the two shafts occur, as in a steering column, the drive being transmitted either by tension-stressed fabric discs or pressurized rubber blocks

◊ **flexible drive** *noun* drive consisting of a cable in an outer sheath, used for mainly light applications such as speedometers, rev counters and windscreen wipers

◊ **flexible (drive) handle** *noun* drive handle with pivoting head for use with sockets, its length giving good leverage and its ability to bend giving access to difficult locations

flexural *adjective* referring to bending; **flexural shock** = sharp shock when bending, which can break plastics

flexure *noun* bending; *see also* STIFFNESS UNDER FLEXURE

flip-top filler cap *noun* quick-release filler cap, as fitted to some sports and racing cars

flitch plate *noun* reinforcing plate for chassis members or wheel arches

float *noun* hollow metal or plastic body that floats on a liquid and operates a valve or a rheostat, as in a carburettor, where it is used to maintain the correct fuel level, or in a fuel tank, where it is used to sense fuel level for the fuel gauge; *(see illustration 11);* **float chamber** *or US* **float bowl** = circular reservoir for petrol forming part of a carburettor, in which a float maintains the desired level by rising as the level of the fuel rises and closing the needle valve in the float chamber cover to shut off the supply; *(see illustrations 11, 12);* **float needle** = needle in the needle valve which rises with the float and shuts off the fuel supply when it reaches its seat

◇ **floating** *adjective* free to move (within prescribed limits); **floating-caliper disc brake** = disc brake with a single piston, in which the caliper itself can move to bring both pads into contact with the disc; **floating cam** = brake cam or other type of expander which is not rigidly mounted in the brake backplate of a drum brake, so that it can exert equal pressure on the two shoes; **floating frame** = frame which holds the cylinder assembly and is supported by the mounting frame, usually made of heavy-gauge sheet steel; **floating piston** = SECONDARY PISTON

flood *verb* to allow too much fuel to enter (the carburettor, the engine); **to flood the carburettor** = to allow extra fuel into the carburettor by pushing down the float with the tickler to give a richer mixture for starting (on older or simpler carburettors); **flooded engine** = engine in which too much fuel has been drawn into the cylinders during attempted starting so that ignition is no longer possible

floor *noun* flat base panel of a vehicle; **floor (gear)change** = gearchange with the gear lever mounted on the floor; **floor mat** = additional loose rubber or carpeting mat on the car floor; *US* **floor shift** = FLOOR (GEAR)CHANGE

◇ **floorpan** *noun* generally synonymous with floor, but can mean the whole platform on which the body is built up *the coupé uses the saloon's floorpan and running gear (see illustration 2)*

flow *noun* passing of liquid or current through something, also the amount conveyed; **flow control** = regulation of the amount of fluid passing through a pump, especially important under changing operating conditions; **flow detachment** = deviation of the gas flow into the cylinder from its ideal path, thus losing its stability, caused by swirl and/or improper combustion chamber design etc.; **flow rate** = amount of liquid conveyed by a pump per unit of time

◇ **flowmeter** *noun* meter indicating the amount of liquid passing through, used for instance to supply information to a fuel consumption indicator

fluid *noun* substance which flows, e.g. a liquid or a gas; **fluid capacities** = amounts of oil, water and fuel required to fill the sump, gearbox, axle, radiator, fuel tank, etc.; **fluid clutch** *or* **fluid coupling** = hydraulically acting coupling by which power can be transmitted, used as an automatic clutch with a driving and a driven rotor revolving in oil which acts as the transmission medium; **fluid flywheel** = kind of fluid coupling in which the flywheel is the driving rotor; **fluid level warning indicator** = warning light on the instrument panel which comes on when the level of hydraulic fluid in the braking system is too low

flush 1 *adjective* level with the surrounding surface *the body glass must be perfectly flush for good streamlining* **flush-mounted speaker** = speaker mounted in a cutout in the interior trim so that it does not project out (NOTE: opposite is **surface-mounted speaker**) **2** *verb* to clean out (the engine, gearbox, radiator, etc.) by running a special liquid through it; **flushing oil** = thin oil for cleaning out the sump, oil ways, etc.

flux *noun* chemical used in soldering and welding to prevent oxidizing

flylead *noun* short lead with a terminal at the end fitted to a component as supplied

◇ **fly nut** *noun* = WING NUT

◇ **flyweight** *noun* weight such as that in a centrifugal advance mechanism which is thrown outwards by centrifugal force as speed increases

◇ **flywheel** *noun* heavy metal wheel that is attached to the crankshaft and rotates with it, helping to smooth out the power surges from the engine power strokes and serving as a mounting for the clutch; *(see illustrations 4, 8)*; **flywheel generator** = small alternator of the rotating magnet type attached to one end of the crankshaft and spinning with it, acting as an additional flywheel; now only used in mopeds or scooters; **flywheel magneto** = magneto mounted in the flywheel of a small engine, often a two-stroke; **flywheel ring gear** = STARTER RING GEAR; **flywheel turner** = special tool used for hand cranking of the engine while working on clutches, gearboxes, etc. or doing jobs that require the crankshaft to be in a specific position; consists of a handle and lever to hook into the starter ring teeth

FM = FREQUENCY MODULATION

foaming *noun* formation of bubbles in the oil of a gearbox, back axle or shock absorber, etc.

Foettinger coupling *noun* torque-converting fluid coupling

fog lamp *noun* **(a)** *(mounted at the front)* lamp giving a wide low beam which penetrates fog, rain, etc. and illuminates the sides of the road **(b)** *(mounted at the rear)* red light of the same intensity as a brake light

folding rear seats *noun* rear seats in a hatchback or estate car which fold forwards into the footwells to give a more or less flat loading area

◇ **folding top** *noun* soft top of a convertible which can be folded away

follow-up spark *noun* secondary spark occurring when a spark is extinguished and re-ignited in the course of the spark duration, especially if the mixture is turbulent

foot brake *noun* main braking system operated by the foot pedal; **foot pedal** = pedal on the floor in front of the driver, especially the brake pedal

◇ **footprint** *noun* = CONTACT PATCH

◇ **foot-pound (force)** *noun* unit of work or energy in the old fps system equal to the force needed to move one pound through one foot

◇ **foot pump** *noun* tyre pump operated by the foot

◇ **footwell** *noun* recess in the floor below the feet of the rear seat occupants, but may also be used for the space used by the feet of people in the front seats

force *noun* any push or pull exerted on an object, measured in newtons (N) in the SI (international system of units), although usage of the superseded units based on feet, pounds and ounces is still frequent

forced circulation *noun* cooling system in which a pump is used to circulate the coolant; *(compare* THERMOSYPHON COOLING)

◇ **forced downshift** *noun US* = KICKDOWN

◇ **forced-feed lubrication** *noun* lubrication system as used in all modern four-stroke engines, in which an engine-driven pump forces the oil through passages in the engine castings, or through external pipes, to the main areas of stress in the engine

forced-induction system *noun* system in which either a conventional supercharger or a turbocharger, or even a combination of both, is used to increase intake pressure and force the mixture into the cylinders; *(compare* NATURALLY ASPIRATED ENGINE)

COMMENT: in hybrid systems, the supercharger supplies low-end boost, and once the engine speed passes a certain limit (e.g. 4000 rpm), the supercharger disengages and a turbocharger takes over

force fit *noun* = PRESS FIT

Ford *noun* second largest car manufacturer in the world (after GM); **Ford-type lug** *or* **terminal** = special type of battery connection consisting of a flat lug with nut and bolt between the battery cables and terminal posts

fore and aft adjustment *noun* ability to move, for example, a seat forwards and backwards

forge *verb* to shape (metal) when hot by hammering or similar mechanical action *forged pistons are capable of withstanding higher loads than cast pistons; forged alloy wheels may consist of one, two, or three pieces*

◇ **forging** *noun* piece of forged metal *alloy forgings are good conductors of heat*

forgiving *adjective* easy to drive because of good handling qualities, so that mistakes can easily be corrected *this car is very forgiving*

forked *adjective* with one end in the shape of a Y; **forked con rod** = special split con rod to take two pistons for uniflow-scavenging two-stroke engines with two pistons per cylinder; **forked rocker (arm)** = rocker arm operating two valves with its forked end

◇ **fork-lift truck** *noun* small vehicle used for loading in factories, warehouses, docks, etc., with two arms at the front projecting forwards which fit into pallets and can be raised and lowered

former *noun* shaped wooden block for use in panel beating, on which a desired shape is produced by hammering

formula *noun* detailed specification, e.g. for a particular class of motor racing; **Formula 1** = formula according to which racing cars are built for the major Grand Prix races counting for the World Championship

Föttinger coupling *see* FOETTINGER

foul *verb* **(a)** to clog or cover (a sparking plug) with deposits *fouling can cause loss of performance and even missing* **(b)** to get in the way of or obstruct (another part) *this projection is fouling the steering arm*

four-cycle *adjective US* = FOUR-STROKE

◇ **four-cylinder engine** *noun* typical engine type used in most small to medium-size cars and commercial vehicles, and in some large and powerful motorcycles

◇ **four-door** *adjective* having two doors on each side, the typical layout for family saloons and executive cars

◇ **four-link rear suspension** *noun* independent rear suspension layout, also used on live rear axles, in which each wheel is guided by two control arms, one mounted longitudinally, the other mounted transversely or almost transversely, thus providing lateral location for the axle

four-spark ignition coil *noun* ignition coil with two primary windings and one secondary winding

| COMMENT: the primary windings are energized by two ignition output stages, and the secondary winding has two diodes at each output, from each of which one high-voltage cable is routed to each sparking plug, two sparks being produced alternately, decoupled by the diodes

four-speed gearbox *or* **transmission** *noun* gearbox with four forward speeds

◇ **four-stroke** *US* **four-cycle** *adjective* operating in accordance with the four-stroke cycle; **four-stroke cycle** = operating principle of most spark ignition and diesel engines, the four strokes which complete the cycle being: induction, compression, power, and exhaust stroke (NOTE: opposite is **two-stroke cycle)**

◇ **four-stroking** *noun* faulty running of a two-stroke engine, firing on every second working cycle only, e.g. when idling or running too rich

◇ **fourth (gear)** *noun* highest gear in a four-speed gearbox, and second highest in a five-speed gearbox

◇ **four-valve** *adjective* (engine or cylinder head) with two inlet and two exhaust valves per cylinder and any number of cylinders

◇ **four-way wheel wrench** *noun* = WHEEL NUT SPIDER

◇ **four-wheel drift** *noun* cornering technique used in motor racing in which the car takes the corner in an intentionally induced sideways slide

◇ **four-wheel drive (4WD** *or* **FWD)** *noun* layout in which all four wheels are driven, giving better traction on slippery surfaces such as mud or grass, making it ideal for off-road vehicles and also giving better adhesion and handling for road use *four-wheel drive car or vehicle* (NOTE: also written **4x4)**; *(see illustration 24)*, **four-wheel drive with constant** *or* **fixed power distribution** = layout in which the amount of power delivered to the front and rear wheels respectively cannot be varied

◇ **four-wheel steering** *noun* steering system which steers the rear as well as the front wheels

FPS *or* **fps** *(short for)* foot-pound-second; **FPS system** = former imperial system of units, superseded by the SI system

frame *noun* structure which is open in the centre, especially a general term referring to the underbody backbone of the car, both for unitary or separate chassis designs; **frame damage** = type of damage to the body that involves damage to the structural members of the car, usually resulting from accident impact; **frame gauge** = measuring instrument for determining car body misalignment

◇ **frameless** *adjective* having no frame; **frameless construction** = unitary construction; **frameless window** = window in an opening door which is not entirely surrounded by a frame

◇ **frame member** *noun* any box-section member which forms part of the structural components of the vehicle chassis

◇ **frame structure** *noun* all structural parts of the car which contribute to the rigidity of the body, both for unitary designs and for cars with a separate chassis

franchised dealer *noun* = AUTHORIZED DEALER

free length *noun* length of a spring, especially a valve spring, when no downward pressure is exerted on it

◇ **free play** *noun* amount of free motion in a gear train, between gears or in a mechanical assembly (NOTE: US English is **lash)**

◇ **free-revving** *adjective (of an engine)* able to accelerate quickly up to high engine speeds

free shape *noun* shape governed by stylistic or functional requirements only; *(compare* FF HEADLIGHT)

> COMMENT: e.g. the shape of a car body, or of headlight reflectors, where the design is dictated exclusively by the requirement to get as much light as possible to the right places in front of the car, a design process feasible only as a result of various high-tech disciplines, such as CAL and advanced thermoplastic injection moulding processes

free travel *noun* distance moved by a pedal before the connected actuating mechanism begins to operate; *(compare* PEDAL TRAVEL)

freeway *noun* American type of multiple-lane motorway without toll charges, with overpasses or underpasses at all intersections and with fully controlled access for intersecting roads, and a speed limit of typically 60 mph

freewheel *noun* device for disconnecting the drive from the engine when coasting, with the aim of saving fuel by reducing the drag from the engine and gearbox; now obsolete and even banned in some countries

◇ **freewheel(ing) hub** *noun* type of hub fitted to the front axle of some four-wheel drive vehicles, in which the drive to the front wheels can be disconnected when the front axle is not being driven

freeze plug *noun US* = CORE PLUG

frenching *noun* shaping the surrounds of headlights, tail lights, number plate frames, etc. into a smooth contour when customizing, so that the actual lights, etc. recede a little towards the interior of the panel aperture and the chrome bezel or other surround looks as though it is part of the body panel; *(compare* TUNNELLING)

Freon (R-12) *noun* refrigerant used in air conditioners; *(compare* REFRIGERANT)

frequency *noun* in relation to a radio station, number of cycles per second expressed in hertz at which it broadcasts; **frequency modulation (FM)** = system of broadcasting using VHF; **frequency range** = BANDWIDTH; **frequency scan button** = button which, when pressed, causes the tuner to scan the frequencies of the preset waveband for stations with sufficient signal strength

◇ **frequency valve** *noun* valve fitted in the fuel distributor of some vehicles with a continuous injection system and catalytic converter, which continually adjusts the air/fuel ratio to varying engine operating conditions, being controlled by a voltage signal supplied by the oxygen sensor and by an ECM

fretting corrosion *noun* corrosion occurring where two surfaces are in contact and friction results, e.g. at mechanical joints in vibrating structures

friction *noun* force which opposes the relative motion of two bodies

◇ **frictional** *adjective* caused by the friction between moving parts

◇ **friction bearing** *noun* = PLAIN BEARING

◇ **friction clutch** *noun* conventional clutch transmitting drive by mechanical friction, as opposed to a fluid coupling

◇ **friction damper** *noun* = FRICTION SHOCK ABSORBER

◇ **friction horsepower (FHP)** *noun* power consumed by frictional losses

◇ **friction lining** *noun* wear-resistant friction material used for clutch and brake linings

◇ **friction losses** *noun* loss of power due to friction between the moving parts of the engine

◇ **friction pad** *noun* = BRAKE PAD

◇ **friction plate** *noun* driven plate of a clutch to which the friction lining is attached

◇ **friction shock absorber** *noun* shock absorber in which friction discs are inserted at the point where the two arms are joined, now no longer used in car suspensions

◇ **friction welding** *noun* welding process in which two surfaces are heated by means of friction; when melting has occurred at the interface, pressure is maintained to consolidate the weld during cooling of the material

frit *noun* partly fused, vitreous substance, ground up and used as a basis for glazes and enamels

frogeye *noun (informal)* nickname for the Series 1 Austin-Healey Sprite produced from 1958-1962, which had the headlamps projecting above the bonnet line

front *noun* **(a)** front seats of a car *to sit in the front* **(b)** = FRONT END

◇ **frontal crash** *or* **impact** *noun* = FRONT-END IMPACT

◇ **front apron** *noun* panel behind and below the front bumper, joining the bottom ends of the front wings

front axle *noun* axle to which the front wheels are attached; **front-axle/rear-axle split** = dual-circuit braking system in which one circuit brakes the front axle only, the other circuit brakes the rear axle only; **front-axle and rear-axle split** = dual-circuit braking system in which each circuit brakes both the front axle and the rear axle

COMMENT: except in front-wheel drive and four-wheel drive layouts, modern vehicles with independent front suspension do not have a front axle as such, even so one finds references to the front suspension assemblies and wheel mountings as 'the front axle'

front bumper *noun* bumper protecting the front of the vehicle, combined in modern cars with a front spoiler or air dam

◇ **front differential** *noun* differential in the front axle of a four-wheel drive vehicle; *(see illustration 24)*

◇ **front disc/rear drum brakes** *noun* typical brake system layout in less expensive cars

◇ **front end** *noun* body area incorporating the leading edge of the wings, the headlights, radiator grille and bumper, i.e. the full area that makes up the frontal appearance of the car; **front-end impact** = impact as the result of a head-on collision

◇ **front engine** *noun* engine located at the front of a vehicle above the front suspension, the most common layout, which may be combined with either rear-wheel or front-wheel drive; *(compare* MID-ENGINE CAR, REAR ENGINE);

◇ **front nose section** *noun* front section of car bodies that use one single structure to make up the front end, i.e. including the radiator grille surround, both wings, front apron, etc.

◇ **front panel** *noun* panel joining the front wings and forming a mounting for the headlamps, grille and air ducts into the engine compartment, which is often identical with the front apron where no separate apron is fitted below the front panel

◇ **front pillar** *noun* = A-PILLAR

◇ **front pipe** *noun* first section of the exhaust system from the exhaust manifold to the silencer (or front silencer where there are two)

◇ **front seat** *noun* seat in the front of the passenger cabin for the front seat passenger; **the front seats** = the front passenger's and driver's seats

◇ **front silencer** *noun* first and main silencer in an exhaust system where there are two; *(see illustration 19)*

◇ **front spoiler** *noun* air deflector on the front of a car, aerodynamically designed to cut the wind resistance around the car, for improved handling control, stability, traction, and better fuel economy

◇ **front suspension** *noun* assembly of linkages and springs supporting the front wheels

◇ **front-wheel drive (FWD)** *noun* configuration in which the drive is taken from the engine to the front wheels, which propel the vehicle; *(compare* REAR-WHEEL DRIVE)

◇ **front wing** *noun* body section covering the front wheels, originally separate but now always faired in and part of the body shell

fsh *(in advertisement)* = FULL SERVICE HISTORY

FTP = FEDERAL TEST PROCEDURE *US* **FTP test cycle** = method of testing automotive emissions for compliance with emission standards by simulating typical driving conditions - which differs from other test cycles such as the European ECE test, so that the results cannot be compared

fuel *noun* substance burned as a source of heat or power, that used in an engine being a liquid or a gas

fuel accumulator *noun* device in the K-Jetronic fuel injection system which serves to absorb the initial pressure surge when a fuel pump starts; *(see illustration 14)*

COMMENT: the control plunger of the metering unit in the fuel distributor is thereby prevented from being forced up before an adequate stable pressure has been established; the fuel accumulator also acts as a reservoir to keep the system under pressure for a short time after the engine has been turned off, in order to prevent vapour lock

fuel additive *noun* preparation added to fuel to improve its properties

◊ **fuel cap** *noun* cap on the top of the tube leading to the fuel tank

◊ **fuel charge** *noun* air/fuel mixture delivered to the combustion chamber

◊ **fuel computer** *noun* = FUEL CONSUMPTION INDICATOR

◊ **fuel consumption** *noun* amount of fuel used, expressed in miles per gallon in Britain and the USA, whereas the international measure is litres per 100 kilometres (NOTE: US English is **fuel mileage**); **fuel consumption indicator** = instrument using a flowmeter to indicate mpg at any given moment on a journey

◊ **fuel cut-off switch** *noun* = FUEL PUMP (SHUT-OFF) SWITCH

◊ **fuel distributor** *noun* device constituting the mixture control unit together with the airflow sensor; *(see illustration 14)*

◊ **fuel economy** *noun* = FUEL CONSUMPTION

◊ **fuel filler flap** *noun* usually locking flap which has to be opened to gain access to the fuel cap; **fuel filler neck** = upper end of the fuel filler tube leading down to the fuel tank, which accepts the fuel hose nozzle at the filling station; **fuel filler tube** = tube leading down to the fuel tank

◊ **fuel filter** *noun* filter in the fuel line intended to prevent any dirt from passing into the carburettor or injection system; *(see illustration 14)*

◊ **fuel gauge** *noun* instrument which shows the amount of fuel in the fuel tank

fuel-injected engine *noun* petrol engine with a fuel injection system rather than a carburettor or carburettors

◊ **fuel injection (FI)** *noun* system used in all diesel engines and most modern petrol engines, in which fuel is sprayed under pressure into the engine, and not sucked as with a carburettor; **fuel injection engine** = petrol engine with a fuel injection system; **fuel injection pump** = pump which receives fuel from the fuel tank (often through the fuel-feed pump in the case of diesel engines) and delivers it under pressure to the injectors

◊ **fuel injector** *noun* injector in a fuel injection system which sprays petrol into the inlet ports, or diesel either directly into the combustion chamber or into a pre-chamber

fuel line *noun* metal, plastic or rubber pipe conveying fuel from the fuel tank to the fuel pump and carburettor or fuel injectors

◊ **fuel mileage** *noun* US = FUEL CONSUMPTION

◊ **fuel pressure** *noun* pressure under which fuel is delivered to the injectors by the fuel pump, governed by the pressure regulator

◊ **fuel pump** *noun* electrical or mechanical device in the fuel system which draws fuel from the fuel tank and delivers it to the carburettor or fuel injection system; *(see illustrations 3, 14)*; **fuel pump (shut-off) switch** = switch which shuts off the electric fuel pump and fuel to the engine in the event of a major collision

◊ **fuel rail** *noun* manifold tube feeding the injectors in a fuel injection system

◊ **fuel return line** *noun* pipe returning surplus fuel to the tank from the carburettor(s) or an injector; *(see illustration 14)*

◊ **fuel starvation** *noun* failure of the fuel system to supply sufficient fuel to allow the engine to run properly, due to a blockage or vapour lock or malfunction of the fuel pump

◊ **fuel supply** *noun* delivery of fuel to the carburettor or injection system; *(see illustration 3)*

◊ **fuel system** *noun* system that delivers the fuel and air to the engine cylinders, comprising the fuel tank and lines, fuel pump, carburettor or fuel injection system, and inlet manifold

fuel tank *noun* reservoir from which fuel is taken for the engine; *(see illustration 14)*; **fuel tank sender** = level sensor in the fuel tank, providing information to the fuel gauge

COMMENT: on cars, the fuel tank may be located almost anywhere, but is usually at the rear, above or behind the rear axle, below or at the side(s) of the boot; on motorcycles it is located between the saddle and the handlebars above the engine; on lorries it is normally an exposed tank mounted on the frame. Originally always made of sheet steel, on cars it is now also made of blow-moulded polyethylene, allowing a much more space-efficient design with considerable increase in capacity, combined with lower weight and greater safety

fuel vapour *noun* **(a)** atomized air/fuel mixture heated in the engine, ready for combustion **(b)** fumes given off by a fuel; **fuel vapour recirculation system** = EVAPORATIVE EMISSION CONTROL SYSTEM

fulcrum *noun* point on which a part pivots, especially a lever; **fulcrum pin** = pin which acts as a pivot, such as a kingpin; **fulcrum ring** = one of two rings on either side of a clutch diaphragm spring, on which it pivots

full bore *noun* = FULL THROTTLE

◊ **full dip treatment** *noun* painting process in which the whole body shell is immersed, used for applying protective primers

◊ **full-flow filter** *noun* filter through which all the oil in the engine passes *a full-flow filter is necessary to trap combustion residues from the circulating oil (compare* BYPASS FILTER) *(see illustration 5)*

◊ **full leather (upholstery)** *noun* car interior in which all the door trim, etc. is covered in leather as well as the seats

◊ **full load** *noun* engine operating conditions where the accelerator is fully depressed, i.e. the throttle is fully open, which does not necessarily mean high engine speed; **full load enrichment** = provision of a richer mixture when the throttle is fully opened; *(see illustration 11)*

◊ **full lock** *see* LOCK (b)

◊ **full panel** *noun* body part that may comprise several other subassemblies and is fairly complex and cumbersome, e.g. a complete bulkhead assembly incorporating the windscreen pillars

◊ **full service history (fsh)** *noun* documents which show all the work carried out on a vehicle, especially the regular services required by the manufacturer

full-size car *noun* largest type of car according to American car categories

COMMENT: a saloon for up to six passengers, 213-235 ft long, roomy but with poor fuel economy. Typical examples are: Buick LeSabre, Cadillac Fleetwood, Chevrolet Caprice, Lincoln Continental, Oldsmobile 98

full-skirt piston *noun* former piston style which had a full-annulus skirt, without the cutaway section of modern slipper pistons

◊ **full throttle** *noun* fully open position of the throttle (NOTE: US English is **wide open throttle**); **at full throttle** = with the throttle

fully open; **to be going full throttle** *or* **full bore** = to be going as fast as one can, with the accelerator fully depressed; **full throttle enrichment** = FULL LOAD ENRICHMENT

◊ **full-time four-wheel drive** *noun* = PERMANENT FOUR-WHEEL DRIVE

fully electronic ignition (FEI) *noun* distributorless, mapped ignition system with cylinder-selective knock control, dwell-angle control, and digital idling speed stabilization

◊ **fully floating axle** *noun* live rear axle assembly in which the axle shafts serve only to transmit torque to the wheel, the total vehicle weight and cornering loads being transferred directly from the wheel bearings to the axle housing; *(compare* SEMI-FLOATING AXLE)

◊ **fully galvanized body** *noun* body shell which, apart from aluminium and plastic parts, is produced entirely of double-sided galvanized steel and galvanized fasteners or which is immersed in galvanizing fluid

fumes *noun* evil-smelling vapours given off by a liquid or a gas, which may be poisonous *fumes from a leaking exhaust had made the driver sleepy*

functional *adjective* **(a)** capable of working *functional components/parts* **(b)** practical, designed not for decoration but solely with a particular use in mind *the severely functional appearance of a racing car*

funnel *noun* cup-shaped object tapering at the bottom to a small hole and a spout, used for pouring oil, fuel or water into relatively small openings

fuse 1 *noun* device containing a thin piece of wire which melts when the current is excessive and thus opens the electrical circuit in which it is placed, to protect equipment in the circuit; **the horn fuse has blown** = the thin wire in the fuse protecting the horn circuit has melted (so that the horn does not work) **2** *verb* **(a)** to melt, and (sometimes) become united in the process **(b)** *(of electrical equipment)* to fail as the result of a fuse blowing *the headlights have fused*

◊ **fuse box** *noun* unit with a removable cover that holds the fuses for the various electrical circuits, which are all routed through it

FWD = FRONT-WHEEL DRIVE *or (less commonly)* FOUR-WHEEL DRIVE

Gg

g *(symbol for)* acceleration of free fall due to gravity *production saloons reach lateral acceleration levels in the order of 0.8 g*

gage *noun US* = GAUGE

gaiter *noun* = BOOT (b)

gal *(short for)* GALLON

GALFAN trademark for a special type of hot-dip galvanized steel sheet with a coating consisting of a zinc alloy containing 5% Aluminium and rare earths

gallon *noun* unit of capacity (NOTE: 1 British gallon (UK gal) = 4.546 litres; 1 US gallon (US gal) = 3.785 litres)

Galvalume trademark for a special type of hot-dip galvanized steel sheet with a coating consisting of 55% Aluminium, 43.4% Zinc and 1.6% Silicon

galvanic *adjective* concerned with an electrical current; **galvanic cell** = cell which converts chemical energy into electrical energy by irreversible chemical reactions; **galvanic corrosion** = corrosion due to the action of a galvanic cell; *(compare* BIMETALLIC CORROSION)

COMMENT: if the coating is damaged, so that a small area of the steel is exposed, the zinc and the steel together with the moisture in the atmosphere will form a galvanic cell

galvanize *verb* to plate with zinc by hot dipping or electrodeposition (to protect from rust); **to galvanize differentially** = to obtain different coating thicknesses on the two sides of the sheet; **galvanized coating** = zinc(-based) coating applied by galvanizing

◊ **galvanizing** *noun* application of zinc coatings on the surface of a metal, by hot dipping or electrodeposition; **galvanizing bath** = bath for hot-dip galvanizing or electrogalvanizing

galvannealing *noun* thermal process which gives improved adhesion to hot-dip galvanized steel sheets

COMMENT: in this process, the hot-dip galvanized sheets are annealed at 600-650°C on leaving the zinc melting pot. This causes the zinc-iron alloy layer to increase, while the pure zinc layer is transformed into an alloy layer

gamma layer *noun* part of the zinc-iron alloy layer on hot-dip galvanized iron and steel containing 21-28% iron

gantry *noun* structure with an overhead beam, used for lifting out an engine; *(compare* ENGINE HOIST)

gap *noun* space between two parts, especially between electric points; *(compare* DOOR GAP, POINTS GAP, SPARKING PLUG GAP); **gap bridging** = formation of carbon or other deposits across the sparking plug gap which shorten the plug; **gap style** = the arrangement of electrodes in a sparking plug

◊ **gapper** *noun US (informal)* = FEELER GAUGE

garage 1 *noun* **(a)** building in which to keep a motor vehicle **(b)** premises on which motor vehicles are repaired or serviced and/or where fuel is sold; *(compare* FILLING STATION) **2** *verb* to keep in a garage

◊ **garaged** *adjective* kept in a garage (NOTE: in advertisements, often abbreviated to **gar'd**)

◊ **garage jack** *noun* powerful hydraulic jack used in garages

garter spring *noun* long, thin coil spring with ends joined to form a ring

gas *noun* **(a)** state of matter, like air, which has no definite shape or volume **(b)** *mainly US (short for)* gasoline; **step on the gas** = put your foot down on the accelerator, i.e. go faster!

◇ **gas chamber** *noun* pressure chamber of a single-tube shock absorber

◇ **gas damper** *noun* gas shock (absorber)

gas discharge headlight *noun* motor vehicle headlight with a gas discharge lamp; **gas discharge lamp** = discharge lamp in which light is generated by gas discharge

COMMENT: produces more light per power input than conventional systems; if start-up and glare problems can be solved, the gas discharge lamp may supersede halogen headlamps

gaseous *adjective* referring to gas; **gaseous discharge headlight** *or* **lamp** = GAS DISCHARGE HEADLIGHT *or* LAMP

◇ **gas flow** *noun* flow of the air/fuel mixture or the exhaust gases in an engine

gas guzzler *noun (informal US)* car that uses a lot of petrol

gasket *noun* seal *the cylinder head gasket is the seal between the cylinder head and engine block* **gasket punch** = tool used to cut out holes in gaskets and other soft materials; **gasket scraper** = scraper with a chisel edge for scraping surfaces clean before installing new gaskets such as water-pump, cylinder head, crankcase or timing chain cover gaskets

COMMENT: typical gasket materials are asbestos and combinations of steel/asbestos or copper/asbestos for hot parts, such as the cylinder head gasket or exhaust manifold gasket, and cork and neoprene/rubber for rocker covers, oil pan, fuel pumps, transmission cover, etc.

gasohol *noun* a gasoline/alcohol blend containing 10% ethanol and 90% unleaded petrol

COMMENT: gasohol has a higher volatility than petrol and may adversely affect starting, drivability and fuel efficiency

gasoline *noun US* = PETROL

◇ **gas pedal** *noun US* = ACCELERATOR

gas prop *noun* gas-assisted strut (e.g. of hatch, tailgate)

gas pump *noun US* = PETROL PUMP

gas shock (absorber) *noun* gas-assisted shock absorber

COMMENT: common design of a single-tube shock absorber, in which a dividing piston separates the working chamber from a pressurized gas chamber (de Carbon principle), or in which the working chamber is filled with an emulsion of oil and gas (Woodhead-Munroe principle)

gas spring *noun* pressurized, nitrogen-filled sphere, used in Hydragas and hydropneumatic suspension systems

gassing *noun* the formation of explosive gas in the form of small bubbles in a battery when charging continues after the battery has been completely charged

gas station *noun US* = FILLING STATION, PETROL STATION

gas-tight *adjective* sealed to prevent the passage of gas

gas welding *noun* welding process widely used in body repair shops (now being gradually replaced by MIG welding) (NOTE: also called **oxyacetylene welding**)

COMMENT: this process uses an acetylene/oxygen mixture supplied from separate bottles. The weld area is heated with a hand-held torch, and the electrode wire is fed in with the other hand to melt off in the weld pool. Heat distortion with this process is greater than with MIG welding

gate *noun* slotted plate in the shape of an H, controlling the movements of a gear lever in a sliding mesh gearbox (pre-1930s)

gauge *US* **gage** *noun* **(a)** tool for checking whether clearances between parts, or the shape and dimensions of pieces being worked comply with specified tolerance requirements **(b)** instrument for measuring a quantity; typical gauges are fuel level, coolant temperature, and oil pressure gauges on an instrument panel and tyre gauge to measure the pressure of air in a tyre **(c)** (i) the thickness or diameter of various materials such as wire or sheet metal; (ii) standard measurement of these

GAWR = GROSS AXLE WEIGHT RATING

G-clamp *noun* screw-activated clamping device in the shape of a G

gear *noun* **(a)** toothed wheel connecting with another wheel of different diameter to change the power ratio of the engine; **gears** = arrangement of gearwheels working together;

(compare SPROCKET) **(b)** one of the combination of gears; *(a)* in a gearbox that a driver selects to impart motion to a car; **do not skip a gear** = do not miss out a gear in sequence when changing up or down; *(see also* FIRST, SECOND, THIRD, FOURTH, FIFTH, REVERSE GEAR) *(compare* TRANSAXLE, TRANSMISSION)

◇ **gearbox** *noun* metal casing for the gear (a) assembly (NOTE: US English is **gearcase** *or* **transmission**); **gearbox input shaft** = shaft which transmits power from the clutch to the gearbox; **gearbox output shaft** = shaft which transmits the drive out of the gearbox

◇ **gearcase** *noun US* = GEARBOX

◇ **gearchange** *noun* process of changing gears (NOTE: US English is **shifting**); **gearchange cables** = cables that in rare cases operate the gearbox; normally a system of rods and joints (linkages) are used; **gearchange linkage** *or* **mechanism** = system of rods and joints used to operate the gearbox

◇ **gearing** *noun* combination or system of gears designed to transmit power

◇ **gear knob** *noun* knob at the end of a gear lever; **gear lever** *or* **gearstick** = stick used by the driver to change gear in a manual gearbox (NOTE: US English is **gearshift, shifter, shift lever)**

◇ **gear oil** *noun* motor oil used in gear boxes and final drives; usually of higher viscosity than engine oil; *(compare* TRANSMISSION FLUID)

◇ **gear puller** *noun* puller with two or more jaws and pressure screw for pulling off gears, bearings, pulleys, etc.

gear pump *or* **gear-type oil pump** *noun* simplest oil pump with two gear wheels; *(compare* ROTOR-TYPE PUMP) *(see illustrations 3, 17)*

> COMMENT: one of the gears is driven by the drive gear, and the other wheel (idler) rotates in mesh; the fluid is conveyed in the spaces between the gear teeth and the pump casing; the gear pump conveys relatively small volumes at high pressure and is, therefore, the typical oil pump in engine lubrication systems

gear range *noun* choice of gears in an automatic gearbox; the typical gear ranges are: P - Park, R - Reverse, N - Neutral, D - Drive, L - Low

gear ratio *noun* the number of revolutions of driving gear required to turn a driven gear through one complete revolution

> COMMENT: for a pair of gears, the ratio is found by dividing the number of teeth on the driven gear by the number of teeth on the driving gear

gear selector *noun* lever that selects the gear in an automatic gearbox; *(compare* GEAR LEVER); **gear selector indicator** = indicator positioned in the instrument cluster or on the centre console shift gate indicating which gear has been selected in an automatic gearbox

◇ **gearshift** *noun US* = GEARCHANGE

◇ **gearstick** *noun (informal)* = GEAR LEVER

◇ **gear tooth** *noun* indentation on the edge of a gearwheel

◇ **gear train** *noun* system of gears that transmits drive from one shaft to another

◇ **gear-type oil pump** *noun* = GEAR PUMP

◇ **gearwheel** *noun* = GEAR (a)

gel 1 *noun* substance like a jelly **2** *verb* to become a gel

◇ **gel coat** *noun* the outer layer of GRP mouldings which gives a smooth surface that may be coloured; **gel-coat resin** = a resin similar to general lay-up resin but with an additive to make it thixotropic, i.e. it does not run on vertical surfaces; used to make the gel coat in mouldings; *(compare* LAY-UP RESIN)

◇ **gelling drier** *noun* drier for PVC sealants

Gemmer steering *noun* = CAM-AND-ROLLER STEERING

general corrosion *noun* in contrast to pitting, a type of corrosion which affects the entire surface of a metal

General Motors (GM) *noun* American vehicle manufacturer; the largest in the world (NOTE: British subsidiary is **Vauxhall** and other European subsidiary is **Opel)**

general purpose lacquer thinner *noun* a type of thinner that may be used for both lacquers and synthetic enamels without causing lifting or other paint faults; *(compare* THINNER, REDUCER)

general purpose pliers *noun* any kind of typical multi-purpose pliers; *(compare* COMBINATION PLIERS)

COMMENT: the most common type of pliers; typically with a flat nose, serrated jaws and a recess for gripping round stock; in Germany and the UK always with a wire cutter, in the USA with or without a wire cutter but always with slip joints; general purpose pliers are also included in automotive on-board tool sets

generate *verb* to produce

◊ **generator** *noun* **(a)** any type of automotive electric power generator, such as an alternator or dynamo **(b)** *US* = DYNAMO

geometry *noun* design, layout or arrangement of parts

girder spanner *noun* adjustable spanner with jaws at right angles to the handle

GL *(short for)* Grand Luxe, meaning more luxurious than a standard model, L (= Luxe); *(compare* CL)

gland *noun* seal that stops fluid under pressure leaking past a rotating or reciprocating shaft or rod

◊ **glandless** *adjective* without a seal

COMMENT: glandless pumps are particularly suitable for handling solvents, abrasives or chemically active fluids, e.g. acids which are not compatible with seals

glare 1 *noun* strong, bright light (e.g. from oncoming traffic) **2** *verb* to shine too brightly; to dazzle

glass *noun* window pane *don't scratch the glass; lift the wiper arm to raise the blade off the glass* **glass area** = the window surface area of a vehicle body; may also refer to the whole area of the body above the waistline; *US* **glass channel** = WINDOW CHANNEL

◊ **glass fibre** *noun* a very thin glass thread, used loosely or in woven form as an acoustic, electrical, or thermal insulating material and as a reinforcing material in laminated plastics

◊ **glass holder** *noun* tool with suction cup(s) to hold and carry glass

◊ **glasspaper** *noun* abrasive paper coated with particles of glass, used for smoothing and polishing; *(compare* SANDPAPER)

◊ **glass reinforced filler paste** *noun* polyester filler that has strands of fibreglass added into the filler paste to increase the rigidity of the repair

◊ **glass reinforced plastic (GRP)** *noun* the basic material for the manufacture of fibreglass body shells and panels; it is made up of several layers of fibreglass mat or cloth and various types of resins *the spoiler is supplied in impact-resistant GRP ready for colour-matching*

Glass's Guide *noun* monthly publication of second-hand car prices

glass seal *noun* a conducting seal in the middle of some sparking plug insulators connecting the top and bottom parts of the central electrode

◊ **glass sphere** *noun* reinforcing filler in the form of particles as opposed to fibres

◊ **glass tampering detector** *noun* part of a vehicle alarm system that detects glass being struck or broken

glaze *noun* smooth, polished surface; **glaze breaker** = CYLINDER HONE

◊ **glazed** *adjective* **(a)** fitted with glass **(b)** with a smooth, polished surface

◊ **glazing** *noun* glass fitted (or to be fitted) in a window; **glazing strip** = moulded rubber strip for mounting windscreens and other fixed glass

gloss *noun* shine on a surface; lustre

glove compartment *US* **glovebox** *noun* small compartment in the dashboard for sundry objects

glow *verb* to burn without flames

◊ **glow coil** *noun* filament in a glow plug

◊ **glow pencil** *noun* pencil-like heating element of a sheathed-type glow plug

glow plug *noun* the most important component in a preheating system of a diesel engine, used to preheat the intake air or the combustion chamber when the engine is cold (NOTE: also called **heater plug**); **glow plug indicator** = monitoring element in a preheater system, which changes the colour of its filament in line with the plug and indicating readiness for starting; **glow plug/ starter switch** = key switch for turning on the preheating system of a diesel engine and starting the car; *(compare* IGNITION SWITCH)

COMMENT: different types of glow plugs are available, but the most common are sheathed-type glow plugs, which have superseded wire glow plugs, to preheat the combustion chamber

glow time *noun* preheating time of a diesel engine

◇ **glow tube** *noun* = GLOW PLUG

glycol *see* ETHYLENE-GLYCOL

GM = GENERAL MOTORS

go dull *or* **flat** *verb* to lose (the) shine *paint that has gone dull may be repolished*

goggles *noun* protective spectacles against dust and glare

gold plating *noun* electrolytic deposition of gold

go off *verb* to begin to harden, the initial phase of the hardening process of plastic body fillers *reduce the amount of catalyst when working in hot weather, otherwise the filler goes off far too soon* (*compare* HARDEN) (NOTE: US English is **kick**)

gooseneck map light *noun* flexible-stemmed map lamp

gouge *noun* a flat, relatively large dent that has no hard contours so it can be reshaped by shrinking using heat or with a hammer and dolly

governor *noun* **(a)** engine speed regulator **(b)** (*automatic transmission control*) transmission regulator

COMMENT: the governor on the output shaft of a hydraulically controlled transmission converts line pressure into governor pressure. In electro-hydraulically controlled transmissions, the governor is replaced by a sensor

governor plate *noun* = CONTACT BREAKER PLATE

◇ **governor pressure** *noun* (*automatic transmission control*) pressure that varies in accordance with vehicle speed and acts on the command valves, where it opposes the control pressure

◇ **governor valve (GV)** *noun* (*automatic transmission control*) valve which converts line pressure into vehicle-speed dependent governor pressure

◇ **governor weight** *noun* (*centrifugal advance mechanism*) = ADVANCE WEIGHT

grab *verb* **(a)** (*brake*) to come on suddenly when the brake pedal is pressed **(b)** (*clutch*) to take up the drive suddenly when the clutch pedal is released (NOTE: also called **snatch)** (*compare* FIERCENESS)

◇ **grab handle** *noun* **(a)** part of a car door interior used to pull the door shut; (*compare* DOOR HANDLE) **(b)** handle on the end of a trailer, used for manual manoeuvring

grade *noun* degree of sandpaper coarseness *use 320 grade sanding paper to sand down old paint* (NOTE: US English is **grit**)

gradient *noun* (i) the slope or inclination of a road; (ii) a measure of this, expressed as the ratio of height (or drop) to horizontal distance; a steep hill might be 1 in 4, whilst a gradual slope might be 1 in 10

graduated tint *noun* tinted stripe at the upper edge of the windscreen

graft copolymer *noun* a copolymer in which polymeric side chains have been attached to the main chain of a polymer of different structure

grain alcohol *noun* = ETHANOL

grain coarsening *or* **grain growth** *noun* roughening of the surface of a material

COMMENT: in the hot regions of exhaust systems, grain coarsening together with the mechanical property effects of high-temperature exposure reduce the mechanical strength of exhaust components by at least 80%

Grand Luxe (GL) *noun* GL model = more luxurious model than a standard

Grand Prix *noun* international car race from which points are scored towards the World Championship

Grand Touring *or* **Gran Turismo** *see* GT

Grand Touring-injection *see* GTi

graph 108 **grit**

graph *noun* diagram showing the relationship between certain numbers or quantities in the form of a line

◇ **graphic display unit** *noun* dashboard panel displaying a plan of the car with illuminated parts representing doors left open, lights switched on, etc.

◇ **graphic equalizer** *noun* unit in a car stereo system that adjusts the audio output signal strength separately for individual frequency ranges; individual frequencies can be emphasized to compensate for specific acoustic conditions

graphite *noun* form of carbon used in making brushes for motors and generators and as a lubricant; **graphite grease** = heavy-duty grease containing graphite, used for brake cables, etc.; **graphitic corrosion** = selective corrosion of grey cast iron, resulting in preferential removal of metallic constituents, leaving graphite

grass (heat) shield *noun* metal shield fitted underneath a catalytic converter to reduce the risk of its heat starting an accidental grass fire

gravel gun *noun* equipment used to hurl crushed stone at objects, such as test panels, to test them for chipping resistance

gravity feed *noun* a fuel supply layout formerly used for two-stroke car engines

| COMMENT: the fuel tank is located above the engine and carburettor level, i.e. the fuel is fed to the carburettor by the force of gravity

gravity-feed spray gun *noun* type of spray gun, in which paint flows downward from a container situated on top of it, thereby reducing the amount of compressed air required

grease 1 *noun* thick, viscous lubricant for machinery made from oil and metallic soaps; **grease gun** = hand pump tool used for lubricating with grease; **grease nipple** = small, one-way valve used for injecting grease into a bearing **2** *verb* to lubricate or coat with grease

greenhouse *noun* (*informal*) = GLASS AREA

green stage *noun* the initial hardening phase during which the resin or filler has

hardened but has not yet set solid; this occurs immediately after the resin or filler has gone off; (*compare* GO OFF)

grid *noun* in a battery, the metal plate with holes, used as a conductor and a support for the active material

| COMMENT: the grid is usually made of a lead-antimony alloy but in maintenance-free batteries, it consists of a lead-calcium alloy which greatly reduces gassing

grid-controlled ignition (system) *noun* microprocessor-controlled ignition system with electronic ignition timing by means of an ignition map stored in the control unit memory

grid dolly *noun* a special shrinking dolly with a large, flat groove; (*compare* SHRINKING DOLLY)

| COMMENT: when stretching metal, the material is beaten down into this groove to reduce stretching effects; may also be used to produce swage lines in body panels with a hammerform

grille *noun* grating that admits cooling air to the radiator; **grille (face) panel** = radiator grille surround

grind *verb* to smooth or polish by friction or abrasion; **grind back to bare metal** = sand down to bare metal

◇ **grinding disc** *noun* abrasive disc; **grinding paste** = abrasive paste used for reseating valves; **grinding wheel** = abrasive wheel used for grinding (usually a composite of hard particles in a resin filler)

◇ **grindstone** *noun* rotating abrasive disc for rubbing away metal and for sharpening tools

grip *noun* adhesion of a tyre to the road surface; important for roadholding and safe braking; **grip in the wet** = a vehicle's roadholding ability in the rain or on a wet surface

grip channel *noun* steel channel spot-welded to the body

| COMMENT: the channel lip, of semicircular cross section, is used to keep rubber seals in place, e.g. around hoods

grip wrench *noun* = LOCKING PLIERS

grit blasting *noun* **(a)** the most popular sandblasting process; grit is used to clean the metal surfaces and is available in various grades for coarse or finer blasting on thin steel **(b)** cleaning the sparking plug electrodes by bombarding them with abrasive particles

grit number *noun* classification of sandpapers by fineness of the grit particles; *see also* P GRIT NUMBERS

grommet *noun* rubber or plastic ring round a hole in metal (to protect a cable or pipe)

groove *noun* **(a)** any machined channel or hollow **(b)** the space between thread ridges

grooved compression ring *noun* scraper-type piston ring

> COMMENT: in addition to its function as a compression ring, the grooved compression ring, due to its groove, also functions as an oil scraper ring

grooving hammer *noun* wide-nose peen hammer

gross axle weight rating (GAWR) *noun US* maximum specified load capacity of an axle

◇ **gross vehicle weight (GVW)** *noun* total weight of a vehicle in any given circumstance (i.e. with or without passengers, luggage etc.); *(compare* DRY WEIGHT, KERB WEIGHT)

◇ **gross weight** *noun* = GROSS VEHICLE WEIGHT

ground *noun US* return path of an electrical system, which in a motor vehicle is provided by the metal body and chassis (NOTE: GB English for this is **earth**)

◇ **ground clearance** *noun* vertical distance between level ground and the lowest fixed item on a vehicle *shorter springs will reduce the ground clearance by up to 40 mm* **ground clearance control** = small lever near the handbrake of cars with hydropneumatic suspension that allows ground clearance to be increased for crossing rough terrain or when changing a wheel; **ground clearance sensor** = instrument that senses the distance between ground and car (for self-levelling air suspension)

◇ **ground contact area** *noun* = CONTACT PATCH

◇ **grounding** *noun* touching the ground (as when a long vehicle goes over a humpback bridge)

growler *noun* electromagnetic device used to find short circuits in coils

grown tyre *noun* tyre that, with use, has slightly increased in size

GRP *noun* = GLASS REINFORCED PLASTIC *GRP body*

grub screw *noun* fully threaded, headless screw; *(compare* SETSCREW)

GT *(short for)* Grand Touring or Gran Turismo, indicating better performance than a standard car model

◇ **GTi** *(short for)* Grand Touring-injection: a GT car model with fuel injection

gudgeon pin *noun* pin in a piston which links the piston to the small end of the connecting rod; *(see illustration 9)* (NOTE: US English is **piston pin, wrist pin**); **gudgeon pin boss** = the material below the piston crown (joined to the skirt) which carries the gudgeon pin; **gudgeon pin circlip** = circlip used to secure the piston ring laterally in the piston; **gudgeon pin end** = connecting rod small end (to which the gudgeon pin is attached)

Guibo coupling *noun* doughnut-shaped type of flexible coupling

guide coat *noun* thin coat of paint designed to highlight imperfections

> COMMENT: applied between two primer coats or after filling, a thin guide coat may be sprayed in a colour differing from that used for the other coats. It is then sanded to reveal body imperfections; the guide coat remains unsanded at low spots, highlighting areas to be worked further

guillotine *noun* bench tool for cutting sheet metal

> COMMENT: a panel is pulled in by two adjustable rollers and is cut at the same time, producing either straight or curved cuts

gull-wing door *noun* roof-hinged door that opens upwards; first used on the Mercedes-Benz 300 SL in the early 1950s

gulp valve *noun* vacuum-controlled valve that admits fresh air to the inlet manifold during deceleration to prevent backfiring in the exhaust system; its vacuum signal is governed by a thermovalve and a solenoid valve to ensure that the gulp valve action does not interfere with cold start enrichment

gum deposit *noun* sticky deposit that occurs if petrol remains unused in the tank for a period of time; the use of detergent in petrol helps prevent it

gun *verb (informal)* to press the accelerator hard *the driver in the next lane gunned his engine as the lights turned to green*

gusset (plate) *noun* triangular plate across an angle, to reinforce the joint

gutter *noun* channel at the edge of a road to carry away rainwater

GV = GOVERNOR VALVE

GVW = GROSS VEHICLE WEIGHT

Hh

H (a) letter on the sidewall of a tyre denoting the maximum speed for which it is designed (210 km/h or 130 mph); *(see* SPEED RATING) **(b)** SI symbol for: HENRY

hacksaw *noun* handsaw for cutting metal, with a narrow blade attached to a frame

hairline crack *noun* tiny stress crack which forms due to strains in the material or extreme temperature differences; as opposed to crazing, a single crack of this type will often occur alone

hairpin valve spring *noun* valve spring formed from a wire or metal strip bent to form two levers emanating from a half-loop or coil; used on some classic cars and bikes

half-moon slip joint pliers *noun* multiple-slip joint pliers with groove joint

half-round body file *noun* body file with domed file surface for working reverse-crowned panels

half-shaft *noun* shaft between the differential and the drive wheel

halftrack *noun* vehicle with caterpillar tracks over the rear wheels to provide motive power but steered by normal front wheels

Hall effect *noun* in electrical conductors where electric current flows perpendicular to a magnetic field, a so-called Hall voltage is produced perpendicular to the direction of current flow and to the magnetic field; **Hall-effect ignition system** = transistorized ignition with Hall generator; **Hall-effect sensor** = HALL GENERATOR; **Hall-effect switch** = HALL VANE SWITCH

Hall element *or* **Hall generator** *noun* pulse generator that makes use of the Hall effect and consists of a rotor with vanes, a conductive element with a permanent magnet and the Hall IC

COMMENT: when the air gap is unobstructed, a Hall voltage is generated; when a vane stands in the air gap, the magnetic flux cannot reach the Hall IC. Hall generators used as ignition pulse generators have as many vanes and Hall windows as the engine has cylinders, dwell being determined by the width of the vanes. Hall generators used in electronic-map ignition systems to provide the engine starting signal have only one Hall window

Hall IC *noun* solid state device with the actual Hall generator and integrated circuits for voltage amplification and potential reversal, producing the pulses for the control unit

◇ **Hall module** *noun* = HALL IC

◇ **Hall sensor** *noun* = HALL GENERATOR

Hall vane switch *noun* 'switch' that makes use of the Hall effect

COMMENT: when the air gap is free, a magnetic field acts on the Hall IC and the Hall voltage reaches its maximum (high). When a rotor vane obstructs the air gap, shielding the Hall IC from the magnetic flux, the Hall voltage reaches its minimum (low). The signal produced is a square wave

Hall voltage *see* HALL EFFECT

halogen *noun* one of the chemical elements fluorine, chlorine, bromine, iodine, or astatine; **halogen bulb** = bulb containing a trace of a halogen, such as iodine; **halogen headlight** = high intensity reflector with inner halogen bulb, precision lens, and 3-prong attachment

COMMENT: the glass of a halogen bulb should not be touched with the fingers as this will cause premature failure. If the glass is accidentally touched, it may be cleaned with methylated spirits on a soft cloth

Hamlin switch *noun* a suspended-mass-type sensor used in new air bag systems; avoids the ecological problems associated with the earlier mercury-type switches

hammer 1 *noun* hand tool with a metal head on a handle, used for beating metal and driving in nails **2** *verb* to hit with a hammer

◊ **hammer drill** *noun* electric hand drill that hammers as well as rotates

◊ **hammerform** *noun* shaped wooden block used in panel beating, on which a desired form is produced by hammering

◊ **hammer welding** *noun* metalworking technique that includes gas welding, preferably without the use of filler rod, followed by hammer and dolly work on the welded joint to smooth out any remaining imperfections

handbook *noun* book which gives instructions or information; *(compare* OWNER'S HANDBOOK)

◊ **handbrake** *noun* brake operated by a hand lever; **handbrake turn** = 180° turn achieved by applying the handbrake (acting on the rear wheels) hard when the vehicle is starting to turn; **handbrake warning light** = light that illuminates when the handbrake is applied; on most new cars it has been superseded by a multifunction brake warning light

◊ **handcrafted** *noun US* built by hand *the Avanti is the only handcrafted production automobile made in America*

◊ **hand drill** *noun* power-driven, hole-boring tool

◊ **handed** *adjective* made to fit on a specific side; **Caution: the axle shafts are handed!** = Beware: the axle shafts are not interchangeable! *left-handed; right-handed*

◊ **hand file** *noun* flat file for shaping metal, with a rectangular cross section, constant blade width and one smooth edge; *(compare* FLAT FILE)

◊ **handle 1** *verb* **(a)** *(of a vehicle)* to react under any given circumstances but especially referring to cornering, roadholding and manoeuvring *the new XYZ handles exceptionally well* **(b)** to deal with *or* to cope with; **the chassis can handle 1,000 bhp** = the chassis is built to withstand the stress of 1,000 bhp **2** *noun* a CB user's code name; **handling (properties)** = the way a vehicle reacts to the actions of the driver (usually with regard to steering) *the new suspension offers precise handling*

◊ **hands-free** *adjective* **hands-free car phone** = voice-operated telephone using microphone and loudspeaker, leaving hands free to drive

◊ **handshaker** *noun* *(informal US)* passenger car with a manual gearbox

hanger *noun* **(a)** flexible ring or strap to hold a pipe, e.g. an exhaust pipe **(b)** mounting bracket, e.g. a spring hanger for a leaf spring **(c)** component of sighting point gauges, used to install the gauge at the vehicle chassis

hangover *noun* a modification of custom cars with separate chassis, e.g. pick-ups, which raises the floorpan and lowers the body, to give the impression that the body has been pulled down over the chassis right down to street level

hard anodic coating *noun* hard, wear-resistant, oxide layer produced in an anodic oxidation process; **hard anodizing** = special type of anodizing adapted to the production of thick, hard, abrasion-resistant films

◊ **hardboard** *noun* board-like building material made of compressed wood chip fibres and sawdust

◊ **hard chromium plating** *noun* electrolytic deposition of a hard, wear-resistant, chromium layer

◊ **hard-dry** *adjective* used of paint when it is hard enough to polish and rub

harden *verb* to set *or* to cure; *(compare* GO OFF)

◊ **hardener** *noun* substance added (as to a paint or varnish) to harden the film

◊ **hardening** *noun* process of a paint becoming hard; *(compare* STOVING)

COMMENT: drying or hardening of the paint film goes through several stages. The first stage is called 'dust-free'; at this stage, the paint has hardened sufficiently to prevent dust from becoming embedded in the paint film. The second stage is called 'touch-dry'; at this point, the paint film can actually be touched with light finger pressure. The third and final stage is referred to as 'hard-dry'; at this point, the paint film is hard enough to polish or rub

hardness *noun* the quality or condition of being hard

COMMENT: the hardness of a plastic material is normally not a value which may be used in design calculations in the way that material properties such as strength and modulus may be used; instead, it is used to indicate whether or not the material is suitable for a particular application

hard rubber *noun* = EBONITE

◊ **hard-sided caravan** *noun* caravan with foldable, hard wall panels; *(compare* SOFT-SIDED CARAVAN)

◊ **hard stop** *noun* hard braking, but not necessarily with locked wheels *several hard stops during running-in are recommended to bed the linings in*

◊ **hardtop** *noun* **(a)** rigid, (sometimes detachable) car roof; *(compare* SOFT TOP); **hardtop stand** = for storage purposes, a foldable stand that holds a detached hardtop in a vertical position **(b)** sports car with a hardtop

◊ **hard trim** *noun* instrument panel mouldings, centre consoles and similar plastic trim; *(compare* TRIM a)

Hardy disc *noun* a disc-style flexible coupling; *(see illustration 22)*

◊ **Hardy-Spicer (universal) joint** *noun* type of universal joint commonly used with prop shafts

harmonic balancer *noun* formerly, two gearwheels carrying an unbalanced weight, mounted in bearings below the middle main crankshaft bearing, driven at twice engine speed and rotating in opposite directions to counterbalance the secondary vibrations in a four-cylinder reciprocating engine

harness *noun* **(a)** belt system used with child seats and in cars, consisting of two shoulder belts and two lap belt portions fastened by a central buckle; **a 4-point racing harness** = safety harness anchored at four points, worn by some racing drivers **(b)** = WIRING HARNESS

hatch *noun* **(a)** = HATCHBACK **(b)** = TAILGATE

hatchback *noun* basically a saloon or coupé with a tailgate; *(compare* FASTBACK)

COMMENT: this body style was popular in the 1960s with cars like the Austin A40 Farina, Autobianchi Primula and Morris 1100, where the rear window area gradually sloped towards the rear end of the rear wings to provide additional interior and luggage space; nowadays hatchbacks are characterized by an almost vertical rear end, with a tailgate hinged at the top

hazard warning switch *or* **hazard flasher** *noun* switch that makes all the direction indicators flash simultaneously, to indicate that the car is a hazard (e.g. is stationary because of breakdown)

HC = HYDROCARBONS

HC engine *noun* high-camshaft engine; the camshaft is located much higher than the crankshaft, (although not in the cylinder head), allowing for the use of shorter pushrods, thus improving the engine's revving ability; *(compare* CIH ENGINE, OHC ENGINE)

HD = HEAVY-DUTY

HDPE = HIGH-DENSITY POLYETHYLENE

head *noun* **(a)** the top part of a tool; the heads designed for use with interchangeable head torque wrenches, for example, come in a variety of shapes, e.g. with open jaw end or ratchet mechanism **(b)** term used to express the increase of energy content in a fluid pumped, expressed in units of energy per unit of mass, usually simply ft (feet) *the head developed in multistage pumps is the head of one impeller multiplied by the number of impellers* **(c)** = CYLINDER HEAD

header *noun* **(a)** part at the top of another part *rear window header* **(b)** *US* = HEADPIPE

◊ **header bar** *US* **header bow** *noun* front bar of a hood which attaches to the top of the windscreen frame; usually made of sheet steel shaped to match the top front edge to the curvature of the windscreen

◊ **header tank** *noun* top radiator tank in a thermosyphon water cooling system; *(compare* BOTTOM TANK, RADIATOR TANK)

head gasket *noun* = CYLINDER HEAD GASKET

heading angle *noun* = YAW ANGLE

headlamp *noun* main light on the front of a vehicle; **headlamp body** = a sheet metal pot welded or screwed to the front wing that provides the housing for the headlamp and its bulbs and wiring; **headlamp bucket** = the headlamp housing of cars having separate headlamps not integrated into the body line, e.g. the Citroën 2CV and most pre-war cars;

headlamp cover = rigid or flexible protection against dirt or stone damage when lights are not being used (may be flush with body); **headlamp mounting panel** = sheet metal panel for rectangular headlamps that is spot-welded to the front section of modern cars where the radiator grille and the headlamps are mounted adjacent to each other; provides the mounting points for the headlamp; **headlamp visor** = attachment between headlamp rim and lens, used on some classic cars only; **headlamp wash/wipe** = system that cleans headlamps with a jet of water and a small wiper (blade)

COMMENT : 'headlamp' refers to the actual unit, whereas 'headlight' is used for the unit as well as for its function and where emphasis is on the actual light produced by the lamp

head land *noun* uppermost piston land, subject to the highest thermal load *note the fractured head land and broken compression ring*

headlight *noun* main light on the front of a vehicle; **headlight beam setting** = alignment of the beam of light from the headlamps; **headlight dipper (switch)** = any type of switch, both stalk or foot-operated, that changes the headlight from main to dipped beam (and vice versa) (NOTE: also called **dipswitch**); **headlight flasher** = by flicking the direction indicator lever upwards against a spring pressure, the headlights flash on and off quickly; *(see Comment at FLASH)*; **headlight levelling** = system that allows the driver to maintain proper headlight beam position regardless of vehicle load; **headlight levelling control** = usually a vertical thumbwheel that adjusts the height of the headlight beam; **headlight on/off delay system** = system with two functions: when activated, it can turn the headlights automatically ON during darkness and OFF during daylight; it can also be set to keep the headlights ON up to approximately three minutes after leaving the parked vehicle; useful in dark, high-risk areas; the system is controlled by a photovoltaic cell on the dashboard; **headlight retractor indicator lamp** = lamp that illuminates when the headlight covers are opening or closing

headlining *noun* soft lining of the inside of a car roof

head-on collision *or* **head-on crash** *noun* the result of two vehicles being driven straight into one another

headpipe *US* **header** *noun* down pipe connecting the exhaust manifold to the front of the silencer or to the connector pipe; *(compare* Y-PIPE*) (see illustration 19)*

headrest *or* **head restraint** *noun* height-adjustable head support, fitted nowadays to both front and rear seats, to minimize the effects of whiplash in a collision

headroom *noun* distance between the top of a passenger's head and the inside of the car roof

head trim *noun* roof lining

head-up display (HUD) *noun* driver information system which displays key information by projection into the driver's visual field in the windscreen area

COMMENT: head-up displays may use LCD technology and holographic combiners to superimpose the projected information on the real scene

heat cracking *noun* pattern of small, irregular cracks (e.g. on brake discs)

heated rear window *noun* rear window fitted with a heating element that demists inside and de-ices outside

◊ **heated tool welding** *noun* welding process in which the parts to be welded are pressed against a heated plate and subsequently pressed together to produce a fusion weld

◊ **heated windscreen** *noun* windscreen fitted with a heating element to facilitate de-icing

heater *noun* system for heating the interior of a vehicle; *(see illustration 15)*

◊ **heater air pipe** *noun* channel section incorporated into the side member or other structural sections that is designed to provide a flow of warm air into the interior of the vehicle, above all into the footwells (e.g. as used on the VW Beetle)

◊ **heater fan** *or* **blower** *noun* electric fan to boost heating and ventilation

◊ **heater flange** *noun* heating element for preheating the intake air in small diesel engines

◊ **heater plug** *noun* = GLOW PLUG; **heater-plug indicator** = GLOW PLUG INDICATOR

heat path *noun* path along which heat passes from the sparking plug tip to the water jacket

◊ **heat range** *noun* measure of ability of a sparking plug to carry away heat; dependent on the length of the insulator nose, electrode shape and material; **heat-range reserve** = the heat-range reserve defines the distance to the start of pre-ignition under further increasing thermal loading of the sparking plug. This reserve is expressed in degrees crankshaft, the amount by which the factory-set ignition timing can be further advanced without pre-ignition occurring

◊ **heat riser** *noun* flapper in the exhaust manifold that is closed when the engine is cold, causing hot exhaust gases to heat the inlet manifold, thus providing better cold engine operation; a thermostatic spring opens the flapper when the engine warms up; *(compare* HOT SPOT)

◊ **heat shield** *noun* sheet metal part, usually reflective, often asbestos-lined; protects heat-sensitive components from heat radiation of the exhaust system; *(compare* GRASS (HEAT) SHIELD)

◊ **heat shrinking** *noun* shrinking dents in panels using a gas welder to heat local areas of the dents

◊ **heat sink** *noun* heat removing component, such as the fins on an air-cooled cylinder

◊ **heat soak** *noun* heat from the engine warming the carburettor and other parts of the fuel system which can cause vapour lock and may make restarting difficult

◊ **heat transfer** *noun* transfer of thermal energy from one material to another by means of thermal conduction, convection or radiation; heat transfer is only possible from a high to a low temperature level

heavy *adjective* **(a)** *(cable, sheet metal)* heavy-duty **(b)** *(paint)* thickly coated **(c)** *(steering, clutch)* having a stiff operation, e.g. requiring considerable effort to turn the steering wheel **(d)** *(traffic)* of great quantity (NOTE: opposite is **light**)

◊ **heavy-duty (HD)** *adjective* designed for heavy loads *an optional heavy-duty cooling system is available if frequent towing is required; for frequent short distance driving, e.g. in a taxi, a heavy-duty unit should be installed when replacing the clutch* **heavy-duty diagonal cutting pliers** = diagonal cutting pliers with a special joint and handle design for extra cutting power; **heavy-**duty end cutting pliers = end cutting pliers with a special joint and handle design for extra cutting power; **heavy-duty (ring) wrench** = heavy-duty single end box wrench for use with a tubular handle; can be used without the handle for quickly running down nuts or, with the handle slipped on, for final tightening or reaching otherwise inaccessible nuts

◊ **heavy film build** *noun* excessive thickness of paint coat

◊ **heavy foot** *noun* **to drive with a heavy foot** = driving at full throttle, especially at high speeds

◊ **heavy goods vehicle (HGV)** *noun* vehicle capable of carrying heavy loads and requiring a special licence to drive *HGV licence*

◊ **heavy phosphating** *noun* application of extremely heavy phosphate coatings

◊ **heavy side pattern** *noun* oval spray pattern that is heavy towards the left or right hand side, i.e. it takes the shape of a crescent oriented towards the right or left. This is often caused by a clogged horn hole at the air cap of the spray gun

◊ **heavy yellow boot** *noun (informal)* = WHEEL CLAMP

heel *noun* **(a)** rubbing block on the contact breaker lever **(b)** = BEAD HEEL

◊ **heelboard** *or* **heel plate** *noun* the vertical transverse sheet metal panel running across the width of the car interior at the front edge of the rear seat well; this panel links the rear seat well to the floorpan and provides rigidity for both panels; *(compare* TOEBOARD)

◊ **heel dolly** *noun* dolly in the form of a heel (of a foot)

HEGO sensor *(short for)* heated exhaust gas oxygen sensor

HEI = HIGH ENERGY IGNITION (SYSTEM)

◊ **HEI-EST** = HIGH ENERGY IGNITION SYSTEM WITH ELECTRONIC SPARK TIMING

height adjustable steering column *noun* steering column whose length or rake may be adjusted to suit the individual driver

◊ **height corrector** *or* **height regulator** *noun* automatic levelling control in hydropneumatic suspension systems

◇ **height hamper pitch control** *noun* = BUMP STOP

helical *adjective* in the shape of a helix; **helical gears** = gears with helical teeth; **helical spring lock washer** = locking device for threaded fasteners; **helical teeth** = curved gear teeth on the edge of a gearwheel, cut at an angle to its axis

Helicoil *noun* proprietary, coil-type thread insert, commonly used to replace a stripped sparking plug thread

helium leak test *noun* pressure test using helium

helix *noun* a spiral, like the thread on a screw or a coil spring in a suspension system

helmet connector *or* **helmet lug** *noun* special type of lug for connecting a battery with tapered terminal posts; *(compare* CABLE CLAMP)

helper leaf *or* **helper spring** *noun* auxiliary leaf spring; *(compare* OVERLOAD SPRING)

hemispherical combustion chamber *noun* combustion chamber with a circular, rounded internal shape to ensure a smooth propagation of the flame front during the combustion process; *(compare* PENT-ROOF COMBUSTION CHAMBER)

henry (H) *noun* unit of inductance, equal to the inductance of a circuit in which the variation of current at the rate of one ampere per second induces an electromotive force of one volt (NOTE: named after US physicist, J. Henry (1797-1878)

herringbone gear *noun* = DOUBLE HELICAL GEAR

hexagonal *adjective* having six sides; **hexagon(al) bolster** *or* **hexagon(al) collar** = tool that allows a screwdriver to be turned with a wrench for extra torque to loosen tight screws; **hexagon bit** *or* **hex bit** = bit with six sides; **hexagon bolt** *or* **hex bolt** = bolt with a six-sided head; **hexagon key** *or* **hex key** = key for hexagon recess screws, 90° offset at one end *an Allen key is a hex key*

h.f.s. *(short for)* heated front seat, (often seen in advertisements)

HGV = HEAVY GOODS VEHICLE

hidden *or* **hideaway wiper** *noun* wiper system with a parking position below normal visibility range

HIF carburettor *noun* type of SU carburettor with a horizontal integral float chamber

highball *noun* US *(informal)* in car sales, the practice of stating a very high trade-in price to a customer who is known or expected to be shopping around, comparing prices; *(compare* LOWBALL)

> COMMENT: when the customer finds that other dealers cannot match the trade-in price, he will return to the original dealer, only to be told that the inflated figure was a mistake (e.g. based on wrong assumptions as to the trade-in's clutch condition, etc.); many customers will then accept a new, lower price because they are tired of shopping around

high beam *noun US* = MAIN BEAM

high-build filler *noun* a spray primer that leaves a relatively thick coat on the panel surface to cover up minor imperfections that would otherwise show up very prominently in the final colour coat

◇ **high-build galvanizing** *noun* galvanizing process in which extremely heavy zinc coatings are applied

high-camshaft engine *noun* = HC ENGINE

high carbon steel *noun* a very hard steel, as opposed to plain carbon steel

high centre rim *noun* raised centre rim design, used in the CTS wheel

high crown panel *noun* panel shape that curves rapidly in all directions, e.g. around the headlamps of older cars (NOTE: opposite is **low crown panel**)

◇ **high crown spoon** *noun* spoon with a broad working surface and a heavily rounded tip that is ideal for using as a dolly or a lever in confined areas, such as headlamp housings or rounded body sections above the waistline

high-density polyethylene (HDPE) *noun* a very tough, chemically resistant thermoplastic, with a 'soapy' touch; e.g. used for blow-moulded parts such as fuel tanks or other mouldings, such as bumpers

high energy battery *noun* innovative battery type developed for electric cars

◊ **high energy coil** *noun* coil which generates higher ignition voltage and/or offers increased spark efficiency; ballasted

◊ **high energy ignition system (HEI)** *noun* ignition system which provides more ignition power (higher voltage at higher amperage) than normal systems; a typical HEI includes an electronic control unit and magnetic pick-up in combination with mechanical ignition timing; **high energy ignition system with electronic spark timing (HEI-EST)** = the HEI-EST system consists of an electronic distributor, with the ignition coil mounted on the distributor cap on 6- and 8-cylinder models or externally on 4-cylinder models; the ignition timing is performed electronically by the electronic control module. (Used on several 1983-88 GM models.)

high gear *noun* fourth or fifth gear, selected for cruising (NOTE: opposite is **low gear**)

◊ **high-geared** *adjective* **(a)** when a small gearwheel is driven by a large one **(b)** when a car's transmission system has higher than usual gearing, to improve fuel economy

high gloss *noun* very shiny, bright appearance *the clear coat gives the paint finish its high gloss and durability*

high leverage diagonal/end cutting pliers *noun* diagonal/end cutting pliers with special joint and handle design for extra cutting power

high/low range gearbox *noun* = DUAL-RANGE GEARBOX

high-mounted brake light *noun* third brake light mounted in the middle of the rear window or on some cars integrated in the trailing edge of the rear deck spoiler

high-performance *adjective* producing better than average results; **high-performance header** = a special exhaust manifold, which is not made of cast iron as usual, but of specially designed, curved and welded steel tubes, to produce a smooth flow

path for the exhaust gases, avoiding any sharp bends; less heavy, less sturdy and more expensive than an ordinary manifold; usually replaces the down pipe

high-pressure *adjective* operating under a lot of pressure, e.g. braking systems or diesel fuel injection; **high-pressure foaming** = process in which plastics are foamed under high pressure (} } 50 bar) (NOTE: opposite is **low-pressure foaming**); **high-pressure relief valve** = located somewhere on the high side of the air conditioning system, often next to the receiver-drier, this valve protects the system against excessive pressure

high revs *noun* towards the top end of the scale of engine revolutions; *(compare* PEAK REVS)

high side *noun* *(of air conditioning systems)* located between the compressor and expansion valve or orifice tube; includes the condenser (NOTE: opposite is **low side)** *(see illustrations 34, 35)*

high speed direct injection (HSDI) *noun* system for rapid injection of fuel into a diesel engine

high spot *noun* raised area on a panel surface

high-tension (HT) *adjective* capable of operating at a relatively high voltage; **high-tension circuit** *or* **HT circuit** = SECONDARY CIRCUIT; **high-tension distributor** *or* **HT distributor** = sometimes used to designate the distributor in electronically controlled ignition systems, which has no controlling functions or advance mechanism; **high-tension lead** *or* **HT lead** = SPARKING PLUG LEAD; **high-tension winding(s)** = SECONDARY WINDING

high-voltage reserve *noun* the difference between the available ignition voltage and the ignition voltage required at a given moment

highway *noun US* any public road outside the cities with a foundation and a hard surface; *(compare* EXPRESSWAY, FREEWAY, MOTORWAY)

COMMENT: the highway is a 'way higher than the ground', e.g. as opposed to stage coach tracks; since similar speed limits exist in the

USA for all types of highways, both single or multilane (usually between 50 and 60 mph), the terms 'highway driving speeds' and 'highway driving' should not be associated with speeds higher than 60 mph

Highway Code *noun* official British code of conduct for all road users

hillholder *noun* mechanically or electromechanically engaged device for preventing accidental rearward movement of a vehicle prior to driving off; found mainly in automatic transmissions

hinge bow *noun* = MAIN BOW

◊ **hinged-caliper disc brake** *noun* old disc brake design formerly used on motor bikes; superseded by sliding-caliper disc brakes

◊ **hinged quarter window** *noun* rear side window between B- and C-posts and/or in the case of estate cars, between C- and D-posts, that is provided with hinges to allow it to be opened

◊ **hinge facing** *noun* part of the door frame that includes the bracing and threaded plate for mounting the hinge to the door (NOTE: not to be confused with the hinge panel that is part of the hinge pillar of the body shell)

◊ **hinge panel** *noun* sheet metal panel spot-welded to the A-post or rear of the front wing that accommodates the hinges for the front door

◊ **hinge pillar** *noun* vertical structural element that carries the front door hinges; the upper end of the hinge pillar is usually the side of the windscreen frame (NOTE: also called **A-pillar**); **hinge pillar reinforcement** = vertical section behind the visible A-pillar

◊ **hinge plate** *noun* reinforcing plate between the hinge and the door panel which distributes the forces acting on the hinge bolts over a larger area of the panel

◊ **hinge post** *noun* = HINGE PILLAR

◊ **hinge tapping plate** *noun* threaded plate housed in a sheet metal cage spot-welded to the hinge pillar or, in some cases, to the door frame; the door is bolted to this plate and may be adjusted within certain limits, as the plate can be moved about in its sheet metal cage

hip belt *noun* = LAP BELT

hitch *verb* to connect or couple up a caravan or trailer to a towing vehicle

◊ **hitch ball** *noun US* = TOWBALL

holdback *noun* a mark-up, e.g. 2 percent, that the dealer pays the manufacturer on each new car that is added to his stock; this amount is rebated to the dealer after the car is sold

hold-in coil *or* **holding coil** *noun* separate relay coil, such as the hold-in winding in a starter solenoid, which is energized by contacts that close when the relay pulls in, to hold the relay in its energized position after the original operating circuit has been broken

◊ **hold-in winding** *or* **holding winding** *noun* part of a relay designed to hold it in the on-position; *(compare* PULL-IN WINDING) *(see illustration 37)*

hole cutting snips *noun* snips with pointed cutting blades for cutting holes in sheet metal material

◊ **hole punch** *noun* pliers used to form holes along the edge of a repair panel; the panel can then be plug-welded to the substructure at these holes

◊ **holesaw** *noun* cylindrical-shaped saw for use with power tools, for cutting holes in sheet metal material, e.g. in car bodies for installation of aerials

hollowing *noun* forming a deeply crowned panel from a piece of sheet steel on a hollowing block or a shot bag, using special mallets and hammers; **hollowing block** = shaped wooden block on which a desired shape is produced by hammering

holographic combiner *noun* semi-reflecting layer embedded in laminated windscreen glass; used for head-up displays

homofocal headlamp *noun* type of headlamp with two reflectors, the inner one being of shorter focal length than the main one

homokinetic joint *noun* = CONSTANT VELOCITY JOINT

homologation *noun* official recognition of a special version of a standard car as a production model, to make it eligible for racing

hone 1 *noun* special tool for use with an electric drill or air tools to smooth and polish engine, clutch or brake cylinders, with a number of honing stones that adjust to different cylinder bore diameters by spring tension **2** *verb* to smooth and polish with a hone *hone the cylinder walls in cases of wear*

honeycomb *noun* a pattern of hexagonal shapes, like bees' cells *the interior of the monolithic converter is a ceramic honeycomb; a honeycomb catalyst support*

honing *noun* precision machining process used to resurface bores and shafts; **honing stone** = tool used for the final smoothing operation, e.g. when repairing a cylinder wall

hood *noun* **(a)** folding roof of a convertible car; **hood bar** *or* **bow** = one of at least four struts that support a hood; usually made of tubular or sheet steel; (*compare* SPRING BAR); **hood stick** = old term for hood bar **(b)** *US* = BONNET

hook up *verb* to connect

horizontal *adjective* lying flat, not upright *three-cylinder horizontal in-line engine*

◇ **horizontal adjuster** *noun* screw for adjusting the sideways aim of the headlight beam

◇ **horizontal draught carburettor** *noun* = SIDEDRAUGHT CARBURETTOR

horizontal keiretsu *noun* a keiretsu system where the keiretsu member companies have shareholdings in each other (NOTE: opposite is **vertical keiretsu)** (*compare* KEIRETSU)

COMMENT: the member companies own relatively small chunks of shares in one another and are each centred on a core bank; the keiretsu system helps insulate company managements from stock market fluctuations and take-over attempts, allowing long-term planning and engagement in innovative projects; it is a key element of the automotive industry in Japan

horizontally opposed engine *noun* engine with horizontally opposed cylinders, set on either side of the crankshaft

horn *noun* instrument on a vehicle that emits a loud warning noise, usually by means of a diaphragm vibrated by an electromagnet; (*compare* AIR HORN); **horn boss** *or* **horn button** = relatively large, round pad in the

centre of the steering wheel which sounds the horn when depressed; **horn button** = (i) relatively small button on the end of the direction indicator lever which sounds the horn when depressed; (ii) horn boss

horsepower (h.p. *or* **HP)** *noun* unit of power

COMMENT: one horsepower is the power required to raise 550 pounds one foot in one second, often expressed as its electrical equivalent, 745.7 watts - which is one brake horsepower

horsepower screw *noun* screw in the cover of adjustable wastegates to adjust spring height, which adjusts boost pressure; screwing down adds HP but may destroy the engine

hose *noun* flexible pipe

◇ **hose clip** *US* **hose clamp** *noun* adjustable steel band (or wire) for securing rubber hoses to metal pipes; **hose clip installer** = special tool for the installation of ear-type clips, used e.g. on some types of CV joint boots, filters, cooling systems, and vacuum lines; **hose clip pliers** = special tool used to remove and install hose clips

COMMENT: hose clips are tightened by spring tension of the clip - as in single-wire clips, by worm screws - as in worm-gear clips, or by screws - as in strap-and-bolt clips

hose pinch-off pliers *noun* special tool to pinch off hoses when servicing the cooling system; pivoting jaws squeeze hoses shut so there is no need to drain the system

Hotchkiss drive *noun* type of live rear axle suspension in which leaf springs absorb the drive torque; (*compare* TORQUE TUBE DRIVE)

hot dip *verb* to coat metal parts by immersion in molten metal, such as tin or zinc *hot-dip zinc coat* **hot-dip aluminizing** = deposition of aluminium coatings by hot dipping; **hot-dip galvanize** = to apply a zinc coating by hot dipping *hot-dip(ped) galvanized steel*

hot gas welding *noun* welding process involving the joining of thermoplastic materials by softening with a jet of hot air, then joining them at the softened points

hot hatch *noun* high-performance hatchback

◇ **hot rod** *noun* car that has been radically modified for increased power

hot sparking plug *noun* sparking plug with a long insulator nose, which absorbs more heat and dissipates it slowly (NOTE: opposite is **cold sparking plug**) *(compare* HEAT RANGE)

hot spot *noun* point of contact below the carburettor, between the inlet manifold and exhaust manifold; *(compare* HEAT RISER)

COMMENT: vaporization of the air/fuel mixture in the inlet manifold is promoted by the heat from the exhaust gases in the exhaust manifold

hot spraying *noun* spray process in which paint is preheated in a paint container so that its viscosity is reduced and it can be atomized without being diluted with a solvent

hot start(ing) *noun* starting a hot engine may be difficult if it has been stopped for a few minutes; the accumulation of petrol vapour in the air filter and inlet manifold, caused by the rise in engine temperature when left standing when hot, can be dissipated by slowly pressing the accelerator right down and turning the engine over until it fires; **hot start enrichment** = fuel mixture enrichment when starting a hot engine; **hot-start pulse relay** = fuel injection component which operates the cold-start valve intermittently to improve starting when the engine is hot; installed in the cold-start valve circuit in some CIS-equipped engines

COMMENT: in Lucas fuel injection systems, hot start enrichment is utilised when the fuel in the fuel rail is too hot to provide a suitable mixture for combustion

hot wax *noun* wax-based material used for hot-wax flooding; **hot-wax flooding** = special cavity-sealing process developed by Volkswagen, which uses a solvent-free wax injected into the cavities of bodies preheated to 60°C; **hot-wax flooding unit** = unit for hot-wax flooding consisting of a preheating zone, a flooding zone and a drip-off zone

hot-wire airflow meter *noun* constant-temperature hot-wire sensing device, used in electronic fuel injection systems, which measures the rate of a mass airflow into the engine by measuring the current needed to keep the hot wire at the same temperature; **hot-wire element** = element in a hot-wire air-flow meter

housing *noun* general term for the casing which encloses or supports bearings, gears, etc.

h.p. *or* **HP** = HORSEPOWER

HSDI *(short for)* high speed direct injection (diesel engine)

HT = HIGH-TENSION; **HT circuit** = SECONDARY CIRCUIT; **HT lead** = SPARKING PLUG LEAD; **HT outlet** = COIL TOWER

hub *noun* central part of any wheel, by which the wheel is attached to or rotatable on a shaft or axle; **hub cap** = **(a)** cover over the wheel hub and bearings **(b)** small metal cap on a front wheel bearing; **hub carrier** = **(a)** part of the suspension system which carries a rear wheel hub on a front-wheel drive vehicle, or on a rear-wheel drive vehicle with independent rear suspension **(b)** = STEERING SWIVEL; **hub plate** = central element of a clutch driven plate which carries the splined hub; **hub puller** = special tool, of both jaw and slide hammer design, used to remove wheel hubs on vehicles by a pulling action

◇ **hubcentric fit** *noun* spigot mounted wheel

HUD = HEAD-UP DISPLAY

humidifying tower *noun* air saturator tower in salt spray test chambers

◇ **humidity chamber** *noun* test chamber for simulating tropical and subtropical conditions

hump *noun* raised portion on the rim bead seat of passenger car wheels, retaining the beads of an insufficiently inflated tubeless tyre on the bead seats, thereby preventing the tyre beads from jumping into the rim well; *(compare* HUMP RIM, SAFETY BEAD SEAT, SAFETY RIM) *(see illustration 33)*

◇ **hump mode** *noun* operating condition where the transmitted torque in a viscous coupling rises to a value several times higher than the value produced in the so-called viscous mode, due to internal clamping, i.e. metal friction of the coupling discs; *(compare* VISCOUS MODE)

◇ **hump rim** *noun* designation for a rim featuring a safety contour (round hump, flat hump, combination hump) either on the outer or on both bead seats; this protection is particularly important with tubeless tyres, where sudden deflation can occur if the tyre beads leave the bead seats and drop into the well; *(compare* HUMP, SAFETY BEAD SEAT)

hundredweight (cwt) *noun* (obsolete) unit of weight measurement, used in some classic-car manuals (NOTE: 1 (GB) cwt = 5080 grams; 1 (US) cwt = 4535 grams)

hunting *noun* uneven running of an engine, due to air/fuel mixture being too rich

◊ **hunting tooth** *noun* extra, odd tooth on a gearwheel, designed to ensure the same teeth do not always mesh together, thus reducing wear

HVAC *(short for)* heating, ventilation and air conditioning (system)

hybrid car *noun* car with a hybrid propulsion system

◊ **hybrid propulsion** *noun* two distinct but interdependent forms of propulsion, such as an electric motor and an internal combustion engine, or an electric motor with battery and fuel cells for energy storage

◊ **hybrid technology** *noun* film circuits combined with integrated circuits, used especially for trigger boxes or electronic control units

Hydragas suspension *noun* = HYDROPNEUMATIC SUSPENSION

hydraulic *adjective* operated by fluid

◊ **hydraulic accumulator** *noun* = ACCUMULATOR (c)

◊ **hydraulic actuators** *noun* hydraulically operated struts which control the movement of the wheels in an active ride suspension system

◊ **hydraulic brakes** *or* **hydraulic braking system** *noun* brakes operated by hydraulic pressure; **hydraulic brake booster** = hydraulic pressure supplied by the power steering pump, or a separate hydraulic pump, which is used to assist in applying the brakes; used on cars and on some lorries

◊ **hydraulic control block** *noun* = CONTROL VALVE ASSEMBLY

◊ **hydraulic fluid** *noun* special oil used in hydraulic systems, such as power steering,

self-levelling suspension, to operate the system of master and slave cylinders; *(compare* BRAKE FLUID, AUTOMATIC TRANSMISSION FLUID)

◊ **hydraulic hood** *noun* convertible top which is raised and lowered by a hydraulic system; depending on engineering, a hydraulic hood can operate fast, silently, and with tremendous power; *(compare* POWER HOOD, TENSILE FORCE)

◊ **hydraulic modulator** *noun* device which regulates hydraulic fluid pressure in an ABS

◊ **hydraulic pressure pump** *noun* engine-driven pump which supplies oil under pressure to operate, e.g. power brakes or power- assisted steering

◊ **hydraulic tappet** *US* **hydraulic valve filter** *noun* small component in the valve train, usually between camshaft and valve, or rocker arm and valve, which maintains zero valve clearance by automatically expanding when a clearance develops; uses the hydraulic principle that liquids cannot be compressed and consists basically of a small check valve, piston and cylinder; *(see illustration 6)*

◊ **hydraulic wedge** *noun* hydraulic jack with ends designed to reach behind dented double panels and to press them back into shape by the hydraulic action of the wedge-shaped ends

hydroactive suspension *noun* = HYDROPNEUMATIC SUSPENSION

hydrocarbon plastics *noun* plastics based on resins made by the polymerization of monomers composed of carbon and hydrogen only

◊ **hydrocarbons (HC)** *noun* generic term for chemical compounds composed only of carbon and hydrogen; one of the three major pollutants in the exhaust of SI engines

hydrodynamic clutch *noun* = FLUID COUPLING

◊ **hydrodynamic torque converter** *noun* = TORQUE CONVERTER

hydrogen embrittlement *noun* process which results in a decrease of the toughness or ductility of a metal due to absorption of hydrogen

Hydrolastic suspension *noun* proprietary suspension system incorporating a conical rubber spring compressed by hydraulic pressure; this system also provides a hydraulic interconnection between front and rear wheels on one side of the vehicle

hydrometer *noun* instrument used (i) to determine the percentage of charge in each cell of a car battery by checking the electrolyte specific gravity; (ii) to test the coolant for the strength of antifreeze

COMMENT: a hydrometer for (i) is available in a ball-type or float-type design and consists of an acid-resistant tube and suction bulb to draw the electrolyte into the tube; the number of balls floating (ball-type) or liquid surface (float-type) gives a direct reading of the specific gravity and the state of charge. A hydrometer for (ii) contains a built-in thermometer to read the antifreeze solution temperature, thus compensating for external temperature variations; it features a tube and bulb for extracting the coolant. The coolant causes a number of balls inside the tube to float; a scale gives a direct reading of antifreeze protection by converting the number of balls floating into strength of antifreeze

hydropneumatic suspension *noun* suspension system using air or gas (nitrogen) under pressure as the primary suspension material, separated from the actuating hydraulic fluid by a diaphragm within a spherical suspension unit

hydropulser *noun* hydraulically operated system that can excite vibrations of various frequencies in a car; serves to find and eliminate noise sources

hydrostatic drive *noun* = HYDROSTATIC TRANSMISSION

◇ **hydrostatic steering** *noun* entirely hydraulic power steering system without mechanical steering links

◇ **hydrostatic test** *noun* pressure test using water

◇ **hydrostatic transmission** *noun* drive by means of hydraulic motors, particularly where the drive is to each wheel of an off-road vehicle

hygroscopic *adjective* tending to absorb moisture

hypoid axle *noun* driving axle with a hypoid gear

◇ **hypoid gear** *noun* type of gear cut in a spiral form where the axes of the driving and driven shafts are at right angles, but not in the same plane; *(compare* SPIRAL BEVEL GEAR)

◇ **hypoid oil** *noun* special lubricant for hypoid gears

Ii

i *(short for)* injection - indicating that the engine is fuel-injected *GTi, EFi, 1.6i*

I&C systems *(short for)* instrumentation and control systems

I-beam *noun* steel beam which in cross section has the shape of an I; **I-beam axle** = RIGID AXLE

ICE = IN-CAR ENTERTAINMENT

IC engine *noun* = INTERNAL COMBUSTION ENGINE

ice scraper *noun* small plastic implement for scraping frost and ice away from windscreens and windows

ID = INSIDE DIAMETER

identical part *noun* = SHARED COMPONENT

identification colour *noun* *(fuse)* particular colour for a specific amperage

IDI = INTEGRATED DIRECT IGNITION (SYSTEM)

idle *verb (engine)* to run slowly with closed throttle and usually with transmission disengaged *start the engine and allow it to idle for 5 minutes (compare* TICK OVER)

◊ **idle air jet** *noun* hole in a fixed-jet carburettor through which air is drawn into the idle system

◊ **idle jet** *noun* carburettor jet within the idle system which supplies a constant amount of fuel for the formation of the idle mixture

idle mixture adjustment screw *noun* tapered adjusting screw (on some carburettors) which controls the volume of air/fuel mixture supplied by the idle system of a fixed-jet carburettor *(see illustration 11)*

COMMENT: turning the screw clockwise results in a leaner mixture, and turning anticlockwise gives a richer mixture

idler *noun* **(a)** gearwheel between a driving and a driven gear in a gear train which may serve to reverse the original direction of rotation of the driven wheel **(b)** free-turning pulley or wheel which serves to maintain tension in a belt drive

◊ **idler arm** *noun (steering system)* similar to the drop arm, but located at the other end of the relay rod, and having a guiding function only; *(see illustration 25)*

◊ **idler pulley** *noun* spring-loaded pulley designed to maintain the tension of the timing belt

◊ **idle speed** *or* **idling speed** *noun* slowest speed at which an engine will run smoothly (about 900 rpm); *(compare* FAST IDLE); **idle speed adjustment** = alteration of the engine tick-over *the idle speed adjustment should always be done with the engine at operating temperature* **idle speed stabilizer** = device which ensures steady engine rpm at idle speed

◊ **idle stop valve** *noun* solenoid-operated valve which cuts off fuel in the idle system of a carburettor and so stops the engine running-on when the ignition is switched off; *(see illustration 11)*

◊ **idle system** *noun* at idle speed, the throttle valve is closed to such an extent that the airflow underneath the plunger no longer forms a sufficient vacuum; the fuel is then supplied via an auxiliary system, the idle system, which consists of the idle jet, the idle air jet and the mixture control screw

◊ **idling** *(engine) noun* turning over at low speed with minimum throttle; **idling circuit** = the passages, jets, etc. in a fixed-jet carburettor which provide idling mixture to the carburettor barrel; **idling drag** = forward motion of a vehicle with automatic transmission, with engine at idle and selector lever in position D (NOTE: also called **creep**)

IFS = INDEPENDENT FRONT SUSPENSION

ignite *verb* to set fire to; to catch fire *the air/fuel mixture is ignited; the air/fuel mixture ignites*

◇ **igniter** *noun (air bag)* bridge igniter with detonator

◇ **ignition** *noun* process which initiates the combustion of the compressed air/fuel mixture in the combustion chamber. In a spark-ignition engine, the mixture is ignited by an electric spark; in a diesel engine, the self-igniting mixture must be preheated by glow plugs when a cold start is performed; *(compare* IGNITION SYSTEM)

◇ **ignition advance** *noun* extent to which the ignition spark is made to occur earlier (NOTE: opposite is **ignition retard)** *(compare* IGNITION TIMING)

◇ **ignition amplifier** *noun* device used to increase the electrical signal in an electronic ignition system

◇ **ignition angle** *noun* angle, measured in degrees crankshaft, by which the ignition is advanced

◇ **ignition cable** *or* **ignition lead** *noun* general term to designate the high-voltage cables of the ignition system, from the ignition coil to the distributor and from the distributor to the sparking plugs

◇ **ignition capacitor** *noun* electrical part which interrupts the primary current with low loss and suppresses most of the arcing between the contact breaker points in conventional coil ignitions

◇ **ignition circuits** *see* PRIMARY CIRCUIT, SECONDARY CIRCUIT

◇ **ignition coil** *noun* = COIL (a); **ignition coil resistor** = BALLAST RESISTOR

◇ **ignition control unit** *noun* general control unit of electronic ignition systems, usually with current and dwell angle control, driver and output stage, in some cases with electronic spark timing functions; *(compare* ELECTRONIC CONTROL UNIT)

◇ **ignition delay** *noun* time lag between ignition triggering and the production of a spark

◇ **ignition disabler** *noun* standard feature of car alarm systems

◇ **ignition file** *noun* tool for filing ignition points and other small objects (NOTE: also called **contact file, magneto file, points file)**

◇ **ignition gauge** *noun* blade or wire-type feeler gauge used to check gaps on ignition systems, such as air gaps between permanent magnet and trigger wheel on electric ignitions

◇ **ignition key** *noun* key used to switch on the ignition

◇ **ignition lag** *noun* in a diesel engine, the time lag between fuel injection and combustion

◇ **ignition lead** *noun* = IGNITION CABLE

ignition map *noun* electronic map stored in the electronic control unit of ignitions with electronic spark timing and containing the most favourable ignition angle/ignition point for every operating point of the engine

COMMENT: spark timing is optimized on the basis of fuel type and consumption, torque, exhaust gas, knock limit, engine temperature, etc.

ignition module *noun* = IGNITION CONTROL UNIT

◇ **ignition oscilloscope** *noun* oscilloscope used especially for ignition tune-ups; usually integrated in an engine tester

◇ **ignition pattern** *noun* display of the waveforms in the primary or secondary circuit of an ignition system in the firing order of the engine; optionally parade or display pattern and stacked or raster pattern

◇ **ignition point** *noun* **(a)** moment of spark firing **(b)** = CONTACT BREAKER POINT; **ignition point file** = IGNITION FILE

◇ **ignition retard** *noun* ignition after top dead centre

◇ **ignition switch** *noun* actuated with the ignition key, the ignition switch closes the primary circuit of the ignition system

ignition system *noun* subsystem of the spark ignition engine, its basic elements being the battery, the ignition switch, the ignition coil, the distributor, the sparking plugs, and the connecting cables; *(compare* ENGINE MANAGEMENT SYSTEM, DISTRIBUTORLESS IGNITION SYSTEM)

COMMENT: the distributor transfers the high voltage induced in the ignition coil to the sparking plugs in the firing order of the engine. From the conventional coil ignition with a a mechanical contact breaker to breakerless transistorized ignition systems and ignitions with electronic spark timing, the evolution shows that individual functions are performed by electronic components to an increasing extent

ignition temperature *noun* = FLASH POINT

ignition timing *noun* maintenance work performed at idle by means of a timing light, to align the timing marks of the engine

COMMENT: speed- and load-dependent ignition timing is achieved by mechanical spark advance mechanisms such as a centrifugal and vacuum advance mechanism or electronically by means of an ignition map

ignition toolkit *noun* set of small tools usually comprising 8 small open-ended spanners (sizes: 3/16 - 7/16 in), a feeler gauge, a small screwdriver and a points file

◇ **ignition transformer** *noun* transforms the primary voltage resulting from the capacitor discharge to the required high voltage

◇ **ignition transistor** *noun* transistor that switches the primary current of a transistorized ignition system

◇ **ignition voltage** *noun* the voltage at which the spark jumps across the electrodes; 30,000 V are quite common today

I-head *noun* US = OVERHEAD VALVE ENGINE

IHP = INDICATED HORSEPOWER

illuminated *adjective* lit up; **illuminated entry system** = additional courtesy lighting system which illuminates the door entry area when the door is ajar; consists usually of lights in the lower door panels and footwells

◇ **illumination control** *noun* = DIMMER CONTROL

imbalance *noun* lack of balance due to uneven weight distribution; *(compare* BALANCE)

COMMENT: improper wheel balance due to uneven weight distribution on the tyre and wheel assembly is one of the most common causes of vibration. When one side of the tyre and wheel assembly is heavier than the other, centrifugal forces try to throw the heavy area outwards as the wheel turns

IMEP = INDICATED MEAN EFFECTIVE PRESSURE

IMI INSTITUTE OF THE MOTOR INDUSTRY British organization for managers in the motor industry

immerse *verb* to dip into or submerge in a liquid

immobile *adjective* unable to move

◇ **immobilize** *verb* to make immobile

◇ **immobilizer** *noun* device that makes something immobile (such as a wheel clamp)

impact *noun* sudden, hard, physical contact; **impact absorber** = an impact-damping element located between bumper and bumper mounting to keep impact energy from propagating into the car body; **impact cushion** = some child seats secure the child by an impact cushion in addition to the seat belt or straps; **impact damage** = damage to the tyre wall caused by contact with the kerb or deep pothole, etc.; **impact pipe** = simplified version of an impact absorber; **impact sensor** = CRASH SENSOR; **impact strength** = ability of a material to resist shock loading strain; **impact stress** = force per unit area imposed on a material by an abruptly applied force

◇ **impact adhesive** *noun* contact glue that provides adhesion when two coated surfaces are pressed together

impact resistance test *noun* determination of the resistance to breakage by flexural shock of plastics, as indicated by the energy extracted from 'standardized' pendulum-type hammers, mounted in standard machines, in breaking standard specimens with one pendulum swing; **impact-resistant** = stiffened (to a certain degree) to resist the force of a collision

COMMENT: the standard tests for these methods require specimens made with a milled notch. In the Charpy and Izod tests, the notch produces a stress concentration which promotes a brittle, rather than a ductile, fracture

impact screwdriver *noun* tool which features a mechanism that converts the impact from a hammer into a powerful torque for loosening (or tightening) threaded fasteners

impact socket *noun* heavy duty socket for use with air or electric power impact tools; **impact swivel ball universal joint** = the swivel ball type universal joint is the most common type for use with impact sockets; **impact wrench** = pneumatic or electric tool for use with impact sockets

COMMENT: impact sockets are designed to stand up to the extreme stress of these tools and can be used in combination with special impact accessories such as extensions, universal joints, and adapters. These accessories are also designed to withstand the stress of air or electric power impact tools

impeller *noun* **(a)** rotating member of a centrifugal pump which is equipped with vanes to convert mechanical energy into fluid energy *it is essential to adapt the type of impeller to the liquid being handled* **(b)** *(fluid coupling or torque converter)* driving member connected to the crankshaft via drive plate and converter cover which generates the fluid flow inside the converter; *(compare* STATOR (c))

◊ **impeller eye** *noun (pump)* inlet area of an impeller

◊ **impeller pump** *noun* centrifugal and side-channel pump

imperial gallon *noun* UK gallon

impermeable *or* **impervious** *adjective* not capable of being permeated, especially by fluids; **impervious to gases** = not allowing the passage of gas

inboard *adjective* located near the vehicle centre rather than at the outside; **inboard brakes** *or* **discs** = brakes mounted on the inner end of drive shafts (a) rather than at the wheel hub; **inboard starter** = Bendix starter; *(compare* OUTBOARD)

in-car entertainment (ICE) *noun* car audio system, typically consisting of a radio/cassette player and perhaps a CD player

COMMENT: the term also includes CB radio, and TV and video on coaches or in the sleeping section of a lorry cab

incipient crack *noun* crack which has just started to form

incline **1** *noun* slope **2** *verb* to slope; **inclined engine** = in-line engine in which the cylinders are inclined to the vertical (NOTE: informally called **sloper)**

◊ **inclinometer** *noun* = CLINOMETER

incomplete thread *noun* thread with incomplete thread profile

increased shank *noun* shank diameter greater than thread diameter

◊ **increasing adapter** *noun* adapter whose male end for the socket is bigger than

the female end for the drive handle (NOTE: opposite is **reducing adapter)**

in-dash gauge *noun* gauge mounted in the instrument panel

indentation *noun* concentrated panel damage or specific dent that may be caused when the car hits a relatively small obstacle, i.e. the towbar of another car; **indentation hardness** = resistance of a metal (or plastic) surface to indentation when subjected to pressure by a hard pointed or rounded tool

independent suspension *noun* separate suspension system for any of the wheels; **independent front suspension (IFS)** = system in which each front wheel is sprung independently; **independent rear suspension (IRS)** = system in which each rear wheel is sprung independently

indicated horsepower (IHP) *noun* theoretical power of an engine calculated from the MEP in the cylinders rather than at the shaft

COMMENT: IHP includes BHP plus the power lost to friction, and pumping needed for the induction of the fuel and air charge into the engine and the expulsion of combustion gases

indicated mean effective pressure (IMEP) *noun* average pressure within an engine cylinder during a working cycle, calculated from an indicator diagram

indicator *noun* **(a)** instrument for recording engine cylinder pressure; **indicator diagram** = cylinder pressure chart, plotted against the working cycle of a piston or engine **(b)** = DIRECTION INDICATOR

◊ **indicator (light)** *noun* lamp on an instrument panel that lights up to show the operation of something, especially the illuminated arrow that indicates the direction in which a vehicle is about to turn *main beam indicator, battery charge indicator (compare* WARNING LIGHT)

indirect damage *noun* type of damage not caused by immediate impact but by the spread of the impact force into other areas of the body, e.g. bulging or dents at the rear of the front wing and the leading edge of the door in the case of direct accident damage to the front edge of the front wing (NOTE: opposite is **direct damage)**

◇ **indirect injection** *noun* fuel injection not into the main combustion chamber but into some kind of prechamber; injection pressures are lower than with direct injection and ignition lag is short; **indirect injection engine** = diesel engine using indirect injection (NOTE: US English is **precombustion engine**)

indium *noun* metallic element (NOTE: symbol is **In**; atomic number is **49**)

induce *verb* to cause *or* to bring about; **to induce a voltage** = to produce a voltage by electromagnetic induction

induction *noun* intake of air and fuel through the carburettor, inlet manifold and inlet ports into the combustion chamber

◇ **induction manifold** *noun* = INLET MANIFOLD

◇ **induction noise** *noun* noise caused by the intake of air by an engine at full throttle

◇ **induction period** *noun* period during the charge changing process of the engine that allows for the intake of the fresh charge into the cylinder while the inlet control, i.e. the valve or port, remains open

◇ **induction pipe** *noun* the duct, typically an alloy manifold, between throttle and cylinder head; the absolute pressure in the induction pipe, the so-called intake vacuum, is indicative of engine load and is used to control many engine-related functions; (*compare* INLET MANIFOLD)

◇ **induction port** *noun* (*2-stroke engines*) the port in the cylinder wall used for admission of the fresh charge into the cylinder; (*compare* INLET PORT)

◇ **induction stroke** *noun* that phase of the 4-stroke cycle during which the inlet valve is open and the piston descends from TDC to BDC, drawing air (in a diesel engine) or an air/fuel mixture (in a SI engine) into the cylinder (NOTE: US English is **intake stroke**)

◇ **induction system** *noun* part of the fuel system in a SI engine, including air filter, carburettor or injectors, inlet manifold, inlet ports and valves

◇ **induction-type pulse generator** *noun* = MAGNETIC PICK-UP (ASSEMBLY)

inductive ignition system *noun* ignition system where the primary energy is stored in an inductor or an ignition coil; (*compare* COIL IGNITION SYSTEM)

◇ **inductive (pulse) pick-up** *noun* = MAGNETIC PICK-UP ASSEMBLY

◇ **inductive winding** *noun* = PICK-UP COIL

inert *adjective* lacking a chemical action; property of the separators used between the plates of a battery

inert arc welding *noun* a family of arc welding processes in the fusion welding category

> COMMENT: the welding pool is surrounded by a layer of inert shielding gas to keep oxygen from the weld; TIG welding is a typical inert arc welding process and is mainly used for repair work

inertia drive *noun* = BENDIX DRIVE; **inertia pinion** = pinion used in an inertia drive

◇ **inertia fuel cut-off switch** *noun* = FUEL PUMP SHUT-OFF SWITCH

inertia reel seat belt *noun* 3-point seat belt with an automatic retractor reel

> COMMENT: this type of seat belt allows the wearer to move whilst the vehicle is stationary or in steady motion but locks to restrain the wearer on sudden deceleration or impact

infant safety seat *noun* = BABY SEAT

infinitely variable transmission *noun* = CONTINUOUSLY VARIABLE TRANSMISSION

inflammable *adjective* capable of being easily ignited and of burning quickly

inflate *verb* to fill with air

◇ **inflation control seam** a system of inflation control seams on advanced air bags to control the inflation speed and inflation characteristics (NOTE: also called **tear seam,** whose negative connotations are perhaps inappropriate in a safety-related context)

◇ **inflation pressure** *noun* = TYRE PRESSURE

inflator (unit) *noun* assembly beneath the folded air bag, consisting of a combustion chamber with a bridge igniter, a detonator and a priming charge surrounded by the solid propellant, and a metal filter

COMMENT: a signal from the trigger unit causes the bridge igniter to fire the detonator, which in turn fires the priming charge and then the solid propellant. The nitrogen thus generated flows through a metal filter and reaches the air bag cleaned and cooled

infrared radiant drier *noun* infrared lamp which accelerates the drying of large areas of fresh paint

◊ **infrared (IR) remote control** *noun* the control of an operation by means of an infrared beam transmitted to a receiver (e.g. garage door, central locking, car alarm system, etc.)

ingress *noun* entry *PVC sealant is applied to the critical seams on a car's underfloor pan and wheel arches to prevent the ingress of moisture*

inhibit *verb* to hinder *or* to prevent *the ability of chromates to inhibit corrosion of ferrous and non-ferrous metals by water has long been known*

◊ **inhibitor** *noun* additive which retards or prevents an undesirable reaction, e.g. phosphates, anti-oxidants (NOTE: opposite is **catalyst (a)**)

inject (with) *verb* to introduce a fluid (into something) under pressure *the box sections in the lower part of the body shell are injected with wax*

◊ **injected engine** *noun* = FUEL-INJECTED ENGINE

◊ **injection-moulded** *adjective* produced by an injection moulding machine or process; **injection moulding machine** = machine used to produce preformed plastic body panels

injection period *noun* the length of time for which fuel is sprayed into the inlet ports or combustion chamber during fuel injection

COMMENT: controlled by the electronic control unit, the injection period depends mainly on engine speed and the amount of induced air and is normally between approx. 1.5 and 9 milliseconds

injection pump *noun* pump which receives fuel from the fuel tank (often through the fuel-feed pump in the case of diesel engines) and delivers it under pressure to the injectors

injector *noun* precision-made device for spraying fuel into the inlet ports or combustion chamber; **injector nozzle** = tip of the injector, either of multi-hole design for direct injection or pintle design for indirect injection; *(see illustration 5)*

COMMENT: in a CIS, the injectors atomize the continuous flow of fuel injected under pressure into the inlet ports of the engine; a valve in the injector nozzle stops the flow of fuel when fuel pressure drops below a certain point; in a CIS, the quantity of fuel is regulated by the fuel distributor's metering unit; in other fuel injection systems, the fuel system delivers a constant supply of fuel at a constant pressure to the injector, and an electronic sensing and control system produces electrical current pulses of appropriate duration to hold open the injector solenoid valves; as fuel pressure is held constant, varying the pulse duration increases or decreases the amount of fuel passed through the injectors

inlet cam(shaft) *noun* the cam responsible for the actuation of the inlet valve in DOHC engines; *(see illustrations 3, 4, 6)*

◊ **inlet line** *noun* pipe or hose on the intake side of a component, through which a fluid is supplied by gravity from a reservoir or tank located at a higher level; e.g. from coolant expansion tank to radiator, or from brake fluid reservoir to master brake cylinder

◊ **inlet manifold** *US* **intake manifold** *noun* the component which guides the intake air to the cylinder head inlet ports; usually an aluminium casting or a GRP moulding, with one inlet opening and as many outlets as there are cylinders in the engine; *(see illustrations 3, 5, 14)*; **inlet manifold heater** = FLAME GLOW PLUG

inlet over exhaust engine (IOE engine) *noun* engine design used on early cars (NOTE: also called **F-head engine**)

COMMENT: inlet and exhaust valves are arranged vertically in a lateral chamber of the combustion chamber and face one another; the side valve (usually the exhaust) is actuated directly by the camshaft, which usually rotates in the cylinder block; the overhead valve (usually the inlet) is located in the cylinder head and actuated via a pushrod and rocker arm

inlet port *US* **intake port** *noun* (of 4-stroke engines) part of the intake system inside the cylinder head, from the inlet manifold flange to the valve ports of the combustion chamber; *(compare* INDUCTION PORT) *(see illustration 6)*

◊ **inlet stroke** *noun* = INDUCTION STROKE

◇ **inlet tract** *noun* a branch of the inlet manifold leading to an inlet port

◇ **inlet valve** *US* **intake valve** *noun* in 4-stroke IC engines, usually a poppet valve, located in the cylinder head, operated directly or indirectly by a camshaft; the inlet valve is usually larger and (on used engines) cleaner than the exhaust valve; it is only open during the induction stroke; *(see illustrations 3, 6)*; **inlet valve closes (IVC)** = mark on a valve-timing diagram; **inlet valve opens (IVO)** = mark on a valve-timing diagram; *(compare* EVC, EVO)

in-line engine *noun* multi-cylinder engine, usually with three or more cylinders that are arranged parallel to one another and are either mounted vertically or at an angle (sloper engine) in one single line; the pistons that reciprocate in these cylinders in turn drive a common crankshaft *in-line four-cylinder engine* (NOTE: also called **straight engine)**

◇ **in-line power steering** *noun* power-assisted steering applied within the steering box or rack

◇ **in-line pump** *noun* pump whose suction and discharge branches are arranged in line for direct installation into the pipework; special foundations are unnecessary, and the absence of shaft couplings eliminates alignment problems

inner attachment face *noun* the part of the brake disc directly fixed to the wheel hub

◇ **inner cone** *noun* small, innermost part of the flame at the tip of a blowtorch, the shape of which indicates the torch adjustment

◇ **inner cylinder** *noun* working chamber of a double-tube shock absorber

◇ **inner dead centre** *see* TOP DEAD CENTRE

◇ **inner headlight** *noun* the inner one of twin headlights (as for BMWs or the Jaguar XJ series); usually for main beam only (NOTE: opposite is **outer headlight)**

◇ **inner liner** *noun* innermost layer of a tubeless tyre which provides an airtight barrier; *(see illustration 32)*

◇ **inner mounting face** *noun* = INNER ATTACHMENT FACE

◇ **inner race** *noun* inner track of a ball bearing

◇ **inner sill** *noun* hidden part of the sill located behind the outer sill panel, which

serves to reinforce the underbody (NOTE: often referred to as the **longitudinal member** or **side member)** *(see illustration 2)*

◇ **innerspring seat** *noun* sturdy, sofa-like seat design using spring coils as damping elements; used mainly by Mercedes-Benz

◇ **inner tube** *noun* inflatable rubber tube inside a tyre (NOTE: nearly all modern tyres are tubeless)

◇ **inner wing panels** *noun* vertical panels mounted to the left and right of the engine bay that provide the mounting flanges for the wings and the top suspension attachment

inorganic *adjective* pertaining to or composed of chemical compounds which do not contain carbon as the principal element, i.e., matter which does not come from plants or animals (NOTE: opposite is **organic)**

input shaft *noun* = CLUTCH SHAFT

◇ **input variable** *noun* the object of measurement and control; e.g. pressure, temperature, etc.

insert *noun* technique of permanently joining plastics and other materials, e.g. embedding steel clips in a moulded plastic cover

> COMMENT: moulded-in inserts are placed into the injection mould cavity so that the melt flows around them during injection; post-moulding inserts may be installed by press-fit or ultrasonic methods

insert socket *noun* socket for use with a slogging ring wrench which raises the wrench above the surface, thus preventing hammer damage to floor or equipment

inside caliper *noun* machinists' caliper used to check inside dimensions

◇ **inside diameter (ID)** *noun* the internal diameter of a cylinder or tube

inside pry spoon *noun* specialized pry bar designed to reach behind brackets and reinforcing bars to pry the metal

> COMMENT: the pointed end of the inside pry spoon is placed at the high point of a dent, which is then forced out

inside spring caliper *noun* inside caliper with spring for accurate setting

insolation *noun* exposure to the rays of the sun

inspection *noun* type of examination which serves to evaluate the operating condition of a component or system; the inspection may identify the need for servicing or repair; *(see also* MOT TEST); **inspection lamp** = mains-powered lamp with a long lead, used in garages to inspect the underside of cars and under the bonnet; **inspection lot** = certain quantity of a particular item chosen at random for quality testing; **inspection mirror** = tool used to inspect hidden areas on automotive parts; **inspection pit** = pit in the floor of a garage providing working space underneath a vehicle

install *verb* to put something in position ready for use

◊ **installation** *noun* putting something in position ready for use (NOTE: opposite is **removal)**

◊ **installed height** *noun* height at which something is placed in position *the installed height of the valve springs must not exceed 820 mm*

instant spare *noun* = EMERGENCY INFLATOR

Institute of the Motor Industry (IMI) British organization for managers in the motor industry

instrument cluster *noun* **(a)** array of separate gauges in one housing; a major component of the instrument panel including analogue or digital instruments and indicators, but no controls except for the trip mileage reset button on some cars **(b)** several gauges integrated into one instrument, making one unit combining several functions, e.g. engine temperature, oil pressure and fuel gauge; if one gauge fails, the entire instrument cluster must be replaced

◊ **instrument panel** *noun* panel below the windscreen which accommodates the instruments and controls *the instrument panel is commendably uncluttered or is trimmed in leather* (NOTE: also called **dash, dashboard, fascia)**

◊ **instruments and controls** *noun* general term covering all gauges, indicators, switches, regulators, and buttons

insulate *verb* to cover with non-conducting material, so as to prevent the transmission of heat, electricity or sound

◊ **insulating cap** *noun* insulated top of the coil tower

◊ **insulating tape** *noun* PVC tape for wrapping round electrical connections

◊ **insulation** *noun* **(a)** the process of insulating **(b)** the material used for insulating

◊ **insulator** *noun* **(a)** material without free electrons which, therefore, is a poor conductor of electricity; *(see illustration 36)* (NOTE: opposite is **conductor) (b)** = SPARKING PLUG INSULATOR; **insulator nose** *or* **tip** = the tip of a sparking plug

insurance premium *noun* regular payment for an insurance policy *after an unprecedented wave of car thefts, insurance premiums are set to rise substantially*

intake manifold *noun US* = INLET MANIFOLD

◊ **intake pipe** *noun* = INDUCTION PIPE

◊ **intake plenum** *noun* = PLENUM CHAMBER

◊ **intake port** *noun US* = INLET PORT

◊ **intake stroke** *noun US* = INDUCTION STROKE

◊ **intake valve** *noun US* = INLET VALVE

integral *adjective* forming part of a whole

◊ **integral body and frame construction** *noun* = UNITARY CONSTRUCTION

◊ **integral colour anodizing** *noun* anodizing process in which the colour is produced by using special electrolytes

◊ **integral moulded seat** *noun* seat with integrated 3-point seat belt

◊ **integral-type power (assisted) steering** *noun* = IN-LINE POWER STEERING

◊ **integrated child (safety) seat** *noun* rear seat that can be converted into a child seat

◊ **Integrated Direct Ignition (IDI) system** *noun* distributorless ignition system consisting of two separate ignition coils, an ignition module, a secondary conductor housing mounted to an aluminium cover plate, a crankshaft sensor, and electronic spark timing

inter-axle differential *noun* = CENTRE DIFFERENTIAL

◇ **inter-cell link** *noun* electric conductor that carries electric current between the adjacent cells of a battery

interchangeable head torque wrench *noun* wrench that does not have the usual square drive for use with sockets, but is designed to accept special interchangeable heads

intercoat adhesion failure *noun* situation in which one coat of finish peels off or can easily be stripped off with masking tape from another layer underneath

COMMENT: this may be caused by excessive bake time of coatings, resulting in too hard a finish, poor flatting of coats, providing poor keying of coats, or very low film thickness

intercooler *noun* heat exchanger of the air-to-air or air-to-water type which lowers the charge air temperature to obtain higher air density and better volumetric efficiency; *(compare* AFTERCOOLER)

◇ **intercooling** *noun* cooling of the charge air between compressor and engine

intercrystalline *or* **intergranular corrosion** *noun* small outbreaks of rust occurring along crystal boundaries of metals or alloys

interference *noun* noise from the ignition system that affects radio and TV reception

COMMENT: suppressors are used to minimize interference and on modern vehicles the main suppressors are the sparking plug leads

interior *noun & adjective* (the) inside (of) a vehicle; **interior light** = COURTESY LIGHT; **interior mirror** = rear-view mirror located centrally near the top of the windscreen; *(compare* EXTERIOR MIRROR); **interior noise level** = level of noise inside the vehicle, typically in the range from 45-90 dBA from idle to full throttle; at 70 mph between 66-87 dBA; **interior trim** = panels, linings, decorative facings, upholstery and covers inside a vehicle

interleaf friction *noun* friction between individual leaves of a leaf spring

interlock 1 *verb (gear train members)* to fit together **2** *noun* device in a change-speed gearbox which prevents two gears being engaged at the same time

intermediate 1 *adjective* between two things or extremes **2** *noun* American car category, with space for 5-6 passengers and a length of 207-215 ins.

◇ **intermediate coat** *noun* any coat of paint between the first coat (primer) and last coat (finish)

◇ **intermediate (drive) plate** *or* **interplate** *noun* disc between the driven plates in a twin plate clutch

◇ **intermediate gear** *noun* any gear between bottom gear and top gear, but usually refers to second or third gears

◇ **intermediate hold** *noun* term dating from the early days of three-speed automatic transmissions; today represented by the position '2' on the selector quadrant

◇ **intermediate rod** *noun* = RELAY ROD

◇ **intermediate shaft** *noun* rotating shaft joining two other shafts

intermetallic compound *noun* alloy of two metals in which a progressive change in composition is accompanied by a progression of phases with varying crystalline structures

intermittent *adjective* occurring at regular *or* irregular intervals *because of the intermittent drizzle I set the wiper control to intermittent* **intermittent fault** = fault which comes and goes (and annoyingly never occurs when the car is taken in to the garage for repair!)

intermittent wiper control *noun* operates the wipers at preset intervals; typically adjustable from 2 to 40 seconds (NOTE: US English is **mist action**)

COMMENT: most often used in conditions of light drizzle or snow, mist, and the spray from other vehicles

internal circlip pliers *noun* special pliers with pointed jaw tips for the installation and removal of internal circlips

internal combustion (IC) engine *noun (compare* EXTERNAL COMBUSTION ENGINE) type of engine in which the fuel is burned within the cylinders of the engine (as opposed to, for example, the steam engine) and the gaseous combustion products serve as the thermodynamic fluid; the spent gases are released into the atmosphere; the term internal combustion engine covers all types of reciprocating and rotary engines, but is typically used with reference to four-stroke petrol and diesel engines

internal damage *noun* damage to the body shell that is not usually visible from the outside

COMMENT: such damage is often caused by rust, as box members and double panels often corrode inside out, i.e. the damage only becomes visible in an advanced state of decay

internal diameter *noun* = INSIDE DIAMETER

◊ **internal gear** *noun* internally toothed annulus gear; *(see illustrations 17, 21)*

◊ **internal gear pump** *noun* gear pump which has one rotor with internally cut teeth meshing with an externally cut gear idler; a crescent-shaped partition is used to prevent liquid from passing back to the suction side of the pump; a typical oil pump, characterized by quiet operation and high capacity; *(see illustration 17)*

◊ **internal micrometer** *noun* micrometer for inside measurements such as distances between two parallel surfaces or inside diameters of cylinder and main bearing bores

internal mix air cap *noun* special type of air cap for spray guns; *(compare* EXTERNAL MIX AIR CAP)

COMMENT: air and material are mixed inside the gun and are ejected through a single orifice. This design is used only for pressure-feed guns, primarily for spraying heavy viscous materials

internal resistance *noun* the resistance inherent in a voltage source, such as a battery

COMMENT: the internal resistance of a battery is made up of several individual resistances, e.g. between the plates and the electrolyte, the plate resistances, the resistance of the electrolyte to ion flow, and internal connectors

internal thread *noun* thread on the inside of a nut or similar into which the external thread of a bolt or screw fits (NOTE: also called **female thread)**

◊ **internal vane pump** *noun* = SLIDING-VANE PUMP

International Standards Organization (ISO) *noun* Geneva-based organization established (in its present form) in 1947 to standardize units of measurement and technical design

interplate *noun* = INTERMEDIATE (DRIVE) PLATE

interruptor *noun* *see* THERMOSTATIC INTERRUPTOR

intersection *noun* road junction

interval operation *noun* intermittent operation

IOE engine *noun* = INLET OVER EXHAUST ENGINE

ion *noun* electrically charged particle formed by losing or gaining electrons; particles of this type make a solution of certain chemicals a conductor of electricity

◊ **ionic-current measuring method** *or* **technique** *noun* measuring the conductivity in the spark gap in order to select a sparking plug of the correct heat range

iridescent *adjective* displaying a spectrum of glittering, shimmering colours; often changing as the position or angle from which they are observed, changes

iron *noun* **(a)** most common metallic element, used for making steel **(b)** *US* = TYRE LEVER

IR remote control *noun* = INFRARED REMOTE CONTROL

IRS = INDEPENDENT REAR SUSPENSION

IRTE = INSTITUTE OF ROAD TRANSPORT ENGINEERS British organization set up to increase the competence and professionalism of vehicle drivers and owners

ISO = INTERNATIONAL STANDARDS ORGANIZATION

iso-octane *noun* liquid hydrocarbon used to determine the octane rating of fuels; *(see also* OCTANE NUMBER)

isolator *noun* item that prevents interaction between two components

IVC = INLET VALVE CLOSES

IVO = INLET VALVE OPENS

Izod method *or* **test** *noun* impact resistance test in which the specimen is held as a vertical cantilever beam and is broken by a single swing of a pendulum, with the line of initial contact at a fixed distance from the specimen clamp and from the centreline of the notch and on the same face as the notch

Jj

jack *noun* mechanical or hydraulic device for raising (part of) a car; **jack stand** = AXLE STAND

COMMENT: jacks come in a variety of shapes; mechanical designs include side-lift jacks and scissors jacks. Bottle jacks and trolley jacks use hydraulic force

jack up *verb* to raise using a jack *when changing a wheel, loosen the wheel nuts before you jack up the car* jacking point = strengthened place on the underbody to put the jack (NOTE: small cars have one point on each side but larger cars may have two)

jackknife *verb (of articulated lorries)* to go out of control when braking harshly so that the trailer slews round at an angle to the cab

jackshaft *noun* = INTERMEDIATE SHAFT

jalopy *noun (informal)* a worn-out old car

jamb switch *noun* push-button light switch located in a door jamb (e.g. for courtesy lights, boot light)

jam nut *noun* = SELF-LOCKING NUT

Japanese lantern-type jacket tube *noun* web-type jacket tube of a steering column which, on impact, folds like a Japanese lantern

Jeantaud axle & steering *nouns* = ACKERMANN AXLE & STEERING

jerking *see* JOLTING

jerk pump *noun* one of the pumping elements of an in-line injection pump

jet *noun* (i) precision-made hole to control the flow of petrol, air or air/fuel mixture, as in a carburettor; (ii) the nozzle containing such a hole; **jet adjuster** = nut that regulates the volume or strength of the air/fuel mixture in a variable-choke carburettor; **jet bearing** = bearing in a Stromberg carburettor; **jet carrier** *or* **jet head** = removable plug in a carburettor containing the jet; **jet needle** = tapered needle in a carburettor jet; **jet tube** = tube that houses the main jet in an SU carburettor; *(see illustrations 12, 13)*

jet process *noun* process by which the thickness of hot-dip galvanized coatings on steel strips can be regulated, allowing the application of coatings of different thicknesses on the two sides of steel strips

COMMENT: on leaving the zinc melting pot, the strip passes two jets through which air, gas or vapour is directed onto the steel strip to remove superfluous zinc. The coating thickness decreases with the strength of the jet

J-flange *noun* most widely used rim flange type for passenger car wheels; the J-flange is 17.3 mm in height

jib-jack *noun* lever-type tower jack

JJD wheel *noun* safety wheel which can be run when deflated

COMMENT: two independently inflated tyres are seated on a double rim consisting of two single rims. The JJD wheel has excellent aquaplaning properties; a reliable tyre pressure control system is required, however, since a defective tyre is not easily detectable

job *noun* particular piece of work; **lube job** = lubrication of an engine; **valve job** = replacing or regrinding old valves

jockey pulley *or* **wheel** *noun* free-turning, spring-loaded idler used to tension the timing belt

joggle 1 *noun* slight step along the edge of a panel to provide a level mounting and welding surface so that it can be overlapped against the adjacent panel for subsequent lap or spot welding **2** *verb* to join by means of a joggle

◇ **joggler** *noun* metalworking tool used for creating a joggle

joint *noun* the interface at which two or more mechanical or structural components are united

◇ **joint splitting tool** *noun* = BALL JOINT SEPARATOR

jolting *noun* effect caused by harsh clutch release: car body jerks repeatedly in a longitudinal direction

joule *noun* SI unit of measurement of energy (NOTE: usually written **J** with figures: **25J**)

COMMENT: one joule is the amount of energy used to move one kilogram the distance of one metre, using the force of one newton

jounce and rebound *noun* = BUMP AND REBOUND

◇ **jounce buffer** *or* **bumper** *noun* compression buffer at the top of the shock absorber or strut; *(see illustration 27)*

journal *noun* the part of a shaft which is supported by a bearing

joyride 1 *noun* a reckless drive in a stolen car **2** *verb* to go for a joyride

◇ **joyrider** *noun* someone who goes for a joyride

jubilee clip *noun* worm-gear hose clip

judder 1 *verb* to shake or vibrate **2** *noun* shaking or vibration **brake judder; clutch judder; wiper blade judder**

juggernaut *noun* a very large goods lorry; *(compare* ROAD TRAIN)

jumper cable *noun US* = JUMP LEAD

◇ **jump leads** *noun* pair of well-insulated electrical cables with crocodile-clip ends, used to connect the two live terminals of a functioning battery to the dead terminals of a flat one to get a car with a discharged battery started

◇ **jump start** *verb* to start a car with a flat battery using jump leads to obtain a charge from a nearby live battery; *(compare* BUMP START)

junk 1 *noun* scrap **2** *verb* to scrap

◇ **junkyard** *noun* place where cars are sent for scrap

just-in-time system *noun* system of production where components are delivered as they are required rather than keeping them in store

Kk

Kadenacy effect *noun* when a port of a two-stroke engine opens abruptly, as is the case with a rectangular exhaust port, the cylinder pressure gives rise to a positive pressure wave transmitted down the exhaust pipe at the speed of sound

KAM = KEEP ALIVE MEMORY

kangarooing *noun (informal)* moving forward in a succession of sudden jerks as a result of improper use of the clutch, (a characteristic of learner drivers)

KD = KICKDOWN

keep alive memory (KAM) *noun* = FAULT MEMORY

keiretsu *noun* Japanese word referring to the large groups of companies that are a characteristic feature of the Japanese economy, especially in the auto industry; *(compare* HORIZONTAL KEIRETSU, VERTICAL KEIRETSU)

> COMMENT: keiretsu companies do business first and foremost among themselves; tight supplier-buyer relationships within the keiretsu system are a barrier to the penetration of foreign goods in Japan because, everything else being equal, keiretsu members prefer to buy from other keiretsu members; the keiretsu system is a controversial issue in US-Japanese trade relations

Kennedy key *noun* two keys in a tangential configuration

kerb *noun* stone edging between the pavement and the road (NOTE: US English is **curb**)

◇ **kerb weight** *noun* weight of a vehicle with fuel, oil and coolant but without occupants, luggage or payload; *(compare* DRY WEIGHT, GROSS VEHICLE WEIGHT)

kerfs *noun* = SIPES

kerosene *or* **kerosine** *noun* **(a)** fuel for jet engines **(b)** *US* = PARAFFIN

key 1 *noun* **(a)** metal instrument for turning locks and key-operated switches **(b)** small peg or wedge that fits into a keyway *the impeller is fixed on the shaft by means of a key* **(c)** L-shaped tool for turning recessed screws (e.g. Allen key) **(d)** roughened surface which provides a basis for subsequent layers of paint or filler *scoring the surface provides a good key for subsequent coats* **2** *verb* to adhere to a lower layer *sand the primer coat to ensure proper keying of the top coat*

◇ **key file** *noun* small file with a length of 100/150 mm for sharpening key holes and other small components, available in standard shapes, e.g. as flat tapered, flat parallel, half round, three square, square or round file

keyless entry system *noun* allows locking and unlocking of the vehicle's doors and boot without using a key

> COMMENT: the system is operated by punching a typically five-digit code into a calculator-style keypad located on the driver's door; if more than five seconds elapse between button pushes, the system will abort, requiring you to start again

keyway *noun* slot cut into a component which accepts the key (b) of another component to ensure such a tight fit that the two components operate as one

K-flange *noun* rim flange type for passenger car wheels; the K-flange is 19.3 mm in height and rarely used today; *(compare* J-FLANGE)

kick *verb US* = GO OFF

◇ **kickdown (KD)** *noun (automatic gearbox)* system that enables a driver to accelerate rapidly, by fully depressing the accelerator pedal to engage a lower gear than the one selected by the automatic gearbox (NOTE: US English is **forced downshift**); **kickdown valve** = mechanically or electrically operated valve which actuates a downward gearchange if the accelerator pedal is fully depressed

◇ **kick panel** *noun* vertical panel wall enclosed by several structural members (e.g. the side panel ahead of the A-pillar that extends up to the sides of the bulkhead and is limited by the floorpan at its bottom end)

◇ **kickplate** *or* **kick strip** *noun* = SCUFF PLATE

◇ **kick start** *verb* to start a motorcycle engine by kicking a pedal downwards

◇ **kickstarter** *noun* pedal lever and ratchet mechanism for kick starting an engine

◇ **kickup** *noun* raised section of the frame and body to provide clearance for the front and/or rear suspension system or axles; **kickup pipe** = exhaust pipe section including the elbow or U around the rear axle; *(see illustration 19)*

kidney dolly *noun* = TOE DOLLY

kilometre (km) *US* **kilometer** *noun* unit of length (1 km = 0.621 miles; 1 mile = 1.61 km); **kilometres per hour (km/h)** = unit of velocity

kilopascal (kpa) *noun* SI measurement of pressure (= 1000 pascals)

kingpin *noun* vertical or inclined shaft about which a steered wheel pivots; **kingpin axis** = centreline of the ball joints in a front suspension system (NOTE: also called **swivel axis**); **kingpin inclination (KPI)** = angle made of the kingpin axis to the perpendicular as viewed from the front (NOTE: also called **swivel-axis inclination**); **kingpin offset** = geometric parameter: 'positive' if the kingpin axis intersects the wheel plane at or below ground level, 'negative' if the point of intersection is above ground level (NOTE: also called **scrub radius**)

kink 1 *noun* twist or sharp bend in a hose **2** *verb* to form a kink *check for kinked, clogged, or damaged hoses*

kit *noun* set of tools, parts, etc. *106-piece tool kit; the lamp kit includes a representative selection of automotive light bulbs*

◇ **kit car** *noun* car that is assembled (often by the DIY enthusiast) from its constituent parts; usually with a GRP body shell

K-jetronic *noun* commonly used mechanical fuel injection system made by Bosch in which the amount of fuel injected continuously under pressure into the inlet ports is controlled by an airflow meter; *(see illustration 14)*

km *(short for)* kilometre; **km/h** = kilometres per hour

knifing stopper *noun* fine grade filler for minor dents and chips

knock *noun* = ENGINE KNOCK

◇ **knock control** *noun* retards the spark advance when detonation occurs

COMMENT: the retard mode is held for a certain time, typically 20 seconds, after which the knock control reverts to normal operation

knocker *noun (informal US)* = PANEL PULLER

knock limit *noun* degree of spark advance before detonation

knock-off/on nut *noun* = SPINNER

◇ **knock-off wheel** *noun* splined-hub wheel with one central locking nut (spinner) which is knocked on and off with a soft-headed hammer

knock resistance *noun* = OCTANE NUMBER

◇ **knock sensor** *noun* = DETONATION SENSOR

knuckle *noun* (i) the joint of a hinge through which the pin passes; (ii) hinged joint between two rods or tubes

◇ **knuckle arm** *noun* = STEERING ARM

◇ **knuckle pin** *noun* = KINGPIN

knurl 1 *noun (on nuts, knobs)* (series of) small ridges to provide a grip for fingers *straight knurl, diamond knurl* **2** *verb* to roughen with knurls; **knurled nut** = thumb nut with knurled sides

◇ **knurling** *noun* roughening with knurls

KPI = KINGPIN INCLINATION

krinkle finish *noun* hard-wearing, usually matt black finish, often used for rocker covers

LI

L (a) *(automatic transmission)* = LOW **(b)** = LUXE

labour *verb (engine)* to struggle to keep turning due to lack of revs or the use of too high a gear

◊ **labouring** *noun (of engine)* having difficulty in turning (NOTE: US English is **lugging)**

lacquer *noun* glossy coating made by dissolving cellulose derivatives in a rapidly evaporating solvent

ladder chassis *US*

ladder frame *noun* chassis layout in which the side members are connected at intervals by cross members, like a ladder; common on coachbuilt designs, obsolete in modern unitary construction designs

lake pipes *or* **Lakes pipes** *noun* nonfunctional side pipes fitted for decorative purposes only

lambda *noun* eleventh letter of the Greek alphabet

◊ **lambda probe** *or* **lambda sensor** *noun* = OXYGEN SENSOR

◊ **lambda window** *noun* narrow range (where lambda = 1), which yields the lowest emission values for CO, NO_x, and HC

laminate 1 *noun* a sheet of material made of several different bonded layers **2** *verb* to make material by bonding together several thin sheets *laminated plastic* **laminated glass** = sandwich-type construction of two or more panes of glass laminated together with an extremely tough, crystal-clear plastic film; on severe impact, laminated glass will crack, but not shatter like ordinary glass, nor craze over like toughened glass; **laminated iron core** = the core of an ignition coil consisting of pieces of soft iron laminations, insulated from one another; **laminated windscreen** =

windscreen made with laminated glass; *(compare* TOUGHENED WINDSCREEN)

◊ **laminating** *noun* covering sheets with a particular layer or covering moulded parts with a specific plastic film

◊ **lamination** *noun* (i) act of laminating; (ii) thin layer; (iii) structure made up of thin layers

lamp *noun* lighting unit; **lamp aperture** = opening in a sheet metal panel for mounting the headlamp or taillight; **lamp blackening** = blackening of a light bulb; gradual blackening of conventional, i.e. non-halogen light bulbs, occurs as a result of metal vapour deposition on the glass envelope which reduces light emission; severe blackening indicates imminent bulb failure; **lamp cluster** = group of lamps behind a cover; the rear lights of most cars are grouped together in clusters; **lamp panel** = panel that encloses part or all of the headlamp or taillight cutout and may extend across the width of the car to include both cutouts; in the latter case, it forms an additional panel to be joined to the smaller front or rear valances; *US* **lamp socket** = BULB HOLDER; **lamp unit** = sealed light unit with reflector and lens all-in-one

land *noun* smooth, open area of a (grooved) surface, such as the bands of metal between the grooves in a piston which carry the piston rings; *(see* PISTON LAND)

landau *or* **landaulet** *noun* classic car style characterized by the fact that only the rear seats were protected by a hard or convertible top, whereas the driver was exposed to the open air in order to be more aware of road and weather conditions; an imitation landaulet style is still found on some American sedans (saloons)

lane *noun* **(a)** narrow road, often in the country **(b)** track on a road, defining lines of traffic *do not change lanes; overtaking lane; three-lane motorway*

lap 1 *noun* **(a)** upper surface of the body from waist to knees when seated **(b)** rotating disc covered with fine abrasive for polishing **2** *verb (valve seats etc.)* to polish with a lap **(b)**

◇ **lap belt** *noun* 2-point belt pulled across the hips, or lap belt portion of a combined lap/shoulder belt; mostly only on the rear centre seat, on some models on all rear seats; *(see* SUBMARINING)

◇ **lap joint** *noun (welding)* simple joint made by overlapping one surface with another and joining them together

lash *noun US* = FREE PLAY

last station memory *noun (audio/ video)* circuit which ensures that when the unit is turned on, the tuner automatically tunes to the station that was received before the unit was turned off

latch *noun* part of the locking mechanism of doors, bonnets, boots, tailgates

COMMENT: consisting of a small metal bar, either mounted on the movable part (always on doors and on some tailgates), or on the car body (always on bonnets and boots), which engages with a striker on the opposite part

latch(ing) pillar *noun* = B-PILLAR

lateral *adjective* relating to the side

◇ **lateral acceleration** *noun* centrifugal force moving a vehicle towards the outside of a curve when cornering

COMMENT: usually measured by driving a car in a circle on a skidpan; production saloons reach lateral acceleration levels in the order of 0.8 g

lateral air passage *noun* passage at the nozzle of a spray gun for shaping the spray pattern to a long or elongated oval; **lateral atomization orifice** = additional passages at the nozzle of a spray gun for supplying additional air to break up the paint into smaller droplets

◇ **lateral grip** *noun* ability of a tyre to maintain its course, or remain under normal steering control, while being subjected to directionally disturbing influences

◇ **lateral impact** *noun* side crash

◇ **lateral runout** *noun* side-to-side wobble (e.g. of wheel, brake disc, rotor); *(compare* RADIAL RUNOUT) (NOTE: the maximum lateral runout of a brake disc should not exceed 0.004 in or 0.1 mm)

◇ **lateral stability** *noun* = LATERAL GRIP

◇ **lateral stiffness** *noun* resistance of a vehicle body structure to lateral impact

lay-by *noun* place at the side of a road where drivers can stop (to rest)

layer of pure zinc *noun* top layer on hot-dip galvanized steel which, in contrast to zinc-iron alloy layers, almost completely consists of zinc

◇ **layer thickness** *noun* coating thickness (indicated in micrometres or millimetres)

laying up *noun* the process of adding several layers of fibreglass mat and resin to form a GRP shell; **lay-up resin** = the resin substance used to laminate GRP parts

COMMENT: the resin available on the do-it-yourself market for fibreglass mat repairs also belongs to this category

Layrub coupling *noun* universal joint using four moulded rubber inserts mounted on a round steel plate

layshaft *noun* intermediate shaft between and parallel to the input and output shafts, carrying the two pairs of gearwheels which provide the required changes in gear ratio (NOTE: US English is **countershaft)**

lazy tongs *noun* (i) any device with extensible arms (often in the form of a series of crossed, hinged bars) for handling objects at a distance; (ii) specifically, a type of pop rivet gun with such arms

LCD *(short for)* liquid-crystal display: an optical, digital display used in the instrument panel

LDC = LOWER DEAD CENTRE

LDPE = LOW-DENSITY POLYETHYLENE

lead[1] *noun* soft, toxic, heavy metal used in starter batteries, and in leaded fuel as an anti-knock agent; **lead-acid battery** = system of lead plates and dilute sulphuric acid; used as a starter battery and as a traction battery in electric vehicles; **lead-antimony grid** *(see)* GRID; **lead deposit** = lead particles that separate from the battery plates during normal operation; **leaded petrol** = petrol to which lead has been added as an anti-knock agent; **lead-free petrol** = unleaded petrol; **lead glazing** = faulty sparking plug condition caused by molten lead salt deposits that solidify into a yellow, brown or green glaze; **lead loading** = the process of filling dents and damaged areas of the bodywork with body lead; **lead peroxide** = poisonous compound used, for example, as an electrode in batteries; **lead sulphate** = chemical compound; poisonous white crystals found in discharged batteries; **lead tolerance** = resistance to leaded fuel; **lead weight** = balance weight on a wheel rim; *see also* RED LEAD

◊ **leadsled** *noun* typical body style of a custom car that became popular in the USA in the 1950s; the term derives from the fact that large amounts of body lead are required to achieve the smooth body lines desired

lead² *noun* **(a)** connection cable for an electric current **(b)** *(bolt,screw)* distance from the thread crest to the adjacent crest of the same thread

lead and lag *noun* terms referring to the time between a valve opening and TDC or BDC (valve lead), and the time between TDC or BDC and a valve closing (valve lag); *(compare* VALVE OVERLAP)

leading *adjective* forward *or* at the front; **leading arm** = front suspension link which supports the wheel in front of the pivot point; *(compare* TRAILING ARM); **leading edge** = forward edge (e.g. of a body panel); *(compare* TRAILING EDGE); **leading shoe** = shoe of a brake drum system which pivots outwards into the approaching drum (NOTE: US English is **primary shoe**) *(compare* TRAILING SHOE)

leaf spring *noun* flat, narrow, metal strip of varying length used as a spring *cantilever leaf spring; semi-elliptic leaf spring*

COMMENT: several strips or leaves are usually bracketed together to form a compound spring, with the longest leaf (main leaf) uppermost and the shortest leaf nearest to the axle; a leaf spring may be either cambered or flat

lean *adjective* of a weak air/fuel mixture that has less petrol than normal (NOTE: opposite is **rich)**

◊ **Lean Authority Limit Switch** *noun* developed by GM to monitor heated carburettor inlet air through an air cleaner TVS and to prevent the control unit from providing the carburettor with too lean a mixture, for better performance when starting from cold

◊ **lean-burn engine** *noun* engine which uses a lean mixture of fuel and air to increase fuel economy and reduce exhaust emissions; *(compare* CACIS)

◊ **lean mixture** *noun* mixture with more oxygen than necessary to burn the fuel contained in the mixture (NOTE: opposite is **rich mixture)** *(compare* STOICHIOMETRIC RATIO)

LED *(short for)* light-emitting diode: a semiconductor device used for digital displays in the instrument panel

left-hand drive (LHD) *adjective* steering system where the steering wheel is located on the left-hand side of the vehicle; used for driving on the right, as in most parts of the world, except for some Commonwealth countries (e.g. the UK and Australia), and Japan (NOTE: opposite is **right-hand drive)**

◊ **left-hand thread** *noun* thread which will accept a nut turned anticlockwise

leftward welding *noun* welding a seam towards the left

legroom *noun* the amount of space available to move one's legs in a vehicle *the capacity of the boot was very generous but legroom in the back was rather cramped*

LE-Jetronic *noun* the LE-Jetronic system incorporates the advantages of direct airflow measurement with the enhancements afforded by electronics

COMMENT: electromagnetically actuated injectors inject fuel onto the intake valves. Each cylinder has its own solenoid injector which is actuated once with every crankshaft revolution. The injectors are opened by control pulses delivered by the ECU; the length of these pulses depend on the quantity of inducted air, engine speed and other parameters. All of these parameters are detected by sensors and processed in the control unit

lemon *noun* a new or used car with many defects

lens *noun* glass or plastic front cover of a headlight through which the light converges or diverges

let in *verb (clutch)* to engage *let the clutch in slowly*

◊ **let out** *verb* to release *let some air out of the tyre if it is overinflated*

level *noun* = SPIRIT LEVEL

◊ **leveller** *noun* component in continuous sheet galvanizing lines by means of which steel strips are stretched and levelled

◊ **level out** *verb* to work on a panel to remove irregularities with the use of hammer and dolly or by filling and sanding, etc.

◊ **level plug** *noun* threaded plug in the side of a gearbox or rear axle to determine if sufficient oil has been used during filling

lever-type shock absorber *noun* spring damper operated by a lever arm from a chassis-mounted hydraulic damper unit; *(compare* TELESCOPIC SHOCK ABSORBER)

levering bar *noun* metalworking tool shaped like a large tyre lever with flat hooked ends for levering bent panels back into position

LH *(short for)* left hand

LHD = LEFT-HAND DRIVE

L-head *noun* L-shaped combustion chamber; **L-head engine** = side-valve engine

COMMENT: intake and exhaust valve are located in a separate lateral chamber of the actual combustion chamber parallel to one another and are both actuated directly by the camshaft located in the cylinder block. This type of valve train was used in the early years of automotive engineering and is no longer found - with some minor minor exceptions - in modern engines

LHM = LIQUIDE HYDRAULIQUE MINERALE

LI = LOAD INDEX

licence *US* **license** *noun* document giving official permission to do something *driving licence; road fund licence*

◊ **license plate** *noun* *US* = NUMBERPLATE

lift *noun* **(a)** amount by which a poppet valve rises when opened **(b)** aerodynamic force caused by greater pressure above the car than below it and having the effect of loss of traction and stability; (counteracted by a suitable spoiler)

◊ **lifter** *noun US* = TAPPET

liftgate *noun US* = TAILGATE

lifting *noun* = ETCHING (a)

lifting platform take-up point *noun* any of the lifting points specified by the manufacturer for supporting the car on a lifting platform

COMMENT: only the points specified provide the rigidity required to lift the car without damaging adjacent components

liftoff effect *noun* in eddy-current testing; severe signal changes associated with small changes in distance between probe and test item

lift pump *noun* = FUEL PUMP

lift-the-dot fastener *noun US* = SNAP FASTENER

light 1 *adjective* **(a)** easy to operate *the steering/clutch is light* (NOTE: opposite is **heavy**) **(b)** weighing relatively little; not heavy *light-alloy cylinder* **2** *noun* **(a)** illumination, as from a lamp **(b)** vehicle window

◊ **light-alloy piston** *noun* = ALLOY PISTON; **light-alloy wheel** = ALLOY WHEEL

◊ **light bulb** *noun* = BULB

◊ **lighter** *noun* electric, push-button device on the dashboard which, when depressed, produces a red-hot filament for lighting cigarettes, etc.

◊ **light-fast** *adjective* unaffected by light

◊ **light-footed** *adjective* used to describe a mode of driving which uses gentle pressure on the accelerator, thus maximizing fuel economy

◊ **light-off temperature** *noun* the temperature at which a catalytic converter achieves a 50% conversion rate; typically near 250°C

◊ **lights-on reminder** *noun* usually a buzzer, chime or voice alert which reminds you that you have left the car lights on

◊ **light truck** *or* **van** *noun* typically a vehicle under 3 tons, which includes pick-ups, passenger vans and most 4wd vehicles and for which one does not need a special licence; *(compare* HGV)

◊ **light unit** *noun* = LAMP UNIT

limit *noun* the performance limit of a car's chassis, tyres, etc.; typically experienced during sharp cornering at high speeds

◊ **limit cycle control** *noun* = CLOSED-LOOP CONTROL

◊ **limited-slip differential** *noun* axle differential or central differential incorporating a locking or slip-limiting mechanism to counter wheel spin

◊ **limiter** *noun* = ENGINE SPEED LIMITER

limousine *or (informal)* **limo** *noun* large luxurious car with a glass partition between driver and passengers

limp-home mode (of operation) *noun* standby circuit which allows a car with electronic system trouble to be driven home slowly

linear (source) lamp *noun* = FESTOON BULB

◊ **linear wiper system** *noun* system in which the wiper arm is attached both at the top and bottom and, instead of describing the usual arc, is guided in a straight line from one side of the windscreen to the other

line pressure *noun* line pressure is fed to the shifting components when they are to be applied; it increases in proportion to engine speed and is the highest pressure in the hydraulic control system

liner *noun* = CYLINDER LINER

line spanner *noun* = FLARE NUT SPANNER

lining *noun* **(a)** interior trim, e.g. of doors, convertible tops **(b)** friction material (e.g. on brake shoes in drum brake, on clutch disc, on brake bands in automatic transmission)

linishing *noun* smoothing sheet metal using power tools, e.g. with an angle grinder and emery belt or grinding disk

COMMENT: typical applications are dressing of weld joints and removal of flaking rust to clean up repair areas prior to welding

link *noun* **(a)** movable, hinged piece connecting moving parts of a machine **(b)** = SUSPENSION LINK

◊ **linkage power steering** *noun* linkage-type, power-assisted steering system in which a conventional manual system is assisted by hydraulic or pneumatic effort applied directly to a steering linkage such as a relay lever or track rod

lip *noun* the edge of a sheet metal panel folded at right angles to the basic panel contours; often used to mount the panel to an adjacent panel, e.g. for spot welding

◊ **lip seal with garter spring** *noun* = RADIAL SHAFT SEAL

liquefied natural gas (LNG) *noun* e.g. methane, possible future alternative fuel for SI engines

◊ **liquefied petroleum gas (LPG)** *noun* by-product of oil refining, mainly butane or propane or a mixture of the two gases, used as a fuel for some SI petrol engines

liquid-cooled *adjective (engine)* cooled by the passage of water or oil (NOTE: opposite is **air-cooled)**

◊ **Liquide Hydraulique Minérale (LHM)** *noun* green hydraulic fluid used by Citroën for some of their suspension systems

◊ **liquid gasket** *noun* room temperature vulcanizing gasket sealer (from a tube)

◊ **liquid paint** *noun* paint which contains solvents and cures at room temperature or by baking

◊ **liquid pump** *noun* machine used to raise liquids from a low to a high energy level by transferring energy to the medium being pumped

list price *noun* the price ex-factory, as quoted in the price list, as opposed to the actual sales price which will include on-the-road charges

little end *noun* small end of the connecting rod; *(see* CONNECTING ROD)

live axle *noun* a power-transmitting axle; *(compare* DEAD AXLE)

L-Jetronic air flow meter *noun* airflow meter used on the L-Jetronic system

◊ **L-Jetronic (fuel injection) system** *noun* electronically controlled fuel injection system

COMMENT: fuel is supplied by an intermittent-action L-Jetronic fuel injection system, which uses engine speed and intake airflow as its main control parameters. Each cylinder has its own solenoid injector, which is opened by control pulses delivered by the electronic control unit; the length of these pulses depends on the control parameters. All of these parameters are detected by sensors and processed in the control unit. This fuel injection system is employed by BMW in the K 75 model

LNG = LIQUEFIED NATURAL GAS

load *noun* **(a)** something to be borne or transported **(b)** amount of material transported **(c)** amount of power carried by an electric circuit **(d)** resistance overcome by an engine when it is driving a machine

◊ **load alteration effect** *noun* reactions in the drive train or, in FWD vehicles, in the steering, due to sudden load alteration; (*compare* TORQUE STEER)

◊ **load-controlled power distribution** *noun* drive torque distribution, as established e.g. by a Torsen differential

◊ **load floor** *noun* (i) cargo-carrying area of a van or lorry; (ii) floor of the luggage area of an estate car or hatchback; **load floor extension** = moulded tray that folds out of the rear luggage area and provides an extended load floor which hangs out over the bumper; (can also be used for picnics)

◊ **load index (LI)** *noun* coded number on the sidewall of a tyre to indicate the maximum load the tyre may carry at a given speed under manufacturer's conditions

◊ **loading** *noun* amount with which something is loaded *the noble metal loading per catalyst is about 2 to 4 grams*

◊ **load overhang** *noun* distance a load extends beyond the rear of a vehicle

◊ **load rating** *noun* = LOAD INDEX

◊ **load resistor** *noun* = BALLAST RESISTOR

load-sensitive proportioning valve *noun* valve which regulates hydraulic pressure to the rear wheels as a function of chassis height-to-axle distance

COMMENT: vehicle weight transfer during hard braking increases this distance and, via a spring or rod linkage, will close the valve to reduce braking pressure at the rear wheels; also, a heavily loaded car will have more braking power at the rear wheels

load transfer *noun* = WEIGHT TRANSFER

lobe *noun* = CAM LOBE

◊ **lobe-type supercharger** *noun* a positive displacement compressor with two lobed rotors; (*compare* LYSHOLM SUPERCHARGER, ROOTS COMPRESSOR)

local cell *noun* galvanic cell resulting from differences in potential between adjacent areas on the surface of a metal immersed in an electrolyte

localized corrosion *noun* corrosion occurring at one part of a metal surface at a much higher rate than over the rest of the surface, e.g. pitting corrosion, crevice corrosion (NOTE: opposite is **uniform corrosion**)

locating dowel *noun* = DOWEL PIN

locating lug *or* **pin** *noun* projection or pin for holding a part in a specific position

COMMENT: all engine bearings have some means of ensuring that they will not shift or move in the housing bore once installed. Most bearings utilize a locating lug, which is simply a small projection that fits into a recess in the housing bore

locating spring *noun* (*of disc brakes*) steel wire clip that secures the cylinder in a floating frame or caliper frame; (*compare* SPREADER SPRING)

lock 1 (a) *noun* device for closing something with a key to prevent unauthorized entry *car door locks can ice up in very cold weather* **(b)** (*steering*) amount by which the wheels of a vehicle are able to turn; **full lock** = the maximum angle attained by the wheels when the steering wheel is turned to its full extent *three steering wheel revolutions from lock to lock; the good lock on this car means a small turning circle* **2** *verb* **(a)** to close with a key *always lock the car in a public car park* **(b)** to fix or become fixed in a certain position *the seat belts locked when the brakes were* *applied suddenly but so did the wheels and the car went into a skid* (c) *(gear train members)* to interlock or couple

◇ **lockable differential** *noun* = LIMITED-SLIP DIFFERENTIAL

◇ **lockable wheel** *noun* wheel that can be secured to the hub with a lock

◇ **lock angle** *noun* = STEERING ANGLE

◇ **lock buster** *noun* = LOCK PULLER

lock cylinder *noun* cylinder in the middle of a cylinder lock that is prevented from turning (locked) by a number of pins (typically five) which penetrate down through the wall of the cylinder

COMMENT: the cylinder is turned by inserting a key which pushes the split pins up to varying heights so that the edge of the cylinder engages with the gap between the two sections of each pin allowing the cylinder to turn

lock facing *noun* the surface of a door to which the lock is attached

◇ **locking bar clamp** *noun* locking clamp with sliding jaw providing extended clamping capabilities

locking clamp *noun* locking pliers with specially shaped jaws for vice work and intricate clamping jobs

COMMENT: locking clamps include, for example, vice grip C-clamps, vice grip pipe clamps, locking bar clamps, welding clamps and sheet metal clamps

locking differential *noun* differential with the facility for locking together the two half shafts, thus putting the differential out of action and greatly improving traction

◇ **locking lug bolt/nut** *noun* anti-theft wheel lug bolt/nut

◇ **locking mechanism** *or* **locking reel** *noun* device which locks the reel of a seat belt when the forward acceleration of the occupant exceeds a certain value

locking pliers *noun* pliers with locking jaws

COMMENT: can be used as pliers, wrench, clamp, or small vice. Closing the handles locks the jaws into position. The jaws are released by pulling a special release lever. Locking pliers with specially shaped jaws for vice work and intricate clamping jobs are called 'locking clamps'

locking synchromesh *noun* common synchromesh mechanism in which the synchromesh pressure is proportional to the gearchange force, thus preventing overriding of the synchromesh action due to hasty operation of the lever; the gear and gearchange sleeve are prevented from engaging until rotational speeds are synchronized

◇ **lock nut** *noun* (i) nut screwed on top of another nut; (ii) self-locking nut

◇ **lock picker set** *noun* set of special tools designed for opening locked cars

◇ **lock pillar** *noun* = B-PILLAR

◇ **lock pin** *noun* = LOCATING PIN

◇ **lock puller** *noun* special door lock picker; attached to the outside of a car door lock, the lock puller rips out the entire lock cylinder

◇ **lock ring pliers** *noun* tool for removing and installing heavy-duty circlips, used e.g. on brakes, transmissions, pedal shafts, and clutch shafts

◇ **lock striker** *noun* = STRIKER

◇ **lock-up clutch** *noun* automatically engaged clutch in a lock-up torque converter which prevents slipping losses; **lock-up torque converter** = torque converter in which the pump can be mechanically locked to the turbine, eliminating any loss through the fluid

locut nut *noun* fastener used to enable sheet metal screws to be used for relatively large holes in panels

long block *noun* the long block consists of the short block plus oil pump and sump, cylinder head(s), camshaft(s) as well as the complete valve train (NOTE: opposite is **short block**)

long block engine *noun* engine with a relatively long crankshaft (NOTE: opposite is **short block engine**) *(compare* BIG-BLOCK ENGINE)

COMMENT: normally, the term long block engine means a 6-cylinder in-line engine (which has a longer block than a 4-cylinder or V-8 engine)

longeron *noun* main side member

long-haul *adjective* long distance *long-haul driving*

longitudinal *adjective* lengthways *the crankshaft runs longitudinally and rotates anticlockwise* **longitudinal engine** = traditional engine layout used on most RWD vehicles with the cylinders lying lengthways from the front to the back (NOTE: also called **north-south layout**; the opposite is **transverse engine**); **longitudinal girder** *or* **member** = SIDE MEMBER

long-nose pliers *noun* pliers with half round and tapered jaws, often with a wire cutter and used for electrical work (NOTE: also called **snipe-nose pliers**); **long-nose self-grip pliers** = locking pliers with extra long reach jaws

◊ **long-reach C-clamp** *noun* self-grip locking clamp with extra long C-shaped jaws

long stroke engine *noun* reciprocating piston engine whose bore diameter is smaller than the stroke; a relatively long stroke produces higher low-end torque at the cost of increased piston speeds and reduced revving ability (NOTE: opposite is **short stroke engine**)

loom *noun* = WIRING HARNESS

loop scavenging *noun* method of scavenging used on two-stroke motorcycle engines

COMMENT: the entering gas streams travel across the piston, up the far side of the barrel and curl over and down to complete the scavenging process; loop scavenging is sometimes used to refer specifically to a special variant of this type of scavenging: Schnürle scavenging

loosen *verb* to make (something) less tight; to slacken *when changing a wheel, loosen the wheel nuts before jacking up the car*

lorry *noun* large motor vehicle for carrying goods (NOTE: US English is always **truck**)

lost-core technique *noun* method of producing thermoplastic inlet manifolds

◊ **lost-foam casting (process)** *noun* casting method using foamed plastic cores, giving the surface of the castings the appearance of styrofoam; used for engine blocks

loud pedal *noun* (*informal*) accelerator pedal

louvre *US*

louver *noun* (**a**) air ventilation slot stamped in several rows into bonnets and bootlids (**b**) = VENT (a)

COMMENT: sometimes louvres have a merely decorative function and do not actually supply additional air to the engine compartment etc.; a fine example of louvres is found on the bonnet of the Morgan roadster

Low (L) *noun* (*automatic transmission*) driving gear ratio for hilly terrain; the top gear is not engaged, and the engine brake takes effect

COMMENT: may be divided into: 3: automatic selection of the three lower ratios for prolonged driving on winding roads or for towing a caravan; 2: automatic selection of the two lowest ratios for long steep slopes or for towing a caravan on difficult roads; 1: locked in first gear for exceptional use on very steep slopes whilst towing a caravan

low-bake booth *noun* closed section in painting lines in a paint shop, in which coats of paint are dried at low temperatures; **low-bake equipment** = equipment for drying coats of paint at low temperatures; **low-bake paint** = respray paint baked at 80°C, giving a high-quality finish but requiring suitable low-bake spray booths/ovens

lowball *noun US* in car sales, the practice of stating a very low price for a new car to a customer who is known or expected to be comparison shopping; (*compare* HIGHBALL)

COMMENT: when the customer finds that other dealers cannot match this price, he will return to the original dealer, only to be told that the price was a mistake; many customers will then accept a new, higher price because they are tired of shopping around

low battery *noun* nearly flat battery

low beam *noun US* = DIPPED BEAM

low-carbon steel *noun* steel containing 0.03 to 0.3 per cent carbon (typically 0.2%)

low crown panel *noun* the predominant shape of modern body panels, e.g. on most side panels such as door skins (NOTE: opposite is **high crown panel**)

low-density polyethylene (LDPE) *noun* a relatively soft, flexible polyethylene, used mainly for plastic film and sheet

low-emission *adjective* generally, releasing relatively few pollutants into the environment *the X model is classified as a low-emission car* (*compare* ZERO-EMISSION VEHICLE)

| COMMENT: in some countries tax relief is available for low-emission cars

lower bending die *noun* lower tool insert of the press brake

lower dead centre (LDC) *noun* = BOTTOM DEAD CENTRE

lower front panel *noun* = FRONT APRON

low fuel indicator *noun* warning light which comes on when fuel is getting low (usually indicating, when the light first comes on, that there is still sufficient fuel to travel at least 25-50 miles)

low gear *noun* first or second gear, used for driving off and climbing steep hills (NOTE: opposite is **high gear)**

◊ **low geared** *adjective* characterized by a small gearwheel (on an input shaft) driving a larger one (on the output shaft), providing a high gear ratio and high torque

low-loader *noun* lorry for heavy loads with a low-level loading platform and often an extension ramp or lift-operated tailboard which can be lowered to street level

low-maintenance battery *noun* battery with removable vent caps that only requires topping-up about once a year; (*compare* MAINTENANCE-FREE BATTERY)

low oil sensor *noun* = OIL LEVEL SENSOR

◊ **low oil warning light** *noun* = ENGINE OIL LEVEL WARNING LIGHT

low-pressure cut-out *noun* device which protects the air conditioning system by switching the compressor off when a pressure loss occurs

◊ **low-pressure foaming** *noun* process in which plastics are foamed under low pressure (1-5 bar) (NOTE: opposite is **high-pressure foaming)**

◊ **low-pressure pump** *or* **low-head pump** *noun* pump used for low total heads; in the case of centrifugal pumps the low-pressure pump has a nominal total head not exceeding 80 m

low-profile air cleaner *noun* usually a circular, flat, chrome-plated air cleaner, mounted on top of the carburettor

low-profile tyre *noun* tyre with a wide tread but no comparative increase in height

| COMMENT: a tyre whose height is 70% or less of its width would be described as low-profile, as opposed to an average tyre of 80%

low rider *noun* customized car lowered to the extreme through body and suspension modifications

low side *noun* (*of air conditioning systems*) side between the expansion valve or orifice tube and the compressor; includes the evaporator; (*see illustrations 34, 35*)

low spot *noun* indentation on a panel surface

low temperature activity *noun* denotes the ability of a catalytic converter to purify exhaust gases in the warm-up phase following a cold start

| COMMENT: this phase is included in most of the current exhaust emission test procedures, as CO and HC concentrations are particularly high when engines are operated below normal operating temperatures

low temperature fouling *noun* = CARBON FOULING

◊ **low temperature phosphating** *noun* phosphating at temperatures around 20°C

low tension *noun* low voltage

low voltage circuit *noun* = PRIMARY CIRCUIT

low zinc technology *noun* technology used in present-day phosphating processes

| COMMENT: normal zinc phosphating baths used as pre-treatment for painting contain approximately 2-4 grams-per-litre (g/l) zinc and approx. 5-10 grams-per-litre (g/l) phosphorus pentoxide. In low-zinc baths, the corresponding values amount to approx.

0.4-1.7 g/l zinc and 12-16 g/l phosphorus pentoxide

lozenged *adjective* used to describe a car chassis which, as the result of an accident, no longer holds its true shape but is rather pushed into the shape of a rhombus or diamond

LPG = LIQUEFIED PETROLEUM GAS

L-section ring *noun* special piston ring characterized by its L-shaped cross-section

COMMENT: used mostly in high-performance two-stroke engines. The L-section ring allows combustion gas to penetrate behind its vertical section and thus uses the gas pressure to increase the pressure of the ring against the cylinder wall

LT circuit *noun* = PRIMARY CIRCUIT

lube *noun (informal)* LUBRICATION; **lube oil** = = LUBRICATING OIL; **lube job** = LUBRICATION

◊ **lubricant** *noun* oily or greasy substance used to reduce friction between parts or objects in relative motion

◊ **lubricate** *verb* to cover or treat with a lubricant

◊ **lubricating oil** *noun* refined crude oil used as a lubricant; **lubricating pressure** = pressure of a lubricating oil

lubrication *noun* covering or treating moving surfaces with oil or grease to keep them apart to reduce friction and wear; **lubrication film** = coat of lubricant to reduce the friction created when two surfaces move on one another; **lubrication point** = place at which to apply lubricant; **lubrication pump** = pump used to supply oil to lubricating points, particularly for plain bearings; **lubrication system** = the system in the engine that supplies engine parts with lubricating oil to prevent contact between any two metal surfaces

COMMENT: until the 1960s, most cars had many lubrication points which had to be lubricated at regular intervals; neglect resulted in rapid deterioration and failure of moving parts; most linkages on modern cars are provided ex-factory with life-long lubrication warranties or with engineering-plastic joints which would even be destroyed when lubricated with petroleum-based grease

lug *noun* **(a)** device mounted on a rotating shaft or component that engages in a recess of a component to be driven **(b)** *(tyre)* solid block of tread (i.e. with no sipes)

luggage *noun* travelling bags or suitcases; **luggage carrier** = rack bolted on top of the boot lid for taking luggage or the spare wheel (often seen on old sports cars where space was at a premium)

lugging *noun US* = LABOURING

lug nut *noun US* = WHEEL NUT

lumbar support *noun* seat support for the lower back *electrically adjustable lumbar supports and side bolsters securely place you in front of the instrument cluster*

luminance *noun* luminous intensity of a surface in a given direction per unit of projected area of the surface, in candela per square metre; not the same as the apparent brightness

lustre *US* **luster** *noun* reflected light; sheen or gloss

luxe (L) *noun* although the word means luxury, on its own it is often used to denote a rather basic model; *(compare* CL, GL*)*

Lysholm supercharger *noun* lobe-type supercharger similar to the Roots compressor, but more efficient and much more expensive

Mm

M+S tyre *noun* mud and snow tyre; winter tyre with a deep tread

machine screw *noun* screw with a thread running the length of the shank and available with a variety of different heads

◇ **machinists' caliper** *noun* measuring tool with two curved arms for inside or outside measurement; the reading taken with the arms is transferred to a steel rule or micrometer to attain the exact value; **machinists' hammer** = BALL PEEN HAMMER

MacPherson strut *noun (suspension)* unitary construction of spring and damper elements with the hub carrier being attached rigidly to the outer tubular member; *(compare* DAMPER STRUT) *(see illustration 27)*; **MacPherson strut tower** = sheet metal panel surrounding the upper mount of the MacPherson strut at the side panels of the engine compartment; it may be a separate panel fitted by spot-welding or a deep-drawn section of the side panel shaped to take the upper strut end; *(see illustration 2)* (NOTE: also called **suspension leg turret**); **MacPherson suspension** = suspension layout incorporating MacPherson struts

macromolecule *noun* any very large molecule, such as a synthetic polymer used in the manufacture of plastic

◇ **macromolecular** *adjective* with very large molecules

MAF = MASS AIRFLOW

mag *noun (informal)* = MAGNETO *(compare* MAGS)

magnesium wheel *noun* = ALLOY WHEEL

magnetic clutch *noun* = ELECTROMAGNETIC CLUTCH

◇ **magnetic (drain) plug** *noun* plug fitted in the sump to collect metal debris

◇ **magnetic field** *noun* the portion of space found in the vicinity of a magnetic body or a current-carrying medium in which the forces due to the body or current can be detected

magnetic pick-up (assembly) *noun* pulse generator consisting of a stator with a permanent magnet and a rotor, which induces an AC voltage in the inductive winding by the periodical change of the air gap between stator and rotor

> COMMENT: magnetic pick-ups attached to the distributor for ignition triggering have as many teeth on the pole piece (stator) and on the trigger wheel (rotor) as the engine has cylinders. Some magnetic pick-ups have a bowl-like rotor with ferrite rods inserted in the walls. Magnetic pick-ups on the crankshaft flywheel act as reference mark sensors

magnetic pick-up (tool) *noun* tool with flexible or rigid shaft and magnetic tip used to retrieve dropped nuts, bolts, and other metal parts from hard-to-reach places; *(compare* PICK-UP TOOL)

◇ **magnetic screwdriver** *noun* screwdriver type tool with a magnetized hexagon socket end to accept and operate hex shank bits and hold them securely; often also with a magazine handle for bit storage

magnetized *adjective* made magnetic

magneto *(informal)* **mag** *noun* small electric generator in which the magnetic field is produced by a permanent magnet; especially used to generate the electric current providing a spark for the ignition

◇ **magneto file** *noun* tool for filing ignition points and other small objects

magneto ignition *noun* compact assembly of a magneto generator, an ignition coil, and a distributor

> COMMENT: ignition voltage is induced within the magneto by the movement of a coil relative to the poles of a permanent magnet.

Requiring no battery, the system is particularly suited for small engines, e.g. motorcycles, outboard engines, etc.

magnet sensor *noun* = HALL VANE SWITCH

mag wheels *or (informal)*

mags *noun* = ALLOY WHEELS

main bar *or* **bow** *noun (soft top)* the bar which carries the main load when the hood is raised and taut, and defines the hinge point for the folding motion

main beam *noun* long-range setting of a vehicle's headlamp; as the beam is directed straight ahead, it will dazzle oncoming traffic if used incautiously; *(compare* DIPPED BEAM) (NOTE: US English is **high beam**); **main beam indicator** = blue indicator light in the instrument cluster which comes on when the main beam is in use

main bearings *noun* bearings bolted to the underside of the cylinder block, that locate and support the camshaft

main combustion chamber *noun* with diesel engines, the fuel may be injected in three different locations: in the prechamber, the swirl chamber, or the main combustion chamber (for direct injection engines), depending on the process used

main jet *noun* main jet in a carburettor through which most of the fuel flows; *(see illustration 11)*

main(line) pressure *noun* = LINE PRESSURE

main member *noun* main chassis rail

main mixture discharge nozzle *noun* jet through which the petrol and air is fed into the carburettor barrel where it becomes the air/fuel mixture; *(see illustration 11)*

main petal *noun* primary petal of a dual-stage reed valve (NOTE: opposite is **subsidiary petal**)

COMMENT: in the case of dual-stage reed valves, the subsidiary petal opens first

main regulating system *noun* the carburettor components are divided into the fuel intake control, the main regulating system, the idle system and the starting aids; the main regulating system includes the main jet, jet needle, needle jet and throttle valve, whose purpose it is to provide an appropriate amount of fuel and air to the carburettor

main shaft *noun* gearbox output shaft

main sun visor *noun* in dual visor systems, the main visor is moved sideways and the secondary visor is flipped down, thus shielding the driver from the sun from both the front and side

maintenance *noun* the work undertaken by a car owner to keep his vehicle in good working order; typically checking the tyres, lights, oil and coolant levels, windscreen wipers and seat belts; *(compare* SERVICE)

◊ **maintenance-free** *adjective* requiring no work in order to be kept operational; **maintenance-free battery** = battery with a permanently sealed top, thus requiring no topping-up

◊ **maintenance manual** *noun* book of instructions detailing routine maintenance

major diameter *noun* diameter measured from the crest of a thread to the corresponding crest on the opposite side of the bolt or screw

male thread *noun* = EXTERNAL THREAD

man *(short for)* MANUAL GEARBOX

manganese phosphate coating *noun* phosphate coating with added manganese to increase resistance to wear and fatigue

manifold *noun* a casting connecting a series of inlets or outlets to a common opening

◊ **manifold absolute pressure (MAP) sensor** *noun* sensor which transmits data referring to the inlet manifold vacuum to the engine controller

◊ **manifold heater** *noun* system used to improve the cold start behaviour of an engine, consisting of heating ducts incorporated into the inlet manifold that are connected to the water cooling system of the engine; alternatively, an electric heater may be used

manoeuvre *verb* to drive or steer a vehicle around obstacles or in a confined space

◊ **manoeuvrability** *noun* the ease with which a vehicle can be manoeuvred

manual 1 *adjective* done by hand **2** *noun* **(a)** book of instructions; *(see* MAINTENANCE MANUAL, OWNER'S HANDBOOK) **(b)** = MANUAL GEARBOX **(c)** *(informal)* car with a manual gearbox

◊ **manual-crank window** *noun* = MANUALLY OPERATED WINDOW

◊ **manual gearbox** *US* **manual transmission** *noun* set of movable gears permitting the speed ratio between input and output shafts to be changed manually and at will; *(compare* AUTOMATIC GEARBOX)

◊ **manually operated window** *noun* window operated by turning a lever by hand; *(compare* ELECTRIC WINDOW)

◊ **manual panel cutter** *noun* cutting tool drawn manually across a panel surface to cut to the desired shape

◊ **manual transmission** *noun US* = MANUAL GEARBOX

◊ **manual valve (MV)** *noun (automatic transmission control)* distributes line pressure to the various control valves and pistons which operate the multi-plate or band brakes or the clutches; operated by the driver via the selector lever

◊ **manual version** *noun* passenger car with a manual gearbox; *(compare* AUTOMATIC)

manufacturer's performance ratings *noun* performance data as specified by the car manufacturer

MAP = MANIFOLD ABSOLUTE PRESSURE

map-controlled *or* **mapped ignition (system)** *noun* microprocessor-controlled ignition system with electronic ignition timing by means of an ignition map stored in the control unit memory

COMMENT: engine speed is sensed by Hall generators at the distributor or magnetic pick-ups on the crankshaft, the load signal being given by pressure sensors which measure the air mass or air per unit of time

map light *noun* interior light to facilitate, for example, map reading

mapping *noun* = CHARACTERISTIC MAP

marbling *noun* producing a special decorative effect with rotating brushes

marker light/lamp *noun* = SIDE MARKER LIGHT/LAMP

Marles steering *noun* form of cam-and-roller steering

marque *noun* 'name' of a car (such as 'MG'), which is an important marketing tool, and inspires customer loyalty

marten *noun* small, weasel-like animal with thick fur and a bushy tail, found in the USA

COMMENT: some martens have acquired a taste for the rubber and plastic materials found in engine compartments and love chewing away at cables, hoses and timing belts; this has resulted in anti-marten systems which make access to modern engines less attractive to both martens and American mechanics

mask *verb* to cover the surrounding area when paint spraying to protect it from splashes

◊ **masking tape** *noun* adhesive tape used to cover surfaces that border an area to be painted, so as to protect them

mass airflow (MAF) meter *noun* device for measuring the mass flow of air into an engine; *(compare* AIRFLOW SENSOR, HOT-WIRE AIRFLOW METER)

◊ **mass damper** *noun* device which reduces or prevents vibrations or oscillations, usually a weight which counteracts (balances) undesirable motions; used on drive shafts of some FWD cars; *(see illustrations 23, 27)*

◊ **mass-produced car** *noun* car which is manufactured in great numbers to a standard pattern and with extensive mechanization

◊ **mass tone** *noun (colour matching)* the tone of a paint as it appears from the colour of the paint in the can; this is required for formulating the ingredients of a paint tone; *(compare* TINT TONE)

◊ **mass transit system** *noun* system designed to transport large numbers of people (or goods)

master con rod *noun* in two-stroke dual piston engines, the connecting rod that is articulated directly on the crankshaft; (*compare* SLAVE CON ROD)

◊ **master cylinder** *noun* large cylinder in a hydraulic system in which the hydraulic fluid is compressed by a piston; (*compare* SLAVE CYLINDER)

◊ **master model** *or* **master pattern** *noun* first precision model of an automobile based on a clay model or CAD-data; essential for the manufacture of prototypes

◊ **master vac (servo unit)** *noun* = VACUUM BRAKE BOOSTER

mastication *noun* reduction of rubber to a pulp preparatory to making tyres *compared with mixing rolls, an internal mixer gives the desired degree of mastication much more rapidly*

mastic seam sealant *noun* soft waterproof sealant for joints

mat(t) *adjective (of a finish)* dull, not shiny

mate *verb* to fit together

◊ **mating** *adjective* fitting together; matching; **mating gears** = gears which mesh together; **mating surface** = surface which interacts perfectly with another *apply a suitable sealer to the crankcase mating surfaces* **mating thread** = thread which engages with a corresponding thread, such as the male and female threads of a nut and bolt

maximum (brake) power *noun* maximum power of an engine as measured by a dynamometer

mean distance to the sun *noun* 240 million miles; used to specify the headroom in convertibles

◊ **mean effective pressure (MEP)** *noun* average pressure on a piston in a cylinder during a power stroke

◊ **mean indicated pressure** *noun* mathematical value that indicates the relation between the effective area of the work diagram of the two-stroke engine and the movement of the piston

mechanic *noun* person who works on engines or machines; **mechanic's creeper** = CREEPER; **mechanic's elbow** = shallow dent in body panels, usually on the top of a wing near the engine compartment; caused

when leaning over into the engine compartment and supporting the body with elbows on the wing; **mechanic's stethoscope** = SONOSCOPE

mechanic's lien *noun* legally recorded claim against property, the term 'mechanic' referring to anyone who has performed work

COMMENT: the purpose of the mechanic's lien is to permit the mechanic (creditor) to seize the property (e.g. a car) and to have it sold in order to obtain the money which is due to him for his labour and any materials used; in the auto repair business, a mechanic's lien is invoked only rarely, e.g. when a customer abandons the car rather than paying the repair bill

mechanical advance *noun* = CENTRIFUGAL ADVANCE (MECHANISM)

◊ **mechanical efficiency** *noun* ratio of brake horsepower to indicated horsepower

◊ **mechanical (face) seal** *noun* shaft seal consisting of two highly polished mating surfaces, one surface being connected to the shaft (rotating element) and the other to the casing (stationary element); *(see illustration 10)*

◊ **mechanical galvanizing** *noun* = MECHANICAL PLATING

◊ **mechanical ignition timing** *noun* centrifugal and vacuum advance; *(compare ELECTRONIC IGNITION SYSTEM)*

◊ **mechanical plating** *noun* deposition of zinc on another material by a cold-peening process, such as tumbling

◊ **mechanical stress** *noun* force acting across a unit area in solid materials in resisting the separation, compacting, or sliding that tends to be induced by external forces

◊ **mechanical surface treatment** *noun* producing a dull or rough surface or a decorative finish by grinding, brushing, polishing or abrasive blasting

megajoule (MJ) *noun* SI measurement of energy (= 1000 joules)

member *noun* general term that refers mainly to the side rails and crossmembers but also to any structural hollow-section part on a car

◊ **member of the gear train** *noun* sun gear, internal gear, and planet carrier are the members of a planetary gear train

memory button *noun* button which operates the position of electric seats, mirrors, etc. and which stores the requirements of a particular driver in its memory

MEP = MEAN EFFECTIVE PRESSURE

mercury switch *noun* safety switch to prevent erroneous deployment of the air bag

| COMMENT: due to ecological problems associated with mercury in automobile waste, mercury switches are being replaced by suspended-mass switches, e.g. a Hamlin switch

mesh *verb* to engage *gears are meshed when the teeth of the two gears are interlaced; the planetary gears mesh with the internal teeth of the annulus* (NOTE: opposite is **disengage**)

◊ **meshing drive** *noun* device for engaging the starter pinion with the flywheel ring gear

◊ **meshing spring** *noun* component of a pre-engaged starter which ensures that the shift lever will move to its final position and that the starter current will be switched on in case of tooth abutment; *(see illustration 37)*

message centre *noun* usually a multi-functional display of a diagnostic system

| COMMENT: typical messages are: NORMAL, DOOR AJAR, TAILGATE OPEN, LAMP OUT, WASHER FLUID LOW, etc.

metal catalyst *noun* catalyst whose active phase is supported by a metal substrate, i.e. sheet steel; *(compare* METAL MONOLITH)

◊ **metal cutter** *noun* bench tool for cutting sheet metal

◊ **metallic** *adjective* referring to or consisting of metal; **metallic drive screw** = THREAD-CUTTING SCREW

metallic finish *or* **metallic paint** *noun* paint type incorporating small metallic flakes which reflect light (NOTE: opposite is **solid paint**)

| COMMENT: the flakes are often of different sizes; when the surface is viewed from different angles, the colour shade seems to vary, since the flakes are all oriented at different angles in the paint and consequently reflect the light differently

metallize *verb* to coat or impregnate a metal or non-metal surface with metal, as by metal spraying or by vacuum evaporation

metallographic examination *noun* test to determine the structural composition of a metal as shown at low and high magnification and by X-ray diffraction methods

| COMMENT: tests of this type include macro-examination, micro-examination, and X-ray diffraction analysis

metal mesh *noun* = WIRE MESH

◊ **metal monolith** *noun* = METAL SUPPORT

◊ **metal shears** *noun* scissor-like hand tool for cutting sheet metal (NOTE: also called **snips**)

◊ **metal spraying** *noun* coating of surfaces with droplets of molten metal or alloy by using a compressed gas stream

◊ **metal support** *noun (in a catalytic converter)* thin corrugated strips of steel alloy rolled up into a tight coil as a support for the catalyst; *(compare* CERAMIC HONEYCOMB)

◊ **metalworking** *noun* forming and shaping metal; **metalworking spoon** = BODY SPOON

meter 1 *noun* device for measuring the quantity of a substance passing through it **2** *verb* **(a)** to measure with a meter **(b)** to supply at a measured rate *the EGR system meters exhaust gas into the induction system*

◊ **metering port** *noun* part of the metering unit in the fuel distributor

metering unit *noun* unit which regulates the quantity of fuel injected in the K-jetronic system

| COMMENT: a lever connected to the sensor plate raises or lowers a stepped control plunger in the metering unit; the position of the control plunger relative to the metering ports in the metering unit varies the flow of fuel to the fuel injectors

metering valve *noun* valve positioned in the hydraulic line to the front brakes, on some cars with front disc and rear drum brakes

| COMMENT: prevents the disc brakes from applying until after the rear brake linings contact the drum: the metering valve closes off pressure to the front disc brakes until a specified pressure level is generated in the master cylinder; this allows pressure in the rear brake circuit to overcome return spring force and air gap before the hydraulic pressure is admitted to the front disc brakes

methacrylate *noun* polymer used in toughening rubber

methanol *noun* used in petrol/alcohol blends, in a variety of concentrations blended with unleaded petrol and solvents; a typical methanol content is 3%; use of petrol blends with methanol will void the new car warranty of most car manufacturers (NOTE: formerly called **methyl alcohol**)

methylated spirits *noun* almost pure alcohol (which has wood alcohol and colouring added to make it unfit for human consumption); used for cleaning

metric thread *noun* one of two commonly used screw threads *metric coarse or fine (pitch) thread (compare* UNC THREAD, UNF THREAD)

metro driving *noun US* = URBAN DRIVING

MF = MULTI-FOCAL; **MF headlight** = conventional headlight with a multiple-focus parabolic reflector

MG *(short for)* Morris Garages; a popular old British sports car marque

microbial corrosion *noun* corrosion associated with the action of micro-organisms present in the corrosion system

microcar *noun* small car, popular in the 1950s, that featured a body offering full-weather protection and mechanics often derived from motorcycle technology, e.g. Goggomobil, BMW Isetta, etc.; *(compare* BUBBLE CAR)

microgalvanic cell *noun* = LOCAL CELL

micrometer *noun* **(a)** instrument for taking very small measurements, such as measuring the width *or* thickness of very thin pieces of metal, etc.; **micrometer (type) torque wrench** = CLICK-TYPE TORQUE WRENCH **(b)** *US* = MICROMETRE

COMMENT: micrometers are used for measuring wear on automotive parts, or the thickness of adjusting shims, or the diameters of components such as crankshafts or camshafts. They are usually graduated in steps of 1/100 mm or 1/1000 in

micrometre *or* **micron** *noun* unit of measurement of thickness (= one thousandth of a millimetre) (NOTE: usually written mm with figures: **25mm**)

micro oil filter *noun* special oil filter designed to trap particles down to 1 micrometre in order to allow extended oil change intervals in the order of 60,000 miles without affecting engine life

microprocessor spark timing system (MSTS) *noun* = MAPPED IGNITION SYSTEM

mid-engine car *noun* car whose engine is located behind the passenger compartment but within the wheelbase; *(compare* FRONT ENGINE, REAR ENGINE)

mid-size car *noun* American car category which encompasses practically all cars which would be considered large outside the USA; some typical examples are: Audi 100/200, BMW 7-series, Buick Regal, Dodge Dynasty, Ford Taurus, Mazda 626, Mercedes S-class (at least prior to 1991), Mercury Cougar, Oldsmobile Cutlass, Pontiac 6000, Volvo 740/940; *(compare* COMPACT CAR, FULL-SIZE CAR)

mid-range *noun* middle of the rev range, around 3000 rpm

midbed *noun* in dual bed catalytic converters with air injection, the plenum between the three-way catalyst and the conventional oxidation catalyst, into which secondary air is injected

midrange torque *noun* pulling power of the engine in the middle of the rev range

MIG *(short for)* metal/inert gas; **MIG welding** = arc welding method in which the electric current is provided by the filler metal wire which is cooled and shielded from the access of air by a stream of chemically inert gas, thus preventing oxidation of the joint; *(compare* TIG WELDING)

migrate *verb (of electrophoretic paint)* to be attracted to car bodies when they are immersed in a bath of paint with an applied polarity across the bath and the bodies

mild steel *noun* type of steel with a low carbon content (0.1-0.25%), widely used in vehicle construction

mileage *noun* **(a)** distance measured in miles, as by a mileometer **(b)** the total number of miles a motor vehicle has travelled **(c)** the number of miles a motor vehicle travels on one gallon of fuel

◊ **mil(e)ometer** *noun* device that records the number of miles travelled; *(compare* ODOMETER)

mill 1 *verb* **(a)** to grind, press or reduce to powder **(b)** to shape or cut metal **2** *noun* **(a)** = MILLING CUTTER **(b)** = MILLING MACHINE

◊ **milled glass fibre** *noun* chopped strands of glass fibre which vary in length from 3 mm to about 50 mm

◊ **milling cutter** *noun* rotating, toothed cutter in a milling machine, used to cut or shape metal

◊ **milling machine** *noun* machine tool with a table on which rests material which is cut by a rotating cutting tool held by a horizontal arbor or vertical spindle

◊ **millsaw file** *noun* flat hand file with round or square edges for sharpening saw blades or machine-cutting knives

milliampere *noun* thousandth of an ampere (NOTE: with figures usually written **mA**)

◊ **milliammeter** *noun* ammeter with a milliampere scale

milligram *noun* unit of measurement of weight (= one thousandth of a gram) (NOTE: with figures usually written **mg**)

millilitre *US* **milliliter** *noun* unit of measurement of liquid (= one thousandth of a litre) (NOTE: with figures usually written **ml**)

millimetre *US* **millimeter** *noun* unit of measurement of length (= one thousandth of a metre) (NOTE: with figures usually written **mm**)

mineral oil *noun* light lubricating oil refined from crude oil

Mini *noun* very successful, small British front-wheel drive car designed in 1959 by Sir Alec Issigonis (1906-88)

miniature offset open-end wrench *noun* very small, open-ended spanner with two jaw openings of the same size set at different angles to the handle, e.g. 15° at one

end and 60° at the other (NOTE: also called **electrical spanner**)

minibus *noun* small, single-decker bus designed to carry around 12-20 people

minicar *noun* very small saloon car, carrying no more than four adults

mini catalytic converter *noun* usually used as a primary catalytic converter and installed close to the engine in the headpipe

miniframe *noun* = SUSPENSION SUBFRAME

mini-grinder *noun* = ANGLE GRINDER

Minilite (alloy wheel) *noun* a true magnesium wheel, developed for the Mini in 1962 by nuclear engineer Derek Power on the basis of experience gathered with magnesium components in nuclear power plants; the Minilite started the boom in alloy wheels

mini spare wheel *noun* = TEMPA SPARE WHEEL

mini tube cutter *noun* compact tube cutter for cutting brass, copper, plastic, or thin steel tubing in confined areas

minivan *noun* minibus-sized van with no side windows, used to transport goods instead of people

Minlon *noun* a mineral-fibre-reinforced polyamide, used for alloy wheels as a rim trim cover that protects the balancing weights

minor diameter *noun* diameter measured from the thread root to the corresponding root on the opposite side of the bolt or screw

mint condition *noun* (in) perfect condition, as brand new

mirror *noun* car mirrors can be either interior or exterior; *(see* DRIVING/REAR-VIEW MIRROR, DOOR MIRROR, WING MIRROR, VANITY MIRROR)

misalignment *noun* general term referring to all types of frame damage caused by accidents

misfire 1 *verb (of the air/fuel mixture)* to fail to ignite properly (often resulting in a backfire) **2** *noun* the act of misfiring

miss *verb* = MISFIRE

mist action *noun US* = INTERMITTENT WIPER CONTROL

mixed-flow impeller *noun* pump impeller which combines radial and axial-flow principles, i.e. liquid flows both along the drive shaft and out through the impeller; pump impellers are classed as mixed-flow when the specific speed is 2,000 to 6,000 rpm; **mixed-flow pump** = centrifugal pump which develops its head partly by centrifugal force and partly by the lift of the vanes on the liquid

◇ **mixing chamber** *noun* **(a)** that part of a carburettor distinct from the float chamber both in function and layout, in which the air and the fuel mix as they meet **(b)** *(of a catalytic converter)* = MIDBED

◇ **mixing head** *noun* head of an oxyacetylene torch by which the mixture of oxygen and acetylene can be adjusted

◇ **mixing rolls** *noun* machine designed for the mixing and mastication of the materials from which tyres are made

mixture *noun* **(a)** air/fuel mixture in an IC engine **(b)** *(two-stroke engine)* mixture of oil and petrol in the fuel tank of a two-stroke engine; e.g. 1:50, i.e. one part of oil is added to every 50 parts of fuel

◇ **mixture control knob** *noun* = CHOKE

◇ **mixture control screw** *noun* adjusting screw which controls the amount of air/fuel mixture supplied by the idling circuit of a fixed-jet carburettor

◇ **mixture control unit** *noun* unit in the K-jetronic fuel injection system which combines the fuel distributor and the airflow sensor; it monitors the rate of airflow and meters the fuel supplied to the injectors

◇ **mixture volume** *noun* the quantity of air/fuel mixture

mobile home *noun US* caravan; *(compare* CARAVAN, MOTOR HOME)

◇ **mobile phone** *noun* cellular telephone

◇ **mobile two-way radio** *noun* receiver/transmitter used for CB communication

mode *noun* way of operating *the system is in normal mode*

model designation *noun* shortened description of a particular model

COMMENT: e.g. 'Toyota Corolla Tercel XLi 1.6 4wd' means: manufacturer Toyota, model Corolla Tercel, version XL (extra luxury or excel), with fuel injection (i), 1.6-litre engine, and four-wheel drive

model year (MY) *noun* a new model year starts after the summer break of the car production plant, during which the assembly lines are altered to accommodate the changes introduced in the cars of the next model year

COMMENT: model year and year of manufacture can, therefore, differ: a car built in October 1994 would belong to model year 1995

modular air strut *noun* = SELF-LEVELLING (SUSPENSION) STRUT

modulator *noun* *(automatic gearbox)* actuator used to transform inlet manifold vacuum into a mechanical motion, which in turn can be used to move the connected modulator valve; **modulator pressure** = pressure controlled by the actuator valve and thus directly related to inlet manifold vacuum; **modulator valve** = valve operated by the modulator to create modulator pressure by means of inlet manifold vacuum

module *noun* electronic control assembly

modulus in shear *noun* measure of a material's resistance to shearing stress equal to the shearing stress divided by the resultant angle of deformation expressed in radians

molecular weight *noun* the mass of a molecule that may be calculated as the sum of the atomic weights of its constituent atoms

mole grips *or* **mole wrench** *noun* locking pliers

molybdenum *noun* metallic element used in alloys, especially to harden and strengthen steels in high temperature applications, like exhaust valves; **molybdenum piston ring** *or* *(informal)*; **moly ring** = piston ring with a molybdenum coating

MON = MOTOR OCTANE NUMBER

monkey wrench *noun* = ADJUSTABLE SPANNER

monobloc casting *or* **construction** *noun* type of engine construction where the cylinders are cast in a single block which incorporates the crankcase

monocoque *noun* unitary design in which body and chassis are all one unit (NOTE: also called **unitary construction**)

Monodex-type cutter *noun* = NIBBLER

Mono-Jetronic *noun* single point injection system developed by Bosch

monolith *noun* single block of material; used to describe the (ceramic) base for the catalyst in one type of catalytic converter; **monolithic converter** = catalytic converter with a catalyst-coated, ceramic honeycomb monolith through which the exhaust gases pass

monomer *noun* a relatively simple compound which can react with itself to form a polymer or with other monomers to form a copolymer

monotube damper *or* **shock absorber** *noun* = SINGLE-TUBE SHOCK ABSORBER

Monroney sticker *noun* window sticker

COMMENT: a US federal law requires that all cars sold in the USA display a Monroney sticker which is required to specify the manufacturer's suggested retail price for the vehicle and all its factory-installed options, a destination charge for shipping from final assembly point (or port of importation) to the dealer, and EPA fuel economy estimates; most dealers add a second window sticker that lists accessories installed at the dealership, as well as other charges

moped *noun* two-wheeled cycle with a low-powered motor (under 50 cc)

moquette *noun* thick, velvety upholstery fabric often used as weatherstrip

MOT *(short for)* Ministry of Transport; **MOT certificate** = certificate awarded when a vehicle passes an MOT test; **MOT test** = annual roadworthiness test for all vehicles over two years old, undertaken by a garage approved by the (currently named) Department of Transport

COMMENT: parts covered by the MOT test are: steering, suspension, transmission, lighting, brakes, tyres and wheels, seat belts, horn, exhaust system (including a metered emission check), vehicle structure

motor *noun* **(a)** electric motor **(b)** engine **(c)** motor car

◇ **motorbike** *noun (informal)* = MOTORCYCLE

◇ **motor car** *noun* a (usually) four-wheeled road vehicle powered by an IC engine and designed for passengers

◇ **motor caravan** *US* **motor home** *noun* a self-powered (motorized) caravan; *(compare* CARAVAN)

◇ **motorcycle** *noun* single-track vehicle usually driven by a two-stroke or four-stroke engine; often air-cooled, less frequently liquid-cooled and usually between 125 cc and 1000 cc

◇ **motor home** *noun US* = MOTOR CARAVAN

◇ **motor insurance** *noun* insurance against damage to or damage caused by a vehicle; *(compare* COMPREHENSIVE INSURANCE)

◇ **motorist** *noun* car driver

◇ **motorized** *adjective* with a motor *a motorized caravan*

◇ **motor mechanic** *noun* car mechanic

◇ **motor octane number (MON)** *noun* fuel octane rating determined by the motor octane test, one of many test procedures; *(compare* OCTANE NUMBER, RON)

◇ **motor oil** *noun* engine oil or gear oil

◇ **motor scooter** *noun* lightweight motorcycle with small wheels, an enclosed engine, open foot platform and leg shields

◇ **motor vehicle** *noun* any automotive vehicle that does not run on rails; usually with rubber tyres; such as cars, trucks, lorries and motorcycles

◇ **motorway** *noun* a multi-lane, main road for fast-moving traffic (speed limit 70 mph in the UK) with a central reservation, and few exit and entry points

MOT test *see* MOT

mottling *noun* spotty, non-uniform, blotchy appearance of metallic paint, characterized by small, irregular areas darker in colour, or spots in solid colour paint

mould *US* **mold 1** *noun* hollow form used to give a certain shape to fluid or plastic material **2** *verb* to shape in a mould

◊ **mouldability** *noun* capacity for being moulded into a particular form

moulded part *or* **moulding** *noun* plastic part produced by injection moulding etc.

| COMMENT: mouldings are parts which have been produced from moulding materials (compounds) by shaping in moulds closed on all sides (e.g. by compression moulding, transfer moulding, or injection moulding)

moulding material *noun* moulding materials are products which can be moulded permanently by a shaping process employing mechanical forces within a given temperature range into moulded parts or semi-finished articles; in some cases moulding materials are used in a preformed state (e.g. pelleted or granulated) without their plastic mouldability being appreciably impaired by such preforming

◊ **mould shrinkage** *noun (of thermoplastics)* the difference in dimension between the cold mould and the cooled moulded part, expressed in % relative to the dimension of the cold mould

Moulton Hydragas suspension *noun* hydropneumatic suspension developed by Leyland; **Moulton Hydrolastic suspension** = Hydrolastic suspension developed by Leyland

mount *verb* to attach something to a support

◊ **mounting** *noun* support to which or by means of which something is attached; **mounting frame** = floating-frame disc brake in which the floating frame is held by a casting which is bolted to the steering knuckle or other suspension part

move off *verb* to start from rest; to begin to drive away

moving contact *noun* component of a solenoid switch; in a starter motor it is designed for switching on the electric circuit in the excitation and armature windings; *(compare* CONTACT BREAKER) *(see illustration 37)*

mpg *(short for)* miles per gallon; measure of fuel consumption

◊ **mph** *(short for)* miles per hour; measure of vehicle speed

MPI = MULTI-POINT INJECTION

MSTS = MICROPROCESSOR SPARK TIMING SYSTEM

mud and snow tyre (M+S tyre) *noun* winter tyre with a deep tread

◊ **mudflap** *noun* flexible rubber or vinyl rear extension to the wheel arch to protect the bodywork from dirt and stones (NOTE: US English is **splash guard**)

◊ **mudguard** *noun* curved part over the wheels of a motorcycle to minimize splashing

muffler *noun US* = SILENCER

Multec (system) *noun* combined fuel injection and ignition system

Multicon connector system *noun* 13-pinned electrical connection system for trailers

◊ **multi-cut file** *noun* = MULTI-PURPOSE FILE

◊ **multi-disc** *adjective* = MULTI-PLATE

◊ **multi-entry** *noun (pump)* = MULTI-SUCTION PUMP

◊ **multi-focal (MF)** *adjective* multiple-focus; **multi-focal headlight** = conventional headlight with a multiple-focus parabolic reflector

multi-function control stalk *noun* a rod-shaped control mounted on the steering column near the steering wheel

| COMMENT: typical multi-function control stalks operate indicators, headlight dipper switch, wiper/washer; some also include speed control or horn button

multigrade oil *noun* if an engine oil meets the viscosity requirements of several different single-grade engine oil types it is referred to as multigrade *use 10W-40 multigrade oil above 32°F*

◊ **multigrip pliers** *noun* pliers with an adjustable head allowing different jaw widths

◊ **multi-hole nozzle** *noun* two-, three- or four-holed injector nozzle in a direct injection engine; *(compare* PINTLE NOZZLE)

◊ **multi-inlet pump** *noun* = MULTI-SUCTION PUMP

◊ **multi-leaf spring** *noun* leaf spring made of several narrow, flat strips (leaves)

◊ **multi-link independent rear suspension** *noun* special multi-link rear suspension design, developed by Mercedes-Benz for the W 201 series; **multi-link rear suspension** = general term for independent rear suspension layouts incorporating several control arms; *(compare* FOUR-LINK REAR SUSPENSION, FIVE-LINK REAR SUSPENSION)

multi-piece rim *noun* rim type incorporating at least one demountable bead seat and/or rim flange to allow tyre mounting (NOTE: opposite is **one-piece rim**)

| COMMENT: the bead seats of all multi-piece rims (except flat base rims) have a 5° taper; rims incorporating the semi-drop centre, the tapered bead seat or the flat base design are multi-piece rims

multi-plate *or* **multiple-plate clutch** *US* **multiple-disc clutch** *noun* clutch with more than one driven plate, usually of the oil-immersed type; frequently used in motorcycle drive trains, in automatic transmissions of cars, in power distribution systems of 4wd vehicles, and as locking elements in limited-slip differentials; *(compare* VISCOUS COUPLING); **multiple-disc limited-slip differential** = limited-slip differential incorporating multiple discs as locking or slip-inhibiting devices

◊ **multiple-point injection** *noun* = MULTI-POINT INJECTION

◊ **multiple-spark (ignition) coil** *noun* = MULTI-SPARK (IGNITION) COIL

◊ **multiplex technology** *noun* in cars, connecting lamps, wipers, horn, etc. to a single power cable via electronically controlled modules, making it easier to diagnose faults and to service

◊ **multi-point injection (MPI)** *noun* petrol fuel-injection system in which only air enters the inlet manifold; as the air approaches the inlet valve, an injection valve opens in the valve port, spraying fuel into the airstream; *(compare* SPI)

◊ **multi-purpose file** *noun* file (usually flat) with faces featuring different cuts, e.g. coarse cut on one side and smooth cut on the other

◊ **multi-reed cage** *noun (two-stroke induction control)* a reed valve which consists of several petals

◊ **multi-spark (ignition) coil** *noun* type of ignition coil used in static high-voltage distribution, designed as a double-spark or four-spark coil

multi-stage pump *noun* pump with two or more stages (impellers/diffusers or other pumping elements) operating in series

| COMMENT: multi-stage centrifugal pumps are employed to operate against higher pressures, where several impellers are built on to one shaft in the same casing

multi-storey car park *noun* car park with many levels

multi-suction pump *noun* centrifugal pump with several impellers connected in parallel; i.e. the flow is separated into two or more partial flows

| COMMENT: multi-suction usually means double suction in practice

mural *noun* customized design airbrushed onto the side panels of vans (and sometimes cars)

mush pot *noun (body soldering)* container used to keep body lead bars in a semi-liquid state to enable them to be spread directly onto the body

mushroom-shaped dolly *noun* dolly with a shank to allow it to be hand-held or clamped in a vice; a more or less rounded head may be fitted to one or both ends of the shank

◊ **mushroom tappet** *noun* tappet shaped like a mushroom located on the underside of a pushrod operating the valves of a four-stroke engine; *(compare* FLAT TAPPET)

◊ **mushroom valve** *noun* = POPPET VALVE

mutual inductance *noun* takes place when a current in one winding induces an EMF in another winding in the same magnetic circuit

MV = MANUAL VALVE

MY = MODEL YEAR

Nn

N *(gear selector)* = NEUTRAL

nail punch *noun* = DRIFT PUNCH

natural frequency *noun* frequency at which an object, circuit or system oscillates or vibrates when set in free vibration

◇ **natural gas** *noun* alternative, environmentally friendly fuel (mainly methane) which can be stored under pressure in the boot as compressed natural gas (CNG)

◇ **naturally aspirated engine** *noun* conventional engine that takes in air at normal pressure, i.e. not turbocharged or supercharged (NOTE: opposite is **forced-induction engine)**

◇ **natural oxide film** *or* **skin** *noun* transparent film which forms naturally on an aluminium surface due to oxidation

◇ **natural rubber (NR)** *noun* rubber which occurs naturally as a product of the metabolism of certain trees and plants, notably trees of the *Hevea brasiliensis* species; *(compare* SYNTHETIC RUBBER)

◇ **natural weathering** *noun* corrosion test by means of which the corrosion resistance of a material is tested in the open air

nave *noun* wheel hub; **nave plate** = hub cap

NCM = NO$_x$-CONTROL MODULE

NCS = NOISE CANCELLATION SYSTEM

NDIR analyser *noun* non-dispersive infrared analyser, used for analysing concentrations of carbon monoxide and carbon dioxide in an exhaust gas sample

NDT method *noun* non-destructive testing method, such as ultrasonic testing, X-ray testing, dye-penetrant testing

nearside (n/s) *noun* the side of a vehicle nearest the kerb (when driving)

necking *noun* when ductile test specimens are subjected to a tensile test, they exhibit necking when the tensile force exceeds the yield strength of the material; necking results in a reduction of area, measured in percent after break of the specimen

needle *noun* **(a)** indicator or pointer on an instrument or gauge **(b)** tapered, needle-shaped pin in a carburettor jet; *(see illustration 12)*

◇ **needle bearing** *noun* roller bearing with long thin rollers; *(compare* ANTIFRICTION BEARING)

◇ **needle-flame test** *noun* test to assess fire hazard by simulating the effect of small flames, which may result from faults within the equipment

◇ **needle-nose pliers** *noun* = LONG-NOSE PLIERS

◇ **needle valve** *noun* (i) valve with a needle-shaped pin that can be moved to control the flow of a fluid; (ii) in a carburettor, valve which controls the amount of petrol flowing from the pump to the float chamber

negative back pressure (modulated) EGR valve *noun* = NEGATIVE TRANSDUCER EGR VALVE

◇ **negative camber** *see* CAMBER (a)

◇ **negative castor** *noun* *(steering geometry)* when an imaginary line extended through the steering axis meets the ground behind the extended vertical axis through the wheel centre; *(compare* POSITIVE CASTOR)

◇ **negative electrode** *noun* = NEGATIVE PLATE

◇ **negative offset** *noun* **(a)** *(steering)* steering geometry layout where the steering axis cuts the wheel axis above the wheel centre plane; *(compare* CENTRE POINT STEERING, POSITIVE OFFSET, SCRUB RADIUS) **(b)** *(wheel)* distance between the mounting face of the disc and the rim centreline; the offset is referred to as negative when the inner attachment face of the wheel disc is shifted towards the the inner side of the wheel (NOTE: opposite is **positive offset)**

◊ **negative plate** *noun* during battery discharge, the grey plate which acts as anode (NOTE: opposite is **positive plate**)

◊ **negative spark** *noun* a spark that jumps from the negative centre electrode to the positive earth electrode of the sparking plug, allowing a reduction in the high voltage required

◊ **negative suction head** *noun* = SUCTION LIFT

◊ **negative terminal** *noun* black battery terminal with a minus symbol indicating negative polarity; *(compare* POSITIVE TERMINAL)

◊ **negative transducer EGR valve** *noun* valve used on engines with a relatively low back pressure to provide the desired opening point and exhaust gas recycling rate

◊ **negative wheel offset** *or* **negative wheel dish(ing)** *noun* = NEGATIVE OFFSET (b)

nerf bar *noun US* type of front bumper guard, typically made of chrome-plated steel tubing; extends horizontally from below front end and is curved upward; a pair of nerf bars is usually braced by a horizontal crossbar (NOTE: in Australia called **roo bar)** *(compare* BULL BAR)

Nernst equation *noun* relationship showing that the electromotive force developed by a dry cell is determined by the activities of the reacting species, the temperature of the reaction, and the standard free-energy change of the overall reaction

neutral 1 *adjective* **(a)** not having any marked characteristics; **neutral handling** = having neither oversteer nor understeer **(b)** having a pH of 7, i.e. neither alkaline nor acid **2** *noun* position of the gearbox in which no gear is engaged; indicated by the letter N on automatic gear selectors

new-old-stock (NOS) part *noun* new genuine spares for older models, referring mostly to spare parts that are normally no longer produced

nibbler *noun* tool used to cut sheet metal without deforming the sheet or causing a burr; works upwards, leaving the hands above the material; allows circular and straight cuts

NiCaSil *noun* nickel-silicon plating used e.g. on the cylinder walls of certain light-weight high-performance engines; reduces weight and friction and improves heat transfer; *(compare* SCANIMET)

◊ **nickel plating** *noun* thin coating of nickel deposited on a surface by electrolysis

nipple *noun* **(a)** *(lubrication)* small, one-way valve used for injecting grease into a bearing **(b)** *(bleeding)* short, steel tube holding a thin rubber or plastic tube used for bleeding hydraulic fluid

nippy *adjective (of a motor vehicle)* small and relatively powerful *the Mini is very nippy, making it ideal for urban conditions*

nitriding *noun (of a steel surface)* hardening by heating for several hours in ammonia gas; used on crankshafts

nitrocellulose paint *noun* paint giving a deep, lustrous finish

COMMENT: used on old Jaguars and prone to crazing and checking; as spraying with nitrocellulose paints creates environmental problems, they are no longer used for volume cars

nitrogen oxides (NO$_x$) *noun* general term for an unknown mixture of nitrogen oxides, usually nitric oxide and nitrogen dioxide

COMMENT: nitric oxide is the main oxide of nitrogen emitted in raw exhaust gas, typically 90%; nitric oxide and nitrogen dioxide are severely toxic gases; without emission controls, the exhaust of an SI engine contains 0.3-1.5 kg of NO$_x$ per 100 litres of petrol consumption

nitrous oxide system *noun* performance system that injects nitrous oxide into the inlet manifold at the press of a button, thereby introducing a quick dose of extra energy and a burst of power

COMMENT: on 6-cylinder or V-8 engines, the nitrous oxide system is intended to add up to 250 HP; it consists basically of a pressurized nitrous oxide bottle as used for welding, solenoids, an injector base plate for the carburettor, and steel pipes; the low vaporization temperature of nitrous oxide (-130°F) cools the A/F charge, dampening detonation and minimizing stress caused by increased load

noble metal *noun* precious metal (such as gold, silver, mercury, platinum) which conducts electricity very well, resists corrosion and is inert; some are used as catalysts in catalytic converters

no-claims bonus *noun* reduction in insurance premiums because no claims have been made

no-cost option *noun* optional extra for a new car at no extra cost (NOTE: opposite is **cost option**)

noise cancellation *or* **reduction** *noun* the reduction of noise by means of anti-noise loudspeakers; **noise cancellation system (NCS)** = ANTI-NOISE SYSTEM (*compare* SOUNDPROOFING MATERIAL)

nominal capacity *noun* = RATED CAPACITY

◇ **nominal diameter** *noun* characteristic value used for pipeline systems to identify parts which belong together such as pipes, pipe joints, fittings, etc; a nominal size for the inside diameter

◇ **nominal engine speed** *noun* = RATED SPEED

◇ **nominal length** *noun* (i) length of the shank of screws/bolts with flat bearing faces; (ii) length of shank plus height of head of countersunk bolts/screws; (iii) overall length of a stud minus the length of the stud end

◇ **nominal pressure** *noun* = RATED PRESSURE

◇ **nominal (thread) diameter** *noun* = MAJOR DIAMETER

◇ **nominal voltage** *noun* = RATED VOLTAGE

non-destructive testing (NDT) *see* NDT METHOD

◇ **non-dispersive infrared analyser** *see* NDIR ANALYSER

◇ **non-ferrous metal** *noun* metal that is not based on iron; includes aluminium, copper, magnesium, etc.

non-self-priming pump *noun* a centrifugal pump which is unable to evacuate and prime the suction line without external assistance (NOTE: opposite is **self-priming pump**)

COMMENT: most centrifugal pumps are non-self-priming and require a flooded suction line

non-servo brake *noun* drum brake design; each brake shoe is anchored, therefore no one shoe can assist in the application of the other; one shoe is self-energizing, the other is not

Nordberg key *noun* round key

Nordic Anti-Corrosion Code *noun* (*for passenger cars*) code developed by the Scandinavian automobile and consumer associations which stipulates that, as of January 1983, all cars must be free of surface corrosion for three years and free of perforation and weakening damage for six years

no rinse treatment *noun* application method of chemical conversion coatings by means of a roll coating system whereby no rinsing treatment is required

normal zinc technology *see* LOW ZINC TECHNOLOGY

◇ **normally aspirated engine** *noun* = NATURALLY ASPIRATED ENGINE

north-south layout *noun* engine layout with the cylinders lying lengthways from the front (north) to the back (south) (NOTE: also called **longitudinal engine**) (*compare* EAST-WEST LAYOUT)

NOS = NEW-OLD-STOCK (PART)

nose *noun* the front end of a vehicle

◇ **nose-to-tail** *noun* driving mode in rush-hour traffic; bumper-to-bumper

◇ **nose-up** *adjective* description of the towing vehicle if the vehicle being towed is too heavy

◇ **nose dive** *noun* = BRAKE DIVE

◇ **nosepiece** *noun* insert for pop-rivet pliers that is used to allow various pop-rivet diameters to be used

nose protector *noun* cover, usually of black soft plastic sheeting with flannel-like backing, that fits around the front end of a car (NOTE: also called **nose bra**) (*compare* STEALTH BRA)

COMMENT: protects the front portion of bonnet and wings against damage caused by flying rocks, road debris and insects; attaches to car with bendable plates, straps or hooks and grommeted edges; sometimes personalized with a vehicle logo; relatively common in rougher terrain in the USA, but rarely found in Europe

noseweight *noun* vertical weight on the centre of the towing ball exerted by the vehicle being towed (on level ground)

COMMENT: this must be within certain limits; generally between 50-75 kilos for car and caravan

no-spin differential *noun* = LIMITED-SLIP DIFFERENTIAL

notch *noun* a V- or U-shaped indentation cut into a test piece, test bar, or into a moulded part *notched bar impact test*

COMMENT: the notch in the Izod specimen serves to concentrate the stress, minimize plastic deformation, and direct the fracture to the part of the specimen behind the notch

notchback *noun* classical saloon car shape with a boot; *(compare* FASTBACK, HATCHBACK)

notchy *adjective (changing of gears)* not smooth, causing a slight crashing of gears; often caused by the clutch failing to disengage fully *a notchy gearbox*

NO$_x$ *(symbol for)* NITROGEN OXIDES; **NO$_x$-Control module (NCM)** = digital ignition control module for retrofitting to cars with Motronic engine control; modifies ignition timing characteristics for lower NO$_x$ emissions

nozzle *noun* jet, hole, or special fitting at the end of a pipe for controlling what comes out

◊ **nozzle restrictor** *noun* restrictor in the fuel filler neck of cars fitted with catalytic converters that prevents filling from leaded petrol pumps, which have larger pump nozzles

NR = NATURAL RUBBER

n/s = NEARSIDE

nucleation site *noun* location where nucleation, i.e. the formation of new crystal nuclei in supersaturated solutions, starts

nudge bar *noun* = NERF BAR

numberplate *noun* plate on the front and back of a vehicle, showing its registration number (NOTE: US English is **license plate**); **numberplate lamp** = lamp providing white illumination of the rear numberplate

nut *noun* small, metal block with a threaded central hole so that it can be screwed on to a bolt, screw, etc.; **nut cracker** *or* **splitter** = tool used to crack open stubborn nuts without damaging the bolt or stud thread; **nut driver** *or* **spinner** = SOCKET DRIVER; **nut end** = the end of a stud onto which a nut is screwed (NOTE: opposite is **stud end**); **nut starter** = tool used to hold nuts for easy placement in tight locations; **nut thread** = internal thread of a nut

nyloc nut *noun* self-locking nut with nylon insert

◊ **nylon** *noun* tough, versatile, synthetic material; can be used in sheet, fibre, or solid form; **nylon hammer** = soft face hammer with a nylon face

Oo

obstruction spanner *noun* bent ring spanner for reaching around manifold and other obstacles to work on parts with difficult access, such as starters or alternators

OC = OVERHEAD CAMSHAFT

ocean liner blast horn *noun* horn which imitates the deep bellow of an ocean liner horn

octagonal (head) bolt *noun* bolt with an eight-sided head

◇ **octagon nut** *noun* nut with eight sides

octane number (ON) *or* **octane rating** *noun* the measure of a fuel's anti-knock rating; the average of Research Octane Number (RON) and Motor Octane Number (MON)

COMMENT: the octane number of a fuel is determined by comparing the behaviour of the fuel in a special test engine with that of the standard iso-octane fuel, which has high anti-knock qualities. The result of this practical comparison is then expressed as a proportion of the 100 which represents the iso-octane fuel

OD = OVERDRIVE, OUTER DIAMETER

odometer *noun* incorporated in the speedometer, the odometer indicates total mileage of the vehicle, in miles or kilometres, either mechanically or electronically; (*compare* TRIP RECORDER)

OE(M) = ORIGINAL EQUIPMENT (MANUFACTURER)

offer up *verb* to bring a part close to or in contact with another, ready to fit the pieces together *then offer up the panel, clamp it in place and weld in*

off-line *adjective* independent of the main production process line; characterized by a separate operation; **off-line painting** =

painting of parts, mostly plastic parts, outside the actual painting line

off-road vehicle *noun* 4wd vehicle with locking differential for use on rough terrain

offset 1 *adjective* set at an angle or to one side *the crankpins are offset by 120°* **2** *noun* **(a)** *(steering geometry)* = SCRUB RADIUS **(b)** *(wheel)* the distance between the centreline of the rim and the attachment face of the wheel disc at the wheel hub; this dimension can either be positive, negative, or zero

COMMENT: the track gauge is determined by the distance over the attachment faces of the wheel hubs and the offset. An incorrect offset dimension may impose excessive stress on the wheel bearings and can alter steering behaviour

offset angle *noun* angle of the offset crankpins in V-engines

offset crankshaft *noun* crankshaft layout whereby the axes of the crankshaft and the piston pin do not intersect

COMMENT: this is because the forces acting on the piston do not act uniformly on the walls of the cylinder through the skirt of the piston but much more on the side affected by the thrust of the con rod during the power stroke. The crankshaft is thus offset, so that the con rod is less inclined during the power stroke than during the compression stroke

offset handle *noun* drive handle for use with sockets, with one end set at 90° to the handle

◇ **offset power steering** *noun* = LINKAGE POWER STEERING

◇ **offset screwdriver** *noun* screwdriver with either straight or cross-head tips or a combination of both, and the two ends set at right angles to the shank

◇ **offset twin** *noun* typical motorcycle engine with the two crankpins offset by 180°

◇ **offset wrench** *noun* L-shaped tool for turning recessed screws

off shade *or* **off colour** *noun* colour mismatch due to wrong paint mixing or application

offside (o/s) *noun* side of the vehicle farthest away from the kerb (when driving)

off-the-car balancing *noun* balancing the wheel after it has been removed from the car (NOTE: opposite is **on-the-car balancing**)

off-the-dolly panel beating *noun* metalworking technique used to hammer out dents in the bodywork

| COMMENT: if the panel has a depression to one side, the dolly is held behind the depression, and the hammer blows are directed on the ridge away from the dolly, i.e. offset to one side of the dolly. This causes a reaction by the dolly, producing an alternating impact on the dent from both sides

OHC = OVERHEAD CAMSHAFT *OHC-engine*

ohmmeter *noun* instrument designed for measuring electric resistance

OHV-engine *noun* = OVERHEAD VALVE ENGINE

oil *noun* the oil used to lubricate an engine (engine oil) is refined from crude oil and apart from reducing friction and wear, cools high-temperature parts like bearings and piston rings (as well as sealing the latter against blow-by) and helps to keep engines clean and free from corrosion caused by combustion gases; *(compare* GEAR OIL)

oil additive *noun* any one of a variety of chemicals added to engine oils to improve their performance

| COMMENT: they include additives to increase viscosity at high and low temperatures; to inhibit corrosion, wear, and foaming; to prevent the formation of breakdown products caused by oil oxidation and to keep these in suspension

oil and water extractor *noun* *(compressor)* = AIR TRANSFORMER

oil breather pipe *noun* crankcase breather pipe used prior to engine emission control systems to remove fumes and pressure from the engine crankcase (NOTE: US English is **road-draft tube**)

| COMMENT: the tube, which was connected to the crankcase and suspended slightly above the ground, depended on venturi action to

create a partial vacuum as the vehicle moved. The method was ineffective below about 20 mph

oil can *noun* **(a)** container with a long, thin nozzle for lubricating machinery **(b)** shallow dent in a panel that causes the panel to warp

| COMMENT: the dent will spring back into its original shape with a characteristic sound if light pressure is applied but will not retain its normal shape once the pressure is released. It must therefore be straightened with body tools

oil change *noun* draining and replacing the engine oil at regular intervals (ideally every six months)

oil circulation *noun* passing of oil round the engine

| COMMENT: the engine oil circulation is maintained by a gear-type pump with an output of up to 35 litres per hour

oil consumption *noun* amount of oil an engine uses *an engine's oil consumption is probably the best indicator of the engine's internal condition*

◊ **oil control orifice valve** *noun* valve located in the feed line between cylinder and cylinder head; **oil control ring** = OIL SCRAPER RING

oil cooler *noun* small, air- or coolant-cooled, radiator-like device designed to decrease the temperature of the oil in the engine to approx. 185°F; **oil cooler bypass valve** = oil-temperature-controlled valve which closes the oil circuit through the oil cooler when the oil is still cold; similar function as the thermostat in the engine cooling system; *(see illustration 18)*

| COMMENT: engine oil is heated to a considerable temperature in engines subject to a high thermal load. This in turn greatly reduces the lubricating ability and the cooling capacity of the oil. Thermostats control the oil volume to the oil cooler, thus ensuring constant temperature of the oil

oil drain plug *noun* = SUMP DRAIN PLUG; **oil drain valve** = valve in an upright oil filter housing which lets oil drain into the sump when the filter element is removed; prevents oil spill

◊ **oil duct** *or* **oil passage** *or* **oil way** *noun* pipe or passage through which oil flows under pressure; *(see illustration 6)*

◊ **oiler** *noun* **(a)** = CAM LUBRICATOR **(b)** = OIL CAN

◇ **oil filler cap** *noun* cap covering the oil filler hole; *(see illustrations 4, 5)*; **oil filler hole** = hole through which oil is poured into the engine (usually situated on top of the rocker cover)

◇ **oil filter** *noun* device for trapping dirt in lubricating or hydraulic oil; usually either a full-flow filter or a bypass filter with the filter element made of pleated paper, gauze, ceramic or fine wire mesh; *(see illustrations 3, 18)*; **oil filter bypass valve** = valve in or near the oil filter which routes the oil unfiltered directly to the lubricating points; it comes into operation when the oil filter is clogged so that pressure across the filter is higher than the pressure needed to overcome the oil filter bypass valve spring; *(see illustration 18)*; **oil filter cartridge** = (i) the type of oil filter usually used on automotive engines which comes complete with filter and housing, and where both components are replaced together; (ii) a paper or textile insert for the oil filter housing (quite commonly used on motorcycle engines where e.g. the main filter is a disposable cartridge, while a filter screen is located on the bottom of the oil pump); **oil filter housing** = case surrounding an oil filter; **oil filter wrench** = special automotive tool for the removal and installation of oil filters; they come in a variety of shapes, e.g. as strap wrenches, chain wrenches, or special cup-style end cap oil filter wrenches

◇ **oil gallery** *noun* passage running the length of the cylinder block through which oil under pressure flows before passing into the bearings (via holes in the cylinder block)

◇ **oil gauge** *noun* = OIL PRESSURE GAUGE

◇ **oil grade** *noun* rating of an oil according to its viscosity

◇ **oil groove** *noun* recess designed to either accommodate or transport lubricant

◇ **oil-immersed clutch** *noun* = WET CLUTCH

◇ **oil level** *noun* depth of oil in sump, gearbox or rear axle; **oil level gauge** = dial on the instrument panel that indicates the oil level; operates when the ignition is switched on and stops shortly after the engine starts to run; **oil level sensor** = sensor mounted in the sump that supplies information on the engine oil level to the corresponding gauge

◇ **oil pan** *noun US* = SUMP

◇ **oil pick-up (pipe)** *noun* pipe or tube from the strainer to the oil pump in the sump; *(see illustration 5)*

◇ **oil pressure** *noun* the lubrication points of the engine will only be lubricated sufficiently if, in addition to the oil quantity required, the oil pressure is also sufficient; the oil pressure is maintained by the oil pump; **oil pressure sensor** = sensor mounted above the oil filter that supplies information on the engine oil pressure to the corresponding warning light; *(see illustration 3)*; **oil pressure switch** = switch which indicates a drop to below the minimum permissible oil pressure by illuminating the oil pressure warning light; **oil pressure warning light** = instrument panel light that illuminates when oil pressure falls below a certain level

◇ **oil pump** *noun* pump which circulates oil under pressure to the moving parts of an engine; normally bolted to the crankcase and located in the sump; usually a gear pump; *(see illustration 17)*; **oil pump strainer** = coarse-mesh metal screen on the bottom of the pick-up pipe that prevents foreign matter (such as lost washers, nuts and bolts) from entering the oil pump; *(see illustration 5)*

◇ **oil rail** *noun* the part of the oil ring responsible for the seal between piston and cylinder wall and thus for the actual 'scraping off' of the oil

oil (scraper) ring *noun* piston ring whose primary function is to control the amount of oil that remains on the cylinder walls

COMMENT: more than enough oil is splashed or thrown onto the cylinder walls, and most of it must be scraped off by the oil ring which consist of up to three separate pieces. The two outside pieces are thin rings (rails), and the inner section of the ring is called the expander ring

oil screen *noun* = OIL PUMP STRAINER

◇ **oil seal** *noun* any seal that prevents the leakage of oil but especially the valve stem seal between the valve and the cylinder head

◇ **oil separator** *noun* wire-mesh filter used to trap oil in the fumes drawn out of the engine by the crankcase ventilation system

◇ **oil sludge** *noun* thick deposits in the sump and elsewhere, of dirt and the products of combustion, partial combustion and oxidation of the oil (e.g. carbon particles, unburned hydrocarbons and oxides)

◇ **oil sump** *see* SUMP

◇ **oil temperature gauge** *noun* gauge which indicates the temperature of the engine oil

◇ **oil trap** *noun* = OIL SEPARATOR

◊ **oil way** *see* OIL DUCT

oleopneumatic suspension *noun* = HYDROPNEUMATIC SUSPENSION

ON = OCTANE NUMBER

on-board computer *noun* electronic component used to control vehicle electrical circuits, etc. and to process data for instrument panel gauges

◊ **on-board diagnostic system** *noun* indicating devices on the car that alert the driver when something is wrong in the system

one-coat finish *noun* finish consisting of a single coat of paint

one-off *noun* a car or spare part of which only a single unit is made

one-piece rim *noun* wheel rim consisting of one part, designed for tubeless tyre mounting; **one-piece rim designation** = coded description of a one-piece wheel rim (NOTE: opposite is **multi-piece rim)** *(compare* PASSENGER CAR WHEEL)

COMMENT: 5° drop centre, 15° drop centre, wide base rims and double wide base rims are one-piece rim designs; one-piece rims are characterized by a cross (x) in the rim designation; e.g.: 13 CH x 4.5J - S, is a one-piece symmetric rim, with a diameter of 13 in , a width of 4.5 in, and a bead seat with a safety combination hump

one-piece wheel *noun* wheel with a rim constructed in one piece incorporating a well formation at or near its centre to enable the tyre beads to be mounted over the rim flanges (NOTE: opposite is **multi-piece wheel)**

COMMENT: cast wheels, one-piece forged wheels and steel wheels having either 5° drop centre rims, 15° drop centre rims, wide base rims or double wide base rims are one-piece wheels

one-way clutch *noun* mechanical clutch which transmits power in one direction of rotation only; when torque is not applied, the driven member rotates freely; used in automatic gearboxes and the old freewheel; *(compare* SPRAG CLUTCH)

◊ **one-way valve** *noun* = CHECK VALVE (a)

on-line *adjective* state in which a piece of equipment or subsystem is directly connected with or incorporated into the main system; **on-line painting** = painting of components within the actual painting line

COMMENT: especially relevant for plastic mouldings, which are fitted to the metal car body after the welding assembly operation; on-line painting means that such plastic parts are painted together with the body and must withstand the bake-in temperatures of about 150°C

on-the-car balancing *noun* balancing the wheel whilst it is still attached to the car (NOTE: opposite is **off-the-car balancing)**

on-the-dolly panel beating *noun* metalworking technique used to tap out dents in the bodywork

COMMENT: the dolly is held directly under the ridge in the panel so that the dolly contour closely matches that of the original panel shape. Hammering is then directed at the peak of the ridge, working along the ridge from end to end in a progressive manner to push the area down gradually to its original shape

on-the-road charges *noun* extra charges, in addition to the list price of a new car, to cover delivery, numberplates and road fund licence (tax disc)

opacimeter *noun* instrument for measuring the content of particulate suspended in a fluid

open coil *or* **open element glow plug** *noun* = WIRE GLOW PLUG

open-deck design *noun* design in which there is no metal at the cylinder head joint face between the cylinder walls and the outer block

open-ended spanner *noun* spanner with open jaws

opening angle *noun* the angle of the timing diagram that indicates how long the port remains open

◊ **opening cam/rocker** *noun* with desmodromic engines, the cam/rocker responsible for opening the inlet or exhaust valve

open-loop *adjective* without feedback from e.g. oxygen-sensor control systems;

open-loop catalytic converter = preset converter which does not use an oxygen-sensor control system and thus operates without feedback (NOTE: opposite is **computer-controlled catalytic converter)**

COMMENT: certain engine management systems deactivate emission control systems (such as EGR and/or oxygen sensor control) under certain operating conditions (e.g. full-throttle driving); i.e. the electronic control module operates in the open-loop mode

opera light *noun US* decorated courtesy light mounted on the central pillar

operating costs *noun* the costs of running a car

COMMENT: includes insurance premiums, tax, depreciation, fuel, oil, maintenance, repairs, etc.; usually expressed in units of currency per mile or kilometre

operating piston *noun (automatic gearbox)* piston which causes its respective clutch(es), band or multi-disc brakes to be applied by converting fluid pressure into mechanical force and movement

opposite lock *noun* turning the steering wheel in the opposite direction to that of the front wheels to counteract the effects of oversteer; i.e. turning the wheel to the left if the result of going round a right-hand bend too fast has caused the rear end of the car to skid

optical check *noun* either a (less thorough) visual inspection or an examination by means of optical instruments

optimize *verb* to set at the best possible value

optional equipment *noun* those parts and systems of a vehicle which are not supplied as standard equipment by the manufacturer, i.e they are not included in the price for a given model (NOTE: opposite is **standard equipment)** *(compare* EXTRAS)

OPUS = OSCILLATING PICK-UP IGNITION SYSTEM

orange peel (effect) *noun (paint fault)* uneven formation on a film surface, similar to that of an orange skin

COMMENT: this is caused by the failure of the atomized paint droplets to flow into each other properly when they reach the surface. This occurs with improper gun adjustment, wrong viscosity or excessive temperatures

orbital sander *noun* flat, cushioned plate covered with abrasive paper, rotated with an elliptical motion by an electric motor and used for fine sanding work like featheredging; *(compare* DISC SANDER)

organic *noun* of chemical compounds, based on carbon chains or rings and containing hydrogen with or without oxygen, nitrogen, or other elements (NOTE: opposite is **inorganic)**

orientation *noun* tendency of plastic molecules if stretched, to align themselves in the direction of the stress

COMMENT: molecular orientation leads to anisotropy of mechanical properties (i.e. having different mechanical properties in different directions). This can be used to advantage in the production of fibres and film or may be the undesirable result of a moulding process

original condition *noun* description of the condition of a car; the car is in the state in which it left the factory; it may be worn but has neither been resprayed nor reupholstered nor has extensive welding been carried out or modern accessories fitted to change its standard specifications

◇ **original equipment (OE)** *noun* parts used in the manufacture of the vehicle, rather than those added afterwards *the catalytic converter is now incorporated in most original equipment exhaust systems* **original equipment manufacturer (OEM)** = original supplier of parts used in the manufacture of a vehicle

O-ring *noun* annular seal, of round or rectangular cross section and almost any diameter; made of rubber, neoprene, etc., or of soft metal, such as copper; *(see illustrations 10, 12)*

o/s = OFFSIDE

oscillating pick-up ignition syst (OPUS) *noun* ignition system where contact breaker and cam are replaced timing rotor, a pick-up module, a amplifier module

oscilloscope *noun* el measurement device used to waveforms or traces of signals; IGNITION OSCILLOSCOPE)

otg = OUTDOOR *or* TEMPERATURE GAUGE

Otto cycle *noun* another name for the four-stroke cycle, named after the German engineer Dr. Nikolaus Otto (1832- 1891) who first patented the design in 1876

outboard *adjective* away from the centre of the vehicle

◇ **outboard contre pente** *noun* *(wheel)* safety contour for tubeless passenger car rims, featuring a contre pente on the outer bead seat; **outboard flat hump** = safety contour for tubeless passenger car rims, featuring a flattened hump on the outer bead seat; **outboard flat pente** = safety contour for tubeless passenger car rims, featuring a flattened contre pente on the outer bead seat; **outboard round hump** = safety contour for tubeless passenger car rims, featuring a round hump on the outer bead seat

outdoor *or* **outside temperature gauge (otg)** *noun* gauge which indicates the ambient air temperature outside the vehicle

outer bulb *noun* = OUTER ENVELOPE

◇ **outer dead centre** *see* BOTTOM DEAD CENTRE

◇ **outer diameter (OD)** *noun* external iameter of a cylinder or tube

outer electrode *noun* **(a)** = OUTER RMINAL **(b)** = EARTH ELECTRODE

ter envelope *noun* *(of gas rge lamps)* bulb which protects and s the arc tube; either filled with gas or d to avoid oxidation of the arc tube

headlight *see* INNER T

ill *noun* sill below the doors he outside; often referred to as s the inner sill is actually the

nal *noun* electrode on the stributor cap, one outer igned to each sparking otor distributes the firing al electrode to the outer pposite is **centre**

n socket on the ding to the outer , to connect the

ytic converter) serves as a

retainer and provides mechanical protection for the insulation

outlet *noun* **(a)** *(of 4-stroke engine)* = EXHAUST PORT (a) **(b)** rear opening of a catalytic converter or silencer **(c)** last pipe of an exhaust system; tailpipe

◇ **outlet pipe** *noun* pump discharge pipe; **outlet side** = that side of the pump or pumping system on which the liquid pumped leaves the pump or system; *(see illustration 17)* (NOTE: opposite is **suction side**)

◇ **outlet valve** *noun* **(a)** = EXHAUST VALVE **(b)** = DISCHARGE VALVE

outline *verb* to mould plastic material around something; *(compare* INSERT)

out of round *adjective* not circular

◇ **out of true** *adjective* inaccurately made or incorrectly adjusted, e.g. of a wheel with side-to-side deviation or wobble

◇ **out of tune** *adjective* poorly tuned *the engine/ignition timing is out of tune*

output speed *noun* speed of the transmission output shaft which is transmitted to the driven wheels via the final drive; as the final drive provides a constant gear ratio, output speed is proportional to vehicle road speed

outrigger *noun* a short angle or box section member that runs across part of the car

COMMENT: on cars with separate frames, outriggers are used to link the main chassis or the longitudinal members with the sill or running board area. An outrigger is far shorter and often of a smaller section than a crossmember

outside caliper *noun* machinists' caliper used to check outside dimensions; **outside spring caliper** = outside caliper with spring for accurate setting

◇ **outside diameter** *noun* the external diameter of a cylinder or tube

oval piston *noun* special piston developed by Honda, able to accommodate eight valves and two sparking plugs

overall gear ratio *noun* ratio of engine revolutions to road wheel revolutions, producing road speed as a ratio of engine speed (sometimes expressed as mph per 1000 rpm)

overaxle pipe *noun* = KICK-UP PIPE

overdrive *noun* **(a)** transmission speed which can be selected manually and gives a ratio of less than 1:1, i.e. the transmission output shaft turns faster than the transmission input shaft **(b)** separate transmission installed in the (rear) drive train giving an overdrive reduction to direct or direct and intermediate gears; usually selected electro-mechanically by means of a button or switch located either in the instrument panel or at the gear lever

COMMENT: once popular as a means of reducing engine wear and improving fuel economy, the overdrive gear has been largely superseded by the fifth gear

overflow hose/pipe *noun* pipe to drain off excess fluid, e.g. between the radiator and the coolant reserve tank, or in the float chamber if the specified fuel level is substantially exceeded due to a leaking needle valve

overhang *noun* distance between the outermost front or rear point of a vehicle and the wheel centres of the respective axle

overhaul *verb* to repair and restore to (near) original condition

overhead camshaft (OC, OHC) *noun* type of camshaft situated over the valves (rather than in the side of the engine)

COMMENT: in single overhead camshaft (sohc) engines, the camshaft is located between the valves and is driven by a chain from the crankshaft; the valves are opened via short rocker arms. In double overhead camshaft (dohc) valve operation, two camshafts are used, one above each valve or bank of valves. The valves are opened via bucket tappets, allowing adjustment by shims. All modern four-stroke motorcycle engines are equipped with double overhead camshafts

overhead valve (OHV) engine *noun* four-stroke engine with the intake and exhaust poppet valves located in the cylinder head and not at the side of the cylinder as in a side-valve engine; the valve stems are either at an angle or parallel and the valve discs face the piston, valve actuation pushrod and swing arm (NOTE: US English is **I-head**)

overheat *verb* to make or become too hot

COMMENT: overheating can effect various parts. Engine overheating could be caused by: a fault in the cooling system caused by a leak, blockage, slipping or broken fan belt; lack of engine oil or an over-lean mixture. Brake overheating can be caused by prolonged use (e.g. when going downhill) leading to brake fade, binding brake shoes, or seized disc pads or pistons

overinflated tyre *noun* tyre which has too much air in it, causing premature wear in the tread centre (NOTE: the opposite is **underinflated tyre**)

overlap *noun* = VALVE OVERLAP

overlay *noun* upper layer of a plain bearing insert

COMMENT: if the overlay is worn, the bearing material beneath it will still allow for a certain emergency operation of the component supported in the plain bearing

overlay paint *noun* special type of custom paint where a design on the painted surface is embedded below a coat of translucent paint, giving the impression that two paints are applied to the car; *(compare* CANDY PAINT JOB)

overload spring *noun (chassis)* spring which acts only under heavy load; prevents bottoming

overrev *verb* to run an engine above th maximum recommended rpm

overrider *noun* short, vertical attachm to the bumper, to prevent interlocking v other bumpers

overrun (a) *noun & verb* a ve travelling with no throttle and the e acting as a brake is said to be 'on the ove or 'overrunning'; *(compare* CC DECELERATION)* **(b)** *verb (of a vehicle)* to travel faster than the vehicle

overrun control valve *noun* va crossover pipe between the co suction and discharge sides c turbocharger systems

COMMENT: when manifold press as during deceleration, the over valve opens and allows compre circulate through the compresso maintains turbo speed on the overrun, minimizing turbo lag when the throttle is re-opened; not to be confused with a safety-relief valve in the compressor discharge line or with a wastegate valve

overrun cut-off/shut-off *noun* = DECELERATION FUEL CUT-OFF

◇ **overrunning clutch** *noun* **(a)** part of a starter motor designed to avoid armature damage caused by severe overrevving; *(see illustration 37)* **(b)** = ONE-WAY CLUTCH **(c)** *(in automatic transmission)* device that disengages the engine on overrun

◇ **overrunning clutch starter** *noun* = PRE-ENGAGED STARTER

oversize piston *noun* piston with a diameter slightly larger than that of the standard piston, used in order to allow for a honing of the cylinder walls

◇ **oversize valve guide** *noun* valve ̄ide with a slightly larger outside diameter ̄n the standard valve guide, used to repair ̄n valve guides after their bores have been ̄ed

spray *noun* undesirable spray ̄s on adjacent panels and car parts ̄ the resprayed area (countered by ̄asking); *(compare SPRAY MIST)*

uare engine *noun* engine where ̄e is larger than the stroke

1 *verb (of a vehicle)* to turn more ̄ the driver intends (possibly ̄r of the vehicle to slide wide) **2** ̄ oversteering (NOTE: opposite

̄ to pass another vehicle ̄direction

̄ add too much thinner to

̄dy who actually owns ̄ title of property *first* ̄*ul owner (compare* ̄**ndbook** = booklet ̄car which briefly ̄ operation of the ̄ ̄itches, as well as ̄ and some

̄ used as an

oxidation *noun* chemical reaction which increases the oxygen content of a compound or in which a compound or radical loses electrons, i.e. in which the positive valence is increased; *(compare REDUCTION)*

◇ **oxide** *noun* chemical compound of oxygen with another element; **oxides of nitrogen** = NITROGEN OXIDES

◇ **oxidize** *verb* to (cause to) combine with oxygen; **oxidizer** *or* **oxidizing agent** = compound which gives up oxygen easily, removes hydrogen from another compound, or attracts electrons; **oxidizing catalyst** = catalyst which decreases CO and HC levels using excess air; *(compare REDUCING CATALYST)*; **oxidizing converter** = converter with a conventional oxidation catalyst that needs a secondary air supply to convert hydrocarbons and carbon monoxide to carbon dioxide and water; does not control NO$_x$ emissions; *(compare SINGLE-BED OXIDIZING CONVERTER)*

oxyacetylene welding *noun* = GAS WELDING

oxygen (O) *noun* gaseous element essential for life and the combustion of fuel

◇ **oxygenates** *noun* oxygen-enriched fuels or anti-knock additives

◇ **oxygen corrosion** *noun* electrochemical corrosion caused by neutral or alkaline electrolytes in which, during the cathodic reaction, oxygen is reduced to hydroxide

oxygen sensor *noun* sensor which measures the amount of oxygen remaining in the exhaust gases (NOTE: usually called a **lambda sensor**)

COMMENT: this information is transmitted to the electronic control unit, where it is used to change the A/F mixture as required to meet varying driving conditions; the oxygen sensor consists basically of a ceramic zirconia body coated with platinum; when heated to temperatures above 300°C, the sensor generates a voltage which varies with the oxygen content in the exhaust gas stream; voltage falls with increasing oxygen content, indicating a lean mixture, and rises with decreasing oxygen content, indicating a rich mixture; typically, the oxygen sensor is located in the exhaust manifold

oxygen sensor system thermo-switch *noun (fuel injection)* usually located in a coolant hose, provides a coolant temperature signal to the ECM

oxyhydrogen gas *noun* highly explosive mixture of oxygen and hydrogen, generated during charging of lead-acid batteries; *(compare* GASSING)

ozone *noun* strong oxidizing agent (often produced by sparking from electrical apparatus, such as arc welding equipment); particularly harmful to tyres

Pp

P (a) *(gear selector)* = PARK **(b)** letter on the sidewall of a tyre denoting the maximum speed for which it is designed (150 km/h or 95 mph); *(see* SPEED RATING)

p/a *(short for)* power-assisted

packed gland *noun (pump)* cylindrical recess that accommodates a number of rings of packing around the shaft or shaft sleeve (NOTE: also called **stuffing box**)

COMMENT: pumps used for high-temperature fluids are provided with jacketed, water-cooled packed glands

pad *(short for)* BRAKE PAD

padding disc *noun* insert in the crankcase area designed to reduce the internal volume of the crankcase and thus to increase the pre-compression ratio; this helps to increase the output of a two-stroke engine

paddle *(short for)* SOLDER PADDLE

◇ **paddling the lead** *noun* filling repair areas by smoothing the body lead layer until a smooth surface is achieved

pad retainer (pin) *noun* pin which locates the brake pad in a disc brake

pagoda(-style) roof *noun* unusual roof design, introduced on the Mercedes-Benz SL Hardtop, which was slightly lower in the centre than at the sides

paint 1 *noun* any pigmented liquid, liquefiable, or mastic composition designed for application to a substrate on a thin layer which is converted to a solid film after application **2** *verb* in an automotive context, painting usually means spray painting

◇ **paint booth** *noun* closed section in a painting line in which coats of paint are applied

◇ **paint chip book** *noun* = COLOUR CHART

◇ **paint colour matching** *noun* determining the correct paint shade with the aid of colour charts and special mixing devices and, in difficult cases, via spectral analysis

◇ **painting line** *noun* route taken (and processes undergone) by the bodywork of a newly manufactured vehicle on its way through the paint shop

◇ **painting robot** *noun* robot used for paint application

◇ **paint refinishing** *noun* the various steps involved in repainting a secondhand car

◇ **paint shop** *noun* **(a)** production stage in an automobile manufacturing plant during which the bodywork is treated with paint **(b)** separate paint repair shop, usually near a body repair shop (i.e. for damaged vehicles)

◇ **paint stripper** *noun* liquid paint remover

◇ **paint system** *noun* the sum of all coats of paint on a work

◇ **paintwork** *noun* overall result of painting; the paint coating or finish

PAIR system *noun* = PULSE AIR SYSTEM

palladium *noun* white, ductile, malleable, noble metal of the platinum family; atomic number 46, atomic weight 106.4; resembles platinum and together with other platinum metals is used as a catalyst in automotive exhaust converters; *(compare* PLATINUM METALS)

pane *noun* sheet of window glass

P&W key *noun* = PRATT AND WHITNEY KEY

panel *noun* **(a)** part made from sheet metal; e.g. door panel **(b)** plastic moulding; e.g. interior trim of doors

◇ **panel beater** *noun* **(a)** person who beats out the dented bodywork of a damaged vehicle **(b)** = PANEL HAMMER

◊ **panel beating** *noun* beating out the dents in damaged bodywork

◊ **panel bonding** *noun* new repair process using a special adhesive to glue body panels in place instead of spot-welding them

◊ **panel contour** *noun* the normal shape of a new, undented body panel as produced by the factory

panel cutter *noun* air-operated tool used to cut out old panels

> COMMENT: it is a relatively coarse tool and is thus suited mainly for cutting sheet metal in areas where minor distortion along the cutting lines does not matter

panel file *noun* = BODY FILE

◊ **panel flanger** *noun* = JOGGLER

◊ **panel hammer** *noun* special hammer for metalworking that has two differently-shaped heads for different purposes, e.g. cross-peen and shrinking hammer

◊ **panelling** *noun* **(a)** a combination of separate sheet metal panels to form a complete assembly, e.g. the outer panels of the body or even the panels surrounding the engine **(b)** plastic moulding; e.g. interior trim of doors; *(compare* CLADDING b)

◊ **panel picking** *noun* straightening very fine indentations or marks of very small diameter on a panel surface with a pick hammer

panel puller *noun* tool with slide hammer and hook or self-threading screw tip to pull dented doors, wings and other sheet metal panels back into place (NOTE: US English is **knocker)**

> COMMENT: after drilling a hole in the deepest part of the dent, the hook or screw tip is inserted to pull out the dent by means of slide hammer impact

Panhard rod *noun* transversely mounted bar between a beam axle and the vehicle body as a lateral location of the axle; *(see illustration 28)*; **Panhard (rod) mounting box** = box section used to mount the Panhard rod of the rear axle

panoramic windscreen *noun* a windscreen style popular in the 1950s and '60s that featured recessed screen pillars, giving a wide, unobstructed view of the road; entry for the front passengers was awkward, since the screen pillar corners projected into the door opening

pantechnicon *noun* large van or lorry, especially one for moving furniture

parabolic reflector *noun* old headlight reflector in the shape of a parabola, now replaced by ellipsoidal reflectors

◊ **parabolic spring** *noun* leaf spring tapered in the shape of a parabola

paraffin *noun* in automotive applications, used as a solvent for removing grease (NOTE: US English is **kerosene)**

parallel 1 *adjective* the same distance apart at every point **2** *noun* two or more electrical components each receiving the same voltage *resistors connected in parallel* (NOTE: opposite is **series) 3** *verb* to connect in parallel

◊ **parallel action locking pliers** *noun* locking pliers with parallel action jaws, e.g. for pinching off hoses when servicing cooling systems

◊ **parallel circuit** *noun* electric circuit in which the individual components are connected between two points, with one of the two ends of each component connected to each point; arrangement used in the vehicle electrical system; *(compare* SERIES CIRCUIT)

◊ **parallelism** *noun* *(of brake discs)* same thickness all the way round

◊ **parallel key** *noun* = FEATHER KEY

◊ **parallelogram steering (system)** *noun* steering system with a drop arm and idler arm (NOTE: opposite is **rack-and-pinion steering)**

◊ **parallelogram suspension** *noun* = DOUBLE WISHBONE SUSPENSION

◊ **parallel trailing link suspension** *noun* front suspension layout used primarily by Volkswagen on rear-engined cars

parallel twin *noun* type of engine usually found on traditional British two-cylinder motorcycles

> COMMENT: the term refers to a four-stroke engine with parallel pistons and crankpins that are not offset. The balance of the oscillating masses is identical with that of a single-cylinder engine

parallel valves *noun* inlet and exhaust valves with parallel valve stems

parent panel *noun* the panel left in place on the car to which a new panel is welded after all the rusted metal has been cut out

park (P) 1 *noun* one of the positions of the gear selector for an automatic gearbox; when engaged (after the vehicle has come to a complete standstill) the driving wheels are locked **2** *verb* to leave a vehicle in a particular place

◊ **parking brake** *noun* mechanically operated brake that is independent of the foot-operated service brakes on the vehicle; set when the vehicle is parked, usually by hand (handbrake) but sometimes by foot on some American cars; **parking brake console** = reinforcing member incorporated in the centre tunnel area of the floorpan to provide the mounting support for the handbrake; **parking brake lever** = *(inside drum brake)* lever which spreads the brake shoes outward; the long end is connected to the parking brake cable, the opposite end to one brake shoe and to a push bar which acts on the other shoe; *(see illustration 30)*; **parking brake lever strut** = push bar between the shoes in a drum brake; **parking brake pedal** = foot-operated pedal for the parking brake

◊ **parking disc** *noun* marker displayed on the inside of a parked car showing time of arrival (or latest permitted time of departure)

◊ **parking heater** *noun* air heating system which operates independently of the engine

◊ **parking interlock** *noun* = PARKING LOCK

◊ **parking light/lamp** *noun* energy-saving vehicle illumination mode for long-term roadside parking; includes only one front sidelight and one taillight; the parking light can be switched to illuminate the LH or RH side

◊ **parking lock (PL)** *noun* lock gear and pawl that lock the transmission mechanically

◊ **parking lot** *noun US* (ground level, outdoor) car park

◊ **parking meter** *noun* coin-operated timing device that indicates how long a vehicle may legally remain parked

◊ **parking space** *noun* parking place reserved for a particular vehicle

◊ **parking ticket** *noun* written fine for a parking offence

◊ **park/neutral safety switch** *noun* = STARTER INHIBITOR SWITCH

part *noun* component

partial flow filter *noun* = BYPASS FILTER

◊ **partial respray** *noun* respraying part of the bodywork (NOTE: opposite is **full** or **complete respray**)

particulate catalyst *noun* pellet catalyst

◊ **particulate emission** *noun* emission of solid particles of carbon and unburnt hydrocarbons from the exhaust system; **particulate emission limit** = weight of particulate emissions in the exhaust of diesel engines, specified in grams per mile

◊ **particulate ignition temperature** *noun* in diesel filtration tests, the exhaust gas temperature at which there is an equilibrium between particulate burn-off and deposit build-up

◊ **particulate matter (PM)** *or* **particulates** *noun* suspended solids of carbon and unburnt hydrocarbons from the exhaust system

part-load operation *noun* operation of systems and components under conditions below full load

part out *verb US* to break up for spares

part panel *noun* = PATCH PANEL

parts catalogue *noun* catalogue listing available spare parts

◊ **part(s) number (p/n, PN)** *noun* reference number attributed to a particular part

part-throttle operation *noun* driving without using full throttle

part-time four-wheel drive *noun* manually selectable four-wheel drive

pas = POWER-ASSISTED STEERING

pascal (pa) *noun* SI measurement of pressure (= one newton per square metre)

pass *verb* to overtake

passenger car *noun* (usually) four-wheeled motor car powered by an IC engine and designed for passengers; **passenger car wheel** = generally one-piece wheels made of sheet steel (rim and disc are welded together) or light-alloy (cast or forged alloy wheels), and designed for tubeless tyres

COMMENT: rims for passenger cars are almost exclusively designed as 5° drop centre rims incorporating a safety bead seat (double hump and combination hump are most common; flat hump designs are less common) and a J-flange. The B-flange type is reduced in height and used on passenger cars with small rim diameter and rim width

passenger compartment *or* **passenger cell** *noun* part of the car in which the driver and passengers sit

◊ **passenger-side air bag** *noun* an air bag restraint system designed to protect the front passenger; introduced on some cars in the early 1990s, it usually occupies the space normally provided for a glove compartment

passivate *verb* to reduce the reactivity of a chemically active metal surface by electrochemical polarization or by immersion in a passivating solution

passive safety *noun* features designed to alleviate the consequences of a crash, such as air bags, collapsible steering column, head restraints, toughened windscreen, etc. (NOTE: opposite is **active safety)**

patching *noun* repair method for welding up local corrosion damage by using smaller panels made up from sheet metal

◊ **patch panel** *noun* small sheet metal panel that is usually made up specially to repair minor rust holes

pattern panel *noun* body panel made by somebody other than the original manufacturer, usually for repair purposes; this also includes panels remanufactured after the spare parts supplies from the factory have been discontinued

pawl *noun* **(a)** an arm pivoted so that its free end can fit into a notch, slot, or groove at certain times in order to hold a part stationary **(b)** catch at the bottom of a lever which connects with a toothed rack to hold the lever in position (e.g. with a handbrake lever or in ratchets) *pawl and ratchet mechanism*

payload *noun* the revenue-earning cargo of a commercial vehicle or the weight of the cargo

pb = POWER BRAKES

PC = PITCH CIRCLE, POLYCARBONATE

pcb = PRINTED CIRCUIT BOARD

PCD = PITCH CIRCLE DIAMETER

PCI = PROGRAMME COMPARISON AND IDENTIFICATION

PCV = POSITIVE CRANKCASE VENTILATION; **PCV valve** = usually located on the cylinder head cover, this valve allows a certain amount of crankcase blow-by gases to be metered into the intake system for burning

COMMENT: the PCV valve is controlled by engine vacuum, i.e. it is closed in the absence of vacuum, such as when the engine is not running; also in case of backfire in the inlet manifold, the PCV valve closes instantly to prevent crankcase fumes from being ignited

PE = POLYETHYLENE, POLYELLIPSOIDAL

peak power *noun* point of maximum torque

◊ **peak revs** *noun* point of maximum engine speed

◊ **peaky** *adjective (of an engine)* only able to deliver useful power at high revs, necessitating frequent gearchanges; *(compare* FLEXIBLE)

pedal *noun* foot-operated lever *fully depress the clutch pedal before changing gear; as you release the clutch pedal, lightly depress the accelerator pedal* **pedal clearance** = the distance between the pedal and the floor, when the pedal is fully depressed; reference points may vary; **pedal free play** = the distance a pedal moves until a slight resistance is felt; **pedal pulsation** = vibration of the brake pedal when depressed, caused by a defective disc or drum (or when ABS is activated); **pedals** = the accelerator pedal, brake pedal and clutch pedal; **pedal travel** = the total stroke of a pedal; *(compare* FREE TRAVEL)

peen *noun* ball-shaped, or narrow wedge-shaped end of a hammer head opposite the flattened striking face; **peen hammer** = body hammer with a peen of triangular section with a fairly sharply shaped end; *(compare* BALL PEEN HAMMER)

◊ **peening** *noun* flattening or shaping with a peen hammer

PE headlight *noun* headlight with a gas discharge lamp and a polyellipsoidal reflector

pein *noun* = PEEN

pellet-type catalytic converter *noun*
the first type of automotive catalytic
converter, introduced in the USA in 1975

> COMMENT: it consisted basically of a sheet
> steel catalyst container surrounded by
> thermal insulation and a sheet steel outer
> shell; the catalyst container was filled with one
> or two beds of ceramic pebbles (pellets)
> coated with a catalyst. This type of catalytic
> converter suffered from poor service life due
> to vibration-induced attrition of the catalytic
> coating; this also produced additional
> particulate emissions and the pellet bed
> caused high exhaust back pressure, resulting
> in poor engine performance. Pellet-type
> catalytic converters have been superseded
> by monolithic converters

pencil-type glow plug *noun* =
SHEATHED-TYPE GLOW PLUG

pendulum impact test *noun* the
standard test methods are the Izod and Charpy
tests; the specimens have a standard notch
machined in them, and the impact energy
absorbed in breaking the specimen is
recorded

penetrating oil *noun* thin oil used to
loosen corroded parts

pent crown piston *noun* piston design
with a sloping, pent-roof shaped piston crown
to improve the flow of the fuel/air mixture and
to increase engine compression

◇ **pent-roof combustion chamber**
noun combustion chamber whose top is
angled like a roof

perfect scavenging *noun* scavenging
parameter of two stroke engines

> COMMENT: in an ideal scavenging process,
> the fresh mixture is considered to push the
> combustion products out of the cylinder
> without mixing or exchanging heat. This
> process continues until all burnt gases have
> been expelled and the cylinder is completely
> filled with fresh mixture

performance *noun* **(a)** the general way a
car (or any other machine or material) handles
(b) specifically, a car's acceleration and top
speed

◇ **performance characteristics of
materials** *noun* specific values for
materials, obtained by standard test methods

and available for the selection of appropriate
materials

◇ **performance handling system**
noun typically consists of front and rear
anti-roll bars, nitrogen-filled gas shock
absorbers, special springs

◇ **performance tuning** *noun* efforts to
improve vehicle performance in general or
engine performance in particular, such as
upgraded suspension, higher engine output
and/or torque, or drag-reducing measures,
such as the addition of spoilers; *(compare
TUNING)*

perimeter frame *noun* type of frame
widely used for American cars that
incorporates separate frames; the side and
crossmembers form a border that surrounds
the passenger compartment

permanent four-wheel drive *noun*
permanently engaged four-wheel drive (with
lockable or limited-slip differentials)

◇ **permanent magnet** *noun* magnetic
material such as hardened steel that has been
strongly magnetized and retains its
magnetism indefinitely; used in electric
machines

personal(ized) numberplate *noun*
numberplate chosen (at a cost) by a vehicle's
owner, rather than one allocated by the
authorities (in the UK, the DVLA)

> COMMENT: for example, one containing the
> initials or even name of the owner (e.g. DAV
> 1S), or a specific message, e.g. HAV 2X - seen
> on the car of an egg producer, or EIEIO -
> indicating the owner to be (a farmer) named
> Macdonald

Perspex *see* POLYMETHYL
METHACRYLATE

petroil lubrication *noun* a lubrication
method for two-stroke engines where the oil
is added to the fuel and lubricates the moving
engine parts as the air/fuel mixture passes
through the crankcase

petrol *noun* liquid blend of hydrocarbons
refined from petroleum, used as a fuel for SI
engines (NOTE: US English is **gasoline** *or* **gas**);
petrol engine = spark ignition engine, using
petrol as a fuel

◇ **petroleum** *noun* the crude oil from
which petrol, lubricating oil, and other such
products are refined; **petroleum jelly** =

whitish jelly-like substance obtained from petroleum, used as a lubricant and as a protection against corrosion

◊ **petrol pump** *noun* pump which dispenses petrol at a filling station (NOTE: US English is **gas pump)**

◊ **petrol station** *noun* filling station (NOTE: US English is **gas station)**

◊ **petrol tanker** *noun* specially equipped lorry for transporting petrol/fuel

PFI = PORT FUEL INJECTION

P grit numbers *noun* standard system of grit numbers applied to sandpapers to ensure identical properties in products made by different manufacturers

phase-locked loop circuitry *see* PLL CIRCUITRY

Phillips screw *noun* proprietary type of cross-head screw; **Phillips screwdriver** = proprietary type of cross-head screwdriver

phosphate coating *noun* conversion coating produced by phosphating; **phosphate section** = section in a painting line in which phosphate treatment is performed; **phosphate treatment** = treatment of metals with a phosphating solution to produce a phosphate conversion coating on the surface

◊ **phosphating** *noun* = PHOSPHATE TREATMENT; **phosphating solution** = solution of phosphoric acid, often enriched with zinc, used during the bodywork production process for cleaning and rust prevention

pH value *noun* measure of the concentration of hydrogen ions in a solution, which shows how acid or alkaline it is

COMMENT: the pH value of an aqueous solution is a number describing its acidity or alkalinity. The pH of a neutral solution is 7.0 at 25°C

pick and finishing hammer *noun* widely used type of body hammer with a pointed end on one side and a shallow domed end for finishing on the other side; **pick hammer** = hammer with a round head for conventional planishing and a small pick-shaped head for working away in sharp or tight corners (NOTE: not to be confused with a bullet-point pick hammer, which has a more blunt pick, nor with a peen hammer)

pickling *noun* removal of oxide or mill scale from the surface of a metal by immersion, usually in an acidic or alkaline solution; **pickling attack** = initial chemical reaction between phosphating solutions and metal surfaces in phosphate treatment

pick-up *noun* **(a)** transfer of material, as between bearing and shaft, caused by friction and heat due to lack of oil; can lead to seizure **(b)** small truck with an open body and low sides (NOTE: called a **utility** or informally **ute** in Australia)

◊ **pick-up coil** *noun* coil in which voltage is induced in a magnetic pick-up assembly; **pick-up module** = trigger-activated device which sends a signal to the ignition unit of an electronic ignition system

◊ **pick-up pipe** *noun* = OIL PICK-UP (PIPE); **pick-up screen** = OIL PUMP STRAINER

◊ **pick-up tool** *noun* tool with a flexible or rigid shaft and a claw type pick-up end; used to retrieve small objects from hard-to-reach areas; *(compare* MAGNETIC PICK-UP (TOOL))

pig iron *noun* produced in blast furnaces, pig iron is the raw material for practically all iron and steel products; contains about 3-5 % carbon

pigtail *noun* = WIRING PIGTAIL

piling *noun* the build-up of metal on a contact breaker point (NOTE: opposite is **pitting)**

pill *noun* jet in the fuel-return line which establishes the mixture

pillar *noun* post between the roof and the waistline; from front to rear, there are A-, B-, C-, and D-pillars; *(see illustrations 1, 2)*

◊ **pillar jack** *noun* = TOWER JACK

◊ **pillar light** *noun* courtesy light mounted on the central pillar

pilot bearing *noun US* = SPIGOT BEARING

◊ **pilot hole** *noun* hole which acts as a guide when drilling a larger hole or for a self-tapping screw

◊ **pilot jet** *noun* jet in the idling circuit of a fixed jet carburettor which measures and admits fuel

◇ **pilot operated absolute** *see* POA SUCTION THROTTLING VALVE *noun*

◇ **pilot shaft** *noun* dummy shaft which is used to align parts and is removed before final assembly of the parts

pin *noun* bar used as a pivot or swivel (e.g. kingpin, swivel pin), or as a fastener (e.g. cotter pin, dowel pin)

pinging *noun US* = PINKING

pinholing *noun* tiny bubbles in the finish that are often grouped together; caused by trapped solvents, moisture or air released from the film; *(compare* SOLVENT POP)

pinion (gear) *noun* a gearwheel which engages with a rack or larger wheel and whose diameter is not much larger than the diameter of its shaft or axle; *(see illustrations 26, 37)*

◇ **pinion shaft** *noun* short drive shaft in the rear axle connecting the prop shaft to the crown wheel via the final drive pinion

pinking *US* **pinging** *noun* metallic, pinging noise caused by detonation or partial detonation in the combustion chamber of a cylinder, usually due to low-octane fuel or over-advanced ignition

pin punch *noun* tool with a parallel shaft for use with a hammer to drive out pins, shafts, rivets, etc.; *(compare* DRIFT PUNCH)

pin slider caliper disc brake *noun* disc brake design with a sliding caliper

| COMMENT: major components are: caliper (a casting with one cylinder and piston), caliper frame (casting), guide pins, Teflon or rubber sleeves/bushings. The caliper floats on the sleeves over the guide pins, the guide pins are threaded or riveted to the caliper frame, and the caliper frame is bolted to the suspension

pinstriping *noun* thin, precisely contoured lines along certain body features; they may extend along the whole car and finish off in elaborate, bouquet-like designs; **pinstriping tool** = painting tool used to apply thin, precise lines on the body, e.g. on motorcycle tanks and to enhance car body contours

| COMMENT: striping usually refers to simple decorative lines, e.g. on motorcycle tanks, while pinstriping mostly refers to custom

work, i.e. more elaborate and sharply curved lines

pintaux nozzle *noun* pintle-type diesel fuel injector nozzle with a hole in the side through which a very small amount of fuel is sprayed when the needle valve is partly opened at low pressure, before the main hole comes into use

pintle *noun* **(a)** the needle of the injection valve in a diesel fuel injector; **pintle nozzle** = injector nozzle containing the pintle **(b)** vertical bolt or pin in a towing bracket, to which the towbar is attached

pin wrench *noun* wrench with a pin that can be fitted into a hole in a nut to exert extra pressure

pipework *noun* system of pipes

pipe wrench *noun* adjustable spanner with serrated jaws

| COMMENT: in GB and the USA the most common type of pipe wrench is the so-called 'Stillson wrench', which resembles a very large heavy-duty adjustable wrench

piping *noun* **(a)** system of pipes **(b)** rubber or plastic strip inserted between two removable panels, i.e. between a bolt-on wing and the body, to cover up the joint and to prevent water getting in; with the piping inserted, only the round bead along the upper edge of the piping is visible

piston *noun* the reciprocating element in a reciprocating piston engine; *(see illustrations 3, 5, 9, 12, 13, 31)*

| COMMENT: the piston moves inside the cylinder, and is attached to the crankshaft via a piston pin and connecting rod; usually made of a light alloy to minimize oscillating masses and the inertial forces that act on the crankshaft, it consists basically of a piston skirt and a piston head with piston rings; during the power stroke, the piston must sustain sudden loads in the order of 4000 pounds (20000 newtons) and temperatures of about 230°C; normally a slipper piston

piston bore *noun* diameter of the bore in the cylinder block in which the piston moves back and forth between top dead centre (TDC) and bottom dead centre (BDC)

◇ **piston charging pump** *noun* either the function of the piston of the two-stroke engine to pre-compress the fresh charge induced into the crankcase, or a separate piston used in earlier two-stroke engine designs to provide a supercharging effect

◊ **piston(-type) compressor** *noun* compressor in an air-conditioning system with one or more pistons arranged in either an in-line, axial, radial or V-configuration

piston crown *noun* the end of the piston facing the valves *install the piston with the arrow on the piston crown facing forward*

COMMENT: the piston crown transmits the pressure created during the ignition of the air/fuel mixture to the piston pin, on to the connecting rod and from there to the crankshaft; the diameter of the piston crown is slightly smaller than the piston skirt

piston damper *noun* small damper piston in an SU or Stromberg carburettor which attenuates the movement of the large air piston in the venturi; *(see illustrations 12, 13)*

◊ **piston diaphragm** *noun* flexible membrane which displaces under pressure, imparting movement to the piston in a Stromberg carburettor; *(see illustration 12)*

◊ **piston engine** *noun* internal combustion engine in which a piston is displaced by thermal expansion of gases; the concept includes reciprocating engines and rotary engines, but is usually used with reference to the common reciprocating engine

◊ **piston extension screw** *noun* stroke limiting screw between the primary piston and secondary piston stop

◊ **piston head** *noun* = PISTON CROWN

◊ **piston land** *noun* the raised portion between two piston ring grooves

◊ **piston lifter** *noun* pin in the base of the piston chamber in an SU or Stromberg carburettor, used to check the strength of the mixture and the free movement of the piston; *(see illustrations 12, 13)*

◊ **piston material** *noun* the materials from which pistons are made are grey cast or light alloys; most light alloys consist of an aluminium-silicon alloy

◊ **piston pin** *noun US* = GUDGEON PIN

piston ring *noun* one of usually three metal rings installed in grooves in the piston which seal the small clearance between the piston and the cylinder wall; *(compare* COMPRESSION RING, OIL SCRAPER RING) *(see illustrations 4, 9)*

piston ring clamp *noun* special automotive tool used for installing pistons

COMMENT: the clamp is slipped over the piston and when tightened, compresses the piston rings into the piston grooves. With the piston rings compressed, the piston can be installed into the cylinder by light tapping

piston ring flutter *noun* oscillations of a piston ring which mainly occur at high engine speed and thus can cause breakage

◊ **piston ring groove** *noun* one of the grooves round the top of a piston into which a piston ring fits; **piston ring groove cleaner** = special automotive tool to remove carbon and varnishes from piston grooves before installing piston rings

◊ **piston ring pliers** *noun* pliers-like special automotive tool used to spread and slip piston rings over a piston for removal and installation

◊ **piston ring stop** *noun* pin pressed into the ring grooves of a two-stroke engine in order to prevent the rings from rotating, which would allow the open ends to become jammed in the ports

piston rocking *noun* = PISTON SLAP

◊ **piston rod** *noun (shock absorber)* rod which operates the piston in a telescopic damper

◊ **piston seal** *noun* fluid seal on a disc brake caliper piston; *(see illustration 31)*

◊ **piston seizure** *noun* sudden stalling of the engine, caused by the piston becoming stuck in the bore; this is often caused by overheating or lack of lubrication and often leaves severe score marks in the cylinders

◊ **piston skirt** *noun* the part of a piston below the gudgeon pin and ring belt area; its temperature can reach 130°C

◊ **piston slap** *noun* audible noise caused by excessive piston play, which allows the piston to tilt in BDC and TDC (when reversing the direction of motion)

◊ **piston speed** *noun* speed of the piston for a given engine rpm

◊ **piston spring** *noun* coil spring in an SU carburettor which counteracts the upward movement of the piston; *(see illustration 12, 13)*

◊ **piston top** *noun* = PISTON CROWN

◊ **piston-valve engine** *noun* two-stroke engine that relies on the ports in the cylinder walls to control admission and exhaust of the air/fuel mixture; it is not equipped with other control elements such as rotary valves

pitch *noun* **(a)** axial distance of adjacent threads measured between corresponding thread points; the pitch of single-start threads equals the lead **(b)** parking space or site for a trailer, caravan, etc.

pitch circle (PC) *noun* the circumference on which the centres of the wheel bolt holes are located; **pitch circle diameter (PCD)** = the diameter of the stud holes/bolt holes for fixing the wheel to the hub

COMMENT: the PC is usually shown as a double number; e.g. 5 - 5.5: the first number indicates the number of holes, and the second, the diameter of the PC

pitman arm *noun US* = DROP ARM; **pitman shaft** = ROCKER SHAFT

pitot tube *noun* tube for measuring the pressure and velocity of a fluid flow; in some CVTs, used in conjunction with a valve arrangement to control ratio changes

pits *noun* **(a)** cavities extending from the surface into the metal as a result of pitting corrosion **(b)** *(at a motor racing circuit)* place where a car stops for servicing, refuelling, tyre changes, etc.

◊ **pitted** *adjective (of contact breaker points)* eroded

pitting *noun* surface damage to a metal in the form of pits or holes *inspect all rocker arms for pitting at the point where they contact the valve stem, pushrod, and cam lobe* (NOTE: in the case of contact breaker points the opposite is **piling**); **pitting corrosion** = corrosion process resulting in pits; **pitting factor** = the ratio of the depth of the deepest pit to the average penetration as calculated from weight loss

COMMENT: material fatigue at the contact faces of two components that run on one another causes the material surface to deteriorate and thus small particles to be torn out of the surface

pivot axis *noun* = SWIVEL AXIS

◊ **pivot pin** *noun* = KINGPIN

◊ **pivot ring** *noun* = FULCRUM RING

PL = PARKING LOCK

plain bearing *noun* cylindrical sleeve friction bearing; most commonly used type of bearing; *(compare* BALL BEARING, NEEDLE BEARING, ROLLER BEARING)

◊ **plain disc wheel** *noun* wheel type without holes or slots in the wheel disc

planetary gear *noun (starter motor)* used in some starters as an intermediate transmission

◊ **planetary (gear) differential** *noun* planetary gear set used as a differential with asymmetric torque distribution, as for 4wd vehicles

◊ **planetary gear set** *noun* comprises a central externally toothed sun gear, an internally toothed outer ring gear, and several intermediate planet gears which are evenly spaced and supported by a planet carrier; they are in constant mesh with the sun gear and the internal gear

◊ **planetary transmission** *noun US* = EPICYCLIC GEARBOX

◊ **planet carrier** *noun* part which revolves around the central axis of a planetary gear set and supports the planet gears; *(see illustration 21)*

◊ **planet gear** *noun (automatic transmission)* gear whose axis is not stationary; it is supported by a planet carrier and revolves around the central axis; *(see illustration 21)*

◊ **planet pinion** *noun* = PLANET GEAR

◊ **planet spider** *noun* common type of planet carrier with a spider or web-style design

◊ **planet wheel** *noun* = PLANET GEAR

planishing *noun* final panel hammering stage for lifting out minor imperfections in a panel surface; part of the panel finishing process; **planishing hammer** = panel beater's hammer

plasma spray process *noun* process in which a very high temperature flame is produced by blowing gas through an electric arc; metal wire or powder is melted by passage through the flame and is projected on the surface to be coated

plastic *noun* a material that contains as an essential ingredient one or more organic polymeric substances of large molecular weight, is solid in its finished state and, at some stage in its manufacture or processing into finished articles, can be shaped by flow

◇ **plastic deformation** *noun* permanent change in the shape or size of a solid body without fracture resulting from the application of sustained stress beyond the elastic limit

◇ **plastic engine** *noun* an automobile engine whose bulk is made of plastic components (e.g. engine block, inlet manifold, water-pump housing, valve covers, sump), the use of metal being limited to parts subjected to extreme mechanical or thermal loads (e.g. combustion chamber, exhaust manifold, pistons, cylinder liners, valve train, etc.)

◇ **plastic filler** *noun* = POLYESTER FILLER

◇ **plasticize** *verb* to soften a material to make it plastic or mouldable by heating, kneading, or adding a plasticizer

◇ **plasticizer** *noun* an additive that gives flexibility to an otherwise rigid plastic

plastics welding *noun* a uniting of thermoplastic, i.e. non-setting plastics of similar or different type using heat and pressure and with or without the addition of plastic of a similar kind (filler material)

COMMENT: welding proceeds within the temperature range of thermoplasticity of the contact surfaces on the parts to be welded; the freely mobile molecular chains in the marginal areas flow together and become interlaced

Plastigage *noun* a soft plastic that flattens out to predetermined widths when subjected to torque; these widths equal a specific clearance

COMMENT: normally used to check main and rod-bearing clearance. It is sold in a paper sleeve that also doubles as the scale on which it is measured (in thousandths of an inch)

plate 1 *noun* **(a)** thin flat sheet of metal *inspection plate; information plate; mounting plate* **(b)** *(battery)* in each battery cell are two lead-alloy plates: one of lead peroxide (positive plate), the other of spongy lead (negative plate); separators are placed between the plates of different polarity **(c)** *(clutch)* = DISC 2 *verb* to coat (a metal) with a thin layer of another metal by electrolysis, chemical reaction, etc.

◇ **plate grid** *noun (battery)* = GRID

◇ **plate group** *noun* assembly of plates of identical polarity (positive or negative) as used in a battery cell

◇ **plate strap** *noun (battery)* the conducting connection between the lugs of plates of like polarity and the cell terminal

◇ **plate support** *noun* support at the bottom of a battery case on which the elements rest; provides space for the sediment chamber

platform frame *noun* underbody construction consisting of a reinforced and fairly flat section that forms the entire lower portion of the car; it includes the floorpans and is bolted to the body; (e.g. Volkswagen Beetle)

plating *noun* (metal) coating

platinum *noun* light-grey, heavy, ductile, noble metal; atomic number 78, atomic weight 195.09; melting point at 1769°C; main member of the so-called platinum metals; together with other platinum metals, is used as a catalyst in automotive exhaust converters

◇ **platinum electrode** *noun (sparking plug)* an electrode made of platinum lasts longer than one of nickel alloy as it can better withstand high temperatures

◇ **platinum metals** *noun* generic term for a family of noble metals found with and resembling platinum; including ruthenium, rhodium, palladium, osmium, iridium, and platinum; used as catalysts in catalytic converters; less than a tenth of a troy ounce is required per converter to produce acres of catalytically active catalyst surface

◇ **platinum sparking plug** *noun* sparking plug with a platinum centre electrode

play *see* FREE PLAY

plenum *noun* an enclosure containing air or gas at a higher pressure than exists outside

◇ **plenum chamber** *noun* **(a)** *(of induction system)* usually a large cast alloy body which connects the throttle body or inlet tube to the cylinder head(s) or inlet manifold; *(see illustrations 5, 14)* **(b)** *(car body)* air compartment formed between the scuttle and the bulkhead, providing a basis for the interior air supply; *(see illustration 1)*

pliers *noun* gripping tool with two hinged arms and serrated jaws

PLL circuitry *noun (radio)* phase-locked loop circuitry which 'locks' the station frequencies to ensure utmost frequency stability

plug 1 *noun* **(a)** stopper which seals a hole **(b)** male electrical connector; *(compare* SOCKET) **(c)** = SPARKING PLUG **2** *verb* to seal with a stopper

◊ **plug gap** *noun* = SPARKING PLUG GAP

◊ **plughole** *noun* hole in a tank or cistern, which can be closed with a rubber plug

◊ **plug spanner** *noun* = SPARKING PLUG SPANNER

plug welding *noun* a number of holes are punched along the edge of the repair section to be welded in; the section overlaps the damaged area to be repaired and is welded to the base metal at the punched holes

COMMENT: this is a convenient way of duplicating the spot welding process used by manufacturers, as spot welding equipment is usually too expensive and cumbersome for repair purposes

plug whiskering *noun* = GAP BRIDGING

plunger *noun* **(a)** any immersing type of piston **(b)** hydraulic tappet component (e.g. in a valve) *sludge, varnish, or metallic particles can cause the plunger to stick or hold the check valve open* **(c)** actuating element in an ignition lock **(d)** piston in a starter solenoid

◊ **plunger principle** *noun* a new ABS control system which offers improved pressure modulation with very small amplitudes even at pressures close to zero; *(compare* VALVE PRINCIPLE)

◊ **plunger pump** *noun* oil pump consisting of a reciprocating plunger in a ported chamber

plunging joint *noun* *US* = SLIDING JOINT

ply *noun* rubber-impregnated layer of cord (made from rayon, nylon, polyester or steel) which forms the basis of a tyre carcass; **ply rating** (**PR**) = index of load-carrying capacity, giving the maximum permitted load for a tyre

PM = PARTICULATE MATTER; **PM trap** = diesel particulate filter

PMMA = POLYMETHYL METHACRYLATE

p/n *or* **PN** = PART(S) NUMBER

pneumatic suspension *noun* = AIR SUSPENSION

◊ **pneumatic trail** *noun* distance between a vertical line through the centre of the wheel and the centre of pressure of the tyre contact patch; most apparent during cornering; *(compare* SELF-CENTRING EFFECT)

◊ **pneumatic tyre** *noun* rubber tyre filled with air under pressure (NOTE: opposite is **solid tyre**)

POA suction throttling valve *noun* stands for 'pilot operated absolute' and is a modification of a suction throttling valve which has a metal bellows with a vacuum instead of a diaphragm; it provides more accurate evaporator pressure control, allowing for lower evaporator temperatures without core icing

pocket (slide) caliper *noun* small slide-type caliper for inside and outside measurement up to about 100 mm or 4 in

pod *noun* housing for a gauge mounted behind the steering wheel

points *noun* = CONTACT BREAKER POINTS; **points file** = thin, fine-toothed file for cleaning and smoothing off the piles on contact breaker points; **points gap** = gap between the contact breaker points when fully open; measured with a feeler gauge

poke *noun* *(informal)* power or acceleration *the XYZ has a surprising amount of poke for its size*

polarity *noun* property of an electric system that has two points with different electric potentials *plates of unlike polarity*

polarization resistance *noun* the transition resistance between the electrodes and the electrolyte; part of the internal resistance of a battery; *(compare* INTERNAL RESISTANCE)

pole *noun* either of two points at which there are opposite electric charges (positive or negative), as at the terminals of a battery

◊ **pole piece** *noun* soft magnetic core of the inductive winding in a magnetic pick-up assembly; stator

◊ **pole shoe** *noun* in an electrical machine, such as a starter motor, a piece of soft iron mounted to the inside of the housing, surrounded by the field coils; *(see illustration 37)*

polishing barrel *noun* barrel used for a polishing process in which the aluminium surface is smoothed in the presence of metallic or ceramic shot by a rotating movement of the barrel

pollutant *noun* in the context of automotive emissions, pollutant typically refers to hydrocarbons, carbon monoxide, and nitrogen oxides *the catalytic converter is an emission control device added to the exhaust system to reduce HC, CO, and NO$_x$ pollutants in the exhaust gas stream*

polycarbonate (PC) *noun* a polyester polymer in which the repeating structural unit in the chain is of the carbonate type; used for bumpers, body and roof panels

polyellipsoidal headlight (PE headlight) *noun* headlight with a gas discharge lamp and a polyellipsoidal reflector

polyester filler *noun* body repair material for smoothing dents in body panels; includes a resin base filler paste and a catalyst which is added to the base filler and hardens by chemical reaction; **polyester powder** = powder used for electrostatic powder coating

polyethylene (PE) *noun* a polymer prepared by the polymerization of ethylene as the sole monomer; very resistant to chemical attack

COMMENT: high-density polyethylene (HDPE) is used, e.g., for blow-moulded parts such as tanks for fuel, coolant, washer and brake fluid; low-density polyethylene (LDPE) is used for plastic film and sheet

polymer *noun* substance consisting of molecules characterized by the repetition of one or more types of monomeric units; **polymer alloy** = a mixture of two or more different compatible polymers

◊ **polymerization** *noun* the bonding of two or more monomers (by chemical reaction) to produce a polymer

COMMENT: plastic parts produced from specific polymer alloys usually give better performance in respect to thermal and mechanical properties as compared to those of parts consisting of the respective individual components

polymethyl methacrylate (PMMA) *noun* thermoplastic polymer derived from methylacrylate; transparent solid with excellent optical qualities and weather resistance; typical automotive applications are the lenses of rear lights (NOTE: also called **Perspex)**

◊ **polyphenylene oxide (PPO)** *noun* characteristics of this plastic are high impact strength, good thermal and dimensional stability as well as excellent flame-resistance

polypropylene (PP) *noun* an extremely versatile plastic, available in many grades and also as a copolymer (ethylene/propylene)

COMMENT: PP has the lowest density of all thermoplastics (900 kg per cubic metre) and is characterized by excellent strength, stiffness, fatigue and chemical resistance; automotive applications are similar to those of polyethylene

polytetrafluoroethylene (PTFE) *noun* the major advantages of this material are its excellent chemical resistance and its extremely low coefficient of friction; automotive uses are parts where these characteristics are relevant, such as in valve stem seals, friction bearings and joints

◊ **polyurethane (PUR)** *noun* thermoplastic material with high strength, good chemical and abrasion resistance; used mainly for foamed reaction injection mouldings and for adhesives, such as for flush-bonded body glass; **polyurethane paint** = type of two-pack paint based on polyurethane substances; **polyurethane powder** = powder used for electrostatic powder coating

◊ **poly-V-belt** *noun* drive belt with multiple Vs; flat, similar to the toothed belts used as timing belts, but with lengthwise V-shaped ribs rather than transverse cogs; used increasingly on new engines instead of conventional V-belts

◊ **polyvinyl chloride (PVC)** *noun* both plasticized and unplasticized PVC types are marked by good weathering resistance, excellent electrical insulation properties, and good surface properties; they are self-extinguishing

poor opacity *noun* paint fault in which the colour of underlying coats or fillers remains visible through the topcoat; may be caused by insufficient paint thickness, overthinning, etc.

popper *noun* = SNAP FASTENER

poppet valve *noun* valve which pops open and shut in a reciprocating motion; consists of a valve stem and valve disc; the typical valve type used in engine cylinder heads (NOTE: also called **mushroom valve** due to its shape)

popping *noun* = SOLVENT POP

◊ **popping back** *noun* = BLOWBACK

pop rivet *noun* type of tubular rivet which initially has a hard steel pin passing through it; when the pop rivet is fitted with a pop rivet gun, the head of the pin expands the inner end of the tubular rivet, closing it; the head of the pin then snaps off; used when a joint can be accessed from one side only

pop-up headlights *noun* = CONCEALED HEADLIGHTS

porcelain enamel *noun* *US* = VITREOUS ENAMEL

pore *noun* small opening in a surface

◊ **porosity** *noun* state or condition of being porous

◊ **porous** *adjective* permeable to air or fluids

Porsche-type synchromesh *noun* sophisticated synchromesh technology depending on the frictional forces created by a spreading synchronizer ring

port *noun* generally, any opening through which air or fluid passes; specifically, the opening in the cylinder of a hydraulic valve and the precision-made hole (jet) in the wall of a carburettor barrel; *(compare* INLET PORT, EXHAUST PORT)

◊ **port area** *noun* used to indicate the cross-section area of the port of a two-stroke engine; this value is one of the factors determining the gas flow and the power of a two-stroke engine

◊ **port bar** *or* **port bridge** *noun* if the ports of the two-stroke engine have to be exceptionally wide, as in the case of the exhaust, a port bar is sometimes formed

vertically across the port to give support to the rings, which might otherwise expand into the port and be jammed and broken

◊ **ported vacuum advance (PVA)** *noun* a series of restriction devices between the distributor advance unit and the carburettor advance port to ensure that there is no vacuum advance during idle, but increasing ignition advance as the throttle opens

◊ **port fuel injection (PFI)** *noun* = MULTI-POINT INJECTION

porthole *noun* a styling accessory popularized by the Buicks of the early 1950s

COMMENT: two or three round chrome surrounds were fitted to the sides of both wings for decorative purposes; this trim detail was soon imitated by other manufacturers and was offered as an option for many models, even in Europe

positive camber *see* CAMBER (a)

◊ **positive castor** *noun* when an imaginary line extended through the steering axis cuts the wheel axis ahead of the extended vertical axis through the wheel centre; *(compare* NEGATIVE CASTOR)

◊ **positive clutch** *noun* = DOG CLUTCH

positive crankcase ventilation (PCV) *noun* introduced in 1963, PCV serves to reduce emissions by recycling crankcase fumes and blow-by gases; *(see also* PCV VALVE)

COMMENT: the crankcase is connected to the inlet manifold; HC-rich crankcase vapours consisting of oil vapours and unburnt combustion gases that leak past the piston rings (blow-by gases) are drawn off by the inlet manifold vacuum via an oil separator, a flame trap, and a PCV valve, and are induced into the combustion chambers together with the fresh A/F mixture; the crankcase vapours are replaced by clean air drawn in via the air cleaner

positive displacement compressor *noun* pump which provides a measured amount of gas or liquid per stroke or cycle and requires some form of mechanical drive arrangement, usually a belt drive from the crankshaft; typical positive displacement compressors are piston compressors, roots compressors and vane-type compressors; *(compare* DYNAMIC SUPERCHARGING)

◊ **positive electrode** *noun (battery)* = POSITIVE PLATE

◊ **positive offset** *noun* **(a)** *(steering)* steering geometry layout where the steering axis cuts the wheel axis at or below the wheel centre plane; *(compare* CENTRE POINT STEERING, NEGATIVE OFFSET, SCRUB RADIUS) **(b)** *(wheel)* the distance between the mounting face of a disc and the wheel centreline; the offset is referred to as positive when the inner attachment face of the wheel disc is shifted towards the outer side of the wheel (NOTE: opposite is **negative offset)**

◊ **positive plate** *noun* during battery discharge the chocolate-coloured plate which acts as cathode (NOTE: opposite is **negative plate)**

◊ **positive terminal** *noun* red battery terminal with a plus symbol indicating positive polarity; *(compare* NEGATIVE TERMINAL)

post *noun* **(a)** pillar between the roof and the waistline; from front to rear, there are A-, B-, C-, and D-posts **(b)** = BATTERY POST

◊ **post-heating** *noun (glow plugs)* heating after the engine is started to prevent blue smoke and misfiring during the warm-up phase

◊ **post-ignition** *noun* ignition of the air-fuel mixture after the electrical ignition point

pot *noun* **(a)** = CYLINDER **(b)** = DASHPOT

pothole *noun* deep hole in the surface of a road

pot joint *noun* universal joint in which the rollers or balls can move freely in an internally grooved cylinder; *(compare* CONSTANT VELOCITY JOINT, SLIDING JOINT)

pour point *noun* the lowest temperature at which an oil can be poured

powder slush moulding *noun* processing technique applied to produce PVC skins

COMMENT: in a preheated rotating mould, a thin layer of PVC dry blend is evenly spread across the mould surface. The mould is transferred to an oven to fuse the PVC skin and is finally cooled in a water-bath

power 1 *noun* the rate at which energy is converted into work **2** *verb* to provide power to *model X is powered by a 3.5-litre engine*

COMMENT: with regard to automotive engines, power was specified in terms of horsepower (hp) [1 hp = 33,000 foot-pounds per minute]; the official unit of power is now the newton, but everyday speech and most specs still use bhp (brake horsepower), e.g. 100 bhp at 6000 rpm

power-assisted brakes *noun* braking system which uses a vacuum brake booster (servo) to reduce the pressure on the brake pedal; *(compare* POWER BRAKES)

◊ **power-assisted steering (pas)** *noun* steering system in which a hydraulic pump powered by the engine helps the driver to turn the steering wheel; *(compare* POWER STEERING)

power brakes (pb) *noun* braking system that uses hydraulic or vacuum or atmospheric pressure to provide most of the force required for braking

COMMENT: includes vacuum brakes, hydraulic brakes and pressurized air brakes but with reference to cars, these terms usually relate to vacuum brakes

power closing *noun* = AUTOMATIC CLOSING SYSTEM

◊ **power cut-off (switch)** *noun* = BATTERY MASTER SWITCH

◊ **power distribution** *noun* specific drive torque distribution between front and rear axles in a 4wd system *a centre differential that provides a 31/69 percent power distribution (compare* ASYMMETRIC POWER DISTRIBUTION)

◊ **power hood** *noun* convertible top which is raised and lowered by an electric motor (NOTE: US English is **electric top)**

◊ **power seat** *noun* seat whose back, height, thigh and lumbar support, etc. can be electrically adjusted

◊ **powershift transmission** *noun US* transmission which can be used without declutching or decelerating

◊ **power steering (ps)** *noun* **(a)** completely hydraulic or pneumatic steering system, allowing the driver little or no 'feel' for the road; not used for road-going passenger vehicles **(b)** *(informal)* = POWER-ASSISTED STEERING; **power steering pump** = pump which supplies hydraulic pressure for the power steering system

power stroke *noun* downstroke of a piston, the third stroke in a four-stroke cycle

COMMENT: in a spark ignition engine: the air/fuel mixture is ignited just before the piston reaches the top of its stroke so that a very large portion of the fuel burns by the time the piston begins descending again. The heat produced by the combustion increases the pressure in the cylinder, forcing the piston down with great force. Diesel engine: as the piston reaches the top of the stroke, the air temperature is at its maximum. A fine mist of fuel is sprayed into the pre-combustion chamber, the swirl chamber, or directly into the main combustion chamber (depending on the process used), where it ignites. The piston is forced downward by the pressure of the expanding gases

power take-off (PTO) *noun* using the crankshaft or gearbox to drive ancillary equipment, such as a pump or generator

◊ **power train** *noun* = DRIVE TRAIN

◊ **power valve** *noun* valve in the enrichment unit, used in some carburettors to provide a richer mixture for extra power under certain conditions; in a typical design, the power valve is a vacuum-controlled ball-type check valve

◊ **power window (pw)** *noun US* = ELECTRIC WINDOW; **power window lock-out switch** = switch that renders inoperable all electric window controls on the individual windows, except for the master controls on the driver's door

Pozidriv screwdriver *noun* proprietary type of screwdriver whose tip resembles the Phillips cross-head configuration but with four additional wedges, making eight flanks altogether, which allows a more positive drive and a higher torque.

PP = POLYPROPYLENE

◊ **PPO** = POLYPHENYLENE OXIDE

PR = PLY RATING

Pratt and Whitney (P&W) key *noun* parallel feather key with round end faces; an end mill is used to cut the keyway; *(compare* SQUARE KEY)

prechamber *noun (of indirect injection diesel engines)* small upper chamber in the cylinder head, connected to the main combustion chamber by a narrow passage; fuel is injected into the prechamber (also called swirl chamber) where it is ignited before spreading to the main chamber

pre-combustion engine *noun US* = INDIRECT INJECTION ENGINE

pre-compounding *noun* process of mixing plastic raw materials with additives

pre-compress *verb* to compress the fueloil mixture first

◊ **pre-compression chamber** *noun* chamber below the pistons in a two-stroke engine in which the fueloil mixture is initially compressed in order to enable more fresh charge to be fed into the cylinder

pre-converter vehicle *noun* a car built prior to the enforcement of emission control standards requiring a catalytic converter to be fitted to every new car

pre-engaged Bendix starter *noun* a combination of Bendix and pre-engaged starter drives

◊ **pre-engaged starter** *noun* starter motor in which the solenoid-operated pinion engages with a flywheel ring gear before the full electric current flows; an overrunning clutch enables the pinion to freewheel before disengaging, once the engine has fired

preheater system *noun* cold starting aid for diesel engines, consisting of glow plugs, a glow-control unit, and a glow plug and starter switch, for preheating the combustion chamber or the intake air up to auto-ignition temperature

preheating zone *noun* section in hot-wax flooding units, in which body shells are preheated to 60°C

pre-ignition *noun* ignition of the air/fuel mixture prior to the electrical ignition point

prelubricator *noun* lubrication system consisting mainly of an electronically controlled pump that circulates pressurized engine oil to an engine's vital parts for about six seconds when ignition is switched on prior to starting of the engine; reduces friction during cold starts and prolongs engine life

prepreg *noun* reinforcing or moulding material already impregnated with a synthetic resin; *(compare* SMC)

preselector gearbox *noun* conventional gearbox with a semi-automatic change mechanism in which a gear is selected before the change is initiated, the change being made by depressing the clutch or auxiliary pedal; *(compare* SEMI-AUTOMATIC TRANSMISSION)

preset station button *noun* button for tuning a radio automatically to a preset frequency, i.e. one radio station can be allocated to each button

press brake *noun* large type of sheet metal folder, built to handle larger panels and thicknesses

◊ **pressed panel** *noun* panel produced with special press tools and dies, as opposed to a hand-made panel

◊ **press fit** *noun* condition of contact between two parts that requires pressure to force the parts together

◊ **pressing plant** *noun* plant specializing in the manufacture of car bodies

pressure accumulator *noun* (usually) spherical pressure tank of about 10 mm diameter in an hydraulic brake booster

COMMENT: a diaphragm separates the pressure accumulator into two chambers, one contains pressurized nitrogen, the other contains hydraulic fluid supplied by the hydraulic pump; pressure inside the accumulator is in the order of 60 bar

pressure differential switch *noun* hydraulic pressure-operated switch (often included in a combination valve) which activates the 'brake failure' warning light when one of the brake circuits (in a dual-circuit system) fails due to a system leak and associated pressure drop

◊ **pressure-feed spray gun** *noun* type of spray gun with a separate paint container (pressure-feed tank) ; it is used mostly for spraying highly viscous materials such as spray putty

pressure limiting valve *US* **proportioning valve** *noun* **(a)** any valve which limits pressure in a system, e.g. in a hydraulic circuit, in automatic transmissions, in pneumatic suspension systems, etc.; *(compare* SAFETY VALVE) **(b)** specifically, the valve used in the rear brake line of some cars with front disc and rear drum brakes

COMMENT: when braking gently, pressure is about equal front and rear; as pedal pressure is increased, the limiting valve controls and finally limits pressure to the rear wheels to

prevent rear wheel lockup during heavy braking

pressure lubrication *noun* **(a)** *(of 4-stroke engines)* = FORCED-FEED LUBRICATION **(b)** *(of 2-stroke engines)* lubrication system with crankcase scavenging

COMMENT: fresh oil is supplied from a separate container and lubricates the engine components as it passes through the crankcase. The oil is ignited along with the air/fuel mixture. With this system, it is no longer necessary to add oil to the fuel when filling up

pressure plate *noun* **(a)** *(brakes)* the plate carrying the brake pad in a disc brake (NOTE: also called **backplate**) **(b)** *(transmission)* the part of the clutch assembly which is pressed against the clutch plate by the clutch springs to transmit the drive

◊ **pressure regulating valve** *noun* **(a)** any valve which maintains pressure at or under a certain pressure; specifically the pressure relief valve of the oil pump **(b)** in a continuous injection system, part of the fuel distributor, consisting basically of a spring-loaded steel diaphragm which serves to keep the pressure drop across the metering ports at a constant 0.1 bar

◊ **pressure regulator** *noun* regulator which governs the pressure of the fuel delivered to the injectors by the fuel pump

◊ **pressure regulator valve** *noun* releases hydraulic fluid if pressure exceeds a preset value

◊ **pressure relief valve** *noun* valve which opens at maximum safe pressure and closes again upon return to normal operating conditions; its main task is to prevent the internal pressure of a component or a system from exceeding a certain set point; *(compare* SAFETY VALVE) *(see illustrations 17, 34)*

◊ **pressure ridge** *noun* work-hardened edge of a damaged panel area that will often remain, even after the area has been smoothed with hammer and dolly; it must then be dressed with hammer and body spoon

◊ **pressure wave** *noun* pulsations or oscillations in the induction and exhaust systems caused by the opening and closing of the valves; **pressure wave supercharger** = COMPREX PRESSURE WAVE SUPERCHARGER

◊ **pressurized** *adjective* working under pressure

primary battery *noun* non-rechargeable battery consisting of one or more primary cells, used e.g. in portable radio receivers (NOTE: opposite is **secondary/storage battery**)

◊ **primary (catalytic) converter** *noun* small converter positioned close to the engine which quickly achieves the necessary operating temperature to reduce exhaust emissions during the warm-up period

◊ **primary cell** *noun* electric cell that converts chemical energy into electrical energy in an irreversible process; unlike a secondary cell, it cannot be recharged

◊ **primary chain** *noun* the chain of a primary drive

◊ **primary circuit** *noun* circuit which comprises the battery, the ignition switch, if ballasted the ballast resistor, the primary winding of the ignition coil, and if breaker-triggered the contact breaker points; *(compare* SECONDARY CIRCUIT*)*

◊ **primary compression ratio** *noun* degree of compression achieved in the crankcase area below the piston of a two-stroke engine when the piston moves down and compresses the mixture supplied into the crankcase

◊ **primary key** *noun* key which operates all the locks of the car; *(compare* SECONDARY KEY*)*

◊ **primary magnetic field** *noun* magnetic field of the primary winding

◊ **primary pattern** *noun* oscilloscope pattern of the primary circuit

◊ **primary piston** *noun* main piston in a tandem master cylinder; *(see illustration 29)*

◊ **primary pump** *noun* engine-driven oil pump feeding pressurized oil to the transmission and hydraulic control system; *(compare* SECONDARY PUMP*)*

◊ **primary seal** *noun* primary piston seal in a tandem master cylinder

◊ **primary shaft** *noun* = CLUTCH SHAFT

◊ **primary shoe** *noun US* = LEADING SHOE

◊ **primary structure component** *noun* any structural component which, if it collapsed, could make the car uncontrollable or would seriously reduce occupant safety in a crash

◊ **primary valve** *noun* valve which controls the primary V-pulley

◊ **primary V-pulley** *noun (CVT)* pulley which is driven by the engine via a clutch; one

of its halves can be slid hydraulically, thus varying the diameter of the steel thrust belt track and changing the transmission ratio

◊ **primary winding** *noun* outer winding of the ignition coil; typically 200 turns of relatively strong wire (NOTE: opposite is **secondary winding**)

prime *verb* **(a)** to apply primer **(b)** to fill a machine (e.g. a pump) with the necessary fluid before starting, in order to improve its sealing qualities **(c)** to put fuel in the float chamber of a carburettor to ease the starting of an engine

◊ **primer** *noun* first coat of paint applied to a bare surface; designed to provide a foundation for the subsequent coats and to ensure rust protection; **primer bath** = bath containing the primer; **primer filler** = special primer used to cover fine cracks; **primer oven** = painting line oven used to dry the coats of primer; **primer surfacer** = material for the resilient coating underneath the top paint coat which provides corrosion protection, protects the paint system from chipping caused by gravel, provides a smooth surface for the top paint coat, and serves as an adhesion promoter

printed circuit board (pcb) *noun* thin plastic insulating board on one or both sides of which the components and connections of an electronic circuit are formed by etching in a metallic coating or electrodeposition

prise off *verb* to lever off *stubborn spring hangers can be prised off the spring shackle bolt with a large screwdriver*

PRNDL = letters denoting the positions on the gear selector of an automatic gearbox, standing for: Park, Reverse, Neutral, Drive, Low (NOTE: Low may be divided into: 3, 2, 1)

probe *noun* a measuring sensor, usually long and thin to gain access to narrow cavities

Procon-ten *noun* safety system developed by Audi which makes use of the relative displacement of the engine during a frontal collision; steel cables pull the steering wheel away from the driver and increase the seat belt tension

production car *or* **model** *noun* car manufactured by a mass-production process; **production line** = system in which the parts of an end product are transported by a conveyor past a number of sites where the parts are modified without stopping the conveyor

◇ **product line** *or* **range** *noun* series of different products made by the same company which form a group (such as different models of cars)

profile *noun* **(a)** side view, shape or outline of an object **(b)** cross-section of a tyre; **profile depth** = TREAD DEPTH *(compare* ASPECT RATIO)

programme comparison and identification (PCI) *noun (radio)* system that identifies a programme (station) and compares programmes so as to find the station which offers the strongest signal

progressive carburettor *noun* = COMPOUND CARBURETTOR

◇ **progressive(ly wound) valve spring** *noun* valve spring with variable spacing between its coils which helps to improve responsiveness and thus to reduce the load on the valve train

◇ **progressive transmission** *noun* transmission in which it is necessary to pass through the gear ratios in a definite order; usage today confined almost exclusively to motorcycles; *(compare* SELECTIVE TRANSMISSION)

projected core/insulator nose *noun* insulator tip that extends beyond the end of the sparking plug shell

◇ **projected spark position** *noun* amount the sparking plug gap projects into the combustion chamber: 1 mm for the slightly projected spark position in older engines and 3 mm for the normally projected spark position in modern engines

projection welding *noun* resistance welding method

promoter *noun* substance embedded in the washcoat on catalyst substrates that serves to enhance catalytic efficiency

propane *noun* colourless, flammable gas used for cooking, heating and as a fuel (see LPG)

propeller (pump) *noun* impeller of a propeller pump, characterized by a small

number of blades of double curvature; propellers are generally axial-flow impellers, seldom mixed-flow ones

◇ **propeller shaft** *noun* generally applicable to the long, jointed shaft between the power unit and differential, usually mounted longitudinally from front to rear on front-engine RWD vehicles; *(compare* AXLE SHAFT) *(see illustrations 22, 24, 28)* (NOTE: US English is **drive shaft)**

proportional load synchromesh *noun* = LOCKING SYNCHROMESH

◇ **proportioning valve** *noun US* = PRESSURE LIMITING VALVE

propshaft *noun* *(informal)* = PROPELLER SHAFT

propulsive power *noun* the force with which a vehicle moves; the pulling force; depends not only on engine power and torque, but also on the amount of friction between driving wheels and road surface

prop up *verb* to fix the bonnet in the open position using the bonnet support stay

protective coat(ing) *noun* layer or layers applied to a surface to provide corrosion protection

◇ **protector washer** *noun* filter disc between the primary piston and primary seal which supports and protects the primary seal when the brake system is under pressure

prototype *noun* a first full-scale and usually functional form of a new type or design of a vehicle; *(compare* CONCEPT CAR)

proud *adjective* projecting up slightly from the surrounding surface; *(compare* FLUSH)

ps = POWER STEERING

psi *(short for)* pound-force per square inch, a measurement of pressure; *(compare* TYRE PRESSURE)

PTFE = POLYTETRAFLUOROETHYLENE

PTO = POWER TAKE-OFF

puckering *noun* *(paint fault)* = WRINKLING

puddle lamp *noun* lamp in he bottom of a luxury car door which illuminates the area into which a passenger is going to step when the door is opened

◇ **puddle welding** *noun* = PLUG WELDING

pull *verb* *(vehicle)* to deviate towards the side

COMMENT: there may be various causes for a vehicle pulling to one side or the other, the most common being: the brakes on either side exerting uneven pressure, incorrect wheel alignment, uneven tyre tread, or a defect in the steering system

pull away *verb* to drive away from a standing start

puller *noun* special automotive tool used to remove gears, bearings, pulleys, wheels and other parts from shafts by a pulling action; *(compare* EXTRACTOR*)*

COMMENT: pulling is either activated by a pressure screw or by means of a slide hammer; the most common type of puller has jaws to grip behind the parts to be pulled off; however, pullers also come in a variety of special purpose designs for removing specific parts on vehicles

pulley *noun* wheel with a grooved rim to carry a belt, chain or rope

pull in *verb* to drive to the side of the road or into a lay-by, etc. (and stop)

pulling beam *noun* hydraulic ram attached securely to the vehicle at strong points; pulling force is then applied to the pulling beam to pull the frame or sheet metal back into place; **pulling post** = post bolted to the shop floor or fixed in a concrete foundation which forms the anchorage for the chain and hydraulic jack assemblies to straighten misaligned bodies

pull-in winding *noun* winding as used in a starter solenoid that does the heavy pull-in work; *(compare* HOLD-IN WINDING*) (see illustration 37)*

pull off *verb* to drive off a road (and stop) *pull off here and let's have our picnic in the field*

pull out *verb* **(a)** to drive away from the side of a road *she pulled out into the traffic*

heading west; the mini pulled out right in front of the lorry **(b)** to drive out from behind a vehicle in front in order to overtake *always indicate before pulling out to overtake*

◇ **pull-out door handle** *noun* door handle which is pulled away from the door skin to open the door from the outside

pull over *verb* to drive to the side of the road (and stop)

pull-type clutch *noun* clutch in which the clutch release bearing is pulled away from the flywheel when the clutch is disengaged; *(compare* PUSH-TYPE CLUTCH*)*

pull up *verb* to stop *the taxi pulled up and a little old lady got out*

pulse air principle *noun* in air induction systems the method of introducing secondary air into the exhaust system by means of aspirator valves actuated by the pressure pulses of the exhaust gas stream; **pulse air system** = air induction system using the pulse air principle

◇ **pulse former** *or* **shaper** *noun* circuit for changing the waveform of a signal

◇ **pulse generator** *noun* = PICK-UP MODULE

pump 1 *noun* machine that transforms mechanical energy generated by a prime mover into the energy of a moving fluid **2** *verb* to add kinetic and potential energy to a liquid for the purpose of moving it from one point to another

COMMENT: a pump receives a flow of liquid or gas at a certain inlet pressure, raises this pressure to a higher value, and discharges the fluid through the outlet; automotive vehicles use various pumps, which may include: engine oil pump, automatic gearbox oil pump, coolant pump, fuel pump, fuel-injection pump, power steering pump, hydraulic pump for suspension, convertible top, etc., washer fluid pumps, secondary air pump, air trumpet pump, and compressors

pump-fed lubrication *noun* = FORCED-FEED LUBRICATION

◇ **pumping chamber** *noun* = PRE-COMPRESSION CHAMBER

◇ **pumping losses** *noun* that part of engine power which is expended on the induction of the fuel and air charge into the engine and the expulsion of combustion gases

◊ **pump power output** *noun* the energy transferred by a pump to the liquid pumped

◊ **pump rotor** *noun* centrifugal pump assembly consisting of the pump shaft, impeller and further rotating components, such as rotating bearing and shaft sealing parts

◊ **pump shaft** *noun* shaft which transmits the driver torque to the impeller(s) of centrifugal pumps or to the displacement element(s) of rotary pumps

punch *noun* tool for making holes or driving out bolts, rivets and pins; *(compare* CENTRE PUNCH, DRIFT)

puncture *noun* hole in a tyre made by a sharp object and causing loss of air pressure; *(compare* BLOW-OUT)

punt chassis *noun* = BACKBONE CHASSIS

PUR = POLYURETHANE

purge *verb* to get rid of impurities; **the carbon filter is purged by a blast of hot air** *(compare* SCAVENGE)

push bar *noun* bar between the shoes in a drum brake; *(see illustration 30)*

◊ **pushrod** *noun* **(a)** steel or aluminium rod linking the tappet to the rocker arm in overhead valve (OHV) engines; **pushrod**

engine = OVERHEAD VALVE ENGINE; **pushrod measuring tool** = tool which measures the length of pushrod needed in an engine; a pushrod of proper length is vital to keep the rocker in the centre of the valve, minimize the risk of breakage and extend the valve guide life **(b)** rod which actuates the primary piston in a master cylinder or power brake servo; *(see illustration 29)*

◊ **push start** *noun* = BUMP START

◊ **push-type clutch** *noun* conventional clutch in which the clutch release bearing is pushed towards the flywheel when the clutch is disengaged; *(compare* PULL-TYPE CLUTCH)

putty *noun* special paste used for repairing minor panel imperfections, e.g. chips or scratches on the filled surface; it is used after normal filling and gives an extremely smooth surface; **putty knife** = tool for scraping off dirt, carbon, and paint or for applying putty

PVA = PORTED VACUUM ADVANCE

PVC = POLYVINYL CHLORIDE; **PVC seam sealing** = the sealing of seams with PVC sealant to prevent the penetration of corrosive agents; **PVC tape** = INSULATING TAPE; **PVC underbody treatment** = treatment of the underbody of a vehicle to protect it from chipping due to gravel or stones and corrosive agents; **PVC underseal (coating)** = protective PVC coating applied to the underbody of a vehicle

pw = POWER WINDOW(S)

Qq

Q letter on the sidewall of a tyre denoting the maximum speed for which it is designed (160 km/h or 100 mph); *(see* SPEED RATING)

QTS = QUARTZ TUNING SYSTEM

quad-cam engine *noun* engine with four camshafts

quadrant *noun* **(a)** *(transmission)* guide which indicates the position of the gear selector of an automatic gearbox **(b)** *(steering)* the V-shaped toothed section of a worm-and-sector steering box

quarter bumper *noun* type of shortened bumper designed to give a car a sporting image

> COMMENT: instead of extending around the full width of the car, short bumper sections around the left- and right-hand corners leave the centre unprotected. This type of bumper was popular on certain sports models manufactured by Opel and Ford in the 1970s

quarter-elliptic leaf spring *noun* cantilevered half of a semi-elliptic leaf spring, rigidly attached to a vehicle at its major section and carrying the axle at its end section

◇ **quarter light** *noun* **(a)** small, roughly triangular, front-door window that swings out on fixed hinges; situated in front of and separate from the main window **(b)** small, roughly triangular window situated behind the main rear-door window

◇ **quarter light filler panel** *noun* a relatively small, roughly triangular panel, usually black, inserted into the rear side-window's rear bottom corner

quarter panel *noun* rear section of the body shell which incorporates the rear wing and usually also the C-pillar; *(see illustration 1)*

> COMMENT: in modern car bodies, the rear wing usually is no longer a separate welded or bolt-on panel, instead it blends smoothly into the bottom of the rear window frame and the rear panel

quartz-halogen bulb *noun* high intensity headlight bulb with a trace of a halogen gas (such as iodine) in a quartz envelope

◇ **quartz tuning system (QTS)** *noun* quartz-controlled tuning system with digital tuning and frequency display; uses microprocessor-controlled PLL circuitry

quattro *(Italian for)* four; indicates that a car has four-wheel drive

quench *verb (spark)* to damp or suppress

◇ **quench zones** *noun* those parts within the combustion chamber of an engine where the temperature of the A/F mixture is lower than necessary for optimum combustion, due to contact with the relatively cold metal surface; incomplete combustion in the quench zones is one of the two major factors contributing to HC and CO concentrations in the exhaust gas

quick take-up valve *noun* residual pressure valve with relief hole in a brake master cylinder

quill shaft *noun* hollow shaft

Rr

R (a) = REVERSE **(b)** letter on a fuel gauge indicating low fuel; when first illuminated it indicates that there is approximately five litres left in reserve **(c)** letter on the sidewall of a tyre denoting the maximum speed for which it is designed (170 km/h or 105 mph); *(see* SPEED RATING)

RAC = ROYAL AUTOMOBILE CLUB

race 1 *noun* inner or outer cylindrical ring holding the balls or rollers in an antifriction bearing **2** *verb (engine)* to run at high speed when not in gear

◊ **racing start** *noun* a start on a normal street, e.g. at traffic lights, using excessive throttle resulting in wheelspin and tyre screeching

rack *noun* long, toothed bar; *(see illustration 26)*

◊ **rack-and-pinion steering** *noun* steering system in which a pinion on the end of the steering shaft meshes with a rack of gear teeth on the major crossmember of the steering linkage (NOTE: opposite is **parallelogram steering**) *(see illustration 26)*

◊ **rack galvanizing** *noun* galvanizing method for objects which can be placed on a rack

rad *(short for)* radiator

radial bearing *noun* bearing designed to absorb the radial forces acting on a pump; *(compare* THRUST BEARING)

◊ **radial clearance** *noun* = RADIAL PLAY

◊ **radial engine** *noun* multi-cylinder engine in which the cylinders radiate from a central crankshaft

◊ **radial-flow pump** *noun* end-suction centrifugal pump with the liquid flowing perpendicular to the pump shaft

◊ **radial play** *noun* bearing clearance in the radial direction

◊ **radial runout** *noun* variation in the radius of the tyre tread from the wheel axis, making the tyre no longer truly round; one of the main causes of vehicle vibration

radial shaft seal *noun* typical seal design used to prevent leaks between stationary parts and rotating shafts and to exclude foreign matter; *(see illustration 4)*

COMMENT: a lip seal, typically of neoprene, is held in a metal retainer and applies a sealing pressure to a rotating shaft, the pressure being provided by an annular garter spring which surrounds the sealing lip; radial shaft seals are used wherever a shaft penetrates a casing, such as on crankshafts, camshafts, water pump shafts, etc.

radial tyre *noun* tyre in which the plies are placed radially, or perpendicular to the rim, with a circumferential belt on top of them; the rubber tread is vulcanized on top of the belt and plies; *(compare* CROSS-PLY TYRE)

radiator *noun* liquid-to-air heat exchanger that transfers engine heat to the outside air; consists of many thin-walled tubes with metal cooling fins that draw off heat from the liquid (predominantly water) inside them; *(see illustration 15)*

◊ **radiator cap** *noun* pressure cap at the top of the radiator

◊ **radiator drain cock** *noun* radiator tap; unlike the radiator drain plug, tools are not required to drain the coolant from a radiator with a drain cock; **radiator drain plug** = threaded closure plug located at the underside of a radiator used to drain the coolant; usually equipped with a hex or Allen head

radiator fan *noun (of water-cooled engine)* crankshaft-driven fan connected via a temperature-sensitive viscous coupling, or driven by an electric motor; *(see illustration 15)*; **radiator fan motor** = electrically operated motor responsible for driving the radiator fan; *(compare* FAN BELT)

COMMENT: an electric motor allows much more freedom in radiator location and engine bay design and permits aftercooling of the engine with the engine switched off; most engines mounted crosswise at the front (as on most front-wheel-drive subcompacts) use electric radiator fans which also lead to reduced power losses, since the vehicle's engine is not also required to also drive the radiator fan

radiator grille *noun* grating that admits cooling air to the radiator; **radiator grille surround** = sheet metal panel for mounting the radiator grille; often combined with the front apron to form a single front panel

◊ **radiator hose** *noun* rubber pipe connecting the radiator to the cylinder block; **radiator hose shark tooth pliers** = special automotive tool for removing and installing radiator and heater hoses; round and toothed jaws securely grip the hose whilst the handles provide leverage to twist the hose free

◊ **radiator support panel** *noun* panel located behind the radiator grille surround which provides a mounting for the radiator and connects the mudguard skirts at their front edge

radiator tank *noun* reservoir containing the coolant in a radiator; *(see illustration 15)*

COMMENT: previously made from sheet metal, typically brass or aluminium, advanced polymer technology and injection moulding processes have made it possible to produce radiator tanks from thermoplastics; since all modern cars use forced circulation systems, there is no need for vertical flow through the radiator; today, therefore, most radiators are horizontally arranged

radio/cassette deck (r/c) *noun* combined radio and tape deck

◊ **radio choke** *noun* electric coil used to prevent static in the radio caused by opening and closing of the contact points in the instrument voltage regulator

◊ **Radio Data System (RDS)** *noun* system which interrupts a radio broadcast with the latest information on e.g. traffic problems

◊ **radio frequency interference (RFI)** *noun* interference generated by the ignition system and other electrical apparatus; counteracted by suppressors

radius arm *or* **rod** *noun* additional suspension link in a beam axle layout providing fore-and-aft location of the axle; *(compare* TORQUE ARM)

◊ **radius seat** *noun* spherical seat that provides positive centring of the wheel bolt head in the wheel (NOTE: opposite is **taper seat**)

ragtop *noun (informal)* convertible

raising *noun* beating a rounded shape out of a flat panel by starting in the centre and working outwards in a spiral to the edge; the metal is shrunk around the edge but remains about the same in the centre

rake (angle) *noun* angle of a slope, e.g. caster angle

ramp *noun* **(a)** equipment used to support a vehicle's front or rear for underbody work **(b)** device used to raise a vehicle in the air *2-post ramp; 4-post ramp*

ram pressure *noun* pressure generated by the deflection of the fluid flow due to the curvature of the stator blades, resulting in a momentum acting on the turbine

range-change *noun* = AUXILIARY GEARBOX

ratchet *noun* **(a)** toothed rack or wheel which is engaged by a lever to permit motion in one direction only *pawl and ratchet mechanism* **(b)** drive handle with ratchet mechanism that permits the socket to rotate in one direction only, i.e. the ratchet releases in one direction, but catches in the other; **ratchet adaptor** = converts a torque wrench or drive handle without a ratchet mechanism into a reversible ratchet tool; **ratchet handle** = RATCHET (b); **ratchet screwdriver** = screwdriver with ratchet mechanism

COMMENT: there are different types of ratchets with round, oval or flexible heads, and large ratchets in particular often have a detachable handle

rated capacity *noun* the quantity of electricity which can be drawn from a fully charged battery for 20 hours by a constant discharging current until cutoff voltage of 1.75 volts per cell is reached; *(compare* AMPERE-HOUR CAPACITY)

◊ **rated power** *noun* the horsepower (or kilowatt) power output of an engine

◊ **rated pressure** *noun* nominal pressure rating applied to vehicle parts

◊ **rated speed** *noun* nominal engine speed at which rated power is obtained

◊ **rated voltage** *noun* the voltage given for electrical equipment or devices which refers to specified operating conditions

rationalization *noun* industrial reorganization primarily aimed at a more cost-effective and time-saving production process

rat-tail file *noun (informal)* round file

Ravigneaux planetary gear set *noun* comprises two sun gears of different diameters, one internal gear, and several planet pinions; *(see illustration 21)*

raw exhaust gas *noun* exhaust gas upstream of any emission control device, e.g. before it passes through a catalytic converter

◊ **raw rubber** *noun* natural rubber which has not been vulcanized

r/c = RADIO/CASSETTE (DECK)

RDS = RADIO DATA SYSTEM

reach *noun (sparking plug)* distance from the sealing washer to the end of the thread

reaction distance *noun* the time needed to respond to a situation, translated into the distance required for this, depending on the speed of travel; braking distance plus reaction distance equals the stopping distance

reaction injection moulding (RIM) *noun* processing technique for the production of large foamed (automotive) components, based on the simultaneous injection of the liquid components and the chemical reaction in the mould; *(compare* POLYMERIZATION*)*

> COMMENT: in some cases, the components are mixed immediately before being injected into the mould. The term 'RIM' is also applied to refer to the plastic material produced by this technique, e.g. 'RIM-PUR'

reaction member *or* **reactor** *noun* *(fluid converter, automatic transmission)* = STATOR (c)

◊ **reactive suspension** *noun* = ELECTRONIC RIDE CONTROL

◊ **reactor one-way clutch** *noun* = STATOR ROLLER CLUTCH

real-time four-wheel drive *noun* automatic four-wheel drive engagement by

means of an electro-hydraulic clutch or a viscous coupling incorporated in the drive train

ream *verb* to enlarge (e.g. worn valve guides) with a reamer

◊ **reamer** *noun* conically or cylindrically shaped tool with longitudinally cut teeth for manual or machine operation, used for precision finishing of bores

rear 1 *noun* the back *the rear of the car slid wildly to the left* **2** *adjective* at the back *rear axle; rear seats*

◊ **rear apron** *noun* = REAR VALANCE

◊ **rear axle crossmember** *noun* tubular frame member at the rear of the body shell that incorporates the mounting points for the rear axle, e.g. on the VW Beetle and the Porsche 911

◊ **rear (axle) differential** *noun* differential situated in the final drive of the transmission assembly in a conventional rear-wheel drive car; *(see illustration 24)*

◊ **rear bulkhead** *noun* vertical panel across the width of the car that extends behind the rear seat backrest and separates the interior from the trunk

◊ **rear bumper skirt** *noun* rear bumper with integral skirt; a large plastic moulding

◊ **rear cabin pillar** *noun* = C-PILLAR

◊ **rear corner panel** *or* **valance** *noun* the bottom corner of the rear wings; for manufacturing reasons, often a separate panel

◊ **rear deck** *noun* the surface of the rear of a saloon which includes the lid of the boot; **rear deck panel** = sheet metal panel extending from the bottom of the rear window to the rear panel and enclosing the cutout for the bootlid, extending sideways to the top of both wings; in some cases this panel covers only the area between the bottom of the rear window and the front edge of the bootlid

◊ **rear end** *noun* the rear part of the body shell, extending approximately from the rear seat pan to the rear apron of the car, incorporating the boot floor; **rear end lift** = tendency of the back of a speeding vehicle to rise, reducing traction; counteracted by a spoiler

◊ **rear engine** *noun* engine located at the rear of a vehicle but outside the wheelbase (i.e. behind the rear wheels); *(compare* FRONT ENGINE, MID-ENGINE CAR*)*

◊ **rear fog light** *or* **lamp** *noun* red light of the same intensity as a brake light

◇ **rear head restraints (rhr)** *noun* back seat head restraints

◇ **rear-hinged door** *noun* older type of door construction that had the hinges at the rear of the door

◇ **rear lamp cluster** *noun* group of lights at the rear corners of a vehicle, commonly comprising: tail lamp, brake lamp, reversing lamp, rear fog lamp, reflector, direction indicator

◇ **rear light surround** *noun* separate panel spot-welded at the juncture between the trailing edge of the rear wing and the rear valance to provide a mounting base for the rear lights

◇ **rear numberplate light** *or* **lamp** *noun* white light illuminating the rear numberplate

◇ **rear panel** *noun* the panel of the body shell set underneath the bootlid; sometimes referred to as the rear valance if the area below the bootlid consists of a single panel only that extends down to the bottom of the body; in many designs, however, the rear valance is a separate horizontal panel that extends from the rear bumper area downwards; *(see illustrations 1, 2)* (NOTE: US English is **back panel**)

◇ **rear quarter valance** *noun* = REAR CORNER VALANCE

rear seat belt *noun* inertia reel belt fitted at each end of the rear seats; a passenger riding in the middle of the rear seats must be satisfied with just a lap belt, which many safety experts regard as inadequate

COMMENT: some manufacturers (notably those from Scandinavia) are tackling the somewhat costly problem and providing secure lap and shoulder belts for all passengers riding in the rear seats

rear shelf *noun* interior shelf extending over the boot at the level of the top of the rear seats

◇ **rear side window** *noun* may refer to various types of side body glass: the side window between the B- and C-posts of two-door saloons, the rearmost side window of estate cars between the C- and D-post, i.e. behind the rear seat backrest, and the third side window found on some four-door saloons behind the rear side doors

rear spoiler *noun* aerofoil mounted on the rear deck, typically made of shock-resistant polyurethane with paintable matt black finish;

effective only at high speeds, but frequently used for the sake of appearance

COMMENT: most sports cars are equipped with front and rear spoilers (air dams and rear spoilers) to improve the aerodynamic performance by reduced lifting force

rear tack strip *noun (soft top)* fixed or hinged bar which holds the rear end of the hood against the rear deck

rear valance *noun* separate panel set below the rear panel which extends approximately from behind the rear bumper downwards to protect the rear end from splashes of mud; *(see illustration 2)*

COMMENT: in designs with a single-piece rear panel that incorporates the rear valance, the whole area is sometimes referred to as the rear valance or rear panel

◇ **rear-view mirror** *noun* mirror that enables the driver to see what is behind him/her without turning round (NOTE: although all the driver's mirrors are rear-view, this usually refers to the interior mirror)

◇ **rear wash/wipe (system)** *noun* electrical system for cleaning the rear window, comprising a water pump, reservoir and wiper

rear-wheel drive (RWD) *noun* configuration in which the rear wheels of the vehicle are driven; **rear-wheel drive transaxle** = rear-wheel drive construction incorporating a transmission-differential unit placed between the rear wheels of a front-engined car; *(compare* TRANSAXLE)

COMMENT: the engine may be a front engine (as in most cars and all trucks), a mid-engine (as in most sports and racing cars), or a rear engine (as in some city cars, the Porsche 911 series, and most buses); RWD ensures good acceleration without wheelspin even on cars with powerful engines; on most small cars, RWD has been superseded by front-wheel drive

rear wheel spat *noun* separate panel used to cover part or all of the rear wheel aperture, available either ex-stock or as an optional extra

◇ **rear window** *noun* central window at the rear of a vehicle (NOTE: US English is **backlight**) *heated rear window* **rear window heating** = heating element that demists inside and de-ices outside (NOTE: US English is **backlight heater system**); **rear window louvres** = plastic moulding attached to the rear window which deflects sun rays to keep the interior cool; usually hinged to lift up for easy window cleaning

◇ **rear wing** *noun* body panel which partially encloses a rear wheel

◇ **rear wiper** *noun* wiper that cleans the rear window

reboard (system) *noun* child restraint system typically installed backwards on the front passenger seat and having the benefit that the child's relatively heavy head is pressed into the back of the child seat instead of being displaced forward in a frontal crash

COMMENT: initially only available for babies, but originating from Sweden, they are increasingly offered for children up to six years old; some reboards cannot be used in conjunction with a passenger-side air bag system

rebore 1 *noun* regrinding cylinder bores *the car needs a rebore* **2** *verb* to regrind worn or damaged cylinder bores before fitting oversize pistons

rebound clip *noun* metal clip that holds the leaves of a multi-leaf spring together

◇ **rebound stroke** *noun* *(shock absorber)* downstroke of a piston in a spring damper; *(compare* COMPRESSION STROKE)

rebuild *verb* to recondition; **rebuilt engine** = engine reassembled using either new parts or reconditioned components

recap *(US and Australia)* = RETREAD

receiver *noun* **(a)** *(e.g. of radio remote control system)* device that receives incoming electrical or radio signals (NOTE: opposite is **transmitter) (b)** *(trailer towing)* steel tubing and channel structure that accepts the ball-mount platform of a removable trailer coupler

◇ **receiver-drier** *noun* device on the high side of an air-conditioning system, somewhere between the condenser and the expansion valve, which stores excess refrigerant and removes moisture from the refrigerant; consists of a tank, a filter, a drying agent, a pick-up tube, and, on some units, a sight glass; *(compare* ACCUMULATOR-DRIER) *(see illustration 35)*

recessed spark position *noun* position where the spark gap is actually in the shell of the sparking plug; used for racing and special engines

rechargeable battery *noun* = STORAGE BATTERY

reciprocating compressor *noun* a positive displacement compressor with reciprocating pistons; rarely used for supercharging, more frequently used for air conditioning

◇ **reciprocating engine** *noun* engine with a piston that moves to and fro, coming to a standstill at each reversal

◇ **reciprocating pump** *noun* = PISTON CHARGING PUMP

recirculating ball steering *noun* special version of the worm-and-nut steering in which ball bearings circulate between nut and worm to reduce friction

reconditioned engine *or (informal)* **recon** *noun* worn engine that has been given a new lease of life by reboring the cylinders, regrinding the crankshaft journals and generally replacing any worn or damaged parts

recreational vehicle (RV) *noun* any vehicle used for pleasure rather than business or transport (e.g. dune buggies); *(compare* SPORT UTILITY CAR)

rectangular-section ring *noun* compression ring with a rectangular cross-section

◇ **rectangular headlamp** *noun* modern shape of headlamp as opposed to the traditional circular headlamp

rectifier diode *noun* *(in alternator)* semiconductor diode that converts alternating current to direct current; *(see illustration 36)*

◇ **rectifier pack** *noun* *(of alternator)* diode heat sink with diodes

recycling car *noun* a car built with recycled materials and designed so as to facilitate recycling

red lead *noun* poisonous, bright-red powder, soluble in excess glacial acetic acid and dilute hydrochloric acid; used for corrosion protection

red line *noun* on a tachometer, the top speed range which is marked red as sign of excessive engine speeds

reduced shank *noun* shank whose diameter approximately equals the effective pitch diameter

reducer *noun* solvent used to dilute synthetic enamels but not compatible with lacquer paints; *(compare* THINNER, GENERAL PURPOSE LACQUER THINNER

reducing adapter *noun* adapter whose male end for the socket is smaller than the female end for the drive handle (NOTE: opposite is **increasing adapter**)

reducing agent *noun (in chemical reactions)* material which adds electrons to an element or compound, i.e. which increases the positiveness of its valence

◊ **reducing catalyst** *noun* a catalyst such as rhodium which converts nitrogen oxides into harmless nitrogen and oxygen in a reducing catalytic converter; *(compare* OXIDIZING CATALYST)

◊ **reducing furnace** *noun* section in continuous galvanizing lines in which the oxygen content of steel surfaces is reduced at 900-980°C by means of hydrogen

◊ **reduction** *noun* chemical reaction in which an element gains electrons, i.e., has an increase in positive valence; *(compare* OXIDATION)

reduction gearbox *noun* gearbox located at the wheels, which reduces the drive speed and may also increase ground clearance; often found on 4wd off-road vehicles

reed *noun* part of a reed valve made of flexible steel, or of glass fibre reinforced resin, attached to the valve case and normally closed

> COMMENT: the reeds are designed to open readily under pressure from the incoming mixture, but will close rapidly once the pressure inside the crankcase reaches that of the surrounding atmosphere; in this way, the maximum amount of mixture is admitted and any back-leakage is prevented

reed stop *noun* component of a reed valve used to limit upward travel of the reed

reed valve *noun* control element which allows the passage of an operating medium into or out of a chamber; **reed valve induction timing** = using a reed valve located in the intake system to control induction timing

> COMMENT: opening and closing of the reed valve is determined by the pressure or vacuum applied; e.g. in a two-stroke engine a vacuum is built up during the upward stroke of the piston; this causes a reed valve to open and to admit a fresh charge into the cylinder; as the piston goes down again, the pressure built up causes the reeds of the valve to close again; reed valves are also used in pulse air systems and in a/c compressors

reface *verb* general term for reconditioning of the interface between valves and their seats in the cylinder head; depending on valve seat condition, refacing may involve lapping, grinding or cutting

reference ignition pattern *noun* oscilloscope pattern of an intact ignition system for comparison purposes

◊ **reference input** *noun* in closed-loop control, the reference input is fed to a controller that changes a controlled variable in a controlled system to achieve a certain output condition or actual value

◊ **reference mark sensor** *noun* magnetic pick-up attached to the flywheel for sensing the crankshaft position and transferring the signal to the electronic control unit, which calculates the ignition point; the reference mark sensor scans a pin or a hole in the flywheel and produces one output signal per crankshaft revolution

◊ **reference temperature** *noun* the temperature at which measuring tools and pieces being worked on must have the specified measurements; the reference temperature 20°C applies to all statements of technical measurements unless the contrary is expressly stated

refinishing paint *noun* paint sold specifically for resprays; many paint formulas used in the factory are not suited for respray equipment, so special paints for the repair trade are required

◊ **refinish system** *noun* complete product lines and product support offered by many paint manufacturers for respray operations in body shops; these include all materials from primers and thinners to the topcoat plus additional respray products; all products are matched for optimum results

reflectance *noun* ratio of reflected luminous flux to that reflected from an ideal, perfectly reflecting surface when similarly illuminated

◊ **reflector** *noun* **(a)** part of a headlamp which receives light from the bulb and reflects it back through the lens **(b)** part of a rear lamp cluster which reflects the light from headlamps behind

refrigerant *noun* *(in air-conditioning systems)* substance used in refrigerating systems; automotive air conditioners now use non-Freon systems as well as the refrigerant R-12 (Freon) as a heat transfer medium; **refrigerant accumulator** = ACCUMULATOR-DRIER

COMMENT: R-12 is non-toxic, non-corrosive, odourless, and harmless to natural rubber components but, being a chlorofluorocarbon, leakage of refrigerants from air conditioning and refrigeration systems contributes to depletion of the earth's ozone layer; a new alternative to R-12 is R-134A, which is less effective but harmless with regard to the ozone layer

refrigeration cycle *noun* *(in air-conditioning systems)* refrigerant in vapour form is pressurized in the compressor, air-cooled in the condenser and becomes a liquid which passes through the receiver-drier into the expansion valve where it expands into low-pressure liquid. It then flows through the evaporator where it expands again and starts to boil, absorbing heat from the core and cooling the air going into the passenger compartment. The compressor draws off the low-pressure vaporized refrigerant and recycles it

regenerative braking *noun* system in which an electric motor can be switched to generator mode when braking, so that the kinetic energy involved may be stored in the battery

register (with) *verb* to align with

COMMENT: the two-stroke piston is provided with cut-outs that line up with the inlet ports as the piston moves up and down in the bore, i.e. they register with the ports. The fresh charge can thus enter the crankcase

registered keeper *noun* the person who keeps the car. i.e. who is registered and pays tax (and insurance) for the car; not necessarily the same as the owner or the driver

◊ **registration** *noun* act of entering the details of a new vehicle in a supervised record; **registration document** = papers giving details of a vehicle, including its manufacturer, date of registration, engine and chassis numbers, and owner's name; **registration number** = unique sequence of letters and numbers assigned to a vehicle when it is registered, usually indicating the year and place of registration, displayed on numberplates on the front and rear of the vehicle; **registration plate** = NUMBERPLATE

regrind 1 *verb* to smooth and polish again (e.g. valve seats) **2** *noun* resin batch material produced by regrinding thermoplastic scrap and waste; such recycled material can be used to produce plastic parts which are not critical in terms of engineering properties or colour, such as wheel arch liners or battery cases (NOTE: opposite is **virgin resin**)

regulated proportioning valve *noun* = LOAD-SENSITIVE PROPORTIONING VALVE

regulator *noun* any device which controls fluid flow, pressure, temperature, voltage, etc.

reinforce *verb* to increase the strength of plastics by filling them with whiskers of glass, metal, fibres, etc.

◊ **reinforced reaction injection moulding (RRIM)** *noun* reaction injection moulding of reinforced plastics (NOTE: the term also refers to the material produced by this technique) *(compare REACTION INJECTION MOULDING)*

relative humidity (RH) *noun* dimensionless ratio of the actual vapour pressure of the air to the saturation vapour pressure

relay *noun* **(a)** automatic device which controls the setting of a valve, switch, etc. by means of an electric motor, solenoid, or pneumatic mechanism **(b)** *(electronics)* electrical device in which a small change in current or voltage controls the switching on or off of circuits or other devices

◊ **relay lever** *noun* *(steering system)* = IDLER ARM; **relay rod** = intermediate rod between the drop arm and idler arm; *(see illustration 25)*

release agent *noun* a substance to prevent a moulding, i.e. a GRP part, from sticking to the mould and to facilitate its removal from the mould; as opposed to release wax, this is marketed in liquid form only

◇ **release bearing** *noun* = CLUTCH RELEASE BEARING

◇ **release button** *noun* button at the end of the handbrake lever which, when depressed, allows the pawl to be released from the ratchet

◇ **release lever** *noun* = CLUTCH RELEASE LEVER

◇ **release wax** *see* RELEASE AGENT

◇ **releasing fluid** *noun* penetrating oil for loosening seized parts

relief passage *noun* = BYPASS (b)

◇ **relief valve** *noun* **(a)** = PRESSURE RELIEF VALVE **(b)** valve in the air pump of an air injection system which dumps part of the air at high pump speeds to prevent pump damage; may be combined with the air gulp valve

◇ **relieved shank** *noun* = REDUCED SHANK

reline *verb* to replace the brake shoes in drum brakes

reluctor *noun (magnetic pick-up assembly)* = TRIGGER WHEEL (a)

re-metalling the bearings *noun* bearing repair method used on pre-war engines with poured bearings instead of Babbitt metal inserts

| COMMENT: the Babbitt metal is poured into the bearing surfaces and is then scraped until a correct bearing surface is established

remote control *noun* **(a)** control of something from a distance **(b)** the device used for this; *(see* INFRARED REMOTE CONTROL*)*; **remote-control locking** = central locking operated by a remote control from outside the car

◇ **remote starter switch** *noun* special automotive tool that allows the ignition switch to be bypassed for cranking the engine

remould *verb & noun* = RETREAD

removable rim *noun* = DETACHABLE RIM

repair *verb* to restore something to working condition, e.g. by reconditioning, rebuilding, replacing **repair manual** *(compare* SERVICE*)*; **repair kit** = kit for the overhaul of parts such as carburettors, generators, pumps, universal joints, etc.; **repair section** = special panel supplied for body repairs that does not include the full panel used for assembling the car but only the most vulnerable areas; i.e. for wings, separate repair sections are supplied for the headlamp area and the bottom wing edges, where damage usually occurs; *(compare* REPLACEMENT PANEL*)*

repeater (lamp) *noun* direction indicator on the side of a vehicle

replacement panel *noun* body panel supplied for repair purposes; sometimes also used to denote a repair section

◇ **replacement vehicle** *noun* a car lent by a dealer to a customer while the customer's car is under repair

replenishing port *noun* port in the master cylinder body which connects the fluid reservoir to the annulus of the primary piston; *(compare* COMPENSATING PORT*)* *(see illustration 29)*

| COMMENT: in a tandem master cylinder, there is one replenishing port for each piston; it is the first port as seen from the pushrod end of the master cylinder and it is always open

replica *or* **reproduction panel** *noun* = PATTERN PANEL

repmobile *noun (informal)* car used by a sales representative

required ignition voltage *noun* maximum high voltage required to produce a spark under particular conditions

RES *(on cruise control, short for)* resume preset cruising speed

research octane number (RON) *noun* fuel octane rating determined by the research octane test, one of many test procedures; *(compare* OCTANE NUMBER, MON*)*

reseat *verb* to recut a valve seat after repeated grinding-in has worn it out of shape

reserve capacity *noun* the time, in minutes, a battery can maintain a discharge rate of 25 amps

reservoir *noun* **(a)** any container filled with fluid *brake fluid reservoir; hydraulic fluid reservoir* **(b)** *(double-tube shock absorber)* the space between the outer and inner tubes of a double-tube shock absorber which takes up the oil squeezed out of the working chamber corresponding to the volume of the piston rod immersed in the working chamber

reshaping *noun* panel beating process for removing dents: the panel is brought roughly into its original shape before detailed work is performed in the finishing stage; may also refer to the process of forming a panel from sheet steel

residual check valve *noun* = RESIDUAL PRESSURE VALVE

◊ **residual exhaust gases** *noun* exhaust gas remaining in the cylinder of a two-stroke engine after the exhaust ports have been closed, i.e. these gases have not been scavenged

◊ **residual pressure valve** *noun* valve mounted in the cylinder outlet between piston and brake lines of drum brake circuits; maintains a certain minimum pressure in the system; disc brakes do not require a residual pressure valve

resin *noun* synthetic, usually organic, material with a polymeric structure which, especially after having been treated with plasticizer, stabilizer, etc., becomes hard when dry *resin adhesive; resin filler*

resist *noun* substance applied onto aluminium pieces before etching; no surface particles are removed where the surface is covered with the protective coating

resistance shrinking *noun* *(bodywork repair)* ripples are removed by shrinking the panel with the aid of heat from an electric current provided by the electrode of a special tool which is brought into contact with the rippled area

◊ **resistance thermometer** *noun* an electrical temperature sensor which, in contrast to a thermocouple, needs an external voltage supply; the actual sensing element is a resistor whose resistance is an accurate indication of temperature

◊ **resistance welding** *noun* a fusion welding method using electric current and pressure; includes spot, seam, projection, and butt welding

◊ **resistivity** *noun* ability of a material not to conduct electricity (NOTE: opposite is **conductivity)**

◊ **resistor** *noun* component that reduces the current in an electrical circuit; **resistor sparking plug** = sparking plug containing a resistor to suppress interference with audio-visual reception

resonator *noun* **(a)** any device that attenuates pressure spikes **(b)** first silencer in a two-silencer system

respray *verb* & *noun* (to add) a coat (or several coats) of paint to the existing finish *a complete respray* (NOTE: it is notoriously difficult to match the colour of a resprayed panel to that of the original paintwork)

restoration *noun* any extensive repair work that is not limited to standard reconditioning but is of far greater scope, including remanufacture of certain parts, stripping to the last nut and bolt and verification of each and every component

restraint system *noun* general term for occupant safety systems such as seat belts, belt tensioners, air bags, child seats, etc.

restrictor *noun* = NOZZLE RESTRICTOR

resurfacing *noun* if the cylinder head is warped due to thermal differences, its mating surface will have to be machined to ensure firstly that a level surface is created and secondly that the engine's compression ratio is not increased to above a tolerable value

retainer (pin) *noun* = PAD RETAINER (PIN)

◊ **retainer plate** *noun* plate which prevents a valve from sliding out of its bore

◊ **retainer spring tool** *noun* special automotive tool used on drum brakes for restraining the shoe retaining springs for removal and installation; comes in a variety of shapes, e.g. as a screwdriver-type tool with a special socket end to grip retaining washers

retard *verb* *(ignition timing)* to cause the spark to occur later (NOTE: opposite is **advance)**

◊ **retarded** *adjective* occurring late *the ignition is (over-)retarded* (NOTE: opposite is **advanced)**

◊ **retarder** *noun* **(a)** additive to decrease the evaporation rate of a thinner or reducer in paint; used to improve viscosity in hot weather **(b)** auxiliary brake used on commercial vehicles and coaches (it is a requirement in some EU countries)

retract *verb* to draw back, pull back or rewind *the seat belt retracts automatically* **retractable aerial** = telescopic aerial; **retractable headlights** = concealed headlights

◊ **retractor** *noun (seat belt)* device which locks the reel of a seat belt when the forward acceleration of the occupants exceeds a certain value

retread 1 *verb* to attach a new tread to a used tyre by vulcanization **2** *noun (informal)* a retreaded tyre (NOTE: called **recap** in the USA and Australia)

retrofit *verb* to equip a vehicle with new parts after manufacture *we recommend retrofitting a lower temperature thermostat in place of the stock unit fitted*

return sweep *noun* body panel section presenting a concave appearance; its most common function is to strengthen loose panel areas such as the finish along the wheel aperture of the wing

rev *(short for)* revolution

◊ **rev counter** *noun (informal)* tachometer

reverse 1 *verb* to drive backwards (NOTE: US English is **to back up) 2** *noun (short for)* reverse gear (R)

◊ **reverse clutch** *noun* clutch which couples the components of planetary gear sets or trains in such a way that the vehicle can be driven backwards

◊ **reversed Elliot axle** *noun* axle design in which the axle beam terminates in an eye, the steering knuckle axis dividing as a yoke or fork-shaped end which straddles the axle beam end; *(compare* ELLIOT AXLE)

◊ **reverse-flow scavenging** *noun* scavenging system for two-stroke engines in which a cylinder has two pairs of transfer ports, at the front and rear respectively, with

two exhaust ports located on either side of the two pairs of transfer ports; the incoming streams of mixture spread out like a fan, are deflected downward and expel the spent gases

◊ **reverse (gear)** *noun* very low gear for driving backwards, denoted by the letter R on a gear knob or gear selector; **reverse inhibitor valve** = valve which prevents the engagement of the reverse clutch in automatic transmissions if the vehicle road speed exceeds 10 km/h

◊ **reverse process** *noun* immersion or combined spray/immersion process employed to apply two protective coatings which, in the case of body shells, replace the dip primer coat and the filler coat (NOTE: the designation derives from the fact that the sequence in which the dip primer coat and the filler coat are applied is reversed) *(compare* ELECTROSTATIC POWDER COATING)

◊ **reverse scavenging** *noun* = LOOP SCAVENGING

◊ **reversible (gear) puller** *noun* puller with two or more reversible jaws, allowing it to be used for inside and outside pulling

◊ **reversing light** *noun* light at the rear of a vehicle which comes on automatically when reverse gear is engaged and illuminates the road behind the vehicle (NOTE: US English is **back-up light); reversing warning signal** = bleeper alarm that sounds when a commercial vehicle engages reverse gear (NOTE: US English is **back-up alarm)**

rev limiter *noun* = ENGINE SPEED LIMITER

◊ **revolution counter** *noun* **(a)** tachometer, which measures the engine speed in rpm **(b)** counter which counts the total revolutions of a shaft (as opposed to rpm)

◊ **revolutions per minute (rpm)** *noun* number of times the crankshaft turns in one minute

RFI = RADIO FREQUENCY INTERFERENCE; **RFI suppressed sparking plugs** = fully shielded and resistor sparking plugs; *(see illustration 4)*

RH = RELATIVE HUMIDITY, RIGHT HAND

◊ **RHD** = RIGHT-HAND DRIVE

rheostat *noun* resistor with variable resistance

rhodium *noun* a silver-white noble metal in the platinum family; atomic number 45, atomic weight 102.905; used in thermocouples and, together with other platinum metals, as a catalyst in catalytic converters; *(compare* PLATINUM METALS)

rhr = REAR HEAD RESTRAINTS

rib *noun* **(a)** structural member for reinforcing bodywork **(b)** ridge on the sidewall of a tyre to protect it from damage on impact with the kerb

◇ **ribbing** *noun* **(a)** solid ribs in castings or mouldings to increase rigidity **(b)** narrow recess stamped into relatively flat body panels, e.g. floorpans, that helps to reinforce the panel and to suppress vibrations in it

rich *adjective* of an air/fuel mixture that has more petrol than normal (NOTE: opposite is **lean**); **rich mixture** = a mixture with more fuel than can be burned by the oxygen contained in the air/fuel charge (NOTE: opposite is **lean mixture**) *(compare* STOICHIOMETRIC RATIO)

| COMMENT: a slightly rich mixture generates the maximum achievable engine power, an overly rich mixture causes sparking plug fouling, loss of engine power and excessive fuel consumption; any rich mixture increases exhaust emissions

ride *noun* degree of comfort, especially with regard to the suspension, experienced by the passengers *the new XYZ offers a much improved ride*

◇ **ride height** *noun* = GROUND CLEARANCE; **ride-height adjuster** = GROUND CLEARANCE CONTROL

◇ **ride levelling** *noun* = AUTOMATIC LEVEL CONTROL (SYSTEM)

ridge *noun* **(a)** the cutting edge of a screw thread (surmounting the flanks) **(b)** *(body damage)* = PRESSURE RIDGE **(c)** *(in wheel rims)* = HUMP

right-hand drive (RHD) *noun* steering system in which the steering wheel is located on the right-hand side of the vehicle; used for driving on the left, as in the UK, Japan, Australia, etc. (NOTE: opposite is **left-hand drive**)

◇ **right-hand thread** *noun* thread which will accept a nut turned clockwise

rigid *adjective* inflexible, without any flexural or elastic characteristic; **rigid axle** =

rear axle which may be either live (in rear-wheel drive cars) or dead (in front-wheel drive cars); **rigid axle connection** = fixed drive

| COMMENT: as opposed to a stiff object, a rigid object will break when subjected to bending stress; a (steel) member is stiff, not rigid; however, the attribute rigid is also used to denote a particularly high degree of stiffness (especially in non-technical usage), and in this sense is also found in connection with axles and body structures

RIM = REACTION INJECTION MOULDING

rim *noun* **(a)** the part of a wheel that connects the wheel disc with the tyre; its basic purpose is to provide support to the lower sidewall; *(compare* WHEEL) *(see illustration 33)* **(b)** *(bodywork repair)* the outer edge of a dented area that is heat shrunk towards the centre of the dent

| COMMENT: the various types of wheel rims are due to various tyre types and to different types of vehicle, i.e. passenger cars, commercial vehicles and agricultural vehicles. An important area of the rim is the rim bead seat. Rims and corresponding tyres are standardized both nationally and internationally and are thus interchangeable

rim bead seat *noun* portion of the wheel rim below the rim flange providing radial support to the bead of the tyre; **rim bead seat taper** = narrowing of the rim width towards the rim well

| COMMENT: the taper must be designed to lock the tyre to the rim and provide a good seal; well-base rims for passenger cars have a 5° taper, those for commercial vehicles have a 15° taper; flat base rims for commercial vehicles have no taper

rim designation *noun* the nominal rim diameter, nominal rim width and any abbreviations and codes for the contour of the rim; *(compare* MULTI-PIECE RIM, ONE-PIECE RIM DESIGNATION)

◇ **rim diameter** *noun* the distance between the intersection of the bead seats and the vertical walls of the rim flanges; *(compare* 13-INCH WHEEL) *(see illustration 33)*

◇ **rim flange** *noun* the part of a rim that supports the tyre bead in a lateral direction; the linear distance between the two rim flanges is termed rim width *lubricate the rim flanges and bead seats to make fitting a tyre easier (see illustrations 32, 33)*

◇ **rim ridge** *noun* = HUMP

◇ **rim size** *noun* comprises the rim width and rim diameter and is measured in inches

◇ **rim type** *noun* depending on the type of tyre, rim types differ according to the rim profile and the number of rim parts; *(compare* MULTI-PIECE RIM, ONE-PIECE RIM, SAFETY RIM)

◇ **rim well (base)** *noun* the portion of the rim with a substantially smaller diameter than the bead seats and located with sufficient depth and width to enable the tyre beads to be forced over the mounting side of the rim flange and bead seat taper for fitting or removal; *(see illustration 33)*

rim width *noun* the nominal distance between the rim flanges

> COMMENT: the width of a rim is an important factor in the handling characteristics of a car: a rim that is too narrow in relation to the tyre width will cause the tyre to distort sideways under fast cornering. Unduly wide rims on an ordinary car tend to give a rather harsh ride because the sidewalls of the tyre have insufficient curvature to make them flex properly over irregularities in the road

ring and pinion *noun* = AXLE DRIVE (b)

◇ **ring belt** *noun* the lands and rings of a piston

◇ **ring expander** *noun* = PISTON RING PLIERS

◇ **ring gap** *noun* the gap between the piston ring ends with the piston installed in the bore

◇ **ring gear** *noun* (a) = ANNULUS GEAR (b) = CROWN WHEEL (c) toothed rim of a flywheel which engages the pinion of the starter motor; *(see illustrations 4, 8)*

◇ **ring spanner** *noun* spanner whose head fits completely round a nut; *(compare* OPEN-ENDED SPANNER) (NOTE: US English is **box wrench)**

rising rate suspension *noun* suspension system that uses variable rate springs which become stiffer under compression

rivet *noun* short metal pin with a head at one end, for joining two or more pieces together; a second head is formed at the other end by hammering it flat, to secure the connection; **rivet gun** *or* **riveter** = tool with pliers-like handles and nose piece to insert rivets; used, for example, in body repair work to rivet sheet metal material together

road-draft tube *noun US* = OIL BREATHER PIPE

◇ **road fund licence** *noun* licence showing that road tax has been paid; *(see also* TAX DISC)

◇ **road hog** *noun (informal)* a selfish, often aggressive driver

◇ **roadholding** *noun* extent to which a vehicle sticks to the road and the course followed by the driver

◇ **road rage** *noun* violent attacks by drivers on other vehicles and drivers, caused by stress

◇ **road speed** *noun* vehicle speed along a road, measured in mph or km/h; *(compare* ENGINE SPEED)

roadster *noun* open two-seater with a folding top made of unlined canvas; *(compare* SPIDER)

> COMMENT: originally a pure driving machine with a minimum of weather protection and a minimum of doors, if any, sliding windows and definitely no roll bar; the original concept is maintained by the Morgan Plus8 but modern roadsters include power features such as power steering, electric windows, etc. (as in the Mercedes-Benz SL)

road tax *noun* annual tax paid in order to use a vehicle on the roads

◇ **road test** *noun* (a) a test to check that a car is roadworthy after repair (b) a test of a car (e.g. a new model) in actual use; for example, by a magazine for comparison with other models; *see also* TEST DRIVE

◇ **road-test** *verb* to give a vehicle a road test

◇ **road train** *noun* several linked trailers pulled by a large truck; common in Australia for transporting stock

◇ **roadworthiness** *noun* being fit to be driven on the roads

◇ **roadworthy** *adjective* mechanically sound, fit to be driven on the roads

robot spraying *noun* application of paint by robots

rocker (arm) *noun* lever which rotates around a shaft pushing down (opening) the valve with one end while the other end is pushed up by the pushrod; the valve is closed again by spring pressure; *(see illustration 5)*; **rocker arm shaft** = shaft on which the rocker arm pivots; *(see illustration 6)*

◇ **rocker box** *or* **rocker cover** *noun* cylinder head cover above the valve train; *(see illustrations 4, 7)* (NOTE: US English is **valve cover**); **rocker cover gasket** = gasket between the cylinder head and the rocker cover; usually either a flat paper or cork gasket or an O-ring; *(see illustration 7)*

◇ **rocker panel** *noun* = SILL

◇ **rocker shaft** *noun* the outgoing shaft of the steering gearbox, to which the drop arm is connected (NOTE: US English is **cross-shaft)**

roll (angle) *noun* angular displacement of a vehicle about its longitudinal axis, i.e. tendency of a vehicle to heel over when cornering or in high cross winds

◇ **roll axis** *noun* axis through the front and rear roll centres

◇ **roll bar** *noun* strong, tubular bar which reinforces the roof of a car, especially one used for racing, rallying, etc. to protect the occupants if the car should overturn; **roll cage** = strong, tubular frame which reinforces the roof of a vehicle, especially one used in rally cars and off-road vehicles, to protect the occupants if the vehicle should overturn

◇ **roll centre** *noun* the theoretical point between the front wheels or back wheels about which the car body rolls when cornering; any centrifugal force causes the body to rotate about the roll centre; *(see* ROLL AXIS)

◇ **roll coating** *noun* application method for organic or chemical conversion coatings using rolls

rolled bead *noun* = BEADED EDGE

roller *noun* non-spherical rolling element in a roller bearing; **roller bearing** = antifriction bearing with non-spherical rolling elements *cylindrical roller bearing; taper rolling bearing (see illustration 22)*; **roller cage** = cage containing the rollers in a roller bearing

Roller *noun (informal)* = ROLLS-ROYCE

roller cell pump *noun* = ROLLER-VANE PUMP

◇ **roller chain** *noun* power-transmitting chain in which each link consists of two

free-moving rollers located by pins connected to sideplates; *(compare* DUPLEX CHAIN, SIMPLEX CHAIN, TRIPLEX CHAIN)

◇ **roller dynamometer** *noun* dynamometer attached to a rolling road

◇ **roller foot lever** *noun* = ROLLER TAPPET

◇ **roller levelling** *noun (in continuous galvanizing lines)* process in which steel strips pass rollers which remove superfluous zinc after the actual immersion process

◇ **roller tappet** *noun* connecting link between the lower end of a pushrod and the camshaft, equipped with one roller to reduce the friction between the pushrod or tappet and the cam during engine operation

◇ **roller-vane pump** *noun* rotary vane pump with rollers as pumping elements which slide against the pump body when the rotor rotates; *(compare* VANE PUMP)

rolling bearing *noun* = ANTIFRICTION BEARING

◇ **rolling circumference** *noun* the circumference of a loaded tyre

◇ **rolling friction** *noun* frictional resistance to rotation in rolling bearings

◇ **rolling radius** *noun* radius of a loaded tyre from its axis to the centre of the contact patch

◇ **rolling resistance** *noun* resistance to motion offered by tyres on a flat road surface, attributable mainly to rolling and mechanical friction and dependant on tyre design, pressure and load; over 50 mph, air resistance becomes more important; *(compare* ROLL RESISTANCE)

◇ **rolling road** *noun* rollers set in the floor of a garage, tuning or inspection centre and designed to simulate road conditions; the rollers can be driven by the driving wheels of a car and connected to a dynamometer for testing the power output of an engine or may be independently powered, e.g. to test the brakes

roll oversteer *noun* oversteer caused by roll when cornering (NOTE: opposite is **roll understeer)**

roll pin *noun* split, tube-like pin made of spring steel for retaining disc pads, gears to shafts in gearboxes, etc.

roll resistance *or* **roll stiffness** *noun* *(chassis)* resistance of a vehicle body to rolling, which depends on the stiffness of the suspension springs and anti-roll bar; *(compare* ROLLING RESISTANCE)

◇ **roll steer (effect)** *noun* effect on a car's steering due to body roll; *(compare* ROLL OVERSTEER, ROLL UNDERSTEER)

roll test *noun* serves to test-drive train functions; may include separate tests for front and rear axle, left- and right-hand sides, noise test; typical duration is two minutes

roll understeer *noun* understeer caused by roll when cornering (NOTE: opposite is **roll oversteer)**

RON = RESEARCH OCTANE NUMBER

roo bar *(Australian for)* NERF BAR

roof box *noun* enclosed, multi-purpose roof carrier

◇ **roof brace** *noun* transverse rail that supports the roof panel; there are usually several roof braces

◇ **roof panel** *noun* the horizontal outer layer of the sheet metal roof panels that is spot-welded along its edges to the top of the roof, door and screen pillars; *(see illustration 1)*

◇ **roof rack** *noun* luggage rack on the roof of a vehicle

◇ **roof rail** *noun* longitudinal side member above the doors to which the roof panel is attached (NOTE: also called **cantrail)**

◇ **roof spoiler** *noun* spoiler attached to the roof of a lorry cab, or vehicle towing a trailer or caravan, to reduce drag and increase stability

room temperature vulcanizing (RTV) sealer *noun* semi-liquid, silicone rubber sealant which is proof against oil and water but not petrol *RTV gasket*

root *noun* lowest point of a screw thread (NOTE: opposite is **crest)**

Roots compressor *or* **supercharger** *noun* typical lobe-type positive displacement compressor; uses two two-lobed or three-lobed internal rotors phased to prevent clashing of the lobes by gears; normally driven from the crankshaft by toothed or V-belts, can achieve speeds up to

10,000 rpm; provides low-end torque and boost without lag but is less fuel-efficient than a turbocharger

rotary disc valve *noun* valve employed as an inlet control in modern two-stroke engines, consisting of a thin steel disc attached to one end of the crankshaft

COMMENT: the inlet port passes through the disc valve assembly, and thus is normally closed off by the disc. To permit induction at the correct part of the engine cycle, part of the disc is cut away, opening the inlet port for the required duration, independent of the piston position

rotary (piston) engine *noun* an engine which uses no reciprocating pistons; instead, triangular rotors revolve in specially shaped housings; the Wankel engine is the only type of rotary engine at present in production

◇ **rotary pump** *noun* pump with rotating members; *(see* ROTOR-TYPE PUMP)

◇ **rotary valve** *noun* engine or pump component forming part of a rotating assembly; may be designed as a cylindrical or a disc valve

◇ **rotary vane pump** *noun* = VANE PUMP

rotating seal ring *noun* rotating element of a mechanical seal

rotation *noun* motion of a body about an axis within the body; *(compare* WHEEL ROTATION)

◇ **rotational atomization unit** *noun* painting unit equipped with rapidly rotating spray bells

rotbox *noun (informal)* = RUST BUCKET

roto cap *noun* device fitted to some engines which turns a valve slightly every time it opens or closes, to prevent the valve sticking or burning (NOTE: also called **valve rotator)**

Rotoflex coupling *noun* one design of a flexible coupling in the shape of a hexagonal rubber ring; *(see* DOUGHNUT COUPLING)

rotor *noun* **(a)** any component which rotates **(b)** rotating part of an electrical machine, such as the armature of a starter motor **(c)** rotating part of the distributor, which distributes the high voltage to the individual sparking plugs; in older systems an oblong shape, in breakerless distributor system usually a disc **(d)** in an alternator, the rotating pole pieces with the electromagnetic winding, which create a rotating magnetic field whose lines of force cut the stationary conductors in the stator; usually of claw-pole design; *(see illustration 36)* **(e)** rotating displacement element of a rotary pump, such as a gear, screw, piston, etc. **(f)** moving part of a pulse generator (NOTE: opposite is **stator**) **(g)** rotating element of a Roots supercharger

◊ **rotor arm** *noun* = ROTOR (c)

◊ **rotor-type pump** *noun* engine oil pump in which an internal rotor, e.g. with four external lobes, is used to drive an eccentric external gear, e.g. with five internal lobe-spaces; operates in a similar way to gear pumps, but has higher pump capacity, and is quieter and more expensive; *(compare* GEAR PUMP, INTERNAL GEAR PUMP) *(see illustration 17)*

rotowelding *noun* = FRICTION WELDING

rotten-egg smell *noun* in cars equipped with catalytic converters, this smell is the result of an excessively rich air/fuel mixture

roughening *noun* mechanical or chemical treatment of a surface to produce minute irregularities

rough *adjective* if an engine sounds rough it is running unevenly, probably caused by misfiring or worn crankshaft bearings

roundabout *noun* road junction where the traffic goes round a raised central circle (NOTE: US English is **traffic circle**)

round file *noun* file in the shape of a round bar, rather than a blade

◊ **round head bolt** *noun* general term including cup head bolts and mushroom head bolts

◊ **round hump** *noun* safety contour on both rim bead seats preventing the tyre from sliding into the rim well; *(compare* HUMP, SAFETY RIM)

route 1 *noun* direction taken (by a cable, etc.) **2** *verb* to lay (something) in a certain direction *to route a cable*

Royal Automobile Club (RAC) *noun* motoring organization in the UK; *(see also* AA)

rpm *(short for)* revolutions per minute; engine speed as measured by crankshaft

revolutions per minute; **rpm sensor** = ENGINE SPEED SENSOR

RRIM = REINFORCED REACTION INJECTION MOULDING

r/seat *(short for)* rear seat

RTV = ROOM TEMPERATURE VULCANIZING

rubber *noun* **(a)** a natural elastomer that at room temperature returns rapidly to approximately its initial dimension and shape after substantial deformation by a weak stress and subsequent release of the stress; **rubber bush** = tubular rubber sleeve for mounting a shaft or rod; **rubber coupling** = flexible coupling using pressurized rubber blocks; **rubber doughnut coupling** = typical flexible coupling, made of vulcanized rubber, shaped like a doughnut; *(see illustration 22)* **(b)** *US (informal)* tyres

◊ **rubberize** *verb* to coat or impregnate with rubber

◊ **rubber mallet** *noun* mallet with a rubber head

◊ **rubber plug** *noun* moulded rubber stopper used to close cutouts or holes in body panels that have to be opened only infrequently, e.g. access holes for rustproofing of box sections

◊ **rubber spring** *noun* element of a rubber suspension system such as Hydrolastic suspension

◊ **rubber squeegee** *noun* special spreader used for filling hollow, concave or rounded body areas; the rubber material adapts better to these surfaces than plastic spreaders and helps to prevent flat spots

rubbing block *noun (ignition)* small block of insulating material on the contact breaker lever

◊ **rubbing compound** *noun* = CUTTING COMPOUND

◊ **rubbing strip** *noun* strip of plastic at the widest point of the body, along doors and wings down each side of the car to protect the bodywork from minor knocks, (as from the open door of a neighbouring car)

Rudge nut *noun* quick-release nut for central-locking wheels

rumble *noun* characteristic, low-pitched noise made by worn main bearings

◇ **rumble seat** *noun US* = DICKEY SEAT

run 1 *noun (paint fault)* the trail of a paint drip; a dribble of paint **2** *verb (of paint)* to form a run

COMMENT: usually caused by moving the spray gun too slowly or spraying too close to the panel surface thus causing an excessive build-up of paint

runabout *noun* **(a)** an open 2-seater, predecessor of the roadster **(b)** small car, especially one for use in town

run channel *noun* U-section rubber used to hold glass parts and other body features in place or to protect panel edges

run-flat properties *noun* the capability of a deflated tyre to operate effectively, i.e. to permit further driving

COMMENT: to achieve this, the following must be fulfilled: the tyre beads must be retained against the rim flanges and on the rim bead seats when the tyre deflates; the tyre must be able to support all possible stresses imposed by deflation; the tyre must remain undamaged by internal friction and heat generated when running flat; the tyre should be able to self-seal any punctures, so that the remaining air will be trapped and heat will be generated to reinflate the tyre within limits

run-flat tyre *noun* tyre which can run for a certain length of time without air in it; *(compare* AH RIM, CTS, DENOVO TYRE, JJD WHEEL, TD WHEEL)

COMMENT: in the inflated state, conventional tubeless tyres perform the task of containing air and rolling. Once deflation occurs, the tyre bead becomes dislodged from the rim bead seat and slides into the rim well. As a result of friction, the tyre will become distorted and the rim may plough into the road, leading to loss of control and giving a potential accident. Run-flat tyres are designed to operate effectively with or without air, providing acceptable handling qualities when deflated and good handling qualities when inflated

run in *verb* to operate new or reconditioned machinery (especially bearings) under light load and at limited speed to avoid excessive friction and heat which would cause uneven bedding in of the component (NOTE: nowadays, new engines do not need to be run in. Note that US English is **to break in)**

running board *noun* foot rest below the doors of a car; common on early motor vehicles, now only seen on VW Beetles, pick-ups and some limousines

◇ **running gear** *noun* the moving components which link the lower part of the vehicle to the wheels, i.e. suspension, including control arms, springs, shock absorbers, steering components, etc.; *(compare* CHASSIS)

running-in *noun* driving a vehicle or running an engine or other mechanical unit at reduced speed and load when new, to prevent pick-up and seizure of the bearing surfaces, and to ensure even initial wear

◇ **running-on** *noun* condition of a SI engine in which fuel continues to burn after the ignition has been turned off, causing the engine to run on (for a few seconds) (NOTE: also called **dieselling**); **running-on control valve** = IDLE STOP VALVE

◇ **run on** *verb (of an engine)* to continue to run after the ignition has been switched off

run-on tyre *noun* tyre with a limited ability to run without air in it; sufficient to pull over safely; *(compare* RUN-FLAT TYRE)

runout *noun* extent to which a part is running out-of-true; *(compare* LATERAL RUNOUT, RADIAL RUNOUT)

rupture *verb* to break, burst or split

rust 1 *noun* oxidized iron or steel, the product of corrosion **2** *verb* to form rust

◇ **rust bucket** *noun (informal)* a badly corroded car

◇ **rust converters** *noun* chemical substances containing phosphoric acid etc. which, according to their manufacturers, transform rust into a stable, firmly adhering iron compound by means of a chemical reaction

◇ **rust eater** *noun* = RUST KILLER

◇ **rusting** *noun* chemical or electrochemical destruction of iron and ferrous metals; *(compare* CORROSION)

◇ **rust inhibitor** *noun* inhibitor which reduces or prevents the formation of rust on iron and ferrous metals; *(compare* CORROSION INHIBITOR)

◇ **rust inspection** *noun* car inspection conducted to detect rust and corrosion damage, usually by means of an endoscope

◇ **rust killer** *noun* substances which, according to their manufacturers, convert rust into a dry mass which can be removed with water; *(compare* RUST CONVERTERS)

◇ **rust neutralizer** *noun* = RUST CONVERTER

◇ **rust pinhole** *noun* early stage of rust penetration of a panel; rust pinholes will often reveal larger rust damage once the surface rust bubbles have been ground away

◇ **rustproof 1** *adjective* resistant to rust **2** *verb* to make resistant to rust

◇ **rustproofing** *noun* making resistant to rust; **rustproofing agent** = anti-corrosion, wax-based sealant

◇ **rust protection** *noun* reducing the possibility of rust forming on iron and steel by coating with protective materials or by

rendering them passive; *(compare* CORROSION CONTROL)

◇ **rust remover** *noun* any chemical substance which removes rust

◇ **rust sealer** *noun* rust converter that provides a coat on metal surfaces to protect them against air exposure and thus to prevent continued corrosion

RV *US* = RECREATIONAL VEHICLE

RWD = REAR-WHEEL DRIVE

Rzeppa-type (universal) joint *noun* constant velocity joint incorporating balls as a means of torque transmission; (named after Alfred Rzeppa, a Ford engineer)

Ss

S (a) *(short for)* Special or Sport, indicating better performance than a standard car model **(b)** letter on the sidewall of a tyre denoting the maximum speed for which it is designed (118 km/h or 113 mph); *(see* SPEED RATING)

Sacco panels *noun* = SIDE BUMPER PANELS

sacrificial anode *noun* an electropositive metal coating, such as aluminium or zinc, that protects the steel of a car body by corroding first when attacked by electrolytic action; **sacrificial protection** = CATHODIC PROTECTION

saddle tank *noun* fuel tank mounted above the rear axle

SAE *(short for)* Society of Automotive Engineers: American professional body which develops standards in automotive (and aeronautical) engineering

SAE gross bhp *noun* old unit of engine power

> COMMENT: in the SAE gross bhp test, a 'bare' engine is used, i.e. an engine equipped with only those accessories that are necessary for its operation, such as the oil pump and fuel pump; water pump, alternator, exhaust system, etc. are not used; this results in a higher power rating than achievable by the same engine under real operating conditions

SAE net bhp *noun* unit of engine power

> COMMENT: a fully-equipped engine (as when installed in a vehicle) is used to determine SAE net bhp figures; as a rough guideline, SAE net is about 70-85 percent of SAE gross

safe stop wheel *noun* = RUN-ON TYRE

safety bead seat *noun* general term for a safety contour on the rim bead seat preventing the tyre bead from sliding into the rim well especially during cornering manoeuvres

tubeless tyres must only be mounted on wheels with safety bead seats (compare HUMP, CONTRE PENTE, SPECIAL LEDGE)

◊ **safety belt** *noun* = SEAT BELT

◊ **safety catch** *noun* catch usually located under the front edge of the bonnet, near the centre, which prevents accidental release of the bonnet if the main cable-operated bonnet lock is activated by mistake

◊ **safety chains** *noun* two, crossed chains linking the trailer and vehicle frame as a safeguard if the towing hitch fails

◊ **Safety Compliance Certification (SCC) Label** *noun US* label which must be attached to the lower half of the left-hand front door lock facing; specifies the VIN and other relevant information

◊ **safety glass** *noun* = LAMINATED GLASS

◊ **safety goggles** *noun* close-fitting glasses or mask to protect the eyes (e.g. during welding)

◊ **safety harness** *noun* = HARNESS (b)

◊ **safety ledge** *noun* = SPECIAL LEDGE

safety rim *noun* rim with small ridges that hold the tyre beads on the wheel during a tyre blow-out (instant rupture and air loss) or flat tyre (slow leak reducing inflation pressure)

> COMMENT: 'small raised lips' on the rim bead seat prevent the tyre beads from sliding into the wellbase, thus improving safety by keeping the tyre from coming off the wheel

safety steering column *noun* = COLLAPSIBLE STEERING COLUMN

◊ **safety valve** *noun* valve that allows fluid to escape when a certain pressure level has been reached

◊ **safety wheel** *noun* general term referring to either a wheel with a safety bead seat or a wheel with run flat properties

sag *verb & noun* (to) bend under weight or pressure

COMMENT: as a result of a front or rear end collision, the frame may develop a sag in the middle, much like a hammock

sagging door *noun* a door that sits too low in the door aperture

COMMENT: often indicated by an uneven door gap that widens towards the rear bottom and front top of the door but narrows down at the rear top and front bottom. This may be caused by faulty setting of the door hinges and lock/striker assembly. On open-top cars, it often pinpoints structural damage, as the chassis then tends to bend in the middle

sags *or* **sagging** *noun (paint fault)* an aggravated condition of paint runs where a curtain of paint runs down vertical or inclined areas of bodywork; caused by excessive build-up of paint, thinners which are too slow-acting, or excessively slow movement of the spray gun

SAI = STEERING AXIS INCLINATION

SALA suspension *noun* = SHORT ARM/LONG ARM SUSPENSION

saloon *noun* two- or four-door car with seating for four or five people (NOTE: US English is **sedan)**

salt spray chamber *noun* test chamber for salt spray (fog) testing; **salt spray (fog) testing** = spray tests with sodium chloride solutions; **salt water splash** = an open-air corrosion test facility

sand *verb* to smooth or clean a surface by rubbing with sandpaper *all rust areas should be sanded back to bare metal to prevent further build-up of rust; this type of filler material sands easily; sand down first, then apply primer and top coat*

COMMENT: sanding usually refers to hand tools such as sandpaper, while grinding always refers to power tools such as angle grinders

sandblasting *noun* cleaning a surface with a jet of sand (or grit) under air or steam pressure

◇ **sander** *noun* power-driven tool with a rotating abrasive disc for smoothing and cleaning surfaces

◇ **sanding block** *noun* rubber or plastic block designed to accept strips of sandpaper for manual sanding

◇ **sandpaper** *noun* abrasive paper coated with sand for smoothing and cleaning; *(compare* GLASSPAPER)

◇ **sand scratching** *noun* paint fault characterized by the paint film appearing low in gloss and showing primer and metal imperfections in the top coat; may be caused by excessively coarse sanding and too thin a paint coat

sandwich construction *noun* composite construction of alloys, plastics and other materials consisting of a foam or honeycomb layer and glued between two hard outer sheets (NOTE: also known as **sandwich laminate)**

satellite *noun* block of controls near the steering wheel rim

SBS = SEAT-INTEGRATED BELT SYSTEM

scab corrosion *noun* scab-like corrosion occurring along a scratch in a coating

scale *noun* solid layer of corrosion products formed on metals at high temperature; **scale rust** = loose, flaking rust

scanimet *noun* nickel-silicon-carbide coating for particularly wear-resistant cylinder walls; *(compare* NICASIL)

scavenge *verb (two-stroke engine)* to clear away, particularly to expel exhaust gas from a cylinder and to fill the cylinder with fresh charge (NOTE: these processes take place simultaneously in a two-stroke engine) *(compare* CHARGE CHANGING PROCESS)

◇ **scavenging jet** *noun* the jet of fresh charge supplied into the cylinder, the shape and direction of which determine the effectiveness of the scavenging process

◇ **scavenging losses** *noun* if the exhaust gases remain in the cylinder, they prevent a full charge of fresh mixture from entering; the power output is thus reduced

◇ **scavenging passage** *noun* the passage inside a two-stroke engine that serves to scavenge the exhaust gas from the engine; in most cases it refers to the transfer passage, as the gas column supplied across the transfer port initiates the scavenging process

◇ **scavenging picture** *noun* in experimental two-stroke engine development, a map of the scavenging air velocity distribution and the scavenging jet orientation inside a cylinder

◇ **scavenging pump** *noun* an oil pump in a dry sump system which returns oil from the crankcase to the main oil reservoir

◇ **scavenging system** *noun* method used to accomplish the charge-changing process in a two-stroke engine

◇ **scavenging valve** *noun* in evaporative emission control systems, a valve in the purge line between activated charcoal canister and inlet manifold which controls the purge air flow that regenerates the charcoal filter

SCC = SPARK CONTROL COMPUTER, SAFETY COMPLIANCE CERTIFICATION

Schnürle scavenging *see* LOOP SCAVENGING

scissor jack *noun* mechanical jack with a scissors-like action

scope *noun (informal)* oscilloscope

scored *adjective (e.g. brake disc)* scratched, grooved, or lined with small cuts *a piston skirt that is scored on both thrust surfaces is an indication of insufficient piston-to-wall clearance*

scrap *noun* waste metal *scrap dealer*

scraper ring *noun* = OIL (SCRAPER) RING

scrapyard *noun* premises of a dealer in scrap metal; *(compare* BREAKER (a)

screen *verb* to shield from electrical interference

screw *noun* threaded fastener, similar to a bolt, but fully threaded and with a slotted, hexagonal head, round head, flat head, fillister head or socket head and often a shank which tapers to a point

| COMMENT: typically used without a nut, i.e. when parts are assembled, the screw passes though a clear hole in one member and screws into a threaded hole in the other; all cap screws 1" or less in length are threaded very nearly to the head; machine screws fulfil

| the same purpose as cap screws, but are used chiefly for small work having thin sections

screwdriver *noun* tool used for turning screws; usually a wooden or plastic handle with a thin shank ending in a cross-cut or flattened square-cut tip; **screwdriver bit** = a hex shank with a screwdriver tip at one or both ends to loosen and tighten recessed screws; designed for use with magnetic or power-driven screwdrivers

| COMMENT: not to be confused with 'bit sockets' which do not have a hex shank, but a female square drive for use with socket drive tools; screwdriver bits can only be used with socket drive tools in combination with a special bit holder

screw extractor *noun* tool for removing broken studs and screws, with a tapered left-hand thread which is screwed into a hole drilled in the piece to be removed

◇ **screw-holding screwdriver** *or* **screw starter** *noun* tool used to hold screws for easy placement in extremely tight places; also appropriate for loosening and tightening

◇ **screw pitch gauge** *noun* measuring tool used to identify thread sizes, featuring a selection of blades with different thread profiles to determine screw pitch

scribe *verb & noun* (to) cut or scratch with a pointed instrument, e.g. (in) a painted surface, for testing purposes or to mark the position of a part

◇ **scriber** *noun* pointed steel hand tool for marking metal

scrubbing *noun* heavy wear on a tyre caused by sliding sideways across the road surface, as when skidding

scrub radius *noun (steering geometry)* geometric parameter: 'positive' if the steering axis intersects the wheel plane at or below ground level, 'negative' if the point of intersection is above ground level

scuff plate *noun* (i) generally, any protective plate; (ii) specifically, the finishing trim on a door sill

◇ **scuff rib** *noun* raised rib on the sidewall of a tyre to protect it from impact with the kerb; *(see illustration 32)*

sculpture line *noun* = SWAGE LINE

scuttle (panel) *noun* the body shell panel directly below the front windscreen; often incorporates the air inlet slots for interior ventilation (NOTE: US English is **cowl**); **scuttle section** = subassembly of the body shell that includes the bulkhead, scuttle, and windscreen pillars; it is preassembled in the factory and spot-welded with the other subassemblies to form the body shell; **scuttle shake** = typical shake exhibited by open cars on rough roads due to lack of torsional stiffness; **scuttle side panel** = vertical panel at either end of the scuttle; *(see illustrations 1, 2)*

seal 1 *noun* flexible ring, disc or washer that prevents the passage of liquid, air, gas or dirt *O-ring seal* **2** *verb* **(a)** to prevent the passage of liquid, air, gas, etc. by means of a seal or sealant (e.g. on seams, joints, flanges) **(b)** to coat a surface (e.g. when undersealing a car) by closing the pores of the anodic oxide layer in order to increase the resistance to staining and its effectiveness against corrosion

◊ **sealant** *noun* organic compounds (such as wax, oil, grease) used to protect seams or surfaces (NOTE: also called **sealer** or **sealing compound**)

sealed-beam headlight *or* **unit** *noun* standard American headlamp design; lens, filament and reflector are sealed into one unit, which eliminates reflector corrosion but when a filament is broken, a new sealed beam unit must be installed

sealing bath *noun* hot water bath for the sealing treatment after anodizing

◊ **sealing smut** *noun* smut which forms after the anodized aluminium pieces are immersed in hot water

◊ **sealing strip** *noun* gas seal to the epitrochoidal surface in a rotary piston engine, with the same function as the piston ring on a conventional piston engine

seam sealing *noun* the sealing of seams, usually using organic compounds, to prevent the penetration of corrosive agents; **seam sealing cell** = flexible manufacturing cell in which seam sealers are applied

seat *noun* **(a)** the part of a vehicle on which you sit *power seats; the seats are well contoured and comfortably padded, but the squabs are too short* **(b)** area into which another part fits securely (such as the seal between a sparking plug or valve and the cylinder head); *(compare* FLAT SEAT, TAPER SEAT, VALVE SEAT)

seat adjuster *noun* knob or lever to adjust the position of the front seats

COMMENT: the fore and aft position is adjusted by a lever or bar usually located under the front edge of the seat, the angle of the backrest is adjusted by a knob usually located on the front edge of the seat near the door, and the angle or height of the seat itself is adjusted by a knob usually located on the front edge of the seat away from the door; power seats may be adjusted in up to 10 different ways

seat belt *noun* webbing belt, usually in the form of a diagonal shoulder belt and lap belt to restrain the wearer in the event of a collision; **seat belt anchorage** = point where the end of a seat belt is attached to the body of a car; **seat belt tensioner** = restraint system controlled by deceleration sensors; **seat belt warning light** = light on the instrument panel which illuminates if seat belts are not properly secured

◊ **seating capacity** *noun* the number of people for which a car is designed

◊ **seat-integrated (seat) belt system (SBS)** *noun* seat belt with all belt elements and deflection points integrated in the seat; this improves occupant restraint in every seating position, but particularly sturdy seats and floorpans are required

◊ **seat pan** *noun* = SEAT WELL

◊ **seat rail** *or* **seat runner** *noun* tracks onto which front seat assemblies are mounted to provide fore and aft seat adjustment; **seat rail console** = mounting panel for the seat rails, spot-welded to the floorpan; the front consoles are usually somewhat higher than the rear ones to produce the desired angle of the seating surface

◊ **seat well** *noun* sheet metal panel to cover up the area below the car seats, especially below the rear seat bench

secondary air *noun* in some exhaust emission control systems, e.g. thermal reactor or two-bed converter, secondary (outside) air is added to the exhaust to ensure sufficient supply of oxygen to promote oxidation of HC and CO, thus converting these pollutants into harmless water vapour and carbon dioxide

◊ **secondary battery** *noun* = STORAGE BATTERY

◊ **secondary braking system** *noun* HGV spring brake system which exerts force when air pressure is released

◇ **secondary cell** *noun* = STORAGE CELL

◇ **secondary circuit** *noun* circuit which comprises the secondary winding of the ignition coil, the distributor, and the sparking plugs; *(compare* PRIMARY CIRCUIT)

◇ **secondary damage** *noun* = INDIRECT DAMAGE

◇ **secondary key** *noun* key which only operates the locks needed for valet parking, i.e. door locks, ignition switch and steering column lock; does not allow access to boot, glove box, etc.; *(compare* PRIMARY KEY)

◇ **secondary pattern** *noun* oscilloscope pattern of the secondary circuit

◇ **secondary piston** *noun (in tandem master cylinder)* floating piston which isolates the two braking circuits from each other and actuates the secondary circuit; *(see illustration 29)*

◇ **secondary pump** *noun* oil pump driven via the gearbox output shaft; *(compare* PRIMARY PUMP)

◇ **secondary seal** *noun* secondary piston seal in a tandem master cylinder; *(see illustration 29)*

◇ **secondary shoe** *noun* = TRAILING SHOE

◇ **secondary visor** *noun* in dual visor systems, the main visor is moved sideways and the secondary visor is flipped down, thus shielding the driver from the sun from both the front and side

◇ **secondary winding** *noun* inner winding of the ignition coil; typically 20,000 to 30,000 turns of very fine wire (NOTE: opposite is **primary winding)**

second (gear) *noun* low gear used to build up speed and for steep hills

section repair *noun* an effective and economical repair method where extensive damage is confined to a specific section of the body shell and an undamaged section is taken from a vehicle which has been written off

sector shaft *noun* = ROCKER SHAFT

sedan *noun US* = SALOON

seed *noun (paint fault)* a uniform distribution of small particles of regular size and pattern in a paint film; caused by contamination of the paint and poor filtration of the air lines

COMMENT: not to be confused with dirt contamination which is caused by dust settling on the painted surface before it has dried

seize *verb* to become stuck; used of moving parts, such as a piston, and commonly caused by lack of lubrication leading to overheating

selective corrosion *noun* corrosion of alloys whereby the components react in proportions differing from their proportions in the alloys

◇ **selective transmission** *noun* transmission layout in which the operator can select any ratio at any time without having to shift through a number of ratios in a definite order; *(compare* PROGRESSIVE TRANSMISSION)

selector fork *noun* part of the selector mechanism of a manual gearbox, shaped like a two-pronged fork, which fits into the groove round a coupling sleeve and moves a sliding pinion forward or back along a selector rod

◇ **selector lever** *noun (automatic gearbox)* lever which permits the driver to adapt the gearchanging processes to particular road or driving conditions (slippery road surface, hilly terrain, towing) by choosing one of the drive ranges; reverse, neutral, and parking lock are also selected by means of the selector lever; **selector lever lock** = locks the selector lever in 'Neutral' or 'Park' unless the driver depresses the brake pedal

◇ **selector rod** *noun* rod running the length of the gearbox, along which the selector fork travels

self-adjusting *adjective* of a mechanism that adjusts itself to compensate for wear or to maintain a certain distance or level (as of heat); *(compare* HYDRAULIC TAPPET)

◇ **self-aligning torque** *noun (of tyres)* the restoring force of a tyre at the centre of the footprint when subjected to a side force, as when cornering; this attempt to reduce the slip angle by the tyre makes the steering feel heavy to the driver

◇ **self-cancelling indicator** *noun* all modern direction indicators switch off automatically when the steering wheel is returned to the straight-ahead position

◇ **self-centring (effect)** *noun (steering geometry)* the forces in a steering system that set the front wheels straight when grip on the steering wheel is released after cornering

◇ **self-cleaning** *noun* the ability of a sparking plug to burn off the deposits of carbon and oil which build up due to tracking across the tip; **self-cleaning limit** = the lower limit of the self-cleaning temperature, generally about 500°C

◇ **self-diagnosis** *noun* test function in electronic engine management systems with a test programme monitoring input and output signals, detecting errors and storing them permanently in a fault memory; *(compare* FAULT READER)

◇ **self-energizing** *see* SERVO BRAKE

◇ **self-ignition** *noun* *(diesel engine)* ignition of the air/fuel mixture caused by high pressure and temperature; *(compare* SPARK IGNITION)

◇ **self-induction** *noun* this occurs when the current in an inductive circuit changes and the magnetic field cuts the conductors; this induced electromotive force opposes the change in current, restricting it if the current is increasing and enhancing it if the current is decreasing; **self-induction back-voltage** = back-voltage produced by self-induction

◇ **self-levelling shock absorber** *noun* = AIR SHOCK ABSORBER; **self-levelling suspension (system)** = AUTOMATIC LEVEL CONTROL (SYSTEM); **self-levelling (suspension) strut** = suspension strut incorporating a shock absorber with a rubber boot filled with compressed air, serving as an auxiliary pneumatic spring

◇ **self-locking nut** *noun* nut with a nylon insert that binds on the thread and resists vibration; *(compare* LOCK NUT)

◇ **self-operating clutch** *noun* = CENTRIFUGAL CLUTCH

◇ **self-parking** *noun* the ability of a car to park automatically, without any input from the driver; introduced by the VW Futura in 1991; **self-parking wiper** = windscreen wiper that automatically returns to the (horizontal) park position when switched off

◇ **self-priming pump** *noun* pump which is able to evacuate and prime the suction pipe *rotary pumps are self-priming* (NOTE: opposite is **non-self-priming pump**)

◇ **self-regulating sheathed-type glow plug** *noun* originally sheathed-type glow plugs with a self-regulating heating coil, now with a heating and regulating coil

◇ **self-starter** *noun* = STARTER MOTOR

◇ **self-tapping screw** *noun* steel screw which cuts its own thread when screwed through a pilot hole into sheet metal

sem *noun* a preassembled fastener, consisting of any type of screw or bolt, furnished with a toothed washer

semaphore indicator *noun* direction indicator used before flashers were introduced, consisting of a lighted arrow that popped out from the side of the car when the turn indicator switch was actuated (NOTE: also called **trafficator)**

semi-active suspension *noun* suspension whose characteristics can be tuned to driving conditions, such as by hydraulic adjustment of spring supports plus electronic correction of the damping rate

◇ **semi-automatic transmission** *noun* transmission in which the clutch is disengaged and re-engaged automatically when the driver actuates the gear lever

◇ **semiconductor** *noun* solid material such as silicon that has a resistivity midway between that of a conductor and a resistor, with properties of both a conductor and an insulator; used as substrates for semiconductor devices such as diodes, transistors, and integrated circuits; *(compare* CONDUCTOR, INSULATOR, SILICON); **semiconductor ignition system** = ignition system that uses semiconductors for the switching operations; *(compare* TRANSISTORIZED IGNITION SYSTEM)

◇ **semi-elliptic leaf spring** *noun* leaf spring with a camber in the form of one half of an ellipse

◇ **semi-floating axle** *noun* live rear axle assembly in which the weight of the vehicle is transferred from the axle housing to the axle shaft, usually by a bearing within the housing, close to the wheel centre plane; the end of the axle shaft facing the differential is supported by the differential bearings, i.e. the axle shaft will carry rotational as well as bending loads; *(compare* FULLY FLOATING AXLE)

◇ **semi-independent suspension** *noun* rear axle design with a torsionally flexible crossmember, the wheels being located on trailing links; *(compare* FLEX ARM SUSPENSION)

◇ **semitrailer** *noun* type of trailer that only has wheels at the rear, the front being supported by the towing vehicle

◇ **semi-trailing arm** *or* **link** *noun* arm of a coil spring, independent rear suspension system which pivots at an angle to the centreline of the vehicle, thus imparting negative camber with increase in load; *(compare* SUSPENSION LINK) *(see illustration 28)*

Sendzimir process *noun* continuous strip galvanizing process, named after its inventor

| COMMENT: the strip is wound from a coil while the oil or grease adhering to it is removed by oxidation. It is then annealed, and the oxides are reduced by ammonia, after which it is cooled to 500°C and immersed in a zinc bath, which is kept molten at about 450°C by the heat from the steel strip. On leaving the bath, the strip is cut and coiled

sensor *noun* any device that receives and reacts to a signal, such as a change in voltage, temperature or pressure; **sensor flap** = part of an airflow sensor which serves as a measure for the induced air volume; a potentiometer converts sensor flap movement into changes in electrical voltage, a form in which these signals can be evaluated by the fuel injection control unit; **sensor plate** = plate in the mixture control unit of a CIS, attached to a lever that operates the control plunger in the fuel distributor; the sensor plate position is governed by the amount of air admitted to the engine via the throttle valve and auxiliary air regulator; *(see illustration 14)*

separate-application adhesive *noun* adhesive consisting of two parts; one part being applied to one face and the other part to the other face and the two faces brought together to form a joint

◇ **separate chassis** *noun* the traditional body and frame design before the introduction of unitary construction; the body was lowered onto the chassis and bolted to it

◇ **separate lubrication** *noun* engine lubrication principle whereby the oil is no longer mixed with the fuel, but is fed by a metering pump from a separate oil tank to the engine components to be lubricated (NOTE: opposite is **petroil lubrication)**

◇ **separation** *noun* after long storage, liquid ingredients of paints and fillers may separate in the can on top of the material; in most cases, this can be overcome by stirring the contents of the can thoroughly before use

◇ **separation line** *noun* = CUTTING LINE

◇ **separator** *noun* **(a)** generally, anything that physically separates one part from another *wheel separator* **(b)** *(of lead-acid battery)* plates of insulating material which physically separate the positive plates from the negative plates **(c)** a filter or trap *oil separator* **(d)** = BEARING SEPARATOR

sequential fuel injection (SFI) *noun* fuel injection system in which bursts of petrol are sprayed into the inlet ports by injectors at timed intervals (NOTE: also called **timed fuel injection)**

◇ **sequential spark** *noun* = FOLLOW-UP SPARK

series *noun* two or more components connected in a circuit so that the same current flows in turn through each of them *the components are connected in series* (NOTE: opposite is **parallel**); **series circuit** = circuit with two or more resistance units so wired that current must pass through one unit before reaching the other

serpentine belt *noun* = POLY-V-BELT

serrated shaft *noun* shaft with V-shaped grooves; *(compare* SPLINE)

serration *noun* series of teeth on an edge (as on a saw)

service 1 *noun* periodic overhaul, usually carried out by a garage; includes changing the oil and oil filter, checking the brakes, tyres, ignition (usually changing the sparking plugs), electrical, fuel and cooling systems, and taking the vehicle on a test run to check the steering, suspension, and transmission systems as well as the performance of the engine and brakes **2** *verb* to carry out a service on a vehicle

◇ **service brake** *noun* foot-operated brake used for retarding, stopping and controlling the vehicle during normal driving conditions

◇ **service interval** *noun* the time or mileage between services (e.g. 12 months or 10,000 miles, whichever should come sooner)

◇ **service life** *noun* the length of time a component or system will remain reliable and safe

◇ **servicing** *noun* carrying out a service

servo *noun* *(informal)* = SERVOMECHANISM

◇ **servo-assisted** *adjective* = POWER-ASSISTED

◇ **servo brake** *noun* a drum brake in which the shoes are arranged so that one shoe helps to apply the other, to create a self-energizing effect in both shoes; *(compare* POWER BRAKES)

◇ **servomechanism** *noun* device that provides power assistance to operate a control (e.g. a brake or clutch)

◇ **servo motor** *noun* small electric motor that supplies power to a servomechanism

set *verb* **(a)** to adjust to a standard *set the gauge to zero* **(b)** *(e.g. body filler)* to harden

setscrew *noun* fully threaded bolt with a parallel shaft, used to secure metal parts together (such as a hub or wheel to a shaft); can have a variety of heads, the most common being hexagonal, round or countersunk; *(compare* GRUB SCREW)

setting *noun* **(a)** adjustment *the idle mixture setting on the carburettor should be checked every 12,000 miles* **(b)** *(e.g. body filler)* hardening

settle *verb* to sink to the bottom (of a liquid)

> COMMENT: the weight of the pigments in a paint varies greatly depending on their colour. Heavy pigments give colour, opacity and specific properties to the paint. Some pigments weigh seven or eight times as much as the liquid part of the paint and because of this, they tend to settle to the bottom of the container

SFC = SPECIFIC FUEL CONSUMPTION

SFI = SEQUENTIAL FUEL INJECTION

shackle *noun* pivoting link between the rear end of a leaf spring and the bodywork or chassis, which moves as the length of the spring varies

shadeband *noun* **windscreen shadeband** = SUNSHIELD

shaft *noun* round bar which transmits turning power from one part to another; *(compare* AXLE); **shaft distributor** = distributor whose drive shaft projects into the engine; the shaft is driven via a gearing system or a coupling (NOTE: opposite is

short-type distributor); **shaft seal** = seal used to prevent leaks between stationary parts and rotating shafts and to exclude foreign matter; **shaft sleeve** = sleeve which protects a shaft from erosion, corrosion, and wear at shaft seals *the shaft can be supplied with a replaceable sleeve* **shaft-to-cage coupling** = viscous coupling design in which the outer disc carrier is connected to the differential cage, while the inner disc carrier is connected to an axle shaft; **shaft-to-shaft coupling** = viscous coupling design in which the outer disc carrier is connected to the left-hand axle shaft and the inner disc carrier to the right-hand axle shaft

shallow pits *noun* corrosion in the form of pits whose diameter is substantially larger than their depth

shammy leather *see* CHAMOIS LEATHER

shank *noun* **(a)** the part of a bolt between the head and the thread *threaded/unthreaded shank* **shank length** = *(of bolts)* the distance from the last full form thread to the bearing face **(b)** the part of a bit which is held in the drill

shape template *noun* a guide or a pattern used in manufacturing items

◇ **shaping** *noun (repair work)* preliminary sanding or forming of the filled surface with coarse grit paper or a body file to establish the approximate body contours; this step is followed by final sanding

shared component *noun* parts or components which are identical in various models of a car family, such as those used on a saloon and its convertible derivative; typical shared components are body panels, suspension components, brakes

shaving (the body) *noun* custom car modification to remove all chrome parts at the front or rear end to achieve smooth contours highlighted only by the paint and the body modifications; in most cases, only a side chrome strip is retained (NOTE: also called **nosing** or **decking)**

shear *verb* to distort or fracture as a result of excess torsion or transverse load *the force of the impact caused the bolt to shear*

◇ **shear (head) bolt** *noun* bolt whose head may (intentionally) be sheared off to make extraction difficult

◇ **shears** *noun* = SNIPS

sheathed-type glow plug *noun* single-pole glow plug having a tubular heating element with a heating coil or a heating and regulator coil enclosed in a thermally conductive insulator ceramic; *(compare* WIRE GLOW PLUG)

◇ **sheath flame** *noun* the outer area of an oxyacetylene flame surrounding the inner cone and the flame feather

shedder drip moulding *noun* metal strip spot-welded below the roof drip rail to deflect rain water away from the door seal

sheet metal *noun* metal (steel) in the form of a thin sheet (pressed to form car body panels); **sheet metal blank** = a flat sheet metal panel as supplied by the trade; used to make repair panels for various body repair purposes; **sheet metal clamp** = lock-grip pliers with wide, flat jaws used to locate sheet metal parts for welding or to bend small sheet metal parts along the edges of the jaws (NOTE: when used for bending sheet metal, may also be referred to as **bending pliers)**; **sheet metal cutter** = any tool used to cut sheet metal; *(see* NIBBLER, SNIPS); **sheet metal folder** = machine used to bend sheet metal along a predetermined using mechanical force; **sheet metal remains** = a strip of metal left on the edges after the bulk of a panel has been cut out; this strip is then removed carefully to ensure that the flanges required on adjacent panels for welding in the new part are not damaged and to avoid cutting out excessive material; **sheet metal roller** = large machine to curve or roll metal in a single plane

COMMENT: the machine is hand-operated and consists of a frame, three rollers and a hand crank. The rollers are arranged as one top and two bottom rollers, and the degree of curvature is controlled by how closely the bottom rollers are set in relation to the top roller. The pressure of the bottom rollers against the top roller causes the metal to curve

sheet moulding compound (SMC) *noun* formerly called prepreg, SMC is supplied as a lightweight, pliable sheet which consists of a mixture of chopped strand mat pre-impregnated with resin, fillers, catalyst, and pigment

COMMENT: a sheet is placed between the halves of a heated mould and under the application of pressure takes up the contours of the mould

sheet wheel *noun* wheel made from aluminium sheet material; *(compare* ALLOY WHEELS)

COMMENT: the manufacturing process of the sheet wheel is comparable to that of the steel wheel but the advantage of the sheet wheel is its reduction in weight (up to 40% compared to a steel wheel)

shelf panel *noun* a deep-drawn steel panel fitted horizontally behind the rear seat backrest of notchback saloons to support the plastic or foam moulding that makes up the rear shelf, visible from the outside; *(see illustration 2)*

shell *noun* structural case or housing *converter shell*

◇ **shell bearing** *noun* type of bearing used for main bearings and big-end bearings, consisting of a circular housing which can be divided into two halves, and which encloses a pair of bearing shells

sherardizing *noun* coating iron objects with zinc powder by tumbling in powdered zinc at about 250-375°C

shield(ing) *noun* = SCREEN(ING)

shift *verb US* to change gear

◇ **shifter** *noun US* gear or selector lever; **shift(er) fork** = selector fork

◇ **shifting** *noun US* = GEARCHANGE

◇ **shift interlock** *noun US* device which prevents different shift forks in the transmission from being moved at the same time, by locking into the inoperative shift fork as the other is being moved; a gearchange cannot be made unless the inoperative shift fork is in its neutral position

◇ **shift lever** *noun* **(a)** *US* = GEAR LEVER **(b)** *(inside an automatic gearbox)* lever which connects the selector lever cable to the manual valve of the control valve body **(c)** component used in pre-engaged starter motors to force the pinion against the flywheel ring gear; *(see illustration 37)*

◇ **shift lock** *noun (automatic gearbox)* = SELECTOR LEVER LOCK

◇ **shift valve** *noun US* = CHANGE VALVE

shim 1 *noun* **(a)** thin packing strip (e.g. between wishbone and frame) **(b)** *(valve* *clearance)* a spacer required for the adjustment of valve clearance in OHC- or DOHC-engines equipped with tappets *an oil film can form between the shim and the top of the valve, which can cause errors in measurement* **2** *verb* to modify by the use of shims *shim the bearing until it is flush with the housing surface*

shimmy *noun* rapid side-to-side vibration of the front wheels

shim pliers *noun* = VALVE SHIM PLIERS

shock absorber *or (informal)* **shock** *noun* any device designed to absorb mechanical shock but especially the spring damper in a vehicle suspension system; *(see illustrations 27, 28)*; **shock absorber tower** = sheet metal panel of hollowed or box-section design that is spot-welded to the body and serves as an anchoring point for the top shock absorber mount

shooting brake *noun* old term for estate car

COMMENT: refers mainly to larger British estate cars with wooden rear and side panels that were popular during the early post-war period, such as coachbuilt models by Daimler, Armstrong-Siddeley, Allard, etc.

shopping car *noun* similar to a city car, may be even smaller

shop primer *noun* coating which temporarily protects a work from corrosion, e.g. during shipment

shore hardness (test) *noun* test method for the determination of indentation hardness of nonrigid plastics

short arm/long arm (SLA) suspension *noun* = UNEQUAL-LENGTH WISHBONE SUSPENSION

short block *noun* engine block complete with crankshaft and piston assemblies but without external parts such as head, sump, oil or fuel pump, etc. (NOTE: opposite is **long block**); **short block engine** = engine with a relatively short crankshaft; *(compare* LONG BLOCK ENGINE)

COMMENT: normally, short block engine refers to a 4-cylinder in-line engine or a V-8 engine which both have a shorter block than a 6-cylinder in-line engine

short circuit *noun* electrical fault whereby the current bypasses part of the circuit and finds a path of low resistance through which an excessive current can flow, causing a fuse to blow, wiring to be overloaded or a flat battery; **short circuit between the plates** = undesirable electrically conductive connection between positive and negative plates within a battery cell; makes battery inoperative

◇ **short circuiting** *noun* occurs during the scavenging process of a two-stroke engine when some of the fresh mixture entering the cylinder may flow across the cylinder and escape via the exhaust ports without producing any scavenging effect

◇ **short engine** *noun* fully reconditioned engine but without external parts such as head, sump, oil or fuel pump, etc.

◇ **short stroke engine** *noun* reciprocating piston engine whose bore diameter is larger than the stroke; a relatively short stroke improves high-end revving ability at the cost of low-end torque (NOTE: opposite is **long stroke engine**)

◇ **short-type distributor** *noun* distributor without a drive shaft; the drive coupling is located directly at the base of the ignition distributor housing (NOTE: opposite is **shaft distributor**)

shot bag *noun* leather bag filled with very fine lead shot over which metal is shaped; similar bags filled with sand are also used

◇ **shot blasting** *noun* blasting process in which rounded particles are impacted onto a surface

shoulder *noun* the part of a tyre between the tread and the sidewall; *(see illustration 32)*

◇ **shoulder belt** *noun (restraint)* belt pulled diagonally across the chest or the shoulder belt portion of a combined lap-shoulder belt; *(compare* 3-POINT (SEAT) BELT, LAP BELT)

shrink-fit *verb* to achieve an extremely close fit, by either expanding the external part by heating, or contracting the internal part by cooling, so that when the parts return to normal temperature they fit tightly together *the valve seat rings and valve guides are shrink-fitted into the cylinder head*

shrinking *noun* body repair technique used to repair locally stretched areas by using heat or special body hammers; **shrinking dolly** = special dolly with a large crowned grid surface, used to facilitate panel shrinking; *(compare* GRID DOLLY); **shrinking hammer** = special hammer with faces shaped to allow for correction of locally stretched sheet metal

> COMMENT: when shrinking metal, the panel is beaten down into the recesses of the grid, which help to reduce stretching

shunt *(informal)* **1** *verb* to crash **2** *noun* a crash, especially one caused by running into the back of the vehicle in front

◇ **shunt firing** *or* **shunting** *noun* *(sparking plug)* short circuit at the firing end, caused by electrically conductive deposits

shut line *noun* line between a closed door and the bodywork

shutter (blade) *noun* curved metal vane of a Hall generator

shuttle valve *noun* valve in which the actuating member shuttles back and forth

SI = SPARK IGNITION

SID = SIDE IMPACT DUMMY

◇ **side aperture panel** *noun* = APERTURE PANEL

◇ **side bumper panels** *noun* large plastic body side mouldings attached to the lower body sides which protect the body against road debris, road salt corrosion and mechanical impact (NOTE: introduced on Mercedes-Benz cars by chief designer Bruno Sacco, thus also called **Sacco panels)**

side curtain *noun* early name for side windows which were made of celluloid in a rigid frame supported by the sides of the body and the doors; some had a hinged flap through which the driver could extend his hand for signalling purposes

> COMMENT: on classic roadsters, the entire assembly of sliding windows and flaps; wedge-type side curtains permit the side curtain brackets to be wedged into the door plates without bolts; regular spring-type side curtains are mounted to the doors by means of thumb nuts or bolts. The curtains can be stored behind the rear seat squab or in a pocket at the back of the front seats

sidedraught carburettor *noun* carburettor with a horizontal barrel so that the air intake is at the side; *(compare* DOWNDRAUGHT CARBURETTOR)

◇ **side electrode** *noun* earth electrode at the side of the threaded part of a sparking plug shell; *(compare* CENTRE ELECTRODE)

◇ **side flasher** *noun* small (amber) direction indicator located in the side of the front wings

◇ **side gear** *noun* = DIFFERENTIAL SIDE GEAR

◇ **side impact bar** *noun* longitudinal reinforcing beam in a car door, designed to withstand side impact; **side impact dummy (SID)** = dummy developed to investigate the effects of side impact crashes; *(compare* ESV)

◇ **sidelamp** *noun* = SIDELIGHT

◇ **side-lift jack** *noun* = TOWER JACK

◇ **sidelight** *noun* low-intensity white front lamp, often incorporated in the headlamp; **sidelight pod** = a design feature of older cars that had their side or parking lights incorporated into a separate sheet metal moulding on top or at the side of the front wings

◇ **side marker light/lamp** *noun* low-intensity lamp mounted on the side of a vehicle to indicate its presence when seen side-on

◇ **side member** *noun* box-section member inboard of the outer sill that often runs from the front to the rear of the car and provides reinforcement of both sides of the floorpan; *(compare* INNER SILL) *(see illustration 2)*

◇ **side panel** *noun* **(a)** quarter panel between the B-pillar and the rear **(b)** = APERTURE PANEL **(c)** vertical panel on the inside of a body shell, e.g. the panel joining the lock pillar to the rear wheel housing

◇ **side pipe** *noun* exhaust pipe running along the side of the car; *(compare* LAKES PIPES)

◇ **side radiator guard** *noun* moulded cover panel fitted to the sides of the radiator to protect it from water splashes

◇ **side rail** *noun* = SIDE MEMBER

◇ **side rod** *noun* = TIE ROD

◇ **side scoop** *noun* air intake for the engine and/or for cooling on mid-engine or rear-engine cars; typically found on sports cars such as the Ferrari range

◇ **side shaft** *noun* = AXLE SHAFT (a)

◇ **side shake** *noun* = END PLAY

◇ **side shift** *noun* damage to the frame when the vehicle has been hit from the side

◊ **side skirt** *noun* extra body panel fitted over the sills (for cosmetic reasons only)

◊ **side step** *noun* (*commercial vehicles*) step plate below the doors to facilitate entry into the relatively high cabin

◊ **sideswipe** *noun* body damage caused by the car hitting an obstacle at an acute angle, causing the panels to be dented over a relatively large area

◊ **side-valve (SV) engine** *noun* engine with the valves to the side of the cylinders; (*compare* L-HEAD ENGINE)

◊ **sidewall** *noun* **(a)** side of a tyre between the bead and the edge of the tread; (*see also* SCUFF RIB) (*see illustration 32*) **(b)** vertical part of the box section of a side member

SI engine *noun* spark ignition engine or petrol engine: internal combustion engine of the reciprocating type in which an air/fuel mixture is compressed and then ignited by an electric spark; (*compare* DIESEL ENGINE)

sight glass *noun* viewing glass or window set in the refrigerant pipe of a car's air-conditioning system, usually in the top of the receiver-drier, which allows a visual check of the refrigerant passing from the receiver to the evaporator (NOTE: the fluid should be clear and free of foam)

◊ **sighting point gauge** *noun* device incorporating a sighting pin, used to measure car bodies for misalignment

silencer *noun* **(a)** (*exhaust system*) device through which the exhaust gases pass and which reduces exhaust noise; (*see illustration 19*) (NOTE: US English is **muffler**) **(b)** (*air duct*) device in an air-conditioning system designed to minimize pumping sounds from the compressor

◊ **silencer shaft** *noun* = BALANCE SHAFT

◊ **silencer-tailpipe tool** *noun* **(i)** chisel-type tool with several cutting edges to cut silencer sleeves without damaging tailpipes; **(ii)** L-shaped tool whose short end is driven between the silencer and tailpipe to break the bond

silent chain *noun* chain with V-shaped teeth

silica *noun* common mineral (silicon dioxide) found as sand, quartz, etc., used in the manufacture of glass, ceramics and abrasives; **silica gel** = form of silica capable of absorbing large quantities of water, used to keep electronic apparatus, etc., dry; **silica sand** = form of silica used for sherardizing or mechanical plating

◊ **silicon** *non* non-metallic chemical element occurring in several forms (principally sand and rock), used in the manufacture of glass and steel (as well as transistors etc.); **silicon carbide** = material of excellent abrasion and corrosion resistance used in bearings and mechanical seals

◊ **silicone** *noun* a silicon compound with a high resistance to heat, water and chemicals, and with good insulating and lubricating properties; used in oils, polishes, sealants, etc.; **silicone brake fluid** = brake fluid which does not absorb water; **silicone-rubber sealant** = semi-liquid sealant which is proof against oil and water but not petrol (NOTE: also called **RTV sealant**)

sill *noun* **(a)** longitudinal box-section member of the body shell at floor level, located below the doors; (*see illustration 1*); **sill cover** = non-structural part covering the sill on its entire length; used on certain designs with separate chassis but also on unitary designs; **sill end piece** = small panel at the front and rear end of the sill that closes off the hollow sill section towards the front and rear wheel arches; (*compare* CLOSING PANEL); **sill membrane** = horizontal stiffening panel between the outer sill and the side member box section; it is ribbed or drilled for extra rigidity **(b)** box-section crossmember just below the lower edge of the bootlid (when closed)

Sillment seal *noun* (*sparking plug*) gas-tight seal between centre electrode and insulator and between insulator and shell

sill stiffener *noun* = SILL MEMBRANE; **sill structure** = refers to the overall design of the sills including outer sills, side member or inner sill and sill membrane

silver-plating *noun* electrolytic deposition of silver

simple tappet *noun* = FLAT TAPPET

simplex chain *noun* chain with only one row of rollers; (*compare* DUPLEX CHAIN, TRIPLEX CHAIN)

Simpson (planetary) gear set *noun* consists of two simple planetary gear sets with a common sun gear and internal gears of different diameter; the planet carrier of one set is fixed to the internal gear of the other set

single-acting *adjective (of a reciprocating engine or pump)* having a piston or pistons that are pressurized on one side only

◊ **single-anchor self-energizing brake** *noun* type of servo brake whose shoes both pivot about one fixed point

◊ **single-bed 3-way catalytic converter** *noun* converter for the control of HC, CO, and NO_x emissions, consisting of one three-way catalyst; in combination with an oxygen sensor, this type of converter yields the lowest emission values; **single-bed oxidizing converter** = converter with one catalyst bed for HC and CO control

◊ **single-circuit braking system** *noun* old form of hydraulic braking system in which a single circuit serves all four brakes (NOTE: not to be confused with **single-line braking system**)

◊ **single-coil twin ignition** *noun* in the early days of straight eight engines, a distributor with two sets of contact points, firing alternately

◊ **single-connector system** *noun* electrical circuit, where only one conductor is laid from the voltage source to the load; return is realized via the vehicle body; *(compare EARTH)*

◊ **single-cut file** *noun* file with teeth in one direction only, used for filing soft material

◊ **single-cylinder engine** *noun* not used on cars but typical for small motorbikes, motocross bikes, and go-carts

◊ **single-decker bus** *noun* bus with one storey or deck

◊ **single-grade (engine) oil** *noun* oil suitable for use within a narrow temperature range; outside this range, its flow characteristics will not allow adequate lubrication; *(compare MULTIGRADE OIL)*

◊ **single-leaf spring** *noun* single element suspension spring in the form of a flexible beam

◊ **single-line braking system** *noun* braking system in which a single line is used to connect towing vehicle and trailer (NOTE: not to be confused with **single-circuit braking system**)

◊ **single overhead camshaft (sohc)** *noun* in a typical sohc engine, the camshaft is located between the valves and is driven by a chain from the crankshaft; the valves are normally opened via short rocker arms; *(compare DOHC)*

◊ **single-piece rim/wheel** *noun* = ONE-PIECE RIM/WHEEL

◊ **single-pivot steering** *noun* steering in which a beam axle is pivoted at its mid-point; rare except on horse-drawn vehicles and trailers; *(compare DOUBLE-PIVOT STEERING)*

◊ **single-plate clutch** *noun* normal type of clutch, with one driven plate; usually dry (i.e. without oil); *(compare MULTI-PLATE CLUTCH)*

◊ **single point injection (SPI)** *noun* petrol fuel-injection system which sprays fuel under pressure into the intake air at one place, usually the throttle body on the inlet manifold; it is less complicated than a multi-point injection system but achieves better carburation than a carburettor; *(compare MULTI-POINT INJECTION)*

◊ **single roller chain** *noun* = SIMPLEX CHAIN

◊ **single-spark ignition coil** *noun* in a distributorless ignition system with an odd number of cylinders, each cylinder requires its own ignition coil; distributor logic on the low-voltage side performs the voltage distribution to each coil; *(compare MULTI-SPARK IGNITION COIL)*

◊ **single-tube shock absorber** *noun* common type of shock absorber with the working cylinder and reservoir contained in one tube; *(compare DOUBLE-TUBE SHOCK ABSORBER, GAS SHOCK ABSORBER)*

◊ **single-wheel suspension** *noun* = INDEPENDENT SUSPENSION

sink in *verb* a tendency of a hardened filler to settle excessively, making the featheredges of the filled area stand out on the painted surface

sinter *verb* to manufacture parts from powdered metals by heating or pressure or both

sipes *noun* fine cuts in a tyre's tread which help to disperse the remaining water from the tread after the grooves and channels have removed the greater part of it; may also reduce tyre noise; *(see illustration 32)*

SIR = SUPPLEMENTARY INFLATABLE RESTRAINT

six-cylinder engine *noun* engine with six cylinders; may be in-line (a straight six) or in a V-layout (a V-6)

◇ **six-light saloon** *noun* old designation of a four-door body style that features another small quarter window behind the rear side doors, resulting in three side windows per side or six windows overall

◇ **sixteen valve (16V) engine** *noun* a four-cylinder engine with four valves to each cylinder

size marking *noun* first part of a tyre marking moulded on the sidewall, giving the tyre's width in millimetres

skeleton construction *noun* modern construction layout of the unitary type, using a skeleton-like assembly as the main structural member, thus relieving stress from the body sheet metal; (*compare* COACHBUILT CONSTRUCTION, UNITARY CONSTRUCTION)

skid 1 *verb* (i) to slide sideways (often out of control); (ii) to slide in a straight line (as after sudden braking with, maybe, locked brakes) **2** *noun* the action or result of skidding; **skid mark** = the mark left on the road surface by the tyres, as a result of emergency braking

◇ **skidpan** *US* **skid pad** *noun* large paved area, usually circular and with various circles painted on it, made deliberately slippery so it may be used to practise controlling skids, lateral acceleration tests, etc.

◇ **skid plate** *noun* = SUMP GUARD

ski flap *noun* flap in the rear bulkhead, for long, thin loads (like skis)

skin *noun* the outer covering surface of a vehicle

skirt *see* PISTON SKIRT, SIDE SKIRT

skylight *noun* pop-up window in the roof of a caravan

SL = SPECIAL LEDGE

slant engine *noun* = INCLINED ENGINE

slapper *noun* (*informal*) = BUMPING BLADE

SLA suspension *noun* = SHORT ARM/LONG ARM SUSPENSION

slatted grille *noun* aerodynamic radiator grille developed by Ford in 1976

COMMENT: the horizontal aerofoil grille elements are shaped like aircraft wings to allow the cooling air to flow towards the radiator at low speeds, whereas excess airflow is directed upwards across the front of the car at higher speeds to produce an effect similar to that of a spoiler

slave con rod *noun* connecting rod of two-stroke dual piston engines which is articulated on the master con rod, not directly on the crankpin; (*compare* MASTER CON ROD)

◇ **slave cylinder** *noun* small cylinder containing a piston which, under hydraulic pressure from a master cylinder, operates the brake shoes or pads in hydraulic brakes or the working part in any other hydraulically operated system (such as a clutch slave cylinder); (*compare* MASTER CYLINDER)

sleeve *noun* **(a)** tube fitted externally over two cylindrical parts in order to join them; (*compare* BUSH) **(b)** = CYLINDER LINER

◇ **sleeve bearing** *noun* any bearing of tubular or sleeve-like construction

slide carburettor *noun* type of carburettor often used in two-stroke motorcycle engines, in which a slide valve modifies the venturi of the carburettor

◇ **slide hammer** *noun* tool with a long round shaft on which a hammer weight slides; the force produced by quickly moving the weight towards the end of the shaft is used for loosening or pulling off tight parts; often used in combination with pullers; (*compare* PANEL PULLER)

◇ **slider** *noun* (*CVT*) device which senses the position of the half of a primary pulley that slides

◇ **slide valve** *noun* valve that slides across an aperture to expose the port or opening

sliding-caliper disc brake *noun* disc brake design with a sliding caliper: (i); (*caliper floats on caliper frame grooves*) major components are: caliper (a casting with one cylinder and piston), caliper frame (casting); the caliper floats on 'ways' in the frame, and the caliper frame is bolted to the suspension; (ii); (*caliper floats on caliper*) *locating pins)* = PIN SLIDER CALIPER DISC BRAKE; (iii); *(with mounting frame)* = FLOATING-FRAME DISC BRAKE *(see illustration 31)*

> COMMENT: sometimes subtle design differences are used to differentiate between 'sliding caliper disc brakes' and 'floating caliper disc brakes', but usually these terms are treated synonymously

sliding contacts *noun (ignition)* assembly developed by Lucas, that causes the moving contact to slide vertically across the face of the fixed contact when the spark is advanced

◇ **sliding friction** *noun* frictional resistance to relative movement of surfaces on loaded contact; *(compare* ROLLING FRICTION)

◇ **sliding joint** *US* **slip joint** *or plunging joint noun* connection in the drive train, of variable length, which permits the drive shaft to change its effective length; *(see* CONSTANT VELOCITY JOINT)

◇ **sliding-mesh gearbox** *noun* obsolete type of gearbox in which the gears on the layshaft are fixed to the shaft rigidly, whereas the gears on the main shaft can slide on it by means of splines but are otherwise in permanent rotational mesh with the shaft; *(compare* CONSTANT-MESH GEARBOX)

◇ **sliding-pillar suspension** *noun* once popular front suspension layout, incorporated for example in Lancia and Morgan cars, in which a carrier-mounted stub axle slides up and down a vertical pillar with enclosed coil springs providing the suspension; less sophisticated versions were used in several pre-war cycle cars

◇ **sliding side window** *noun* window style of classic roadsters, consisting of aluminium frames with tracks for two sliding window panels made of clear Plexiglas, and with draught seals; on some cars, also furnished with flaps; *(compare* SIDE CURTAIN)

◇ **sliding T-bar** *noun* drive handle with square drive sliding on round bar for T-handle turning operation

sliding-vane pump *noun* positive displacement pump in which an eccentric rotor revolves in an eccentric or circular case; *(compare* EXTERNAL-VANE PUMP)

> COMMENT: the pumping element consists of multiple blades which slide in slots in the rotor and divide the crescent-shaped fluid space

into variable volumes; some sources state that in the sliding-vane type, vanes do come into contact with the casing, whereas in 'vane-type pumps' a clearance of about 0.004 inches is maintained between vanes and casing

sliding weight *noun* functional part of a sliding hammer that provides the inertia required for the pulling force

slip *noun* relative motion between driving and driven parts; *(see* CLUTCH SLIP, WHEELSLIP)

◇ **slip angle** *noun* angular difference between the direction in which a tyre is effectively rolling and the wheel plane

◇ **slip friction** *noun* = SLIDING FRICTION

◇ **slip joint** *noun* **(a)** *US* = SLIDING JOINT **(b)** connection in an exhaust pipe; *(see illustration 19)*

slipper piston *noun* piston design developed for short-stroke engines; a cutaway section on opposing sides of the piston skirt saves weight; *(compare* FULL-SKIRT PISTON)

slip ring *noun* in an alternator, the rings that form a rotating connection between the armature windings and the brushes; **slip-ring end bracket** = cover housing the bearing at the slip-ring end of an alternator (NOTE: opposite is **drive end bracket)** *(see illustration 36)*

slip roll *noun* = SHEET METAL ROLLER

slipstream 1 *noun* stream of air behind a moving vehicle **2** *verb* to drive closely behind another vehicle in order to benefit from the decreased wind resistance immediately behind it

slip the clutch *verb* to operate the clutch so that it partially disengages, as when keeping up the revs when driving off; causes wear on the clutch; *(compare* CLUTCH SLIP)

sloper *noun (informal)* = INCLINED ENGINE

sloping headlamp *noun* old headlamp type used on the VW Beetle prior to 1967

slot *noun* a narrow channel or aperture, especially the groove in the head of a screw which receives the tip of the blade of a screwdriver

◊ **slotted piston** *noun* = SPLIT SKIRT PISTON

slow charging *noun (battery)* charging using a charging current which corresponds to 10% of the battery capacity; *(compare* FAST CHARGER)

SLOW DOWN indicator *noun* indicator light in the instrument panel that warns the driver to slow down in the event of excessive catalytic converter temperature

COMMENT: a protective warning circuit causes the indicator initially to flash if the catalytic converter becomes overheated; if the temperature increases beyond a certain second level, the lamp will glow continuously

slow-running *noun* = IDLING

sludge *noun* = OIL SLUDGE

sluggish *adjective* unresponsive; functioning at below normal rate or level

slushbox *noun (informal)* = AUTOMATIC GEARBOX

slush moulding *noun* thermoplastic casting in which a liquid resin is poured into a hot, hollow mould where a viscous skin forms; excess slush is drained off, the mould is cooled, and the moulded product is stripped out

small block engine *noun* an American V-8 engine with typically 289 cu.in. displacement; still very powerful, but not quite as gargantuan as the big block; *(compare* SHORT BLOCK ENGINE)

◊ **small end** *noun* top of a connecting rod, attached to the gudgeon pin; *(see illustration 9)*; **small end bearing** = the smaller bearing of the two on a connecting rod and through which the piston is attached; usually fitted with a plain bearing or a needle-roller assembly

SMC = SHEET MOULDING COMPOUND

SMMT = SOCIETY OF MOTOR MANUFACTURERS AND TRADERS

smoke *noun* the visible product of combustion; a common problem with diesel

cars on starting or pulling hard, caused by too much fuel (black smoke) or oil (blue smoke); **smoke meter** = instrument which measures the density of (especially diesel) exhaust smoke

Sn *symbol for* tin

snake *verb (caravan or trailer)* to swing from side to side when being towed too fast

snap fastener *noun* fastener with a projecting knob on one part that snaps into a hole on another part, used on some roadsters to attach the convertible top or tonneau cover to the rear deck and/or windscreen header (NOTE: US English is **lift-the-dot fastener)**

snap ring *noun US* = CIRCLIP

snatch *verb* = GRAB (b)

snipe-nose pliers *noun* = LONG-NOSE PLIERS

snips *noun* tool used to cut straight, circular and irregular patterns in sheet metal material; available in various designs for straight, left- or right-hand cut

snow chains *noun* chains which are wrapped around tyres to provide extra traction in snow or ice; **snow chain switch** = signals the ASR system that snow chains are fitted to the drive wheels

◊ **snow tyre** *noun* = WINTER TYRE

snubber *noun* = BUMP STOP

soaking time *noun* time required before a dry-charged battery is ready for use after being filled with acid

Society of Motor Manufacturers and Traders (SMMT) *noun* official organization of the British motor industry

socket *noun* **(a)** any recess formed for the purpose of receiving a spigot or other part, especially one into which an electrical connector may be inserted **(b)** cylindrical spanner head with one end shaped to fit over the head of a nut or bolt, and a female square drive at the other end to accept the drive tool; **socket bit** = bit for use with socket drive tools; **socket driver** = screwdriver-type handle for use with sockets; **socket spanner** = spanner with socket end(s) or a drive tool combined with a socket

sodium-cooled exhaust valve *noun* the exhaust valves of some high-performance engines are filled with sodium to improve the heat dissipation from the valve stem to the valve guide, since the exhaust valve is subject to higher thermal loads than the inlet valve

◇ **sodium-sulphur battery** *noun* new type of battery, with higher energy density than conventional batteries such as the lead-acid battery; developed for use in electric powered vehicles

softening agent *noun* = PLASTICIZER

soft face hammer *noun* tool for striking objects without marking; usually has replaceable screw-in faces made of plastic, nylon, or rubber

◇ **soft paint** *noun* paint fault apparent when the paint surface can be marked easily even after full drying has been allowed; caused by excessive film thickness or, in the case of two-pack paints, an insufficient quantity of catalyst

◇ **soft-sided caravan** *noun* caravan with canvas or other fabric walls, which folds compactly to the size and shape of a small trailer whose light weight and low profile result in low wind resistance and fuel consumption; *(compare* HARD-SIDED CARAVAN)

◇ **soft top** *noun* a convertible with a roof made of fabric rather than metal

◇ **soft trim** *noun* = TRIM (a)

SOHC *or* **sohc** = SINGLE OVERHEAD CAMSHAFT

solar car *noun* lightweight electric vehicle powered by solar generators

◇ **solar collector** *noun* heat exchanger that transforms solar radiant energy into heat; typical solar collectors are flat-plate collectors and concentrating collectors

◇ **solar generator** *noun* a panel-shaped array of photovoltaic cells designed to transform solar radiant energy directly into electric energy; installed on car roofs, they can be used to recharge the batteries of electric-powered cars

solder 1 *noun* alloy which is melted to form a joint between two metal surfaces; typically,

soft solders are alloys of lead and tin, whilst hard solders are alloys of copper and zinc **2** *verb* to join together using solder

◇ **soldering iron** *noun* tool with a handle attached to a copper or iron tip which is heated, electrically or in a flame, and used to melt solder to make joints

◇ **solder paddle** *noun* tool made of maple or beech, designed for spreading body solder over the surface of a panel

◇ **solder paint** *noun* paste used to prepare the area to be leaded so the body lead will stick to the metal surface; consists of a flux in which powdered lead is held in suspension

solenoid *noun* an electrically energized coil of insulated wire which produces a magnetic field within the coil, usually used to pull a movable iron core/plunger to a central position within the coil; used as an actuating device, e.g. for valves; **solenoid starter switch** = solenoid-operated starter motor switch; **solenoid valve** = valve actuated electrically by means of an electromagnet, or 'solenoid'; *(see also* STARTER SOLENOID)

solid *adjective (of brake discs)* unventilated

◇ **solid disc wheel** *noun* = PLAIN DISC WHEEL

◇ **solidify** *verb* to become solid, compact, or hard

◇ **solid injection** *noun* = DIRECT INJECTION

◇ **solid paint** *noun* paint of one uniform colour, not metallic; *(compare* METALLIC PAINT)

◇ **solid phase pressure forming** *noun* special type of thermoforming of polypropylene sheeting

◇ **solid propellant** *noun* propellant in pellet form, used to inflate air bags

◇ **solid-state ignition (system)** *noun* = DISTRIBUTORLESS IGNITION (SYSTEM)

◇ **solid tyre** *noun* solid rubber tyre that is not inflated by air (NOTE: opposite is **pneumatic tyre)**

soluble anode *noun* positive electrode of a galvanic cell at which metal ions pass into solution

◇ **solution** *noun* single, homogeneous liquid, solid, or gas phase that is a mixture in which the components (liquid, gas, solid, or combination thereof) are distributed uniformly; **solution pressure** = measure of the tendency of hydrogen, metals, and certain non-metals to pass into solution as ions

◊ **solvent** *noun* liquid which can dissolve another substance to form a solution *solvent-based adhesive; solvent-free adhesive* **solvent pop** = small bumps in a paint film which, under close inspection, can be seen to have small holes in the top; caused by excessive film depth being applied in one coat, preventing the thinners from escaping properly

sonic idling *or* **sonic throttling** *noun* system developed by Ford, for a fixed-jet carburettor which uses air at the speed of sound to atomize fuel supplied by the idling circuit; makes idling smoother and reduces exhaust pollution

sonoscope *noun* diagnostic tool used to listen for noises in engines and identify trouble spots such as faulty valves, worn gears and water pump, bearing knock, damaged gaskets or piston slap (NOTE: also called a **mechanic's stethoscope)**

sooted *or* **sooty plug** *noun* carbon-fouled sparking plug

sound absorption *noun* the weight and space restrictions of modern cars call for sound absorption using thin-walled materials, whose thickness is small in relation to the wave length of the sound to be absorbed

sound metal *noun* metal panel not substantially weakened by rust that provides a basis, for example, for welding on repair panels

soundproofing material *noun* any material used to deaden the sound from surfaces which transmit or generate noise; (e.g. felt lining on the underside of a bonnet); *(compare* ANTI-DRUM COMPOUND)

souped up *adjective (informal)* modified or tuned for greater power

space frame *noun* type of strong, steel chassis construction used for sports cars; *(compare* TUBULAR FRAME)

◊ **spacer** *noun* generally, anything that separates one part from another; **spacer plate** = VALVE BODY SEPARATOR PLATE; **spacer ring** = EXPANDER SPACER

space-saving spare wheel *noun* wheel with a cross-ply tyre folded together on the rim; in the event of a puncture or a badly damaged wheel, the tyre is inflated by a compressor (NOTE: US English is **collapsible spare tire)**

COMMENT: compared to conventional spare wheels, space-saving spare wheels offer a weight reduction of 30-40% and a space saving of up to 50%; their maximum permitted speed is 60 mph and they are only for temporary use

space wagon *noun* a vehicle category introduced in the USA in 1983 with the Chrysler Voyager, and in Europe at the end of the 1980s with the Renault Espace; a multi-purpose vehicle for everyday and recreational use that combines the handling and luxury of a saloon with the space and headroom of a van; usually with three rows of seats for at least six people and with a sliding door on the side

spalling *noun* flaking of the surface of a bearing

spangles *noun* crystal structure on hot-dip galvanized metals

spanner *noun* steel hand tool with jaws or a hole of particular shape at the end, designed to fit round a nut or bolt head in order to turn it

spare *noun* **(a)** = SPARE PART **(b)** = SPARE WHEEL

◊ **spare part** *noun* a replacement part, either available from a dealer or carried with the vehicle (like bulbs, fuses, plugs, etc.)

◊ **spares car** *noun* = DONOR CAR

◊ **spare tyre/wheel** *noun* additional wheel which allows for the replacement of a defective wheel or a punctured tyre; **spare tyre carrier** = on light commercial vehicles, the spare wheel is usually mounted below the loading area in a horizontal rack near the rear axle; **spare wheel well** = indentation in a flat boot floor that houses the spare wheel in a horizontal position

spark *noun* electric spark that jumps across the sparking plug gap to initiate the combustion of the air/fuel mixture *to advance/retard the spark; a goodstrong spark*

◊ **spark advance** *noun* = IGNITION ADVANCE

◊ **spark air gap** *noun* gap between the electrodes of a sparking plug; *(compare* SURFACE GAP)

◊ **spark angle** *noun* = IGNITION ANGLE; **spark-angle map** = IGNITION MAP

◊ **spark breakaway** *noun* end of spark duration

◊ **spark control computer (SCC)** *noun* electronic control unit with electronic spark timing

◊ **spark current** *noun* current that flows across the electrodes of a spark gap at a particular point in time

◊ **spark discharge voltage** *noun* = IGNITION VOLTAGE

◊ **spark duration** *noun* burning time of the arc following the initial flashover between the sparking plug electrodes until the residual energy decays

spark gap *noun* = SPARKING PLUG GAP; **spark gap coil tester** = tester providing a spark gap or neon tube to provide a comparison for the coil being tested

COMMENT: the coil to be tested is connected to the spark gap of the tester, and the length of the spark it produces is measured; a good coil is used as a standard of performance

spark head *noun* displayed as a firing spike on an oscilloscope pattern

◊ **spark ignition** *noun* ignition initiated by an electric spark in a spark ignition engine; *(compare* SELF-IGNITION); **spark ignition angle** = IGNITION ANGLE; **spark ignition engine** = SI ENGINE

sparking plug *noun* device screwed into the cylinder head of spark ignition engines (one sparking plug per cylinder) which initiates fuel combustion by an electric spark arcing from the centre electrode to the side electrode; typically consisting of a steel shell with a hexagon and a thread with the welded-on side electrode, a ceramic insulator and the centre electrode; *(see illustrations 4, 5, 6)*

COMMENT: the sparking plug must withstand extremely high electrical, mechanical, chemical and thermal stress to seal the combustion chamber gas-tight at any time; gas-tight sealing between centre electrode and insulator as well as between insulator and shell is achieved by different materials, depending on manufacturer. Sparking plugs differ in type, heat range, gap style and shielding

sparking plug body *noun* = SPARKING PLUG SHELL

◊ **sparking plug boot** *noun* moulded rubber or plastic insulator which fits over a sparking plug terminal; **sparking plug boot puller** = special automotive tool for the safe removal and installation of sparking plug boots

◊ **sparking plug brush** *noun* hard, compact brush for removing carbon from sparking plug electrodes

◊ **sparking plug cable** *noun* high-voltage cable from the distributor to the sparking plug; *(compare* IGNITION CABLE) *(see illustration 4)*; **sparking plug cable cover strip** = connecting system that integrates the sparking plug connectors, sparking plug leads, distributor cap, distributor connector, high-voltage cable, and ignition coil connector; **sparking plug cable loom** *or* **separator** = typically, a T-shaped and sometimes chrome-plated steel holder with cable guide holes and plastic inserts; keeps cables neatly in place and eliminates ignition leakage; **sparking plug cable markers** = numbered snap-on C-clips which identify the firing order

◊ **sparking plug condition** *noun* visual appearance of the sparking plug electrodes and insulator

◊ **sparking plug electrode** *noun* the two electrodes in a sparking plug are the centre electrode and the side (or earth) electrode

◊ **sparking plug gap** *noun* the shortest distance between the centre and side electrodes of a sparking plug where the spark jumps over (approx. 0.6-1.1 mm) *to set the sparking plug gap; to arc across the sparking plug gap*

◊ **sparking plug gauge** *noun* tool used for checking sparking plug gaps; usually with metal feeler blades or calibrated wire feelers; often includes an electrode adjusting tool for altering the gap between the electrodes

◊ **sparking plug insert tap** *noun* tool used to enlarge and tap new threads in damaged sparking plug holes in order to accept sparking plug inserts

◊ **sparking plug insulator** *noun* highly stressed part of the sparking plug, usually made of alumina ceramic, which serves to insulate the centre electrode and the terminal stud from the shell; its material must have high dielectric, mechanical and thermal strength as well as good thermal conductivity

◇ **sparking plug lead** *noun* = SPARKING PLUG CABLE

◇ **sparking plug pliers** *noun* pliers-like tool with specially shaped jaws to securely grip sparking plug boots for removal and installation, and insulated handles for shock-proof grip

◇ **sparking plug shell** *noun* metal body of the sparking plug which encloses the lower part of the insulator

◇ **sparking plug tester** *noun* screwdriver with a bulb inside the handle, which lights up if a spark is present when the blade is touched against the outside insulation of the sparking plug cable

◇ **sparking plug spanner** *noun* spanner for removing and installing sparking plugs; come in a variety of shapes, e.g. with swivel or T-handle, and many have rubber inserts to prevent damage to the fragile insulating porcelain

sparking rate *noun* the sparking rate per minute in a spark ignition engine is the number of cylinders multiplied by half the engine speed

◇ **sparking voltage** *noun* = IGNITION VOLTAGE

◇ **spark knock** *noun* = ENGINE KNOCK

◇ **spark map** *noun* = IGNITION MAP

◇ **spark plug** *noun* = SPARKING PLUG

◇ **spark position** *noun* the position of the spark gap in the combustion chamber *recessed spark position*

◇ **spark retard** *noun* = IGNITION RETARD

◇ **spark timing** *noun* = IGNITION TIMING

◇ **spark voltage** *noun* **(a)** voltage required to maintain the spark after reduction of the firing voltage **(b)** voltage measured at the electrodes of a spark gap at a particular point in time **(c)** = IGNITION VOLTAGE

spatter *noun* sparks produced during the welding process; more pronounced if the welding parameters are not correctly set or if impurities are present on the welded area

spec *noun* (*informal*) = SPECIFICATION

special body *noun* a body not supplied by the car manufacturer or by an approved body supplier in the case of manufacturers that do not build their own bodies, but rather by an independent coachbuilder who produces a body different from the standard body

COMMENT: a 'one-off body' refers specifically to a body of which only one example is made, whereas in general, 'special' or 'coachbuilt bodies' may be produced in small-scale series

special ledge (SL) *noun* safety bead seat contour mainly used on passenger cars of American make

specific activity *noun* the conversion rate of a given catalytic converter per unit volume; it is desirable to have a high specific activity, i.e. a small but efficient converter

◇ **specification** *noun* detailed technical description of a part, piece of machinery, plan or proposal

◇ **specific fuel consumption (SFC)** *noun* the amount of fuel consumed by an engine for each unit of energy produced; measured in kilograms-per-megajoule or -per-kilowatt-hour or pounds-per-bhp-hour

specific speed *noun* an index which provides information on the general profile or shape of the impeller of a pump

COMMENT: the specific speed is the speed in revolutions per minute at which an impeller would run if reduced in size to deliver 1 gallon per minute against a total head of 1 ft; impellers for high heads usually have low specific speeds and impellers for low heads usually have high specific speeds

specular finish *or* **specular gloss** *noun* a mirror-like finish of high reflectivity

speech synthesizer *noun* electronic device which simulates speech to warn the driver of something wrong (such as an unclosed door); (*compare* VOICE ALERT SYSTEM)

speed *noun* **(a)** rate of movement *road speed* **(b)** (*transmission*) gear or gear ratio *three-/four-/five-speed gearbox*

◇ **speed brace** *or* **speeder** *noun* drive handle in the shape of a crank; appropriate for fast operation but not having sufficient leverage for large nuts and bolts

◇ **speed category** *noun* = SPEED RATING

◇ **speed control (system)** *noun* = CRUISE CONTROL; **speed control vacuum**

advance = system which cuts off vacuum ignition advance when a car is cruising at low speeds, typically under 35 mph; for this purpose, a solenoid-operated valve is hooked into the distributor advance vacuum line, which is governed by a speed-dependent signal from a switch mounted on the transmission

◊ **speed limit** *noun* the maximum allowable vehicle speed at any given point

◊ **speed nut** *noun* a self-locking device used especially to secure sheet metal screws; consists of a small steel plate with a hole and two arched prongs that engage with the screw thread; used extensively to attach plastic parts to a steel car body

◊ **speedometer** *or (informal)* **speedo** *noun* dashboard instrument showing speed of travel in mph or km/h; *(compare* ODOMETER, TACHOMETER); **speedometer (drive) cable** = cable carrying the drive from the gearbox, or a front wheel, to the speedometer

speed rating *noun* the maximum driving speed for which a tyre is designed, indicated by a letter in the tyre designation on the sidewall

COMMENT: the speed rating evolved gradually and is thus not directly proportional to the alphabetical order; hence: P = up to 150 km/h or 95 mph; Q = up to 160 km/h or 100 mph; R = 170 km/h or 105 mph; S = up to 180 km/h or 113 mph; T = up to 190 km/h or 118 mph; U = up to 200 km/h or 125 mph; but H (high-speed) = up to 210 km/h or 130 mph; and V (very high speed) = over 210 km/h or over 130 mph

speed ratio *noun* ratio of the speed of the driving member of a mechanical drive to the speed of the driven member

◊ **speed-sensitive steering** *noun* type of power-assisted steering which is light at low speeds and increasingly heavier at higher speeds, giving the driver more feel; **speed-sensitive wiper system** = system which increases blade pressure on the windscreen as the car gathers pace

◊ **speedster** *noun* a fast, sporty car model

◊ **speed symbol** *noun* = SPEED RATING

spent gas *noun* the gases burnt during the previous firing cycle that remain in the combustion chamber of a two-stroke engine after the charge changing process has been completed and the ports have been closed by the piston

COMMENT: an excessive proportion of spent gas in the cylinder weakens the mixture available for combustion

spherical combustion chamber *noun* the combustion chamber of an internal combustion engine equipped with reciprocating pistons is ideally very compact in design, i.e. without gaps, grooves, edges, etc.; the most favourable design would thus be a sphere but the valves of a four-stroke engine make this impossible. The combustion chamber in diesel engines, however, is located in the piston crown, where it is in fact spherical

SPI = SINGLE POINT INJECTION

spider *noun* **(a)** a roadster with more amenities, such as doors, windows, boot, folding top (unlined); may also have two emergency rear seats, power steering, electric windows, etc. **(b)** central crosspiece linking the two yokes of a universal joint; *(see illustration 22)* **(c)** cross-shaped wheel spanner with a different-sized box socket head on each of the four legs **(d)** = WHEEL SPIDER

COMMENT: the term used at (a) is derived from an 18th-century 2-seater coach, whose wide wheelbase and large, thin wheels had a spider-like appearance; typical spiders are the Alfa Romeo Spider and the Fiat 124 Sport Spider

spigot *noun* short, cylindrical projection on one part designed to fit into a hole in another part, for location or retaining purposes (as for road wheels); **spigot bearing** = small bearing in the centre of the flywheel end of the crankshaft, which carries the forward end of the clutch shaft (NOTE: US English is **pilot bearing**); **spigot mounting** = unlike stud-mounted wheels, spigot-mounted wheels incorporate a centre hole in the wheel disc which is machined to provide a close-tolerance fit on the hub spigot for location

spindle *noun* rotating rod that acts as a shaft; **spindle cap** = small metal cap on the front wheel bearing

spine-back *noun* = BACKBONE CHASSIS

spin galvanizing *noun* hot dip galvanizing process for small objects

COMMENT: the objects are immersed into the molten zinc in a perforated basket which, once the coating forms, is centrifuged at high speed so that the spinning action throws off the surplus zinc and ensures a clean profile

spin imbalance *noun* = RADIAL RUN-OUT

spinner *noun* knock-off/on nut for central-locking wheels

COMMENT: originally developed by the British company Rudge-Whitworth to enable racing car wheels to be changed quickly by knocking on and off the nut with a soft-headed hammer; the wheel is positioned by matching tapered faces within the wheel centre and on its hub, the splines enabling driving or braking forces to be transmitted from hub to wheel; the spinner is a self-tightening nut with a left-hand thread for LH-side wheels and a right-hand thread for RH-side wheels; modern cars use large hexagon nuts

spinner handle *noun* screwdriver-type handle for use with sockets, used to quickly tighten and loosen fasteners

spiral bevel gear *noun* bevel gear with curved teeth in the final drive

COMMENT: unlike hypoid bevel gears in which the axis of the pinion is offset, in spiral bevel gears the pinion axis passes across the centre of the crown wheel; different designs are usually named after their respective manufacturers, i.e. Gleason-, Oerlikon- or Klingelnberg-type

spiral casing *noun* = VOLUTE CASING

◊ **spiral-type glow plug** *noun* glow plug having an exposed coil with a high number of turns

spirit level *noun* tool for testing if a surface is level (or vertical) using a glass tube containing an air bubble

splashed graphics *noun (custom paint)* paintwork resembling paint drops and splashes on the body which look as if a can of paint had been spilled over the car; also available as stickers

splash guard *noun US* = MUDFLAP

◊ **splash lubrication** *noun* oil from the crankshaft journals, under pressure from the oil pump, is splashed onto the cylinder bores and gudgeon pins to provide lubrication

◊ **splash panel** *noun* vertical closing panel mounted inside the wheel arch ahead of

the rear edge of the front wing and/or hinge area to protect these areas from splash water and road dirt

◊ **splash shield** *noun (of disc brakes)* plate which protects the inner surface of a disc from water and dirt

◊ **splash zone** *noun* sections of a car body subject to extreme corrosion loads due to water splash

splayed crankpins *noun* the slight spreading apart of a crankpin in a V-type engine so that each rod has its own crankpin; this reduces vibration in some V-6 engines that have a 90° angle between the banks

spline *noun* any one of a series of narrow slots cut down the length of a shaft (external splines) that fit into corresponding grooves in a mating part (internal splines); used to prevent movement between two parts, especially in transmitting torque *splined shaft*

◊ **splined hub** *noun* the hub of a driven plate in a clutch which is splined so that it can move along the gearbox input shaft

split bearing *noun* = SHELL BEARING; **split bearing attachment** = BEARING SEPARATOR

◊ **split collar** *noun* = COLLET

◊ **split-friction road surfaces** *noun* differing road surfaces (such as ice and tarmac) offering differing tyre adhesion

◊ **split electrode sparking plug** *noun* sparking plug with a V-shaped side electrode

◊ **split (folding) rear seats** *noun* rear seats which may be folded down in two sections, thus combining some extra luggage space with the possibility of a passenger sitting in the back of the car

◊ **split pin** *noun* metal pin for securing a nut or rod, whose ends are bent backwards after insertion

◊ **split propshaft** *noun* = DIVIDED PROPSHAFT

◊ **split screen** *noun* divided windscreen on the original Morris Minor

◊ **split skirt piston** *noun* precursor of the modern solid piston skirt, with a narrow slot in one side of the piston to allow for expansion

◊ **split spray** *noun* incorrect setup of a spray gun, giving a spray pattern that is heavy at the top and bottom but narrow in the middle

◇ **split-system master cylinder** *noun* = TANDEM MASTER CYLINDER

◇ **splitting chisel** *noun* extremely flat chisel used for body work and panel beating

◇ **split washer** *noun* = SPRING LOCK WASHER

◇ **split-window Beetle** *noun* the original VW Beetle with a 2-part rear window split vertically; produced up to 1953

spoiler *noun* generally, a wing-shaped device designed to reduce lift at high speed, but may take various forms and may be attached to the vehicle in various places; *(compare* EAR, FRONT SPOILER, REAR SPOILER, ROOF SPOILER, WHALE TAIL)

spoke *noun* **(a)** part connecting the hub of a wheel to its rim; the number and size of steering wheel spokes have been reduced over the years to improve the view of the instrument panel **(b)** = WIRE SPOKE

spoke wheel *noun* a styled, cast or forged alloy wheel with a wheel spider which incorporates a spoke design

COMMENT: spoke wheels can be distinguished according to the respective number of spokes; many alloy spoke-type wheels, however, have a wheel spider with 28, 30, 32 or 34 spokes which are arranged in different angles and in a criss-cross pattern: these are referred to as cross-spoke wheels

sponge rubber valve *noun* a sponge-rubber-lined valve plate attached to a bimetallic strip, which controls the air intake temperature to the carburettor in some BL cars

COMMENT: the bimetallic strip moves the plate up or down according to temperature, in its extreme positions, the sponge rubber seals either the cold air intake or the hot air intake

spongy lead *noun* pure lead which serves as the active material in the charged negative plates of a battery; *(compare* LEAD PEROXIDE)

spoon *noun* = BODY SPOON

sports car *or* **sportster** *noun* usually a relatively low-profile two-seater, sometimes with two spare seats in the back; emphasis is on handling and performance rather than on smooth ride

COMMENT: originally, sports cars were faster than saloons; today, many saloons can easily outperform sports cars in terms of top speed as well as acceleration; typical sports cars are roadsters and many spiders, as well as some GT models

sport utility car *noun* a new kind of recreational vehicle; combines features of buggies, off-road 4wd vehicles, and stylish sports cars for a 'life-style-conscious' market segment; first launched in the USA in 1990; *(compare* RECREATIONAL VEHICLE)

spot lamp *noun* long-range, narrow-beamed light used in addition to the headlamps

spotting in *noun* the respraying of very small areas *spotting in is a tricky business since the edge must be invisible once the paint has dried*

spot welding *noun* type of resistance welding in which two pieces of metal are joined at a series of points (spots) by means of heat (usually electrically generated) and pressure; the most important welding method in auto body construction

◇ **spot-weld drill** *noun* = SPOT-WELD REMOVER (a)

◇ **spot-welded flange** *noun* sheet metal strip forming a flange at the edge of panels joined by spot welding

◇ **spot-weld remover** *noun* **(a)** special drill bit used to drill out weld spots on sheet metal material without damaging the sheet metal material; **(b)** tool for use with a hand drill; features reversible cutting blade to cut out weld spots without damaging the sheet metal material; the cut depth can be varied, e.g. to release the upper panel only

spout *noun* = TAILPIPE

sprag clutch *noun* type of one-way clutch using spring-loaded locking cams; found in automatic gearboxes, overdrives and freewheels

spray bell *noun (painting)* dome-shaped, rotating spray element

◇ **spray coating** *noun* application method for chemical conversion coatings

◇ **spray gun** *noun (painting)* apparatus shaped like a gun which delivers an atomized mist of liquid; **spray gun nozzle cleaning unit** = special cleaning unit for paint shops which holds several spray guns in such a position that the nozzle is soaked in thinners

◊ **spray(ing) booth** *noun* closed section in a painting line in which paint is sprayed on workpieces or body shells

◊ **spraying viscosity** *noun* the viscosity required to make a paint suitable for spraying, i.e. neither too thick nor too thin

◊ **spray mist** *noun* fogging caused in the course of spray painting; part of this settles as overspray on adjacent panels and nearby objects; *(compare* OVERSPRAY, MASK)

◊ **spray pattern** *noun* the shape of the jet of spray leaving a spray gun

spread *noun* = OVERALL GEAR RATIO

spreader *noun* **(a)** hand-held tool used to apply body filler to a damaged area prepared for filling **(b)** hydraulic jack with ends designed to reach behind dented double panels and to press them back into shape by the hydraulic action of the wedge-shaped ends

◊ **spreader spring** *noun (of disc brakes)* usually cross-shaped part made of spring steel sheet which applies radial pressure to the brake pads to prevent rattling (NOTE: also called **anti-rattle springs)**

spring *noun* a coil, strip or disc of special steel, a block of rubber or a gas (e.g. air spring) which is elastic enough to absorb and give back energy

◊ **spring bar** *or* **bow** *noun (soft top)* in 5-bar hood mechanisms, an additional bar between the main bar and the rear window; spring loaded, it assists the main bar in shaping the hood; a similar effect can be achieved by spring-steel leaves embedded in the canvas

◊ **spring beating** *noun* metalworking process for removing pressure ridges in body panels in which a spring beating spoon is laid on the ridge area and is gradually moved across the ridge while the spoon surface is hammered with a body hammer; **spring beating spoon** = a light pressed-steel blade designed specially for beating on ridges; the spoon is placed directly on the ridge and sharp blows with a hammer are delivered to the back of the spoon, spreading the force over a large area

◊ **spring-biased** *adjective* = SPRING-LOADED

◊ **spring bracket** *noun* = SPRING HANGER

◊ **spring clip** *noun* **(a)** fastening device made of an incomplete circle of spring steel, e.g. for covers **(b)** rebound clip which holds the spring leaves of a leaf spring together **(c)** fastener used to provide a screw hole for a sheet metal screw; certain variants of this fastener may be moved slightly at their mounting to provide a certain degree of adjustment; *(compare* SPEED NUT)

spring compressor *noun* tool used to restrain coil springs for safe removal and installation

COMMENT: available in a variety of shapes, as manual or hydraulic designs; the most common type consists of two steel jaws running on a threaded screw which securely hook into the coil spring; turning a nut reduces the distance between the jaws and compresses the spring. This type of spring compressor is always used in pairs, e.g. to remove MacPherson strut springs

spring divider *noun* divider with a spring for accurate setting

◊ **spring eye** *noun* cylindrical hole formed by bending the end of a leaf spring round, for attachment to the vehicle

◊ **spring hanger** *noun* rubber-bushed bracket on a vehicle chassis onto which a leaf spring eye is mounted; *(compare* SHACKLE)

◊ **spring-loaded** *adjective* held in position by pressure from a spring

◊ **spring lock washer** *noun* a toothed, spring steel washer used as a locking device *spring lock washer with square ends or tang ends (see illustration 7)*

◊ **spring mounting** *noun* = SPRING HANGER

◊ **spring rate** *noun (of springs or tyres)* ratio of the load on a spring to the amount it moves (deflects), measured in newtons per millimetre; *(compare* RISING RATE SUSPENSION)

◊ **spring seat** *noun (suspension strut)* recessed mounting to accommodate a coil spring

◊ **spring shackle** *noun* = SHACKLE

◊ **spring washer** *noun* a warped-looking washer, typically used to prevent rattling by spring-loading certain movable threaded connections

◊ **spring wind-up** *noun* spring deformation under hard acceleration or deceleration

sprocket (wheel) *noun* wheel with teeth which engage in a drive chain, e.g. a timing chain

sprung mass *or* **weight** *noun* the weight of those parts of the car that are supported by the suspension system; *(compare* UNSPRUNG MASS)

spur differential *noun* differential in FWD vehicles incorporating spur gears rather than bevel gears, since input and output shafts are not at right angles; *(compare* BEVEL DIFFERENTIAL)

◊ **spur gears** *noun* gearwheels with straight teeth in line with their shafts (NOTE: also called **straight-cut gears)**

spyder *noun* = SPIDER (a)

squab *noun* a seat's backrest; **squab panel** = panel supporting the rear seat squabs, separating the passenger compartment from the luggage space; **squab shelf** = rear parcel shelf

square engine *noun* type of engine design in which the bore and stroke are the same measurement; **square-four engine** = four cylinder engine in which each cylinder axis forms one corner of a square

COMMENT: this represents a way of doubling parallel twin cylinders to make a four-cylinder unit, with two separate parallel crankshafts connected by gears or chain. This arrangement allows the engine width to be kept to that of a twin cylinder unit with only a small increase in length, thus providing the advantages of an in-line four without the problem of width. Applied in four-stroke and two-stroke motorcycles; in two-strokes mainly to permit rotary valve induction

square key *noun* parallel feather key with square end faces; a plain milling cutter is used to cut the keyway for the square key

squat *noun* dipping of a car's rear end occurring during hard acceleration, due to a load transfer from the front to the rear suspension; *(compare* ANTI-SQUAT SYSTEM, BRAKE DIVE)

squib *noun* device for detonating the air bag

squirt box *noun (informal)* carburettor

squish band *or* **zone** *noun* narrow section of a combustion chamber in which the fuel charge is more compressed by the piston than in the rest of the chamber; designed to help direct the flow of the fresh charge and to improve scavenging

sr = SUNROOF

SRS *(short for)* supplementary restraint system; air bag; **SRS warning light** = air bag warning light

SR sheathed glow plug *noun* = SELF-REGULATING SHEATHED-TYPE GLOW PLUG

SS = STAINLESS STEEL

SSC = STRESS CORROSION CRACKING

stab braking *noun* = CADENCE BRAKING

stabilize *verb* to make or keep stable

stabilizer (bar) *noun* = ANTI-ROLL BAR

◊ **stabilizer belt** *noun (of belted radial tyres)* belt consisting of cords (usually fine steel wire) embedded in rubber directly beneath the tread and above the radial cord body plies

◊ **stabilizer link** *noun (suspension)* link which connects the anti-roll bar to the lower wishbone

stainless steel (SS) *noun* type of steel containing nickel and chromium, which is resistant to corrosion; **stainless-steel exhaust system** = more hard-wearing and therefore more expensive system than one made of mild steel; **stainless-steel mesh** = WIRE MESH

stake *noun* a panel-beating tool formed like a dolly, but with a shaft attached allowing it to be clamped in a vice

◊ **staked nut** *noun* nut secured to a bolt with a metal tab (e.g. a wheel bearing adjusting nut)

stalk *noun* = CONTROL STALK

stall *verb (of an engine)* to stop unintentionally

COMMENT: usual causes of stalling are: sudden increase in load without an accompanying increase in fuel flow (often occurring when a driver engages the clutch to drive away without increasing the engine speed) and braking to a very low speed without disengaging the clutch

stall speed *noun* test characteristic of a fluid converter; result of the stall test

◇ **stall test** *noun (automatic transmission)* short-time (5 seconds) full throttle operation with the vehicle brakes fully applied and the selector lever in 'D' position; the test results in an engine speed (stall speed) that indicates the performance of the fluid converter

◇ **stall torque ratio** *noun* torque conversion in fluid converters on taking up drive, i.e. when the turbine is still stationary; stage of maximum torque multiplication

standard equipment *noun* those parts and systems of a vehicle supplied by the manufacturer at no extra cost, i.e. they are included in the basic price for a given model *alloy wheels are provided as standard equipment on the XYZ* (NOTE: opposite is **optional equipment**); **standard wheel** = original wheel on a vehicle supplied by the car manufacturer (NOTE: opposite is **custom wheel**)

standing start *noun* one method of acceleration testing in which the vehicle starts from rest

Stanyl *noun* a new proprietary polyamide with unusual temperature stability, mechanical strength, and resistance to oil and grease

start *verb* to use the starter motor to crank the engine until it fires and runs on its own; **start boosting** = bypassing the ballast resistor of an ignition system when starting the engine; **start bypass** = bypass of the ballast resistor

starter (motor) *noun* powerful electric motor that engages with the flywheel to turn an internal combustion engine which begins the induction of fuel and the ignition cycle

COMMENT: invented in 1911, the starter replaced manual crank-starting by an electric motor and thus made it easier for women (and men!) to start and drive cars

starter inhibitor switch *or* **starter interlock** *or* **starter lockout** *noun* switch which prevents starting of the engine

unless certain system conditions are fulfilled; e.g. on cars with automatic transmission, the selector lever must be in Neutral or Park

◇ **starter punch** *noun* tool used to start the removal of pins, shafts or rivets by breaking them loose; longer and thinner than a drift punch

◇ **starter ring gear** *noun* a gear fitted around the flywheel that is engaged by teeth on the starter drive to crank the engine

◇ **starter solenoid** *noun* assembly of a pre-engaged starter used first to engage the pinion teeth with the flywheel ring gear and then to switch on the starter current; *(see illustration 37)*

◇ **starter switch control cable** *noun* mechanical cable to the starter switch on vehicles without a starter solenoid (e.g. Fiat 500)

◇ **start from rest** *verb* to drive off from a standing start

◇ **starting carburettor** *noun* usually a simple slide carburettor which works in parallel with the main carburettor and acts as a starting aid

◇ **starting handle** *noun* cranked handle for turning an engine over manually

◇ **starting interlock** *noun* = STARTER INHIBITOR SWITCH

◇ **starting switch** *noun* on certain classic cars, separate switches are used to turn the ignition on and to operate the starter; on such cars, the starting switch was a push button, often located in the centre of the dashboard; on modern cars, the starting switch is integrated in the ignition and starter switch

star wheel *noun* adjusting nut on a drum brake or clutch

static balancing *noun* checking a wheel's balance by seeing if it stops in the same position when rotated; if it does, a small weight is attached to the rim opposite the heavy area (i.e. opposite the bottom of the wheel when it stops rotating). A tyre and wheel assembly is in static balance when the weight of the wheel is evenly distributed around the axis of rotation (NOTE: opposite is **dynamic balancing**)

◇ **static belt** *noun* seat belt with no automatic belt retractor and whose length is manually adjusted; *(compare* INERTIA REEL SEAT BELT)

◇ **static friction** *see* STICTION

◊ **static high-voltage distribution** *noun* high-voltage distribution achieved without a rotary distributor, using multi-spark ignition coils or one coil per sparking plug

◊ **static (ignition) timing** *noun* now obsolete timing procedure carried out by rotating the engine until the timing marks are aligned and then connecting a test lamp or a voltmeter between the negative coil terminal and earth; when the points open, the test lamp lights up or the voltmeter registers battery voltage (NOTE: opposite is **dynamic** or **stroboscopic ignition timing**)

◊ **static seal** *noun* oil seal between two stationary parts (NOTE: opposite is **dynamic seal**)

station wagon *noun US* estate car

stator *noun* **(a)** *(of an alternator)* the stationary windings in which electric current is generated; located between drive end and slip-ring end fittings, consisting of a stator frame with windings in three circuits to generate three-phase current which is then rectified by diodes; *(compare* ROTOR (d)) *(see illustration 36)* **(b)** *(magnetic pick-up assembly)* self-contained unit of the magnetic pick-up, consisting of a permanent magnet, an inductive winding and the pick-up core; the stator can be a disc-shaped pole piece with stator tooth or a simple pole piece **(c)** *(fluid converter, automatic transmission)* wheel with curved blades (sometimes adjustable) mounted on a one-way clutch; it serves as a reaction member, i.e. it multiplies the torque output of the turbine by increasing the momentum of the fluid flow acting on the latter; *(compare* IMPELLER (b), TURBINE WHEEL)

◊ **stator roller clutch** *noun (fluid converter)* holds the stator stationary as long as its blades are struck by the fluid flow against the rotational direction of pump and turbine; if the fluid flows in the direction of rotation, the stator starts running

Stealth Bra *noun* nose covering composed of composite materials that absorb microwaves emitted by radar devices and significantly diminish the return signal, making a car less detectable to police radar; ineffective against speed cameras or light-operated speed guns; *(compare* NOSE PROTECTOR)

steam clean *verb* to clean the engine with a high-pressure jet of steam

◊ **steam injection system** *noun* based on the same principle as water injection systems, the steam injection system uses engine exhaust heat and a boiler to pre-heat and boil the water before it is injected into the inlet manifold as steam

steel *noun* an alloy of iron containing a small percentage of carbon *steel belted radial tyre* **steel backing** = the supporting part of a plain bearing insert; **steel strip** = sheet steel less than 600 mm wide; **steel thrust belt** = a large number of steel plates with slots in each side to receive the two composite steel bands which hold them together; transmits torque between two pulleys; **steel wheel** = consists of a steel disc and steel rim which are welded together to provide better impact-resistance, lower price, and higher weight than alloy wheels; *(compare* ALLOY WHEELS, SHEET WHEEL)

steering *noun* general term encompassing all components of the steering system or the steering function of a vehicle; *(see illustration 25)*

◊ **steering angle** *noun* horizontal angle between the plane of a steered wheel when cornering, and the plane when adjusted straight ahead *steering angle sensor*

◊ **steering arm** *noun* a forged lever attached to the steering knuckle and to one of the tie rods; *(see illustrations 25, 26)*

◊ **steering axis** *noun* = KINGPIN AXIS; **steering axis inclination (SAI)** = KINGPIN INCLINATION (KPI)

◊ **steering box** *noun* the part of the steering system that is located at the lower end of the steering shaft; changes the rotary movement of the steering wheel into the linear motion of the front wheels for steering; *(see illustration 25)*

◊ **steering column** *noun* shaft between the steering wheel and steering box or rack and pinion; **steering column controls** = consist mainly of control stalks for some or all of the following: lights, windscreen wipers and washers, direction indicators and horn; **steering column gearchange** = COLUMN GEARCHANGE

◊ **steering damper** *noun* a shock-absorber-like bump stop which absorbs vibrations in the steering system

◊ **steering gear** *noun* (i) the whole mechanism by which a vehicle is steered; (ii) the gears in this mechanism; **steering gear arm** = DROP ARM; **steering gearbox** =

STEERING BOX; **steering gear shaft** = the rotating, torque-transmitting part of the steering column; *(see illustrations 25, 26)*

◇ **steering geometry** *noun* the geometric arrangement of the components and linkages of a steering system, incorporating various steering angles

◇ **steering kickback** *noun* sharp and rapid movements of the steering wheel as the front wheels encounter obstruction in the road; the shocks of these encounters 'kick back' to the steering wheel

◇ **steering knuckle** *noun* the part of the front suspension on which a front wheel is mounted; strictly speaking, an assembly or single component comprising stub axle and steering arm, stub axle often being used to describe the steering knuckle itself; *(see illustrations 26, 31)*; **steering knuckle arm** = STEERING ARM

◇ **steering linkage** *noun* all parts conveying movement from the rack or steering box to the steering swivels (e.g. track rods and steering arms)

◇ **steering lock** *noun* **(a)** lock that stops the steering wheel being turned when the ignition is switched fully off **(b)** = LOCK (b)

◇ **steering ratio** *noun* the number of degrees that the steering wheel must be turned to pivot the front wheels one degree

◇ **steering support (structure)** *noun* mounting locations and reinforcements for fitting the steering box to the bulkhead or side member

◇ **steering swivel** *noun* = STEERING KNUCKLE; **steering-swivel axis** = SWIVEL AXIS; **steering-swivel inclination** = = KINGPIN INCLINATION

◇ **steering system** *noun* = STEERING

◇ **steering wheel** *noun* wheel which is turned by the driver to control the direction of the vehicle; *(see illustrations 25, 26)*; **steering wheel and brake lock** = anti-theft device in the form of an extendable steel rod that engages in a spoke of the steering wheel and the brake or clutch pedal; when locked, neither wheel nor pedal can be operated; **steering wheel balance** = measures the steering wheel angle in an automatic steering wheel centring system; **steering wheel centring** = adjusts the steering wheel and steering system so that the wheel is in its centre position when the front wheels are pointing straight ahead; **steering wheel damper** = STEERING DAMPER; **steering wheel puller** = special puller for removing steering wheels

Stellite *noun* proprietary range of very hard, wear-resistant alloys containing cobalt, chromium, carbon, tungsten and molybdenum; used for tools, castings, valve seat inserts, coating exhaust valves, etc.

stem seal *noun* valve stem seal between the valve and cylinder head

step *noun* ledge formed by an edge setter in a sheet metal panel to provide a level mounting and welding surface with the adjacent panel

◇ **step feeler gauge** *noun* feeler gauge with metal feeler blades; the thickness of the blade increases from one end of the blade to the other

◇ **stepless transmission** *noun* = CONTINUOUSLY VARIABLE TRANSMISSION

◇ **stepped compression ring** *noun* = L-SECTION RING

◇ **stepped piston** *noun* an obsolete design of two-stroke pistons; the diameter of the lower part of the piston was larger than the top diameter; it ran in a similarly stepped bore and was said to give better compression of the incoming mixture

◇ **stepped planet gear** *noun* planet gear with different diameters

◇ **stepper motor** *noun* on some carburettor cars, stepper motors are used to adjust the air/fuel mixture; they are controlled by the ECM

◇ **step plate** *noun* **(a)** small step for climbing into a vehicle (e.g. on an ATV or RV) **(b)** = SCUFF PLATE

◇ **step steering input** *noun* rapid change in steering angle, for example when a steered wheel hits an obstacle

sticker price *noun US* manufacturer's suggested retail price (as displayed on an affixed sticker), usually subject to a negotiable discount

sticking *noun (welding)* fusing of the electrode to the surface of the piece being worked on, mainly at the beginning of the welding cycle

stick shift *noun US* gearchange with a gear lever

sticky clutch *noun* = CLUTCH DRAG

stiction *noun* shortened form of static friction; the frictional force which must be overcome to set one object in motion when it is in contact with another *driven plate stiction*

stiff *adjective* not easily bent or turned

COMMENT: as opposed to a rigid object, a stiff object does not break when subjected to bending stress, and implies a certain degree of flexibility; a bridge, for example, is stiff, not rigid, and steel panels are inherently stiff; however, a particularly high degree of stiffness, e.g. when steel panels are shaped to a load-carrying structure, is sometimes referred to as rigid

stiffness under flexure *noun* a measure of the resistance offered by a test specimen to its tendency to bend under the action of forces (own weight)

◊ **stiff nut** *noun* = SELF-LOCKING NUT

still-air pocket *noun* area of relatively turbulence-free air immediately behind the windscreen of convertibles with the hood down

Stillson wrench *noun* very large heavy-duty adjustable wrench

stink-bomb smell *noun* = ROTTEN-EGG SMELL

Stirling engine *noun* an external combustion engine that uses air or an inert gas as the working fluid operating on a highly efficient thermodynamic cycle

COMMENT: the heat released from the burning fuel is transferred to the confined gas (such as hydrogen) which activates the pistons; named after the Scottish engineer, Robert Stirling (1790-1878)

stirring paddle *noun* component of the agitator of a paint power mixer

stirrup bolt *noun* = U-BOLT

stock car *noun* production car (usually a saloon) modified for a form of racing in which the cars often (deliberately) collide

stoichiometric *adjective* having the exact proportions for a particular chemical reaction; **stoichiometric ratio** = in a spark-ignition engine, the ideal air/fuel mixture ratio of 14.7:1, which must be maintained on

engines with dual-bed and three-way catalytic converters; *(compare* AIR RATIO)

stone chip damage *noun* paintwork defect caused by gravel or stones

◊ **stone deflector** *or* **stone guard** *or* **stone shield** *noun* separate panel fitted below the front bumper or on the leading edge of the rear wing to provide protection from rocks, dirt, etc.

stop *noun* component which limits the motion, travel or stroke of a moving part (NOTE: a more informal word for **abutment)**

◊ **stop light** *noun* **(a)** = BRAKE LIGHT **(b)** red light on a traffic signal indicating that vehicles should stop

stopper *noun* filler or putty used for filling holes, dents, etc.

◊ **stopper plate** *noun* = REED STOP

stopping distance *noun* the total amount of time (translated into distance) a vehicle and driver need in which to come to a halt; the shortest stopping distance is the reaction (or thinking) distance (of the driver) added to the braking distance (of the vehicle)

storage battery *noun* a rechargeable single cell or connected group of two or more storage cells such as the type used in vehicles (NOTE: opposite is **primary battery)**

◊ **storage cell** *noun* an electrolytic cell for generating electric energy; rechargeable by sending a current through it in the opposite direction to the discharging current

stove *verb* to dry a coat of paint in heat

◊ **stoving** *noun* process of drying or curing a paint coating by the application of heat; immediately after stoving, the paint film is still soft, taking some time to harden

straight-cut gear *noun* = SPUR GEAR

◊ **straightedge** *noun* rule-type tool without graduation for checking, e.g. warp of cylinder block and head

◊ **straight eight** *noun* an eight-cylinder in-line engine

◊ **straightened panel** *noun* a panel brought into its original shape with hammer and dolly or straightening equipment

◊ **straight engine** *noun* = IN-LINE ENGINE

◇ **straightening bench** *noun* workbench or fixture equipped to hold single panels such as doors or bonnets for straightening and metalworking jobs; **straightening kit** *or* **set** = power jacks used to straighten localized body damage, essentially comprising special ram cylinders, pumps, attachments, and extensions

◇ **straight-line stability** *noun* = DIRECTIONAL STABILITY

◇ **straight pattern snips** *noun* snips with cutting blades designed for straight cuts on sheet metal material

◇ **straight six** *noun* a six-cylinder in-line engine

◇ **straight-through side styling** *noun* = ALL-ENVELOPING BODY

◇ **straight-through silencer** *noun* type of absorption silencer with a single perforated tube surrounded by sound-absorbing fibre which creates less back pressure and consequent loss of power than other types

◇ **straight weight (engine) oil** *noun* = SINGLE-GRADE (ENGINE) OIL

strainer *noun* wire mesh filter, as used in an oil pump strainer in the sump

strain in the drive train *noun* strains resulting from the different track arcs travelled by the four wheels of a vehicle when cornering with centre or axle differentials locked up

strand *noun* one of a number of wires twisted together to form an electrical conductor or cable *7-strand sparking plug lead*

strangler *noun* (*informal*) old name for choke

strap drive *noun* drive transmitted from the clutch cover to the clutch pressure plate in diaphragm spring and coil spring clutches, using flexible spring-steel straps attached to the clutch cover

◇ **strap wrench** *noun* tool for loosening and tightening round or irregularly shaped objects such as oil filters, featuring a strap which is wrapped around the object, and a lever or key by means of which the object is turned

stratified charge *noun* in a SI engine, an air/fuel charge which consists mainly of a lean mixture and a small layer or pocket of rich mixture; the rich mixture is ignited first, then ignition spreads to the leaner mixture filling the rest of the combustion chamber *stratified charge engine*

straw *noun* convenient DIY tool for blowing debris from the sparking plug recess before plug removal

streak *noun* a long thin trace of dirt *a damaged wiper blade will leave streaks and smears on the windscreen*

streamline *verb* to design the shape of a car body or lorry cab so that it reduces air resistance to a minimum

street car *noun US* = TRAM (CAR)

◇ **street version** *noun* a detuned version, usually of a racing car

strength *noun* the stress at which material ruptures or fails; (*compare* BENDING STRENGTH, TENSILE STRENGTH)

stress *noun* force causing deformation or strain *stress and strain diagram* **stress concentration** = a condition in which a stress distribution has high localized stresses; usually induced by an abrupt change in the shape of a member (often in the vicinity of notches etc.); **stress corrosion cracking (SSC)** = cracking due to stress corrosion, a process involving joint corrosion and straining of a metal due to residual or applied stresses; **stress cracking** *or* **fracturing** = damage of parts, especially body panels, subject to constant overload caused by improper mounting; this introduces strain into the panels, causing them eventually to crack

stretch limo *noun* (*informal*) limousine that has been lengthened to provide extra seating and more legroom

striker *noun* the mating part of door lock or bonnet latch mechanism which is secured to the body; the striker itself has no mechanism and provides only the anchor for the door or bonnet latch; typical strikers are stud or U-shaped; **striker plate** = anchor plate to which the striker is attached

◇ **striking blow** *noun* dent removal technique in which the hammer does not hit the panel straight on but is drawn to one side on hitting the surface, thus spreading the impact over a larger area

strip *verb* to tear off or break the thread from a screw, bolt, etc. or the teeth from a gear

striper *noun* = PINSTRIPING TOOL

strobe lamp/light *noun (informal)* = STROBOSCOPE

◊ **stroboscope** *noun* = TIMING LIGHT

◊ **stroboscopic ignition timing** *noun* = DYNAMIC IGNITION TIMING

stroke 1 *noun* **(a)** any of a series of continuous, often reciprocating, movements; a cycle **(b)** in a reciprocating engine, the distance between the highest and lowest points reached by the piston **2** *verb* to modify the stroke of an engine, by using a different crankshaft to increase or reduce displacement; stroking normally refers to an increase in cc *the engine was stroked from 1.8 to 2 litres*

Stromberg carburettor *noun* a type of variable venturi carburettor; *(see illustration 12)*

structural part *noun* any part of a vehicle that plays a role in ensuring the rigidity and integrity of the vehicle as a whole and that, if it collapses, could make the vehicle unsafe

strut *noun* **(a)** a structural member, especially as part of a framework, used to stiffen, give strength or carry weight **(b)** = SUSPENSION STRUT **(c)** bar that connects the lower control arm to the car frame; used when the lower control arm is attached to the frame at only one point **(d)** = GAS PROP

◊ **strut rod** *noun* = PUSH BAR

stub axle *noun* short axle that carries one of the front wheels and has limited angular movement about a kingpin

◊ **stubby screwdriver** *noun* = CHUBBY SCREWDRIVER

stud *noun* **(a)** threaded fastener without a head; similar to a grub screw, but with an unthreaded portion roughly in the middle; typically used for nut and stud assembly of alloy parts, e.g. to attach manifolds to alloy cylinder heads or to secure the cylinder head to the cylinder block. The stud is screwed into a threaded hole until the run-out threads in the metal of the stud jam in the first thread in the hole; studs should never reach the bottom of the hole; *(see illustration 7)*; **stud end** = opposite end of a stud to the nut end; **stud extractor** *or* **remover** = tool like a socket spanner for the removal (and installation) of studs **(b)** bolt projecting from a plate, like a wheel stud; **stud hole** = hole in a wheel through which the wheel studs pass; *(see illustration 33)* **(c)** projecting pin or peg attached to the tread of a snow tyre to improve traction *studded tyre*

stuffing box *noun* = PACKED GLAND; **stuffing-box packing** = sealing element of a stuffing box consisting of rings of tissue (e.g. cotton) or metal rings

STV = SUCTION THROTTLING VALVE

subassembly *noun* an assembled unit designed to be fitted to a larger unit of which it is a component; e.g. the steering gear and front suspension or the final drive and rear suspension

subcompact (car) *noun* American car category with an overall length less than 14ft 7in and a wheelbase less than 8ft 4in; FWD or 4wd; *(compare* COMPACT CAR*)*

COMMENT: subcompacts range from tiny, economical commuter cars to plush, sporty convertibles; nearly all have 4-cylinder engines, a few have 3-cylinder engines and some are available with a V-6. Some typical subcompacts are: Audi 80, BMW 3 series, BMW 850 coupé, Mercedes-Benz 190, Suzuki Swift

subframe *noun* a strong, detachable assembly that is mounted to the underbody of the car to support the engine, accessories, drive train and/or running gear

submarining *noun* sliding under the lap belt in a frontal collision

subplate *noun* = DISTRIBUTOR BASEPLATE

subsidiary petal *noun* secondary petal of a dual-stage reed valve (NOTE: opposite is **main petal**)

substrate *noun* surface or layer on a material serving as a base for another layer or coat; e.g. base material or base metal *the filler is applied as a substrate for the top paint coat* *(compare* CATALYST SUBSTRATE*)*

substructure *noun* = UNDERBODY (STRUCTURE)

SU carburettor *noun* widely used type of variable venturi carburettor; *(see illustration 13)*

COMMENT: named after Skinners' Union, a long-established manufacturer of variable venturi carburettors; the first SU carburettor was patented in 1905 by George Herbert Skinner who went on to found a company with his two brothers to manufacture SU carburettors

suction chamber *noun* space above the piston in the piston chamber of a variable venturi carburettor *suction chamber cover (see illustrations 12, 13)*

◊ **suction cup dent puller** *noun* = VACUUM SUCTION CUP

◊ **suction-feed spray gun** *noun* type of spray gun with a paint pot mounted underneath

suction lift *noun* *(pump)* the vertical distance, in feet, from the liquid supply level to the pump centreline, the pump being above the liquid level

COMMENT: suction lift should not exceed the recommended maximum limit and when viscous fluids are being pumped, they should be avoided altogether

suction line *or* **pipe** *noun* pipe on the suction side of a pumping system leading from the suction tank to the pump; *(compare* INLET LINE)

◊ **suction side** *noun* that side of a pumping system or pump at which the liquid to be pumped enters the suction line or pump casing; *(see illustration 17)* (NOTE: opposite is **discharge side)**

suction throttling valve (STV) *noun* valve located at the evaporator outlet which controls evaporator pressure and temperature

COMMENT: when evaporator pressure rises, the STV releases pressure into the low-pressure vapour line to the compressor, thereby preventing core icing; a modification of the STV is the POA suction throttling valve

suction valve grinder *noun* = VALVE GRINDING TOOL

suicide door *noun* *(informal)* a rear-hinged door

sump *noun* metal bowl (usually of sheet steel or cast alloy) attached to the bottom of the crankcase, into which oil drains to form a reservoir; typically carries one gallon of motor oil; *(see illustrations 3, 5)* (NOTE: US English is **oil pan**); **sump (drain) plug** = short fat bolt for draining the sump (when removed); **sump gasket** = gasket fitted between the cylinder block and the sump; **sump guard** = shield fitted under the engine to protect the sump

sun car *noun* *(informal)* = SOLAR CAR

◊ **sun gear** *or* **sun wheel** *noun* central spur gear in a planetary gear set meshing with the planet gears; *(see illustration 21)*

◊ **sunroof (sr)** *noun* panel (often translucent) in the roof of a car which may be tilted or slid open, either manually or electrically to provide extra light and/or ventilation *electric sunroof (esr); pop-up or sliding sunroof (see illustration 1)*; **sunroof aperture panel** = panel which accommodates the sunroof guide rails and draining channels and fits below the roof panel; *(see illustration 1)*; **sunroof deflector shield** = shield or visor that can be attached to the front of the sunroof to deflect the wind; **sunroof top** = a folding canvas sunroof

◊ **sunshield** *noun* tinted strip of transparent vinyl attached to the top of the windscreen to cut glare from the sun (NOTE: also called a **windscreen shadeband)**

◊ **sun visor** *noun* **(a)** hinged flap above the windscreen that can be pulled down to shield the driver's or front seat passenger's eyes from sunlight; often contains a vanity mirror on the inside **(b)** body accessory mounted on the outside of the windscreen on pick-up trucks, lorries, RVs; in the 1960s a short-lived fad on cars - not at all aerodynamic

◊ **sun wheel** *see* SUN GEAR

super *noun* petrol with a high octane rating, typically 98

supercharge *verb* **(a)** to increase the intake pressure of an internal combustion engine with a supercharger *supercharged engine* **(b)** *(pressure-wave effect on two-stroke engines)* to tune the exhaust pressure in such a manner that the pressure wave propagating back to the exhaust port arrives there as soon as the transfer ports close, thus pushing the final amount of fresh charge that has already escaped into the exhaust back into the cylinder

◊ **supercharger** *noun* device such as a positive displacement compressor or dynamic compressor used to improve the volumetric efficiency and power output of internal combustion engines by raising the intake pressure, thus increasing the amount of air drawn in; *(compare* ROOTS SUPERCHARGER) (NOTE: largely superseded in cars by the **turbocharger)**

supplementary inflatable restraint (SIR) *or* **supplementary restraint system (SRS)** *noun* air bag

suppressor *noun* electrical device used in car circuits to damp out and filter out radio or TV interference caused mainly by the ignition system and battery circuit

surface discharge plug *noun* = SURFACE GAP SPARKING PLUG

◇ **surface gap** *noun* spark gap of a surface gap sparking plug in which the sparks glide over the insulator-filled gap (NOTE: opposite is **spark air gap**); **surface gap sparking plug** = type of sparking plug in which the spark is fired across the insulator surface between the centre electrode and the shell; there is no side electrode

◇ **surface ignition** *noun* ignition initiated by hot spots in the engine cylinder rather than by a timed spark

◇ **surface-mounted speaker** *noun* speaker mounted on top of the bearing surface (NOTE: opposite is **flush-mounted speaker)**

◇ **surface resistance** *noun* the electrical resistance of the surface of an insulator

◇ **surface spoon** *noun* special body spoon with a relatively long, smooth working surface set at a steep angle to the handle

surface tack *noun* a condition occurring after filler is applied to a panel surface, characterized by the fact that the filler will not cure in certain places

COMMENT: this may be caused by improper mixing of the filler paste with the hardener, insufficient curing time or insufficient hardener being used

surface-type filter *noun* filter design in which particles accumulate on the surface, e.g. of a folded paper element; typical design of air and cartridge-type oil filters

surge *noun* unevenness in the power output of an engine caused by: (i) irregular fuel supply due to the clogging of a filter or a main jet, or to too lean an air/fuel mixture; (ii) an ignition fault due to misfiring

suspension *noun* **(a)** system of springs, arms and dampers which supports the body of a vehicle and insulates it and its occupants from road shocks transmitted by the wheels *active suspension; air suspension; double wishbone suspension; four-/five-link rear suspension; hydropneumatic suspension; independent suspension; rising rate suspension; sliding-pillar suspension* **(b)** mixture of fine, non-settling particles of any solid within a liquid or gas

COMMENT; the particles are the dispersed phase, while the suspending medium is the continuous phase; used engine oil, for example, is a suspension with suspended combustion residues which produce a blackish appearance

suspension aids *noun* accessories designed to reinforce the rear suspension when carrying heavy loads or towing caravans or trailers; they include: extra, single-leaf springs, coil springs, and heavy duty spring dampers

◇ **suspension link** *noun* any arm which links the chassis to the axle; *(compare* LEADING ARM, SEMI-TRAILING LINK, TRAILING ARM, TRANSVERSE LINK, WISHBONE)

◇ **suspension mounting** *noun* sheet metal parts, bores, etc. on the underbody designed to locate the axles and springs on the body

◇ **suspension sphere** *noun* pressurized, nitrogen-filled sphere used in hydropneumatic suspension systems

◇ **suspension strut** *noun* unitary construction of spring and damper elements; depending on whether the hub carrier is mounted to the spring or the damper element, the suspension strut is referred to either as a damper strut or as a MacPherson strut

◇ **suspension subframe** *noun* suspension layout absorbing noise and vibration, in which all suspension elements are mounted on an insulated, detachable suspension subframe

◇ **suspension turret web** *noun* reinforcement supporting the MacPherson strut at the lower side of the strut tower panel; this allows the strut to rest against the top strut mounting from below

SV engine *noun* = SIDE-VALVE ENGINE

SW *(short for)* switch; to be found on the coil terminal connected to the ignition switch

swage line *noun* narrow profiled line in outer body panels, e.g. above the upper edge of the wheel cutouts, that helps to enhance the flowing lines of the bodywork

swash plate *noun* a rotating disc or face plate on a shaft that is inclined at an oblique angle to the axis of rotation and either imparts reciprocating motion to push rods or plungers parallel to the shaft axis, as in a swash plate pump or, conversely, converts reciprocating motion to rotation (replacing the crankshaft), as in a swash plate motor

sway bar *noun US* = ANTI-ROLL BAR

sweeper *noun* a type of seal used along moving surfaces, e.g. door windows, that is often provided with a lip to ensure sealing; *(compare* WINDOW WEATHERSTRIP)

swelling *noun* **(a)** *(paint fault)* condition that occurs when an excessively rapid thinner is used in a paint and the soft paint sinks into cuts **(b)** *(of plastics)* an increase of volume conditioned by the absorption of liquids, vapours or gases in the coating film

swept volume *noun* that part of the cylinder capacity that is swept by the pistons on their up and down strokes, i.e. the volume through which a piston moves in one stroke, formed by the bore diameter and the piston stroke

swing arm suspension *or* **swing axle** *noun* independent suspension system in which each axle pivots near the centre of the vehicle and the movement of the axle changes the angle of camber

◇ **swinging caliper** *noun* a type of floating caliper with wedge-shaped disc pads (only one of which is activated by hydraulic pressure from the piston, the other being fixed), which can pivot on its hinge pin to equalize the pressure on both pads

◇ **swinging shackle** *noun* = SHACKLE

swirl *noun* rotary or swirling motion given to the charge mixture as it enters a cylinder by offsetting the inlet tract; **swirl chamber** = small chamber or cavity in the cylinder head to promote swirl in the indirect injection combustion system of a diesel engine *swirl-chamber diesel engine*

◇ **swirl marks** *noun* circular pattern produced by an orbital sander on a paint surface; it must be hand-sanded with a sandpaper of finer grit, otherwise it will remain visible through the respray coat

swivel 1 *verb* to turn or swing about a point **2** *noun* = STEERING KNUCKLE

◇ **swivel angle** *noun* = KINGPIN INCLINATION

◇ **swivel axis** *noun* = KINGPIN AXIS; **swivel axis inclination** = KINGPIN INCLINATION

◇ **swivel pin** *noun* = KINGPIN

symmetric rim *noun* rim type in which the rim well is located symmetrically on the wheel centreline (NOTE: opposite is **asymmetric rim)**

synchromesh *noun* device in manual gearboxes that automatically matches the rotating speeds of transmission gears as they are about to mesh; *(compare* CONSTANT-MESH GEARBOX, LOCKING SYNCHROMESH)

synchronize *verb* to make two things happen at the same time, or to move at the same speed

◇ **synchronizer** *noun* device which synchronizes

synchronous motor *noun* an alternating-current motor that runs at a speed that is equal to or is a multiple of the frequency of the supply (e.g. the drive motor of electric powered vehicles)

synergetic *or* **synergistic effect** *noun* protective effect occurring as a result of the combination of a metallic and an additional organic coating

synthesizer *noun* device which generates quartz-controlled frequency steps in a PLL circuit

synthetic engine oil *noun* non-petroleum based oil; more expensive than mineral oil but more resistant to breakdown at high temperatures and less viscous at low temperatures

◇ **synthetic rubber** *noun* synthetic products with properties similar to those of natural rubber, including elasticity and ability to be vulcanized; usually produced by the polymerization or copolymerization of petroleum-derived olefins or other unsaturated compounds

system pressure regulator *noun (K-jetronic)* basically a pressure relief valve located on the fuel distributor; *(see illustration 14)*

◇ **system scanner** *noun* = MESSAGE CENTRE

Tt

T letter on the sidewall of a tyre denoting the maximum speed for which it is designed (190 km/h or 118 mph); *(see* SPEED RATING)

tab *noun* **(a)** small projecting part as on a tab washer, or on a gasket where it engages with another seal **(b)** not a continuous flange as provided at the top mounting of a wing, but a short flange section to provide localized fitting of one panel to another

◇ **tab washer** *noun* washer with a tab that may be hammered against a flat side of a nut, or into a hole in the surface, or over an edge, in order to secure the nut to the surface on which it bears

TAC = THERMOSTATIC AIR CLEANER

tachograph *or (informal)* **tacho** *noun* a tachometer that produces a graphical record of its readings, especially used to record the speed and distance covered by a heavy goods vehicle (thus theoretically making it easier to check on a driver's speed and the length of time spent driving between rest periods)

◇ **tachometer** *or (informal)* **tach(o)** *noun* instrument in the instrument panel, electronically operated by the ignition system, which indicates engine rpm with an analogue or digital read-out; red areas indicate dangerous engine operating speeds; *(compare* SPEEDOMETER) (NOTE: also informally called a **rev counter**)

tack cloth *or* **tack rag** *noun* special cloth used to wipe sanded panels prior to spraying in order to remove even minute dust particles and other foreign substances from the panel surface

◇ **tack welding** *or* **tacking** *noun* attaching a panel provisionally by placing a few spots of weld along its outline; final spot or seam welding is only carried out afterwards

TAC system *noun* contact breaker ignition system developed by Lucas, controlled by two transistors, one serving as a power output transistor

tail *noun* the rear

◇ **tailboard** *noun* board at the rear of a lorry or pick-up that can be removed or let down on a hinge; *(compare* TAILGATE)

tail fin *noun* vertical fin on the back of the rear wings

| COMMENT: stimulated by a Lockheed P38 fighter plane, Cadillac introduced tail fins on a coupé in 1948; they were a fashion until the 1960s

tailgate *noun* estate cars and most hatchback saloons feature a large rear lid that includes the rear window and opens to give access to the whole interior; *(compare* TAILBOARD) *(see illustration 1)* (NOTE: US English is **lift gate**)

| COMMENT: 'tailgate' is applicable to all versions, irrespective of the location of the hinges, i.e. at the top, bottom or side; it also refers to pick-ups; a hatch refers to hatchback saloons and coupés only, not to pick-ups or estate cars

tailgating *noun* driving so close to the vehicle in front as to be affected by its slipstream; a very dangerous practice as available reaction time is reduced to a minimum

◇ **tail heavy** *adjective* description of the towing vehicle if the vehicle being towed is too heavy

◇ **tail lift** *see* BRAKE DIVE

◇ **tail light** *or* **lamp** *noun* red rear light that illuminates as soon as the lights are switched on, to indicate the presence of a vehicle from the rear

tail light box *noun* a deep-drawn panel spot-welded into the tail light aperture to take the complete tail light cluster; **tail (light) panel** = REAR PANEL; **tail light surround** = REAR LIGHT SURROUND

| COMMENT: a tail light box provides better corrosion protection for the electrical connections of the tail light than would be

possible by installing the tail light with a rubber seal into the open light aperture

tailpipe *noun* last pipe of the exhaust system which fits behind the silencer and extends to the rear of the vehicle *insert the probe into the tailpipe; tailpipe extension (see illustration 19)*; **tailpipe expander** = special automotive tool used for reshaping and expanding tailpipes evenly, to assure a tight fit and prevent exhaust leaks

◊ **tailshaft** *noun* = GEARBOX OUTPUT SHAFT

take up *verb (clutch)* to begin to transmit the drive when the clutch is engaged *a fierce clutch tends to take up suddenly*

◊ **take-up** *noun* the act of taking up *a sharp take-up of the drive causes a sudden jerk*

talc *noun* a soft mineral; a basic magnesium silicate usually occurring in foliated, granular, or fibrous masses, used in the manufacture of electrical insulators

talking warning system *noun* using the car radio speakers, this microprocessor-based system tells the driver the source of the problem in a clear, pleasant (female) voice; if the radio is on at the time of the alert, the computer automatically turns down the volume so the warning can be heard

tamperproof carburettor *noun* a carburettor with factory-adjusted idle speed, sealed idle speed adjustment screw, and provisions to ensure that exhaust emission levels remain within specified limits over an extended period of time

tandem axle *noun* type of axle in which two axles are closely coupled, usually not more than one metre apart

◊ **tandem master cylinder** *noun* master cylinder with two pistons; when the brake pedal is pressed, the pushrod activates the primary piston which in turn moves the secondary piston; necessary for dual-circuit braking systems; *(see illustration 29)*

tang *noun* device mounted on a rotating shaft or component that engages in a recess of a component to be driven

tangential-flow scavenging *noun* = LOOP SCAVENGING

tank *noun* any container for liquid or gas *petrol tank; radiator tank*

◊ **tanker** *noun* lorry designed to carry liquid in bulk *petrol tanker*

tap *noun* tool used to cut inside threads, e.g. in a hole; *(compare* DIE*)*; **tap and die set** = selection of tools such as taps, tap holders, dies and die stocks for cutting inside and outside threads

taper *noun* gradual reduction in size of a long round object towards one end (e.g. of a bore, piston, journal)

◊ **taper-breaking tool** *noun* = BALL JOINT SEPARATOR

◊ **taper cutter** *noun* tool used to ream, deburr, align, and enlarge holes, e.g. on car bodies (NOTE: also called **tapered reamer)**

◊ **tapered compression ring** *noun* upper compression ring which, due to its tapered cross-section, requires a reduced running-in period thus ensuring a tight seal quickly

◊ **taper(ed) leaf spring** *noun* = PARABOLIC SPRING

◊ **tapered punch** *noun* = DRIFT PUNCH

◊ **taper roller bearing** *noun* bearing consisting of a cone (which includes the rollers and the cage) and a cone-shaped, stationary race or cup; can accept axial thrust as well as providing shaft location

◊ **taper seat** *noun* **(a)** conical seat that provides positive centring of a wheel bolt head in the wheel (NOTE: opposite is **radius seat) (b)** *(sparking plug)* seal without a gasket achieved by mating the conical surface of the sparking plug shell and the cylinder head

tap holder *noun* tool used to hold and drive taps, reamers, and screw extractors with two long handles to provide high leverage for turning operation

tappet *noun (in valve gear)* usually cup-shaped element (one for each valve) which slides on the cam lobes and converts the rotary motion of the camshaft into the reciprocating motion of the valves; the tappets actuate either pushrods, rocker arms, or valves directly (NOTE: US English is **(valve) lifter)** *remove all of the tappets and shims, keeping them separate for installation in their original locations* **tappet adjusting screw** = VALVE ADJUSTING SCREW;

tappet gasket = ROCKER COVER GASKET; **tappet wrench** = wrench designed for adjusting valve clearances on OHV-engines with bucket tappet assembly that use an adjusting screw instead of valve shims for adjustment; *(compare* VALVE SHIM)

tapping plate *noun* = HINGE TAPPING PLATE

tap ratchet *noun* tool with ratchet mechanism used to hold and operate bits such as taps, drills, reamers, or screw extractors; **tap spanner** = TAP HOLDER

targa bar *noun* a type of roll bar made of a relatively wide band of sheet steel rather than of tubing; made popular by the Porsche 911 Targa; **targa top** = rigid, removable roof section between the windscreen and targa bar

tarnish *verb* to discolour due to the formation of a thin film of oxide, sulphide, or some other corrosion product

COMMENT: even precious metals like gold and silver tarnish in time, and this is a form of corrosion

tax disc *noun (informal)* road fund licence disc displayed on the windscreen to show that road tax has been paid

taxi(cab) *noun* car in which passengers are carried for a rate which is usually recorded by a meter; **taxi rank** = place where taxis wait to be hired

t.b. = TOWBAR

T bar roof *noun* roof with a T-shaped bar connecting windscreen and rear section of roof

TBI = THROTTLE BODY INJECTION

TC = TORQUE CONVERTER; TWIN CARBURETTORS

TCI = TRANSISTORIZED COIL IGNITION
◇ **TCI-H** = TRANSISTORIZED COIL IGNITION WITH HALL SENSOR

TCM = TRANSMISSION CONTROL MODULE

TCS = TRANSMISSION CONTROLLED SPARK

TC sparking plug *noun* = THERMOCOUPLE SPARKING PLUG

T-cut *noun* proprietary rubbing compound used to give a finish to dull paintwork

TDC = TOP DEAD CENTRE

TDI = TURBO DIESEL ENGINE WITH DIRECT INJECTION

TD rim *noun* wheel rim which incorporates two grooves running around the circumference of the bead seats; the tyres have specially extended bead toes which fit into these grooves; **TD wheel** = safety wheel incorporating a TD rim with run-flat properties, which in case of a puncture allow further driving of up to 20 miles at a maximum speed of 40 mph

COMMENT: in the event of deflation, the reinforced bead toes are held firmly in place by the grooves, thereby preventing the tyre from sliding into the rim well. The width and diameter of both tyre and rim are given in millimetres, to prevent the fitting of a normal tyre to a TD rim or conversely of a TD tyre to a conventional wheel. Rim marking 150 TD 365 stands for a rim measuring 150 mm in width and 365 mm in diameter and having a TD contour

tear seam *noun* = INFLATION CONTROL SEAM

Teflon *noun* = POLYTETRAFLUOROETHYLENE

TEL = TETRAETHYL LEAD

telescopic shock absorber *noun* a tubular spring damper operated by rod and piston; the most common type of shock absorber; *(compare* LEVER-TYPE SHOCK ABSORBER)
◇ **telescopic steering column** *noun* steering column that collapses in on itself on impact

tempa spare (wheel) *noun* spare wheel type with considerably reduced overall dimensions (rim width: 3.5-4.0 in), designed to operate at a higher inflation pressure than the standard tyre and wheel unit

COMMENT: the tempa spare saves weight (up to 40%) and space in the boot (up to 50%) and although it has the same load capacity as standard wheels, may only be operated at speeds of up to 50 mph; the VW Golf and Audi 100 series have tempa spares as standard equipment

temper *verb* thermal treatment of finished products (metals, alloys, plastics) to remove internal stresses

temperature compensator *noun (in some SU carburettors)* wax-type thermostat contained in a housing at the base of the jet head; with increasing temperature, the wax expands and pushes the jet upwards, thereby reducing the effective area of the jet and restoring the correct fuel flow

COMMENT: as underbonnet temperature increases, fuel viscosity is reduced, resulting in increased fuel flow through the carburettor jet and an air/fuel mixture which is too rich; as this causes excessive emissions, particularly during idling, some SU carburettors feature a capstat temperature compensated jet

temperature control element *noun (in oil filter bypass valve)* a temperature-controlled valve spring bias regulator which controls the bypass valve as a function of oil temperature; *(see illustration 18)*

◊ **temperature-measuring sparking plug** *noun* = THERMOCOUPLE SPARKING PLUG

◊ **temperature of deflection under load** *noun* ability of a test specimen to preserve its shape up to a given temperature under a given dead load; characterized by the temperature at which the specimen supported at both ends and heated continually and uniformly in a liquid heat-transfer medium is deformed by a given amount when the load is applied midway between the supports

◊ **temperature valve** *noun* = THERMOVALVE

temper rolling *noun* rolling for the purpose of removing spangles on hot-dip galvanized steel sheet

template *noun* thin metal or card sheet, used as a pattern for cutting pieces of wood, metal, etc. to an exact shape

temporary spare wheel *noun* = SPACE-SAVING SPARE WHEEL

tensile force *noun* the stretching force that acts on the windscreen header to keep the hood taut; **tensile strength** = measure of a material's ability to withstand tension or stress

COMMENT: a high tensile force reduces wind noise when driving with the top up and increases the force needed to close and lock the top; typical convertibles with manually operated tops have a tensile force of about 200 newtons, the Mercedes Benz SL cars introduced in 1991 have a tensile force of 1000 newtons and need a hydraulic system to close the top

tension (a) stretching force **(b)** = VOLTAGE *high-tension lead*

◊ **tensioner** *noun* device designed to maintain the tension of a timing belt or chain; *(compare* JOCKEY PULLEY)

◊ **tensioning spring** *noun* spring designed to maintain tension in a drum brake

terminal *noun* (i) one of the connecting points in an electric circuit; (ii) a conducting device by which current enters or leaves at such a point *battery terminal (see illustration 36)*; **terminal post** = BATTERY POST; **terminal reamer** = tapered reamer-type tool used to remove corrosion from the inside of battery cable clamps

◊ **terminal tower** *noun* sockets on the distributor cap for connecting the ignition cables; *(compare* OUTER TOWER)

◊ **terminal voltage** *noun* the sum of the individual battery cell voltages *the battery has a terminal voltage of 12 volts*

test bar *noun* test specimen with the shape of a bar as used in the impact resistance test

◊ **test-bed** *noun* area equipped with instruments, used for testing machinery, engines, etc., under working conditions

◊ **test current for low temperatures** *noun* specification for assessing battery starting behaviour at low temperatures and under given conditions; indicated in amps on the battery case

◊ **test drive** *noun* a trial drive of a car after it has been repaired, or of a new car to decide if one likes it enough to buy it

◊ **test-drive** *verb* to take a car for a test drive before purchasing it

◊ **test lamp** *or* **light** *noun* automotive tool used to test powered circuits on 6-24 volt systems such as headlights, horns, directional or tail lights

COMMENT: consists of a handle with a bulb and sharp probe and a lead with a crocodile clip. The sharp probe is used to pierce the insulation on the wire leading to the defective part; if the bulb glows, the circuit is complete. Simpler designs do not feature a probe, but come in a standard screwdriver shape

tetraethyl lead (TEL) *noun* anti-knock fuel additive

◊ **tetramethyl lead (TML)** *noun* anti-knock fuel additive

t/glass *noun* = TINTED GLASS

THC = TOTAL HYDROCARBONS

T-head *noun* **(a)** *(type of cylinder head)* in side valve engines, the valves are either adjacent and parallel or installed on opposite sides of the piston in a configuration resembling a 'T' *T-head engine; T-shaped combustion chamber* **(b)** type of screw or bolt head shaped like a 'T'

theft protection *noun* = ANTI-THEFT SECURITY SYSTEM

thermactor *noun* = THERMAL REACTOR

thermal conduction *noun* heat transfer within a substance or to another substance by direct contact

◊ **thermal convection** *noun* heat transfer by the combined mechanisms of fluid mixing and thermal conduction

thermal efficiency *noun* the ratio of useful work available from an engine to the heat supplied from the fuel

COMMENT: even the most thermally efficient normally-aspirated or turbocharged petrol engine does not exceed a thermal efficiency of about 30%; positive displacement supercharged engines have less, diesel engines better thermal efficiency

thermal head *noun* initial temperature of exhaust gas upstream of a catalytic converter

◊ **thermal radiation** *noun* heat transfer from one substance to another by means of electromagnetic waves

◊ **thermal reactor** *noun* device installed in the exhaust manifold of some air injection systems to promote HC and CO oxidation by providing long exhaust gas residence times in a localized area

◊ **thermal time valve** *noun* valve which senses temperature, typically the temperature

under the bonnet, and gives full vacuum advance when the temperature is below 10°C; above this temperature, the thermal time valve allows distributor vacuum to be controlled by the thermal vacuum switch; includes a delay of typically 20 seconds to allow full spark advance for better hot starting

thermal vacuum switch (TVS) *noun* measures either air/fuel temperature, underbonnet temperature, or coolant temperature, or a combination of any two to regulate the EGR valve accordingly; **thermal vacuum valve (TVV)** = valve with the same function as a thermal vacuum switch

COMMENT: TVS units, which serve to interrupt exhaust gas recirculation when the temperature is too low, are located in the vacuum line between EGR valve and inlet manifold or carburettor

thermocouple *noun* an electrical temperature sensor; **thermocouple sparking plug** = sparking plug with a thermocouple in the centre electrode, used to measure the temperatures in the individual cylinders as a function of engine speed and load in order to select the correct heat range

COMMENT: as opposed to a resistance thermometer, the thermocouple operates without an external voltage; it consists basically of two conductors of dissimilar metals, typically copper/constantan, iron/constantan, nickel-chromium/nickel, which are connected at their ends; one joint, the hot junction, is exposed to the temperature to be measured, the other joint, the cold or reference junction, is held at a fixed, known temperature; a thermoelectrical voltage is developed between the two junctions which is proportional to the temperature difference between the junctions

thermoforming *noun* shaping of a polymer sheet while heating

thermoplastic *noun* plastic material with long chain-like molecules that can repeatedly be softened by heating and hardened by cooling; most plastic parts used on vehicles are made of thermoplastics; **thermoplastic elastomers** = materials which are rubbery at room temperature but which on heating melt to viscous liquids that can be moulded and otherwise processed; the change is reversible; on cooling, the melted material reverts to a solid material having rubbery properties

thermosetting *adjective* (polymer) which sets at the same time as it is being moulded *epoxy resin is a thermosetting resin*

thermostat *noun* temperature-controlled valve located in the hot leg between engine and radiator, often mounted on the cylinder head; *(see illustration 15)*

COMMENT: by controlling the flow of coolant through the radiator and regulating heat dissipation, the thermostat allows the engine to reach its operating temperature as quickly as possible; this reduces oil dilution, cylinder bore wear, fuel consumption, exhaust emission, and improves the efficiency of the heating system; typical thermostat designs are the aneroid-type and the wax-type thermostat

thermostatic air cleaner (TAC) *noun* air cleaner which also controls the temperature of the air entering the engine

COMMENT: temperature control is necessary to optimize the air/fuel ratio with regard to minimum exhaust emissions; typically, the TAC regulates air intake temperature at about 27-46°C by means of a control damper that mixes pre-heated air from an inlet at the exhaust manifold with air from a cold air inlet; designs for actuating the damper range from simple thermostatic action to vacuum-motor and stepper-motor control

thermostatic interruptor *noun* a bimetallic circuit breaker in lighting circuits which switches to an alternative circuit in the event of a fault or short circuit

thermosyphon cooling *noun* natural cooling, utilising the fact that two columns of liquid at different temperatures possess natural circulation because the hotter column weighs less on account of its lower density; thus the hot engine must be located at a lower level than the cool radiator; *(compare* FORCED CIRCULATION)

thermo-time switch *noun* a switch in a continuous injection system that interrupts current from the starter solenoid to the cold-start valve solenoid when the engine is hot or after the starter has been operated for more than a few seconds, in order to prevent flooding; *(see illustration 14)*

thermovalve *noun* valve which opens and closes as a function of temperature

thermowell *noun* space which accommodates a temperature sensor (NOTE: the term is sometimes used with reference to the temperature sensing point or sensor rather than to the well itself)

thin *verb (paint)* to add thinners to a paint in order to adjust the viscosity

◊ **thin needle-nose pliers** *noun* needle-nose pliers with thin extra long reach jaws without a wire cutter

thinner *noun* substance used to dilute lacquer or acrylic products, as opposed to reducers used for synthetic enamel products

COMMENT: thinners and reducers are not normally interchangeable, i.e. the corresponding type of thinner/reducer must be used for each type of paint; however, some general-purpose thinners are available

thinning (out) *noun* tendency of liquid paint to form much thicker coatings near the edge of a steel sheet, thereby causing the paint film thickness on the side opposite this edge to decrease

◊ **thin-wall casting** *noun* used, for example, as a weight-saving measure on oil filter housings

third (gear) *noun* intermediate gear used for increasing speed, climbing hills and sometimes for overtaking

◊ **third motion shaft** *noun* = GEARBOX OUTPUT SHAFT

third port induction *noun* a design feature of two-stroke engines that relies on the piston position to control induction of the fresh charge

COMMENT: a feature of this design is the use of the third port, i.e. the transfer port, to complement the inlet and exhaust ports, e.g. as opposed to two-stroke diesels that have valve-controlled inlets and do not need transfer ports

third scavenging port *noun (loop scavenging)* an additional transfer port located opposite the exhaust port of a two-stroke engine cylinder and connecting through the piston skirt to the region above the gudgeon pin and below the piston crown

thixotropic *adjective* having the property (of certain resins and paints) that prevents them from running off vertical surfaces

thrash *verb (informal)* to push an engine to its limits

thread *noun* helical ridge along the body of a screw, bolt, etc., formed by a die or lathe tool (male or external thread); (ii) helical groove in a cylindrical hole, nut, etc., formed by a tap or lathe tool (female or internal thread); **thread angle** = the angle between the adjacent flanks of a thread; **thread crest** = highest point of a screw thread, opposite the root; **thread-cutting screw** = a self-drilling fastener that drills its own hole, taps a mating thread, and then fastens, all in a single operation; **thread diameter** = diameter measured from the crest of a thread to the corresponding crest on the opposite side of the bolt or screw; **thread file** = tool for restoring internal or external threads by filing; **thread gauge** = SCREW PITCH GAUGE; **thread height** = distance from root to thread crest, measured perpendicular to the axis of the thread; **thread insert** = screw-thread system that allows the use of high-strength cap screws and studs in light soft metals, such as aluminium and magnesium, through the use of a phosphor bronze or stainless steel coil which is screwed into a threaded hole; the thread insert can also be used to repair damaged threads; **thread pitch** = PITCH (a); **thread pitch gauge** = SCREW PITCH GAUGE; **thread root** = lowest point of a screw thread, where the thread joins the body (opposite the crest)

three-chamber system *noun* test installation consisting of a salt spray chamber, a cold chamber and a climatic chamber

◇ **three-door** *adjective* typical design of subcompact hatchbacks with two side doors and one tailgate

◇ **three-piece alloy wheel** *noun* type of forged alloy wheel with a wheel spider or wheel disc and a divided rim consisting of an outer and an inner rim well; the rim is bolted to the spider or the disc

◇ **three-point seat belt** *noun* combined lap-shoulder belt fastened at three points, usually with an automatic retractor

◇ **three-port engine** *noun* the traditional two-stroke engine design incorporating the inlet port connecting the crankcase to the atmosphere, the transfer port connecting the crankcase to the combustion chamber, and the exhaust port to evacuate the spent gas from the combustion chamber (NOTE: the term is used even if the three-port types are used in pairs)

◇ **three-quarter floating axle** *noun* rear axle assembly in which the weight of the vehicle is borne by the outer bearings of the axle shafts, mounted between the hubs and axle housing

◇ **three-speed gearbox** *or* **transmission** *noun* a gearbox with three

forward speeds; the usual arrangement for automatic gearboxes

◇ **three-valve (engine)** *noun* engine with two intake valves and one exhaust valve per cylinder; a four-cylinder three-valve engine is also called a '12-valve engine'

three-way catalyst (TWC) *noun* catalyst for the simultaneous conversion of the three exhaust pollutants HC, CO, and NO_x; **three-way catalytic converter** = catalytic converter for the simultaneous control of HC, CO, and NO_x emissions

COMMENT: used as a single-stage converter with a 3-way catalyst, or as a two-stage system consisting of an oxygen-sensor-controlled 3-way catalyst in series with an oxidation catalyst, or a reduction catalyst and an oxidation catalyst in series, or two three-way monolithic catalysts in series

three-wheeler *noun* a light car with three wheels; formerly made popular by, for example, the Morgan, the BSA and the Coventry Victor, now embodied by the Reliant Robin

throat depth *noun* an indicator of the reach of welding clamps such as C-clamps

◇ **throaty** *adjective (exhaust pitch)* rough-sounding

throttle *noun* **(a)** = THROTTLE VALVE **(b)** the accelerator pedal used to control the throttle valve

◇ **throttle body injection (TBI)** *noun* = SINGLE POINT INJECTION

◇ **throttle gauge** *noun* tool with straight calibrated measuring pins for measuring throttle and choke valve gaps

◇ **throttle position sensor (TPS)** *noun (fuel injection)* switch with two contacts for the two end positions of the throttle valve, which sends a signal to the electronic control unit when the throttle valve is closed (idle) or wide open (full load)

◇ **throttle return spring** *noun* spring which forces the throttle valve closed when pressure is taken off the accelerator pedal; *(see illustrations 11, 12)*

◇ **throttle shaft** *or spindle noun* shaft on which the throttle valve disc pivots in a carburettor barrel or inlet tract; *(see illustrations 11, 12, 13)*

throttle solenoid *noun* a solenoid which operates mechanically on the throttle lever;

when energized, the solenoid stem extends and opens the throttle to establish the preset idle speed

COMMENT: since the early 1970s, most manufacturers have used a throttle solenoid to prevent 'run-on', or dieselling

throttle valve *noun* **(a)** *(in air intake, e.g. in carburettor)* a butterfly valve in the inlet tract, designed to provide control of power output by limiting the amount of fresh mixture induced; *(see illustrations 11, 12, 14)* **(b)** *(automatic transmission control)* modulator valve actuated via either the accelerator pedal, or the vacuum in the engine inlet manifold, or the carburettor throttle; it converts line pressure into an engine-load dependent pressure, which is directed to various valves

◊ **throttle (valve) switch** *noun* = THROTTLE POSITION SENSOR

◊ **throttling** *noun* reducing the power output of an engine by closing the throttle, thus restricting airflow through the carburettor or inlet tract

through bolt *noun* (i) generally, any bolt which is inserted through the parts of an assembly and secured on the other side by a nut; (ii) specifically, one of the two long bolts that holds the starter or alternator assembly together; *(see illustration 36)*

throwing *noun* elongating certain sections of a panel by hammering (NOTE: opposite is **tucking**)

COMMENT: when making a section rounded along the inner and outer edges that is to be folded along the outer edge, the length of the outer edge must be increased. This is achieved by regular hammering, which causes the edge of the panel to stretch, reducing its thickness by spreading the metal

throwout bearing *noun US* = CLUTCH RELEASE BEARING

◊ **throwout fork** *or* **lever** *noun US* = CLUTCH RELEASE LEVER

thrust bearing *noun* a low-friction bearing on a rotating shaft that resists axial thrust in the shaft; usually consists of a collar which bears against a ring of well lubricated stationary and sometimes tilting pads; *(compare* RADIAL BEARING)

◊ **thrust plate** *noun* = DRIVEN PLATE

◊ **thrust washer** *noun* an axially loaded washer, e.g. of a shaft bearing; *(see illustration 8)*

thumb nut *or* *thumbscrew noun* a nut or screw with projections enabling it to be turned by thumb and forefinger; a wing nut/screw

◊ **thumbwheel** *noun* small wheel for adjusting, which can be turned by using the thumb and forefinger

thyristor *noun* silicon-controlled rectifier which converts alternating current to a unidirectional current; **thyristor ignition** = CAPACITOR DISCHARGE IGNITION (SYSTEM)

TI = TRANSISTORIZED IGNITION

◊ **TI-B** = BREAKER-TRIGGERED TRANSISTORIZED IGNITION (SYSTEM)

tickler *noun* carburettor starting aid

COMMENT: when starting at low temperatures, the float may be pushed below the fuel level in the float chamber by depressing the tickler, so that more fuel is supplied than is required for normal operation

tick over *verb* to run at low speed with the throttle control closed and the transmission disengaged; to idle

◊ **tick-over** *noun* the speed of an engine when it is ticking over

tie rod *noun* **(a)** generally, any connecting rod or bar, usually under tension **(b)** specifically, the link between the drop arm and the steering-knuckle arm; a track rod; *(see illustrations 25, 26)*; **tie rod end** = steering ball joint at the outer end of a tie rod; *(see illustration 26)*; **tie rod puller** *or* **separator** = special automotive tool for forcing out joints on tie rod ends by screw action; *(compare* BALL JOINT SEPARATOR)

TIG *(short for)* tungsten/inert gas; **TIG welding** = an inert arc welding method using a tungsten electrode

◊ **TI-H** = TRANSISTORIZED IGNITION WITH HALL GENERATOR

◊ **TI-I** = TRANSISTORIZED IGNITION WITH INDUCTIVE PICK-UP

tilt column *noun* a steering column that can be adjusted for height

◊ **tilt/slide sunroof** *noun* a sunroof, made of steel or glass, that slides and tilts and is operated either manually or electrically

◊ **tilt steering wheel** *noun* a steering wheel that can be adjusted for height

time delay relay *noun* a relay which responds to a signal with a certain delay; (*compare* DELAY VALVE)

> COMMENT: in some ignition systems, a time delay relay allows for full vacuum advance 20-30 seconds after start-up, after which control is again taken up by the TCS; some cars have an additional time delay relay which delays vacuum advance about 30 seconds after the transmission has been shifted to high gear

timed (fuel) injection *noun* = SEQUENTIAL FUEL INJECTION

timer core *noun* (*magnetic pick-up assembly*) = TRIGGER WHEEL (a)

timing *noun* the setting of a mechanism so that it acts at exactly the right moment; **to set the timing** = to adjust the firing of the sparking plug so that it coincides with the piston; (*see* IGNITION TIMING; VALVE TIMING)

◊ **timing belt** *noun* plastic toothed belt with steel cord or fibreglass reinforcements, used to drive the camshaft of a four-stroke engine (NOTE: also called **camshaft belt** or **cam belt**); **timing belt tensioner (pulley)** = spring-loaded jockey pulley or idler pulley designed to take up the slack in the timing belt

◊ **timing chain** *noun* a single or double roller chain at the engine front that transmits crankshaft power to the camshaft; typically used in OHC-engines (NOTE: also called **camshaft chain** or **cam chain)**

◊ **timing diagram** *noun* a diagrammatic representation of the engine timing, i.e. the times during which the inlet and exhaust valves are open and closed

◊ **timing light** *noun* stroboscopic light used to set the ignition timing; (*see* DYNAMIC IGNITION TIMING)

◊ **timing mark** *noun* **(a)** (*ignition timing*) timing indicator or pointer on the engine block and rotating timing mark on the flywheel for basic ignition timing **(b)** (*valve timing; for camshafts*) alignment or indexing mark on a timing gear or camshaft pulley which must be lined up with another mark to give the correct position

◊ **timing rotor** *noun* rotating part of the pick-up assembly, in the form of a drum with ferrite rods embedded vertically in the outer edge, used instead of a trigger wheel

◊ **timing shaft** *noun* = DISTRIBUTOR SHAFT

◊ **timing window** *noun* window through which it is possible to see the timing marks *the crankcase is equipped with a timing window to facilitate ignition adjustment*

Timken (roller) bearing *noun* type of taper roller bearing

tin immersion treatment *noun* formation of a thin tin deposit before electroplating

◊ **tinmen's shears** *noun* = SNIPS

◊ **tinning** *noun* (*bodywork repair*) pretreating sheet metal before the application of body lead

> COMMENT: to ensure that the body lead adequately covers and takes to the area to be repaired, a flux and a thin coating of tin or a special solder paint are applied

tinted glass *or* **tinted windows** *or* (*informal*) **tints** *noun* glass that has been specially coloured to reduce glare from the sun

◊ **tint tone** *noun* (*colour matching*) a shade produced when a small amount of colour is mixed with a large amount of white; this is required for formulating the ingredients of a certain paint tone; (*compare* MASS TONE)

tin(ners') snips *noun* = SNIPS

tip *noun* the end of a sparking plug insulator, nearest the electrode

TML = TETRAMETHYL LEAD

toeboard *noun* the front vertical panel that provides support for the pedals and for the front passenger's feet, usually inclined towards the front and spot-welded to the floorboard at its bottom end and to the bulkhead at its upper end; (*compare* HEELBOARD)

◊ **toe dolly** *noun* a flat slab of metal thinned down at one end and with a curved surface; useful for getting into awkward and narrow corners

◊ **toe-in** *noun* slight inward inclination of the leading edge of the front wheels to improve steering and equalize tyre wear; **toe-in angle** = angle formed by each front wheel plane and the longitudinal axis of the car, usually expressed as the difference in distance between right and left wheel rims at front and rear, measured at hub level

◊ **toe-out** *noun* slight outward inclination of the leading edge of the front wheels

tolerance *noun* difference between the permissible maximum size and the permissible minimum size of a measured quantity

toll *noun* money charged for the use of a road or bridge *toll bridge; toll road* **toll sticker** = sticker displayed on the windscreen denoting payment of a toll

tommy bar *noun* short bar used as a lever to provide torque for tightening a box or socket spanner (NOTE: US English is **crossbar**)

tonneau cover *noun* detachable horizontal cover to protect the seating area of an open car; may include a zipped compartment that can be removed to reveal the driver's seat

toothed belt *noun* positive-action reinforced rubber or plastic belt in which parallel teeth engage with grooves in a driving and a driven wheel; commonly used for the valve timing gear as an alternative to a roller chain *do not turn the camshaft mounting bolt, since this will stretch the toothed belt* (*compare* POLY-V-BELT)

top *noun* **(a)** a car roof, especially that of a convertible **(b)** (*short for*) top gear

◊ **top carriers** *noun* typically, square steel bars with sturdy clamp-on gutter brackets, used to secure loads on a car roof, such as bulky containers or bicycles

top chop *noun* modification of the roof of custom cars

> COMMENT: the roof pillars are cut off and shortened; when the roof is welded back on, the roof line is far lower than before and the screen and side window height may have been reduced to a minimum. Due to problems of rigidity and finding suitable glass parts, this modification is extremely difficult

top coat *noun* final paint coat; **top coat drier** *or* **oven** = oven for drying or stoving the final paint coat

◊ **top dead centre (TDC)** *noun* the position when the piston has reached the upper limit of its travel in the cylinder and the centre line of the connecting rod is parallel to the cylinder walls; **before top dead centre (BTDC)** = the period before a piston reaches TDC; the time when ignition occurs; **after**

top dead centre (ATDC) = the period after a piston has reached TDC and begins to descend; maximum thrust is developed between 10° and 15° ATDC (NOTE: opposite is **bottom dead centre (BDC)**; the corresponding point (to TDC) in a horizontally opposed or 'flat' engine is that closest to the combustion chamber, also called **inner dead centre)**

◊ **top electrode** *noun* (*sparking plug*) earth electrode protruding above the centre electrode, either full coverage type or set back slightly from the far edge of the centre electrode

◊ **top end** *noun* the upper range of engine revolutions *top end power*

◊ **top end gasket set/kit** *noun* set which includes all the seals, O-ring and gaskets required for the assembly of the cylinder and cylinder head

◊ **top feed gun** *noun* = GRAVITY-FEED SPRAY GUN

◊ **top gear** *noun* the highest available gear

◊ **top hat section** *noun* basically a structural sheet metal member of U-section, but incorporating flanges for welding or assembling the section to a flat mating panel

◊ **top land** *noun* = HEAD LAND

◊ **top-of-the-range model** *noun* the most powerful and expensive model in a particular manufacturer's range

◊ **top speed** *noun* the maximum speed of a vehicle

◊ **top tints** *noun* tinted stripe at the upper edge of the windscreen

◊ **top up (with)** *verb* to raise the level of a liquid in a container to the required level; **top up with distilled water** = add distilled water to the battery so that the plates are covered *topping up should not be carried out if the outside temperature is below the freezing point of water*

torpedo body *noun* early type of touring car with a streamlined torpedo-like body

torque 1 *noun* mechanical force that causes rotation **2** *verb* (*informal*) to tighten with a torque spanner

◊ **torque arm** *noun* T-shaped extrusion of the rear axle casing to take up forward thrust of the driven axle; (*compare* TORQUE TUBE, RADIUS ARM)

◊ **torque converter (TC)** *noun* type of coupling device used with most automatic gearboxes, consisting of rotating and static vane assemblies, by which torque can be transmitted to a fluid held in a sealed container, which in turn drives a rotor; *(compare* FLUID COUPLING); **torque converter drive plate** = DRIVE PLATE; **torque converter housing** = BELL HOUSING; **torque converter (lock-up) clutch** = automatically engaged clutch in a lock-up torque converter; prevents slipping losses

◊ **torque curve** *noun* graph which shows engine torque as a function of engine speed *two-valve engines usually have a flatter torque curve than four-valve engines*

◊ **torque limiter** *noun* tool used in conjunction with a plug spanner which allows the controlled tightening of sparking plugs by releasing automatically once a preset torque setting is reached

◊ **torque   screwdriver**   *noun* screwdriver with a device that measures the amount of torque being applied

◊ **torque spanner** *noun* spanner with a device for measuring the amount of torque applied on a nut or bolt; used for threaded fasteners with a critical tightening torque, such as cylinder head bolts, alloy wheel lugs, suspension links, etc.

◊ **torque split** *noun* distributing torque between wheels on the same axle or between front and rear axles in a 4wd vehicle; *(compare* POWER DISTRIBUTION)

◊ **torque steer** *noun* on some FWD cars, a pulling force felt in the steering wheel during acceleration; can be caused by drive shafts of unequal length

torque tube *noun* hollow forward extrusion of the rear axle casing incorporated in early live rear axle designs, both enclosing the drive shaft and providing a forward location of the driven axle, pivoting about a spherical joint either at the rear end of the gearbox or at the chassis frame; *(compare* TORQUE ARM); **torque tube axle** *or* **drive** = a live rear axle layout with a divided drive shaft and a T-shaped axle housing, the hollow forward extrusion of which carries the rear half of the divided drive shaft; *(compare* HOTCHKISS DRIVE)

COMMENT: the forward thrust of the axle is taken up by a stressed ball joint located near the centre of the vehicle, where a high-speed universal joint couples the two halves of the drive shaft

torque   wrench   *noun*   =   TORQUE SPANNER

◊ **torquey** *adjective* of an engine which develops high torque (i.e. it pulls well) at low speeds, relative to its power

Torsen   differential   *noun*   'torque-sensing' differential system incorporating a worm and roller mechanism; **Torsen four-wheel drive** = permanently engaged four-wheel drive incorporating a Torsen differential

COMMENT: based on the principle that a worm gear can drive a roller but not vice versa, the Torsen differential balances different wheel speeds due to different travel distances, whereas speed differences due to differing adherence situations are not balanced

torsion *noun* the strain on a part or component produced by torque

torsional stiffness *noun* resistance against torsional loads, specified in newton-meter per angular degree of body twisting

COMMENT: on vehicles with a frame-type chassis, the torsional stiffness is governed by the stiffness of the frame only; in unitary body construction, the overall body structure, in particular the roof, determines the torsional stiffness; it is an inherent problem of convertibles

torsional vibration damper *noun* (i) generally, any device that reduces torsional vibrations; (ii) specifically, the small flywheel on the front end of a crankshaft

◊ **torsion bar** *noun* metal bar attached at one end to the body and at the other to the axle, which acts as a torsional spring when twisted by the movement of the car

◊ **torsion damper** *noun* = TORSIONAL VIBRATION DAMPER

TORX *noun* refers to a special star-shaped screw recess (internal TORX) or screw head top (external TORX) with six rounded corners to set the tool

COMMENT: the TORX configuration on tools allows a very tight fit on the fastener and the application of high torque. The rounded corners also reduce wear of both the fastener and the tool

total   hydrocarbons   (THC)   *noun* measurement of all hydrocarbons emitted by the exhaust system

◊ **total-loss   lubrication**   *noun* the components of the conventional two-stroke engine with crankcase scavenging are lubricated by the oil added to the fuel; since the oil is burnt along with the fuel, fresh oil is constantly fed to the lubrication points inside the engine

touch-dry *adjective* describes the condition after respraying a body when the paint coat has dried to an extent that foreign substances will not stick to the surfaces and light finger pressure will not leave any marks; the coat has not yet hardened completely, however, i.e. it cannot yet be sanded or polished

◊ **touch up** *verb* to repair minimal blemishes in the paintwork, e.g. those caused by stone chippings or scratches

toughened windscreen *noun* windscreen made of toughened glass which, on impact, will not shatter like ordinary glass but fractures into small pieces and crazes over; laminated glass is nowadays the preferred material; *(compare* LAMINATED WINDSCREEN)

touring car *or* **tourer** *noun* an early type of convertible, often with a folding top, seating five or more passengers

tow *verb* (i) to pull a trailer or caravan behind a vehicle by means of a towing hitch; (ii) to pull a disabled vehicle behind another vehicle by means of a rope, cable or rigid bar *the XYZ must be towed with the front wheels off the ground*

◊ **towable** *adjective* capable of being towed: (i) description of a car after an accident; (ii) description of the condition of a car purchased for restoration or spares; the car is a non-runner, but brakes, tyres, and steering work sufficiently to allow the car to be towed

◊ **tow away** *verb* to remove unauthorized (e.g. illegally parked) vehicles, thus incurring a hefty fine for the owners

◊ **towball** *or* **towing ball** *noun* metal ball on a towing bracket onto which a trailer or caravan is coupled (NOTE: US English is **hitch ball)**

◊ **towbar** *noun* **(a)** crossbar of a towing bracket onto which the towball is mounted **(b)** rigid bar used for towing disabled vehicles short distances; *(compare* TOWROPE) **(c)** = DRAWBAR

tower jack *noun* tower with a solid foot and an arm at right angles which fits into a slot

in the side of a car and is wound up the tower to raise the vehicle

towing bracket *noun* structure attached to the rear of a car to enable a trailer or caravan to be towed; consists of one or two brackets, a towbar and towball

◊ **towing eye** *or* **towing lug** *noun* steel ring fitted to the chassis of a car to which a towrope can be attached

◊ **towing hitch** *noun* inverted cup on the drawbar of a trailer or caravan which fits over a towball

◊ **towing jaws** *noun* coupling attachment on the rear of a lorry cab into which the drawbar eye of a trailer fits to lock with a coupling bolt

◊ **towrope** *noun* rope, or textile- or plastic-covered cable, usually no longer than 5 metres, used for towing another vehicle

Toyota *noun* the largest car manufacturer in Japan and the third largest in the world (after GM and Ford)

TPP = TREAD PATTERN PERCENTAGE

TPS = THROTTLE POSITION SENSOR

track *noun (vehicle geometry)* distance between the centres of the contact patches of two wheels on a common axle (NOTE: US English is **tread)**

◊ **track arc** *noun (steering)* the path travelled by a road wheel during a turn

◊ **track bar** *noun* = PANHARD ROD

◊ **track control arm** *noun* = TRANSVERSE LINK

◊ **tracking** *noun* **(a)** correct alignment of the wheels; adjusted by means of the track rods; *(compare* DIRECTIONAL STABILITY) **(b)** *(sparking plug)* = SHUNT FIRING **(c)** = CARBON TRACKING

◊ **tracking mark** *noun* telltale sign on the distributor cover or ignition cables indicating a leakage of current

◊ **track rod** *noun* one of the transverse bars connecting the steering system to the steering arms; the link between the drop arm and the steering-knuckle arm (NOTE: also called **tie rod**) *(see illustrations 25, 26)*

traction *noun* **(a)** pulling force **(b)** adhesive friction between the tyre and the road surface; gripping power

◊ **traction avant** *(French for)* front-wheel drive

◊ **traction control system** *noun* = ANTI-SPIN REGULATION

◊ **traction differential** *noun* = LIMITED-SLIP DIFFERENTIAL

◊ **tractive conversion** *noun* = STALL TORQUE RATIO

trade-in price *noun* the price of one's old car when selling it in part exchange for another one

traffic *noun* vehicles travelling along a road or street *heavy traffic; rush-hour traffic*

◊ **trafficator** *noun* = SEMAPHORE INDICATOR

◊ **traffic circle** *noun US* roundabout

◊ **traffic island** *noun* raised area in the middle of a road designed to separate two flows of traffic and to provide a safe temporary stopping place for pedestrians crossing the road

◊ **traffic jam** *noun* a number of vehicles stopped behind one another on a road

◊ **traffic light** *noun* red, amber, and green lights on a traffic signal placed at junctions to regulate the flow of traffic

trail *noun* = CASTOR (b)

trailer *noun* **(a)** a, usually two-wheeled, vehicle designed to be towed behind a car **(b)** the goods-containing part of an articulated lorry that is drawn by the cab **(c)** *US* caravan

trailing arm *or* **link** *noun* rear suspension link which supports the wheel behind the pivot point; *(compare* LEADING ARM) *(see illustration 28)*

◊ **trailing axle** *noun* a dead axle

◊ **trailing edge** *noun* rear edge (e.g. of a body panel); *(compare* LEADING EDGE)

◊ **trailing shoe** *noun* shoe of a brake drum system whose activated end faces away from the approaching drum (NOTE: US English is **secondary shoe**) *(compare* LEADING SHOE)

tram(car) *noun* electrically driven public transport vehicle which runs on rails laid in the surface of the road and which is usually powered by an overhead cable (NOTE: US English is **streetcar**)

◊ **tram gauge** *noun (alignment tool)* basically, a long bar that has two or three parallel pointers extending at right angles and attached so that they can be moved to any position along its length

◊ **tramline** *or* **tramway** *noun* the rails along which a tram runs

◊ **tramlining** *noun* the tendency of a vehicle's tyres (often when of low profile) to follow a ridge or rut in the road's surface

tramp *noun* = AXLE TRAMP

tranny *noun US (informal)* = TRANSMISSION

transaxle *noun* combination of transmission and differential typical of FWD cars with transverse engines; *(compare* REAR-WHEEL DRIVE TRANSAXLE); **transaxle housing** = usually an aluminium casting for the transaxle; *(see illustrations 23, 24)*

transfer (gear)box *or* **transfer case** *noun* gearbox that transfers an input drive between two shafts, e.g. between front and rear axle in four-wheel drive vehicles

◊ **transfer passage** *noun* the passage connecting the crankcase of a two-stroke engine with the combustion chamber

◊ **transfer plate** *noun* adapter plate in the control valve assembly of automatic transmissions, used to direct the fluid flow between adjacent valve bodies

◊ **transfer port** *noun* port in the cylinder of a two-stroke engine through which the compressed combustible air/fuel mixture enters the combustion chamber from the crankcase; *(compare* SCAVENGING PASSAGE); **transfer port cover** = the transfer passages of most two-stroke engines are accessible from the outside to allow for maintenance, they are covered by the transfer port covers for regular engine operation

transistorized coil ignition (TCI) (system) *noun* = TRANSISTORIZED IGNITION (SYSTEM); **transistorized coil ignition with Hall sensor (TCI-H)** = TRANSISTORIZED IGNITION WITH HALL GENERATOR; **transistorized ignition (system) (TI)** = ignition system using a transistor as a power switch; available as breaker-triggered TI with contact breaker or as breakerless TI with magnetic pick-up or Hall generator; **transistorized ignition**

system with inductive pulse generator = TRANSISTORIZED IGNITION WITH INDUCTIVE PICK-UP; **transistorized ignition with Hall generator (TI-H)** = there are two types of TI-H: in one version, the dwell angle is determined by the width of the rotor vanes in the distributor; the other version contains a circuit for automatic dwell angle control incorporated in the electronic control unit; **transistorized ignition with inductive** _or_ **magnetic pick-up (TI-I)** = transistorized ignition system with a magnetic pick-up in the distributor and an electronic control unit for signal processing, with current and dwell angle control

transmission _noun_ **(a)** the transference of motive force or power **(b)** the drive train system from clutch to final drive **(c)** _US_ gearbox; _(compare_ AUTOMATIC TRANSMISSION)

◊ **transmission controlled spark (TCS)** _noun_ system to reduce the emission of nitrous oxides by which a vacuum solenoid and a switch in the transmission system prevents the distributor's vacuum advance mechanism from operating in the lower gears and at low speed

◊ **transmission control module (TCM)** _noun_ electronic automatic transmission control unit which computes data on the actual operating conditions of the vehicle and generates corresponding signal pulses for the solenoid valves of the hydraulic control system; may also exchange data with other electronic control units

◊ **transmission control system** _noun_ hydraulic or electro-hydraulic system which controls the changes of ratio in automatic transmissions corresponding to engine load, vehicle speed, positions of the selector lever, and shift mode button

◊ **transmission cover** _noun_ a removable part of the floorpan usually located at the front end of the centre tunnel in cars with a longitudinally mounted engine; provides better access to the top of the gearbox for maintenance and adjustment purposes

◊ **transmission extension (housing)** _noun_ rear-wheel drive transmission housing enclosing an extended main shaft, sometimes accommodating the gear lever and associated mechanism

◊ **transmission governor** _noun_ = GOVERNOR (b)

◊ **transmission housing** _noun_ housing containing the gearbox and final

drive on front-wheel drive cars with transverse engines in which housing and clutch are at opposite ends of the engine

◊ **transmission tunnel** _noun_ a semi-circular or oval bulge along the longitudinal axis of the floorpan to accommodate the propeller shaft and, at its front end, the transmission, enabling the shaft and transmission mounting position to be raised to the floorpan level, thus providing better protection for the drive train against road dirt and obstacles

transmitter _noun (e.g. of radio remote control system)_ device that transmits electrical or radio signals (NOTE: opposite is **receiver**)

transplants _noun_ strictly speaking an overseas production plant; in most cases, the term refers to automotive vehicles produced in Europe at Japanese-owned factories

| COMMENT: some European car manufacturers insist such transplants should be considered Japanese and should be subject to the quota system for Japanese imports; Japanese firms argue that transplants should be considered European cars

transporter _noun_ large articulated lorry for transporting several cars (on two or three decks)

transverse engine _noun_ the typical engine arrangement on FWD subcompact cars with the engine mounted across the car, which reduces the length of the engine compartment, resulting in more space for the passenger compartment; introduced in 1959 by the British design engineer Sir Alec Issigonis on the BMC Mini (NOTE: also called **east-west layout;** the opposite is **longitudinal engine)**

◊ **transverse (flow) scavenging** _noun_ = CROSS SCAVENGING

◊ **transverse leaf spring** _noun_ usually a semi-elliptic leaf spring mounted across the car for either front or rear suspension, with radius arms being necessary to locate the axle

◊ **transverse link** _noun_ any suspension link that provides lateral support for wheels; on front suspensions, a typical design is the Y-shaped wishbone; _(compare_ WISHBONE) _(see illustration 27)_

◊ **transverse rod** _noun_ = PANHARD ROD

trap _noun_ a filter or separator _flame trap, oil trap_ **trap oxidizer** = in diesel particulate filters, a means of burning the particulate charge trapped in the filter element, to prevent the filter from clogging and to restore filtration capacity; usually a catalyst coating that promotes oxidation of carbon particulates to harmless carbon dioxide

◇ **trapped volume** *noun* = CLEARANCE VOLUME

◇ **trapping efficiency** *noun (of two-stroke engines)* the mass of fresh charge in a cylinder actually retained, divided by the mass of fresh charge supplied per cycle; *(compare* CHARGING EFFICIENCY)

travel *noun* the distance moved by a mechanical part when performing an operation; e.g. the stroke of a piston

tray table *noun* table that folds out of the back of the front seat (similar to those found on aeroplanes)

TR-Denloc rim, wheel = TD RIM, WHEEL

tread *noun* **(a)** the part of the tyre that makes contact with the road; it is the thickest part of the tyre and is cut with grooves to provide traction for driving and stopping; *(see illustration 32)* **(b)** *US* = TRACK

◇ **tread bar** *noun* a block of tyre tread between two grooves *the sipes go down to the edge of the tread bar (see illustration 32)*

◇ **tread depth** *noun* the depth of the grooves in a tyre tread; 1.6 mm across three-quarters of the tyre width is a legal requirement; **tread depth gauge** = simple compact device for measuring the depth of tread, consisting of a spring-loaded plunger calibrated in millimetres

◇ **tread groove** *noun* one of several channels cut in the tread that disperses water when the road is wet; *(compare* SIPES) *(see illustration 32)*

◇ **tread pattern** *noun* tread patterns differ according to the manufacturer of the tyre but they all have in common the aim of dispersing water from the road to enhance grip and to avoid aquaplaning, the dispersion of heat and the reduction of noise and wear; **tread pattern percentage (TPP)** = the percentage of grooves and sipes to the overall surface of the tread; car tyres have a TPP of about 30%

◇ **tread profile** *noun* the shape of the tread as seen in cross section

◇ **tread rib** *noun* = TREAD BAR

◇ **tread wear indicators (TWI)** *noun* raised bars at the bottom of the grooves at several places round the tyre to indicate when the tread has worn down to the legal limit; may be indicated on the sidewall by a symbol or the letters TWI

triangular earth electrode *noun* earth electrode having three bridges attached to its end points, which form a link to the threaded shell

◇ **triangular safety reflector** *noun* = WARNING TRIANGLE

tricar *noun* old name for a three-wheeler

trichlorethene *or* **trichlorethylene** **(C$_2$HCl$_3$)** *noun* cleaning solvent

trickle charge *noun* continuous charging of a storage battery at a low rate to keep it in a fully charged condition for a period when no current is drawn from it; **trickle charger** = small, mains-operated battery charger, typically delivering less than five amperes

trigger box *noun* = IGNITION CONTROL UNIT

◇ **triggering device** *or* **unit** electronic control unit that triggers the air bag in a crash, containing a deceleration sensor, a Hamlin switch and a check circuit

◇ **trigger wheel** *noun* **(a)** rotor of a magnetic pick-up integrated into the distributor, with as many teeth as the engine has cylinders; *(compare* TIMING ROTOR) **(b)** *(Hall generator)* rotor with an outer ring interrupted by one or several Hall windows, depending on its purpose

trim *noun* **(a)** a car's interior decoration, including the upholstery, roof and door linings (NOTE: also called **soft trim**) *(compare* HARD TRIM) **(b)** a car's exterior decoration, including wheel trims, rubbing strips, bezels

◇ **trim panel** *noun* decorative interior panel; **trim panel release tool** = fork-like tool used to pry out fasteners on interior panels without breaking them or damaging the car

trip computer *noun* computer with a multifunction display; supplies the driver with trip information such as range, ETA, distance to destination, time, fuel economy, fuel consumption, average speed, accumulated trip miles, elapsed time since last reset

triplex chain *noun* a chain with three rows of rollers; *(compare* DUPLEX CHAIN, SIMPLEX CHAIN)

trip meter *or* **trip mileage counter** *noun* = TRIP RECORDER

tripod joint *noun* widely used constant velocity joint with three balls engaged in curved grooves

trip odometer *noun* = TRIP RECORDER

◇ **trip recorder** *noun* incorporated in the speedometer, the trip recorder indicates the mileage (in miles or km) covered during a particular journey (trip), either mechanically or electronically; trip figures can be reset to zero by turning or pushing a reset button; *(compare* ODOMETER)

trolleybus *noun* electrically powered public transport bus that takes its power from overhead wires

◇ **trolley jack** *noun* hydraulic jack with swivel wheels

troy weight *noun* system of measurement of weight used for gold and other metals, such as silver and platinum; **troy ounce** = measurement of weight (= 31.10 grammes) (NOTE: in writing, often shortened to **troy oz.** after figures: **25.2 troy oz.**)

> COMMENT: troy weight is divided into grains, pennyweights (24 grains = 1 pennyweight), ounces (20 pennyweights = 1 ounce) and pounds (12 troy ounces = 1 pound). Troy weights are slightly less than their avoirdupois equivalents; the troy pound equals 0.37kg or 0.82lb avoirdupois

TR rim *noun* safety rim developed by Michelin with a flattened rim flange and run-flat potential; *(compare* TD RIM)

Truarc retaining ring *noun* internal or external circlip of rectangular cross section with holes for easier installation and removal

truck *noun* a large lorry

true *adjective & adverb* accurately made or correctly adjusted; **the wheel runs true** = the

wheel rolls straight without any wobble or deviation from side to side (NOTE: opposite is **out of true**)

◇ **true up** *verb* = DRESS

trunk *noun US* boot

tube *noun* **(a)** long hollow cylinder for carrying liquids or gas; **tube bender** = tool for bending tubing without collapsing it, e.g. pipe bending pliers; **tube cutter** = tool with cutting wheels for cutting off tubing evenly at right angles **(b)** = INNER TUBE

◇ **tubed** *adjective (of a tyre)* having an inner tube *tubed tyre*

◇ **tubeless** *adjective (of a tyre)* having no inner tube; **tubeless tyre** = tyre with no inner tube, whose air pressure is maintained by an air-tight seal between the outer casing of the tyre and the wheel rim

◇ **tubing reamer** *noun* tool used to remove burrs on tubes, e.g. after a tube cutter is used when servicing the brake line system

◇ **tubular** *adjective* in the shape of a tube; cylindrical; **tubular backbone frame** = a backbone chassis with a tubular central spine; **tubular frame** = frame construction that features members of tubular cross section; often used for racing cars, as this layout allows for weight-saving design with the use of aluminium; **tubular nut driver** *or* **spinner** = nut driver with handle and tubular shank for driving hexagon nuts and bolts

tucking *noun* reducing the length of certain sections of a panel (NOTE: opposite is **throwing**)

> COMMENT: when making a panel with rounded edges that has to be folded along the inner edge, the radius along this edge must be increased and its length reduced; this is done by thickening the material in certain areas

tumblehome *noun* the inward sloping of a car's body above the waistline; *(compare* TURN-UNDER)

tumbling *noun* the smoothing of an aluminium surface by tumbling it in rotating barrels with metallic or ceramic shot but without any form of abrasive

tuner *noun* that component/circuit of a radio which tunes to the frequencies of radio stations; (tuner + amplifier = receiver)

tune (up) *verb* to adjust an engine to obtain optimum performance; e.g. adjustment of the ignition timing, valve clearances and the carburettor's idling circuit, and servicing of the distributor and sparking plugs *a well-tuned, properly maintained vehicle will deliver better fuel economy than a neglected vehicle*

◊ **tuned header** *noun* = HIGH-PERFORMANCE HEADER

◊ **tune-up** *noun* adjustments made to an engine to improve its performance; **tune-up decal** *or* **label** = VEHICLE EMISSION CONTROL INFORMATION

tungsten *noun* hard, malleable, greyish-white element used in lamp filaments, electrical contact points and, alloyed with steel, in high-speed cutting tools; **tungsten-halogen bulb** = a quartz-halogen bulb with a tungsten filament

tuning *noun* the adjustment of carburettor, ignition timing, etc. to improve performance

tunnel drier *or* **tunnel furnace** *noun* heated tunnel through which body shells are passed in painting lines, e.g. to dry their phosphate coatings

◊ **tunnelling** *noun* moving a component deeply into its surrounding sheet metal to give the appearance of being recessed, e.g. headlights, tail lights and aerials; *(compare* FRENCHING)

turbine *noun* machine which produces power by the action of water, steam, gas, etc. turning a wheel with blades

◊ **turbine housing** *or* **casing** *noun* the casing enclosing a turbine; *(see illustration 10)*

COMMENT: turbochargers use almost exclusively a radial-inflow turbine with a single or twin entry internal volute tract which directs and accelerates the exhaust gas through the turbine; the turbine housing gradually changes the angle of gas flow from tangential to axial (at the outlet nozzle); most turbine housings are cast in spheroidal graphite (SG) nodular iron; for heavy-duty housings, a high-nickel cast iron is used

turbine wheel *noun* **(a)** *(of a turbocharger)* wheel driven by exhaust gases, the turbine wheel spins at speeds up to 160,000 rpm and drives the compressor which is located at the opposite end of the turbine shaft; wheel and shaft are usually inseparable; *(see illustration 10)* **(b)** *(of a torque converter)* driven member which

transmits multiplied engine torque to the transmission input shaft; *(compare* IMPELLER, STATOR)

turbocharged engine *noun* engine fitted with a turbocharger

turbocharger *or (informal)* **turbo** *noun* a centrifugal compressor or supercharger driven by exhaust gas energy; *(see illustration 10)*

COMMENT: the typical turbocharger consists of a radial inflow exhaust gas turbine with a diameter of about 50 mm (for a 2000 cc engine), surrounded by a vaneless turbine housing. The turbine drives a centrifugal compressor which is mounted at the opposite end of the turbine shaft; between turbine and compressor is a bearing housing; operating speeds are about 100,000 rpm, operating temperatures of the turbine as high as 1,000°C, service life may cover up to 100,000 miles before overhaul. Advantages: low weight, small size, high efficiency, no wear, good fuel economy, low emissions; disadvantages: requires high engine rpm, no improvement of low-end torque, turbo lag

turbocharging *noun* a method of extracting more power from an engine of a given capacity by means of a turbine unit driven by exhaust gases and rotating at very high speed

COMMENT: with a greater volume of air entering the combustion chamber during each induction stroke, a correspondingly greater amount of fuel can be admitted and burnt, thus producing more power

turbo diesel (engine) *noun* a diesel engine which is turbocharged; **turbo diesel engine with direct injection (TDI)** = directly injected turbo diesel engine (NOTE: opposite is **swirl-chamber diesel engine**)

◊ **turbo gauge** *noun* boost pressure gauge of turbocharged engines

◊ **turbo lag** *noun* the time it takes a turbocharger to respond after the accelerator pedal has been depressed

◊ **turbo-supercharger** *noun* = TURBOCHARGER

turbulence *noun* = SWIRL

turnbuckle *noun* metal sleeve with opposite internal threads at each end for the threaded ends of two rods or for ringbolts, forming a coupling that can be turned to tighten or loosen the rods or wires attached to the ringbolts

◇ **turning circle** *noun* the smallest circle in which a vehicle can turn, i.e. with the wheels on full lock; **turning radius** = the radius of the turning circle

◇ **turn-in rate** *noun* the way a car steers into a bend; the roll-steer effect

◇ **turn into the skid** *verb* to turn the steering wheel in the same direction as that in which the rear of the car is sliding, in order to counteract the skid

◇ **turnpike** *noun US* toll road, especially one that is an expressway

◇ **turn signal indicator** *noun* = DIRECTION INDICATOR

◇ **turn-under** *noun* the inward sloping of a car's body below the waistline; *(compare* TUMBLEHOME)

TVS = THERMAL VACUUM SWITCH

◇ **TVV** = THERMAL VACUUM VALVE

TWC = THREE-WAY CATALYST

tweak *verb (informal)* to tune an engine for peak performance

twelve-cylinder engine *noun* an engine with twelve cylinders, e.g. a V-12

twelve-valve (engine) *noun* three-cylinder engine with four valves per cylinder (e.g. Daihatsu), or a six-cylinder engine with two valves per cylinder, or a four-cylinder engine with three valves per cylinder, i.e. two inlet valves and one exhaust valve

TWI = TREAD WEAR INDICATORS

twin A-arm suspension *noun* = DOUBLE WISHBONE SUSPENSION

◇ **twin axle** *noun* = TANDEM AXLE

◇ **twin barrel** *or* **twin choke carburettor** *noun* carburettor with two identical barrels to feed two banks of cylinders

◇ **twin cam(shaft) engine** *noun* = DOUBLE OVERHEAD CAMSHAFT ENGINE

◇ **twin carburettors (TC)** *noun* two carburettors on an engine, mechanically coupled and balanced

◇ **twin diaphragm pump** *noun* diaphragm pump with two diaphragms; if one fails the other takes over its function

◇ **twin exhaust system** *noun* exhaust system with two tailpipes; either a complete exhaust system, as on performance cars and cars with V-engines, or simply two tailpipes emanating from the rear silencer (NOTE: US English is **dual exhaust system)**

◇ **twin front pipe** *or* **twin header** *or* **headpipe** *noun* = Y-PIPE

◇ **twin headlamp** *noun* headlamp arrangement containing two headlights; the outer lights provide the main and dipped beams, the inner lights are for main beam only

◇ **twin ignition (system)** *noun* distributor with two sets of contact points, each of which operates with its own coil in a separate primary circuit; the contact points open alternately, each set firing half of the cylinders

◇ **twin overhead camshaft** *noun* = DOUBLE OVERHEAD CAMSHAFT

◇ **twin-piston engine** *noun* now obsolete two-stroke engine design featuring two cylinder barrels plus two pistons per cylinder; the pistons are linked to the crankshaft via a forked con rod or a master/slave con rod assembly

◇ **twin planets** *noun* two planet gears in mesh; one meshes with the sun gear and the other with the internal gear

◇ **twin-plate clutch** *noun* clutch with two driven plates separated by an intermediate drive plate; gives higher torque capacity

◇ **twin plug** *or* **twin spark ignition** *noun* = TWIN IGNITION (SYSTEM)

◇ **twin swirl combustion chamber** *noun* special design of a four-stroke engine, in which the intake valves are arranged in such a way as to ensure that the gas flow ends in two separate swirls; this design improves swirl and thus enhances combustion of the fuel/air mixture within the cylinder

◇ **twin-tube damper** *noun* = DOUBLE-TUBE SHOCK ABSORBER

◇ **twin wheel** *noun* **(a)** a double-rimmed wheel with two independently inflated tyres; has good aquaplaning and run-flat properties; *(compare* JJD WHEEL) **(b)** with two wheels fitted to one hub (as in HGVs)

twist-beam rear axle *noun* = SEMI-INDEPENDENT SUSPENSION

◊ **twist drill** *noun* drill bit having two helical grooves running from the point along the shank

twisted frame *noun* type of frame damage often encountered as a result of the car rolling over

COMMENT: the left-hand and right-hand frame members are then no longer parallel and on a level when viewed from the side; instead, they are offset as if they had been turned on a horizontal axis at right angles to the frame members

two-coat system *noun* = BASE AND CLEAR SYSTEM

◊ **two-cycle engine** *noun* = TWO-STROKE ENGINE

◊ **two-door** *adjective* having one door on each side; a body design typical of all two-seater sports cars (such as roadsters, spiders) and many subcompact cars *a two-door hatch(back)*

◊ **two-pack filler** *noun* all polyester fillers in use today comprise a basic filler paste and a hardener or catalyst; **two-pack paint** = paint prepared by mixing two constituents, such as pigment and an acrylic resin

◊ **two-piece (forged) alloy wheel** *noun* wheel which consists of the rim and the wheel disc or spider bolted together (NOTE: 'forged' is optional, since multi-piece alloy wheels are always forged and not cast; compare CAST-ALLOY WHEEL)

◊ **two-speed** *adjective* having two speed settings (e.g. fan, windscreen wiper); **two-speed gearbox** = DUAL-RANGE GEARBOX

◊ **two-stage carburettor** *noun* = COMPOUND CARBURETTOR; **two-stage pump** = generally a centrifugal pump with two impellers and diffusers arranged in series

two-stroke cycle *noun* operating principle of an internal combustion engine characterized by the fact that the inlet, compression, combustion and exhaust phases overlap and require only two cycles; used mainly by small motorcycle engines (NOTE: opposite is **four-stroke cycle)**; **two-stroke engine** = an engine operating on the two-stroke cycle

COMMENT: on cars, the two-stroke engine was never very popular and was never produced in the USA; a new two-stroke engine concept with separate lubrication system and a valve system similar to four-

stroke engines may combine the benefits of both the 2-stroke and the 4-stroke systems

two-tone horn *noun* two horns whose diaphragms cause a column of air to resonate at two different frequencies; **two-tone paint** = paint colour of two different shades *the two-tone paint scheme sets off the body lines to good effect*

◊ **two-valve engine** *noun* engine with two valves per cylinder; **two-valve head** = cylinder head with two valves per cylinder

◊ **two-way catalyst** *noun* = OXIDIZING CATALYST; **two-way (catalytic) converter** = OXIDIZING CONVERTER

◊ **two-way system** *noun* turbocharging system in which, as long as the charging pressure is insufficient, the air is drawn in from a prechamber via a diaphragm valve; with rising charging pressure, the valve closes and the turbocharger delivers air via the surge tank connected to a pressure regulator

◊ **two-wheel drive** *noun* the normal drive for a vehicle in which two of the four wheels (either front or rear) are driven; *(compare* FOUR-WHEEL DRIVE); **two-wheel driven** = of a vehicle with two-wheel drive; also written '4x2'

type approval certificate *noun* certificate issued by the Department of Transport denoting that a particular vehicle type meets official requirements

◊ **type designation** *or* **symbol** *noun* sparking plug designation indicating seat and thread type, version, heat range code number, reach, spark position, and electrode material

tyre *noun* the casing-and-tread assembly that is mounted on a wheel to provide pneumatically cushioned contact and traction with the road *(see illustration 32)*

◊ **tyre bead** *noun* the part of a tyre which is shaped to fit the rim and rests on the rim bead seat; made of steel wires, wrapped and reinforced by the plies of the tyre; *(compare* BEAD BASE, BEAD HEEL, BEAD SEAT, BEAD TOE, SAFETY RIM) *(see illustration 32)*; **tyre bead lock** = the tyre bead and rim of a TD rim are designed so that an enlarged and reinforced toe on the tyre bead engages in a small circumferential groove in the bead seat area of the rim; the bead thus remains locked in position under both inflated and deflated conditions

◊ **tyre body** *noun* = CARCASS

◊ **tyre chains** *noun* = SNOW CHAINS

◇ **tyre contact area/zone** *noun* = CONTACT PATCH

◇ **tyre gauge** *noun* = TYRE PRESSURE GAUGE

◇ **tyre iron** *noun* = TYRE LEVER (NOTE: the term **tyre iron** is occasionally used to denote a wheelbrace with a flat end and a socket end)

◇ **tyre kicker** *noun (informal)* in car sales jargon, a person who is just looking, not buying

◇ **tyre lever** *noun* special automotive tool used to remove and install tyres by lever action or to prize off parts (NOTE: US English is **iron**)

tyre pressure *noun* manufacturer's recommended pressure for a tyre, dependent on load, speed, etc., usually given in bar, or pound-force per square inch (psi); **tyre pressure gauge** = instrument for measuring air pressure in a tyre; *(compare* OVERINFLATED TYRE, UNDERINFLATED TYRE)

COMMENT: 1.8 bar = 26 psi; 2 bar = 29 psi; 2.2 bar = 32 psi; 2.4 bar = 35 psi; 2.7 bar = 39 psi

tyre rotation *noun* = WHEEL ROTATION

◇ **tyre scuff** *noun* = TYRE WEAR

◇ **tyre size (designation)** *noun* specified on the tyre sidewall; e.g. P 205/60 R 15, where: P = Passenger car; 205 = tyre width in millimetres; 60 = tyre section height to width ratio; R = radial ply; 15 = nominal rim diameter in inches

◇ **tyre slip angle** *noun* = SLIP ANGLE

◇ **tyre squeal** *noun* noise made by the tyres when suffering sudden acceleration or braking or when cornering too fast

◇ **tyre tread gauge** *noun* = TREAD DEPTH GAUGE

◇ **tyre valve** *noun* the function of the tyre valve is to admit air under pressure to the tyre chamber formed between the casing and the rim, and to release air for pressure-adjustment purposes or for tyre removal; car tubeless tyres use a snap-in valve; *(compare* VALVE HOLE, VALVE SLOT)

◇ **tyre wear** *noun* the amount by which, for example, the tread of a tyre is worn down, or the sidewall damaged by impact with the kerb; *(compare* FEATHERING, OVERINFLATED TYRE, SCRUBBING, SCUFF RIB, UNDERINFLATED TYRE)

◇ **tyre width** *noun* the width of a tyre, measured across the carcass

Uu

U-bolt *noun* metal bar in the shape of a U, threaded at both ends and often with a bridging piece to close the circle; used to secure leaf springs, exhaust pipes, ring bolts, shackles, etc.

U-cylinder engine *noun* = TWIN-PISTON ENGINE

UDC = UPPER DEAD CENTRE

UJ *or* **U-joint** = UNIVERSAL JOINT

ultrasonic welding *noun* a high-tech welding procedure used for metals (e.g. in wire bonding of integrated circuits) and plastics

COMMENT: pressure is applied to the parts to be joined and ultrasonic vibrations are transmitted through the materials; frictional heat at the materials interface causes localized melting and coalescence; ultrasonic welding is fast and produces precise, strong welds

unburnt hydrocarbons *noun* pollutant (basically petrol vapour) released into the atmosphere as an exhaust gas, due to incomplete combustion

uncluttered *adjective (instrument panel)* ordered, neat, free of irrelevant detail *the fascia is commendably uncluttered*

UNC thread *noun* Unified National Coarse thread; one of the screw threads used on British cars; *compare* UNF THREAD

underbody *noun* the underside of a car; **underbody coating** *or* **underbody protection** = coating of the underbody of a vehicle, usually with organic coating materials (plastic, wax, bitumen-based products), to protect it from mechanical damage and corrosion; **underbody sealing compound** = UNDERSEAL; **underbody structure** = the structural members and flat panels of the bodywork on the chassis level (NOTE: may also be called **substructure)**

◇ **underbonnet area** *noun* the engine compartment

◇ **undercarriage** *noun* = UNDERBODY STRUCTURE

undercoat *noun* **(a)** any preliminary coat of paint applied prior to the top coat **(b)** *US* = UNDERSEAL

COMMENT: undercoats are used to build up the thickness of a paint film, cover the primer and filler and give opacity to the colour of the finish coats, as well as providing a smooth surface for their application where a high gloss is required

undercut *noun* recess either cut or moulded into the underside of an object so as to leave a lip or protuberance at the top

◇ **underfilm corrosion** *noun* = CREEPAGE

◇ **underfloor** *noun* the underside of a car; **underfloor mid-engine** = new design, introduced on the Toyota Previa minivan, where the engine is located below the passenger compartment, between front and rear

◇ **underframe** *noun* general term referring to the underbody backbone of a car, both for unitary or chassis designs

◇ **underhead collar** *noun* washer fitted under the head of a bolt or screw

◇ **underinflated tyre** *noun* tyre which has too little air in it, causing increased wear at the tread edge (NOTE: opposite is **overinflated tyre)**

◇ **underpowered** *adjective* of a car whose engine provides less power than is necessary for acceptable performance; especially noticeable when accelerating, overtaking or going uphill

◇ **underseal 1** *noun* rustproof coating with sound-deadening properties applied to the underbody (NOTE: US English is **undercoat) 2** *verb* to apply underseal

◇ **under seat panel** *noun* = SEAT WELL

undershield *noun* body accessory panel made from tough, oil-resistant plastic for fitting on cars that do not have a standard wheel house panel

COMMENT: it is designed to protect the upper inside area of the wing and the door hinge area from splashes of water and mud deposits; it is also used as standard equipment on some modern cars to replace the traditional steel wheel house panel

underside *noun* the lower side of the underbody, i.e. the surfaces that face the road surface; **underside panelling** = smooth covers on the underside of a car for improving aerodynamics below the vehicle, e.g. on the Porsche 911 and 928

◊ **under sill panel** *noun* a separate closing panel or section used on cars where the inner sill or side member consists of several separate parts; it forms the bottom of the inner sill and connects the sill area to the floor panel

◊ **underslung** *adjective* suspended below a supporting member, e.g. of a chassis suspended below the axles *underslung leaf spring* **underslung frame** = frame design of the pre-war era whose characteristic feature is that the frame members run below the axles

◊ **undersquare engine** *noun* = LONG STROKE ENGINE

◊ **understeer 1** *verb (of a vehicle)* to turn less sharply than the driver intends **2** *noun* action of understeering (NOTE: opposite is **oversteer)**

◊ **undertray** *noun* the bottom panel of multi-layer or complex underbody panel assemblies, which faces the road surface

◊ **undertread** *noun* = BREAKER (b)

unequal-length wishbone suspension *or (informal)* **unequal wishbones** *noun* double wishbone suspension system in which the upper wishbone is shorter than the lower one, with both converging slightly at the wheel hub; reduces tyre wear due to variations in track and camber angle when cornering

UNF thread *noun* Unified National Fine thread; one of the screw threads used on British cars; *compare* UNC THREAD

unibody (construction) *noun* = UNITARY CONSTRUCTION

unidirectional (flow) scavenging *or* **uniflow scavenging** *noun* scavenging process of two-stroke engines

COMMENT: one of the characteristic features is that the flow of fresh charge does not follow a path opposed to that of the burnt charge; scavenging and exhaust ports are not located at the same stroke end of the piston but rather are staggered, i.e. the fresh charge flows along the length of the cylinder without its direction being reversed. This process is widely used in large engines, e.g. for ships

Unified National Coarse thread *see* UNC THREAD

Unified National Fine thread *see* UNF THREAD

uniform corrosion *noun* corrosion occurring over the entire exposed surface (NOTE: opposite is **localized corrosion)**

union nut *noun* nut used to secure the connection between pipes or rods

uni-servo brake *noun* a servo brake with one single-end wheel cylinder and two self-energizing brake shoes

unitary construction *noun* modern chassis layout with no separate frame, using the sheet metal parts of the vehicle body or floorpan as structural members which also carry all suspension parts; introduced by Citroën in 1934, by GM/Opel Olympia in 1935 (NOTE: also called **monocoque)** *(compare* COACHBUILT CONSTRUCTION, SKELETON CONSTRUCTION)

unit engine *noun* a term used for motorcycles where engine and gearbox are accommodated in one common housing

universal joint (UJ) *noun* **(a)** a form of coupling between two rotating shafts allowing freedom of movement in all directions; general term for a family of universal joint designs; *(compare* CARDAN JOINT, CONSTANT VELOCITY JOINT, FLEXIBLE COUPLING, YOKE) *(see illustrations 22, 24, 28)* **(b)** *(tool)* accessory which allows a socket to be turned through an angle; **universal joint socket** = socket with universal joint to reach into cramped working areas

◊ **universally jointed shaft** *noun* = CARDAN SHAFT

◊ **universal sparking plug socket** *noun* sparking plug socket with universal joint for reaching hard-to-get-at sparking plugs

unleaded petrol *noun* petrol to which no lead has been added

COMMENT: unleaded petrol must be used in cars fitted with a catalytic converter as the lead destroys the catalyst

unloader valve *noun* = DELIVERY VALVE

unsprung mass *or* **weight** *noun* the weight of those parts of the car which are not carried by the suspension system, but are supported directly by the tyre and wheel assembly and considered to move with it *wheels have to be light in order to reduce the unsprung weight of the car* (NOTE: opposite is **sprung mass/weight**)

updraught carburettor *noun* carburettor in which the air/fuel mixture is drawn in from below; a rather unusual type (NOTE: opposite is **downdraught carburettor**)

upper dead centre (UDC) *noun* = TOP DEAD CENTRE

up-stroke *noun* the ascending stroke of a piston, from BDC to TDC

urban driving *noun* driving in towns, in built-up areas (NOTE: US English is **metro driving**)

urban (test) cycle *noun* driving cycle that simulates driving in a town

U section *noun* a sheet metal section often used on underbody structural members; it differs from a box section in that the fourth wall of the box is missing, i.e. its cross section more or less resembles the letter U

ute *(informal) (Australia)* = UTILITY TRUCK

utility (truck) *noun* = PICK-UP

UV absorber *or* **stabilizer** *noun* any substance that absorbs ultraviolet radiation, then dissipates the energy in a harmless form; used in plastics and rubbers to decrease light sensitivity

Vv

V (a) *see* V-ENGINE **(b)** *(short for)* valve *16v engine* **(c)** *(short for)* volt **(d)** letter on the sidewall of a tyre denoting the maximum speed for which it is designed (over 210 km/h or over 130 mph); *(see* SPEED RATING)

V-4, V-6, V-8, V-10, V-12 = V-FOUR, V-SIX, V-EIGHT, V-TEN, V-TWELVE ENGINE

vacuum *noun* in carburation terms, pressure below the atmospheric pressure

◊ **vacuum advance (mechanism** *or* **unit)** *noun* vacuum control unit for advancing the spark (NOTE: opposite is **vacuum retard unit**)

◊ **vacuum brake booster** *noun* device directly connected to the master cylinder and mounted on the engine side of the bulkhead, which uses engine manifold vacuum to produce additional braking force (NOTE: also called **master vac** *or* **vacuum servo**)

◊ **vacuum capsule** *or* **chamber** *noun* *(ignition timing)* pneumatic actuator that converts air pressure differences into a regulating short-stroke movement; the circular, flat capsule has a spring-loaded diaphragm with a lever attached; *(compare* VACUUM CONTROL UNIT)

◊ **vacuum control** *noun* load-dependant mechanical ignition timing, controlled by the inlet manifold vacuum; *(compare* VACUUM ADVANCE, VACUUM RETARD)**; vacuum control switch** = switch that monitors the vacuum signal enabling the ECU to recognize open or closed throttle (idle) operation; **vacuum control unit** = assembly for load-dependent ignition timing controlled by the inlet manifold vacuum, consisting of a vacuum capsule with a spring-loaded diaphragm linked to the breaker plate; *(compare* VACUUM CAPSULE)

◊ **vacuum filter** *noun* filter which removes electrical noise from the vacuum signal sent from the vacuum sensor to the ECU

◊ **vacuum gauge** *noun* instrument for measuring engine depression *hook up the vacuum gauge between the EGR valve and carburettor and check the vacuum*

◊ **vacuum hose** *noun* pipe which connects the inlet manifold to the vacuum brake booster

◊ **vacuum ignition-timing control** *noun* = VACUUM CONTROL

vacuum modulated EGR *noun* exhaust gas recirculation in which the amount of exhaust gas admitted to the inlet manifold depends on a vacuum signal controlled by throttle position

> COMMENT: when the throttle is closed, at idle or during deceleration, there is no vacuum signal to the EGR valve; as the throttle is opened, a vacuum signal is supplied causing the EGR valve to open

vacuum reducer valve (VRV) *noun* valve used to limit the amount of vacuum governing the ignition advance mechanism of the distributor; on some ignition systems, a VRV is used to reduce inlet manifold vacuum when the coolant temperature is above 104°C, in order to prevent detonation

◊ **vacuum retard (unit)** *noun* vacuum control unit for retarding the spark (NOTE: opposite is **vacuum advance unit**)

◊ **vacuum sealing apparatus** *noun* component in continuous zinc vapour deposition lines through which steel strips enter the deposition chamber and which prevents a build-up of pressure within the chamber

◊ **vacuum sensor** *noun* sensor which detects changes in manifold pressure; such changes indicate the need for an adjustment in A/F mixture and electronic spark timing to maintain efficient engine operation

◊ **vacuum servo** *noun* = VACUUM BRAKE BOOSTER

◊ **vacuum solenoid** *noun* on some engines, a vacuum solenoid controlled by an electrical sensor switch is used to control the EGR valve

◊ **vacuum suction cup** *noun* hand tool for pulling out shallow body dents and for lifting flat, heavy objects such as windscreens or sheet metal

◇ **vacuum timing control** noun = VACUUM CONTROL

◇ **vacuum unit** noun = VACUUM CONTROL UNIT

valance noun panel used to conceal structural detail or to provide extra protection; (compare REAR VALANCE)

valet parking noun the parking of one's car by a parking attendant; (compare SECONDARY KEY); **valet switch** = on some alarm systems, a switch to override the alarm system for valet parking, car washes, etc.

valve noun (a) any device that starts, stops, regulates or controls the flow of a fluid, gas, etc. (b) (in cylinder head) valve which opens the respective ports during the induction and exhaust strokes and seals the compression chamber during the compression and expansion strokes *engine with two valves per cylinder* (compare POPPET VALVE) (c) = TYRE VALVE

◇ **valve adjusting screw** noun screw at the end of a rocker which bears on a pushrod; used to tilt the rocker and thus adjust the valve clearance *the feeler gauge should fit with a slight drag; if it does not, loosen the valve adjusting screw until it does* (see illustration 6)

◇ **valve angle** noun a segment of the full circle of a rotary disc valve cut out to admit the fresh charge into the cylinder

◇ **valve aperture** noun = VALVE HOLE

◇ **valve block** noun = CONTROL VALVE ASSEMBLY

◇ **valve body** noun part of the valve assembly containing plungers, pistons, springs, etc.; **valve body housing** = housing which incorporates the bores in which the valve spools slide and the canals which channel the oil flow; **valve body separator plate** = plate sandwiched between two gaskets which separates the upper and lower parts of the valve body

◇ **valve bounce** noun bouncing of a valve on its seat due to the valve spring resonating at very high engine speeds

◇ **valve bushing** noun = VALVE GUIDE

◇ **valve cap** noun screw-on cap for a tyre valve to prevent the entry of dirt and dust

◇ **valve clearance** noun the operating clearance between the rocker arm and the valve stem tip in an overhead valve engine

engines equipped with hydraulic tappets only very rarely need adjustment of the valve clearance (see illustration 6); **valve clearance depression** = recess in the piston crown

◇ **valve cover** noun US = ROCKER COVER

◇ **valve crown** noun = VALVE HEAD

◇ **valve cut-out** noun on some four-valve engines at low speed the main rocker arms open only two valves per combustion chamber in order to keep the energy of the gases at a high level; with increasing rpm, the energy of the gases becomes sufficiently strong for the remaining two valves to be opened via hydraulic locking bolts

◇ **valve diameter** noun inlet valves can be distinguished by their larger diameter

◇ **valve float** noun = VALVE BOUNCE

◇ **valve gear** noun mechanism that operates the inlet and exhaust valves; includes the cams, pushrods, rocker arms, etc. but not the valves themselves; (compare VALVE TRAIN)

valve grinder or **valve grinding tool** noun special automotive tool consisting of a wooden shaft and rubber suction cup(s) for hand grinding valves; (compare VALVE LAPPER); **valve grinding compound** = an abrasive compound used for refacing valve seats *raise the valve from the seat and apply a small amount of valve grinding compound to the valve seat*

COMMENT: the suction cup is placed on the valve head and the valve is pressed into the seat; turning the handle between one's hands will grind the valve into its seat; always use with grinding paste. Not to be confused with 'valve seat cutter' which is used to cut worn valve seats to a specific angle

valve guide noun replaceable tubular sleeve through which the stem of a valve passes; designed to keep the valve in proper alignment and to absorb the lateral forces on the valve stem as well as dissipating the heat of the valve stem to the surrounding cylinder head; (see illustration 6); **valve guide driver** = tool for installing valve guides; **valve guide reamer** = tool used to ream worn valve guides to accommodate oversized valve stems; **valve guide remover** = drift punch for driving out valve guides; **valve guide seal** = VALVE STEM SEAL

COMMENT: if a valve guide is worn, it will not guide the valve in a straight line, causing burnt valve faces or seats, loss of compression, and excessive oil consumption

valve head *noun* the disc at the end of the valve stem which performs the sealing operation in a poppet valve

valve hole *noun* the hole in the rim of a wheel for mounting tubeless tyres; *(compare* VALVE SLOT) *(see illustration 33)*

COMMENT: tubeless car tyres commonly have a snap-in valve consisting of a rubber moulding bonded to the metal stem casing. The rubber moulding has a groove formed at the base; when the valve is pulled through the valve hole, the pliable rubber base snaps into position. Commercial vehicle valves for tubeless tyres are all metal; they are attached to the rim and the valve hole by an extended thread formed at the base and secured by a nut. Airtight sealing is achieved by either an O-ring or a flat and flanged rubber washer. Commercial vehicle valve stems may have a single, double, or triple bend to accommodate different rim profiles and single and twin wheel combinations

valve keeper *noun* fastener for the valve stem in the upper valve retainer, e.g. a collet *remove the valve keepers, collars, and valve spring (see illustration 6)*

◇ **valve lapper** *noun* special automotive tool for grinding (lapping) valves into valve seats; some types are power-operated, thus allowing faster grinding compared with standard suction-type valve grinding tools; **valve lapping compound** = VALVE GRINDING COMPOUND

◇ **valve lash** *noun* = VALVE CLEARANCE

◇ **valve lift** *noun* the distance a valve is lifted from its seat by a cam, usually about a quarter of the diameter of the port

◇ **valve lifter** *noun* **(a)** any tool that compresses valve springs for removal and replacement **(b)** *US* = TAPPET

valve overlap *noun* short period between the opening of the inlet valve and the closing of the exhaust valve, when both valves are open

COMMENT: usually expressed in degrees of crankshaft rotation and determined by the valve timing, valve overlap is necessary for the efficient flow of gases in and out of the combustion chamber

valve plate *noun* = VALVE BODY SEPARATOR PLATE

◇ **valve port** *noun* the inlet or exhaust port of a four-stroke spark ignition engine

◇ **valve principle** *noun* the original method of ABS control using an electrically operated valve to control the air pressure; *(compare* PLUNGER PRINCIPLE)

◇ **valve rotator** *noun* = ROTO CAP

valve seat *noun* that part of a valve, or the part of the cylinder head against which it seats, which contacts the matching part; **valve seat cutter** = special automotive tool with cutting blades for use with power tools; used to cut worn valve seats with 30° or 45° angles; **valve seat face** = annular part of a valve head located at the valve seat of the cylinder head; **valve seat insert** *or* **ring** = ring-shaped insert of a harder metal than that of the cylinder head; the use of valve seat inserts dispenses with the need for lead in the fuel to act as a lubricant between the valve head and seat; *(see illustration 6)*

COMMENT: 'valve seat' often refers to the cylinder head half rather than the valve itself; the valve seat angle is usually 45°, less commonly 30° and many valve seats are renewable. For even cutting action, valve seat cutters are always used in combination with pilots. Two further valve seat cutters are used for the final cutting of valve seat edges to 15° and 75°. Not to be confused with a 'valve grinding tool', which is not used to cut worn seats, but to grind valves into seats

valve shim *noun* calibrated shim used to adjust valve clearance on OHV engines with bucket tappet assembly; for adjustment, a calibrated valve shim is placed or removed from between tappet and cam; **valve shim pliers** = special automotive tool for removal and installation of valve shims

◇ **valve slot** *noun* tube-type tyres require a valve slot instead of a valve hole to allow the tyre valve to be removed from the rim; a thread adaptor is moulded to a circular rubber patch vulcanized to the inner tube; the valve stem casing is then screwed onto the tube adaptor; *(compare* VALVE HOLE)

◇ **valve spool** *noun (in automatic transmission)* sliding cylindrical internal part of a valve with one or more sections of reduced diameter

◇ **valve spring** *noun* a coil spring used to close the valves and to keep the exhaust valve closed during the induction stroke, thus acting against the vacuum created in the cylinder; *(see illustrations 3, 6)*; **valve spring cap** *or* **collar** = retaining cap (of inlet/outlet valves) which secures the valve keeper on the valve stem; *(see illustration 6)*; **valve spring compressor** = special automotive tool used to compress valve springs for removal and replacement; the most common type is a

C-shaped clamp; **valve spring depressor** = lever-type tool used to depress valve springs, e.g. for removal and installation of valve stem seals; **valve spring lifter** = pliers-type tool with two expanding jaws, used to lift and compress valve springs for removal and replacement; **valve spring retainer** = VALVE SPRING CAP; **valve spring seat** = seat retaining the bottom of the valve spring (opposite to the valve spring cap); *(see illustration 6)*

◇ **valve stem** *noun* narrow cylindrical rod which supports the valve head and moves up and down in the valve guide; **valve stem seal** = oil seal between the valve and the cylinder head which prevents excessive oil leakage from the top of the cylinder head into the combustion chamber; *(see illustration 6)*; **valve stem seal installer** = sleeve-type tool used to push down valve stem seals for installation; **valve stem seal pliers** = special pliers for removing valve stem seals on overhead camshaft engines

◇ **valve timing** *noun* the valve timing of four-stroke engines state at what crankshaft position with respect to the dead centres of the pistons the inlet and exhaust valves open and close *valve timing index mark*

◇ **valve train** *noun* the entire mechanism from camshaft to valve that is involved with the operation of a valve; the valve and its valve gear *if the vehicle runs well and there is no audible clicking in the valve train, leave it alone*

van *noun* (a) a covered road vehicle for carrying goods (b) a recreational vehicle based on the body of a commercial van, usually with comfortable, plush interior trim, often with a bed

vane *noun* a blade or plate on a wheel or hub, especially the stator blade in a turbine

◇ **vane-in-rotor pump** *noun* = SLIDING-VANE PUMP; **vane-in-stator pump** = EXTERNAL VANE PUMP

◇ **vane pump** *noun* type of rotary pump with either a slotted rotor and sliding vanes or a rotor with hinged vanes; typically used for air pumps in secondary air injection systems, as a compressor in air conditioning systems, and in some transmission systems; *(compare* ROLLER-VANE PUMP, SLIDING-VANE PUMP)

◇ **vane switch** *noun* = HALL VANE SWITCH

◇ **vane wheel impeller** *noun* impeller with straight radial vanes

vanity mirror *noun* mirror on the inside of a sun visor

◇ **vanity plate** *noun* = PERSONAL(IZED) NUMBERPLATE

vaporize *verb* to turn into vapour

vapour *noun* the gaseous form of a liquid (usually caused by heating); **vapour canister** = ACTIVATED CARBON CANISTER; **vapour degreasing** = type of cleaning procedure to remove grease, oil, and loosely attached solids from metals; a solvent such as trichlorethylene is boiled, and its vapours are condensed on the metal surfaces; **vapour deposition** = production of a surface film of metal on a heated surface, usually in a vacuum, either by decomposition of the vapour of a compound at the work surface, or by direct reaction between the work surface and the vapour; **vapour lock** = blockage in a pipe caused by a bubble of gas, especially that in an overheated fuel line leading to the carburettor

COMMENT: vapour lock occurs on hot days, usually because fuel lines are too close to hot parts of the engine; fuel actually begins to boil in the fuel lines and the resulting bubbles block the flow of fuel. Vapour lock is recognizable when the engine stops running or does not start when hot; the cure is simply to let the engine cool

vapour recovery *or* **recycling** *noun* an emission control system used by petrol stations

COMMENT: a special filler nozzle seals the gap between the pump filler nozzle and the car's filler opening, preventing benzene vapours from escaping into the atmosphere; instead, they are recycled into the petrol station's own fuel tank; the same system is also used when the petrol station receives a new delivery of fuel from a petrol tanker

variable belt transmission *noun* continuously variable transmission using rubber V-belts on expanding-contracting pulleys, depending on engine speed and load; originally developed by van Doorne for DAF and then used on the Volvo 340

◇ **variable-choke carburettor** *noun* = VARIABLE-VENTURI CARBURETTOR

◇ **variable dwell** *noun* = DWELL-ANGLE CONTROL

◇ **variable hole cutter** *noun* a drill bit with a stepped cutting head used to drill holes into sheet metal and to enlarge the radii gradually by advancing from one step diameter to the next on the same drill bit

◇ **variable limited-slip axle/centre differential** *noun* limited-slip axle/centre differential with an electronically operated multiple-disc clutch as a slip-inhibiting device

◇ **variable rate springs** *noun* springs which become stiffer under compression; variable rate gas springs are a feature of air suspension systems

◇ **variable ratio steering** *noun* steering ratio characteristics in power steering systems providing different ratios for small and large steering angles

◇ **variable valve timing** *noun* advancing and retarding valve timing to increase efficiency by precisely controlling the amount of valve overlap

◇ **variable-venturi carburettor** *or* **VV carburettor** *noun* the characteristic feature of this carburettor is the vacuum-operated piston which adjusts the cross-sectional area of the venturi and moves a jet needle in and out of a needle jet; typical designs are the SU and Stromberg carburettors; *(see illustration 12)*

Variomatic transmission *noun* = VARIABLE BELT TRANSMISSION

varnish *noun* **(a)** a hard, glossy transparent coating **(b)** a product of oil oxidation which is deposited on pistons and piston rings at high temperatures

V-band clamp *noun* clamp which connects the turbine housing and bearing housing; *(see illustration 10)*

◇ **V-belt** *noun* drive belt with a V-shaped cross section, for transmission of low to moderate forces; typically used to drive generators, water pumps, air pumps, air conditioner compressor units and power steering pumps; *(compare* TOOTHED BELT*) (see illustration 4)*; **V-belt drive** = type of friction drive in which forces are transmitted from belt to pulley or vice versa by friction

VBRA = VEHICLE BUILDERS AND REPAIRERS ASSOCIATION

VC = VISCOUS COUPLING

VECI = VEHICLE EMISSION CONTROL INFORMATION

Vee-belt *noun* = V-BELT; **Vee-eight** = V-EIGHT; **Vee-engine** = V-ENGINE; **Vee-four** = V-FOUR; **Vee-six** = V-SIX; **Vee-ten** = V-TEN; **Vee-thread** = V-THREAD; **Vee-twelve** = V-TWELVE

vehicle *noun* **(a)** any form of transportation but especially one with wheels; *(compare* MOTOR VEHICLE*)* **(b)** = BINDER

◇ **Vehicle Builders and Repairers Association (VBRA)** *noun* British trade association

◇ **Vehicle Emission Control Information (VECI)** *noun* a label in the engine compartment, e.g. pasted to the radiator fan cover, providing information about the engine and emission controls

vehicle identification number (VIN) *noun* chassis type and identification number punched on a permanent structure, such as the engine compartment bulkhead; *(compare* ENGINE IDENTIFICATION NUMBER*)*

COMMENT: on cars made to US specifications, the VIN is also found on a small stamped plate located on the left front corner of the instrument panel pad, visible from the outside of the vehicle through the windscreen

vehicle registration document *noun* document which specifies the registered keeper(s) of a vehicle

◇ **vehicle tax** *noun* = ROAD TAX

V-eight engine (V-8) *noun* an engine with eight cylinders in the form of a V; the type of engine typically used on US automobiles of the 1950s and '60s was a large displacement V-8

velocity stack *noun* device mounted on the carburettor, typically made of polished or gold anodized aluminium, with or without a wire mesh filter; it looks good, provides greater air intake and increases engine performance but reduces engine life due to the intake of unfiltered or badly cleaned air

V-engine *noun* engine in which two banks of cylinders are set at an angle to each other (usually 60° or 90°) so that the axes form the letter V with the crankshaft in the middle *V-four engine; V-six engine; V-eight engine; V-twelve engine; V-engine with offset crankshaft*

vent 1 *noun* **(a)** small opening for the passage of air or gas **(b)** *US* small triangular window for letting air into the passenger compartment **2** *verb* to expel through a vent; e.g when bleeding air (through a vent valve or bleed screw) out of a diesel fuel system after running out of fuel

> COMMENT: air vents (which are also used for heating and are sometimes called 'louvres') are usually situated at the top of the dashboard (pointing upwards towards the windscreen), in the centre of the dashboard (directing the airflow out into the middle of the passenger compartment), on each side of the dashboard (sending the air back along the sides to the rear of the vehicle), and in the centre underneath the dashboard (directing air into the front footwells)

ventilate *verb* to provide with (fresh) air; **ventilated discs** = two discs in a disc brake system separated by ribs and channels to allow cooling air to disperse the heat between the discs

◊ **ventilation** *noun* provision of a free or controlled circulation of air; **vent(ilation) slot** = gaps in the wheel disc which allow the passage of air to assist brake cooling; *(see illustration 33)*

◊ **ventiport** *noun* = PORTHOLE

◊ **vent port** *noun* = COMPENSATING PORT

venturi (tube) *noun* a short tube with a constricted passage that increases the velocity and lowers the pressure of a fluid conveyed through it; *(see illustration 11)*; **venturi vacuum** = vacuum in the venturi of a carburettor which increases with the speed of the airflow passing through it; an exception are VV carburettors

> COMMENT: the venturi, or 'choke tube', in a carburettor is used to suck the fuel from the float chamber through a discharge nozzle (fixed jet carburettor) or main jet (variable choke carburettor) into the barrel

vernier (caliper *or* **gauge)** *noun* a short graduated scale that slides along a longer graduated instrument and is used to indicate fractional parts of divisions, as in a micrometer

VERTAC-process *noun* process in which car bodies are transported horizontally through the surface treatment plant

vertical keiretsu *noun* a keiretsu system with a production-oriented close partnership between a major company (such as Toyota)

and many small suppliers which work exclusively and/or constantly for their giant customer within the just-in-time concept (NOTE: opposite is **horizontal keiretsu)** *(compare* KEIRETSU; JUST-IN-TIME SYSTEM)

veteran car *noun* a car constructed before 1919, especially one made before 1905 (NOTE: only the latter are permitted to take part in the London-Brighton Commemoration Run) *(compare* VINTAGE CAR)

V-four engine (V-4) *noun* an engine with four cylinders in the form of a V

vgc *(in advertisements, short for)* very good condition

VI = VISCOSITY INDEX

vibration damper *noun* = TORSIONAL VIBRATION DAMPER

Vicat softening temperature *noun* the temperature at which a flat-ended needle of 1 mm^2 circular cross section will penetrate a thermoplastic specimen to a depth of 1 mm under a specified load, using a selected uniform rate of temperature rise; **Vicat test method** = determination of the softening temperature of plastics

vice *US* **vise** *noun* clamping device with adjustable jaws (usually mounted on a workbench) used to grip an object to be worked on; **vice grips** = LOCKING GRIPS

VIN = VEHICLE IDENTIFICATION NUMBER

vintage car *noun* a car constructed in the period 1919-1930; *(compare* VETERAN CAR)

virgin resin *noun* new resin material which has not been recycled before; needed for high-quality parts (NOTE: opposite is **regrind)**

visco-control unit *noun* = VISCOUS COUPLING

◊ **visco-differential** *noun* = VISCOUS COUPLING DIFFERENTIAL

viscoelastic materials *noun* the most characteristic features of viscoelastic materials are that they exhibit a time-dependent strain response to a constant stress (creep) and a time-dependant stress response to a constant strain (relaxation). In addition, when the applied stress is removed the materials have the ability to recover slowly over a period of time

viscosity *noun* resistance to flow *low-viscosity/high-viscosity fluids*

viscosity cup *noun* special cup of conical shape with a calibrated bore at the bottom

> COMMENT: when filled with paint, the paint will flow out at the bottom of the cup in a determined time. To adjust the viscosity, thinners are added to the paint until the cup contents flow out in the number of seconds indicated in the paint manufacturer's instructions

viscosity index (VI) *noun* measure of how the viscosity of a liquid (especially oil) changes with temperature: the higher the VI, the smaller the change of viscosity with temperature; **viscosity index improver** = oil additive which reduces thinning at high temperature, thus improving the VI

◊ **viscous** *adjective* thick and sticky; **viscous coupling (VC)** = a type of multi-disc clutch used in some 4wd vehicles; the discs rotate in a special fluid whose viscosity increases sharply whenever there is a difference in input and output shaft speeds; installed in the drive train between front and rear axles, the VC smoothly engages rear-wheel traction whenever the front wheels (and, as a result, the propeller shaft to the VC) rotate faster than the rear wheels; *(see illustration 24)*; **viscous coupling differential** = limited-slip differential using viscous couplings as slip-inhibiting devices; **viscous mode** = operating condition in a viscous coupling with inner and outer parts rotating at different speeds, in which a torque is transmitted through the coupling, which corresponds to the value of the resultant shearing velocity; *(compare* HUMP MODE); **viscous transmission (VT)** = four-wheel drive with a viscous centre differential

vise *noun US* = VICE

visor *noun* = SUN VISOR (a)

vitreous enamel *noun* glassy material obtained by melting a mixture of inorganic materials; this can then be applied in one or more layers on a metal surface to which it is firmly bonded after firing; typical automotive applications are for badges and trim (NOTE: US English is **porcelain enamel**); **vitreous enamelling** = application of a glass coating to a metal by covering the surface with powdered glass frit and heating it until fusion occurs

voice alert (system) *noun* system in a car which announces warning messages to the driver, e.g. 'Warning! Oil pressure too low'; *(compare* SPEECH SYNTHESIZER)

◊ **voice recognition** *noun* the ability of a computer to recognize a command spoken by the user; enables a driver to use a car phone without using his hands

volatility *noun (e.g. of fuels)* the ability readily to change into a vapour

Volkswagen (VW) *noun* German car manufacturer

voltage *noun* electromotive force, or difference in electrical potential, expressed in volts; **voltage regulator** = electric or electronic device which regulates the voltage output from a dynamo or alternator which is affected by engine speed, the power required by the circuits and the state of the battery; **voltage reserve** = HIGH-VOLTAGE RESERVE; **voltage tester** = screwdriver for testing electrical current, with an insulated blade and handle; a bulb inside the handle lights up if the blade touches a live terminal; **voltage transformer** = assembly for increasing the voltage supplied to the air bag system to 12 volts in case of a drop in battery voltage

◊ **voltammeter** *noun* dual-purpose instrument for measuring either voltage or amperage

◊ **voltmeter** *noun* instrument for measuring voltage

volume *noun* cubic capacity

◊ **volume car** *noun* mass-produced car

◊ **volume control screw** *noun* adjusting screw which controls the amount of air/fuel mixture supplied by the idling circuit of a fixed-jet carburettor; *(see illustration 11)*

volumetric efficiency *noun* (a) the ratio of air or air/fuel mixture drawn into the cylinder of an internal combustion engine to the volumetric displacement of the piston (b) number of horsepower (hp) per cubic inch displacement *the volumetric efficiency of SI engines is considerably greater than that of diesel engines*

COMMENT: in practice, a normally aspirated car engine does not take in an amount of air equal to the displacement, it passes only about 80% of the theoretical charge; i.e. volumetric efficiency is 80%; this can be increased by supercharging

volute *adjective* having the form of a spiral; **volute casing** = a progressively expanding pump casing proportioned to reduce the liquid velocity gradually so that some of the velocity energy of the liquid is converted into static pressure

V-pulley *noun* pulley with a pair of adjustable cup-shaped discs, used on belt transmissions, to permit adjustment of the effective pulley diameter and transmission ratio

VR engine *noun* new engine design: a combination of in-line and V-engine, the V-angle being reduced (VR) to about 15°; this results in a block which is shorter than a four-cylinder unit of similar capacity. Unlike conventional V-8 engines, the VR engine is topped by a single cylinder head

VRV = VACUUM REDUCER VALVE

V-six engine (V-6) *noun* an engine with six cylinders in the form of a V

VT = VISCOUS TRANSMISSION

V-ten engine (V-10) *noun* an engine with ten cylinders in the form of a V

V-thread *noun* triangular screw thread

V-twelve engine (V-12) *noun* an engine with twelve cylinders in the form of a V

vulcanization *noun* chemical reaction which changes the physical properties of elastomers

◊ **vulcanize** *verb* *(of tyre production)* to treat rubber with sulphur or sulphur compounds under heat and pressure to improve elasticity and strength

VV carburettor *noun* = VARIABLE-VENTURI CARBURETTOR

VW = VOLKSWAGEN

Ww

waddle *noun* side to side rocking movement of a vehicle in motion, caused by suspension or tyre damage or excessive lateral runout

wad punch *noun* tool with round cutting edge for cutting out holes in gaskets or other soft materials

wagon *noun* = STATION WAGON

waistline *noun* an imaginary or moulded horizontal line below the bottom of the side window that separates the roof area from the bottom of the body (NOTE: US English is **belt line**)

wander *noun* tendency of a vehicle to stray from its steered course; a fault caused by incorrect tyre pressure, worn steering linkage, etc.

Wankel engine *noun* a rotary engine which uses no pistons; instead, triangular rotors revolve in specially shaped housings (NOTE: named after the German engineer, Felix Wankel 1902-88)

warding file *noun* = KEY FILE

warm up *verb* to run an engine until it reaches normal operating temperature; *(K-jetronic)*; **warm-up control unit** = unit that produces the richer mixture needed for cold running and modulates fuel system pressure according to engine temperature; the unit includes an electrically heated thermostatic spring, which reduces the force on a spring-loaded control diaphragm; *(see illustration 14)*; **warm-up enrichment** = reduced enrichment of the air/fuel mixture following cranking and after-start enrichment

COMMENT: in the past warming up an engine was thought to be good practice but nowadays manufacturers recommend that motorists drive off immediately, as this is the quickest way of heating up the engine and preventing oil being washed off the

cylinder walls by partially burnt rich mixture (which causes engine wear)

warning lamp *or* **light** *noun* small lamps on the instrument panel that light up if there is a problem; *(compare* SPEECH SYNTHESIZER)

COMMENT: typical lamps warn of battery malfunction, lack of fuel, coolant, oil, or hydraulic pressure, brake pad wear, handbrake on, door open, choke out, etc.

warning triangle *noun* triangular red safety reflector that must be carried on all vehicles and be placed at the side of the road to warn of an obstruction ahead, such as a broken-down vehicle

warp 1 *noun* **(a)** bending or twisting out of shape **(b)** threads in cloth that run along the length of the material *the longitudinal cords of the tyre ply consist of several warp threads* **2** *verb* to bend or twist out of shape

warranty *noun* formal written declaration of good quality by the manufacturer of an article, including an agreement to repair or replace it if it is found to be defective within a certain period of time *the car will be repaired free of charge because it is still under warranty*

washcoat *noun* oxide layer on the catalyst substrate which increases with the active surface area

washer *noun* flat disc or ring of metal, rubber, leather, etc., fitted under a nut to even out pressure and prevent damage to the part on which it bears, or to lock the nut in place, or used for spacing or as a seal

washer fluid *noun* fluid added to the water in the windscreen washer and rear screen washer reservoirs/bottles to improve the cleaning action and lower the freezing point

◇ **wash/wipe switch** *noun* switch on the instrument panel that operates the rear screen wash/wipe system (NOTE: the windscreen washer system, which includes an intermittent wipe, is usually located on the windscreen wiper control stalk) *(compare* HEADLAMP WASH/WIPE)

wastegate *noun* a valve located on the exhaust side of the engine, with three connections: to the engine exhaust manifold, turbine, and silencer; most wastegates have a control line to the inlet manifold

COMMENT: the wastegate controls turbocharger speed and boost pressure to protect the turbocharger and, in particular, the engine; it may be operated manually or by inlet manifold pressure or by a servo motor; when the wastegate opens, some of the exhaust flow can bypass the turbine, thus reducing turbine speed and resulting boost; the bypass flow goes 'overboard', i.e. directly into the silencer

waste spark method *noun* in distributorless ignition systems, dual-spark coils fire two sparking plugs at the same time; one of these sparks is in a cylinder during its exhaust stroke, where the spark has no effect (waste spark); the other spark occurs in the cylinder near the end of the compression stroke

water-cooled *adjective (engine)* cooled by the passage of water (NOTE: opposite is **air-cooled**)

◊ **water cooling system** *noun* the normal cooling system used on most cars and lorries to keep the temperature of the engine down to a desirable level; engine heat is removed via water acting as a coolant which surrounds the cylinders in a water jacket; the system typically includes water passages, coolant pump, thermostat, hoses, and radiator; *(see illustration 15)*

water injection (system) *noun* system that prevents detonation in high-compression engines by injecting metered amounts of water into the inlet manifold where it mixes with the air/fuel charge entering the engine; there the water spray turns to steam, cooling combustion and cleaning out old carbon deposits

COMMENT: the system typically consists of a water tank with pump, similar to those of windscreen washers, an electronic control unit, hoses and mounting parts; water injection systems are frequently used in connection with bolt-on turbocharging systems

water jacket *noun* the channels between the inner and outer shells of the cylinder block

or head, through which coolant circulates to prevent overheating of the engine; *(see illustrations 3, 15)*

◊ **water marking** *noun* stains on the paintwork caused when a drop of water evaporates, leaving behind an outline of the drop; *(compare* WATER SPOTTING)

◊ **water passage** *noun* passage within the water jacket designed to prevent the formation of pockets of steam; *(see illustration 6)*

◊ **water pump** *noun* in the cooling system, the mechanism that circulates the coolant between the water jacket and the radiator; usually a centrifugal pump, located preferably in the cold leg of the circuit (to reduce the risk of cavitation); *(see illustration 4)*

◊ **water spotting** *noun* stains on the paintwork that occur when a drop of water evaporates from the painted surface and leaves a white spot behind; *(compare* WATER MARKING)

◊ **water temperature gauge** *noun* gauge on the instrument panel which indicates coolant temperature

Watt linkage *noun* a means of reducing or eliminating lateral movement of a beam axle relative to the vehicle body, consisting of an upright member at the centre of the axle whose top and bottom are connected by rods to the sides of the body

waveband *noun* series of wavelengths forming a group

wax 1 *noun* a substance resembling beeswax in appearance and character, and in general distinguished by its composition of esters and higher alcohols, and by its freedom from fatty acids; used for underbody sealing, cavity sealing, and paintwork care **2** *verb* to treat with wax

◊ **waxing** *noun* the formation of wax crystals in diesel fuel in freezing conditions, thus clogging the fuel filter and stopping the engine; avoided by the use of a fuel heater or fuel additives

◊ **wax injection** *or* **lancing** *noun* the injection of corrosion-inhibiting wax into car body cavities

◊ **wax-type thermostat** *noun* thermostat in which the expansion of melting paraffin wax (in a rigid cylinder) deforms a moulded rubber membrane and displaces a piston/pin from the cylinder; this has the advantage of being insensitive to sudden temperature fluctuations or to the pressure in the system; *(compare* ANEROID-TYPE THERMOSTAT)

WD-40 *noun* proprietary water-repellent spray

weak *adjective (of A/F mixture)* = LEAN

wear *noun* the progressive loss of substance from the operating surface of a body occurring as a result of relative motion at the surface; rubbing away; **wear bars** = TREAD WEAR INDICATORS; **wear pattern** = pattern of wear visible at the point where two parts touch; **wear resistance** = ability to withstand conditions which cause a progressive loss of substance; **wear ring** = *(pump)* ring used to prevent costly wear of the casing and impeller at the running joint; (fitted on both the casing and the impeller)

weathering *noun* physical disintegration and chemical decomposition of materials on exposure to atmospheric agents

◊ **weather resistant** *adjective* able to withstand natural climatic conditions which cause surface deterioration

◊ **weatherstrip** *noun* a rubber seal fitted to the body, e.g. along a door aperture or bootlid, to prevent water, air and moisture from getting into the interior of the body

web *noun* **(a)** internal reinforcement between panels **(b)** = CRANK WEB

◊ **webbing** *noun* woven nylon strap used for seat belts; **webbing grabber** = device in an inertia reel seat belt that grips the belt webbing tightly in the event of sudden braking or impact

wedge combustion chamber *noun* wedge-shaped chamber with the valve in the longer sloping surface and the sparking plug in the shorter; the tapered part of the wedge forms a squish zone

◊ **wedge end** *noun* the flat peen of a peen and finish hammer, shaped like a wedge

◊ **wedge expander** *noun* part of a mechanical drum brake system which forces the shoes apart into contact with the drum

weighbridge *noun* device for measuring the weight of vehicles (especially lorries),

consisting of a metal plate set into the road surface

weight *noun* **(a)** *see* DRY WEIGHT, GROSS VEHICLE WEIGHT, KERB WEIGHT **(b)** = BALANCE WEIGHT **(c)** = ADVANCE WEIGHT

◊ **weight per unit area** *noun* indicates the thickness of metallic paint coatings in grams per square metre of surface area

◊ **weight transfer** *noun* the transfer of load from one end or side of the vehicle to the other when accelerating, braking or cornering; *(compare* BRAKE DIVE, SQUAT)

Weissach axle *noun* special double wishbone rear suspension developed by Porsche for the 928S to minimize the problems of oversteering

welch plug *noun* **(a)** disc-shaped metal plug used to seal holes **(b)** = CORE PLUG

welding *noun* joining pieces of metal or plastic together by heating them to suitable temperatures, with or without the application of pressure, and with or without the use of filler material; **welding clamp** = locking clamp with U-shaped jaws (which allow more visibility and working space), used to hold panels, bars, tubes, etc. for welding; **welding jig** = a special type of frame gauge used to establish the correct position of structural parts on the body prior to welding them in; **welding rod** = *(gas/arc welding)* welding electrode supplied in individual lengths; **welding wire** = *(MIG welding)* welding electrode fed into the handset from a reel

COMMENT: among the approximately 40 different welding methods, the resistance welding processes, and especially spot welding, are most relevant for automobile production, whereas arc welding methods are most relevant for servicing and repair

weld-through primer *noun* special paint used along spot welds or seams; it does not burn off during welding and thus offers good protection on the back of welded panels that would normally be inaccessible once welding is completed

well *noun* = RIM WELL

◊ **well-base rim** *noun* wheel rim with a central channel or recess into which one side of the tyre bead can drop; the other side can then be forced over the rim for fitting or removal; **well-base wheel** = ONE-PIECE WHEEL

COMMENT: wheels with well-base rims are commonly used on passenger cars because they enable easy installation and removal of the tyre; the seats of the rim on which the tyre sits (rim flanges) have a 5° taper so that, as the tyre is inflated, the beads are forced up the taper to give a wedge fit and a good seal for tubeless tyres; safety bead seats must also be incorporated, however

welting *noun* = PIPING (b)

W-engine *noun* a rare engine design, basically similar to a V-engine, but using three instead of two cylinder rows

COMMENT: the W-engine is less perfectly balanced than a V-engine, but this is compensated by balancer shafts; the main advantage of the W-engine is its short crankshaft which results in a very short block; the compact construction permits a 12-cylinder W-engine to be installed transversely in a mid-engine sports car

wet clutch *noun* friction clutch that uses an oil bath to dissipate heat

◊ **wet galvanizing** *noun* galvanizing method in which the flux is deposited in molten form on the zinc bath, and the metal to be galvanized is introduced into the bath by passing it through this layer of flux (NOTE: opposite is **dry galvanizing)**

◊ **wet grip** *noun* roadholding ability of a tyre on a wet surface

◊ **wet liner** *noun* cylinder liner that is in direct contact with the coolant (NOTE: opposite is **dry liner)**

◊ **wet motor** *noun* pump whose motor compartment is filled with liquid; submersible pumps are generally classified as wet motor types; *(compare* CANNED MOTOR PUMP)

◊ **wet-on-wet application** *noun* paint application by which a second coat of paint is applied over a first coat before it is dried or stoved; in the case of metallic paint systems, the clear coat is applied over the wet base coat

◊ **wet sanding** *noun* sanding with wet-and-dry sandpaper that has been wetted with water to prevent the paper from clogging; commonly used for final sanding

◊ **wet sleeve** *noun* = WET LINER

◊ **wet sump lubrication** *noun* the usual engine lubrication system in which the oil is carried in a sump below the crankshaft;

such a system relies on gravity draining the circulated oil and needs no return pump; *(compare* DRY SUMP LUBRICATION)

whale tail *noun (informal)* large, rear spoiler

wheel *noun* **(a)** a rotating, load-carrying member between the tyre and axle consisting of a rim and a wheel disc or spider; a wheel must be designed to support the tyre while withstanding loads from acceleration, braking and cornering; as part of the unsprung mass of a car, it must be light *when the tyre is off the wheel, check the rim for dents or cracks (see illustration 33)* **(b)** the whole wheel and tyre assembly upon which a vehicle rolls **(c)** *(informal)* = STEERING WHEEL

◊ **wheel adapter** *noun* spacer ring that adapts hubs to wheels with a different number of lugs, e.g. 4-lug hubs to 5-lug wheels

◊ **wheel alignment gauge** *noun* gauge used to measure the distance between the rims of the front wheels; *(compare* TOE-IN, TOE-OUT)

◊ **wheel arch** *noun* the edge of the wing around the wheel cutout; sometimes also used with reference to the entire wheel housing; *(see illustration 1)*; **wheel arch extension** = a roughly square extension of the wheel arch; the areas in front of and behind the wheel cutout, as well as a strip above the cutout, are angled sharply outwards to increase the width of the wheel arches to allow wider tyres to be fitted; *(compare* WING ARCH); **wheel arch protector** = UNDERSHIELD

◊ **wheel assembly** *noun (turbocharger)* comprises the compressor, shaft and turbine wheel

◊ **wheel balancer** *or* **wheel balancing machine** *noun* a machine capable of locating static and dynamic wheel imbalance and determining the mass of the balancing weights required; *(compare* BALANCING)

◊ **wheelbase** *noun* distance between the centrelines of the front and rear wheels; for lorries with tandem rear axles, the rear centreline is considered to be midway between the two rear axles

◊ **wheel bearings** *noun* the bearings in wheel hubs: ball bearings for drive shafts and taper roller bearings for driven hubs

◊ **wheel bolt** *noun* bolts which are screwed into threaded holes in the wheel hub or at the axle flange; common on passenger car wheels and one-piece commercial vehicle wheels; *(compare* WHEEL NUT)

◇ **wheelbrace** *noun* a cranked socket spanner for wheel nuts

◇ **wheel camber** *noun* = CAMBER (a)

wheel changing *noun* changing a defective wheel; *(compare* WHEEL ROTATION)

COMMENT: important steps are: stop the car on firm, level ground and put the handbrake on; loosen the wheel bolts or nuts before jacking up the car; after replacing the old wheel on the hub with a new (or spare) one, tighten the bolts or nuts evenly, giving them a final tightening once the jack has been removed

wheel chock *noun* wedge-shaped block put under a wheel to prevent a vehicle from rolling

◇ **wheel clamp** *noun* device attached to the wheel of a parked car to prevent it being driven away; used as an anti-theft device if attached privately, and a means of ensuring payment of a fine (to the authority to have the device removed) if parked illegally (NOTE: US English is **Denver boot)**

◇ **wheel cover** *noun* metal or plastic disc fitted to the centre of a road wheel

◇ **wheel cutout** *noun* the open area described by the wheel arch, which determines to what extent the wheels are visible

◇ **wheel cylinder** *noun (drum brake)* hydraulic brake actuating device; major parts are cylinder body, spring, cup expander, cup or piston seal, piston, dust boot, bleeder valve; *(see illustration 30)*

◇ **wheel disc** *noun* part of the wheel that connects the rim to the hub; its design is governed by specific rim type, axle connection, brake contour, brake cooling, hub cap fixing, load capacity and attractive styling; *(see illustration 33)*

◇ **wheel dolly** *noun* = DOLLY (b)

◇ **wheel flutter** *noun* = WHEEL WOBBLE

◇ **wheel hop** *noun* = WHEEL PATTER

◇ **wheel house** *or* **housing** *noun* the inner area behind the wing described by the inner and outer wing panels; the term is occasionally used for the inner wing panel; **wheel house panel** = a steel panel inside the wheel housing that is shaped similar to the wheel cutout and protects the upper inside

areas of the wing from splashes and gravel; *(compare* UNDERSHIELD) *(see illustration 2)*

◇ **wheel hub** *noun* = HUB

◇ **wheelie** *noun (informal)* manoeuvre in which the front wheel(s) is/are lifted off the ground on sudden acceleration; originally practised on motorbikes; **wheelie bar** = bar incorporating little wheels, mounted behind the rear axle of a dragster to reduce the effect of a wheelie

◇ **wheel imbalance** *see* IMBALANCE

wheeling machine a special shop tool used to shape steel and aluminium panels

COMMENT: no electric, pneumatic or hydraulic power is used; the base takes the form of a large C and the parts used to do the shaping are fastened at the open end of the frame. A flat-faced steel wheel is bolted to the top of the C; the lower wheels, called anvils, are smaller in diameter and have a curved surface. To shape the metal, the steel sheet is moved back and forth between the two wheels

wheel judder *noun* = SHIMMY

◇ **wheel load** *noun* that part of the vehicle weight resting on a single wheel; *(compare* AXLE LOAD)

◇ **wheel lock** *noun* **(a)** condition in which the wheels stop turning as a result of excessive braking; leads to a skid; *(compare* ABS) **(b)** any anti-theft device for expensive (alloy) wheels

◇ **wheel marking** *noun* all disc wheels are marked (generally on the front side of the disc in the stud hole area) with the manufacturer's trademark, the wheel number, rim size, and date of production

◇ **wheel mounting** *noun* the fitting of a wheel onto a hub

wheel nut *noun* one of several nuts which hold the wheel and tyre assembly on the car and are screwed on the studs (NOTE: US English is **lug nut); wheel nut spider =** cross-shaped spanner with four socket heads; *(compare* WHEEL BOLT)

COMMENT: the inner face of the wheel nut is tapered (conical nut) to help centre the wheel. On modern wheels for passenger cars, wheel nuts and corresponding studs are less frequently used than bolts. On commercial vehicles, however, wheel nuts are very common

wheel panel *noun* the panel area around the wheel cutout in the wing; this term often also refers to a repair section for this area, as this is a favourite rust spot on many cars

◇ **wheel patter** *noun* vertical oscillation of a wheel making it hop up and down rapidly, either because of imbalance or because the tyre is faulty or badly fitted

◇ **wheel rim** *noun* the outer part of the wheel on which the tyre is mounted

◇ **wheel rotation** *noun* swapping wheels around to compensate for unequal tyre wear and increase tread life; moving them from front to rear is generally recommended and is the only safe method on vehicles fitted with directional tread tyres

◇ **wheel shimmy** *or* **shudder** *noun* = SHIMMY

◇ **wheelslip** *noun* = WHEELSPIN

◇ **wheel spacer** *noun* disc between hub carrier and wheel that widens the track

◇ **wheel speed sensor** *noun* electronic device for picking up the rotational speed of a wheel in order to inform the processing unit of an ASR or ABS system

◇ **wheel spider** *noun* part of a cast/forged wheel which connects the rim and the wheel hub and incorporates a spoke design

◇ **wheelspin** *noun* effect of too much throttle making the driven wheels turn too fast to grip the road surface; easily done on a wet or icy surface and leaves a telltale trace of rubber on a dry one; *(compare* RACING START*)*

◇ **wheel stud** *noun* one of several threaded bolts projecting from the wheel disc to which the wheel is secured by a wheel nut

◇ **wheel tramp** *noun* = RADIAL RUN-OUT

◇ **wheel tree** *noun* a special stand for wheels, e.g. for a complete set of summer or winter tyres, designed to prevent condensation and tyre deformation over extended storage periods

◇ **wheel trim** *noun* = WHEEL COVER; **wheel trim emblem** = plastic emblem with logo; self-adhesive backing adheres to hub cap or wheel cover centre cap; **wheel trim rim** = aluminium or stainless steel recessed ring, chrome-flashed or polished for added lustre; improves the looks of old steel wheels

◇ **wheel tub** *noun* that part of the wheel housing visible on the inside of the car body to either side of the rear seats

◇ **wheel type** *noun* generally refers to the styling of the wheel disc: e.g. disc wheel with

holes, plain disc wheel, styled disc wheel with ribs, disc wheel with flange openings, spoke wheel, rim type

◇ **wheel weight tool** *noun* special automotive tool for use when balancing wheels; installs, trims and removes all types of clip-on wheel weights with a hammer head and pliers for installation and removal and a cutter for trimming

◇ **wheel well** *noun* = RIM WELL

◇ **wheel wobble** *noun* oscillation of the front wheels caused by unbalanced wheels, defective steering gear, etc.

whip aerial *noun* long, thin, flexible aerial

whiplash injury *noun* neck injury resulting from a violent forward and backward jerking of the head, as in a vehicle collision

whipping *or* **whirling** *noun (of a drive shaft)* tendency of a long rotating shaft to bend at high speed, like a bow or whip

white metal *noun* any of various (tin-based) alloys, such as Babbitt metal, still occasionally used for bearings

◇ **white lithium grease** *noun* type of grease that will not freeze, melt or wash off; used for speedometer and brake cables, door and bonnet hinges, door stop latches, boot springs, seat slide tracks, distributor cams, windscreen wiper mechanism, etc.

◇ **white rust** *noun* loose, porous oxidation products formed on zinc when a lack of carbon dioxide occurs and water condenses on the surface of the work

◇ **whitewall rings** *or* **whitewall toppers** *noun* narrow or wide rubber rings that snap on between tyre and rim to give the effect of a whitewall tyre; **whitewall tyre** = a tyre with white sidewalls

wide-nose peen hammer *noun* a peen and finish hammer with an extra-wide wedge end well suited to shaping of sharp corners and beads in panels

◇ **wide open throttle (WOT)** *noun US* = FULL THROTTLE

widget *noun* any small gadget, device or mechanism that is unknown or temporarily forgotten; a car is full of them

Wilson gearbox *noun* an early pre-selector epicyclic gearbox still used in buses

(NOTE: named after British inventor Walter Gordon Wilson, 1874-1957)

wind deflector *noun* = AIR SHIELD

windlace *noun* a type of piping covered with fabric; often used along the outlines of hoods, etc.

window channel *noun* U-shaped draught excluder, often fitted with a steel core, along wind-up door window edges inside the door frame (NOTE: US English is **glass channel**)

◊ **window etching** *noun* a security measure whereby the glass panes of a car's windows are permanently marked by etching a number (such as the registration number) into the glass surface

◊ **window line** *noun* = WAISTLINE

◊ **window weatherstrip** *noun* rubber or moquette sealing strip fitted in the gap on either side of a sliding door window to seal the door gutter and prevent water getting into the interior of the door frame

◊ **window winder** *noun* handle on the inside of a door panel with which the window is manually wound up and down

windscreen *US* **windshield** *noun* forward-facing front window of a motor vehicle

◊ **windscreen aperture** *noun* the open area into which the windscreen fits, determined by the windscreen panel

◊ **windscreen corner panel** *noun* a separate panel that extends the scuttle to the left-hand and right-hand top rear corners of the wings and closes off the area towards the bottom windscreen corners; on many cars, it is part of the one-piece scuttle extending from the left-hand to the right-hand wing

◊ **windscreen header (panel)** *noun* box-section or double panel at the front end of the roof panel above the windscreen aperture that helps to reinforce the roof frame; *(see illustrations 1, 2)*

◊ **windscreen mounting flange** *noun* the spot-welded flanges of the panels which together form the windscreen aperture

◊ **windscreen panel** *noun* the panel around the windscreen that links the roof panel above the windscreen to the scuttle below the screen

◊ **windscreen pillars** *noun* the front posts of the body shell which together with

the scuttle and header panel form the windscreen aperture

◊ **windscreen shadeband** *noun* = SUNSHIELD

◊ **windscreen support panel** *noun* = SCUTTLE

◊ **windscreen surround** *noun* moulded rubber insulating strip round the windscreen

windscreen washer *noun* a person who washes windscreens; *(compare* WINDSCREEN WASH/WIPE SYSTEM)

COMMENT: as a form of private enterprise, the original idea was to wash a car's dirty windscreen while it is waiting at a red traffic light but in many places, the windscreen washer is perceived as a sort of mugger who uses a dirty sponge and bucket as a begging tool and leaves a windscreen, whether formerly clean or not, in a streaky mess

windscreen wash/wipe system *noun* system operated by the same lever on the control stalk that operates the wipers, which directs a jet of water onto the windscreen and activates the wipers for a short period

◊ **windscreen wiper** *noun* electrically operated arm with a (renewable) rubber or plastic blade that wipes a windscreen clear of rain, snow, etc.; activated by a switch or lever on the instrument panel or control stalk

windshield *noun US* = WINDSCREEN

wind tunnel *noun* tunnel-like chamber in which a current of air can be maintained at a constant velocity and in which motor vehicles (and aircraft, etc.) are tested to determine their aerodynamic properties and the effects of wind pressure

wind-up window *noun* window that is manually operated with a winder; *(compare* ELECTRIC WINDOWS)

wing *noun* the car body panel that covers a road wheel and provides protection against splashes of mud, etc.; *(see illustration 1)* (NOTE: US English is **fender**); **wing arch** = a smoothly shaped, rounded widening of the wheel arch area to extend the wheel arch further from the body and allow wider tyres to be installed; *(compare* WHEEL ARCH EXTENSION); **wing beading** = a strip used to cover the seams between wings that are not normally detached and adjacent body panels;

in most cases, this strip is chromed and permanently fixed, i.e. it is destroyed when it is removed and cannot be reused; **wing bumping hammer** = body hammer with a one-sided, fairly long head that is lightly curved and terminates in a rounded section; it is used to reach wing curves from the inside; **wing extension** = smaller panel in the bottom front area of the front wing that extends the wing towards the front panel and the wheel housing; **wing landing section** = horizontal flange at the top of the flitch plates that provides the seating for the wings; in most cases, it also includes the mounting threads or spot-welds for fitting of the wings; **wing mirror** = rear-view mirror mounted on the wing; once common but now replaced by door mirrors; **wing mounting** = the top flange of the sidewalls in the engine compartment and its vertical extensions at the front and rear; the wing is welded or bolted to this edge along its entire length

wing nut *noun* nut with two flat projections like wings so that it can be easily turned by hand

wing punch *noun* a hole punch with a specially shaped head to fit over awkward wing panels, rain gutters and wheel arches

◇ **wing shield** *noun* small curved panel in front of the front side window which deflects wind and reduces draught with the window open; typically made of transparent acrylic, clear or smoked

◇ **wing splash apron** *noun* panel on the inside of the wing to prevent splash water from reaching certain areas of the wing, wheel house and A-post; as opposed to wheel house panels, it is usually flat and mounted in an upright position behind the front wheels

◇ **wing strengthening buttress** *noun* horizontal closed section of triangular shape in the upper rear edge of the inner wing area that adds rigidity to this area, e.g. on the MGB

◇ **wing support bracket** *noun* sheet metal brace used to attach the bottom edge of the wing to the body, to keep it from flexing and vibrating

winker *noun* (*informal*) = DIRECTION INDICATOR

winter tyre *noun* a tyre with a deep tread suitable for winter conditions

wiper *noun* short for windscreen wiper, rear wiper, headlamp wiper; **wiper wing** = moulded attachment to the back of the windscreen wiper arm, intended to increase the pressure of the wind on the blade to provide effective cleaning at high speeds

wire brush *noun* brush with wire bristles for removing loose paint, dirt, carbon, or rust from metal surfaces

> COMMENT: wire brushes come in a variety of shapes, e.g. with an extremely thin head for cleaning parts in very tight places (such as brake rotors or calipers), or they can be attached to power tools to remove carbon and deposits from cylinder heads, transmissions, etc. e.g. as knotted or crimped rotary wire brushes, wire cup brushes, or wire end brushes

wire feeder *noun* the handle and gas nozzle through which the steel wire electrode is fed by an electric motor in a MIG welding system

◇ **wire glow plug** *noun* double-pole glow plug with an unsheathed wire loop; now superseded by sheathed-type glow plugs

◇ **wire loom** *noun* = SPARKING PLUG CABLE LOOM

◇ **wire mesh** *noun* in catalytic converters with a ceramic monolith, a stainless-steel fabric used as a shock-absorbing support for the honeycomb

wire spoke *noun* part which connects the hub of a wire spoke wheel to the rim

> COMMENT: all loads are transmitted from the rim to the hub by steel spokes; individually, they have little resistance to bending stresses and therefore have to be laced in a complex criss-cross pattern. Due to their complicated design (each spoke is hooked at one end into the hub, and the other end is pushed through a hole in the rim, where a tapered nut is screwed down to pull the spoke tight) and their reduced stiffness and poor stress resistance (if the spokes are too loose or too tight, the relatively flimsy rim will distort), wheels with wire spokes are expensive and rarely used

wire (spoke) wheel *noun* wheel designed in such a way that its rim is joined to the centre member by a series of wire spokes

> COMMENT: the stiffness of the wheel is obtained by a relatively wide hub with two or three sets of spokes arranged at different angles and in inclined pairs, so that they form a series of relatively rigid triangles. Only tubed tyres are suitable for this type of wheel

wire strippers *noun* pliers used for removing insulating material from the ends of electrical wire; **wire stripper/crimper tool** = multi-purpose electricians' pliers for cutting and stripping wire and crimping insulated or non-insulated solderless terminals when servicing the electrical system

◊ **wiring an edge** *noun* rolling the edge of a panel, e.g. a wheel opening of a wing, around a wire to provide additional stiffness of the panel edge

◊ **wiring harness** *or* **wiring loom** *noun* vehicle wiring bound in a protective sheath, which aids installation as an integrated unit

◊ **wiring pigtail** *noun* short length of wire, usually with connector, permanently attached to an electric component, such as an oxygen sensor

◊ **wiring trough** *noun* longitudinal moulding that guides and conceals wiring

wishbone *noun* transverse link shaped like an A or wishbone (NOTE: US English is **A-arm**)

COMMENT: due to its wider base, the wishbone can accommodate lateral forces as well as longitudinal ones; a double-wishbone suspension is especially effective, but needs much space and is used mainly on sports and racing vehicles

withdrawal fork *noun* = CLUTCH FORK

wobble *noun* side-to-side vibration; lateral runout

◊ **wobble extension (bar)** *noun* special extension with a unique male end that enables the user to drive the socket up to 15° from vertical

◊ **wobble plate** *noun* = SWASH PLATE

wood alcohol *noun* = METHANOL

woodie *noun (US informal)* shooting brake

Woodruff key *noun* semicircular key (b) that slots into a curved keyway in a shaft to prevent rotational movement between the shaft and a hub or pulley; *(see illustration 36)*

working cycle *noun* recurring sequence of events in the combustion process, e.g. a four-stroke cycle

◊ **working cylinder** *noun* inner cylinder of a double-tube shock absorber

worm *noun* short, rotating shaft on which a helical groove has been cut, as in a gear arrangement in which such a shaft meshes with a toothed wheel; **worm-and-lever steering** = CAM-AND-LEVER STEERING; **worm-and-nut steering** = steering system in which rotation of the worm causes a nut, which encloses it, to move up or down, thus turning the rocker shaft; **worm-and-peg steering** = CAM-AND-LEVER STEERING; **worm-and-roller steering** = CAM-AND-ROLLER STEERING; **worm-and-sector steering** = type of steering system in which rotation of the worm moves a V-shaped section of a toothed wheel at the top of the rocker shaft; **worm gear** = device consisting of a short, threaded shaft (worm) that mates with a gearwheel (worm wheel) so that rotary motion can be transferred between two shafts at right angles to each other; **worm wheel** = gearwheel driven by a worm

WOT = WIDE OPEN THROTTLE

wrapround *adjective* curving round in one continuous piece; **wrapround bumper** = modern bumper style that extends around the front and rear of the body right up to the wheel cutouts to offer maximum protection of the body panels; **wrapround dash design** = instrument panel design introduced on volume cars by BMW which, in contrast to the classic flat panels, is curved to provide optimum driver access to all controls; **wrapround windscreen** = PANORAMIC WINDSCREEN

wrench *noun* a spanner, especially one with adjustable jaws

wrinkling *noun (paint fault)* the top coat tends to wrinkle to a smaller or greater degree if the outer paint coat dries too rapidly, preventing the underlying coats from drying properly; this also occurs if the paint film is too heavy

wrist pin *noun US* = GUDGEON PIN

write off *verb* **(a)** to damage a car beyond repair or, for insurance purposes, so as to be not worth repairing **(b)** *(insurance assessor)* to consider (a car) to be a total loss

◊ **write-off** *noun* a car damaged beyond repair or so badly damaged as to be not worth repairing for insurance purposes

Xx Yy Zz

xenon *noun* colourless, odourless gas used in electric luminescent tubes to provide a bright light; a xenon stroboscope for ignition timing is strong enough to use in daylight

X-flow cylinder head *noun* = CROSSFLOW CYLINDER HEAD

X-type frame *noun* a frame design shaped like an elongated letter X that narrows to a strong junction at the centre section; it usually has three or more crossmembers to provide torsional stability but there are no crossmembers in the centre section of the vehicle

yaw *verb* to move or rotate about a vertical axis; **yaw acceleration** = a steady increase in the yaw angle; **yaw angle** = angle of deviation between a vehicle's longitudinal axis and its true direction of motion, i.e. the difference between the direction a vehicle is pointing when cornering and the direction in which it is actually moving

Y-belt *noun* Y-shaped belt design used to restrain babies in a baby seat

◇ **Y-configuration** *noun* Y-shaped connection of the three stator windings of an alternator; *(compare* DELTA CONFIGURATION)

yellow shoe *or* **boot** *noun (informal)* = WHEEL CLAMP

yoke *noun* forked parts of a U-joint connected by the spider (b); *(see illustration 22)*

Y-pipe *noun (exhaust system)* Y-shaped down pipe connecting a two-branch exhaust manifold to a single exhaust pipe; *(see illustration 19)*

Z-axle *noun* a rear axle introduced with the BMW Z1 in 1988, consisting of a trailing arm, one upper lateral link, one lower diagonal link, and a coil spring at each side; also included is an anti-roll bar

zebrano *or* **zebrawood** *noun* striped hardwood used for interior trim as a cheaper alternative to burr walnut

Zener diode *noun* voltage regulator diode in electronic ignition and alternator output circuits

zero-emission vehicle (ZEV) *noun* vehicle which itself produces no emissions, such as electric powered vehicles

COMMENT: the concept does not take into account the fact that electric cars use the electric power of batteries that are normally charged by power supplied by electric power plants (which generally do produce certain emissions); Californian laws require that from 1998, 2% of new cars must be ZEVs

zero offset *noun* = CENTRE POINT STEERING

ZEV = ZERO-EMISSION VEHICLE

zinc *noun* metallic element used in galvanizing metals, die-casting, as a constituent in various alloys, as a battery electrode, etc.; **zinc alloy** = alloy whose main component is zinc; **zinc bath** = GALVANIZING BATH; **zinc-electroplating** = ELECTROGALVANIZING; **zinc immersion treatment** = pretreatment before electroplating; a thin zinc deposit forms by immersion of aluminium in a zinc solution which prevents further oxidation of the aluminium and provides a key for the galvanic coating; **zinc-iron alloy layer** = alloy layer formed on iron and steel during hot-dip galvanizing as a result of the diffusion of atoms from the molten zinc into the work and vice versa; **zinc phosphate coating** = zinc-rich conversion coating produced by phosphating; **zinc plating** = application of a zinc coating by galvanizing or electrogalvanizing; **zinc-rich paint/primer** = paint containing an extremely high proportion of metallic zinc dust in the dry film (about 95% by weight), applied to iron and steel as an anti-corrosive primer; the application of zinc-based primer may be regarded as a less durable form of cold galvanizing

◇ **zincrometal** *noun* trademark of a special type of coil-coated steel sheet with plastic and zinc dust coating, which is proving increasingly useful in automobile manufacture

zinc spraying *noun* process for applying zinc coatings to iron and steel

COMMENT: particles of molten zinc are sprayed onto the surface to be coated; the coating metal, usually in the form of wire, is fed into a spray gun, in which it is melted by the combustion of a fuel gas, e.g. a mixture of oxygen and acetylene. The molten metal is atomized by compressed air and precipitated onto the surface to be coated at high velocity

zinc vapour deposition (ZVD) *noun* process in which zinc vapour is deposited in a vacuum on the pieces being worked on

zirconia (ZrO₂) *noun* zirconium oxide, used in enamels and ceramic coatings

zirconium *noun* metallic element (NOTE: symbol: **Zr**; atomic number: **40**)

ZVD = ZINC VAPOUR DEPOSITION

SUPPLEMENT

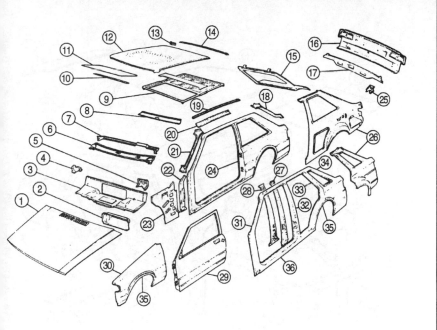

: Body Parts 1

1	bonnet	18	rain channel
2	plenum chamber	19	drip moulding
3	scuttle panel	20	roof rail reinforcement
4	wiper motor support panel	21	A-pillar reinforcement
5	steering column bracket	22	hinge pillar reinforcement
6	scuttle top	23	scuttle side panel
7	dash panel	24	aperture panel, quarter panel
8	windscreen header (panel)	25	bumper bracket
9	sunroof aperture panel	26	inner quarter panel
10	air shield	27	B-pillar reinforcement
11	sunroof	28	B-pillar inner panel
12	roof panel	29	door
13	hinge brace	30	front wing
14	rear window header	31	A-pillar
15	tailgate	32	B-pillar
16	rear panel	33	C-pillar
17	rear panel reinforcement	34	D-pillar

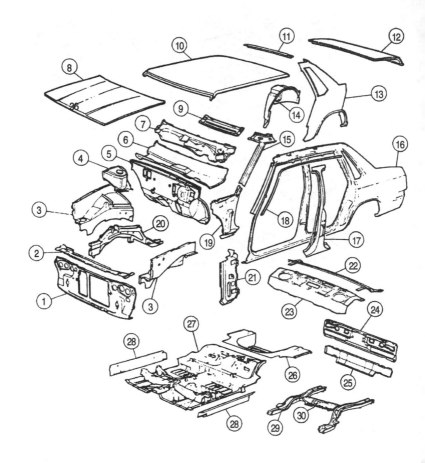

2: Body Parts 2

1	radiator support panel	16	aperture panel
2	tie bar panel	17	B-pillar outer panel
3	engine bay side panel	18	drip moulding
4	MacPherson strut tower	19	scuttle side panel
5	bulkhead	20	front side member
6	scuttle panel	21	hinge pillar reinforcement
7	scuttle top	22	rain channel
8	bonnet	23	shelf panel
9	windscreen header reinforcement	24	rear panel
10	roof panel	25	rear valence
11	rear window hear	26	rear floorpan
12	bootlid	27	front floorpan
13	inner quarter panel	28	inner sill
14	wheel house panel	29	side member
15	A-pillar reinforcement	30	crossmember

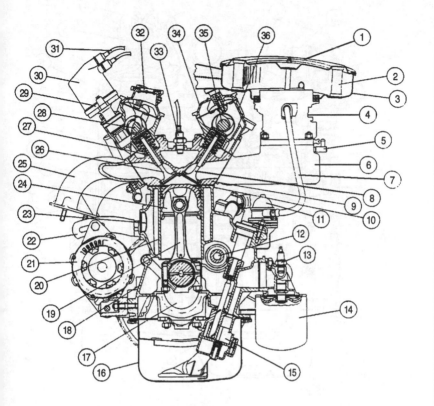

4-cylinder Double Overhead Camshaft Engine (cross-section)

1	air filter cover	19	connecting rod
2	air filter element	20	cylinder with water jacket
3	air filter body	21	alternator
4	carburettor	22	adjusting link
5	EFE connection	23	core plug
6	inlet manifold	24	piston
7	fuel supply line	25	exhaust manifold
8	inlet valve	26	exhaust valve
9	cylinder head	27	valve spring
10	engine block	28	exhaust camshaft
11	fuel pump	29	distributor
12	auxiliary drive shaft	30	distributor cap
13	oil pressure sensor	31	sparking plug cable
14	oil filter	32	oil filler cap
15	gear pump	33	engine temperature sensor
16	sump	34	rocker cover
17	crankshaft	35	inlet camshaft
18	crankcase	36	camshaft housing

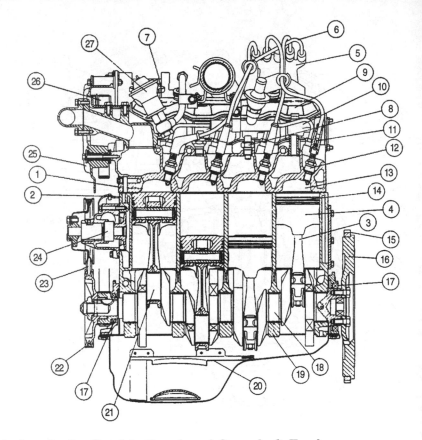

4: 4-cylinder Double Overhead Camshaft Engine (longitudinal section)

1	cylinder head	15	ring gear
2	engine block	16	flywheel
3	connecting rod	17	radial shaft seal
4	piston	18	crankshaft journal
5	distributor cap	19	crankshaft main bearing
6	sparking plug cable	20	baffle
7	oil filler cap	21	crankpin
8	engine temperature sensor	22	crankshaft pulley
9	rocker cover	23	V-belt
10	camshaft housing	24	water pump
11	RFI suppressor	25	timing cover
12	sparking plug	26	cam wheel
13	combustion chamber	27	EGR valve
14	piston rings		

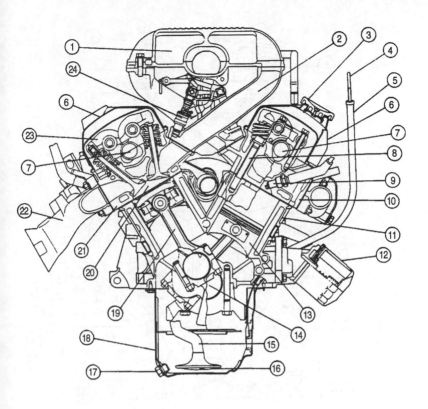

5: V-6 SOHC Fuel Injection Engine (cross-section)

	plenum chamber	13	piston
	inlet manifold	14	crankshaft
	oil filler cap	15	oil pick-up (pipe)
	dipstick	16	oil pump strainer
	dipstick tube	17	sump plug
	valve cover	18	sump
	camshaft	19	connecting rod
	cylinder head bolt	20	combustion chamber
	sparking plug	21	RH cylinder head
0	LH cylinder head	22	exhaust manifold
1	engine block	23	rocker arm
2	full-flow filter	24	injector

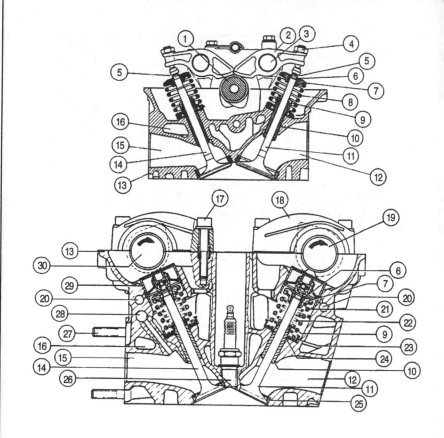

6: OHC and DOHC Cylinder Heads

1	camshaft	16	water passage
2	rocker arm	17	screw
3	rocker arm shaft	18	bearing block
4	valve adjusting screw	19	inlet camshaft
5	valve clearance	20	oil duct
6	valve keeper	21	outer valve spring
7	valve spring cap *or* collar	22	inner valve spring
8	valve spring	23	valve spring seat
9	valve stem seal	24	circlip
10	valve guide	25	valve seat insert *or* ring
11	inlet valve	26	sparking plug
12	inlet port	27	stud
13	cylinder head	28	air injection duct
14	exhaust valve	29	hydraulic tappet
15	exhaust port	30	exhaust camshaft

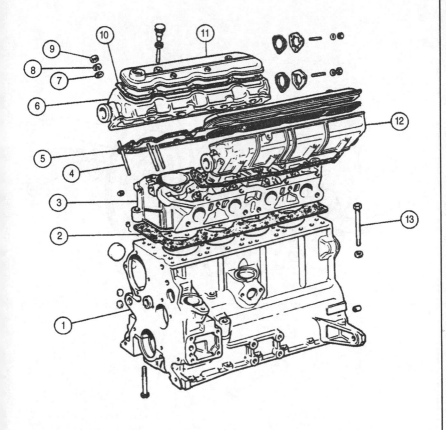

: Static Engine Components

1	engine block	8	spring lock washer
2	cylinder head gasket	9	nut
3	cylinder head	10	rocker cover gasket
4	stud	11	rocker cover
5	gasket	12	camshaft housing
6	camshaft housing	13	cylinder head bolt
7	washer		

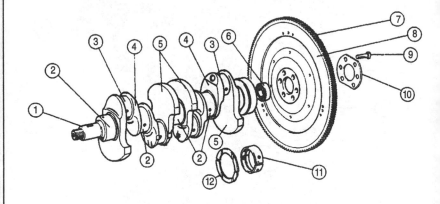

8: Crankshaft and Flywheel

1	crankshaft	7	ring gear
2	crankshaft journal	8	flywheel
3	crankpin	9	screw
4	crank web	10	plate
5	counterweight	11	main bearing
6	bearing	12	thrust washer

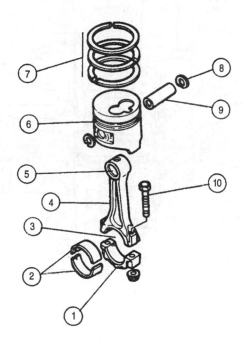

Piston and Connecting Rod

bearing cap		6	piston
connecting rod bearing shells		7	piston rings
big end		8	gudgeon pin circlip
connecting rod		9	gudgeon pin
small end		10	strength bolt

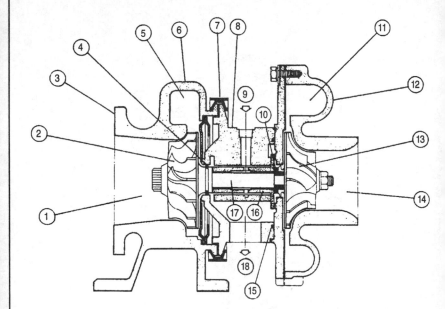

10: Turbocharger

1	exhaust gas out	10	mechanical (face) seal
2	turbine wheel	11	air discharge
3	flange	12	compressor housing
4	seal	13	compressor impeller
5	exhaust gas in	14	air intake
6	turbine housing	15	O-ring seal
7	V-band clamp	16	floating bearing
8	bearing housing	17	shaft
9	oil inlet	18	oil outlet

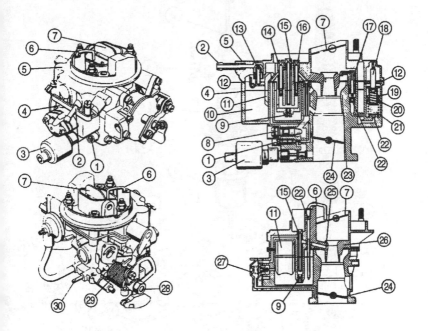

: Downdraught Carburettor

	idle mixture adjustment screw	16	idle mixture jet
	fuel supply	17	accelerator pump injection nozzle
	idle stop valve	18	accelerator pump push rod
	carburettor body	19	accelerator pump piston
	float chamber cover	20	cup seal
	full load enrichment	21	accelerator pump spring
	choke valve	22	ball valve
	volume control screw	23	venturi
	main jet	24	throttle valve
	float chamber	25	main mixture discharge nozzle
	float	26	inner venturi
	cover gasket	27	enrichment unit
	float needle valve	28	throttle shaft
	starter air jet	29	throttle return spring
	air correction jet	30	distributor vacuum port

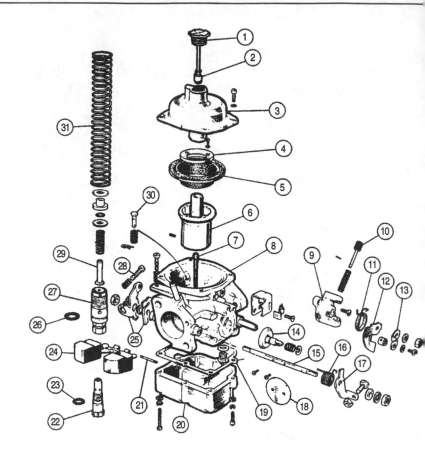

12: Stromberg carburettor

1	damper screw	17	lever
2	piston damper	18	throttle valve
3	suction chamber cover	19	gasket
4	diaphragm retaining ring	20	float chamber
5	piston diaphragm	21	float hinge pin
6	piston	22	jet adjuster
7	needle	23	O-ring
8	throttle body	24	dual float
9	starter housing	25	lever
10	stop	26	O-ring
11	spring	27	jet bearing
12	cam	28	throttle adjustment screw
13	lever	29	jet
14	starter valve	30	piston lifter
15	throttle shaft *or* spindle	31	piston spring
16	throttle return spring		

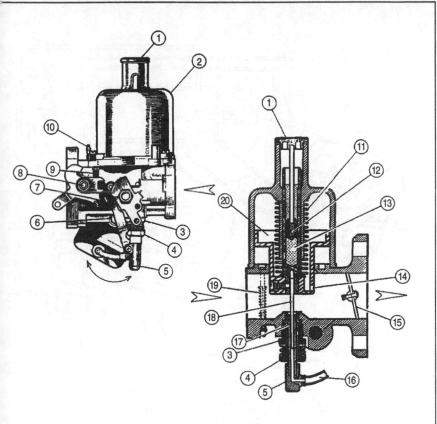

: SU Carburettor

	damper screw	11	piston spring
	suction chamber cover	12	piston damper
	jet locking nut	13	oil
	jet adjuster	14	vacuum port
	jet head	15	throttle valve
	float chamber attaching screw	16	float bowl connection
	fast idle screw	17	jet
	throttle shaft	18	needle
	throttle stop screw	19	piston lifter
	distributor vacuum port	20	piston

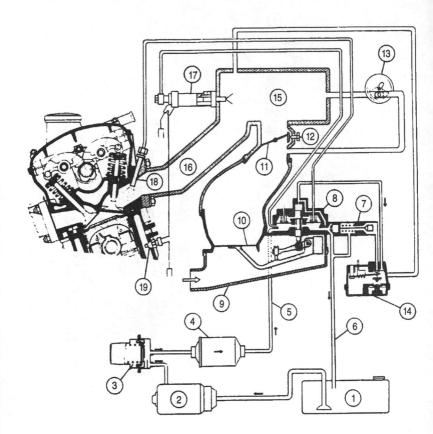

14 K-Jetronic Fuel Injection System

1	fuel tank	11	throttle valve
2	fuel pump	12	idle speed adjuster screw
3	fuel accumulator	13	throttle bypass valve
4	fuel filter	14	warm-up control unit
5	fuel supply line	15	plenum chamber
6	fuel return line	16	inlet manifold
7	system pressure regulator	17	cold start injector
8	fuel distributor	18	fuel injector
9	airflow sensor	19	thermo-time switch
10	sensor plate		

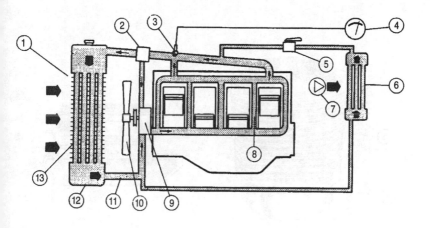

5 Cooling System

1	radiator	8	water jacket
2	thermostat	9	coolant pipe
3	temperature sensor	10	radiator fan
4	coolant temperature gauge	11	hose
5	heater control valve	12	radiator tank
6	heater core	13	core
7	heater fan		

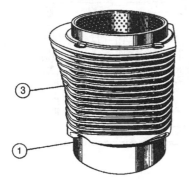
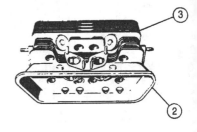

16: Air-cooled Cylinders

1	air-cooled barrel	3	cooling fins
2	cylinder head		

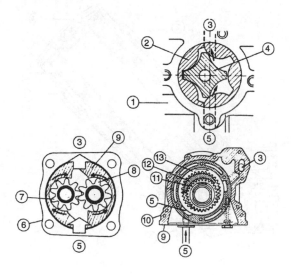

: Oil Pumps

	rotor-type pump	8	driven gear
	outer rotor	9	pump housing
	outlet side	10	internal gear pump
	inner rotor	11	internal gear
	suction side	12	crescent
	gear-type oil pump	13	outer gear
	drive gear	14	oil pressure relief valve

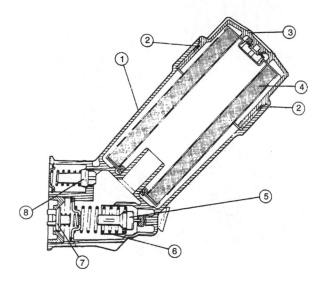

18: Oil Filter

1	oil filter housing	5	temperature control element
2	O-ring	6	sliding cup
3	screw cap	7	oil cooler bypass valve
4	filter element	8	oil filter bypass valve

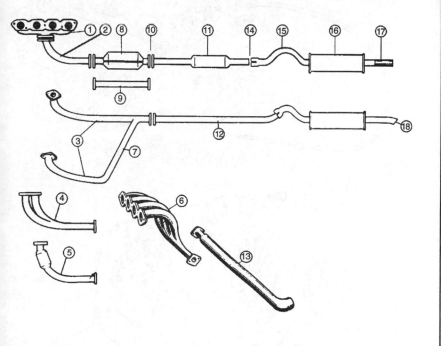

9: Exhaust System

	exhaust manifold	10	flange joint
	headpipe	11	front silencer
	dual headpipe	12	connector pipe
	Y-pipe	13	side pipe
	headpipe with mini-converter	14	slip joint
	high-performance headpipe	15	kickup pipe
	cross-over pipe	16	rear silencer
	catalytic converter	17	tailpipe
	converter test pipe	18	spout

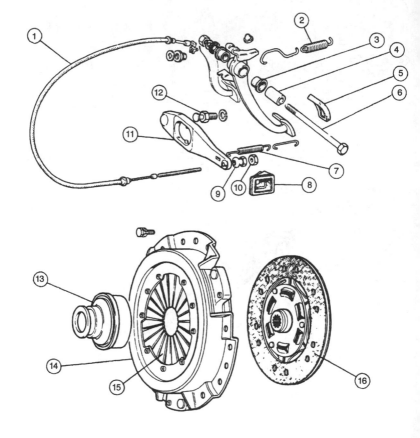

20: Clutch

1	clutch cable	9	pedal free travel adjusting nut
2	pedal return spring	10	locking nut
3	pivot bush	11	clutch release lever
4	sleeve	12	lever pivot
5	rubber pad	13	clutch release bearing
6	kingpin	14	clutch pressure plate
7	lever return spring	15	diaphragm spring
8	dust boot	16	clutch plate

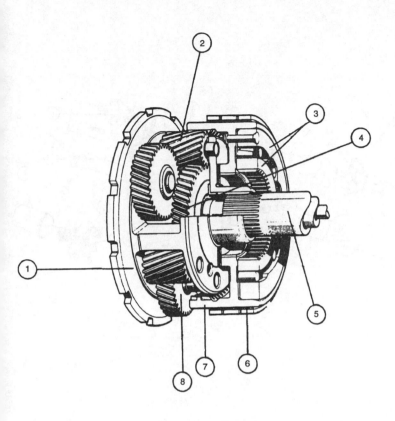

1: Ravigneaux Planetary Gear Set

	planet carrier	5	output shaft
	long planet gear	6	brake band
	free wheel	7	internal gear
	sun gear	8	short planet gear

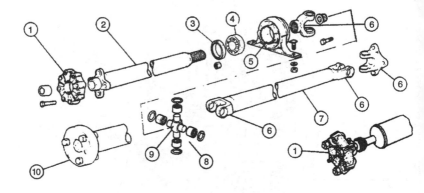

22: Propeller Shaft (rear-wheel drive)

1	doughnut coupling	6	yoke
2	front propeller shaft	7	rear propeller shaft
3	dust boot	8	universal joint (UJ)
4	roller bearing	9	spider
5	centre support	10	Hardy disc

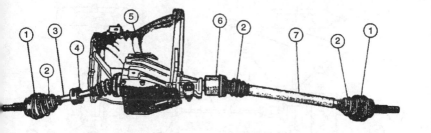

: Drive Shaft System (front-wheel drive)

	CV joint	5	transaxle
	dust boot	6	CV joint
	left drive shaft	7	right drive shaft
	mass damper		

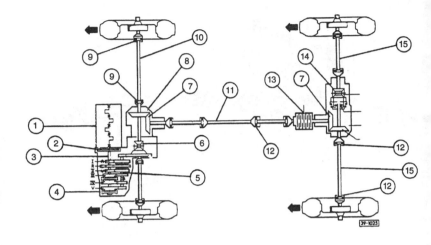

24: Four-wheel Drive

1	engine	9	CV joint
2	clutch	10	front-wheel drive shaft
3	input shaft	11	propeller shaft
4	transaxle	12	universal joint (UJ)
5	output shaft	13	viscous coupling (VC)
6	front differential	14	rear differential
7	bevel gear	15	rear-wheel drive shaft
8	bevel gear system		

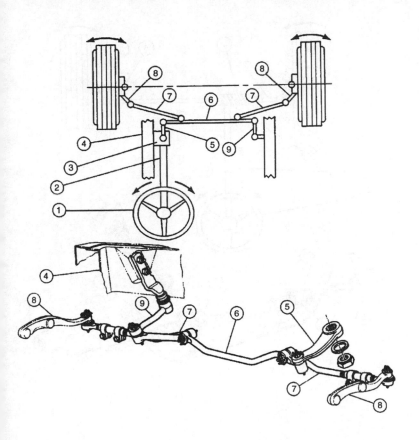

5: Steering

1	steering wheel	6	relay rod
2	steering gear shaft	7	tie rod *or* track rod
3	steering box	8	steering arm
4	frame	9	idler arm
5	drop arm		

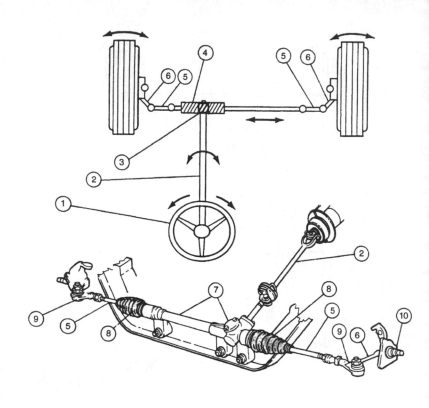

26: Rack-and-pinion Steering

1	steering wheel	6	steering arm
2	steering gear shaft	7	steering gear
3	pinion	8	gaiter
4	rack	9	tie rod end
5	tie rod *or* track rod	10	steering knuckle

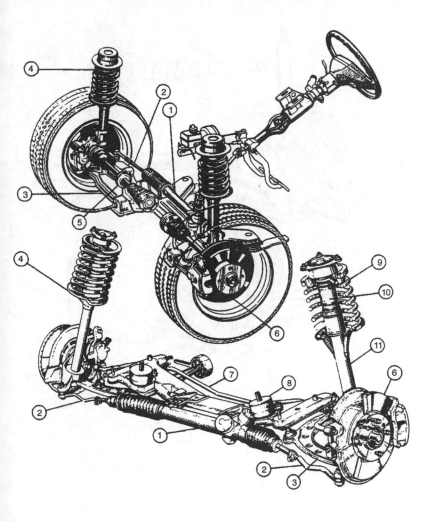

: Front Axle
) Front-wheel drive
) Rear-wheel drive

1	rack-and-pinion steering	7	anti-roll bar
2	tie rod	8	engine mounting
3	transverse link	9	coil spring
4	MacPherson strut	10	jounce buffer
5	drive shaft with mass damper	11	shock absorber
6	disc brake		

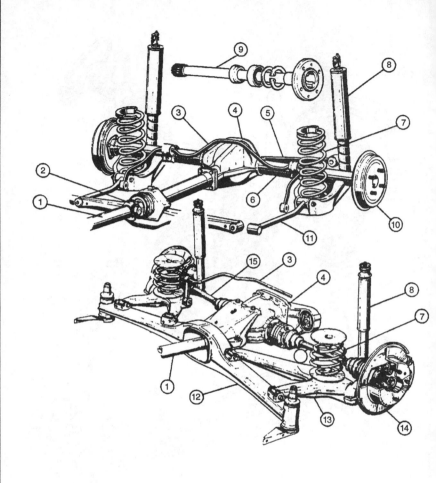

28: Rear Axle

1	propeller shaft	9	axle shaft
2	universal joint (UJ)	10	drum brake
3	anti-roll bar	11	trailing arm *or* link
4	differential	12	crossmember
5	Panhard rod	13	semi-trailing arm *or* link
6	live axle	14	disc brake
7	coil spring	15	drive shaft
8	shock absorber		

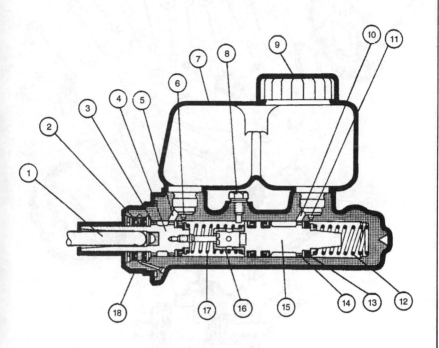

9: Tandem Master Cylinder

1	pushrod	10	replenishing port
2	secondary seal	11	compensating port
3	bleeder hole	12	secondary piston return spring
4	primary piston	13	primary cup
5	replenishing port	14	bleeder hole
6	compensating port	15	secondary piston
7	brake fluid reservoir	16	stop sleeve
8	stop screw	17	primary piston return spring
9	cap	18	body

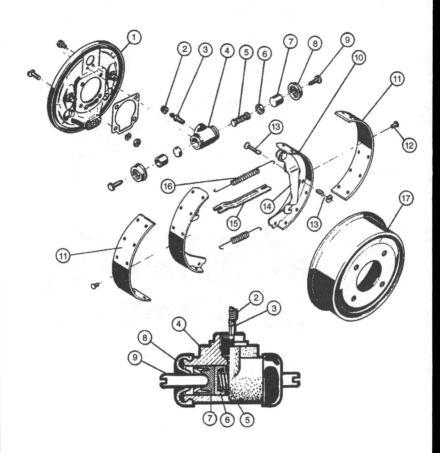

30: Drum Brake

1	backplate	10	brake shoe
2	cap	11	brake lining
3	bleeder screw	12	rivet
4	wheel cylinder	13	brake shoe hold-down
5	expander spring	14	parking brake lever
6	cup seal	15	push bar
7	piston	16	brake shoe return spring
8	dust boot	17	brake drum
9	link		

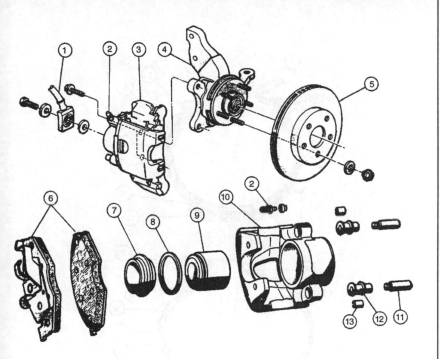

1: Sliding-caliper Disc Brake

1	brake hose	8	piston seal
2	bleeder screw	9	piston
3	brake caliper	10	brake caliper
4	steering knuckle	11	caliper pin
5	brake disc	12	sleeve
6	brake pads	13	pin bush
7	dust boot		

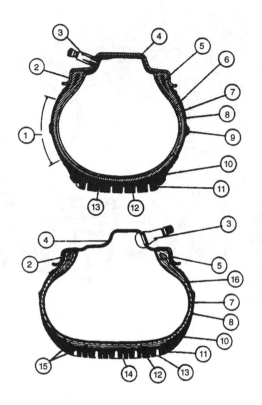

32: Tyres

1	flexing zone	9	scuff rib
2	rim flange	10	shoulder
3	valve	11	tread
4	drop centre well	12	tread bar
5	tyre bead	13	tread groove
6	tube	14	sipes
7	carcass	15	belt
8	sidewall	16	inner liner

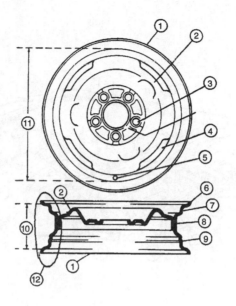

33: Wheel

1	wheel	7	bead seat
2	wheel disc	8	rim well
3	stud hole	9	hump
4	ventilation slot	10	width of rim
5	valve hole	11	diameter of rim
6	rim flange	12	rim

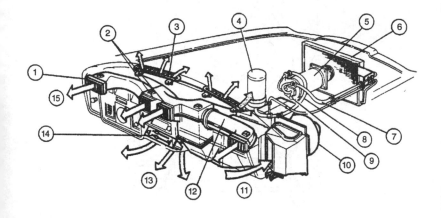

34: Heating, Ventilation, Air-conditioning

1	air outlet	9	pressure relief valve
2	centre air outlet	10	fan
3	demister nozzle	11	air intake
4	accumulator-drier	12	air duct
5	compressor	13	floor heating
6	condenser	14	controls
7	high side	15	airflow
8	low side		

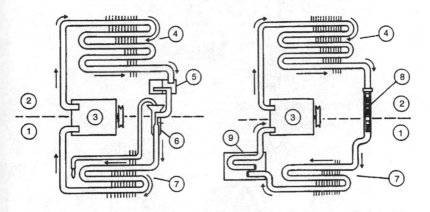

35: Air-conditioning System
(A) Receiver-drier System
(B) Accumulator-drier System

1	low side	6	expansion valve
2	high side	7	evaporator
3	compressor	8	expansion tube
4	condenser	9	accumulator-drier
5	receiver-drier		

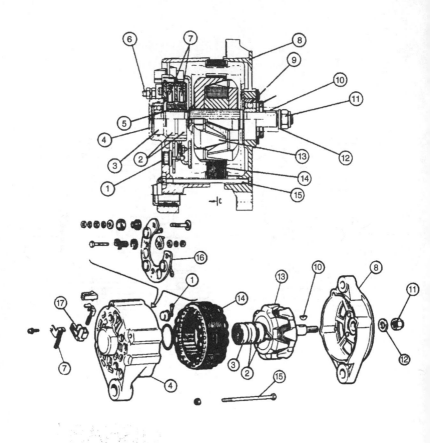

36: Alternator

1	rectifier diode	10	Woodruff key
2	slip rings	11	nut
3	slip-ring end bearing	12	washer
4	slip-ring end bracket	13	rotor
5	insulator	14	stator
6	terminal	15	through bolt
7	carbon brushes	16	diode heat sink
8	drive end bracket	17	brush holder
9	drive end bearing		

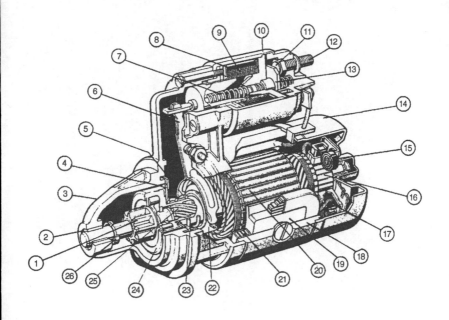

37: Starter Motor

1	pinion	14	commutator end frame
2	bush	15	carbon brush spring
3	drive end bracket	16	commutator
4	brake disc	17	carbon brush
5	meshing spring	18	starter frame
6	shift lever	19	pole shoe
7	return spring	20	armature
8	hold-in winding	21	field winding
9	pull-in winding	22	collar
10	starter solenoid	23	stop ring
11	contact	24	overrunning clutch
12	terminal stud	25	armature shaft
13	moving contact	26	stop collar